The American Exploration and Travel Series

*Pedro Vial and the Roads to Santa Fe*

+++

# PEDRO VIAL AND THE ROADS TO SANTA FE

*by Noel M. Loomis*
*and Abraham P. Nasatir*

UNIVERSITY OF OKLAHOMA PRESS : NORMAN

*Library of Congress Catalog Card Number:* 66–13422

 Composed and printed at Norman, Oklahoma, U.S.A., by the University of Oklahoma Press. First edition.

+++

# *Acknowledgments*

My obligations for assistance with the materials presented here are numerous, and many of them have been acknowledged by name in other works; therefore I simply offer grateful thanks to the many archivists and friends in Spain, in Mexico, in Santa Fe, and in Washington, and especially to my colleague in the Foreign Language Department of San Diego State College, Leslie P. Brown.

ABRAHAM P. NASATIR

## *Further Acknowledgments*

Most of the source material for this book was handed to me by Professor Nasatir, and in those cases where I needed something more, the problem was alleviated by Eleanor B. Adams, University of New Mexico; Mary H. Estes and Eugene C. Barker, Texas History Center at the University of Texas; J. Robert Feynn, Historical Society of New Mexico; Robert W. Hall, New York Public Library; Concha Romero James, Library of Congress; Myra Ellen Jenkins, New Mexico State Records Center; Wm. Kaye Lamb, Dominion Archivist of Canada, and D. Wurtele, at Montreal; David C. Mearns, Library of Congress; Rupert N. Richardson, Hardin-Simmons University; E. R. Smith, United States Bureau of Land Management, at Santa Fe; James H. Thompson, University of North Carolina Library; Dorman H. Winfrey, University of Texas Library; and Mrs. Helen Harding Bretnor, at the great Bancroft Library at Berkeley, who helped me with microfilm and photostats from the archives of Mexico and Spain and a number of other items.

The work of gathering the material of which this book is compounded, however, was done over a period of thirty-six years by Abraham P. Nasatir, my colleague in San Diego State College. At the Bibliothèque Nationale, at the Archives Nationales, and at other libraries in Paris in 1924, 1930, and 1950; at the Archivo Histórico Nacional at Madrid and the Archivo General de Indias at Seville in 1924, 1925, and 1930–31; at the Archivo General y Público de la Nación in Mexico City in 1941; in the Manuscript Division of the Library of Congress and in the National Archives in Washington many times; in the Jefferson Memorial Library of the Missouri Historical Society in St. Louis many times; in the Archives of New Mexico at Santa Fe in 1940; and in a dozen other places (even in Santiago, Chile, in 1959) he has looked indefatigably for material.

Now, searching for documents that may or may not exist in ancient archives that often are cold, badly lighted, and dusty, is not a chore for a small boy, and when a man continues month after month, he must have a tremendous drive and a fairly good constitution. There is also, on occasion, a need for great diplomacy to obtain permission to examine archives that still are classified in 1960 because they were *reservada* in 1660, and it is desirable to secure the co-operation of librarians and archivists not always accustomed to the sound of human voices in those great, stone caverns, and then there is the mechanical problem of arranging for some sort of duplication. A good deal of this material was obtained before the days of the easy accessibility of photocopy devices, and therefore many of the early documents were copied by hand. On one occasion Nasatir set up a Leica and made microfilm by the light that came in through the windows.

One who has not handled and tried to read Spanish documents of the 1700's can have no adequate conception of the problem of finding, among millions of papers, the ones that will be useful to him. The armchair researcher can get a taste of the problem by going to the National Archives in Washington—one of the better handled archives—and asking for papers about a specific person or occurrence (say, Major Price's conduct in the campaign in the Texas Panhandle in 1874, and events leading to his court-martial). The researcher will soon find that the emphasis is on "search," for there is no big book or card index to which he can turn to find the pertinent papers. Each subject presents a different problem, and each problem is involved and requires the help of the staff archivist, for the vast quantity of material imposes an indexing problem that so far has been insurmountable; the only practicable answer is to work with someone thoroughly familiar with that section of the archives. How much more difficult, then, it must be in archives that have many times more material but whose allocations for sorting and for physical care have been far less than those in Washington.

A few men—Roscoe R. Hill, working on the Cuban papers deposited in Seville; J. A. Robertson, concerned with Spanish documents of which copies are readily available in the United States; William R. Shepherd, in Simancas, Madrid, and Seville; Charles E. Chapman, concentrating on the Archives of the Indies at Seville; Luis Marino Pérez, in the Cuban archives; Herbert E. Bolton, with his very useful coverage of the Mexican archives; and Mrs. N. M. Miller Surrey and others, including Nasatir himself, who have worked with French archives—have spent months and years in those foreign repositories, have made rough translations and have compiled calendars or guides or finding aids and indexes; each succeeding reseacher uses the work of those who have gone before, and not infrequently finds occasion to invoke some sort of blessing.

One should read the introductions to their various works to obtain some idea of the monumental problems of such research. In some cases, thousands of documents have been piled in a heap on an attic floor (it has happened in this country too) and shoveled about with a grain scoop; in other cases, old documents have been sold by the truckload as waste paper (and that also has occurred in the United States).

Nasatir searched for materials relating to French and Spanish activities in the area west of the Mississippi River, especially in Spanish Illinois, in the Southwest, and in California. Over the years he must have examined several million folios of ancient documents, for he has, in his own private library, copies of over 200,000 pages. His collection is the result of an enormous amount of work.

While Nasatir was looking for materials on certain subjects, other subjects began to emerge. Even though the trained historian is usually not greatly concerned about small affairs unless they affect the course of history (thereby missing, in the layman's mind, some of the most interesting items), a good historian, however, responds to interesting bits as well as significant bits, and Nasatir turned out to be responsive to human qualities. He began to watch the slowly emerging pictures of men and to accumulate a considerable mental file of names, and consequently took everything he could find that bore those names. Thus, his left hand was busy gathering one type of material while his right hand gathered something else.

Eventually, then, he found himself hopelessly submerged in a large number of interesting and worthy topics for books—so many that he would never have time to write half of them, and when I arrived on the scene in 1958, he approached me with a catch-line that he knew would coincide with my special interests. Since I had come into historical work through the side door with *The Texan-Santa Fé Pioneers* (University of Oklahoma Press, 1958), which showed my interest in the Southwest, and since I had written some forty Western novels, he said, "I can give you some material on the greatest frontiersman of them all."

Which shows that a historian does not attain a position of eminence by thinking with his feet.

After that, it was fairly simple. He took me to his home, sorted through the 200,000 pages of material, set up a three-foot shelf of books for me to read, told me his idea of the project, and said, "It's all yours. Take it home. Handle it any way you want to." And all I had to do was sit down with a bushel basketful of transcriptions (typewritten and handwritten), photocopies and microfilm of original documents, and study the books and bibliographies, and try to put them all together to make sense—interesting sense. It has been quite a job, but a fascinating one—and a bushel basketful of documents can very well take over an entire house, especially when it is added to, about once a week, by installment after installment.

Nasatir did not, in succeeding months, try to tell me what to do; he never bothered me except to ask hopefully, "How are you getting along with Vial?" and it was a great satisfaction when I could not only report progress but also show him a sizable amount of copy. Then his work began again.

The ten unpublished journals all came from him with complete generosity; most of the translations were done by him; the proofreading of those documents in various stages was done by him; the final versions were meticulously checked by him.

One must realize that Spanish documents often had many copies. There may be an original, a copy or several copies (often included as part of a letter), an informal copy known as a draft, and a certified copy or several certified copies. The number of copies was not always prescribed, and their distribution was often involved, depending on the subject matter—but it was never haphazard.

From the governor of New Mexico, for instance, the original would normally find its way to the commandant-general of the Interior Provinces; that official would in turn send a copy to the viceroy; the viceroy might on some occasions send a copy to the Audiencia of Santo Domingo, and that in turn to the Council of the Indies. The viceroy often sent a report directly to the king's minister in Spain or to one of his cabinet officials. Also, it was common practice, and was encouraged by the officials in Spain, for New World officials down to the level of governor-general to send direct reports to Spain—and that was done constantly. Still other copies might go to any official who might be interested; if the matter involved smuggling across the Louisiana-Texas border, a copy might go from the governor of New Mexico to the governor of Texas, one to the French commandant at Natchitoches, one to the governor at New Orleans, and even on occasion to the captain-general at Havana. Such a matter might well move the commandant-general at Chihuahua also to send a report to the governor at New Orleans and another to the captain-general at Havana. Therefore, in spite of the bewildering number of copies, one presently discovers—as I did when Professor Nasatir pointed it out—that there actually was an organized method that will today help a researcher who wants to locate a missing document.

A good series to show the sequence of reports is one from 1806 concerning incidents and fears arising from reports of Anglo-Americans in Louisiana and the Interior Provinces. This sequence began February 4, 1806, when Governor Antonio Cordero of Texas wrote Nemesio Salcedo, commandant-general of the Interior Provinces, that he had been informed by Captain Sebastian Rodríguez, commandant at Nacogdoches, that he had been chased away from the vicinity of Nacogdoches by an American officer (among other items). Cordero's letter is missing, but we gather these details and others from Salcedo's report to the viceroy, Yturrigaray, on February 23. The viceroy sent a report to Miguel Cayetano Soler in Spain on March 27, and the king acknowledged receipt of the information and news of the steps taken, in a letter dated November 17.

In the meantime, however, other things had been happening. On February 14 Cordero had written Félix Calleja, commandant of the Tenth Brigade, at San Luis Potosí, and told him the same story that he had told Salcedo; presumably Calleja was the one to whom Cordero was to appeal for military aid under certain conditions. Calleja sent a copy of Cordero's report to the viceroy; that letter is missing, but we have a copy of Calleja's answer to Cordero—a copy that was sent to the viceroy. On March 7 the viceroy acknowledged it.

Meanwhile, the Marquis of Casa Calvo, previously governor of Louisiana but in 1806 captain-general at Havana, wrote a letter on the same general subject to Spain, enclosing material from the *Kentucky Gazette* that had been sent to him by Casa Yrujo, the Spanish minister at Philadelphia. On February 1 Casa Calvo wrote similarly to the viceroy, indignantly passing on an amount of gossip; perhaps Casa Calvo was annoyed because he had been requested to leave New Orleans with the Spanish members of the boundary commission.

The viceroy's answer to Casa Calvo is not at hand, but on March 1 the viceroy wrote to Calleja, enclosing a copy of his letter of the same date to Salcedo and a copy of one of the letters from Casa Calvo. On the same day he also wrote Salcedo, advising him that Calleja had sent him a copy of Cordero's letter of February 14; the viceroy also sent a copy of a letter from Casa Yrujo.

This particular series of letters is drawn from a duplicate of the viceroy's letter to Soler in Spain, March 27, 1806, and all the letters except that of March 27 and the king's acknowledgment, are from copies that the viceroy enclosed with his letter to Soler.[1]

Very often an official letter is nothing but a quotation from an *oficio* from somebody else, who is quoting in turn from somebody else. Also, there are many kinds of draft. Besides the original, signed by the author, there are originals unsigned; then there are copies certified and signed by the copyist, and there are copies signed by the original author; and there are just plain drafts: copies, usually unsigned by anybody, but

[1] Yturrigaray to Soler, No. 989, March 27, 1806, in Archivo General de Indias (hereinafter cited as A.G.I.), Sección, Audiencia de Santo Domingo, leg. 2600.

of course with the original signatures copied—and sometimes a copy with no signature whatever.

Many, many documents exist only in copies; many others exist only as references in other documents, and not even copies can be located. These latter may have been lost or destroyed, and undoubtedly many are still in existence in the massive archival deposits of the New World and the Iberian Peninsula—sometimes, too, in Paris or London or Washington.[2]

When several copies of a document are found, the texts seldom are identical, and sometimes they vary substantially, as will appear in the diary of Pedro Vial from Santa Fe to St. Louis, where an important paragraph was omitted from the version of this diary once published, but now appears in this work for the first time, taken from a different copy.

There are now three major depositories—at Simancas, Madrid, and Seville; by modern plans, material to 1750 is to be some day gathered in Simancas, that after 1750 in Madrid, with colonial material in Seville. Most documents relating to colonial matters did go to Seville, but those sent by top officials, for determination of policy and other high-level decisions, went to the Consejo at Madrid. And those three: the Archivo General at Simancas, the Archivo Histórico Nacional at Madrid, and the Archivo General de Indias at Seville—those three are the important archives in Spain.[3]

A thorough reading of the introductions to the guides to Spanish and Mexican archives will throw considerable light on the use of those immense deposits, and is recommended whether or not the reader has any expectations of going to Spain or Mexico.[4]

[2] See Charles E. Chapman, *Catalogue of Materials in the Archivo General de Indias, for the History of the Pacific Coast and the American Southwest,* 1–5.

[3] William R. Shepherd has an excellent discussion of political organization in his *Guide to Materials for the History of the United States in Spanish Archives,* 10–12.

[4] The best guides in English are: Chapman, *Catalogue of Materials*; Shepherd, *Guide to Materials*; Herbert Eugene Bolton, *Guide to Materials for the History of the United States in the Principal Archives of Mexico*; Roscoe R. Hill, *Descriptive Catalogue of the Documents Relating to the History of the United States in the Papeles Procedentes of Cuba Deposited in the Archivo General de Indias at Seville*; Luis Marino Pérez, *Guide to the Materials for American History in Cuban Archives;* and James Alexander Robertson, *List of Documents in Spanish Archives Relating to the History of the United States, Which Have Been Printed or of Which Transcripts Are Preserved in American Libraries.*

In making a book of such archival materials, the most important fact was that the many documents were present, in my hands—which made the task considerably easier than it would have been if I had had to look for them in the first place. It was also vital that I have someone at hand with a knowledge of the over-all situation to furnish a reason for the book, and with an encyclopedic knowledge of sources and of ways to get at them—which for this work was present in the person of Professor Nasatir, whose knowledge is comprehensive.

In translations into current English, sometimes the formal meaning of a word actually loses its original meaning if given literally. Thus, *reservada* in the old Spanish documents means *reserved*—but *reserved* does not mean today what it must have meant in those documents. It means *reserved for the eyes of certain persons*, but today, under a different cultural structure, the word *reserved* loses force; today it has a colloquial meaning, *confidential* (or even *classified*), which must give today's reader a better idea of its meaning in 1786. Sometimes, in my own efforts, I went too far, but Nasatir is an intelligent translator, and he watched me carefully and offered a dissent whenever he was not satisfied.

The general plan of this book, the divisions, the manner of presentation of these priceless documents, is on my shoulders. I am a lone worker; I like to find out all I can about a subject, then go home and write the book. I cannot work with anybody looking over my shoulder. Let us hope that this is not the time it will work to anyone's disadvantage.

Both of us give our combined and separate thanks to Ida Nasatir and to Dorothy Loomis. It takes a very special breed of woman to live with a writer or a historian and like it; apparently these two do. And Ida is the one who always had the right answer when I raised my head from a box of musty documents and asked, "What do I smell cooking?"

Noel M. Loomis

*April 20, 1966*
*San Diego State College*

+++

# *Introduction*

America has had many great frontiersmen. A few, of considerable merit, have been elevated to the level of folk heroes; a few of no great merit have been elevated anyway; and a few of substantial merit have remained unknown.

Aside from the few who have become household bywords—Manuel Lisa, the Chouteaus, the Sublettes, Jedediah Smith, the Robidoux and the Bents; Boone, Crockett, and Bowie; Earp, Slaughter, and Tilghman (barely to start an endless roll call)—the great body of Western pioneers followed their paths of duty quietly and without fuss or feathers, not seeking or expecting immortality: the mountain men, the missionaries, the soldiers, the sheriffs, and the great cattlemen—and were satisfied to be able to meet the problems that came to hand.

Among them are the many who have been forgotten, who were unknown to those of the Western era and who are equally unknown to us today, but who earned their small niches in the infinite hall of fame by reason of their exploits and their significance to the growth of the continent and the spread of Western civilization. Such a man was Pedro Vial. For one hundred and forty years, his name and the story of his almost unbelievable travels were buried deep in the musty archives of Mexico City, of Havana, of Seville, of Madrid, and of Santa Fe.

Pedro Vial, or Pierre Vial, was a native of Lyons, in the southeast part of central France. He has left some remarks that indicate that he was on the Missouri River before the Revolutionary War, but he first appears actively on the scene in the Southwest in 1786 as an explorer who was sent to open a trail from San Antonio to Santa Fe. He was a loner; on that first historic trek, he traveled with one man only: Cristóbal de los Santos; he became ill and spent weeks in the tipi of a chief in a Tawakoni (Wichita) village; he followed the Red River to the village of Chief Zoquiné of the Comanches,[1] where he stayed for some time; and finally he went on to Santa Fe to make his report to the governor of New Mexico and to draw two maps, one of which still exists.

For twenty years thereafter, Pedro Vial traveled the wilderness around Santa Fe, San Antonio, Natchitoches, and St. Louis, seemingly at will. It was something of a feat to journey safely among Apaches, Utes, Kiowas, Comanches, Kansas, Osages, Otos, Missouris, Iowas, Sioux, Arapahos, Pawnees, and other tribes known to be indefatigable gatherers of scalps—and not lose one's own hair.

For at least two hundred years, Santa Fe's only direct connection with the rest of the world had been through Chihuahua, some six hundred miles south of Santa Fe. There had been no other road. Vial, however, remedied that situation emphatically by opening up three new roads that were direct routes from Santa Fe to the outside world—one to San Antonio in Texas, one to Natchitoches in Louisiana, and one to St. Louis in what is now Missouri.

It was a little over one year after Vial reached Santa Fe from the Texas village of San Antonio on his first big excursion that he made a trip from Santa Fe eastward across the Texas Panhandle, down the Red River to Natchitoches to establish a route that led eventually from Santa Fe to New Orleans, and then back to San Antonio (Bexar, it was often called by the Spanish), and then again to Santa Fe. On that trip he made a total journey of 914.5 leagues (2,377 miles) in one year and two months (less four days), having spent the winter in San Antonio.

When Vial started the trip to Natchitoches, he was accompanied by several men, one of whom was Santiago Fernández, who kept a journal as far as the Jumano (Wichita)[2] villages in the vicinity of present-day

[1] Rupert N. Richardson, *The Comanche Barrier to South Plains Settlement*, 70, says that when the Spaniards said "Comanches," they meant Penatekas, or Southern Comanches. If they meant the Kotsotekas—the other big Comanche division—says Richardson, they called them "Cuchanticas."

[2] The Wichitas were a large group of Caddoan stock, known as Black Pawnee or Pani Piqué, and by other names; they included tribes now known as Wichita, Taovaya,

Ringgold, east of Wichita Falls, and then returned to Santa Fe while Vial continued east. Francisco Xavier Fragoso also had been keeping a journal, and after Fernández' departure, Fragoso took the full burden and continued it to Natchitoches and San Antonio and on to Santa Fe. Perhaps the Spanish officials were tired of translating Vial's poor French.[3]

In 1789, while he gathered himself in San Antonio for the final portion of that memorable trip, Vial was not entirely idle, for he was sent from San Antonio to take presents to the implacable Comanches. After that side trip, Vial left for Santa Fe and for at least the fifth time traveled through Comanche country, arriving at Santa Fe with no undue delay.

In 1792–93 Vial made the first transit in history of the Santa Fe Trail, by traveling the 876.5 leagues (2,279 miles, his distance for the round trip) in successive summers. On the way to St. Louis, he and his men were captured by Kansas Indians, threatened with death, and held naked for six weeks but Vial later told Zenon Trudeau, the commandant at Fort St. Louis of the Illinois country, that he could have made the trip in twenty-five days if he had not been delayed by the blood-thirsty savages.

It was the speed of that trip that brought realization to the Spanish at high levels of authority[4] that Santa Fe was not as far from the United

Tawakoni, Waco, and others. The Jumanos were encountered in Coronado's time on the Río Grande and were usually allied with or enemies of the Apaches, and sometimes were considered to be Apaches. Bolton says ("The Jumano Indians in Texas, 1650–1771," *Southwestern Historical Quarterly,* Vol. XV, No. 1 [July, 1911]—erroneously cited in *After Coronado)* that while the Wichitas or Taovayas who came from the north to settle on the Red River seem sometimes to have been called Jumanos, the names are not interchangeable.

[3] In examining the documents in Mexico, Archivo General y Público, Sección de Historia (hereinafter cited as Historia), Vol. 43, in Mexico City, Professor Nasatir found this note appended to the entry in the index to Vol. 43, pertaining to Vial's diary of 1792: "Which is repeated because the translations differ from the original French in which the author wrote; besides varying in some things, there is also added now the return trip." This note was included with a letter of transmittal to the viceroy; Nava to Revillagigedo, Chihuahua, January 9, 1794; Historia, Vol. 43, No. 19.

[4] Zenon Trudeau to Carondelet, St. Louis, October 7, 1792; Papeles de Cuba, leg. 2362; Provincias Internas, Vol. 183, and elsewhere (printed in Louis Houck, *The Spanish Régime in Missouri,* I, 351). He advised the governor that Vial could have made the trip in twenty-five days if he had not been waylaid by the hostile Kansas Indians. Three years later (July 4, 1795), Trudeau again mentioned the matter to Carondelet,

States as the Council of the Indies might have wished. Already the restless Anglo-Americans, as the Spaniards called them,[5] were beginning to probe the rivers and explore the plains that led to the great and unknown West. From turbulent New Orleans, from the tiny outpost of Natchitoches, from the wicked river town of Natchez, from the Indian village of Chickasaw Bluffs (some day to be known as Memphis), from the war-born settlement of Louisville (resulting from the expedition of George Rogers Clark), and from Pittsburgh (jumping-off place on the Ohio River), coonskin-capped Americans took their steel traps in tow-sacks and their rifles on their shoulders and set out to see what lay beyond the next hill or the next range of mountains—and somehow the mountains always seemed to be the Rockies,[6] and what lay beyond was not really beyond the mountains at all, but nestled in among them: the tiny, fabled village of Santa Fe, entrepôt of all northern Mexico[7] and the key to the rich and massive Southwest.[8]

The whole West was fair game. From the time of Estevâncio, Friar Marcos de Niza, Coronado, and The Turk, it had been reputed to be a land of rich mines of silver, gold, and turquoise; moreover, beyond argument in 1793 it was the home of vast bands of wild horses—and horses were negotiable. They had been in great demand during the Revolutionary War, and later Thomas Jefferson had encouraged the

---

saying that the same Vial had traveled from Santa Fe to the Pawnees in eight days, and that traders regularly traveled from the Pawnees to St. Louis in ten days (printed in Abraham P. Nasatir, *Before Lewis and Clark*, I, 330).

[5] Some writers say that United States citizens should not call themselves Americans, that it is presumptuous, because the Spaniards also were Americans—but see Lawrence Kinnaird's comments in "American Penetration into Spanish Louisiana," *New Spain and the Anglo-American West*, I, 211. See Manuel Muñoz to the governor, February 15, 1795; Pedro de Nava to the governor, July 30, 1795; Salcedo to the governor, April 25, 1807; Manrrique to Salcedo, March 31, 1810; Melgares to Conde, July 9, 1819—in all of which they referred to "Americans." They also, of course, used the term "Anglo-Americans," and often *ingleses* (English), for the Revolutionary War was barely over.

[6] Variously called the Stony Mountains, the Shining Mountains, the Spanish Mountains, the Mexican Mountains, and the Anáhuac Mountains.

[7] Max Moorhead, *New Mexico's Royal Road*, v. Taos also was a port of entry, but the real business for the movements of goods south, was done with the governor at Santa Fe.

[8] The Southwest in those days was everything south and west of the Missouri River.

frontiersmen to bring them in; and Philip Nolan, responding to the direct interest of the President, made a stomping-ground out of Texas. There was the technicality that all soil west of the Mississippi River (or, after 1803, all soil west of the Missouri and all west of the Sabine) belonged to Spain, but that bothered nobody. The great flood tide of continental migration had set in, and nothing could have stopped it.

These facts do not imply that the Spaniards were hostile toward the migrators. Far from it. The Spaniards were uneasy, for they knew the Americans were vigorous and uninhibited, but Spanish resistance was largely token and without sustained direction or determination. In fact, during the Revolutionary War a man named Oliver Pollock financed George Rogers Clark and enabled him to hold the western country (the Ohio River Country) for the United States; Pollock not only put up money, but he also persuaded the Spaniards to sell him many thousands of pounds of gunpowder and to allow him to ship it north on the Mississippi River.

Once the Revolution was over, however, it was Santa Fe toward which the restless Anglo-Americans began to push their way. It was strange that the seven-thousand-foot-high village of adobe huts and barking dogs became the target for so many adventurers. Few people even knew where Santa Fe was located except that it lay somewhere to the west and south.

Somewhere north and east of Santa Fe was St. Louis. Toward the east, far down the Red River, was Natchitoches, an equally small outpost; and while Santa Fe was an outpost of New Mexico, Natchitoches was an outpost of Louisiana. Southeast of Santa Fe was San Antonio in Texas, much closer to Santa Fe than was Natchitoches in Louisiana. South of Santa Fe were El Paso del Norte, Chihuahua, and Durango. Chihuahua actually was the farthest outpost of civilization for the Spanish Empire in Mexico, and in that town lived—at times—the governor of the province of Chihuahua and the commandant-general of the Interior Provinces.[9] Far southwest of Santa Fe, in Sinaloa on the Gulf of California, was Guaymas, which was to become an important

[9] The political structure of the Interior Provinces changed frequently, as did the location of the capital. Often two or more functions of government were combined in one man, and that fact perhaps influenced the location of the capital—which at various times was at Saltillo, Durango, Chihuahua, Arizpe, and perhaps other places—a fluid situation.

point of entry for British ships (and sometimes for smugglers). Far, far west of Santa Fe was a new establishment, San Diego de Alcalá, the first presidio and mission in Alta California.[10]

Aside from those vague directions and distances, not much was known about the outside world by those in Santa Fe, or about Santa Fe by those in the outside world, and for a good reason: for nearly three centuries the Spanish rulers of New Spain had felt their northern colony secure by the very reason of its isolation. At the time of Pedro Vial, Louisiana was considered to be a strong buffer on the north and east, and therefore the Spanish officials in the Interior Provinces had not been concerned enough to do anything except issue routine warnings to one another.

But suddenly, when Pedro Vial showed them how close Santa Fe was to the long rifles of Kentucky and the Trans-Allegheny West, they felt less complacent—almost defenseless. They realized that they were terribly exposed to the driving Anglo-Americans, and Spanish officials in St. Louis, in New Orleans, in Havana, in Natchitoches, in San Antonio, in Santa Fe, in Chihuahua, in the City of Mexico, and in Madrid took cognizance of the danger abruptly created—or at least revealed—by Pedro Vial's statement that if he had not been captured by Indians, he could have made the trip from Santa Fe to St. Louis in twenty-five days.

The new danger was not Vial's responsibility, and probably he did not give it much thought. In making the trip, he had acted under orders and had done what he was paid to do—as he had always done in the service of Spain.

After that trip, Vial continued to explore and to make trips in Indian country for the governor of New Mexico; he was listed as an interpreter at six *reales*[11] a day. Probably he used the sign language[12]

[10] While California was not prominent at that time in the problems of the Spaniards at Santa Fe, nevertheless many references to it appear in the documents of those years.

[11] About 75 cents.

[12] Sign language had long existed among North American Indians, and, contrary to some writers, was not confined to Plains Indians. Cabeza de Vaca encountered it in Florida in 1528 and used it clear across the continent (see F. W. Hodge, *Spanish Explorers in the Southern United States*, 26: "We . . . received their answers by signs, just as if they spoke our language and we theirs"; and similarly on page 107). Coronado encountered the use of sign language among the Querechos in eastern New Mexico in

and he must have spoken many Indian tongues, for he dealt with the Taovayas (Wichitas), Comanches, Jicarilla Apaches, Pawnees, Osages, Kansas, and a number of other tribes, probably including some tribes known to the Spanish by names that no longer mean anything to anyone but a historian.[13]

A curious item turns up here: Vial was said by the governor of Texas on his first trip to have lived and traded among the Texas Indians many years; on that first trip, from San Antonio to Santa Fe, Vial spent some time with the Comanches and must have been able freely to communicate. Later he was sent from San Antonio to the Comanches with presents; but yet, when he made the trip from Santa Fe to Natchitoches, he was provided with a Comanche interpreter. Perhaps bureaucracy is older than we think.

Five years after the St. Louis trip—in 1797—Vial "deserted" the Spanish and went to the Comanches. In 1799 he was a resident of Portage des Sioux, just north of St. Louis.

On July 4, 1803, Vial returned to Santa Fe, and apparently was forgiven, for in 1805 he went back to the Missouri under Spanish orders on what was ostensibly an expedition to the Pananas (Pawnees), Mahas (Omahas), Otos, Lobos, and other tribes, but which in reality was a counteraction to the Lewis and Clark expedition. The reports at that time were that the Americans and French[14] had "seduced"[14a] the In-

1541 (see George Parker Winship, "The Coronado Expedition," *Fourteenth Annual Report*, Bureau of American Ethnology, 504: "Although they conversed by means of signs they made themselves understood so well that there was no need of an interpreter.")

[13] Herbert E. Bolton, Frederick W. Hodge, Alfred B. Thomas, and others deal with various names that have become extinct: Cuampes (some say Comanches, some say Kiowas; Lansing Bloom says they were a division of the Faraon Apaches); Carlanas, Chilpaines, Faraones, Jicarillas or Xicarillas, Llaneros, Natagés, Palomas, Pelones, Perrillos, and Vaqueros (all Apache tribes); Penxayes, Quartelejos, and Sierra Blancas (all Apaches, says Thomas); Padoucahs (George Hyde says they were Kiowa-Apaches, but the preponderance of evidence now leans toward Comanches; Bolton says they were a Comanche division); Laitânes or Naitanes (Comanches); Ietans (Comanches); A's or Aas or Eyeish (Caddos); Guaguaches (Osages); Jumanos (Taovayas or Tawakonis, tribes now known as Wichitas); and many others. All tribes had numerous divisions, and those divisions constantly split, changed, were exterminated, joined other divisions, or changed their names; consequently an Indian name might mean one tribe today, another tomorrow. Also, each tribe had a different name for every other tribe and for itself; and English, Spanish, and French names often were different for the same tribe.

[14] "French" at that time meant French-Canadians.

[14a] *Seduce:* To entice from the right, to draw aside from duty.

dian tribes with more generous presents than the Spanish had offered them. Vial took a fair-sized body of soldiers—unusual for him—and, strangely enough or significantly enough, encountered serious trouble. He was attacked by Indians (whose tribal affiliation he did not know) and lost much property—and that turn of events made it seem that the Spanish fear of American penetration was well founded (as it was).

In the following year, Vial led another and stronger expedition to the Pawnees, but his men deserted, and again he returned unsuccessful.

There is, in the correspondence of the governor of New Mexico, mention of a Vial diary that has not yet turned up, and Vial made two or three other trips for which no journal has been found; undoubtedly there were still others, for there are records of payments made to him for his function as an interpreter—sometimes for one month, sometimes for several months. He could not write Spanish,[15] but wrote rather badly in his native French, and the several documents now preserved are not in his original handwriting but have been translated into Spanish by someone else. Vial's signature, however, appears on the Spanish version of his trip from Santa Fe to St. Louis; probably that was done to legalize the translation, and it may explain why, on one occasion (the completion of his first trip to Santa Fe), he signed his journal some weeks after his arrival.

The Spaniards made one more effort to consolidate their outposts in Texas and New Mexico, but it did not occur until 1808, when they were moved by the expedition of Zebulon Montgomery Pike and alarmed by the increasing frequency of unwelcome American visitations in or toward Santa Fe. At that time, they sent Francisco Amangual, a lieutenant in the service of the king, with two hundred soldiers, from San Antonio to Santa Fe, and back to San Antonio by way of El Paso.[16] They seemed at last to feel the definite need of consolidating communications with Santa Fe and setting up some sort of defense. But they had dallied too long, for the Americans were already on the move.

In that same year of 1808, oddly enough, Vial was issued a license to hunt (trap) on the Missouri, by William Clark, United States Indian agent. That William Clark was the red-headed Clark of the Lewis

[15] See *infra*, Concha's instructions to Vial, May 21, 1792, paragraph 8.

[16] Now Juárez, across the Río Grande from El Paso.

and Clark expedition, which Vial had been ordered to stop only three years before.

In 1814 Vial died in Santa Fe and was buried there. His will, signed in a manner that seems to indicate infirmity, shows that he had some property and a number of small debts, so presumably he had not left Santa Fe more than temporarily. Although his liquid assets were not enough to pay his debts, he left his property to María Manuela Martín, and one wonders if she was the sister or widow of Alejandro Martín, who had often traveled with Vial and who had been an interpreter also for José Mares. In 1795 Vial was said to have some children, but in his will, in 1814, he said that he had never been married. One wonders if perhaps María Manuela was their mother. No children are mentioned in his will.

Pedro Vial and those who kept the various journals that now have a bearing on the genesis of the Santa Fe Trail were not alone in Santa Fe. Indeed, there were times when the drowsy little hamlet seemed to be a bright lodestone attracting explorers from all over America—from the entire world. Seldom were there more than one thousand inhabitants of the mud-walled pueblo, and it was roughly one thousand miles from anywhere, but it seemed that if you could behave yourself and stay out of Spanish jails long enough, you might meet almost anybody in the plaza before the governor's palace.

There were a good many Frenchmen such as Vial, and some Spaniards, and some who may have been either: Alejandro Martín, the Comanche and Kiowa interpreter; the ubiquitous José Chalvert, who offered to work as interpreter at half-price if the governor would let him stay in Santa Fe (and it appears his offer was accepted); Juan Lucero, one of Vial's most faithful companions; the fast-talking Jean Baptiste Lalande and his companion, Laurenzo Durocher, both from St. Louis, who fought a marathon battle with the Spanish authorities for their expenses to Chihuahua, where they had been taken as prisoners.

And there were those Americans who made the penetration from the Mississippi—naturally through Missouri, Arkansas, or Louisiana, but predominantly in the lower region: as early, possibly, as 1785, when the mustang hunter Philip Nolan began to roam through Texas (eventually he lost his ears), and as late as 1804 and thereabouts, when the matter-of-fact Dunbar, the self-promoting Sibley, and the impractical Dr. Hunter contributed their bits to early American history.

Two or three years later, Americans began to swarm across the Great Plains from St. Louis: dissembling Zebulon Montgomery Pike, who professed to have mistaken the Río Grande for the Red River; John McKnight, who was sent to Chihuahua and stayed in jail for ten years, until his own offal was up to his shoulders; his brother Robert, who later made a fortune in the copper mines in Santa Rita in the Chiricahua Apache country of southern New Mexico; James Baird, the fur trapper; and the dumb but fearless Jacques d'Eglise. D'Eglise was the first known traveler up the Missouri to the Mandans; he lost money at everything he tried, but since he was said to have died a wealthy man, perhaps he was smarter than some of his early actions would lead us to think; he was heinously murdered, and the governor of New Mexico got special permission from the Audiencia of Guadalajara to hang his murderers on a public road for two days as a lesson to others.[17] Other Americans included the conniving and indefatigable Auguste Pierre Chouteau and his partner, Jules DeMun; the always-fighting, always-moving, always-aggressive Manuel Lisa, who outsmarted Pike even as Pike was leaving St. Louis with his interesting party on his trip to Santa Fe;[18] and the fabulous, hard-driving Jacques Clamorgan, who startled the Spanish out of their *gente de razón* complacency by making the first profitable trip from the United States to Santa Fe (from the Platte River in 1807), and who in 1808 made a fast return trip across Texas from Chihuahua, reaching Missouri with some of his profits at the age of seventy-five. Clamorgan died in St. Louis in 1814, leaving his property to his four natural children, to none of whose mothers he had ever been married.[19]

There are many men of the Southwest whose stories are yet to be told, and many contemporaries who deserve a small paragraph in the

[17] For the story of Jacques d'Eglise, see Nasatir, "Jacques D'Eglise on the Upper Missouri, 1791–1795," and "Spanish Exploration of the Upper Missouri," *Mississippi Valley Historical Review*, Vol. XXIV, No. 1 (June, 1927), 47–71; and Nasatir, *Before Lewis and Clark*. For his death, see Lansing B. Bloom, "The Death of Jacques D'Eglise," *New Mexico Historical Review*, Vol. II, No. 1 (October, 1927), 367–79.

[18] A full-scale treatment of Manuel Lisa by Professor Nasatir is contained in his edition of W. B. Douglas, *Manuel Lisa*.

[19] Nasatir, "Jacques Clamorgan: Colonial Promoter of the Northern Border of New Spain," *New Mexico Historical Review*, Vol. XVII, No. 2 (April, 1942), 101–12.

Southwestern Book of History. But of them all, perhaps none is better qualified for immortality than Pedro Vial. He was not a man of high position; he was a foreigner in the service of Spain. He did not write Spanish well enough to keep his journals in that language; he did not marry into a good family. But quietly, without fanfare and apparently without any tangible reward (although it was promised to him) except six reales a day, he traveled at will through the wild and savage Southwest, on foot or on horseback, usually without escort. He it was who blazed the trail that was followed a few years later by William Becknell, James Wiley Magoffin, Doctor Connelly, Josiah Gregg, George Frederick Ruxton, and all that great galaxy of prairie men who ramrodded the big wagons through the Osage-Pawnee-Comanche-Apache no-man's-land that later became Kansas; who sold their goods in Santa Fe or Chihuahua or San Juan de los Lagos at four times their cost; who danced at the *fandangos* and knife-fought over the black-eyed girls; and who later married those same girls and settled down. All those men, and all their giant adventures, owed a small debt to Pedro Vial, who had shown that it could be done.

## Contents

✠✠✠

# *Illustrations*



## MAPS

*Pedro Vial and the Roads to Santa Fe*

# I

# *Major Thrusts into New Spain*

In the early sixteenth century the Hapsburgs of Austria had control of the Spanish throne and began manipulations of Spanish destiny typical of a set of professional monarchs. Charles V and Phillip II were kings of Spain during the sixteenth century, and gave Spain an efficient government but involved the country in European problems. They threw Spain into conflict with England on the sea and with France on land, and those two countries later reduced Spain to a second-rate power, for England whipped her in 1588 with the defeat of the Spanish Armada; in the early 1700's the French Bourbon kings took over, and in the early 1800's Napoleon guided Spain's affairs to suit his own desires.

Plagued with inferior kings and looted by political ambitionists, wracked by opportunists under the cloak of religion, hamstrung by an economic system that took everything possible from the people to maintain an increasingly top-heavy aristocracy—Spain for three hundred years looted the New World to stave off liquidation, but the great damage had been done, and the final acts—one of which was the retrocession of Louisiana to France in 1800—were little more than formalities.

Some individuals in the Spanish hierarchy saw the possibilities of the Western Hemisphere on a long-time basis, but Spain officially had a more immediate view: a vision of gold, silver, furs, and taxes. And so there evolved a massive structure designed to rule the New World—not with the objective of putting anything permanent into it, but in such a manner as to get the most out of it. By the middle of the eighteenth century, a large part of the American continents was bogged down in decrees of distant councils whose members had never seen the new hemisphere; by a cumbersome, duplicating, almost authorityless system of government that was primarily concerned with positions and salaries for its own members and with collectible taxation to maintain those members and to satisfy the royal government on the Iberian Peninsula.

Actually, there were six or seven forms of interlocking governmental authority in Mexico: administrative, military, ecclesiastical, judicial, fiscal, political, and royal; there were also secret societies. Any of those agencies or interests might function at any place where it could foresee a chance for success—and profit; in other areas, it might be totally absent. In most cases, there was conflict among different interests within one department—as, for instance, over designating the fund out of which certain expenses would be paid, or the long conflict among many elements in the ecclesiastical division (not the least of which was the turmoil caused by the Jesuit priests). Often, too, the conflict was between different divisions, as between the judicial and the ecclesiastical, or the ecclesiastical and the military, or the military and the judicial.[1]

In its intensive search for revenue, the crown had developed (theoretically) rather complete control of all possible activities. One-fifth of all the gold and silver produced in the New World belonged to the

[1] For a not untypical example of such a quarrel, see France V. Scholes, "The Supply Service of the New Mexican Missions in the Seventeenth Century," *New Mexico Historical Review*, Vol. V, No. 2 (April, 1930), 196ff. The viceroy demanded that officials of the Franciscan order discipline Fray Ramírez, *procurador-general* who had charge of the delivery of supplies to New Mexico every three years; the viceroy gave some of Ramírez' prerogatives to Mendizábal, governor of New Mexico, and Ramírez quarreled with Mendizábal, who was arrested by the Holy Office of the Inquisition. With Ramírez under fire, Fray Posada was appointed *custodio* of New Mexico in Ramírez' place, and also commissary of the Inquisition in that area; Posada went after Mendizábal and then Peñalosa, who succeeded Mendizábal, but Peñalosa retaliated against Posada by arresting him. Ramírez, meantime, was in hot water. The church, the treasury, and the Audiencia were all involved in the scrap, and, before it was over, Spaniards were treated to the spectacle of a three-cornered fight wherein the officials of the Holy Office were trying to prosecute one of their own men, while the man was defended by the Audiencia, and the treasury pleaded for more time so he could adjust his accounts. Mendizábal died in the prison of the Inquisition after one year's time. Ramírez was reprimanded but eventually restored to grace. Posada was tried finally by the Holy Office. Peñalosa was fined and forced to walk the streets as a penitent, then was expelled from the viceroyalty; he had already been expelled from Peru.

king; bars of those metals were stamped with the king's imprint when the tax was paid, and were not legally usable without the stamp. Even after the tax was paid, use of the ingots was subject to restrictions. For instance, the ingots could not legally be exported, nor could they be exchanged for goods from other countries; they could not even be used to buy goods from other provinces of New Spain. Spanish policy was to keep out foreign goods and keep in Spanish gold, to force that gold to flow to Spain. It was quite an attraction to the venturous, and had much to do with building up one of the most extensive contraband trades ever developed.

The crown's need for income, however, was not the only factor in the stifling of trade. The avarice of Spanish merchants played a large part, especially in the prohibition of trade between provinces and foreign countries, and between provinces themselves. The merchants of Chihuahua, for instance, went to the annual fair at Taos, sold their goods at big prices, manipulated the exchange according to their whims,[2] and rode their mules back to Chihuahua with as much as thirty thousand dollars at a time in the saddlebags. This was a bureaucracy, where wealth and power were in the hands of a few, where the people paid or went without.

The sale of playing cards and of gunpowder were licensed. The sale of tobacco was taxed, and its cultivation was restricted to certain areas, and then by permit only, so that the citizens of New Mexico used *punche*, a black weed not the same as "real tobacco" and therefore not subject to taxation[3]—but in 1776 even the planting of *punche* was prohibited.[4]

Vendors of melons and carriers of packed snow from the mountains

[2] Bancroft explains, in *History of Arizona and New Mexico, The Works of Hubert Howe Bancroft*, Vol. XVII, 277–78, one way in which the merchants took advantage of the *peones:* inasmuch as there were no coins, the merchants invented four imaginary currencies: *pesos de plata*, worth 8 reales to the peso; *pesos de proyecto*, 6 reales to the peso; *pesos antiguos*, 4 reales to the peso; and *pesos de la tierra*, 2 reales to the peso. Needless to say, they bought from the natives at pesos of the land, and sold them at pesos of silver when they could. See also R. L. Duffus, *The Santa Fé Trail*, 26–29, and Moorhead, *New Mexico's Royal Road*, 50–51, for discussion of Chihuahua merchants' stifling the trade of New Mexico.

[3] Leslie A. White, "Punche: Tobacco in New Mexico History," *New Mexico Historical Review*, Vol. XVIII, No. 4 (October, 1943), 390ff.

[4] Bancroft, *History of Arizona and New Mexico*, 276.

paid a tax. Almost everything was subject to taxation, and there was taxation upon taxation. Some of the taxes were the *almojarifazgo* (an import duty), the *sisa* (an excise on foods), the *quinto* (the royalty on bullion), the *derecho de fundidor* (which was originally a smelting charge but evolved into the *quinto*), the *alcabala* (a sales tax), the *palmeo* (a trade tax based on the bulk of the goods), the *encomendero* (a capitation tax paid by every male Indian), tithes (collection of which was granted to the crown), the *bula de santa cruzada* (a tax on indulgences), the tax for the *armada de barlovento* (to fight pirates), the *derecho de unión de armas* (to maintain a fleet to protect Atlantic trade), the *mesada* (a tax on appointive offices that evolved into the *media anata,* half of the first year's salary), and many others. High officials regularly sold public offices; the right of collection of the capitation tax on male Indians was sold to the highest bidder; officials confiscated gold and silver that reached Seville and issued annuity certificates for it; they borrowed from estates that had not been probated.

Unavoidably, in the ultimate analysis, taxes came from the common people, for they were the only ones producing. And eventually the entire structure went the way of all governments in which those at the top put their energy into collection rather than production: it went down in bankruptcy.[5]

Strangely enough also—or perhaps by design—Mexico and Louisiana and all the vast territory of Spain in what is now the continental United States was almost without artisans of any kind. Beyond a few miners, smelters, iron workers, leather workers, and jewelers, the New World Spaniards—especially in New Mexico—lived simply and crudely, with almost no tools to do those things that are usual even in a primitive country.

In 1788 Brigadier General Jacobo Ugarte y Loyola urged that artisan instructors be sent to New Mexico,[6] but apparently without result. A few years later, a rather large number of Frenchmen had

[5] An excellent discussion of taxation in New Spain is found in C. H. Haring, *The Spanish Empire in America,* 276–99; see also Bancroft, *ibid.,* 275ff.; and Herbert I. Priestley. "The Reforms of José de Gálvez in New Spain," in Herbert E. Bolton and H. Morse Stephens, eds., *The Pacific Ocean in History,* 349–59; and Lillian Estelle Fisher, *Background of the Revolution for Mexican Independence.*

[6] Bancroft, *ibid.,* 276.

entered New Spain, a good many of them brought by Spanish officials who wanted good cooks and barbers.[7]

In 1812, wrote Pedro Baptista Pino, there was no physician, no surgeon, and no pharmacist for civilians in the entire province of New Mexico; 121 soldiers were served by one "surgeon,"[8] who diagnosed ailments, treated patients, and dispensed medicines, undoubtedly in addition to his surgical work, which at that time probably consisted of wound dressing, bone setting, and blood letting. Apparently the same doctor made trips to other towns and presumably treated civilians, but when he was ill, the nearest medical practitioner was 260 leagues away in Chihuahua.

In 1843, says Josiah Gregg, there was not even a lawyer in New Mexico, and Gregg also notes the primitive state of agriculture, furnishings, and clothing.[9] Cabinet work and the building of homes were done without a real ax to make lumber, to say nothing of augers, drawknives, or saws. Spinning and weaving were almost entirely of wool, and with only the crudest of equipment.

As late as 1856 there was still not a native physician in New Mexico, and few carpenters, blacksmiths, and jewelers.[10] Those who worked with their hands continued to work with their hands, and were satisfied with the status quo, whatever it was. It was this lack of artisanship that created the great demand for goods in the 1820's, and perhaps it was the real reason for the continual attempts at penetration by the French and the Yankees before the days of William Becknell and the mule-trains on the Trail. As far back as 1749, the laws against foreigners had been relaxed to permit the settlement of three Frenchmen, one of whom was a barber, blood-letter, and tailor, and the other two of whom were car-

[7] John Rydjord, *Foreign Interest in the Independence of New Spain*, 136–37.

[8] H. Bailey Carroll and J. Villasana Haggard, *Three New Mexico Chronicles*, 94.

[9] Josiah Gregg, *Commerce of the Prairies* (Max Moorhead, ed.), 142, 143, 146, 148.

[10] W. W. H. Davis, *El Gringo*, 193, 211. Even at a meeting of the Supreme Consejo de Estado in November, 1795, it was said that artisans in Louisiana were "indispensable"; Abraham P. Nasatir and Ernest R. Liljegren, "Materials Relating to the History of the Mississippi Valley, from the Minutas of the Spanish Supreme Council of State, 1787–1797," *Louisiana Historical Quarterly*, Vol. XXI, No. 1 (January, 1938), 57 (hereinafter referred to as "Minutas").

penters.[11] The Spaniards themselves made nothing beyond absolute necessities, and into that vacuum—where scissors were priceless, where a packet of needles would bribe one's way out of prison or would obtain a woman to share one's cell—aggressive nationals probed without let-up.

### *Six Major Threats to Spanish Territory*

When there is a market, somebody will try to supply it, and even though Spain laid down many restrictions, the market was still there, and any attempt of foreigners to supply goods to it was an inherent danger to Spain, for trade always brought taxation, regulation, resentment, and finally conflict. It was a classic pattern: foreigners brought goods, officials taxed them, the foreigners resented it and fought back, the officials tried to enforce the regulations, and finally the foreigners appealed to their own nation for protection. It was a process with which the Spaniards were familiar, and the dangers of which were not often far from their minds. The strange thing is that they did not protect themselves by supplying the market. The solution seems simple at this distance, but in imperial Spain there were no simple answers. Spanish toes would have been stepped on, and so it could not be done. They all went along, each one watching the others feed the tiger, each one hoping that he would somehow escape its jaws.

From the Spanish viewpoint, the first item in the defense of New Mexico was the Indian menace. Whether it was entitled to the importance usually allocated to it in the Spanish problems of defense is not easy to determine. Certainly there were threats and depredations; there were numerous tribes, and most of them were hostile; they harassed the Spaniards from all sides. The Popé Rebellion of 1680 caused the Spaniards to leave northern New Mexico for a few years; even the Spanish missions on the Neches River in Texas were abandoned in 1693 under pressure from the Indians. There were the raids of Cuerno Verde about one hundred years later, and the Indians did not

[11] The three men were Febre, Satren, and Riballo. Vélez (governor of New Mexico) to the viceroy, June 19, 1749, and the viceroy's answer, cited in Bolton, "French Intrusions Into New Mexico, 1749–1752," in Bolton and Stephens, *Pacific Ocean*, 395. Revillagigedo, Gálvez, Bucareli, Croix, and De Mézières all had Frenchmen in their personal service. Rydjord, *Foreign Interest*, 137.

actually quit raiding in New Mexico until the Chiricahua Apaches under Geronimo and Nachez were subdued in 1886.

Spanish documents indicate that the Indians were considered a very serious problem, and on the basis of statistics they were undeniably so. There are many examples: in the five-year period 1744–49 in the village of Pecos, east of Santa Fe, 150 residents were killed by Indians;[12] in 1771–78, in New Vizcaya, 1,963 persons were killed and 68,873 head of stock stolen;[13] in three months in 1777, the Apaches and Comanches killed 61 persons in New Mexico.[14] However, to list the damage is to say that these things happened; it is not to say that they were unavoidable.

Yet the total damage done by Indians was small compared to the casualties of a full-scale war, and it may be wondered if the lack of a determined and consistent Spanish effort was not the major factor in the failure to solve the Indian problem, since the impatient Anglo-Americans moved the same Indians to a position of suppliance in about eighty years—from 1803 to 1886. The Spanish rulers, however, were hampered by red tape, official orders, thorough incompetence, and lack of money—for it was not always easy to find a fund that would stand the expense of an Indian expedition, as Spanish documents repeatedly testify.

In 1727 Rivera, as inspector, decided against the establishment of a presidio in northeast New Mexico because of the cost, and thereby opened up the central region to the Comanches; his decision is quoted later. In 1766–68 Marqués de Rubí made a long inspection, and his engineer, Nicolas de la Fora, drew up a plan for a line of presidios from Texas to California—but it stayed on paper because of the expense.

In 1777 Teodoro de Croix, commandant-general of the Interior Provinces, wrote Antonio María de Bucareli, the viceroy, saying that in New Vizcaya from 1771 to 1776 there had been 1,674 persons murdered and 68,256 head of livestock stolen by the Indians (figures remarkably similar to those reported from New Vizcaya by Governor

[12] Alfred B. Thomas, "Antonio de Bonilla and Spanish Plans for the Defense of New Mexico, 1772–1778," *New Spain and the Anglo-American West*, I, 209.

[13] Thomas, *ibid.*, I, 183.

[14] Thomas, *ibid.*, I, 184; Bolton, "French Intrusions Into New Mexico, 1749–1752," in Bolton and Stevens, *Pacific Ocean in History*, 392.

Felipe Barri). Croix pointed out that the 1,500-mile frontier of northern Mexico was patrolled by fewer than 2,000 soldiers, and asked for 2,000 more to bring the Indians under control,[15] but Bucareli answered that he was shocked at the request, which, he said, would have cost 600,000 pesos annually.[16]

In the meantime, of course, there were some effective campaigns against the Indians: Hugo O'Conor successfully campaigned against the Apaches in 1773 and 1775; Juan Bautista de Anza brought the Comanches to subjection in 1779 and carried out a successful campaign against the Moquis in 1780; and Juan de Ugalde, 1781–83, made three devastating campaigns against the Apaches and closed the Bolson de Mapimí[17] to the Indians. The Indians remained subdued, however, only as long as they knew they would be punished for aggressions. As soon as the official who had whipped them was replaced by a new and naïve man who started a policy of kindness, it was all to do over again.

In 1779, two years after Bucareli had been shocked at Croix's request for 2,000 additional soldiers, the already small sums allotted to defense in northern Mexico were partially diverted to the Spanish war against England, and the Comanche menace grew steadily until 1783.[18] The conclusion is inescapable that Spanish policy as a whole never came to grips with the Indian problem in a manner that had a chance of success.

Rivalry from other nations, however, was a more serious problem.

[15] Measurement indicates that the 1,500-mile frontier followed roughly the present international boundary between the United States and Mexico, and Rubí had so described it in 1766–68—from the Gulf of California to Bahía del Espíritu Santo (Donald E. Worcester, ed., *Instructions for Governing the Interior Provinces of New Spain, 1786, by Bernardo de Gálvez*, 9). La Fora, the engineer with Rubí in 1766, also followed that line (Lawrence Kinnaird, *The Frontiers of New Spain*, 42, note 29—and Kinnaird notes that the line had been established in 1772). Obviously such a line of defense contemplated New Mexico as an outpost area—as indeed Rubí suggested by noting that both Santa Fe and San Antonio were beyond the line, and would require some troops. A loop to include Santa Fe, Taos, and San Antonio would have involved another one thousand miles of frontier. Croix's proposal for 2,000 men envisaged 150 for New Mexico (Alfred B. Thomas, *The Plains Indians and New Mexico*, 55, 212–13); Rubí's plan had suggested 960 soldiers for the frontier, with 160 at Santa Fe and San Antonio (Kinnaird, *Frontiers of New Spain*, 38).

[16] Alfred B. Thomas, *Teodoro de Croix*, 25–30.

[17] An unhabited desert occupying the eastern half of the state of Chihuahua and the western half of Coahuila.

[18] Alfred B. Thomas, *Forgotten Frontiers*, 71.

The first period of international rivalry for the trade of New Mexico and northern Mexico started about 1714 with the activities of Louis Juchereau de St. Denis, known at St. Denis the Elder, and was characterized by several attempts of the French to reach Santa Fe from Lower Louisiana. Some of those attempts were motivated by thoughts of profit, but many also were inspired by the ambitions of imperial France. Nearly all the thrusts were aimed at Santa Fe, and some of them reached that town, but no commercial relations were established, and the threat ended technically in 1763 when Louisiana became Spanish in name. Interestingly enough, however, Spaniards in the Southwest (New Mexico, Texas, and present Chihuahua) still considered the French a threat, and directed considerable worry toward Louisiana, which was a huge Spanish colony but not one to be trusted.[19] They knew that entrance might be made from Natchitoches, near the Louisiana-Texas border, or up the Red or Arkansas River; and from the Missouri River or one of its many tributaries: the Osage, the Republican, the Platte, the Yellowstone, and others. The two points from which a thrust might start were New Orleans in Lower Louisiana and St. Louis in Upper Louisiana (or Spanish Illinois). The two principal routes were considered to be the Red and the Missouri, with the Arkansas a sort of boundary line between New Mexico and the Illinois country.

The Spanish fears were not totally unjustified, for the French Revolution occurred in 1789, and only four years later a plot was afoot, directed toward the Southwest, involving Citizen Genêt of France and George Rogers Clark of the United States.

The second threat was from the British. Although this threat had been present for some time, it gained new life in 1763, when the British took Canada from the French, and continued rather actively until 1783, when the British relinquished their technical claim to the Ohio River area in Ohio and Pennsylvania and to all the land up to the Mississippi River. However, the British continued to threaten Louisiana through Prairie du Chien in Wisconsin, via the St. Peter's and Des Moines rivers, and from posts on the Missouri and even on the Platte. They entered Texas and went up the Red or Arkansas River in Lower Louisiana; they had a number of traders in East Texas and

[19] In spite of the fact that Rubí, after his inspection trip of 1766–68, recommended a chain of trading centers at Natchitoches, Arkansas Post, Santa Fe, and Taos.

Arkansas in that period, and, considering the well-known British habit of success, they were a constant threat.

Coming from Canada, the Hudson's Bay Company and the North West Company (both British) were firmly established in the Mandan area—Dakota and western Minnesota. During the Nootka Sound controversy on the northwest coast in 1790–91, the Spaniards feared British invasion of Illinois (from British posts in the Canadian Great Lakes area), and subsequent British-United States pressure—but the Nootka trouble was settled without its breaking out in Louisiana.[20]

The American threat from the Missouri River, 1783–1807, was more serious. This might be called the Lewis and Clark period, and the most determined American efforts originated in St. Louis, then a small town near the confluence of the Missouri and the Mississippi that acted as outfitting point and wholesaling center for the great Missouri River country. St. Louis was conveniently situated to receive goods shipped down the Ohio River from Pittsburgh, a historic shipping point; also, it was accessible to Kentucky and the great flood of pioneers who had moved into Kentucky from Virginia but were already restless again.

This era of movements toward Santa Fe received great impetus from the Lewis and Clark expedition, and it is worth noting that the Spaniards had started saying back in the 1790's that an American expedition was intended to do exactly that: open the road to Santa Fe; they continued to say it when the expedition got under way, but they did not take positive action to stop it.

Although this entrance was an American penetration, until after Lewis and Clark's trip most of those who went into Spanish territory from the Missouri had French names: Clamorgan, the Chouteaus, D'Eglise, Chalvert, Lelande, Durocher, and others. Nevertheless, both Illinois and Louisiana were American territories after 1803, and all such expeditions traveled under American sponsorship or protection.

From the lower Mississippi after 1783 the *entrada* was substantially Anglo-American, springing from Kentucky, Tennessee, and Nat-

[20] The best discussion of this affair is W. R. Manning, "The Nootka Sound Controversy," in American Historical Association *Annual Report for 1904*, 279–478; for its relation to Louisiana, see Arthur P. Whitaker, *The Spanish-American Frontier, 1783–1795*, chap. X.

chez, Mississippi, and after 1803 starting from New Orleans and Natchitoches. Philip Nolan initiated it by going into Texas, presumably to gather mustangs; Nolan's base was Natchez, and before long he made contact in Nacogdoches with William Barr, an Anglo-American merchant who had become a naturalized Spanish citizen.[21] Nolan was followed by Sibley and his peripatetic activities as Indian agent, and by two groups traveling at the instance of President Jefferson himself: the Freeman and Dunbar parties. None of those parties established trade between Santa Fe and New Orleans, but they caused the Spaniards a great deal of anxiety.

From about 1807 to 1821, there flourished a fifth period that might be called the Pike era. Actually it was an extension of the Lewis and Clark period, but it received great impetus from Pike's explorations and his copious writings, and the Spaniards gave it unwitting publicity with their traditional fumbling methods: they threw many of the venturesome Americans into the royal hoosegow—James Purcell, Jacques Clamorgan, and the members of the famous McKnight party; McLanahan, Baird, and Sprague; Chouteau and De Mun; and David Meriwether, who later became territorial governor of New Mexico.

As had happened before, and has happened since, such imprisonment did not aid the Spaniards, but created resentment and antagonism in the United States and drew the attention of more and more persons to their adobe-hutted jewel, Santa Fe. Perhaps the Spaniards should have been more considerate—but it is hard to say. The likelihood is that any move they might have made would have been wrong.

Santa Fe, aside from itself offering a market for a large quantity of goods, also was the gateway to northern Mexico, down what Max Moorhead calls the Chihuahua Trail.[22] New Mexico itself had a population, in that period, of something like forty thousand persons,[23] largely living along the Río Grande from Taos to El Paso; from El Paso to the south another three hundred miles (six hundred from Santa Fe) was Chihuahua, the center of a vast area in which the people were hungry for all kinds of goods. South of Chihuahua along the trail to

[21] Barr in 1798 became associated with Peter Samuel Davenport in a firm that later became famous as Barr & Davenport.

[22] Moorhead, *New Mexico's Royal Road*, 3.

[23] Bancroft, *History of Arizona and New Mexico*, 342.

the capital of New Spain were Durango, Zacatecas, San Luis Potosí, Guanajuato, and Querétaro, and at the end was Mexico City. That huge area grew progressively denser in population toward the south, and it likewise was a big market—but governmental regulations were more strictly enforced as one approached the capital.

It is interesting to speculate on the outcome if the rulers of Spain had been more farsighted, had been willing to make as strong an effort to put something into the New World—goods—as they were to take gold and silver out of it. If they had supplied their own market, the Americans would have had little reason to go into Spanish territory.

Also from the Missouri River—for the third time—were the Anglo-Americans from 1821 to 1846. The year 1821 ended the probing era, for Mexico revolted from the Spanish crown and established a new ruling hierarchy. In the first flush of their new power, the Mexicans indicated friendliness toward the Americans, and in that year William Becknell took his mules from Boone's Lick, Missouri, to Santa Fe, loaded with goods. He got through the Comanches, reached Santa Fe and sold his goods, survived the *fandangos,* said good-by to the black-eyed girls, and went back to Independence. There the great, booted, bearded men threw rawhide bags of silver pesos into the streets and cut them open with axes, and let the big silver doubloons scatter carelessly in the mud. They struck a spark that traveled through the United States like wildfire and burned for twenty-five years—the Santa Fe Trail era that had been first prepared for by Pedro Vial.

In that winter of 1821–22 the Santa Fe Trail was a commercial success; money was brought back, and the thrill of adventure and the lure of a foreign land drew men from all over the United States—from a country newspaper in Georgia, from a broker's house on Wall Street. In the summer of 1822, Becknell was only one of many who went down the trail, but Becknell that time had wagons that carried a great deal more goods and launched the real commercial phase of the Santa Fe Trail.

A large number of Anglo-American merchants—Albert Speyer, Kelly, Dr. Connelly (who later became territorial governor of New Mexico), the Aulls, Solomon Houck, and many others—and a number of Chihuahueños made a business of wagon-training between Chihuahua and St. Louis (or Independence), and a rather large number of Anglo-

Americans settled in Chihuahua, went into business, married Mexican girls, and took out citizenship papers. Some of the more venturesome took their goods almost to Mexico City, looking for the highest dollar.

Many others, known and unknown, went down the trail to fame and fortune. In 1831 it was Josiah Gregg, who wrote a great textbook on the Santa Fe trade; in 1844, on the eve of the trail's end, it was Josiah Webb, who left a valuable book on those last few years; and in between were the Magoffins and the Corderos and the Bents, and Chavez and Caldwell and Olivarez, and all the little men who made no records but left their scalps and their lives beside the stagnant, green-scummed water-holes. The greatest market in the world plus the most venturesome road plus the most restless men—these combined to keep the Santa Fe Trail the greatest highway known to western history until Kearny and his Army of the West in 1846 followed that same trail, entered Santa Fe, used Philip St. George Cooke and James Wiley Magoffin to take New Mexico from Armijo without firing a shot, and went on to California.

Nearly all the North American continent between Mexico and Canada and west of the Louisiana Purchase had now come under the rifle, ax, and lariat of the restless Anglo-American pioneer, and Spain's fumbling days were over, ended as inauspiciously as they had started more than three hundred years before. From the wild tales of Marcos de Niza, who had seemed somehow to see into the bedrooms of the Zuñi Indians from miles away, to the defection of the bombastic Armijo, who left Santa Fe in the face of Kearny's army in such great harassment that he was able to take seven wagonloads of precious cotton goods with him—from Niza to Armijo was three centuries during which the Spaniards had not made much progress. The American movement had begun with the adventure of John Peyton in 1773 and had been continued by John Purcell in 1805. Now, by 1846, the Americans had taken over, and the aggressive Anglos marched on westward to their destiny.

# II

# *The Indian Menace*

One of the greatest barriers to Spanish domination of the American Southwest—and one not always easy to comprehend—was the Indian threat.[1] It is not to be thought of as an organized attack, or even as organized opposition, for the Indians were extreme individualists and not subject to more than a suggestion of concerted effort. It is sometimes astonishing that the Spaniards did not send out a war party and wipe them out and get rid of that threat. Certainly the Spaniards had guides and interpreters who knew the Indians. The fact is, however, that seldom did the governor of New Mexico have over 150 soldiers at his command to patrol the entire New Mexico frontier, which reached far into Arizona, Colorado, Kansas, Texas, and Oklahoma.

On rare occasions the Spaniards did carry out such a campaign—under O'Conor, Croix, and Anza, to name three—but such campaigns were never followed up by succeeding officials, and, as far as the Indians were concerned, were chastisements to be respected only as long as they were forthcoming.

Perhaps one reason for the Spanish ineptness in handling the Indian problem lies in the reason for the Spanish merchants' discouragement of trade between the province of New Mexico and any other province or nation: avarice. Perhaps the Spaniards did not want to rid New Mexico of the Indian menace, for the Indians went to the Taos fair and traded furs for trinkets, and it seems that most of the Indians

[1] For discussions on the earlier Indians, see France V. Scholes; on the Navahos, see Frank D. Reeve; on the Apaches, see Donald Worcester; for a summary of Indian activities in the seventeenth century, see Jack Forbes, *Apache, Navaho, and Spaniard.*

made periodic trips to the settlements to conduct fairs of their own. The Indians were easily cheated, so why chase them too far away?

Throughout the seventeenth century, the Apaches encircled what is now, roughly, the state of New Mexico: Navahos on the northwest, Cuartelejos and Jicarillas (and others) on the northeast, Faraones and others on the east, Mescaleros on the southeast, and Chiricahuas on the southwest. They caused trouble from the time Oñate led his settlers along the del Norte in 1598.

During the 1600's an unforeseen factor entered into the relations between the Spaniards and the Indians, and affected Oñate's attempt to colonize New Mexico. Droughts were frequent in that region, and during a period of drought the Spaniards took food and supplies from the Indians (whose supplies were scanty anyway). Naturally the Indians resisted those levies but could hardly stop them. In 1665, however, the entire region suffered from a severe and prolonged drought, and the Apaches' scanty yield of corn became much scantier. The Apaches raided the Pueblos, who were sedentary and agricultural and usually had corn; then, when the Pueblos' supplies were gone, the Apaches raided the Spaniards. Altogether, it was a ten-year series of raids that caused great damage to the Spaniards.

At some time after 1664 Juan de Archuleta led one of the first Spanish expeditions into Colorado when he took a force of soldiers to El Cuartelejo, an Apache village in southeastern Colorado or western Kansas, to bring back Pueblo Indians who had fled from the raids of the Apaches and the levies of the Spaniards. A short time later the drought and the oppression from the Spaniards and Apaches inspired the Popé Rebellion of the Pueblo Indians in 1680, which forced the Spaniards to retire from central and northern New Mexico.

Governor Diego de Vargas reconquered the province in 1692, and in 1693 Spain abandoned her Texas settlements—in unrelated moves. Other developments accompanied or followed Vargas' reconquest, however, for when Spain reconquered New Mexico, the Comanches emerged on the Plains, and almost simultaneously the French appeared in the northeast. In 1694 it was said that the Navahos were accustomed to raid the Pawnees and French, so it seems the French (from Canada) were along the Missouri River and the Platte River that early; they had been among the Osages and Missouris in 1694.

Three years later, in 1697, the report was that the French and Pawnees had severely defeated the Navahos and apparently put a permanent end to their raiding in western Kansas and perhaps Nebraska. The Navahos did not hear about that, however, and made a highly successful retaliatory raid the following year—but that seems to be their last big appearance in that area.

In 1696 Governor Vargas made the second sizable New Mexican expedition among the Indians when he pursued some Taos and Picuris who had fled to join the Apaches—possibly the same ones who had been pursued by Archuleta. Vargas captured eighty-four of the party and charitably gave them out as servants to his officers.

In 1702 Governor Pedro Rodríguez Cuberó made a successful campaign against the Faraones. The Navahos broke the peace that year on the other side of Santa Fe, and Cuberó went after them with a party of soldiers, but the Navaho chief stopped him by making amends. Two years later Cuberó died while chasing the Faraones again.

In 1706 Juan de Ulibarrí made the third Spanish trip to El Cuartelejo to return to New Mexico some rebellious Pueblos of Taos and some Picuris; the Spaniards were slow to take a hint.

From 1702 until 1719 New Mexican Spaniards were severely raided by the Navahos, eastern Apaches, Utes, and Comanches; and those tribes were treated to equally devastating punitive raids by the Spaniards. In 1705 Roque de Madrid went northwest against the Navahos and defeated them severely, but the Navahos carried out many raids from 1708 to 1710. They attacked Spanish settlements again in 1714, and Madrid again ravaged their country.

The Utes had been friendly to the Spaniards until sometime after 1694 and before 1706, when their attitude changed and they became allied with the Comanches; the two tribes appeared in northern New Mexico and in 1706 made a combined attack on the Jicarillas. They continued to be allies until 1747.

Between 1707 and 1712 the Utes and Comanches sought peace. In 1716 they raided Taos, and were punished by Captain Serna; in 1717 they raided the Jicarillas; in 1719 they raided Taos and Cochití. Governor Valverde y Cosio led another big expedition to El Cuartelejo to punish them—and also to determine the location of the French to the northeast.

In 1712 Governor Juan Ignacio Flores Mogollón went against the Faraones, and again in 1714 Captain Antonio Valverde y Cosio went against them, but in 1715 the Faraones made severe attacks on the Picuris and Taos pueblos—which probably explains why the Taos and Picuris were constantly retreating. After the 1715 attacks, Juan Paez Hurtado went after the Faraones, but without success.

There were, of course, many smaller raids, which increased in number and violence as the bigger and better-organized war parties carried out their extensive raids on the towns. It was not unusual, in the larger raids, for three or four hundred Indians to descend on a town and kill or carry off several hundred head of livestock, and sometimes a large number of New Mexican captives (women and children).[2]

In 1719 the Comanches and Utes harassed the Apaches, but the Spaniards were worrying about the French, and it was in 1720 that Pedro de Villasur was sent to the northeast with a substantial force to locate the French traders on the Platte; he was accompanied by Jean de l'Archevêque, who had been with the men who murdered La Salle. Villasur's force was massacred on the Platte by the Pawnees with the advice and assistance of some Frenchmen; out of forty-two Spanish soldiers, thirty were killed, including Villasur and L'Archevêque.

In the same year a presidio was ordered established at El Cuartelejo, but the New Mexicans wanted it closer, at Jicarilla.[3]

In 1726 Rivera inspected New Mexico and recommended against the establishment of a presidio among the Jicarillas; instead, he suggested the Jicarillas be moved to Taos to save them from attack by the Comanches. The viceroy ordered his recommendation carried out because Rivera said that the expense of a presidio would be too great.[4] The removal, however, had an effect that Rivera had not anticipated: it created a wide-open avenue for the Comanches into the central area

[2] These items are told in some detail by Thomas, *After Coronado.*

[3] Jicarilla or La Jicarilla apparently was a Jicarilla village thirty-seven leagues (one hundred miles) northeast of Taos. Bancroft, *History of Arizona and New Mexico*, 229. Cuartelejo or El Cuartelejo, says *Kansas Historical Collections*, Vol. VI (1900), 126–27, is shown by excavations to be in the Beaver Creek valley in Scott County, Kansas, about twelve miles north of Scott City, or about two hundred miles east by north of Pueblo, Colorado; however, it is placed by Henri Folmer about fifty miles east of present Pueblo (*Franco-Spanish Rivalry in North America, 1524–1763*, 281).

[4] Rivera said: "If every proposal for the founding of a presidio were acceded to, the treasury of Midas would not suffice." Thomas, *The Plains Indians*, 13.

of New Mexico. In 1727 there were Frenchmen at El Cuartelejo, but from that time until 1739 the Frenchmen were conspicuous by their absence because the Comanches prevented their traveling there; the Comanches did not want French rifles in Apache hands. The French, of course, were well occupied with the Fox Indians in the Wisconsin area, and perhaps did not push the Comanches as hard as they might have.

The Comanches had made big medicine with Bourgmont in 1724, but, being Comanches, they did not stay softened up, and they would not let the French go through their country to other tribes because they did not want the other tribes to get firearms. The Comanches were particularly aggressive during that period. In 1725–45 they fought the Jumanos and the French, the Apaches (especially the Jicarillas), and the Pueblos. Inasmuch as the Spaniards had withdrawn their support of the Jicarillas and would not let them have firearms, the Apaches were well defeated by the Comanches by 1739, and withdrew from northeastern New Mexico, thus eliminating the Spaniard's buffer against the Comanches. During that period, the French, though they did not make serious efforts to enter Spanish territory, represented a threat because of their selling of guns to the Indians. The Comanches, on the other hand, drove the Kansas Plains Indians south to prevent their getting rifles, and at the same time drove the Jicarillas south, opening up the eastern frontier of New Mexico from Albuquerque north, to their own terrific raids of the 1740's, which literally depopulated the frontier.

In 1739 the Mallet brothers broke through the Comanche barrier, but in the 1740's the Comanches raided the Indians in eastern New Mexico and the Spanish New Mexicans, causing a general exodus from the north.

In 1746 the French made a treaty with the Comanches and Jumanos, which to a certain extent cleared the way for French traders.

The Comanches were not idle, however, for, in the period 1744–49, they raided Pecos and killed 150 Spaniards; then Governor Codallos with 500 men overtook them beyond Abiquiú and killed 107, captured 206, and took 1,000 horses.[5] The next year a presidio was again urged at the Jicarilla site, but in that same year the Comanches were

[5] Bancroft, *History of Arizona and New Mexico*, 249.

admitted to the Taos fair; and by April, 1749, the Utes and Comanches were deadly enemies—perhaps because the Apaches, who had been their common enemy, were no longer there. In that year Bernardo de Bustamente y Tagle pursued the Comanches down the Arkansas to the Jumano villages in Oklahoma. By 1750 the Comanches and Jumanos were waging cruel attacks against all the tribes east and southeast of Santa Fe: Carlanas, Palomas, Chilpaines, Natagées, and Faraones. After 1750 the Utes and Apaches joined forces against the Comanches.

In 1751, three hundred Comanches attacked Galisteo after the Taos fair; Tomás Velez Cachupín overtook them near the Arkansas, set fire to the woods, and killed 101 and captured 44.[6] Thereafter, garrisons were established at Pecos and Galisteo, for both towns were on the eastern frontier of New Mexico and were bearing the brunt of Comanche attacks.

In 1760 the Comanches became overly bold; they raided Taos, killed all the men, and carried off fifty women, and in 1761 they came back to trade as if nothing had happened! They were refused admission to the fair, but in December they returned again and were so contrite that they offered to give up seven of their captives if the Spaniards would allow them to trade. But Governor Manuel Portillo Urrisola finally got his back up and took out after them, and killed, he said, four hundred of them.[7] In 1762 the Comanches put their marks on a peace treaty, and for a while were only moderately destructive.

In 1766 and 1767 the Marqués de Rubí was sent to make an inspection of the northern frontier, accompanied by Nicolás de la Fora, an engineer. After an extensive tour, Rubí recommended that the northern posts be arranged to form a cordon from La Bahía in Texas to the Gulf of California in the west, and he made a number of specific recommendations for Texas (including removal of the capital to San Antonio, and removal of the settlers to that area). His report went to the king,

[6] Cachupín to Revillagigedo, Santa Fe, Nov. 27, 1751. Thomas prints this report in *The Plains Indians*, 67–76, and cites it in Mexico, Archivo General y Público de la Nación, Sección de Provincias Internas (hereafter referred to as Provincias Internas), Vol. 102. Bolton lists reports by Cachupín in his *Guide*, but apparently includes this one with others dated ten years later. See also Bancroft, *History of Arizona and New Mexico*, 256; Urrisola, Santa Fe, June 27, 1762, in Provincias Internas, Vol. 161, No. 34.

[7] Bancroft, *ibid.*, 257.

and in 1772 many of his recommendations were adopted. The most noteworthy feature, as far as New Mexico was concerned, was that Santa Fe remained far outside the defensive cordon.

Rubí also urged peace with the Norteños (which would include the Comanches). Santa Fe still had its 1762 treaty with those Indians, but in 1771 Governor Mendinueta signed another treaty with them. He should have known better. In 1773 the Comanches made a severe raid on El Valle, fifteen leagues from Santa Fe; in 1774 they made five raids on Spanish settlements, including one at Pecos and two at Albuquerque.[8] Altogether there were one thousand Comanches invading the Chama district, but in August they came to the Taos fair as if nothing had happened and were permitted to return captives for ransom and to sell livestock. In September, Governor Mendinueta, with 60 men, killed 250 Comanches.

But the Indians were just getting warmed up. During the year 1775 the Comanches, Gileños, and Navahos raided at will. Several hundred Comanches attacked Taos (without success, for once); others killed thirty-three Pueblo Indians, were pursued, but escaped; Comanches invaded Pecos; four hundred Comanches attacked Galisteo but were repulsed; the Gileños raided Laguna, Belem, and Tomé; the Navahos raided six times. So many mares were stolen that the Spaniards could not breed more horses.

In 1777, when continued colonization of the province was beginning to appear uncertain, there were fifteen Comanche and Apache raids, but the number of casualties decreased. In one raid twenty-three persons were killed; in another, four hundred Comanches killed fourteen —but there was an average of four Spanish casualties per raid. Commandant-General Teodoro de Croix of the Interior Provinces sent thirty-eight lightly armed soldiers, one sergeant, and a standard bearer to New Mexico while he was trying to work out a system of defense.

In 1778 the Comanches were led by the great Chief Cuerno Verde, who hated the Spaniards because his father had been killed by them. He raided settlements with impunity; he was cruel, insolent, and seemingly invincible. In one series of raids the Comanches killed or captured 127 persons.[9] But Cuerno Verde was about to meet a Spaniard

[8] Thomas, *Forgotten Frontiers*, 61–62.

[9] Thomas, *Teodoro de Croix*, 111.

who was more than a match for him: Juan Bautista de Anza, who had become governor of New Mexico under the new system established by Croix.

Anza did not fool with the Indians; he gathered a force of men and went after Cuerno Verde. They had a great battle that the Spaniards won and in which they took a great deal of loot—but not Cuerno Verde. Anza kept after him, however, and, in a day-long battle near Greenhorn Peak, Colorado, Cuerno Verde and his oldest son, four other Comanche chiefs, and an Indian priest (medicine man?) who had preached that he was immortal, were slain. Anza was promoted to colonel—and properly so, for he had the one thing the Comanches respected: strength.

In 1785, four hundred Comanches sought peace at Taos, but Anza declined to grant it until all the Comanches were in agreement. In 1786 a great Comanche council was held on the Arkansas River at Casa de Palo. Ecueracapa, who had succeeded Cuerno Verde as chief of the Comanche tribes, went to Santa Fe and signed a Comanche-Ute peace pact that was to last a generation. Anza had shown what could be done with fortitude and resolution.

The Spaniards suffered also from tribes not considered inhabitants of the New Mexico area. In 1787 a party of 250 Piegan warriors traveled from near the Canadian border and captured a pack train of silver and a large number of horses and mules from the Black Men (Spaniards).[10] It is quite a stretch from the Upper Montana Rockies to the Chiricahua Mountains.

Perhaps that report makes a little more credible the apparent fact that the Osages, normally considered residents of the Missouri-Arkansas area, raided Santa Fe in 1790.[11] The Osages, of course, ranged over a wide territory, and sometimes shifted their home area a great distance. In July, 1770, according to De Mézières, the Osages, the Ishmaelites of the plains, were subjected to so much pressure that they moved their home camping ground from its ancient location to an area "far distant" on the Arkansas River. Inferences from other documents make the distance 250 leagues. The airline distance from Ar-

[10] J. B. Tyrrell (ed.), *David Thompson's Narrative of His Explorations in Western America, 1784–1812*, 370–71.

[11] Peyroux to Miró, April 7, 1790, in Papeles de Cuba, leg. 203.

kansas Post to the point where the Arkansas River crosses the Colorado state line is approximately seven hundred miles—barely more than 250 leagues, so it would seem that for a while, at least, the Big Osages may have lived in proximity to New Mexico (though most of the Osages lived near St. Louis). In 1782 or 1783 the Osages routed a caravan guarded by troops and "brought to their nation ingots of silver and mules, and committed murders and insults of all sorts continually on these rivers."[12] Therefore, it is not difficult to believe the report of Peyroux, commandant at Ste. Geneviève, that, in 1790, the "Osages carried off 800 horses from Santa Fe,"[13] though it is not clear just how Peyroux learned of the raid.

Six months later, the governor of Louisiana spoke of the Osages in more general terms: "The said nation [Osage] is extremely unfaithful . . . various incursions against the establishments of Santa Fe, capital of the kingdom of New Mexico."[14] It is not a matter of wonder that Louisiana officials continued to receive news of the Osages, because those Indians went regularly to St. Louis to get their annual presents.

After 1790 there are no more reports of the Osages around Santa Fe, but there is a suggestion-after-the-fact that the Osages were not strangers in New Mexico, for Delassus, the former governor of Louisiana who was staying in St. Louis as an observer after the Americans took over, wrote that two Osages related that "several years ago a party from their nation went to Mexico and surprised a caravan; that the troop submitted and they pillaged horses and mules loaded with that *white metal* (silver) (the deed is verified as your Excellency knows" [italic in document].[15] (Apparently there had been some previous report of the same event.)

After 1790, however, the Spanish policy was directed away from the Indians and toward the Americans, for the Spaniards recognized

[12] De Lassus to Salcedo, St. Louis, May 13, 1802, in Papeles de Cuba, leg. 77.

[13] Peyroux de la Coudrenière to Monsieur [Miró], Ste. Geneviève, April 7, 1790, in Seville, Archivo General de Indias, Sección, Papeles de Cuba (hereafter cited as Papeles de Cuba), leg. 203. The reply is dated May 10, 1790: "Manuel Perez . . . also informs me [of the bad effects of the Osages]."

[14] Miró to Las Casas, New Orleans, October 6, 1790, in Papeles de Cuba, 1440.

[15] Delassus to Casa Calvo, Confidential, St. Louis, August 10, 1804, in Papeles de Cuba, leg. 141; printed in Nasatir, *Before Lewis and Clark*, II, 744–45.

the inherent threat and turned their attention to the Missouri River. In 1794 Spain even tried to instigate Indian resistance against the Americans by giving some arms to the Taovayas, Tawakonis, Comanches, and others, with appropriate suggestions as to where those arms might be directed. It was a radical departure for the Spaniards, but it will be observed that they were still cautious: they gave the Indians *some* arms.[16]

A few years after 1790, some of the Choctaws, pushed out of their ancestral lands east of the Mississippi, were living in Louisiana and caused considerable trouble among the Indians around Nacogdoches, until the Spaniards feared that the British and Americans were trying to alienate the Choctaws from the Spaniards.[17]

And west of Santa Fe, as late as 1805, Lt. Antonio Narbona severely punished the Navahos in Chelly Canyon, killing "94 bucks" and taking a number of women and children as prisoners.[18]

It is evident from this recital, which is little more than a skeleton outline, that until the time of Pedro Vial, Indians of various tribal affiliations had been harassing the Spaniards in New Mexico for approximately two hundred years. During the same time, some of the other provinces of northern Mexico were punished by the Indians more severely and with even more impunity. Certainly if New Mexico's experience is typical, it seems that most Spanish officials handled the Indian problem with all the understanding and efficiency of complete amateurs at the game of war and Indian-fighting.

Teodoro de Croix himself said: "I do not know whether the greatest enemy of them [the provinces] is the savage Indians or the impression which conjectural opinion and mistaken reports have made."[19]

Determined punitive raids by the Spaniards in a particular area generally brought peace for several years, but it was fantastic to expect two hundred (at the most) soldiers to protect such a large area as New

[16] Elizabeth Ann Harper, "The Taovayas Indians in Frontier Trade and Diplomacy, 1779–1835," *Panhandle-Plains Historical Review*, Vol. XXVI (1953), 14.

[17] Nava to Godoy, No. 17, Chihuahua, September 5, 1797, in Seville, Archivo General de Indias, Sección, Papeles de Estado, Mexico, leg. 37 (hereafter cited as Estado, México).

[18] Bancroft, *History of Arizona and New Mexico*, 285.

[19] Croix to Galvez, No. 105, Confidential, Durango, October 11, 1777; quoted in Thomas, *Teodoro de Croix*, 30.

Mexico, to patrol 1,600 miles of border (one man for every eight miles). On occasions when a governor did set out to punish the Indians with six hundred men, most of those six hundred were armed settlers and friendly Indians, but several commanders showed that such a force could be effective.

What, then, was the real difficulty? Perhaps two words can describe it: stupidity and paternalism. A new governor would come in and would observe that the Indians were well in hand, and would then embark on a policy of sweetness and kindness. If it happened—as it sometimes did—that the viceroy was trying to save a few pesos for whatever viceroys saved them for, then it did not take the Indians more than a few months to ascertain that they had a live one in front of them.

When things became extremely bad, the viceroy would send an inspector, and the inspector, knowing what the viceroy wanted to hear, let him hear it. More than once the governor asked for firearms to fight with and horses to ride, and received 10 per cent of his needs or none at all.

Seldom, in Indian warfare, were Spanish casualties very big, and never did North American Indians carry out any sort of unified or concentrated campaign against the whites. Not even the hate-filled Cuerno Verde or the great Ecueracapa, or, a hundred years later, Gall or Crazy Horse visualized any sort of campaign in terms of more than a single raid. The Indians were not even capable of waging guerrilla warfare; they were magnificent at guerrilla tactics, but not at anything that resembled a sustained drive.

The Indian was an individual strange to Caucasians. He was the world's greatest individualist—so individualistic that he lacked the concept of working with others, of depending on his fellows. For that reason, Indians almost never made anything resembling a frontal attack.

He was almost wholly free in many of the aspects of life—love, marriage, even murder—but he was bound by an incredibly vast and intricate network of admonitions, superstitions, fears, taboos, and egotistical standards. He was the supreme individualist, but in the very act of being so, he found himself bound by standards of conformity unknown to the cultured person of today. He might kill his wife for adultery with comparative impunity, but not the man involved; from him he had to demand and collect payment of property —usually horses—not because he had been injured, but because his standing as a man required it.

When the Indian violated a taboo, it was not his medicine that killed him for violating a rule that he himself had invented, but his knowledge that he had violated it, and his childish belief that he would be punished.

Against such an enemy, it seems that even a half-hearted attempt would prevail. Probably three hundred soldiers with reasonably determined leadership would have secured all the borders of New Mexico—but the soldiers would have had to remain alert.

Short-sightedness, avarice, paternalism, confusion of responsibility, absence of moral integrity, and a large portion of stupidity—all those played an important part in Spain's futility in New Mexico; all contributed to the invasions that teased New Mexico for hundreds of years. With that kind of defense, it is no wonder that the Indian threat dominated New Mexican thinking for so long.

It seems significant that the final conquest of New Mexico was accomplished by Kearny without the firing of a single shot.

# III

# *Early French Intrusions*

For one hundred and forty-five years the Spaniards had New Mexico to themselves. The first European in the area was Alvar Núñez Cabeza de Vaca, who was shipwrecked on the Texas coast and spent eight years reaching the Pacific Ocean. When he arrived at Culiacán in 1536 he brought tales of the gold and precious stones of Quivira, and, in consequence, in 1540 Francisco Vásquez de Coronado set out with several hundred young seekers of fortune, and assorted women, children, Indians, and Negro slaves to bring the natives of the Southwest into the fold of Roman Catholicism and under the protective aegis of his Holy Catholic Caesarian Majesty, Charles V.

Coronado's expedition found little gold, but he and his men discovered some interesting geographical features such as the Grand Canyon and the Llano Estacado, as well as a few zoological curiosities: the wild turkey, the prairie dog, and the buffalo. Coronado failed to find the lords who were transported in forty-oared boats and who fanned themselves under trees hung with tinkling golden bells and performed their ablutions with golden sweat-scrapers—but hardly anybody suspected that Quivira was a myth.

Coronado's report discouraged exploration for several decades, but the enthusiasm for golden treasure remained and led to a new series of explorations. In 1581 (Rodríguez), in 1582 (Espejo), in 1590 (Sosa), and in 1594 (Leyva and Humaña) Spanish expeditions went into New Mexico.

In 1598 Juan de Oñate, of an illustrious family and married to a granddaughter of Montezuma, went north to colonize New Mexico, but he encountered much difficulty. He was too harsh toward the Indians, and scanty rainfall resulted in a severe shortage of food supplies. The trouble with the Indians, it appears, was largely of Oñate's own making. On one occasion Oñate's men levied on the Indians at Ácoma but were resisted. When finally some eighty male Indians were captured, Oñate ordered their right feet cut off in punishment and sentenced each man to twenty years' servitude. Forced to resign, Oñate left New Mexico in April or May, 1608, as soon as his successor became established. Oñate was tried and found guilty of a number of charges arising from his conduct of the New Mexican venture, ranging from implied unnecessary execution of Indians and one army officer to concubinage with army women, and was perpetually exiled from New Mexico and fined four thousand ducats. Oñate seems to have tried diligently for the rest of his life to have his crimes expunged from the record—apparently with some success.

The Spaniards during this time settled along the Río Grande, which runs north and south through the middle of New Mexico, and the center of population has always been in the north central area, in the region of Santa Fe and Albuquerque. Santa Fe was founded in 1610, and the Spaniards had no one except the Indians to contend with for seventy-five years.

However, Peñalosa, who had gotten into a fight in New Mexico, who had run afoul of the Inquisition, who had been tried and convicted and exiled, proposed to the French government to attack, with French help, the rich northern provinces. His proposition to France became known to the Spaniards, who were not surprised when in 1664 and 1665 Peñalosa made definite proposals to take Durango, the capital of Nueva Vizcaya,[1] with the idea of marching eventually on Mexico City.[2]

In 1678, Spain signed a treaty with France, but within twelve years the two countries were at war again—but long before the out-

[1] Nueva Vizcaya included present-day Chihuahua and Durango.

[2] The proposals of Peñalosa are found in Pierre Margry, ed., *Découvertes et Établissements des Français,* III, 44–45; see William Edward Dunn, *Spanish and French Rivalry*, 13–20. For a full treatment of this affair, and especially of the turmoil centered around Peñalosa, see Charles W. Hackett, "New Light on Don Diego de Peñalosa," *Mississippi Valley Historical Review*, Vol. VI, No. 3 (December, 1919), 313–35.

break of hostilities, definite plans had been afoot to attack northern Mexico with French forces. Father Hennepin, with La Salle, had ascended the upper Mississippi River in 1680—at which time he had located the Pawnee Indians on the Platte River—some distance from the Mississippi.

By 1683 La Salle was in France to put before the king a proposition similar to Peñalosa's. La Salle, however, proposed to use 15,000 Indians as his principal military force.[3]

Peñalosa's proposals were then dropped, but La Salle's plans were modified and accepted. La Salle was placed in sole charge, and apparently planned to march to the Pacific Ocean to cut off northern Mexico. Then possibly, he intended to recruit more forces and march on Mexico City itself. This was an ambitious project, involving the establishment of a colony—for which purpose La Salle took four ships, four hundred colonists, considerable equipment, and a large quantity of supplies. The ships anchored in Matagorda Bay in 1685, and La Salle and his men built a fort on Garcitas Creek—the first definite thrust at the rich mining district of northern Mexico.

When news of La Salle's landing reached Spain, it set off a great deal of activity. One Spanish ship left Havana under Juan Enríquez Barroto and Antonio Romero but ran into storms. In northern Mexico the Marquis of Miguel de Aguayo, governor of Nuevo León, was ordered to look for La Salle's colony—and that expedition was to be the beginning of Spanish colonization in Texas. The troops went under command of Alonso de León but returned without having located La Salle's little settlement. Eight months later, Aguayo sent a second expedition under León, but again without success. Another expedition, under Marcos Delgado, was sent out from Florida, but it failed to reach the Mississippi River. Then two ships set out from Vera Cruz under Antonio de Iriarte and Martín de Rivas, with Barroto and Romero acting as pilots. They found the wreckage of a French vessel, signs of the settlement at Matagorda Bay, and a stranded French vessel. In the meantime, two more ships under Andrés Pez and Francisco de Gamarra were sent to rescue Iriarte and Rivas; they fairly well duplicated the voyage of the first two. These two last voyages indicated that the French settlement had been abandoned, but the desire to find a Briton

[3] La Salle's proposals are in Margry, *ibid.*, II, 356–69.

named Ralph Wilkinson, accused of piracy, spurred the Spaniards to send another expedition under Pez and Barroto. All these marine expeditions missed the mouth of the Mississippi River, even though one of their objectives was to locate a great river that ran into Espíritu Santo Bay (now Matagorda Bay). (Perhaps that confusion arose from La Salle's original plan to locate his settlement on the Mississippi, and there still is disagreement as to whether he missed that river accidentally or intentionally.)

Wilkinson, incidentally, was later sentenced to hard labor in the galleys—presumably for piracy.

In 1688 Alonso de León, who had become governor of Coahuila (Nueva Estremadura), made a trip across the Río Grande and brought back a Frenchman who was chief of an Indian tribe. The Frenchman, examined several times, told many stories—but obviously he was a Frenchman in Spanish territory. Whether his name was Juan Enrique, Jan Jarri, Jean Géry (the name by which he is usually known), or something else has not been documented, but his conflicting testimony of a town or settlement spurred the Spaniards to make a fifth exploration by sea.

Rivas and Pez made that expedition, but again the result was negative—and late in the year Juan de Retana set out by land from Nueva Vizcaya to see what he could find. He was met by Juan Xaviata, or Sabeata, chief of allied tribes at the Conchos and Río Grande (two hundred miles below El Paso), who told Retana that the Indians had massacred the French settlers and destroyed the settlement—and Retana returned.

In the meantime, León had been ordered to make another exploration from Coahuila to obtain a definitive answer to the questions aroused by the countless rumors. With one hundred soldiers, two priests, and seven hundred horses and mules, guided by Jean Géry, who was no longer believed to be entirely sane, León left in March, 1689, crossed Texas, many of whose rivers he named, and learned that the French settlement had indeed been abandoned. At long last he reached Garcitas Creek, where he found six small huts, falling into ruin, with all the evidence of an Indian massacre—broken guns, torn books, and mutilated ecclesiastical ornaments. He found three skeletons—two men and one woman.

Through loss of ships, poor management, bad administration, illness, desertions, and trouble with the Indians, the ambitious colony had come to destruction within two years. La Salle had been assassinated, the colony had been destroyed, and fewer than one dozen persons survived—all or most of them scattered among the Indians.

León went on down the creek to Matagorda Bay, where an Indian courier brought him a letter from Jean de l'Archevêque, of Bayonne, who had been with La Salle. Presently L'Archevêque, along with Jacques Grollet, joined the Spaniards; both denied knowing Jean Géry. The two Frenchmen, examined at length, fully verified the various reports of the fate of La Salle's colony.[4]

Thus, eleven expeditions were sent by the Spaniards to find La Salle's colony near Matagorda Bay. León made a fifth trip in 1690, for on his 1689 expedition he had been accompanied by one Father Massanet, and in 1690 he returned with Massanet to establish a mission among the Indians—the first missionary activity in East Texas—with the approval of the viceroy.[5] Father Massanet was not able to maintain the missions very long, however; they were abandoned in 1692 and 1693. In effect, all of Texas was given back to the Indians, and four Spaniards, including José de Urrutia,[6] stayed with the Indians. Thus ended the first French threat to Santa Fe and the extensive Spanish answer to it.

From that time on, however, the French continued to probe toward Santa Fe—at first unofficially and haphazardly. Certainly the movements toward Mexico's far-flung outpost did not appear to be parts of an over-all pattern—but the Spanish were realists, and all appear-

[4] The Spanish search for La Salle is detailed by Dunn, *Spanish and French Rivalry*. L'Archevêque and Grollet were imprisoned in Spain until 1692, then returned to New Spain. L'Archevêque was killed with Villasur on the Platte River in 1720.

[5] Massanet resented León's organization of the expedition as primarily a military venture, because it tended to reduce Massanet's importance, and eventually León was replaced by Domingo Terán de los Ríos, who became Texas' first governor, 1691–92. On the 1690 expedition, León rescued from the Indians five children, survivors of the colony: Pierre Talon, Pierre Meusnier, and Robert, Lucien, and Marie Madelaine Talon—the latter three brothers and sister.

[6] *The Handbook of Texas* says he was born in 1678, but that would make him pretty young. Henri Folmer, in *Franco-Spanish Rivalry*, 218, calls him a captain, and says he was later a captain at Bexar. He died in 1740, and was succeeded at Bexar by his son, Toribio, who was commandant there at the time of the San Saba massacre.

ances of Frenchmen were duly reported by the governor of New Mexico to his superior—before 1776, usually the viceroy; after 1776, usually the commandant-general. Sometimes Frenchmen reached Santa Fe but were not named in official documents; very often their penetrations were known in Santa Fe by hearsay only, having gotten into official records through the reports of Indians or by the appearance of French goods in Indian villages.

In Texas, the Spaniards, with the Arroyo Hondo at their backs, faced the French from Los Adaes; on the north, across the Arkansas River; and in the far north they faced the French in the Minnesota area and in the Dakota area. But in 1763 the boundary changed from east of the Sabine and from the upper Arkansas to the Mississippi River itself, and after 1763 the Spaniards found themselves facing the British in British Illinois. Twenty years later, in 1783, they were facing the Americans in Kentucky and Tennessee, and the British were infiltrating across the upper Mississippi and through the Mandan area. From New Orleans to Prairie du Chien, the Spaniards faced Americans and British with whom they were not equipped to cope. Then in 1803 the Spaniards suddenly found themselves facing the Americans the full length and breadth of Louisiana: from across the Sabine and Arkansas rivers, from behind the Rocky Mountains.

At that time the Arkansas River was roughly the dividing line between Illinois and New Mexico, and Illinois was the key to Santa Fe.

It seems astonishing that there was no sort of military expedition toward Santa Fe from 1685 to 1806 (from the time of La Salle to the time of Pedro Vial), but this inactivity may be explained in part by the fact that during that period (between 1700 and 1763) Spain and France three times united to fight wars against England, and Spain and France fought each other in America. From 1763 to 1803, of course, Spain's ownership of the vast buffer territory of Louisiana involved distances great enough to discourage military ventures. In the early part of the period, there were some official parties to Santa Fe, but their object always seemed to be the establishment of trade relations.

In 1694 French traders, coming down from Canada, had traded among the Osages and the Missouris, and in that same year a curious chain of events got under way, causing great alarm in Santa Fe for some time: a party of Navahos returned from Quivira, in western

Kansas, with some captured children, and when the Spaniards refused to ransom the children, the Navahos beheaded them. That brutal action so horrified the Spaniards that they presently notified the Navahos that they would ransom such hostages, and in 1697 the Navahos went back to Quivira on what must have been a gigantic raid. However, the Navaho raiding party must have met an equally huge force of French and Pawnees, for they lost four thousand warriors. (The figure may be exaggerated, but even four hundred would have been a heavy loss.) The following year, however, the Navahos returned and annihilated three Pawnee settlements and a "fortified post" (a French fort?). They returned to the 1699 Taos fair laden with spoils: slaves, jewels, carbines, powder flasks, sword belts, waistcoats, shoes, brass pots, and cannons![7]

Perhaps in connection with the same sequence of events, a Spanish priest in 1698 ransomed two small French girls from the Navahos.

Along with these various incidental portents that the French *coureurs de bois* were coming down from Canada and going up the Missouri from Illinois to trade in the Platte River region, the second serious French threat to Santa Fe began in Lower Louisiana in 1699. Biloxi was founded east of present New Orleans by D'Iberville, and the French immediately began to look toward the west.

In the year 1700 the Apaches reported that Frenchmen had destroyed a town of the Jumano Indians, presumably somewhere in Oklahoma or Kansas,[8] and certainly the trend of all these events was to put the Spaniards on notice that the Frenchmen were close, were numerous, and were belligerent. It would seem logical, then, that the Spaniards should send an expedition eastward against the Faraon Apaches in 1702, for nearly every Spanish expedition had as one of its objectives the obtaining of information on the whereabouts of Frenchmen. This expedition went further, however: it reported that its Pecos Indian allies killed a "Francisco" with the Jumanos.[9] Presumably that was a Frenchman.

[7] Thomas, *After Coronado*, 13–14, gives this excellent summary, as he does of affairs connected with other Indian tribes.

[8] *Ibid.*, 14.

[9] There would be nothing inconsistent between this report and that of the destruction of a Jumano town by the French. Loyalties changed rapidly; likewise, it seems obvious that it was common for a Frenchman to go to live with an Indian tribe, and such a man might not hear of a French-Indian enmity until it had been resolved, or if

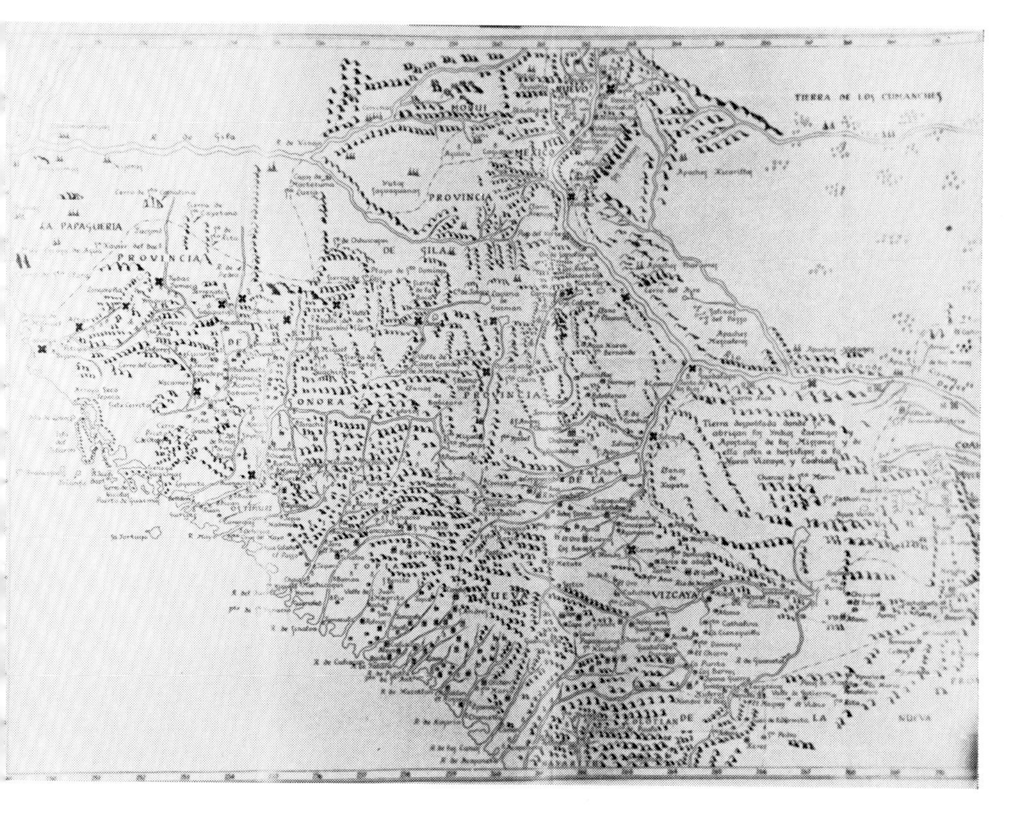


*The Map of the Spanish Borderlands drawn by the engineer La Fora in 1771 for the Marqués de Rubí.*

*The military plaza of San Antonio around 1850.*

From William H. Emory, *United States and Mexican Boundary Survey*

*The church and plaza at El Paso, 1851.*

From John Russell Bartlett, *Personal Narrative*

*The presidio of San Elzeario in 1851.*

From John Russell Bartlett, *Personal Narrative*

*The church in Santa Fe about 1846.*

From *Report of Lt. J. W. Abert*

*The big Comanche village west of the Taovaya villages on the Red River.*

From George Catlin, *North American Indians*

*Manuel Gayoso de Lemos, commandant at Natchez.*

From Louis Houck, *The Spanish Régime in Missouri*

*Bernardo de Gálvez, governor of Louisiana, 1777–85.*

From Louis Houck, *The Spanish Régime in Missouri*

In the following year, 1703, twenty Canadians (Frenchmen from Cahokia, in Illinois, across the river from St. Louis), were found or reported trying to reach the New Mexican area.[10] Three years later, Ulibarrí in El Cuartelejo was shown the scalp and firearm of a Frenchman. It turned out that the Frenchman had been one of a party of Pawnees and Frenchmen coming to attack the Cuartelejo village during the Apaches' absence on their annual buffalo hunt; the Frenchman's wife (undoubtedly Indian) was pregnant and had fallen behind, perhaps to give birth, and the Frenchman had stayed with her. The Cuartelejos had found them and killed them both, and the French war party, discovered, had gone back to the Pawnee country.[10a]

In 1706 or 1707 a man named Derbanne is reported to have made an exploration of the upper Missouri River; how far he went, or the exact year, is hazy from the various documents, but Derbanne was subsequently commandant at Natchitoches, which would suggest that his exploration of the Missouri might have had some kind of governmental sanction.[11] (Interestingly enough, an individual named Derbanne was associated with St. Denis in 1717—probably the same man.[12]) And by 1724 Étienne de Bourgmont was exploring the Missouri with the Indian *sauvagesse* for whose love he had deserted his post at Fort Detroit.

The second important French thrust was led by a dashing young

he should hear of it, he might decide to ignore it, for by that time he would have at least one wife and a number of children. Also, there is a suspicion here that more than one tribe of Indians was called Jumanos by the Spaniards.

[10] N. M. Miller Surrey, *The Commerce of Louisiana During the French Régime, 1699–1763*, 415.

[10a] With all these movements of the French toward Santa Fe, it seems there was no unanimity of antagonism toward the Frenchmen, because in 1711 Father Francisco Hidalgo sent several letters from East Texas to invite French traders to settle among the Texas Indians to buy horses and cattle. (Folmer, *Franco-Spanish Rivalry*, 230). Perhaps Father Francisco needed an outlet. It will be seen later that in 1739 Father Santiago Roybal of Santa Fe actually sent a letter to New Orleans with a list of desired goods and a promise to pay them for them in silver.

[11] Gilbert J. Garraghan, *Missouri Historical Review*, Vol. XXXV, No. 3 (April, 1941), 374. We have not found a reference to Derbanne as commandant at Natchitoches. There were many interim commanders, and records are woefully fragmentary. Nasatir treats Derbanne in *Before Lewis and Clark*, I, 9.

[12] Folmer, "Contraband Trade Between Louisiana and New Mexico in the Eighteenth Century," *New Mexico Historical Review*, Vol. XVI, No. 3 (July, 1941), 254.

cavalier who was already a figure on the Franco-Spanish frontier—Louis Juchereau de St. Denis.[13] St. Denis had been with Bienville on an abortive mission in 1700 to search for mines and map New Mexico. And again five years later St. Denis had traveled across Texas, reaching the presidio and mission of San Juan Bautista on the Río Grande.[14]

His more significant activities, however, commenced in 1713, when he entered East Texas to trade with the Indians. Then in 1714, loaded with trade goods and accompanied by three white companions and several Tejas Indians, St. Denis set out on the seven-hundred-mile trek to San Juan Bautista, which he had visited nine years earlier.

On reaching their objective, St. Denis and his companions were made prisoners by Captain Diego Ramón, the commander of the presidio. The Frenchmen did not find their incarceration irksome, however, for they were surrounded by persons of culture and breeding; there was linen to eat from, silver to drink from, and there were white women—among whom was the captain's granddaughter, said to be the "most beautiful girl in all the northern provinces of Mexico"; her name was Emanuelle—hardly a Spanish name—and she was engaged to the governor of Coahuila, who was Ramón's superior. Emanuelle, however, was part French, and very much aware that the governor of Coahuila was a fat widower, while St. Denis was young and handsome.

However, St. Denis was taken to Mexico City in chains in April, and he requested permission to carry out trading activities—ably seconded by Emanuelle's uncle. His blandness puzzled the Spaniards, and, though

[13] St. Denis (sometimes known as St. Denis the Younger) was of a distinguished family of French jurists; his grandfather migrated to Canada in 1634; his father was granted nobility by the French king. Louis Juchereau was the eleventh of twelve children; he was twenty-one years old in 1700; he was educated in Paris, enjoyed many escapades in that city, and inspired many legends of love affairs and duels. He was commandant at Natchitoches for many years, and in 1729 he directed a massacre of Natchez Indians who had moved and settled northwest of Natchitoches. He and his wife, Emanuelle, reared a large family, and he died at Natchitoches in 1744 and received one of the largest funerals ever held on the frontier. It is St. Denis of whom Governor Boneo of Texas said in effect: "St. Denis is dead, thank God; now we can breathe easier!" See Ross Phares, *Cavalier in the Wilderness* (Baton Rouge: Louisiana U. Press, 1952).

[14] No records have turned up, but the trip is referred to in statements made in his declaration in Mexico City on June 22, 1715. See Castañeda, *Our Catholic Heritage*, II, 17. San Juan Bautista had been established in 1700 below present Eagle Pass, Texas, on the south side of the river and a few miles inland.

his request was denied, he won favor in the viceroy's court and was even placed in charge of an expedition to East Texas to establish a mission there. Before long, however, he was back in San Juan Bautista and married Emanuelle. He and his new father-in-law set out for Mobile, returning in 1717 with 30,000 pesos worth of trade goods. St. Denis was jailed in Mexico City, but escaped and returned to Natchitoches, and somehow got the beautiful Emanuelle there with him. She had already borne him one child, but she was to bear him seven more, and his descendants were still in Natchitoches in the 1760's when the Spaniards took over Louisiana—as rambunctious as St. Denis if not as clever.

St. Denis' bold crossings of Texas with trade goods had alarmed the Spaniards, and after his 1715 appearance in Mexico City they sent an expedition that established six missions and the presidios of Los Adaes and Dolores.

Henry Folmer thinks that St. Denis may have given to Le Page du Pratz the famous account of the French trader in Spanish country: "I went with two pack mules, loaded with merchandise, . . . a tall man, . . . the only garment he had was a pair of trousers. . . . Do you have there, he asked me, merchandise that deserves to be seen? . . . I saw a woman, crouched to make fire; . . . She was pretty and had a graceful smile . . . the only garment, a corsage and skirt, . . . the corsage was so torn that her breasts were entirely visible." (It rather sounds like St. Denis.) He observed two children, naked. He was entertained at dinner with the most primitive furniture and eating equipment. He observed a doublet and green velvet trousers and a sword on the wall, and sold them some yard goods and some red silk embroidered stockings. "Finally, the strong box was opened; there was a pile of about five or six hundred dollars in a corner of the box, covered with a large deerskin."[14a]

The significance, of course, is in the extreme poverty of goods and the rather large supply of cash in these primitive surroundings, which suggests that an active market existed for enterprising traders—a fact of which the Spaniards in Mexico City were keenly aware.

Until 1717 the Spaniards spent most of their combative energy against the Indians, but perhaps St. Denis' brash crossing with goods stirred them to action, and they sent the expedition under Ramón to

[14a] *New Mexico Historical Review,* Vol. XVI, No. 3 (July, 1941), 251–52. Folmer cites Le Page du Pratz, *Histoire de la Louisiane,* II, 273–78.

establish six missions and the presidio of Dolores between the Neches and the Red rivers in Texas, and the presidio of Los Adaes east of the Sabine River, to hold back the French. That was the answer to the second thrust.

In the meantime, however, a third movement was developing along the Red River. At that time there were, in French minds, two principal roads to New Mexico: first, along the Red and the Canadian; second, along the Missouri and the Platte. The Arkansas might be used in conjunction with the Red River approach, or it might serve as a leg on the Missouri River approach.

The French had a number of ambitions: to establish a trade route with Santa Fe; to gain access to the mines of northern Mexico; to establish trade with the Indians on a wider scale; and to find a route to the Western Sea and thus open a route to Japan, China, and India. The search for a road to the Western Sea, however, did not develop its full importance until later in the century; in the first half of the 1700's, most French efforts were aimed at Santa Fe.[14b]

In 1705 a Frenchman named Laurain said that he had been up the Missouri, had visited the Indian tribes on the river, and had gone as far as the frontier of New Mexico.[14c]

Meanwhile, another French threat was developing along the Red River. In 1719 Jean Baptiste Bénard de la Harpe,[15] commissioned by Bienville to open trade relations with New Mexico, established a

[14b] The Western Sea, Vermillion Sea, or Pacific Ocean, was for a long time in French minds. In 1673 Father Marquette hoped to reach it via the Missouri River (Nasatir, *Before Lewis and Clark,* I, 3); in 1715–16 the Spaniards were aware that the French wanted to reach the South Sea (*ibid.,* 15); in 1742 Father Charlevoix suggested several possible routes to the Western Sea (*ibid.,* 31); in 1738 La Vérendrye made a visit to the Mandans—and foremost in his mind since at least 1726 had been the search for the Western Sea (*ibid.,* 33–34); in 1753 Macarty predicted the route to the Western Sea via the Missouri and the Columbia (*ibid.,* 49); and many others.

[14c] Pierre Margry (ed.), *Découvertes et Établissements des Française dans l'Ouest et dans le Sud de l'Amerique Septentrionale,* 1614–1754. *Memoirs et Documents Originaux Recueillis et Publiés par Pierre Margry,* VI, 181.

[15] La Harpe had been a governor in France and a captain in the coast guard. He received a land concession northwest of Natchitoches and established a trading post and fifty settlers there in 1718, from which point he was very active with tribes on the lower Canadian River. He tried to make a settlement at Galveston Bay in 1721, but the Indians drove him away. He left New Orleans in December, 1721, and made a trip up the Arkansas River, and retired to France in 1723. Bolton, *Athanase de Mézières,* I, 30–31, 45–46; *Handbook of Texas.*

trading post among the Nassonite Indians near present-day Texarkana, one hundred leagues above Natchitoches, and boldly sent a letter to the Spanish missionaries in Texas, suggesting that they tell their friends of New Mexico, New Vizcaya, and New León that he was in business. He offered the missionaries a 5 per cent commission. Alarcón, governor of Texas, ordered La Harpe to withdraw, but La Harpe answered that La Salle had taken possession of Texas in 1687 and that St. Denis had renewed the claim! Alarcón had no forces to spare, and the trading-post was a long way off. The priest of the mission at Nacogdoches apparently liked the percentage offered, and gave La Harpe assurance although he did advise caution.

La Harpe's geographer, Du Rivage, had already left on an exploration trip up the Red River, which he ascended for 180 miles. Two months later La Harpe himself explored the Canadian River, traveling northwest up into Oklahoma until he reached a settlement of Tawakonis, Taovayas, and Yscanis,[16] with whom he made a treaty.

La Harpe's explorations are important because they produced much information on topography, soil, products, posts, and prices—all of which was of interest to both France and Spain. Entitled "Memoire qui regarde la Louisiane," his account of his explorations has been preserved in several different forms, one translation of which presents the following wide variety of information:

## Memoir Concerning Louisiana[17]

In order to place this colony in an advantageous position, it could

[16] These tribes were usually considered the vanguard of the Wichita, or Quivira, tribes on the march toward the south under pressure of the Comanches, Kansas, and Pawnees. The Jumanos were first reported at the junction of the Conchos and the Río Grande in Chihuahua (in the region of present Presidio, Texas) as early as 1535, when they were semi-agricultural and lived in grass houses. They were also called Patarabueyes, and, because they were tattooed, were called Rayados or perhaps Flechas Rayadas east of the Río Grande in New Mexico in 1598. They were for a while on the plains of Texas, later in Kansas, and became associated with—or perhaps were—the Wichitas. Sometimes they were called Choumans. It seems that in Texas they were called Tawehash, and eventually Wichitas. F. W. Hodge, "The Jumano Indians", *Proceedings of the American Antiquarian Society at the Annual Meeting, April, 1909*. See also Carroll and Haggard, *Three New Mexico Chronicles*, 163.

[17] Paris, Archives Nationales, Colonies, $C^{13}A$, vol. 43, ff. 361 vo.-364 vo. (hereafter cited as A.N.C.). Another copy is: La Harpe, St. Malo, August 8, 1763; A.N.C., $C^{13}B$, vol. 1. These two copies have phrases identical and many similarities, but each has material not in the other. In this fashion the French left their accumulated information to the Spaniards.

be suitable that the king give his orders to form an establishment on the banks of the Arkansas River; to have constructed there a regular fortress. The rock, the slab proper for making limestone, sand for the bricks, and slate are found in its environs.

The entrance of this river is situated about 38 degrees latitude, 200 leagues above the capital, following the windings of the river. Ordinarily it takes 40 to 45 days to go from New Orleans there in boats or pirogues, and 12 to 14 days to descend the river to New Orleans.[18]

The Ohio River, a branch of the Ouabache, is 70 leagues above the Arkansas on the east. It is by this river [the Ohio] that the English have the greatest facility for going to the banks of the Mississippi. From the Ohio to the entrance of the Missouri River, a great river in our western district which falls into the Mississippi 5 leagues above the Kaskaskia or Illinois, . . .

This post of Arkansas fortified, one should expect that the nations of Canada, having been always attached to the French, will no longer send their skins to Montreal and to Quebec. They will descend in pirogues to the Arkansas, where they will find the colonists, charged with power of attorney for their correspondents from France, with assortments of goods in their warehouses in the environs of a regular fortress constructed by men in the business, to which colonists will be joined not only all the French of the eastern district but also the savages of the country who will not wish to remain under the domination of the English [but] will withdraw themselves to the Western district under the domination of France.

There remain in Canada more than 60,000 French people of all sexes, a number of whom do not have habitations. Learning of the establishment in question in a temperate climate, the land of which is fertile in wheat and other grains, abundant game, fur-trade free for all the inhabitants, sure of having free concessions of land, extensive protection by the government, more than 6,000 of these good Canadians and traders will go there, which will render this post within a few years in a position to form a *ville* of considerable proportions, to receive from New Mexico and from [?] the troops that his Catholic Majesty [the Spanish king] is going to send there [?] [*dans peu d'anneé en état de former une ville de consideration de recevoir du nouveau Mexique des secours des troupes que sa M. C. vat y faire passer*] after having constructed a regular fortress at the Arkansas,

[18] The memoir in C[13]B, vol. 1, says 196 leagues from New Orleans, or forty days ascending the river, twelve to fifteen days descending.

in which it will be suitable to maintain a 200-man garrison in time of peace and to reinforce it when there is an appearance of war, to furnish it with artillery and abundant munitions of war, appointing a commandant for this post who is a wise and honest man to whom the Court would send directly the presents destined for the chiefs of the tribes, and who will not follow the too-common abuse of having them pay for them in skins.

This colony, established in this fashion, should not fear the English. It will be maintained by the numerous [Indian] nations of the country. Although quite some distance away, one might be able to engage his Catholic Majesty to give his orders to the commandants on the frontier of New Mexico to engage the tribes that are their allies to make peace with those of our frontiers, and it would be easy to engage our Indians in this matter. In this matter, the Arkansas will aid by their correspondence with New Mexico.

It would be interesting to construct a good redoubt near the entrance of the great Missouri River in 43° latitude, distant by land from the Arkansas about 100 leagues; to maintain there a garrison of 25 men; to make for this effect presents to the chiefs of these nations. This small establishment would serve to favor the trade in beaver and other kinds of furs which are very considerable there.[19] Moreover, between the Missouri and the Arkansas there is a country abounding in various metals. This small establishment, where several Canadians would come to establish themselves, is the means of preventing the English from crossing to there from the Illinois, they not being [un?] scrupulous enough to disregard such a considerable establishment although this river is situated in the western district that belongs to us.

The knowledge that I have of the lands and of the tribes of this district to the west of Louisiana comes from having established a post in 1720, 200 leagues above the Red River,[20] then penetrated into the land with a small detachment of troops 60 leagues to the northwest, crossed several mountains, woods, rivers, and prairies covered with wild oxen, deer, and other animals, met by roving Indians on horseback, mines of lead, copper, [and] pit-coal, quarries of the most beautiful marble, granite, found in the land several pieces of rock crystal and in a stream some shellfish in which there were some seed-

[19] Thus does La Harpe, in 1763, guess at the relative importance of Arkansas Post (two hundred men) and the future St. Louis (twenty-five men).

[20] This is the post that La Harpe established among the Nassonites northwest of Natchitoches. It is also mentioned by Laurain.

pearls.[21] At the end of this route I found six fine villages speaking different languages. They are situated on the upper part of the Arkansas River, 38½ degrees latitude, 190 leagues from the Mississippi. Returning from these discoveries, I tried to charge myself with discovering whether this Arkansas River was navigable for pirogues as far as the tribes discovered and even as far as New Mexico by making alliance with the nations that I would be able to discover.

From New Orleans I left with three large pirogues, a detachment of troops and two officers to be next in command under me. After having re-ascended the river about 190 leagues, I advanced into the Arkansas River 120 leagues, and according to my estimate I did not have 50 leagues to go in order to reach the six villages discovered in 1722 [*sic*], but one of my pirogues in which there was food and presents for the savages having been destroyed on a reef, I was forced to return, which caused me much pain. The river commenced to rise, which proves that it is at all times navigable, always being 8 to 10 feet deep and not less than 250 to 260 feet wide. One can judge how much such a river would aid the commerce of the Arkansas [country].

I did not obtain any advantages from this discovery except to have looked over a very beautiful country, prairies covered with oxen and other animals whose skins are valuable. Turtles are very good there. There are birds of all kinds there. Turkey-hens and black bears are common there. Also common there are trees suitable for clapboards, all very fine, and others [trees] of fruit, wild vines, and white mulberry trees.

In the environs of this river is a chain of mountains that extends to the west northwest. The tribes in the environs assure us that various minerals are found there. It is situated between the Missouri and Arkansas rivers. Sieur Dumont de Montigny, lieutenant of the infantry who was with me, found in this river some grains of gold of little value, as he makes mention in his relation of the Mississippi printed 1753.

On account of the great extent of this country, one can judge that in order to make the best of it within a few years, is to send there a large number of colonies, to aid them, and to send there *farines* [millers?] (the Illinois will no longer furnish them), wines and *eau-de-vie*, munitions of war and dry merchandise (goods); not to levy any duty until they are well established; fortify New Orleans

[21] It would be a long time before the pearl excitement would subside in Arkansas.

and make some redoubts opposite this capital; and finally (or in short), do not bother in any way the liberty of the trade of this province.

There remain two observations to add to this memoir: the proximity [close relationship] of the English with Vera Cruz and via the Mississippi with the richest provinces north of Mexico [of northern Mexico], should engage France and Spain to maintain themselves in their possessions. For this, it would be best for the welfare of this colony that the king appoint a consul of France at Havana. In the time of King Philip V there was one from St. Malo who was Sieur Jouche [?]. Since his decease, no other has been appointed. Has not the time arrived when it is necessary to anticipate the *relaches* [putting into port] of the French vessels [as] very useful, and the aid that can be drawn from there necessary; that there be sent to this island a subject who knows Louisiana, who speaks the language of the country, and who is a good Frenchman. That can only effect a great good.

The second article [of observation] is known by all France: our colonists can scarcely be maintained without a navy; the finances to re-establish it will not be lacking; but people are necessary to conduct it. There are no *gardes-de-marines*, and they take their recruits from the merchant marine, and you will then have business men of this district, whom they seek as much as possible to draw into the English navy. There are good officers in the navy of the king. It is necessary to conserve them, but there is no order in the list that is given for merit; [let] that subordination be established, and you will have a navy. Upon which depends the safety of your colonies and the honor and strength of the state.

Thus wrote La Harpe forty-three years after his trip onto the Great Plains. At the time of the writing, Louisiana had just been ceded to Spain, but it seems doubtful the Spaniards followed any of La Harpe's advice. It might even be thought that they deliberately went against it.

The Red River was not the only avenue to be explored in the time of La Harpe, for in 1719 Charles Claude du Tisné had led a trading expedition into the Illinois country, attempting to reach the Pawnees (along the Platte) via the Missouri. The Osage Indians stopped him, however, and in the following year he went up the Missouri and branched off on the Osage, where he found some Osage villages. He proceeded southwest to a Pani village in Oklahoma, where he almost lost his life when the Indians plotted to kill him and his men and take their stock of trade goods.

But it seems that Du Tisné, who was only seventeen years old, had already learned their language and was prepared for them. Completely bald from childhood, he wore a wig, and when the Indians advanced to kill them, Du Tisné terrified them by removing it, and apparently they were only too pleased to do business by negotiation. He made an alliance with the Panis and traded all the goods he could spare. He wanted to go on to the Padoucahs (Comanches), but when the Panis would not allow him to continue, he returned to Illinois and finally to Quebec with a fine load of furs.[22] A remarkable trip—and he probably would have reached Santa Fe if the Panis had not interfered.[23]

War had been declared between France and Spain, and a French force from Natchitoches marched seven leagues and took over Los Adaes, which was then only a mission and presidio (soon it would be the capital of Texas). The Spaniards withdrew to newly founded San Antonio. All property at Los Adaes was destroyed, but it is not clear whether the action was official or unofficial.[24] Certainly the commander at Natchitoches, Blondel, had a plan to pursue the Spaniards to San Antonio—a plan that had been approved by many French officials but which for some reason never was consummated.[25]

But a further prong developed along the Texas coast, and an impor-

[22] Thus, Du Tisné, who had been rejected by the French army because he was too small, overcame that handicap. He enlisted in the Canadian army, which obviously was not as exacting, as a cadet at 12 or 13, and upon his return from the Missouri River the governor made him an ensign, and later the royal court made him a lieutenant; he was a commander at the post of Natchez, and a captain in 1719 of troops in the Illinois country. Other sources say that he was made a captain in 1724, and that in 1736 he became a prisoner of the Chickasaw Indians and was tortured and burned to death. Folmer treats him more fully in "French Expansion Towards New Mexico in the Eighteenth Century," unpublished master's thesis, University of Denver, 1939, and translates many passages from Le Page du Pratz and Margry.

[23] This is substantially the relation of Le Page du Pratz, with a number of factual details supplied by Nasatir. In *Before Lewis and Clark*, I, 18–19, Nasatir gives a somewhat different and better authenticated version; he says that Du Tisné went to Mobile with Bienville, and had undertaken several missions among the Indians for Bienville; that he was commandant at Natchitoches in 1714; that he made the trip up the Missouri at Bienville's order, going back to Kaskaskia to winter. It is a more plausible story if for no other reason than that it hardly seems reasonable that Du Tisné could have learned the Pani language in a few days.

[24] Hubert Howe Bancroft, *The North Mexican States and Texas*, I, 618–19.

[25] Folmer, "Report on Louis de St. Denis' Intended Raid on San Antonio in 1721," *Southwestern Historical Quarterly*, Vol. LII, No. 1 (July, 1948), 84.

tant one, for it would play a major part in motivating the powerful Aguayo expedition from Mexico.

In 1718 a ship had sailed from France with more colonists for the Texas coast—troops and convicts—but an epidemic broke out, and an officer named Bellisle and four other officers either went ashore or were abandoned. All but Bellisle died of starvation; he fell in with the Attakapas, a cannibalistic tribe, but survived until St. Denis rescued him in 1721.

In 1720, a man named Béranger was sent to explore the Bay of Espíritu Santo[26] and to make a settlement there. He found a bay and left some men, but the location probably was south of Espíritu Santo.

In the following year, La Harpe, who had been appointed commandant of the Bay of Espíritu Santo, set out to take possession of the bay; if the Spaniards were there, he was to get rid of them, by force if necessary. He entered Galveston Bay but did nothing more startling than to seize a dozen Indians and take them back to Mobile.[27]

By that time, the Spaniards were thoroughly excited, and one prong of their answer to the third thrust of the French was the Villasur expedition to the Platte River in 1720. In answer to the report that six thousand Frenchmen were within 180 miles of Santa Fe,[28] Valverde, governor of New Mexico, was ordered to carry through the long-delayed establishment of a post at El Cuartelejo and to make a reconnaissance to the northeast to locate the French. Valverde wrote back to urge that the fort be located at Jicarilla instead of Cuartelejo, and his recommendation was granted. Meanwhile, the expedition had been organized, and instead of the governor, Don Pedro de Villasur[29] was in command, and they marched northeast with forty-two seasoned soldiers, three settlers, sixty Indians, and a priest. With them was Juan l'Archevêque as interpreter—but they traveled three hundred leagues

[26] The French called it the Bay of St. Bernard.

[27] The affairs along the coast are taken from Bancroft, *North Mexican States*, I, 619–22.

[28] Governor Cruz to Viceroy Valero, Parral, December 11, 1719; printed in Thomas, *After Coronado*, 147.

[29] Villasur, a native of Castile, had been an officer at El Paso, alcalde at Santa Barbara in Nueva Vizcaya, an official at other points, and alcalde at Chihuahua. He was in New Mexico by 1719, and when he was killed seems to have been a colonel or lieutenant colonel. He was also rated as "lieutenant-general" under the governor of New Mexico, who was also captain-general of New Mexico. Thomas, *ibid.*, 272.

without needing L'Archevêque, for they found no sign of Frenchmen.

The party reached the Río Jesús María[30] and crossed it; discovering Pawnees ahead, they crossed the San Lorenzo,[31] not far above the junction of the two rivers. There were several indications that should have warned him, but Villasur ignored them, and the Pawnees, with Frenchmen leading them or among them, attacked at daybreak and accomplished a full-scale massacre. Villasur, L'Archevêque, the priest, twenty-four soldiers, a captain and four servants, a guide, and eleven Indians were slaughtered.[32] The survivors fled to El Cuartelejo and eventually returned to Santa Fe. Valverde reported the disaster and begged for replacement troops immediately.[33]

The other prong in answer to the third French thrust was made in Texas by the Marquis of San Miguel de Aguayo,[33a] a hard-headed career man who knew a great deal about St. Denis but liked little of what he knew. He was appointed governor of Texas by Zúñiga, the same viceroy who had sent the Villasur expedition from Santa Fe, and he was ordered to drive the French from Texas. Aguayo at his own expense raised 500 men and bought 6,600 horses, with huge supplies of food and munitions. In April, 1720, the many detachments began assembling in Coahuila. A very severe drought caused them much difficulty, and their horses, finding no pasture, began to die; only 560 horses reached Monclova. By the end of September they had 3,400 more horses, but all were in poor condition; later, they received 600 mules. But Spain and France had signed a truce by that time, and

[30] The South Platte.

[31] The North Platte.

[32] The massacre took place near the present town of North Platte, Nebraska, on the south side of the river. Thomas, *After Coronado*, 278–79.

[33] *Ibid.*, 39–42.

[33a] Joseph de Azlor y Virto de Vera was born into a distinguished Spanish family and married into the title of Marquis of Aguayo (the title passed through the female line by special dispensation of the king). In 1712 he and his wife went to Mexico to live on one of their haciendas; in 1719 he was appointed governor and captain-general of Coahuila and Texas, and in 1720 made the expedition to reoccupy the East Texas missions and presidios that had been abandoned in 1719. His expedition strengthened Spain's claim to Texas so that it was not again seriously challenged by the French. He resigned as governor because of ill health resulting from the expedition's hardships, and in 1724 he was made field marshal. He died in 1734, after having built up, through his marriage to an Urdiñola and through his personal wealth and his efforts, one of the greatest landed estates of the New World.

Aguayo was ordered to fight only if attacked. He marched north, and the next summer St. Denis came to meet him at the Neches River.

Aguayo re-established five missions and a presidio and crossed the Sabine River to build, under protest from the ad interim commander at Natchitoches, a presidio at Los Adaes. He received fresh horses and mules a number of times, as well as two hundred mules loaded with flour, four hundred sheep, and three hundred head of cattle. But a heavy sleet storm felled two thousand trees and killed many horses and mules; he started for Bexar, but the great cold killed many more animals, and he reached Bexar with only fifty out of five thousand horses and one hundred out of eight hundred mules. He was hard on stock, but he was the governor and apparently got by with it. At Espíritu Santo he established a fort later known as La Bahía, and then, broken in health, resigned his commission. It was one of the more determined efforts of the Spanish viceroys, and it was eminently successful, for it pushed the French back to Natchitoches and kept them there. The expense, however, had been heavy—considerably more than the $250,-000 originally allotted, and such lavish spending was bound to have repercussions in vice-regal councils.[34]

During the 1720's, the French and Spanish had been fighting a rather traditional type of war at sea. Little blood was shed, but it was always a see-saw. Meanwhile, French producers in Louisiana tried to send their produce to Spanish ports in Mexico, and offered (and indeed hoped) to trade for Spanish goods.[35] The Spanish commanders at the ports usually had orders to prohibit such trade, but occasionally they did admit a French ship, and the French captains became adept at the manufacture of excuses, sometimes anchoring outside the port and claiming illness made it impossible for them to put to sea. On occasion, Spanish ships went to Louisiana or Florida, but on the whole the French vessels did not enjoy a good reception. Then in 1723, from fear of the

[34] Bancroft, *North Mexican States*, I, 622–29.

[35] The French vessels brought for sale rice, buffalo wool, indigo, hemp, catskins, hides, deerskins, and some merchandise from France. From Mexico they wanted wheat, farm animals, flour, tobacco, sugar, tanned skins, cocoa, logwood and Brazil wood, sarsaparilla, vanilla, sugar, and cochineal. Not a very handsome offering from the French side. Spanish vessels, when permitted, often went to Louisiana with goods and with money, expecting to buy French-manufactured goods, but frequently found nothing worth buying. Surrey, *Commerce of Louisiana*, 388–406.

plague then current in Europe, Spanish officials issued orders to port commanders to oblige French ships to put to sea or be sunk. Any official allowing them entrance would be subject to the death penalty. One thing may be said for the Frenchmen: they tried.

But in 1723 a fourth thrust began to develop on the Missouri when Bourgmont,[36] who in 1714 had described the Missouri River as far as the Arikaras (the last stop before the Mandans), was appointed commander on the Missouri River. He ascended that river for the French Company of the Indies and made definite and positive attempts to reach Santa Fe.[37]

Bourgmont was ordered to construct a fort to forestall any more expeditions such as that of Villasur. He was to make friends with all the tribes between Illinois and Santa Fe—especially the Comanches, so as to open a trade route. He was also to determine the truth of reports that the Spaniards were about to advance from Santa Fe, presumably to avenge the massacre of Villasur's command and certainly to make an

[36] Étienne Véniard de Bourgmont was from an old Norman family, and became commandant at Fort Detroit in 1706, replacing Tonty. He was a capable officer, once withstanding an attack by Fox Indians. He lived with the Missouri Indians for a number of years, and during that time he explored the Missouri River and its tributaries and became acquainted with the country and with the various tribes of Indians that inhabited it. In September, 1718, Bienville asked for him the Cross of St. Louis. There are unflattering stories, such as the one that he had an Ottawa chief beaten to death for defending himself against Bourgmont's dog. It is hard to know. Certainly Bourgmont was extremely susceptible to women, for he eloped with a married woman, Madame Tichenet, at Fort Detroit in 1707 and went to live in the forest with other deserters. Fifty men went after them and brought them back; Bourgmont was court-martialed but acquitted. He fell in torrid love then with La Charesse, an Indian girl, and possibly with her—but more likely with another Indian girl—deserted the army again, and lived with the girl among her Missouri tribesmen for several years. He was with the Indians until 1718, and explored the Missouri River country, apparently as far as the Arikaras—wherever *they* were at that time. He went to France for a few years and married a very rich widow, but in 1723 he returned to the Missouri and began rebuilding Fort Orléans at once. It was 1724 when he went to meet the Padoucahs, and in 1725 he went back to France with a new Missouri mistress. He was made a nobleman in 1725, and presently retired, but the details of his death are unavailable. Folmer, "Étienne Véniard de Bourgmond in the Missouri Country," *Missouri Historical Review,* Vol. XXXVI, No. 3 (April, 1942). Folmer spells it "Bourgmond."

[37] Most of our information concerning Bourgmont's activities comes from Folmer's thesis, "French Expansion Towards New Mexico," which cites primarily Villiers du Terrage, *La Découverte du Missouri.*

alliance with the Apaches against the French.[38] Goodness knows, the Spaniards had reason for that.

As a matter of fact, the talk of a Spanish advance was not unfounded, for in October, 1723, the viceroy advised the governor of New Mexico, Juan Domingo de Bustamante, that he had learned that the people of New Mexico had bought 12,000 pesos worth of goods from Louisiana, and that such contrabanding must be stopped. Then Bustamante, in November, took an expedition to Jicarilla, northeast of Taos—but no presidio was established.[39] Bustamante held a council of war the following April, and ten substantial citizens of the area swore under oath that they had never heard of any New Mexicans' trading with the French.[40]

In that same year, Bourgmont built a post at Fort Orléans (in present Carroll County), across the river from the Missouri Indian village of his wife's people.[41] The Missouris were glad to see him and his half-Missouri son, who apparently had been with him from the time he had left the Missouris; nothing at all is said about his wife.[42] The following spring he traveled west on the river, intending to go to Santa Fe, but was delayed by illness and did not contact the Comanches' principal village near present Ellsworth, Kansas, until October. There Bourgmont held many palavers, and the big chief of the Padoucahs said to him in late October: "Soon a great number of warriors will leave to go to the Spaniards to buy horses." That statement reminds us that there were other items of commerce than silver and furs in New Mexico—and a very important one was horses.

[38] Folmer, *Franco-Spanish Rivalry*, 284.

[39] Thomas, *After Coronado*, 197–201.

[40] *Ibid.*, 245–55.

[41] Two miles west of the Wakenda River, on the north bank of the Missouri, in present Carroll County; see Gilbert J. Garraghan, "Fort Orléans of the Missoury," *Missouri Historical Review*, Vol. XXXV, No. 3 (April, 1942), 373. Near Cranberry Island, says Folmer (*Franco-Spanish Rivalry*, 287)—which would be some seventy miles northwest of Jefferson City. Thus Fort Orléans was within a few miles of the Missouri village where Pedro Vial would live about 1773. Bourgmont kept a diary in 1714, printed in Villiers du Terrage, *La Découverte*, 44ff., and translated by Folmer, 104ff.

[42] It was not unusual for a white man to return to civilization and take a favorite child with him; the wife may have died, but more likely she was left behind, and acquired another husband as soon as Bourgmont left. The stern necessities of existence made any other course impracticable, for men were the hunters.

To Bourgmont, the Comanche chief also complained of Spanish treatment, saying the Spaniards would sell the Comanches only a few bad axes, whereas the French traders would provide them with rifles, powder and bullets, kettles, axes, knives, blankets, awls, and other merchandise. And the Comanche chief assured him that "If you need two thousand warriors, you have only to speak." So, while Rivera was whimsically making decisions to save pesos for the viceregal treasury, the Comanches had already offered to support a major invasion of New Mexico. Perhaps the Lord does protect fools, but sometimes He must get a little weary of sheer stupidity.

Bourgmont made a firm alliance with the Comanches and presented them a French flag. He was only twelve marching days from Taos,[43] he was told, but he did not go there because it was too late in the season (November). Before returning to Fort Orléans, Bourgmont held a big peace conference with the Padoucahs, Otos, Osages, Iowas, Kansas, Omahas, Missouris, and Illinois. The Padoucahs, Iowas, Otos, Missouris, and Omahas accepted peace with one another and all solemnly promised to keep their word; the others were more vague, but generally inclined toward friendship. The Kansas chief offered him as wife a girl of thirteen or fourteen years, but he chivalrously declined; the chief then offered her to Bourgmont's son, who was probably younger than the girl, but Bourgmont suggested they postpone the liaison.[43a]

He left the Indians—especially the Comanches—many tokens in the form of trade goods and souvenirs which must have been readily identifiable as of French origin, and which would soon be known to the officials in New Mexico. He returned to Fort Orléans in late 1724, having cleared the way for trading. Of course, the trading would be contraband—but that was a detail.[43b]

The desire to increase trade was not entirely one sided, for in 1723

[43] The airline distance is something like 450 miles, which would mean a march of about thirty-seven miles a day if the trip was made in twelve days.

[43a] Before we credit Bourgmont with moral impulses that actually would be somewhat foreign to the frontier, if not to Bourgmont, we might reflect that perhaps there were practical considerations, such as the fact that the Comanches were the dominant tribe.

[43b] With all the Spanish apprehension over French intrusion into New Mexico, it is interesting to note that the French Indies Company had instructed Bourgmont to build Fort Orléans to keep the Spaniards out of Missouri! Folmer, "French Expansion Toward New Mexico," 125–26.

the directors of the French Company of the Indies learned that the Spaniards of New Mexico had "gone to buy as much as twelve thousand pesos of European merchandise from the French of the new colony of Louisiana."[44]

In 1725 Bourgmont took some Osages to Paris, and among them was a "Missouri princess" whose presence in Paris, it seems safe to suppose, was not intended altogether for the delectation of Parisian anthropologists. Presumably Bourgmont's French wife was not complacent over Bourgmont's *jeune sauvagesse*, however, for the Missouri girl married one of Bourgmont's sergeants in the cathedral of Notre Dame, and they returned to the Missouri.[44a]

In 1726, with the Franco-Spanish war having ended six years previously in Europe, the threats of invasion from Louisiana seemed less real to the viceroy, and it was at that time that Pedro de Rivera made his inspection of New Mexico and Texas. He ordered Valverde brought to trial for not personally accompanying the Villasur expedition; he issued an opinion that the building of a presidio at either La Jicarilla or El Cuartelejo would be an unjustifiable expense; he recommended that the Apaches be moved to Taos (one of the most serious strategic mistakes ever made in New Mexico); and he recommended that the number of soldiers in Texas (267) be cut in half. After Aguayo's splurge, the customary viceregal parsimony would come back into its own.

As for the French, the Louisiana traders did not immediately take advantage of Bourgmont's trade opening, even though in 1727 six Frenchmen apparently settled in El Cuartelejo and built houses near that village. There were many other instances of French intrusion,[45] but from 1727 to 1739 the Comanches, in spite of their friendship for Bourgmont, were a barrier because they were at war with other tribes,

[44] King to Casafuerte, Aranjuez, May 10, 1723, in A.G.M., Historia 298, *ff.* 178–80; cited in Hackett, "Policy of the Spanish Crown Regarding French Encroachments from Louisiana, 1721–1762," *New Spain and the Anglo-American West*, I, 111.

[44a] Folmer covers a good many of Bourgmont's activities in his thesis, citing Margry, *Découvertes;* De Villiers, *La Découverte;* Charlevoix, *Histoire et Description de la Nouvelle France;* Bossu, *Nouveaux Voyages* (Paris, 1768), other printed sources, and a number of French documents.

[45] Folmer, "Contraband Trade Between Louisiana and New Mexico in the Eighteenth Century," *New Mexico Historical Review*, Vol. XVI, No. 3 (July, 1941), gives many instances.

and they did not want their enemies to get rifles. (They were in conflict with the Jumanos, who had some Frenchmen with them, and with the Apaches, Spaniards, and Pueblos, and could not afford mistakes.) There was also turmoil caused by the Fox wars that affected tribes along the lower Missouri and that deterred the French because the Fox Indians were traditional enemies of the French. The *coureurs de bois*, however, remained friendly with the Comanches, supplying them with rifles and ammunition in their struggle against the Apaches—whom the Comanches began to roll back as soon as the Jicarillas were moved to Taos and the northeast frontier of New Mexico left unprotected.[45a]

French traders were constantly engaged in contrabanding, and while some of that activity may well have been directly with persons of Spanish nationality, probably more of it was through intermediary Indian tribes. Any introduction of non-Spanish goods into Spanish territory, of course, was contraband, and between 1718 and 1732 Spanish officials issued repeated orders to stop or prevent contrabanding. Then, between 1732 and 1735, there was a lull in Franco-Spanish contacts, but that ended in 1735 when the French commandant moved Natchitoches to the west side of the Red River to secure the Red River as the boundary between Louisiana and Texas; Spanish officials protested the move, but St. Denis did not back down, and the fort seems to have stayed there at least until 1753.[46]

Folmer says that after Bourgmont left the Missouri country in 1725, the Frenchmen in Illinois began to believe that no one could reach New Mexico via the Missouri River and that this belief grew, and the country between the Missouri and New Mexico was considered an uncrossable wilderness.[47]

But finally, in 1739, a French party got through. Pierre and Paul Mallet led a party of nine Canadian traders up the Missouri, looking for the road to Santa Fe.[47a] When they found they were going in the

[45a] George B. Grinnell, *The Cheyenne Indians*, I, 36; Margry, *Découvertes*, VI, 453.

[46] See Hackett, "Policy of the Spanish Crown Regarding French Encroachments from Louisiana, 1721–1762," *New Spain and the Anglo-American West*, I, 118.

[47] Folmer, *Franco-Spanish Rivalry*, 297.

[47a] Personal information on the Mallets is elusive. In Wisconsin Historical *Collections*, XVI, 424, is a reference by the younger brother of Tonty to a Montreal merchant named Pierre Maillet (Mallet) whose wife wanted to "go down" with her

wrong direction they retraced their route and struck out across the plains of Nebraska, Kansas, and southwestern Colorado. They lost their pack trains and goods in a stream but reached Santa Fe in good health and were well received; they were held there for several months, and then were allowed to go home. Two, however, stayed in Santa Fe; three went to Illinois, and four to New Orleans.[48]

News of the kind treatment of the Mallets by the Spaniards soon reached New Orleans and set off another flurry of expeditions—a development not entirely unexpected by the Spaniards.[48a] As a matter of fact, Governor Bienville got behind the next move. For some reason he appointed a nincompoop named Fabry de la Bruyère[49] to lead an ex-

husband and children in 1720 or 1721. The letter, dated January 10, 1723, contains frequent references to the Marquis of Vaudreuil, who was not governor-general of Louisiana until 1743. The Mallet brothers seem to have been experienced frontiersmen, although they could not use a compass (if Bruyère is to be relied on). They both were with Bruyère in 1741, and were blamed heavily by Bruyère for his failure. Pierre Mallet in late 1750 or early 1751 guided the Boyce-Ojofrion-Roc (spelled variously: e.g., Boyer-Gionfrio—Roque) party toward New Mexico. That party was taken to Mexico City, and there Pierre (recorded by the Spaniards as Pedro Malec) testified that he was a native of Montreal but had been in New Orleans seventeen years; he was a trader, forty-seven years old (Pierre Mallet, above, was married in 1698), and a widower; in 1740, he said, he had lived in Missouri, where there had been a garrison of soldiers. Each of the other three men on the 1751 expedition was a native of Montreal. It appears that Sarvé and possibly others of the 1739 or 1740 expedition were also in prison in Mexico in 1751, and asked to testify. Their route in 1739 was from New Orleans up the Mississippi and the Missouri to some point considerably above the Platte; then overland to the Platte, overland to the Arkansas, up that river to the Purgatoire, to Santa Fe, and back down the South Canadian and the Arkansas rivers—thus establishing the value of the Arkansas River route to Santa Fe and short-cutting the Missouri River route from New Orleans.

[48] Folmer, "The Mallet Expedition of 1739 Through Nebraska, Kansas, and Colorado to Santa Fé," *The Colorado Magazine*, Vol. XVI, No. 5 (September, 1939), 163–73.

[48a] One reason for it was a letter that the Mallets took back to New Orleans with them, from Father Sant Iago de Ribald, vicar of Santa Fe, to Father Beaubois of New Orleans, requesting him to send merchandise according to an enclosed list, to the extent of 4,000 piasters, which he promised to pay in silver. Folmer, "Contraband Trade Between Louisiana and New Mexico in the Eighteenth Century," *New Mexico Historical Review*, Vol. XVI, No. 3 (July, 1941), 262–63. One should remember that the priest's proposed trade would have been contraband and illegal.

[49] Bruyère was a strange choice, it seems, to lead this expedition. He was an inexperienced naval clerk—but perhaps he was expected to make a reliable map. He does not seem to have been a leader, because he made poor decisions at times, and could not get along with the Mallets, who, it appears from Bruyère's own words, were

pedition that set out in 1741 to find the Western Sea and to explore the lands bordering on it, which were thought also somehow to border on China and Grand Tartary. His instructions do not mention Santa Fe, but they do say that if he should happen to be caught on Spanish soil, he should present to the authorities a letter asking their assistance; perhaps the most interesting feature of the letter is that it is addressed to "the governor of Santa Fe."[50]

Bruyère was to ascend the Arkansas and Canadian rivers, but it was September and the water was too low for the boats. Four men from the Mallet party (including Pierre and Paul Mallet) were with him, but it did not help. In spite of the opposition of the Mallets, Bruyère fumbled again and again. He was afraid to move at flood-stage, and he could not move when the river was low. He refused to buy horses, and finally, after almost a year of his ineffectual leadership, with the expedition still on the Arkansas River, the Mallets left him and struck out on foot for Santa Fe. Bruyère blamed the Mallets for the failure of the expedition, but one need not look past Bruyère himself.[51]

The French had failed again, but the failure was in execution, not in purpose, for Bruyère said in his own account: "In consequence of the orders of Messrs. de Bienville and Salmon[52] . . . Mr. Andre Fabry de la Bruyère, ordinary clerk of the marine . . . left from New Orleans . . . to attempt to discover the route to Santa Fe in New Mexico."[53] And even though Bruyère's trip had failed, it would be tried again several times before the end of French control in Louisiana.

Fort Orléans, established by Bourgmont in the vicinity of the village

---

capable explorers. De Vaudreuil had given Mallet permission to hunt with the Pawnees and Comanches, to try to find some hunters who owed him (Mallet) some money, and to go on to Santa Fe. Bruyère contradicts himself more than once in his account, and his repeated charges against the Mallets seem ill founded. He was vain and stubborn, and the expedition was a failure, but he continued in the king's service.

[50] Folmer, "French Expansion Towards New Mexico," 251, citing Margry, *Découvertes,* VI, 471–72.

[51] Folmer, *ibid.*, 248–68, covers Bruyère's misadventures.

[52] Edme Gatienne Salmon, counsellor of the king, commissary of the marine, was the French *ordonnateur*, or intendant, of Louisiana in the 1730's and 1740's under Bienville.

[53] Folmer, "French Expansion Towards New Mexico," 252. After the failure, both Salmon (266) and the Count de Maurepas, French minister of the marine (267), spoke of it as the attempt to reach Santa Fe.

that would later be Pedro Vial's home, had lasted only a few years and had been abandoned about 1728. Fort Cavagnolle was established farther west—near present Kansas City—primarily to deal with the Osage and Kansas Indians. The frontier was moving west, and the Bruyère fiasco was only the beginning of a flurry of attempts to reach Santa Fe.

In 1744, Jacques Velo (or Belleau or Bellot) deserted from the French service in Illinois, struck out across the Great Plains, and reached Pecos (Coronado's village of Cicuye, east of Santa Fe), and was escorted to Santa Fe, where a new governor ordered him sent to Nueva Vizcaya.[54]

Two or three years later there was an event that might have opened up the route to the strangely attractive little town, for in 1746 or 1747 the Comanches made peace with the Jumanos;[55] whether or not they had assistance from the French is unknown, but the Comanches relaxed their barrier against the French, who wasted no time heading for Santa Fe. In February, 1748, thirty-three French traders entered a Comanche village on the Jicarilla River,[56] and two of them wanted to accompany the Comanches to the Taos fair. In the spring of 1749, three Frenchmen—perhaps different ones, perhaps some of the same—actually did attend the Taos fair, and were taken on to Santa Fe. They were Luis Febre, Joseph Miguel Raballo, and Pedro Satren, and they all had deserted Arkansas Post because of harsh treatment. The three were qualified in the trades of carpentry, tailoring, barbering, and bloodletting, and the governor of New Mexico secured permission from the viceroy for them to remain in Santa Fe to ply their various trades. Those three had been originally a party of twelve.[57]

In 1750 seven Frenchmen arrived in Santa Fe at different times, probably via the Arkansas River. One was Felipe de Sandoval, who had come through the Jumano villages on the middle Arkansas. Sandoval said the Jumanos were at war with the Pawnees and that he had

[54] New Mexican Archives, I, 149; II, 214.

[55] Herbert Eugene Bolton, *Texas in the Middle Eighteenth Century*, 67.

[56] Thomas, *The Plains Indians*, 17.

[57] Folmer, "Contraband Trade Between Louisiana and New Mexico in the Eighteenth Century," *New Mexico Historical Review*, Vol. XVI, No. 3 (July, 1941), 266–68; and Bolton, "French Intrusions Into New Mexico, 1749–1752," *Pacific Ocean*, 394.

seen them eat two of their captives; apparently six Frenchmen left the Jumano village with him, and they or some of them made their way to Taos and were taken to Santa Fe. Later the viceroy ordered six men sent to Sonora.[58] There may have been many more.

Soon the Jumanos made peace with the Pawnees and effected an alliance of the Comanches with the Pawnees and with the Ais; all those tribes were fighting the Kansas and Osages, but the French continued to go through.

October 2, 1750, the French minister commented on somebody's proposed trip to Santa Fe: "Vaudreuil [the governor of Louisiana] has not yet sent permissions that you tell me he has given—one to go to Santa Fe, the other to go to trade in cattle at Natchitoches."[59] He may have been referring to Sandoval's trip, for sometime in late 1750 or in 1751 Sandoval was back in Santa Fe with four other Frenchmen. But in 1751 a royal Spanish order arrived, saying in effect that Frenchmen who should enter New Mexico or Texas without authority would not be allowed to return to Louisiana.[60]

Meantime, apparently, four Frenchmen who had made the trip and were still enjoying the hospitality of Santa Fe became caught in the viceregal net and were sent to Mexico City: Pedro Malec,[61] Juan Batista Boyce, Pedro Ojofrion, and Batista Roc. In Mexico City they gave extensive testimony concerning themselves,[62] Malec saying that he had been among the ten soldiers whom Bienville had sent to New Mexico in 1740.[63] They had gone up the Red River, and Sarvé, who must have been with them, had gone to San Antonio. Four others who had fallen ill were left behind. Francisco Sarvé was there to testify for himself, but the result was the same for all: they were ordered sent to Spain as prisoners.[64]

[58] Folmer, *ibid.*, 268–69.

[59] [Minister] to Michel, Versailles, October 2, 1750, in Archives Nationales, Col. B 91, *ff.* 403 *et vo.*

[60] Bolton, "French Intrusions Into New Mexico, 1749–1752," *Pacific Ocean*, 405.

[61] The Spaniards listed him as Pedro Malec, but Hackett identifies him as Pierre Mallet (Charles W. Hackett, *Pichardo's Treatise*, III, 298), and that identification seems rather certain from the information "Pedro Malec" gave about himself.

[62] A long series of documents and letters concerning these men appears in Hackett, *ibid.*, III, 298–370.

[63] A reference to the Mallet party.

It is now evident that the two original avenues for the French advance—through Texas and via the upper Missouri River—had merged on the Arkansas River, which was convenient to New Orleans and which lessened the likelihood of encountering Spanish troops, who did not often, if ever, venture beyond the Red. The French, impelled by the desire for silver and for horses, both of which they thought could be obtained in New Mexico, now renewed their efforts to set up commerce with Santa Fe. In 1751, Pierre Mallet, with three other Frenchmen, ascended the Missouri River from New Orleans and reached New Mexico, but all were arrested and sent to Spain under the new regulation.

Spanish officials were watching developments carefully in 1751. Captain Fernández Sánchez Salvador, of Sonora and Sinaloa, thought the French would soon reach the Colorado (that is, the Colorado of the West) and descend it to the Pacific Ocean unless they should be impeded.[65]

These apprehensions were justified, for in 1752 there arrived in New Mexico two Frenchmen with an ominous document: a trading license issued by the commandant at Fort Chartres, across the Mississippi River in Illinois, "to make the discovery of New Mexico and to carry the goods that they may think proper."[66] Thus the expedition—and the goods—were official. That particular expedition was led by Jean Chapuis and Louis Feuilli, from Illinois; they reached Pecos and threw the Spaniards into a tizzy—not the least part of which was the orthographic difficulty encountered by the priest who wrote the governor, for he spelled their names Jean Xanxapij and Luis Fxuij. It is no wonder Spanish officials were opposed to French intrusions.

Chapuis and Feuilli had reached Pecos after ten months' travel. Their reception was somewhat less than cordial, and shortly after their arrival they were imprisoned and conducted to Chihuahua and later sent to Spain.[67]

[64] Pichardo's *Treatise*, III, 333 note. Pedro Malec's testimony indicates that he had made three trips toward Santa Fe.

[65] Bolton, *Texas in the Middle Eighteenth Century*, 68. He does not cite the document.

[66] Bolton, "French Intrusions Into New Mexico, 1749–1752," *Pacific Ocean*, 400–403.

[67] Bolton discusses this case at length in *loc. cit.*, 400–404.

Certainly the Spaniards had every right to be wary, for Chevalier de Kerlérec,[67a] governor of Louisiana, wanted to open trade with the interior parts of northern Mexico,[67b] and in 1753 proposed to the French king that they break through the Apache barrier (presumably in southwestern Texas) by obtaining an alliance between the Apaches and their enemies on the east, so they (the French) could establish a base in Apache country, with a view to taking the mines of Coahuila and Nuevo León in case of war. Kerlérec spoke of getting control of the road to Santa Fe[68] and at one time proposed to take Texas and the Mexican silver mines from the Spaniards.[69] Apparently nothing was done about the proposal, but the fact that it was made shows the seriousness of French intentions.

Kerlérec was only one French official with designs upon northern Mexico; the fact that many of the incidents have an earlier origin seems to point to Vaudreuil also. In 1751 a Frenchman, M. Massé, was living quietly, and presumably trading, on the Río Flores near Los Adaes, and nearby was M. Cortablau.[70] But others had been near Los Adaes and even deeper into Texas before Massé and Cortablau.

Chapuis and Feuilli were sent to Spain in 1754, and in that same year Joseph Blancpain was arrested at the mouth of the Trinity River on the East Texas coast, and with him were two Frenchmen, Elías

[67a] L. Billouart, Chevalier de Kerlérec, was born in France in 1704; was in the marine guards at 17, served in twenty-three campaigns; promoted to captain in 1751, and appointed governor of Louisiana in 1753, and was governor during the Seven Years' War with England, but left the colony in good condition in 1764 when he returned to France. He was then accused by subordinate officers and an officer's widow of abuse of authority and excess severity; he was exiled in 1769 but appealed, and was gathering testimony as to his ability and integrity when he died. He was a strict martinet, and many were the severe punishments during his administration: burning at the stake, breaking on the wheel, sawing in two in a coffin. He lived in a raw country, and those punishments, while certainly severe, were not as bad then as they would be today. He spent a great deal of money, but there was no evidence that he pocketed it.

[67b] Bolton (*Texas in the Middle Eighteenth Century*, 69) cites *"Projet de Paix et d'Alliance Avec les Cannecis," Journal de la Société des Americanistes de Paris*, Nouvelle Série, Vol. III, 67–76.

[68] Bolton, *Athanase de Mézières*, I, 64.

[69] Folmer, *Franco-Spanish Rivalry*, 303; Bolton, *Texas in the Middle Eighteenth Century*, 359–63.

[70] Isaac Joslin Cox, "The Louisiana-Texas Frontier," *Southwestern Historical Quarterly*, Vol. X, No. 1 (July, 1906), 21.

George and Antonio de la Fars, and two Negroes. Blancpain had been living there for two months, and he apparently owned cabins in the area. He said he had been trading, probably out of New Orleans, with the Indians for twenty-five years, and that he had a trading house at Natchitoches. He had a license from the governor of Louisiana to buy horses from the Attakapa Indians among whom he was living; he also appears to have been selling firearms. The Indians at El Orcoquizac, some reports say, were expecting fifty families of settlers and a minister from New Orleans.

It would have been difficult for any man to have violated more laws of the land, of the Spanish crown, and of the Holy Inquisition. The Spaniards gave his cabins to Chief Calzones Colorados (Red Drawers) of the Orcoquiza Indians (who apparently were Blancpain's hosts while he traded with the Attakapas), and sent him and his men to Mexico City. Blancpain died in prison, and his companions were sent to Spain for disposal by the Casa de Contratación, the powerful commerce-regulating board of the Spanish colonies.[71]

Kerlérec protested the arrest of Blancpain, at the same time claiming the mouth of the Trinity for Louisiana.[72] If Spanish officials had not been so concerned with budgetary matters, they probably would have taken more positive steps. And in at least one case the Spaniards themselves were profiting from the trade in contraband: beginning in about 1751 the governor of Texas, Barrios y Jáuregui,[73] had monopolized the contraband trade in his area, securing goods at Natchitoches and selling them where he could get the best prices.[74]

All this time the Taovaya Indians had been moving south, and 1760 found them with several villages in Texas. The Taovayas, the great traders of the southern plains, seem to have had their villages in a triangle: one cluster was at present-day Ringgold on the Red River, one north of Mineola, and one a little later at Waco. The villages north

[71] Bolton, "Spanish Activities on the Lower Trinity River, 1746–1771," *Southwestern Historical Quarterly*, Vol. XVI, No. 4 (April, 1913), 348–49.

[72] Bolton, *Texas in the Middle Eighteenth Century*, 73.

[73] Jacinto de Barrios y Jáuregui was a lieutenant-colonel of cavalry, was appointed governor and captain-general of Texas in 1751; during his time, the mission and presidio at San Saba were founded. Until 1759 he made much money by obtaining goods from the French in Natchitoches and trading them to the Indians, then marketing the furs in Natchitoches. He was later governor of Coahuila.

[74] Bolton, *Texas in the Middle Eighteenth Century*, 65.

of Mineola apparently were moved to the upper waters of the Brazos River by 1778, but in 1760 Father Calahorra found five French houses near the Taovaya villages north of Mineola, and in 1763 he reported seeing a French flag. Four years before, in 1759, Parrilla had said the Ringgold Taovayas had been led by Frenchmen, and there was a report that the Taovayas were on the Sabine.[75] Despite the difficulties of pinpointing Indian locations, it seems definite that the Taovayas (Jumanos, Wichitas) had moved south into Texas and that the French traders had come a great distance up the Red River to meet them.

In 1755 a French priest named Disdier and a man named Masé (the same as M. Massé?) asked Spanish permission to settle among the Orcoquisac Indians, but it was not granted.[76]

French efforts to penetrate Spanish territory abated in 1754, when France was fighting with England a war that eventually was to lose North America for them, and we have no more actual records of French attempts to reach Santa Fe.

In 1758 and 1759 the French appeared in Texas after two thousand Comanches and allied Indians massacred the Spaniards at the mission at San Luis de las Amarillas (commonly known as San Saba). The Indians, who carried French weapons, killed ten persons at the mission (of Santa Cruz), and Captain Parrilla[76a] pursued the raiding party with more than six hundred men and several cannon. He brought the Indians to bay (or did they bring him to bay?) at the Taovaya villages on the Red River near present Ringgold. The Indians made a stand and then counterattacked! Showing a French flag, using French weapons, and possibly using tactics directed by French minds, they whipped him soundly. Parrilla lost fifty-two men and at least two cannon—one of the worst defeats ever suffered by the Spaniards in the Southwest.[77]

[75] *Ibid.*, 91.

[76] Folmer, *Franco-Spanish Rivalry*, 304–305.

[76a] Diego Ortiz Parrilla served in the Spanish army against the Moors, then in Cuba, and at Vera Cruz as commander of Dragoons. He was governor *ad interim* of Sinaloa and Sonora, and became commandant of the San Sabá presidio in 1756, but was never enthusiastic about the location. After the massacre by Indians in 1758, he led some six hundred men on the northern expedition—which was considered a major disaster. He was governor of Coahuila in 1765. He surveyed the Texas coast from La Bahía to the Río Grande, and in 1769 met the governors of Coahuila and Texas in San Antonio to plan a campaign against the Norteños. He was promoted to brigadier by 1780.

The Seven Years' War (or French and Indian War) broke out in 1754 between France and England over the Ohio country; Spain did not fully align herself with France until 1762, when Prussia joined England. The war ended with England victorious, and final settlement was made by the Treaty of Paris, in which England received Spanish Florida in exchange for Havana. In a separate treaty, France ceded Louisiana to Spain to keep it out of British hands. When the smoke cleared away, the boundary of the Interior Provinces had jumped to the Mississippi River.

The Seven Years' War ended in 1763, but the transfer of authority in Louisiana was slow to reach local levels, and there was considerable resistance on the part of the Frenchmen in Louisiana, so that permanent control of Louisiana by the Spaniards did not become an actuality until about 1769.

In the meantime, a Mr. Brevel might have been up the Red River to Santa Fe and considerably beyond; he describes the country in very general terms, and speaks of the flora and fauna, not omitting the "white bears" (or grizzly bears) that Lewis and Clark were to note. Little more came of Brevel's trip, but Sibley reports that Brevel attempted, in 1782, to make a trip from San Antonio to Santa Fe but turned back for lack of water. Brevel's trip in 1782 was four years before Pedro Vial's first journey. However, not much reliance can be placed on the Brevel stories without further substantiation.[78]

After 1763, Louisiana was no longer a menace—for one important reason: Louisiana was now owned by Spain; and the territory was now in as great need of trade goods as was any part of New Spain. There

[77] Bolton, *Texas in the Middle Eighteenth Century*, 87–89. An interesting sidelight is the fact that Father Serra and Father Palóu were assigned to San Sabá, but following the report of the massacre they were reassigned to California, where Serra became the founder of the California mission system and Palóu became the great historian of that period. See Fray Francisco Palóu, *Historical Memoirs of New California* (Herbert E. Bolton, ed.).

[78] The Brevel story is told in a letter from John Sibley, Indian agent at Natchitoches, to General Henry Dearborn, Secretary of War, April 10, 1805, and appears in *American State Papers, Indian Affairs*, Vol. I, 725–30. Sibley says that Mr. Grappe, who had been long in the area and was was an interpreter and informer for the French, along with the American merchants at Nacogdoches, told Sibley that whatever account Brevel might give him could be relied upon. Pichardo, on the other hand, is vehement (perhaps too vehement) in maintaining that Brevel was a liar. See Hackett, *Pichardo's Treatise*, II, 73–76.

would continue to be disputes between New Spain and residents across the Sabine, but for practical purposes the rivalry was over.

The year after the cession of Louisiana, St. Louis was established (in 1764) as a fur-trading post by Pierre Laclède Liguest[79] and his stepson, Auguste Chouteau.[80] They were not aiming then at the Santa Fe trade but at the rich fur trade of the Osages to the southwest, only a fraction of the distance to Santa Fe; of the Pawnees to the west; of the Omahas and Otos up the Missouri. Liguest and Chouteau were given the right to trade along the entire Missouri River.

With Spain's borders now reaching to the Mississippi River, the complexion of Spanish defense was considerably changed. New Mexico no longer actively feared France, but she did fear Britain, which now owned Canada and all the North American continent east of the Mississippi River except the island of Orlèans, so the Spaniards began to use Louisiana as a buffer colony to keep the English out of New Mexico.

One aspect of the Spanish defenses—and it would seem to be a good one—was the acceptance of French governing officials into the service.

[79] Pierre Laclède Liguest (who in later life dropped the name Liguest) was born in the Pyrenees in France, and went to New Orleans in 1755, and in 1757 formed a union with a highly respected married woman, Marie Thérèse Chouteau, who, with her son, René Auguste Chouteau, left her husband for him. In 1762 Laclède became a partner in a trading firm, Maxent, Laclède & Co., and got an eight-year monopoly of trade with the "savages of the Missouri." In early 1764 he had his stepson, who was fourteen, start the village soon to be named St. Louis. Laclède was the sole ruler in Upper Louisiana for eighteen months (the French had ceded Louisiana in 1763), but was a benevolent dictator. He became entangled in debt to his firm and spent two years in New Orleans straightening out his accounts. On the way home in 1778 he died near the mouth of the Arkansas. He was the founder of a great family that does not bear his name, because under French law his descendants bore the legal name of his undivorced wife. One of his sons was Jean Pierre, born in 1758, and Jean Pierre had two sons: one named Pierre, born 1789, and Auguste Pierre, born in 1786.

[80] René Auguste Chouteau (generally known as Auguste), stepson of Pierre Laclède Liguest, was born in 1749, and went with his mother when she joined Liguest in 1757; she alleged gross cruelty on the part of her husband. When Auguste was fourteen, Laclède sent him in charge of a party of thirty men to begin the building of the village that was to be St. Louis. Auguste was Laclède's chief lieutenant until Laclède's death; he held councils with the Osages in the 1780's and had a monopoly on Osage trade from 1794 to 1802, acquiring a fortune. He was one of the first three judges of Louisiana under the United States, and in 1808 was made colonel of the St. Louis militia. Married in 1786, he died in 1829, leaving a widow, four sons, and three daughters. He was a man of great energy, ability, and tact, and of "incorruptible integrity." He was of medium height, had light-brown hair and a straight nose, was smooth shaven, quiet and grave.

Spain's multi-echeloned hierarchy in the New World, already plagued with Alejandro Oreilli,[80a] Hugo O'Conor,[80b] and the Flemish Baron de Riperdá, now had to digest Gallic tongue-twisters like Athanase de Mézières and Nicholas de Lassige.[80c] It therefore followed with logic that in Louisiana and even in East Texas (influenced by De Mézières), the Spaniards adopted the French policy of Indian control by the fur-traders-and-presents method (instead of the New Mexico and California pattern of mission-and-presidio),[81] perhaps influenced by the

[80a] Alexander O'Reilly (the Spaniards spelled his name in many ways) was born in Ireland about 1735, fought for Spain, Austria, and France. As major-general for Spain, he went to Havana in 1762, then saved Charles III's life in the Madrid insurrection of 1765. When the maladroit Antonio de Ulloa, the first Spanish governor of Louisiana, was expelled by insurrectionists in 1768, O'Reilly was sent to inflict punishment and restore order with 2,056 of the flower of the Spanish army. He was decisive, believed in inexorable justice, and almost immediately executed five Creoles who had been involved, thereby incurring the enmity of the Frenchmen, who labeled him "Bloody O'Reilly." Nevertheless, he restored order in six months, turned the government over to Unzaga, and returned to Spain. He was gentle, mild, courteous, and suave, but with an indomitable will; he was a capable administrator, and instituted in Louisiana a system of regulated trade. He died in 1794.

[80b] Hugo O'Conor, who started life as O'Connor but eventually signed "Oconór," was inspector-general of the Interior Provinces of the East, went to Texas in 1765 to investigate trouble between Navarrete and Pacheco; he became governor in 1767, when Texas was in very bad condition because of Indian raids. From 1772 to 1776 his task, as commander-inspector of the northern provinces, was to reorganize the frontier line of presidios in accord with Rubí's recommendations, and at the same time keep the Indians cowed along a two-thousand-mile front. He was a favorite of Bucareli, the viceroy, but his task was not easy. In 1775 he began an offensive war against the Apaches with one of the largest bodies of troops ever brought together to fight those Indians, and in general seems to have been a capable man, but he made his task more difficult by making accusations against a number of governors and comparable officials; he attacked De Mézières for his work among the Indian tribes, he attacked Riperdá for supporting De Mézières. In 1776 he said he was broken in health, and received a lighter post as governor of Guatemala, where apparently he recovered his health. His flaming red hair caused the Indians to call him the Red Captain.

[80c] Nicolas de Lassige or Lassize was a "notable" who signed several documents, one a treaty with the Taovayas and Cadodachos. Bolton, *Athanase de Mézières*, I, 259, 262.

[81] Bolton, *Athanase de Mézières*, I, 69–74. Apparently that change of policy did not come immediately, however, for thirty years later it was still a subject of discussion, when the governor of Louisiana wrote the commandment at Nacogdoches, saying: "In all the provinces of Louisiana and Florida it [furnishing of arms and munitions] is open and free with all the Indians. . . . After all, one must adopt the method that is followed in these provinces [those outside his command] if the Indians are to be contained, and to stop in time the vast designs of the Americans." Letter, unsigned, to Bernardo Fernández, New Orleans, January 10, 1797, Papeles de Cuba, leg. 124.

recommendations of the Marquis de Rubi,[82] following his 1766–68 inspection of the Texas area.

That recommendation was merely part of a considerably larger plan for reorganization of the entire northern frontier to provide a cordon of fifteen posts from Bahía to California, roughly along the line of the present international border. There would be a trading center and military post at Natchitoches, another on the Arkansas River, and establishments at Santa Fe and Taos, but all these would be beyond the cordon of presidios recommended. Rubí considered the cost of establishing a frontier line to include those points prohibitive, and therefore he felt the defense line should be farther south while there would be consolidations at those few points outside the area to be defended. He also recommended abandonment of the weak defenses in East Texas, now that Texas was no longer the frontier, and concentration of all missions (as well as all presidios) at San Antonio and Bahía del Espíritu Santo.[83]

His recommendations were ordered carried out, and East Texas was abandoned for a few years, but in 1773 Antonio Gil Ybarbo[84] led a revolt of the settlers who had been removed from East Texas, and the plan was departed from.

[82] Cayetano María Pignatelli Rubí Corbera y Saint Clement, Baron of Llinas, Marquis of Rubí, was already a field marshal in the Spanish army when he was appointed to inspect the defenses of the Interior Provinces in Texas and elsewhere. In 1766 he was joined by Nicolás de Lafora, engineer and map maker (who kept a diary). He was in Texas from August, 1767, to February, 1768, and his *Reglamento e Instrucción*, published in 1772, called for fifteen presidios forty leagues apart, and became part of a royal order providing abandonment of all Texas missions and presidios except those at San Antonio and Goliad, and aiming at friendliness toward the Norteños and extermination of the Apaches.

[83] Bolton, *Athanase de Mézières*, I, 66; Bolton, *Texas in the Middle Eighteenth Century*, 103–10; Thomas, *Teodoro de Croix*, 16; Kinnaird, *Frontiers of New Spain*, (1958), 1–42.

[84] Antonio Gil Ybarbo (or Ibarvo) was born at Los Adaes in 1729, to colonists sent from Spain. The ranch which he established there apparently was a fairly large operation. When the settlers were moved from East Texas by O'Conor following Rubí's recommendation, Ybarbo led the fight to return. In 1774 the settlers were allowed to return to the Trinity River and establish Bucareli, but after a disastrous Comanche raid in 1779, they removed to the site of Nacogdoches. Ybarbo was made lieutenant-governor and captain of militia and judge of contraband, but on the complaint of many persons that he was contrabanding, he resigned as governor. He was cleared of charges but exiled to Louisiana. He returned to Nacogdoches and died at his ranch there in 1809.

On the whole, after 1763 Spanish officials rested more easily, although they did not lose sight of the French menace, and in 1772 Riperdá, the governor of Texas,[85] proposed that a line of presidios be established from the Mississippi River to New Mexico. The *fiscal* in Mexico City,[86] however, did not seem very enthusiastic about the proposal but recommended that the matter be considered in council.[87]

In 1776 the Revolutionary War broke out, and in 1783, twenty years after France had a war with England, England in turn lost to the United States. Another shifting of boundaries occurred, and this time the Spaniards were faced with new and more vigorous threats, for when the Treaty of Versailles was signed, Spain found herself looking across the Mississippi at United States territory, and the Spaniards, who had faced numerous threats before, now had some new ones with which to contend.

They knew the restless character of the Anglo-Americans. In New Orleans, which was in Spanish territory, they called the Americans Kentuckians, and it was a dull week that did not bring a rumor that the Kentuckians were about to descend the Mississippi River and take over New Orleans. The coonskin-capped frontiersmen were constantly demanding free use of the river as a waterway for their bacon, flour, and whisky, and James Wilkinson, an officer in the United States Army, was promoting Wilkinson. Nobody knew better than did the Spaniards the

[85] Juan María Vicencio de Riperdá (or Ripperdá—sometimes without the accent) was Flemish but a native of Madrid. He was the first Spanish governor of Texas to make headquarters in San Antonio; Indian hostility was depopulating the country, and he had to threaten the settlers to get them to stay. In 1772 the capital of Texas was moved from Los Adaes to San Antonio, and there was a resultant expulsion of Texans from East Texas; they were supposed to go to San Antonio, but under the opposition of Gil Ybarbo were allowed to establish Bucareli on the Trinity River. Riperdá worked closely with De Mézières on the Indian problem, and they did much to pacify the Indians. Riperdá was governor until 1778, spent eleven months in Mexico, then was governor of Honduras, where he died in 1780.

[86] The *fiscal* was a sort of royal watchdog or attorney who defended the king's interests wherever they might appear—especially in cases affecting the exchequer, the church, and the rights of the Indians. There was a *fiscal* attached to the Council of the Indies and sometimes two *fiscales* attached to an *audiencia* (one for civil cases, one for criminal cases); usually a *fiscal* was attached to the viceroy's office, and he offered advice on administrative matters (as he did also to governors). Haring, *Spanish Empire*, 130.

[87] Areche to viceroy, Mexico, July 31, 1772, in Provincias Internas, Vol. 20, No. 7; printed in Bolton, *Athanase de Mézières*, I, 277–82.

seething nature of the country between St. Louis and the Cumberland Gap; Wilkinson[88] was in the Spanish pay and reported frequently to Spanish officials after 1787.

By 1785 it appears that both Spaniards and Frenchmen had tempered their ideas of hills of gold and lakes of pearls somewhere in the vast lands between Santa Fe and the Mississippi, but there were other products that had come to be valuable. One of them was horses. By that time, the droves of wild mustangs in Texas numbered countless thousands.

Documents of the 1760's and 1770's are replete with references to horses. In 1770 De Mézières,[89] who licensed all traders out of Natchitoches, was ordered to forbid trade in horses, mules, and slaves.[90]

[88] Wilkinson was born in Maryland in 1757 and took part in the Revolution. He was involved in the Conway Cabal against Washington; as clothier-general, his accounts were irregular. He resigned from the army but re-entered, becoming a brigadier general in 1792, commander-in-chief in 1796, and governor of Louisiana in 1805. After investigation by a court of inquiry in 1815, he moved to Mexico, where he died. He was a troublemaker, engaged in treasonable activity at least as early as 1787, and in the 1790's he was constantly embroiled in plans to separate Kentucky from the Union and attach it to Spain—for which purpose he was in the Spanish pay. He made a good impression on Miró; he was a hard-drinking man with a passion for intrigue and a greed for money. He was so devious that he sometimes wrote letters anonymously and sent them to himself. He became involved in the Burr conspiracy to set up a republic in Texas, and was court-martialed in 1811 for his part in the plot after he had revealed Burr's machinations to the government—presumably to save his own skin. Many thought Wilkinson was the originator of the entire scheme. He was acquitted for lack of evidence that has turned up since. Wilkinson was courteous, captivating in manner, and open, mild, and intelligent in appearance; firm, manly, and erect in carriage; accommodating and popular. He was a close friend of Gayoso and an employer of Philip Nolan.

[89] Athanase de Mézières was a native of Paris, went to Louisiana about 1733, and was in Natchitoches by 1743. In Natchitoches he was a captain of the army by 1756, and at that time was lieutenant commander of the post. He was a trader and planter of some substance. He was promoted to lieutenant colonel in 1773, received the Cross of St. Louis, and was appointed governor of Texas just before he died in 1779. He made a number of trips among the Indians of Texas, and was relied upon by men like Teodoro de Croix for information of those tribes. He was a man of culture, breeding, and education, and yet vigorous enough to recommend a campaign to exterminate the Apaches. Riperdá said De Mézières knew more than anyone else about Louisiana and Texas, and he is known as the man who established Spanish rule in the Red River Valley. He married first a daughter of Louis Juchereau de St. Denis, but that wife died in 1748; later he married again, but his wife and a son and a daughter died in an epidemic, all in the same week. See Bolton, *Athanase de Mézières.*

(That put the Taovayas on the spot, for they had little else to trade.)

The Spaniards objected to the trade in horses especially because the Indians built up their trading stock by stealing from the Spaniards, but when normal commerce with the Natchitoches traders was stopped, the Taovayas traded elsewhere. In 1773, J. Gaignard, on a good-will mission to the Comanches and Taovayas, found the Taovayas were selling their slaves and horses to the *contrabandistas* from Arkansas Post. Governor Elguezábal[91] of Texas tried to stop the contrabanding, but he reported that sometimes one thousand head of stock a month were moving into Louisiana.[92] Not only did the traders want horses, but the consumers in Louisiana also needed them, for in 1778 a captain of militia at Attakapas was on his way to Bexar for horses and mules for his troops.[93]

Horses were needed for farming, for exploring, and for waging war, and in 1785 the governor of Louisiana said: "All the wealth of the Indians on the Missouri consists in having many horses which they get from the Laytanes or Apaches . . . [who] live on the border of New Mexico." And it is hardly necessary to emphasize the fact that none of the Plains tribes were horsebreeders.

It has been pointed out that the term Illinois indicated land north of the Arkansas River, and it should be emphasized that Illinois was considered the key to Mexico by all who were interested.[94] It should be remembered that Miró also reflected the general view when he said that the Missouri River cut the Rocky Mountains north of the Río Grande; most of the maps of that time show the Missouri turning down the west side of New Mexico to about the latitude of the present United States-Mexico boundary. Also, the Missouri River was con-

[90] O'Reilly to De Mézières, January 23, 1770, in Papeles de Cuba, leg. 188–1, no. 26; printed in Bolton, *Athanase de Mézières*, I, 135.

[91] Juan José Elguezábal was born in San Antonio in 1781, but spent most of his public life in Coahuila as an army captain and commandant of the Río Grande and as adjutant-inspector of presidios in Coahuila and Texas. He was ad interim governor of Texas in 1834 and 1835 and was captured by Texans in 1835 and sent back to Matamoros, where he died in 1840.

[92] Mattie Austin Hatcher, "Conditions in Texas Affecting the Colonization Problem," *Southwestern Historical Quarterly*, Vol. XXV, No. 2 (October, 1921), 91.

[93] Bolton, "The Spanish Abandonment and Reoccupation of East Texas, 1773–1779," *Southwestern Historical Quarterly*, Vol. X, No. 2 (October, 1905), 104.

[94] Nasatir, *Before Lewis and Clark*, I, 78.

sidered the gateway to the Pacific Ocean,[95] and it was thought that one could ascend the Missouri, turn south, and reach Santa Fe with comparative ease. These geographical assumptions were commonly accepted by men in official positions until Lewis and Clark made their trip in 1804, 1805, and 1806.

One might think the Spaniards were through with the French menace when the French gave them Louisiana in 1763, but they never seemed to feel secure, and their misgivings were justified when, soon after the birth of the French Republic, Citizen Genêt came to the United States and violated United States neutrality by arming privateers and recruiting men. He tried to develop a plot, with George Rogers Clark, to march on New Orleans and against Santa Fe and Florida, but his actions became obnoxious to the United States, which demanded Genêt's recall in 1794.

Spain, on the other hand, for a number of years entertained a serious hope of separating Kentucky from the Union and attaching the western country (west of the Allegheny Mountains) to Spain. The Spanish intrigues commenced in 1787 under Governor Miró,[96] and involved James Wilkinson from the first; they subsided in 1791 when Carondelet[97] became governor, but in 1794 Wilkinson stirred the embers of Spanish hopes by advising Carondelet that the time was ripe

[95] *Ibid.*

[96] Esteban Rodriguez Miró was born in Catalonia in 1744 and entered the Spanish army at sixteen. He came to America in 1769 and was aide-de-camp to Bernard de Gálvez. Later promoted to colonel, he became acting governor when Gálvez left Louisiana in 1782, governor in 1785, and brigadier general in 1789. When Miró was charged with intriguing with Wilkinson to make $2,000 annually on tobacco, he went to Spain to defend himself. He was later appointed field marshal and died in 1795. As governor, Miró was popular, and his administration calls for respect. His intrigues with Wilkinson were carried on under instructions from Madrid. He was a mild administrator, encouraged commerce and agriculture, opposed the Inquisition, restored New Orleans after the great fire of 1788, and encouraged immigration and the partial opening of the Mississippi. He married Celeste C. C. Macarty, daughter of a wealthy Creole family. He knew French well, English less well.

[97] François Louis Hector, Baron of Carondelet, was born in 1748 in Flanders and was a colonel in the Spanish army and governor of San Salvador when he was appointed to succeed Miró in 1791 as governor and intendant of the provinces of Louisiana and West Florida. He was a brother-in-law of Las Casas, the captain-general at Havana, and is often criticized, but seems, all in all, to have been a rather good governor during trying times—the great period of the intrigues against Louisiana. In 1797 he left New Orleans to become president of the Audiencia of Quito.

(and requesting 200,000 pesos as expense money). Gayoso de Lemos,[98] governor of Natchez, got into the act and requested appointment to Philadelphia to conduct the intrigue, but Carondelet did not accede, undoubtedly knowing that such a position would put Gayoso into a position of too much importance. Carondelet did, however, write Godoy, urging the separation of Kentucky as a royal policy; the Consejo did not agree, but left Carondelet free to work on his own.

Carondelet sent Gayoso upriver, and after a complicated series of maneuvers during which Gayoso entertained William Clark but got no encouragement for his scheme of separation, Gayoso returned to Natchez, and the intrigues ended in 1796 because the Kentuckians got what they wanted in the Pinckney Treaty (Treaty of San Lorenzo).[99]

Spanish officials in Louisiana (many of them French by birth) were keenly aware of the violence that accompanied the French Revolution, and Carondelet voiced their fears when he wrote the viceroy in 1795:

> Our situation becomes each day more critical; each day arrive new songs, anonymous incendiary papers, etc., directed to make the officials odious and to familiarize the common people with the idea of guillotining us, of hanging us, and of committing the other atrocities which have afflicted France; we discover a conspiracy among the Negroes to kill their masters, . . . There reigns within these last two months a distrust, and many indications are observed which denote

[98] Manuel Gayoso de Lemos was born in 1752 in Portugal, educated in England, and entered the Spanish army, becoming a sub-lieutenant in 1772, lieutenant colonel in 1786, and colonel and governor of Natchez in 1789. In Natchez he was to administer the new Spanish policy of assimilation of Anglo-American settlers. In 1797 he succeeded Carondelet as governor-general of Louisiana, and he died as governor in 1799 at the age of forty-eight. He was energetic and able; mild, honest, likable, and a polished gentleman. He was a drinking friend of Wilkinson, and it will appear later that he was not entirely discreet in his dealings with Wilkinson. He married first in Spain; second in 1793, when Elizabeth Watts became his wife. She died within three months, and he married her sister, Margaret Cyrille, 17. He had a son by his Spanish wife and one by Margaret. He was a convivial spendthrift and died a poor man.

[99] For a discussion of Carondelet's interest in the project, of Gayoso's machinations in Illinois, Wilkinson's demands for money, and a mention of Philip Nolan's acting as Wilkinson's agent, see Frances Ellen Coughlin, "Spanish Galleys on the Mississippi: 1792–1797," unpublished master's thesis, Claremont Graduate School, 421–90. For a discussion with special emphasis on Carondelet, see Arthur Preston Whitaker, *The Spanish-American Frontier, 1783–1795*, 153–70. For Philip Nolan, see *infra*.

an insurrection . . . houses with wooden roofs have been purposefully set afire at night on various occasions. . . .[100]

In 1795 Spain and the United States signed the Pinckney Treaty, providing that the men from Kentucky (as they were called colloquially) could use the Mississippi River and could deposit their goods on the river bank at New Orleans (the right of deposit), and the Spaniards hoped that the granting of this new privilege would alleviate the threat from the Kentucky country. But Carondelet was taking nothing for granted; in 1795 he sent Gayoso de Lemos up the river to find out the temper of the inhabitants. Gayoso made an extensive report in November, assuring the governor that the people of Illinois were loyal and peaceful and of good intentions toward the government. He said also: "I consider it [Illinois] the most direct passageway to the kingdom of Mexico," and he reassured Carondelet by mentioning many of the prominent men of St. Louis and affirming their loyalties.

Immediately following Gayoso's report (and perhaps written without knowledge of the report) there was a letter from Revillagigedo[100a] to the governors of Nuevo Santander and Nuevo León,[101] warning them that the French might attack the Texas coast.[102]

[100] Carondelet to Branciforte [the viceroy], New Orleans, April 25, 1795, Madrid, Archivo Histórico Nacional (hereafter referred to as A.H.N.), Sección de Estado, carpeta 7, no. 7, cuaderno 12, f. 55 *passim.* See Ernest R. Liljegren, "Jacobinism in Spanish Louisiana, 1792–1797," *Louisiana Historical Quarterly*, Vol. XXII, No. 1 (January, 1939).

[100a] Juan Vicente de Güemes Pacheco de Padilla, second Count of Revillagigedo, and the second Revillagigedo to be a viceroy, was one of the great viceroys of New Spain. He succeeded Manuel Antonio Flores in 1789, and was a superior administrator and left an impression upon the prosperity of the country. He was eccentric but had endless energy and outstanding ability. He cleaned the filth out of Mexico City and was the first to light the streets there; he ordered that Indians be not compelled to pay tribute to the priests. The many craft guilds had suppressed training of workmen until Revillagigedo pointed out their decadence through monopoly and restriction of competition—which led to stagnation and a dearth of artisans; he expressed strong disapproval of the practice of selling public offices to the highest bidder. He was succeeded in 1794 by Branciforte. See Haring, *The Spanish Empire in America.* "The greatest of the nineteenth-century viceroys," says Priestley in *José de Gálvez;* of superb vigor and energy, he pushed the revenue to its highest figure of colonial times, and cleansed and beautified the city. The new king, Charles IV, began to oppose him, however, and ended his usefulness.

[101] Nuevo León was the district east and south of Coahuila of which Monterrey was the capital. Nuevo Santander was the region on the Gulf Coast of Texas south of the Nueces River.

The very real Spanish fear of the French was highly dramatized in the Spanish reaction to a book published in Philadelphia, entitled *El Desengaño del Hombre* (*The Undeceiving of Man*). The book, though containing a plea for realism and liberty, hardly seems to merit the great attention given it by the Spaniards, or the great fear that it engendered in Spanish minds. However, the documents of the late 1700's are replete with references to this volume and its iniquitous and subversive contents, and there are many admonitions to guard against its introduction into Louisiana.[102a]

It was in 1795 that the famous order went out to Spanish officials to "arrest all Frenchmen," and by the time of Revillagigedo's letter to the governors of Nuevo Santander and Nuevo León, there were 110 French prisoners in Mexico.

Less than one year later Carondelet had something specific about which to be worried, for he had arrested General Victor Collot of the French Republic,[103] who had come down from the Ohio country, where he had been traveling with an engineer, making detailed sketches of the country and the fortifications of the Ohio and of the Mississippi from St. Louis to Natchez, and perhaps of other portions of the country. He told Carondelet that it was advisable for France to

[102] Revillagigedo to governors, No. 7 (in Gómez), Mexico, December 18, 1795, A.H.N., Sección Estado, leg. 4177, carpeta 7.

[102a] James Puglia was the author of *El Desengaño del Hombre* (Philadelphia, 1794), which dealt with the controversy between Thomas Paine (*The Rights of Man*) and Edmund Burke, the great British writer in the field of political reasoning. Puglia was a Spanish instructor in Philadelphia, and the book was intended for Latin-American readers; three hundred copies were supposed to be sent into New Spain through New Orleans. Dr. Nasatir has read *El Desengaño del Hombre* and has not found it particularly noxious, even though Branciforte called it "extremely abominable" and thought it had been written by Frenchmen—"pernicious characters." There is a copy in the Library of Congress.

[103] George Victor Collot was born in France in 1751; he became a major general and chief of staff of the Army of the North in 1792. He transfered his allegiance to the Republic, and became governor of Guadeloupe in 1793. Made a prisoner-of-war by the British in 1794, he was paroled to the United States. He died in Paris in 1805, and his book, *A Journey in North America* (2 vols. and atlas), was published in Paris and London in 1826. For more on Collot, see Liljegren, "Jacobinism in Spanish Louisiana, 1792–1797," *Louisiana Historical Quarterly*, Vol. XXII, No. 1 (January, 1939); and Lloydine Della Martin, "George Victor Collot in the Mississippi Valley, 1796," unpublished master's thesis, University of California, 1935.

obtain the return of Louisiana to counteract England in Canada.[104] (At that time, war had broken out between England and Spain—in October, 1796—but the news did not reach Louisiana until early 1797.) Collot believed that the states west of the Allegheny Mountains would declare themselves independent if they could obtain support by either Spain or France. Carondelet, however, believed that the establishment of such a republic would put the kingdom of Mexico in much greater danger than ever before. It was only seven years after the French revolution, and Carondelet, an aristocrat, thought anything better than another revolution. When he reported to Havana he had placed Collot under arrest, and he informed the captain-general that more than two million pesos would be needed to put the province on a war footing.[105] Perhaps it was the mention of such a large sum of money that influenced Spain to return Louisiana to France.

Soon afterward (February 18, 1797), Godoy, the king's minister, wrote Yrujo,[106] the Spanish minister in Philadelphia, ordering him to send reports on Collot with all haste to Madrid and to include all maps and plans that might be used to settle the boundary dispute favorably.[107] On the same date, Yrujo wrote Godoy, saying that Collot had been arrested but freed, and that he had left the United States, also that Collot and the French minister had offered copies of all maps and other material made on Collot's trip.[108]

[104] Carondelet to Las Casas, No. 163, confidential, New Orleans, Nov. 1, 1795, in Papeles de Cuba, leg. 1447.

[105] *Ibid.*

[106] Carlos Martínez de Yrujo was born in Cartagena in 1769. In 1785 he was made secretary of the Dutch legation, and in 1787 an official of the London embassy. In 1795 he became minister to the United States. In 1802 he discovered the Blount conspiracy against Louisiana and the Floridas and defended the interests of Spain against Thomas Pickering, who favored the English. Yrujo was ambassador until 1807 and continued in public service until 1818, when he became *Secretario del Despacho de Estado* in which position he served almost one year. See Miguel Gómez del Campillo, *Relaciones Diplomáticas Entre España y los Estados Unidos*, I, *lxxxi* ff.

[107] Endless were the arguments about the boundaries of Louisiana, and in 1803 Napoleon told Livingston and Monroe the United States would have to accept the boundaries as they had been received from Spain. For practical purposes, however, Louisiana may be considered to have been bounded on the east by the Mississippi River, on the south by the Gulf of Mexico, on the west by the Sabine River, the Red River, the Arkansas River, and the Continental Divide.

[108] Yrujo to Godoy, No. 34, Philadelphia, February 18, 1797, A.H.N., Estado, leg. 3889; Godoy to Yrujo, annexed to No. 34.

During the 1790's, then, the Spanish had little easement of their fears, but instead walked a constant tightrope, trying to get along with the Americans without giving them too many advantages or too many invitations. And all the time, the English were infiltrating northern Louisiana through the Mandan area and through Prairie du Chien on the Mississippi River. The Spanish fear of the Americans was perhaps more vivid, but their fear of the British was more deep seated.

# IV

## *The British Threat*

From the time of the Mallet brothers, the Spaniards had tried to restrain French traders from reaching Santa Fe, but in 1763 they suddenly found that the French threat to New Mexico had disappeared when England had won Canada from France and France had ceded Louisiana to Spain to keep it out of British hands. When France no longer had a hold on continental North America, Spain found the former no-man's-land between the Arkansas and the Missouri no longer a barrier between nations but actually Spanish territory, so Spanish sovereignty moved into the Mississippi Valley and took up an uneasy occupancy across the river from England.[1] By no means did Spain breathe more easily, for in place of the aggressive and successful French came the more aggressive, more successful, and more feared British.

It was not a new fear for the Spaniards, for the Britons had long worried the Spaniards in Santa Fe and Texas. They had been in the habit of coming down from the Hudson's Bay country in the north, of entering the Arkansas country from Carolina on the east, of dabbling around on the Texas coast.

Nor were the British blind to the proximity of the Spaniards, for as early as 1754 Anthony Hendry took a vacation trip from Hudson's Bay and turned up among the Blackfeet Indians, where he found Spanish horses with Spanish brands, Spanish bridles, and Spanish bits, which

[1] The region north of the Arkansas River and west of the Mississippi River then became known as Spanish Illinois. See Nasatir, "The Anglo-Spanish Frontier on the Upper Mississippi, 1786–1796," *Iowa Journal of History and Politics*, Vol. XXIX, No. 2 (April, 1931), 156.

the Britons translated into terms of the nearness of New Mexico and the world-famous silver mines.[2]

Nine years after Hendry's trip, England ousted France from Canada and also from the area enclosed by the Mississippi River, the Ohio River, and the Great Lakes. That area, to be known as British Illinois, was not immediately occupied by the British because of the conspiracy of Pontiac, the Ottawa chief, but England soon established her rule, and her aggressive traders, coming down from Canada through Michigan and the Great Lakes, traded goods to the Indians for furs—with no particular respect for established boundary lines. From that time on, the Anglo-Spanish frontier was at the Mississippi River, and Spain had a set of new and different problems.

With Spain and England facing each other across the Mississippi, various complications arose because not only did English traders cross to the west, but Spanish traders also crossed to the east side, and Indians living on the shores of Lake Michigan went to St. Louis for their annual presents. This sort of wide-open enterprise led to the Ducharme incident of 1773.

Jean Marie Ducharme in 1772 obtained a license to trade in the Illinois country, using two canoes, seventeen men, and £1,500 worth of merchandise. Obviously such a license, issued by a British official, was good only in British Illinois—but sometime in October or November, 1772, under this license or a similar one, Ducharme took his company across the Mississippi and up the Missouri to the Little Osage Indians, where he stayed for four or five months.

Pedro Piernas,[3] lieutenant-governor of Spanish Illinois, learned of Ducharme and heard that he was subverting the Osages and inspiring in them "sentiments totally opposed to the maxims of Christianity and of good conduct." The Osages had long been bad actors, and it was poor etiquette for a foreigner to stir them up, so Piernas dispatched Pierre Laclède Liguest and a detachment of men in canoes (all without ex-

[2] [ ] to Vaudreil, Versailles, October 2, 1750, in A.N.Col., B 91, f. 405.

[3] Pedro Piernas was sent to Upper Louisiana by Ulloa where he took charge in 1769. He returned to New Orleans and was re-appointed by O'Reilly; afterward he became lieutenant-governor of St. Louis and was ordered to investigate the conduct of Francisco Ríu. He became the first Spanish commandant of Upper Louisiana, at a salary of 327 pesos annually. He actually took charge in St. Louis in 1770, and in 1775 he was succeeded by Francisco Cruzat.

pense to his Majesty) to apprehend the intruder. Ducharme and some of his men were taken into custody, along with a considerable amount of goods. The goods were awarded to the men of the expedition under Laclède, thereby saving the royal treasury considerable expense—but Ducharme escaped, and one month later at Montreal he received another license to trade with the Indians.[4]

Spain was aware at an early date that England was a far more dangerous foe than Bourbon France had been. And as Louisiana became Spanish, an important change took place in the strategy of defense for New Mexico, because that province was no longer a frontier barrier but an integral part of New Spain's inner defenses, while Louisiana now formed the outer barrier to foreign penetration. From 1763 to 1800, Louisiana was regarded as the key to the defense of New Spain (which was considered more valuable than Louisiana itself), and Louisiana's occupation was considered necessary primarily to forestall infiltration by English and American pioneers and traders who would promptly move on to Santa Fe.[5] Louisiana was a big land, and its size would act as a barrier, the Spaniards reasoned. Perhaps, too, a defensive line could be established from the Gulf of Mexico to Canada to protect the rich Mexican silver mines.[6]

In accordance with the new strategy, and to prevent the entry of British traders into Louisiana, military defenses were diverted from East Texas to the Mississippi River (and some were pulled back to San Antonio),[7] Francisco Ríu[8] was sent to construct a fort at the con-

[4] See Nasatir, "Ducharme's Invasion of Missouri," *Missouri Historical Review,* Vol. XXIV, No. 1 (October, 1939); Ducharme remained in the Indian trade until he died at Sault St. Louis in 1791 at the age of eighty-one.

[5] Bolton, *Athanase de Mézières,* I, 66–67.

[6] Nasatir, *Before Lewis and Clark,* I, 59–60; see Redon de Rassac, 1763, A.N.C., C[13]A, Vol. XLIII, ff., 380–86, in which is discussed the building of a fort at two hundred leagues "above the post of Missouri," and nine others among the Panis, Kansas, Cadodaquis, and others, to form a chain of forts to protect the north and east districts of Mexico.

[7] Bolton, *Athanase de Mézières,* I, 66–67.

[8] Francisco Ríu was sent by Ulloa in 1767 to build two forts in Upper Louisiana. St. Ange de Bellerive, the French commandant at Fort Chartres, was in actual command of Illinois and Upper Louisiana at that time and remained there, acting as Ríu's adviser on Indian affairs. Ríu, however, was maladroit and incompetent, and disliked by soldiers and citizens; Pedro Piernas, sent to investigate him in 1770, actually took over the command of the forts from St. Ange.

fluence of the Missouri and the Mississippi,[9] and a lieutenant-governor was appointed, with headquarters at the recently established village of St. Louis, to administer the vast upper Mississippi-Missouri valley.

Long before the end of the French and Indian War, Spain had feared that the English would cross the Mississippi and the Missouri, and had actually feared that England might take over western Louisiana.[10] And although that dreaded situation had not developed, England had occupied the area east of the Mississippi, and now Spain feared that British traders would seduce the Indians across the river from them. Therefore, Spain's attitude toward the Plains Indian tribes also changed. Previously the Spaniards had maintained a precarious peace with whatever tribes seemed subservient and had used those tribes to fight other tribes. But now the Jumanos, Pawnees, Kansas, Comanches, and Osages could be as effective a barrier against the English as they had been against the French—but this time it would be better organized, and the Indians would receive more assistance from the Spaniards. So Spain changed her policy toward the Indians and went to the traders-and-presents system.

The specific objectives were several: to win and hold the allegiance of the Indian tribes of Louisiana (including all the great warrior tribes of the Plains); to keep those tribes hostile to all foreigners, especially the English; to exclude unlicensed traders; to stop all trade with Indians in horses, mules, and slaves; to encourage friendly tribes to pillage French traders; to induce friendly Indians to cross the Mississippi from the east, and to establish posts to encourage those crossings; to control the Indians through carefully regulated trade, and to keep them in a peaceful frame of mind toward the Spaniards, partly by the distribution of liberal annual gifts in the name of

[9] Ulloa to Ríu, January 7, 1769, in Houck, *Spanish Régime,* I, 20. Antonio de Ulloa was born in Seville in 1716 and entered the Spanish navy in 1733. A scholar, he worked thirteen years on a commission to measure an arc of the equatorial meridian. He was once captured by the British, who later released him. In 1762 he became the first governor of Louisiana, but he was too mild and gentle to administer the colony after the transfer of authority. An insurrection caused his withdrawal in 1769, when he was succeeded by O'Reilly. He served in the navy but interested himself in scientific matters to the detriment of the navy. He married the beautiful Peruvian Marchioness d'Abrado (see Gayarré, *History of Louisiana,* II, 173–86), and died in 1795.

[10] Bolton, *Athanase de Mézières,* I, 68; Bjork, "The Establishment of Spanish Rule," chap. X.

the king; to provide enough trade goods to keep the Indians satisfied (a very important item); and to give them an outlet for their furs and surplus crops. Under the new system, traders would be governmental agents as well as private businessmen, for they were permitted to enter the trade only under definite governmental restrictions designed to promote the best interests of Spain. Foreigners were to be excluded from Spanish Indian country, and intoxicating liquor was not to be given or sold to the Indians.[11]

To further the new system, the Spaniards sent special agents to various tribes and encouraged native chiefs to visit Spanish posts; they used friendly Indians as intermediaries between the Spaniards and hostile tribes. Cajolery and flattery and the liberal distribution of medals among Indians were used to keep as many tribes as possible friendly to Spain. Finally, the Spaniards increased their Mississippi and Missouri river posts in number and strength and began policing the Mississippi River.

For the execution of the new policy, Spain depended to a large extent on officials of French heritage who had elected to remain in the Spanish service. As a network of posts or distribution centers for presents, they designated Natchitoches in the south, and posts on the Arkansas in the mid-east, St. Louis in the northeast, and Santa Fe and Taos in the west; Nacogdoches also was used in northeast Texas.[12]

But with the tremendous expansion of the northern frontier, still other reforms were called for—the most important of which involved setting up an entirely new government for the northern provinces of Mexico. It had long been recognized that those provinces, all large in land area, and all at a great distance from Mexico City, presented problems that could not be adequately handled from Mexico City. Therefore, at the instigation of José de Gálvez,[13] Spain's great *visitador*

[11] Bolton, *Athanase de Mézières*, I, 68–73, 149.

[12] *Ibid.*, I, 74; this entire thing, of course, arose from Rubí's inspection.

[13] José de Gálvez, who started in life as a shepherd boy, rose in the ruling circles of Spain through a good legal education, a fortunate French marriage, and a secretaryship under Grimaldi, the minister of state. In 1765 he was sent to New Spain by Charles III as visitor-general of the royal treasury. He was intelligent and capable and was able to fit his administration to the times. In Guanajuato in 1767 he punished those taking part in a rebellion by executing 85, lashing 73, banishing 117, and imprisoning 674. But in his six years' visitorship, he checked official corruption and rapacity and increased the royal income. He antagonized the viceroy of Mexico by sending a warship

*general* in Mexico, a sweeping reform was made: the creation of the commandancy-general of the Provincias Internas (the Interior Provinces). Under that system, the northern provinces were separated from the rest of Mexico under a military government headed by a commandant-general independent of the viceroy. New Mexico and Texas were included in the Interior Provinces, but Louisiana was left outside, attached to a captaincy-general at Havana, which also was independent of viceregal authority. Northern Mexico and Louisiana, then, were two very large areas, each independent of the viceroy and each independent of the other.

From Louisiana, the traders-and-presents policy extended into Texas, while in South Texas and in New Mexico, the mission-and-presidio system continued. Presumably the new governmental setup was expected to lead to co-operation and harmony between New Mexico and Louisiana—but actually it did not. Instead, it created conflicts in frontier policy that contributed later to the practical isolation of each area from the other.[14]

Under the new plan, Teodoro de Croix became the first commandant-general. He was to study the archives in Mexico City and to inspect the provinces in person; at Arizpe, Sonora, he would establish a capital and a mint; he would have jurisdiction over the departments of justice, policy, treasury, and war; he would maintain a bodyguard; and his salary would be 20,000 pesos a year.[15]

Croix promptly called councils of governors and military men in

to capture French and English smugglers, and in the process he uncovered a number of dishonest Spanish officials. The viceroy, Cruíllas, complained bitterly and was recalled and replaced by Francisco de Croix, the uncle of Teodoro. Gálvez and Croix worked well together and carried out the Jesuit expulsion of 1767; Gálvez was in charge of the settlement of San Diego and Monterey in Alta California. Gálvez and Croiz worked out the intendent system to eliminate many evils of government, but it was not fully utilized until Revillagigedo established it after Gálvez' death. Gálvez became minister-general of the Indies in about 1771, and it was in that capacity that he established the Interior Provinces—much to the displeasure of most viceroys. Gálvez died in 1787. He was a man of incredible energy, great nervous force, towering ambition, and malignant vindictiveness. See Herbert I. Priestley, "The Reforms of José de Gálvez in New Spain," *Pacific Ocean History,* 349–59. José's brother, Matías de Gálvez, was viceroy, 1783–84, but died in office and was succeeded by his son (José's nephew), Bernardo de Gálvez, who had been governor-general of Louisiana.

[14] Bolton, *Athanase de Mézières,* I, 75–76, 105, 107.

[15] Thomas, *Teodoro de Croix,* 20.

Monclova, San Antonio, and Chihuahua, and out of those meetings came a well-articulated defense program that included protective measures for the entire frontier of the Interior Provinces. Whereas O'Conor had fought Indians with efficiency but had neglected the rearrangement of the presidios and the disposition of his forces of defense against the Indians (the principal feature of the Rubí plan), and had thereby contributed to a further decline of the Interior Provinces, Croix planned rearrangement of the presidios, establishment of a secondary defense system in principal pueblos, frontal attacks upon Apache bands, and alliance with various groups of Comanches.[16] The Spaniards' primary concern, as always, was the Indian threat.

The defense plan that was established seems almost the same as Rubí's plan, although the new plan was concerned only with the Interior Provinces and Louisiana. It is noticeable, however, that although the acquisition of Louisiana had caused the reorganization, Louisiana did not enter very strongly into the strategy for northern Mexico.

The Lipan Apaches at that time constituted a greater problem than did other Indian tribes because of Comanche pressure against them from the north. Deprived of their usual victims, and especially cut off from their trading contacts with the Taovayas, the Apaches had turned on the Spanish inhabitants of Texas—especially those in the region of San Antonio—and Rubí (who had made the long inspection of 1766–68), had suggested a union with the Comanches against the Apaches because he believed the Comanches would better observe a treaty than would the Apaches.

At the time of Croix's activity, New Mexico was in the middle of her Indian problems, and she especially was more concerned with the Indians than with the British, who were a long way off.

One of Croix's plans was to unite three or four hundred frontiersmen of Louisiana with the military forces of the Interior Provinces to wipe out the eastern Apaches (Lipans)—a proposal made by Ripperdá in 1772, and probably originated by Athanase de Mézières. The plan was feasible in 1777–78 only because of Croix's friendship for Bernardo de Gálvez, governor of Louisiana.[17]

[16] Bolton, *Athanase de Mézières*, II, 220–24.

[17] Bernardo de Gálvez, nephew of José de Gálvez, had one of the most meteoric careers in New Spain—partly explainable by the influence of his uncle, José, who

De Mézières, at the time of Croix's becoming commandant-general (1776), was well recognized as an authority on Texas Indians, and Croix called on him for help. The council at Monclava recommended that he be called to Texas to cultivate the Norteños and to work out a plan for using them in the proposed campaign. Though De Mézières was not a member of the council at Monclova or the following one at San Antonio, he was in San Antonio within two months of the meeting of the council and had prepared a plan to exterminate the Apaches.[18] Then De Mézières was sent on an extended trip to the Wichitas and Tonkawas, and during that trip wrote Croix sixteen long and detailed letters on the Indians; when he returned to Natchitoches, he continued to write Croix, and the council of war at Chihuahua recommended that the governor of Louisiana be asked to permit De Mézières to be transferred to Texas.

Spain was about to get into war with England, however, and the plan to wage war on the Apaches had to be postponed. Croix asked Gálvez for the loan of De Mézières as ad interim governor of Texas, but Cabello[19] arrived, and De Mézières instead made another trip among the Texas Indians.

was second only to King Charles III, but also in large part by his own great ability. He was in the war with Portugal, fought Apaches in Nueva Vizcaya in 1769, 1770–72, and was a close friend of Teodoro de Croix. He went to Louisiana in 1776, as a colonel, and became governor in 1777, succeeding Unzaga. In 1784 he became captain-general of Cuba and governor of Louisiana and the Floridas; in 1785 he succeeded his father, Matías (older brother of José), as viceroy, and for a while ruled Cuba, the Floridas, Louisiana, Mexico, and the Interior Provinces. As viceroy, he was made a count. However, in November, 1786, he was stricken with fever, and died at the age of thirty-eight. He had not the intellectual attainments of Ulloa, the military reputation of O'Reilly, or the executive experience of Unzaga, but he was no callow youth; he was dynamic, attractive, personable, and a leader of men, and he possessed his own attributes of greatness that made him equal to the needs of his time. He and his wife Felicita were charming and very popular, and he was commended by the king. A daughter was born eight days after his funeral. See John W. Caughey, *Bernardo de Gálvez in Louisiana, 1776–1783*.

[18] His plan for the campaign against the Apaches was opposed by the king and never carried out.

[19] Domingo Cabello, born in Castile, was a sub-lieutenant in the army in 1741, governor of Nicaragua in 1762, and a colonel in 1777. In 1778 he succeeded Riperdá as governor of Texas, and in 1786 he commissioned Pedro Vial to explore a route from San Antonio to Santa Fe (diary printed *infra*). In that year he was transferred to Havana and was succeeded in Texas by Rafael Martínez Pacheco.

A major problem of the Spaniards in connection with the acquisition of Louisiana was the cost of Louisiana's administration—an item that hit Texas especially hard because of its problem with the Apaches. Spanish officials were economizing, as usual, and that fact alone prevented any real unification of the outlying territory. Plagued by unruly Indians, harassed by the British threat on the east, and uncomfortable because of lack of funds, the Spaniards found themselves in a dilemma, and unfortunately the formation of the Interior Provinces did not by any means solve all their problems—especially those created by the British.

As soon as the British had taken over from the French in 1763, British traders had swarmed through Prairie du Chien on the upper course of the Mississippi River. The post at Prairie du Chien had long been a convenient meeting place for Indians and traders in the upper Mississippi area. Probably at first the traders from British Illinois merely congregated there and did business with the Indians who met them, but that state of affairs did not last long, and Prairie du Chien soon became an official port of entry into northern Louisiana as well as a trading center.[20]

From Prairie du Chien by 1776 the British were ascending the Missisipi and St. Peter's rivers to the rich fur areas of Minnesota, where they traded with the Indians in violation of international and Spanish laws—encouraged by British officials and unmolested by Spanish officials. From Prairie du Chien also they crossed into the Iowa country via the Turkey, Iowa, and Des Moines rivers. In truth, the movement through Prairie du Chien was the beginning of an economic war between Spain and England for the control of the upper Mississippi Valley.[21]

With the British moving in through Prairie du Chien, the Spaniards feared that England would attempt the physical conquest of New Mexico from the north. Certainly England wasted no time establishing contact with the Plains Indians when the French withdrew from Lou-

[20] Prairie du Chien is five hundred miles above St. Louis, at the mouth of the Wisconsin River, and was a great meeting place in the 1780's. See Nasatir, "The Anglo-Spanish Frontier," *Iowa Journal of History and Politics,* Vol. XXIX, No. 2 (April, 1931), 157.

[21] Nasatir, *Before Lewis and Clark,* I, 79.

isiana. As a matter of fact, Englishmen had been trading far west of the Missouri before 1763; shortly after that time, Britons from the north began to follow the trail blazed by the Vérendryes[22] in 1738; traders from the Hudson's Bay Company followed the southern tributaries of the Assiniboine River, and those from the North West Company's posts on the Assiniboine and on the Red River of the North began to cross overland to trade with the Mandans and Arikaras on the upper Missouri. In Iowa and Minnesota, both the St. Peter's (the Minnesota River) and the Des Moines rivers led toward the Missouri, and British traders from Prairie du Chien followed those rivers, portaged across the Iowa hills or the Dakota prairies, and then ascended the Missouri.

In that struggle for the upper Mississippi and upper Missouri valleys, the English had a number of advantages over Spain, as England had had them over France: superior organization for trading; less governmental restriction; more aggressive, more efficient, and more clever traders, trappers, and *voyageurs;* greater governmental encouragement and protection; more and better merchandise at lower prices; a more adequate supply of money; and a better market for furs.[23] With those

[22] Pierre Gaultier de Varennes, Sieur de la Vérendrye, was born in Quebec in 1685, went into the French army in Europe, and fought in three campaigns in Canada against the English. In 1712 he was made an ensign in Canada by recommendation of the wife of Vaudreuil, then governor of Canada. He established a trading post near Three Rivers, but after a few years he began to think about going toward the Pacific Ocean. In 1731 he went into partnership in the fur trade, and with three sons and a nephew he traveled west from Grand Portage. In 1738–39 he visited the Mandans on the Missouri River (though some authorities do not agree that he went that far), preceding David Thompson, F. A. Larocque, Charles Mackenzie, Alexander Henry, and Lewis and Clark, who were later followed by Brackenridge, Bradbury, Catlin, and Maximilian. In 1742 two of Vérendrye's sons tried to reach the Pacific Ocean and went considerably southwest of the Mandans—far enough to receive descriptions of Spaniards (perhaps from Kiowas); they were on the road about ten months. Vérendrye prepared a map that does not show either the headwaters of the Missouri or that river's connection with the Mississippi. He died in Montreal in 1749 after a lifetime of struggle against debt. See Lawrence J. Burpee, *Journals and Letters of Pierre Gaultier de Varennes de la Vérendrye and His Sons.*

[23] See Surrey, *The Commerce of Louisiana,* 49–52, 58–59, 62, 65, 346; Nasatir, *Before Lewis and Clark,* I, 86n., 182, 401, 433, and especially Trudeau to Carondelet, St. Louis, May 20, 1793, on pp. 174–79; also Nasatir, "The Anglo-Spanish Frontier on the Upper Mississippi, 1786–1796," *Iowa Journal of History and Politics,* Vol. XXIX, No. 2 (April, 1931), 159, 163, 219.

advantages, the British traders from Montreal and Michilimackinac[24] not only were able to compete with their Spanish rivals but also were able to win away from them a large share of the trade and friendship of the Indian tribes, and they even, before it was over, sold British goods to Spanish merchants in St. Louis.

Actually, there was nothing new about the English penetration of Louisiana, for one early account relating British intentions against the French and Spanish lands dates back to 1716, and although the source is French, it reflects the British threat without equivocation:

> The English, being very strong in Carolina and Virginia, besides observing with a covetous eye the French mastery of Louisiana, are endeavoring seriously to turn to [their own] account this beautiful and charming country, which is a barrier that prevents their penetration of Mexico, the riches of which are a great temptation to them.[25]

The French had tried to stem the English infiltration but failed. The Indians under Pontiac kept the Englishmen out of the Ohio country from 1763 until 1765,[26] but as soon as the Britons overcame the Indian resistance and reached the Anglo-Spanish frontier on the Mississippi, English traders and merchants began to move up the Missouri and up the Platte. That forced the Spaniards to act. Up to that time, they had delayed their effective occupation of Louisiana, but now,

[24] Michilimackinac was at about the site of the present Mackinaw, Michigan, on the south side of the Straits of Mackinac, which separates Lake Michigan from Lake Huron and was one of two important posts between Montreal and the fur country: Detroit and Michilimackinac. Traders and *voyageurs* brought supplies in canoes up the St. Lawrence from Montreal, through Lake Ontario and Lake Erie to Detroit, then through Lake Huron to Michilimackinac, then south through Lake Michigan or west on the Wisconsin rivers; or from Michilimackinac west through Lake Superior and the Grand Portage. Michilimackinac was about the site of the present Mackinaw, Michigan, on the south side of the Straits of Mackinac.

[25] [Minister] to Vaudreil, Versailles, Oct. 2, 1750; A. N. Col., Vol. B 91, 405 *et vo*. It should be understood that the many references to the silver mines of New Mexico were partly true but partly arose from geographical misunderstanding. There were mines near Chihuahua and in northern Sonora, and since the geography of that entire area—and especially of New Mexico—was not at all definite, and especially since, from the standpoint of nations looking that way from the north and east, Santa Fe was the outpost, it rather appears that New Mexico and the silver mines tended to merge.

[26] Nasatir, "Ducharme's Invasion of Missouri, an Incident in the Anglo-Spanish Rivalry for the Indian trade of Upper Louisiana," *Missouri Historical Review*, Vol. XXIV, Nos. 1, 2, 3 (October, 1929, January and April, 1930), 5.

while the French marked time, waiting for the Spaniards to take actual control, Englishmen were arriving to foment trouble among the Indian tribes. In spite of Ríu's fort and the governorship at St. Louis, the English advanced westward, and there were frequent Spanish complaints against them, offset either seriously or contentiously by numerous English complaints that Spanish traders were invading eastern Louisiana across the Mississippi! In present-day Missouri and Illinois, both sides were active, but neither seemed to be dominant; in the Iowa-Minnesota area, British traders were in control.

During that period, several ominous events occurred. Ducharme traded with the Osages in 1772 and 1773. Peter Pond went into Iowa in 1773, and Jonathan Carver, a British captain, entered Spanish territory from Prairie du Chien in 1776.[27] In 1786 also Colonel Francisco Bouligny[28] reported to José de Gálvez, then secretary of state for the Indies, that since 1764 the commerce of Louisiana had been $600,000 a year, of which sum only about $15,000 a year had gone to Spain—the rest to England.

In 1777 the English were trading with the Sioux via the Des Moines River.[29] In the following year (1778), in the period from April 13 to June 4, no fewer than twelve persons or firms received British licenses to trade in the Illinois country, on the Mississippi River, and from Prairie du Chien.[30] In that year, however, the Spaniards were able to counter the British in the Mississippi Valley, and perhaps to have an edge on them, for the American Revolution had diverted British attention to the Atlantic Coast, and Spain found herself able to check the physical advances of the British. She defeated a British attack on St. Louis and countered with a lightning attack on the British post of St. Joseph; in the south, she won back the Floridas, which she had ceded to England in 1763.

[27] Nasatir, "The Anglo-Spanish Frontier in the Illinois Country," *Journal* of the Illinois State Historical Society, Vol. XXI, No. 3 (October, 1928), 295.

[28] Francisco Bouligny to José Gálvez, August 10, 1786 (cited in Gayarré, *History of Louisiana,* III). Francisco de Bouligny was colonel of the Louisiana Regiment, succeeding Pedro Piernas; in 1785 he was relieved of the commandancy of Natchez at his own request. When Gayoso died in 1799, Bouligny was for a short time the military commandant of Louisiana, but he died soon after Gayoso. His descendants have been prominent in Louisiana.

[29] Houck, *Spanish Régime,* I, 145.

[30] See *Wisconsin Historical Collections,* XI, 99.

In 1780 two British flags were somehow introduced among the Missouri Indians in Spanish territory, and a Sioux chief returned to Spanish territory from Michilimackinac with British presents.[31] In 1793 the English traded with the Mandans;[32] in 1795 they traded with the Omahas and built a fort in Omaha country.[33] In 1795, while the Hudson's Bay Company traded along the Canadian border, "traders from Montreal" built a fort among the Mandans and occupied it continuously;[34] in the following year (1796) the English had a settlement on the Platte River;[35] and in that same year the Welshman, John Evans, destroyed the British fort among the Mandans,[36] and also offered to destroy the British fort on the Platte.[37]

Although Britain encroached upon Spanish territory, the Spaniards, with their defeat of the Britons at St. Louis and in the Floridas and their successful attack on the British post at St. Joseph,[38] might have seemed to have the upper hand—but eventually those meager successes were reversed. The Spanish commandant at St. Louis could not obtain supplies for his posts and for the Indians, and again Spain lost control of the upper Mississippi and even of the upper Missouri, and her long frontier was penetrated at will by both English and American traders. British traders monopolized the trade of the Iowa-Minnesota area as before, and of the Great Bend region of the Missouri as

[31] Houck, *Spanish Régime,* I, 175–76.

[32] Burpee, *Journals . . . a la Vérendrye,* 11.

[33] Houck, *Spanish Régime,* II, 187, 190. Diary of James Mackay, apparently reporting from the neighborhood of present Sioux Falls. Mackay was a Scotsman, one of the first English-speaking settlers of Upper Louisiana. As a fur trader, in 1795 he made a voyage of discovery up the Missouri, for which he was made commandant of the post of St. Andrew and granted 30,000 arpents of land.

[34] *Ibid.,* 254.

[35] *Ibid.,* 181.

[36] *Ibid.,* 207, 254.

[37] Carondelet to Godoy, New Orleans, June 3, 1796, in Nasatir, *Before Lewis and Clark,* I, 355.

[38] An important British post, apparently about where St. Joseph, Michigan, is now, on the east side of Lake Michigan near the south end; they went up the Illinois River from St. Louis 80 leagues, and then overland 130 leagues. It was in the dead of a severe winter, but the attack was successful, and they destroyed a large quantity of supplies apparently intended for an invasion of Spanish territory. See Nasatir, "The Anglo-Spanish Frontier in the Illinois Country During the American Revolution, 1779–1783," *Journal* of the Illinois State Historical Society, Vol. XXI, No. 3 (October, 1928), 332.

well, and British firms supplied Spanish merchants from their stocks in Illinois, Michilimackinac, and Prairie du Chien.[39] Incredibly enough, Harry Gordon, a Scotsman, in the spring of 1766 took goods from Kaskaskia all the way down the Mississippi River to New Orleans.[40]

Nineteen years later the trade still continued, for James McGill, a fur trader in British Illinois and partner of the redoubtable Isaac Todd,[41] wrote Lieutenant-Governor Hamilton:

> Upper country trade in general as now carried on from this place [Montreal] is extended as far south as the mouth of the Ohio, to the westward as far as the Rivers falling from that side of the Mississippi will carry Canoes including from the River of [blank in document] in latitude 33 [Is this the Arkansas? The thirty-third parallel falls about evenly between the Arkansas and the Red]; to the sources of the Mississippi and to the Northwest as far as Lake Arabaskas [Athabaska] including the whole north side of Lake Huron and Superior, . . .[42]

The pressure of Britain and the uneasiness of the Spaniards resulted in an episode on the west coast, before there was any land con-

[39] There is considerable documentation for the British supplying of Spanish merchants. See Nasatir, "The Anglo-Spanish Frontier on the Upper Mississippi, 1786–1796," *Iowa Journal of History and Politics*, Vol. XXIX, No. 2 (April, 1931), 162–63, 164, 175, 195–96, 207, 209–10, 211; 190; (the commander of Michilimackinac said in 1793 that trade had been going on for years); 191 (where we find that Spanish merchants from St. Louis made trips to Michilimackinac to buy goods); 219 (St. Louis merchants had long traded with Michilimackinac and with American merchants in Illinois). Perhaps the most convincing note of all is Carondelet's letter of January 23, 1793, to Trudeau, in which he advised Trudeau to buy goods from the British (173).

[40] C. W. Alvord and C. E. Carter, *The New Régime, Illinois Historical Collections*, Vol. XI, 67n.

[41] Isaac Todd was one of the original partners in the North West Company in 1779, but in 1784 he went into partnership with James McGill as Todd, McGill & Company, which withdrew from the northwest trade to work in the Lake Michigan and the Mississippi River areas.

[42] James McGill to Lieutenant Governor Hamilton, Montreal, August 1, 1785; London, Public Records Office, Colonial Office Papers (hereafter cited as C.O.), series 42, Vol. 48, f. 207, published in *Canadian Archives Report, 1890*, 56–68. McGill was the partner of Isaac Todd in Todd, McGill & Co.; Henry Hamilton was lieutenant-governor at Detroit for the British and was captured by George Rogers Clark at Vincennes in 1778. He was a lieutenant-governor of upper Canada in 1785. Mr. McGill took in a large territory.

nection between St. Louis and the Pacific Ocean, that became known as the Nootka Sound Controversy.

Nootka Sound is a bay on the west side of Vancouver Island, just south of fifty degrees latitude, and it had been visited many times by British, Spanish, American, Russian, and other ships. In 1789, however, the viceroy of New Spain, Flores, becoming concerned over reports of Englishmen and Russians on the northwest coast, sent two vessels to claim the country for Spain, to establish a colony, and to prepare to defend it. There was a good deal of traffic in and around Nootka Sound when the Spaniards got there, and they took possession of the *Iphigenia*, a British ship that also had Portuguese registry—but the Spaniards changed their minds and restored the vessel to its captain. The Spanish commander, Martínez, took possession of the port; shortly thereafter the schooner *North West America* appeared and was seized and sent on a trading adventure for Martínez and his American friends. A British ship, the *Argonaut*, arrived and was seized by the Spaniards, and they also seized her escort, the *Princess Royal*. During these events, the Spaniards maintained cordial relations with Americans in the area, and it appeared that Martínez had legal justification for seizing the various British ships—but the entire affair precipitated action on a higher level.

Spain had always claimed the northwest coast by right of discovery and by the right of the papal bull (the line of demarcation); if her claim was valid, then the British ships were properly seized, but if England could successfully challenge Spain's claim by one means or another, the outcome might very well be that the British flag would fly over the northwest coast. England's protest was harsh, and Spain immediately retreated from the strong position she had taken. The vessels by that time had been restored by the viceroy, and Spain was willing to forget the incident. But England demanded satisfaction in the way of damages, declaring the right of her subjects to trade or settle on the northwest coast without interference from Spain. These diplomatic thrusts and counter-thrusts occurred in 1790, and the threats of war soon began to be an upsetting factor in European councils, though it was understood that Spain did not want war, and in October the Spanish council accepted a proposition that gave England free access to the northwest coast above San Francisco for commerce, navigation, and settlement. The agreement was verified in Madrid and in London—a triumph for England, a humiliation for Spain. Exact interpretation of the agreement was a matter of discussion later at various times, but for the moment the Spanish had tried to dislodge the British but had failed, and the scene of further conflict returned to the Illinois country.[43]

The Spaniards were not a factor in the northern trade of Louisiana until 1791, when Jacques d'Eglise went up the Missouri to the Mandans—and by that time the English intrusion had started from the Mandans. It is interesting to note that when D'Eglise discovered the Mandans,[44] he found a Frenchman, Menard, who had lived with the Mandans for fourteen years (since 1777).[45] D'Eglise also found the Mandans in constant communication with the British, who had established posts only fifteen days to the north. At that time, also, the Kiowa Indians, whose home was still in the Black Hills of South Dakota, were intermediaries between the Englishmen on the upper Missouri and the Spaniards of New Mexico, and D'Eglise is one of those who saw Spanish saddles and bridles among the Mandans.[46]

From the time of that first trip of D'Eglise to the Mandans, the Spaniards tried to establish control of their northeastern frontier (the Missouri-Mississippi area), and temporarily, through the activities of the Missouri Company and Andrew Todd,[47] they forced the English traders to withdraw from the Mandan villages.

The Spaniards commenced a major trading offensive to force British merchants out of the Iowa country, and at the end of the century they made a determined effort to oust British and American traders from the west bank of the Mississippi by sending spies, traders, and armed galleys up the Mississippi River. Spanish traders, supplied from St.

[43] See W. R. Manning, "Nootka Sound Controversy," in American Historical Association *Annual Report for 1904*, 281–478.

[44] D'Eglise was the first Spaniard to reach the Mandans from St. Louis, but it will appear later that perhaps Pedro Vial was at the Mandan villages somewhat earlier.

[45] Nasatir, "Jacques D'Eglise on the Upper Missouri, 1791–1795," *Mississippi Valley Historical Review*, Vol. XIV, No. 1 (June, 1927), 47–49.

[46] Nasatir, *Before Lewis and Clark*, I, 82.

[47] The Missouri Company, a fur-trading firm, was organized in 1793 by Jacques Clamorgan and St. Louis merchants (later joined by Andrew Todd), with the blessing of Spanish officials, who hoped it would counteract the British in the north. Its official title was The Commercial Company for the Discovery of the Nations of the Upper Missouri. See Nasatir, "The Formation of the Missouri Company," *Missouri Historical Review*, Vol. XXV, No. 1 (October, 1930).

Louis, also tried repeatedly to ascend the Missouri, eject British traders from the area, and reach New Mexico and the Pacific Ocean, and the Spaniards still were considering ringing the northeastern frontier of New Spain with forts, for in 1792 the captain-general at Havana was keeping the proposition under advisement.[48] Apparently the forts were needed, for in 1793 Zenon Trudeau, the commandant at St. Louis,[49] reported thirty-six British canoes from Machilimackinac had gone to various Indian tribes to trade.[50]

The Spanish stiffening took another interesting form when in 1795 Governor Carondelet offered a prize of three thousand pesos to the first person to reach the Pacific Ocean via the Missouri River;[51] not only did they want to find out what lay behind the mountains, but they also recognized the great strategic value of a chain of posts or forts from St. Louis to the Pacific Ocean to join the Spaniards on the Pacific Coast and consolidate Spanish defenses against the British and also against the Russians, who were active in Alaska.[52] Later that same year, therefore, the Missouri Fur Company sent a man named Lecuyer up the Missouri, expecting him to reach the ocean by spring, 1796;[53] James Mackay, who had been with the British in the north, also was employed to reach the Pacific Ocean; and John Evans was instructed to cross the continent to the Pacific.[54]

48 Houck, *Spanish Régime,* I, 322. Also in Carondelet's "Military Report on Louisiana and West Florida," printed in James Alexander Robertson, *Louisiana Under Spain, France, and the United States,* I, 335. Suggested by Pérez, December 1, 1788, Papeles de Cuba, leg. 2361; printed in Nasatir, *Before Lewis and Clark,* I, 73; also *ibid,* I, 80, a manuscript of April 5, 1791, in the Bancroft Library. Carondelet to Las Casas, November 24, 1794, in Robertson, is also in *Before Lewis and Clark,* I, 225.

49 Zenon Trudeau was born in New Orleans in 1748. He was well educated and became a lieutenant colonel in the Louisiana Regiment. He was appointed lieutenant-governor of Upper Louisiana in 1792 and declined to retire in 1797 because of the war with England. He was succeeded by De Lassus in 1799, and accepted a pension and retired in 1803. He died some years later in St. Charles Parish, Lower Louisiana.

50 Nasatir, *Before Lewis and Clark,* I, 81.

51 The offer itself seems to be missing, but the Consejo approved it on May 27, 1796 (Minuta del Acta del Supremo Consejo de Estado, Archivo Histórico Nacional). Clamorgan and Rheile spoke of the line of forts to the Pacific Ocean in a letter printed in Houck, *Spanish Régime,* II, 173–78. See Nasatir and Liljegren, "Minutas," *Louisiana Historical Quarterly,* Vol.. XXI, No. 1 (January, 1938).

52 Nasatir, and Liljegren, "Minutas," *ibid.,* 66.

53 Nasatir, *Before Lewis and Clark,* I, 91.

54 *Ibid.,* 96–98.

For wealth, goods, and contacts, the key man in all those efforts to reach the ocean was Andrew Todd,[55] but he died of yellow fever in 1797, bringing an end to that series of efforts—although three or four years later Jacques Clamorgan, the promoter, made a last effort by sending Hugh Heney to discover a route to the Pacific.[56] (Heney was stopped by the British.)

That surge of activity did not open the route to the ocean, however, or close the area to the British. As a matter of fact, in 1796 the English took twelve pack horses with goods to the Platte to trade with the Panis and Abenaquis,[57] and by that year it was actually difficult for the Spaniards to reach the upper Missouri because the lower tribes, especially those at the Platte, had been well indoctrinated by the English.[58] As a matter of fact, the Spanish efforts were futile, as Lewis and Clark discovered in 1804 when they found the upper Missouri Indian trade under the control of British traders carrying on the rivalry between the Hudson's Bay Company and the North West Company—the English using the Kiowa Indians as before.

While after 1763 the Illinois country struggled against the British, the Arkansas country had problems also, farther south. The English had penetrated the Arkansas River Valley long before and were never checked, and the Spaniards had graphic fears of English penetration to the interior mines of northern Mexico—an old story.

The Spanish post in the Arkansas country was known as Arkansas Post, near the confluence of the Arkansas and the Mississippi rivers, but it was never a very effective barrier, especially against the English, who repeatedly tried to win over the Quapaws in Arkansas, tried to pro-

[55] Andrew Todd was a young Irishman, a British subject and trader at Machilimackinac. He supplied Spanish merchants in St. Louis, and was raided by Trudeau in 1793. Jay's Treaty, under which the British agreed to abandon their posts in the Northwest, threatened to ruin his business in 1795, and he turned to the Spaniards. A man of considerable ability and great influence, Todd joined the Missouri Company, putting up $8,000 for a substantial block of stock in the company. He traveled to New Orleans in an attempt to obtain special trading privileges; while there, he contracted yellow fever and died—a blow to Spanish trading on the Missouri.

[56] Nasatir, *Before Lewis and Clark*, I, 108.

[57] Carondelet to Branciforte, New Orleans, June 7, 1796, A.G.I., Estado Mexico, leg. 6; printed in Nasatir, "The Anglo-Spanish Frontier on the Upper Mississippi, 1786–1796," *Iowa Journal of History and Politics*, Vol. XXIX, No. 2 (April, 1931), 179.

[58] Nasatir, *ibid.*, 206.

mote a war between the Chickasaws and the Quapaws, and encouraged the Choctaws to cross the Mississippi into Spanish territory. To facilitate those efforts, the English established a small post between the White and the Arkansas rivers and plied the Indians with *eau de vie,* and it was well known that the Englishmen would supply the Indians whenever Spanish supplies were lacking or Spanish presents were late. The English even went so far as to found a strong-house and refuge at El Cadrón, near present Little Rock, far west of Arkansas Post, in 1777.[59]

The Englishmen had no compunction; they would use any means they could devise to undercut Spanish traders, and the Spanish fears that the English might penetrate Mexico were never allayed. During the American Revolution, De Villiers, commandant at Arkansas Post, was greatly concerned about the influence of English traders over the Arkansas Indians, and he was warned by Governor Bernardo de Gálvez not to allow any Englishmen on the frontier.

The difficulties at Arkansas Post, however, were extensive, and De Villiers did not find easy the carrying out of Gálvez' suggestion. The Osage Indians were dominant in the Arkansas country, and they played the Spaniards at Arkansas Post against the Spaniards at St. Louis, and the cupidity of the Spanish traders at Arkansas Post against that of the Spanish traders at St. Louis. The Osages received their annual presents at St. Louis, and it was from St. Louis that the licenses to trade with the Osages were granted; therefore it would seem that Arkansas Post had very little influence over the Indians.

As a matter of fact, the Spaniards planned a full-fledged war against the Osages in 1793 but the plans were soon dismissed, partly because of fear of the French and George Rogers Clark.

When the Osages were not busy keeping De Villiers busy, the *contrabandistas* were, for English and American smugglers carried on an extensive trade from Arkansas Post to the Taovaya villages on Red River.[60]

The British had become especially active in the contraband trade

[59] Nasatir, "Indian Trade and Diplomacy in the Spanish Illinois" (unpublished doctoral thesis, University of California, 1926), 93; Bolton, *Athanase de Mézières,* II, 141.

[60] See Isaac Joslin Cox, "The Louisiana-Texas Frontier," *Southwestern Historical Quarterly,* Vol. XI, No. 1 (July, 1906), 31, 36.

after 1763, when they became established at Natchez[60a] and other points on the east bank of the Mississippi; they introduced firearms into the Taovaya villages in Texas via the route through Oklahoma, but at the same time they were active in other parts of Texas as well.

South and west of Arkansas Post, and east of the Taovayas (who were in north-central Texas), the key Spanish post of Natchitoches on the Red River was a source of worry to the Spaniards, for there, too, they could not seem to stop English travel across Spanish territory. In 1769 four Englishmen were living at or near Natchitoches,[61] and there was little doubt concerning their occupation. By 1772 British firearms were present among the Taovayas (whose villages were a target for traders at both Arkansas Post and Natchitoches),[62] and English merchants were at Opelousas south of Natchitoches.[63] In October, 1773, English traders were crossing the Mississippi toward Natchitoches in spite of all that could be done by Spanish officials.[64] A man named Hamilton along with other Englishmen went to the Trinity River in Texas to buy horses and mules from Indians who had stolen them from the Spaniards as far west as San Antonio.[65] In 1778 Croix, commandant-

[60a] Natchez has a wild history. The French built Fort Rosalie there in 1716, but the fort was destroyed in a massacre by the Natchez Indians in 1729. In 1763 it went to the British, who settled in some numbers; in 1779 the Spaniards took possession. After 1783 the English and Americans settled there, and in 1798 the Americans took it over.

[61] De Mézières, to Unzaga, No. 187, February 1, 1770; Papeles de Cuba, leg., 110; printed in Bolton, *Athanase de Mézières*, I, 77, 136–37. Luis de Unzaga y Amezaga was taken by O'Reilly to be governor of Louisiana, and was the first governor-general. He had gone into the army in 1735, had served in Spain, Italy, and Africa, and twenty-six years in America. In 1775 he was made brigadier general. He was governor from 1769 to 1775, and he married a daughter of St. Maxent, partner of Laclède. When he was succeeded in Louisiana by Miró, Unzaga became captain-general of Caracas. He was generally mild and conciliatory and tried to enforce the laws although he closed his eyes to infractions of commercial regulations; he was impartial even to his own father-in-law. See Caughey, *Bernardo de Gálvez*, 43.

[62] De Mézières even urged the Wichitas, Taovayas, and Tawakonis to move inland for protection from the British and Osages, in 1772. Bolton, *Athanase Mézière*, I, 97.

[63] Bolton, *ibid.*, I, 19, 77; Bolton, *Texas in the Middle Eighteenth Century*, 397–98.

[64] Bolton, *Athanase de Mézières*, I, 76, 77.

[65] Bolton, *ibid.*, I, 77, 105; II, 105; Bolton, *Texas in Middle Eighteenth Century*, 407–408.

general of the Interior Provinces, wrote that he was opposed to letting the Indians have firearms, but he knew that if such trading should be prohibited, the Indians would get arms from the English.[66] (The same type of intrusion was taking place in Upper Louisiana, and was complained about by Piernas and by De Leyba,[67] lieutenant-governors at St. Louis.[68]) The following year Athanase de Mèziéres wrote Croix, expressing his fear of being defeated by the aggressive English.[69]

As early as 1768 Ulloa, governor of Louisiana, had written O'Conor, governor of Texas, to say that the Yatasí Indians would not lack means to go to the English frontier to get what they wanted,[70] and in the same year De Mézières had reported that tribes along the Louisiana-Texas border were buying goods from Englishmen,[71] and two years later Spanish-licensed traders were instructed that no English merchants or merchandise were to enter Spanish territory.[72] In another two years, Riperdá, governor of Texas, notified the viceroy of Mexico that the Indians were getting goods from the English, and that the English traders provided better and cheaper arms. It was then that Riperdá proposed an outer line of presidios from Mississippi to New Mexico—a hopeful, if familiar, proposal.[73]

In the same year (1772), Areche, *fiscal* to the viceroy, said the Indians were stealing horses and that they used them to obtain goods from the English, and he advised that it was necessary to keep the

[66] Croix to José de Gálvez, Chihuahua, September 23, 1778, Provincias Internas, Vol. 182, f. 10, published in Bolton, *Athanase de Mézières*, II, 222–23; also in this volume (I, 270), see Riperdá to viceroy, April 28, 1772.

[67] Fernando de Leyba, born in Spain, became a captain in the Louisiana Regiment. He succeeded Cruzat as lieutenant-governor at St. Louis in 1778, dying in office in 1780. He was not popular with the people of St. Louis; he was said to lack tact and discretion, to be penurious and intemperate; one writer characterizes him as drunken, voracious, and feeble-minded—but this writer seems to have been biased. Leyva strictly enforced trade regulations and tariffs that Cruzat had quietly ignored.

[68] Piernas to Unzaga, July 4, 1772, and April 21, 1773; Leyva to Gálvez, November 16, 1778; see Bolton, *Athanase de Mézières*, I, 79.

[69] De Mézières to Croix, October 7, 1778, published in Bolton, *ibid.*, II, 294–97.

[70] Ulloa to O'Connor, December, 1768, published in Bolton, *ibid.*, I, 128–29.

[71] *Ibid.*, I, 76–77.

[72] Instructions for Traders, February 4, 1770, in Papeles de Cuba, leg. 110, published in Bolton, *ibid.*, I, 148.

[73] Riperdá to viceroy, April 28, 1772, published in Bolton, *ibid.*, I, 270. De Mézières to Riperdá, July 4, 1772, in Bolton, *ibid.*, I, 303.

Indians loyal to Spain as a bulwark against the English.[74] At almost the same time, De Mézières reported to Riperdá that the Indian nations of Texas knew about the English traders; that the Pani-Mahas, recently migrated to the Red River,[75] were telling the Taovayas the advantages of trade with the Englishmen (and Riperdá told the viceroy that the English were supplying arms to the Indians through the Pani-Mahas near the Missouri River[76]); De Mézières told Riperdá that it was easy for the English to penetrate Texas and New Mexico, that it was necessary to establish a cordon of settlements to extend to the New Mexican mountains to keep out the English, and that the Missouri River had been navigated for a long time but that its sources were not known.[77] Twelve days later De Mézières reported to the viceroy that the English were trading with the Taovayas;[78] at about the same time it was reported that Englishmen were at the mouth of the Trinity, cutting wood for houses.[79]

It was then that De Mézières mentioned the fact that the English were highly skilled at using rivers to go into any territory that took their eye, and he pointed out that they could use the tributaries of the Mississippi to reach New Mexico—one more worry.[80]

De Mézières' apprehension was duly reflected in the higher levels of the Spanish ruling hierarchy. On July 6, 1772, Riperdá wrote the viceroy of his fears of the Norteños (Indian Nations of the North—Comanches, Tonkawas, and Taovayas[81]), who, he said, were fond of the Englishmen who were supplying them.[82] Sometime that year, also, an Indian known only as Joseph, who had been at the fall of Quebec,

[74] Areche to viceroy, July 31, 1772, Provincias Internas, Vol. 20, f. 7; published in Bolton, *ibid.*, I, 277.

[75] In 1772 or 1773.

[76] Riperdá to Bucareli, Bexar, December 2, 1772; Pichardo, *Limits of Louisiana and Texas*, I, 393.

[77] De Mézières to Riperdá, July 4, 1772, published in Bolton, *Athanase de Mézières*, I, 301.

[78] Bolton, *ibid.*, I, 115; and I, 77, 330; II, 19, 207, 228.

[79] Bolton, *Texas in the Middle Eighteenth Century*, 407–408.

[80] De Mézières to Riperdá, July 4, 1772; published in Bolton, *Athanase de Mézières*, I, 302.

[81] *Ibid.*, I, 68. The Taovayas are now more commonly known as Wichitas. The Pani-Mahas also soon became known as Norteños.

[82] Riperdá to viceroy, July 6, 1772, in Provincias Internas, leg. 20, f. 26, and published in Bolton, *ibid.*, I, 329–30.

lived with the Taovayas and told them of the great strength of the British—and probably had considerable influence with the Indians.[83]

Arriaga,[84] secretary of the Indies, finally took cognizance of the situation and wrote Unzaga, the governor of Louisiana, in 1774, ordering him to stop English traders' intruding themselves among the Indians as Unzaga had reported they were doing the previous October.[85] This news filtered to the king himself, and he ordered De Mézières to get the English out of Spanish territory. This order perhaps was to an answer to De Mézières' report that English traders were among the Nachcitos (in the Natchitoches area), planning to trade with the Caddos.[86]

Three months later (in 1774), De Mézières wrote Unzaga that English traders were going to the mouth of the Trinity River (on the Texas coast) to buy horses and mules from the Indians;[87] and by 1777 the situation had not improved, for in September of that year, De Mézières wrote Gálvez that a band of Englishmen was at El Cadrón on the Arkansas River with a great quantity of merchandise;[88] and in February, 1778, he advised the viceroy that the Spaniards should explore the Missouri, that the English were considering it.[89] The following April he wrote Croix, commandant-general of the Interior Provinces, to say that the Taovayas had asked for Spanish traders to settle among them. If that request should be granted, De Mézières said, it would be a master key to the north; the Spaniards could deal with friendly nations, and the Comanches and Osages could be won over. The Spaniards could secure information about remote tribes; they could prevent any new English invasion; and there would be easy access to

[83] Harper, "The Taovayas Indians . . . (1769–1779)," *Southwestern Historical Quarterly*, Vol. LVII, No. 4 (October, 1953), 181; see also Bolton, "The Spanish Abandonment and Reoccupation of East Texas, 1773–1779," *Southwestern Historical Quarterly*, Vol. IX, No. 2 (October, 1905), 92; Bolton, *ibid.*, I, 301.

[84] Julian de Arriaga was general minister of the Indies.

[85] Arriaga to Unzaga, Aranjuez, May 30, 1774, published in Bolton, *Athanase de Mézières*, II, 104.

[86] *Ibid.*

[87] De Mézières to Unzaga, June 30, 1774, published in *ibid.*, II, 105.

[88] De Mézières to Gálvez, September 14, 1777, Papeles de Cuba, leg. 2358, published in Bolton, *ibid.*, II, 141.

[89] De Mézières to viceroy, February 20, 1778, Historia, Vol. 28, f. 228–38, published in Bolton, *ibid.*, II, 182.

and communication with Natchitoches, Illinois, New Mexico, and Bexar.[90] On the same date but in another letter, De Mézières said that two Englishmen had come via the Arkansas River to entice the Taovayas.[91]

By no means was De Mézières the reporter of all the unpleasant information in Texas during those years. In 1777 Gil Ybarbo, the champion of East Texas, made a trip to the mouth of the Sabine River, returning with the following ominous items: an English vessel had been at the mouth of the Neches River in 1774, and its crew had stayed long enough to sow a crop there (he found the abandoned vessel in Sabine Lake); another vessel was reported on the Trinity; and he found a lost and naked Englishman, Bautista Miler, who had been in Texas for seven months.[92]

In 1778, De Villiers at Arkansas Post urged Governor Gálvez to build a fort on the banks of the Arkansas, because, he said:

> An establishment on this river seems of great importance either to protect our hunters, who, if they are not disturbed by the Osages and the Taovayas, pour into the province large amounts of tallow, fresh oil, and furs of all sorts, or [it would be of importance] to be on guard against the enterprises of the English, who in time of war might penetrate as far as the frontiers of New Mexico. . . . No one ignores the fact that these savages will belong to those who give them the most; that, not receiving anything—or practically nothing—from Spain, they will go to the English in an instant, which makes felt the necessity of forming a respectable establishment on this river.[93]

[90] De Mézières to Croix, April 19, 1778, Provincias Internas, Vol. 138, published in Bolton, *ibid.*, II, 205.

[91] De Mézières to Croix, April 18, 1778; published in Bolton, *ibid.*, I, 207.

[92] Bolton, *Texas in the Middle Eighteenth Century*, 424–26.

[93] De Villiers to Gálvez, June 11, 1778, Papeles de Cuba, leg. 192. Captain Balthazard de Villiers said in 1778 that in the previous twenty years he had commanded almost every post in Louisiana (he had been at Natchitoches and Point Coupée, among others). He was comparatively well educated and always in debt—as were most frontier officers. He had once to return to Natchitoches to straighten out his debts, and in 1778 asked Gálvez to allow him to stay longer at that "most disagreeable hole in the universe" (Arkansas Post) so that he could become solvent. His wife handled his money and traveled considerably between Arkansas Post and New Orleans. He longed for glory and advancement, and did capture Concordia from the British in 1780, but was friendly to Americans. In 1782 he became ill and went to New Orleans, but died the day after an operation. See Marjorie Oletha Thomas, "The Arkansas Post of Louisiana, 1682–1763," unpublished master's thesis, U. of California, 1942, chapter VIII.

De Villiers was hoping for a stronger fort than the Arkansas Post.

After 1783 and the end of the American Revolution, the Spanish administration was building (or trying to build) forts, patrolling the Mississippi, befriending the Indians—and also inviting Americans to come over to settle on Spanish land, while the invitation to the Americans was loudly protested by Spanish commandants at Arkansas Post, St. Louis, and elsewhere. While officials of the higher echelons in Spain considered Louisiana's value merely that of a bulwark to protect the valuable interior mines of New Spain, those actually in Louisiana had a sharp understanding of the threat posed by American penetration. Even Carondelet, effeminate nepotist in New Orleans, said: "Louisiana ought to be considered now as a frontier province which covers the vast dominions of His Majesty in America," and he speaks of the menace of the Americans;[94] that fear was expressed by many Spaniards: by the Women of St. Louis in 1790,[95] by Governor Miró in 1792,[96] and many others.

The French had understood British intentions as early as 1776, when the Marquis Vergennes wrote to D'Ossun: "[Louisiana] is the forward wall of New Mexico . . . where the English could well be tempted to go one day to look for the compensation of their southern colonies, if they [the colonies] escape from them."[97] Fourteen years later Philip Nolan reported to the governor of Louisiana that General

[94] Carondelet (unsigned) to Las Casas, No. 158, New Orleans, April 15, 1796, Papeles de Cuba, leg. 153A.

[95] Petition of Women of Illinois, undated [1790], Papeles de Cuba, leg. 2362.

[96] Miró to Cruzat, New Orleans, March 8, 1785, Papeles de Cuba, leg. 3; cited in Nasatir, *Before Lewis and Clark,* I, 72, 393n. Francisco Cruzat was born in Navarre in 1738, and went to Louisiana with O'Reilly; he became lieutenant-governor of Illinois in 1775. He was popular but incurred the displeasure of Bernardo de Gálvez. He was succeeded in 1778 by De Leyba, who died in office, and Cruzat again became lieutenant-governor in 1780, until he was succeeded by Pérez in 1787. His wife had died in 1786, and two daughters had died in the epidemics. Cruzat, a lieutenant colonel, died at Pensacola in 1790 at the age of fifty-one. See Nasatir, "The Anglo-Spanish Frontier in the Illinois Country During the American Revolution, 1779–1783," *Journals* of the Illinois State Historical Society, Vol. XXI, No. 3 (October, 1928), 228.

[97] M. le Marquis Vergennes (not signed) to D'Ossun, No. 11, Versailles, March 15, 1776, Paris, Archives des Affaires Étrangères, Section Correspondance Politique, Espagne, Vol. 579, f. 310–12; printed in Henri Doniol, *Histoire de la Participation de la France à l'Établissement des Etats-Unis d'Amérique,* I, 338–40; D'Ossun was the French minister at Madrid.

Morgan of Virginia thought the British would possess themselves of the Spanish settlements on the Mississippi, and Nolan said he believed that as soon as war should be declared, the British from Canada would descend upon Louisiana, for which purpose, he believed, the British already had the necessary supplies at Detroit.[98] And again in 1797 General Victor Collot gave an opinion on the matter:

> Upper Louisiana captured, Lower Louisiana will necessarily fall . . . [and] in the hands of the English or the Americans opens the door to New Mexico . . . I repeat these things, that if Upper Louisiana falls into the hands of the English or Americans, Santa Fe will be pillaged and ravaged, the surrounding country ravaged, because those two nations will always be in accord as long as it is a question of making money.

And he goes on to say that this matter should be taken up, not with Secretary of State Timothy Pickering, "whose deceit is quite well known to the two allied powers," but with the President of the United States.[99]

Complicating the situation was the fact that in that period New Orleans was a free port for the West Indies and for some European nations but not for England.[100]

And by no means to be overlooked was the great fear held by the Spaniards during the Nootka Sound controversy (1790), that the British would invade Spanish Illinois from Canada.[101]

Whatever those on the ground thought, high Spanish officials insisted on the concept of an Indian buffer state (rather than a frontier province), held firm by a system of trading and a chain of military posts. It rather seems that the distant officials held to the view that it would

[98] Nolan to Miró, New Orleans, August 17, 1790, Papeles de Cuba, leg. 2362.

[99] Collot to the Spanish minister, Philadelphia, March 1, 1797, Paris, Affaires Étrangères, Section Correspondance Politique, Etats-Unis, Supplément, Vol. 28, f. 111–17. Timothy Pickering, a noted Anglophile, was born in Salem, Mass., in 1745; was adjutant-general and quartermaster-general during the Revolution: postmaster-general, and, in 1795, Secretary of War and Secretary of State (held the latter office until 1800). He served in the Senate afterward; was a violent Federalist, and even went so far as to plot disunion.

[100] Harper, "The Taovayas Indians in Frontier Trade and Diplomacy," Part III (1779–1835), *Panhandle-Plains Historical Review*, Vol. XXVI (1953), 9.

[101] Nasatir, "The Anglo-Spanish Frontier on the Upper Mississippi, 1786–1796," *Iowa Journal of History and Politics*, Vol. XXIX, No. 2 (April, 1931), 171.

be of no particular disadvantage to lose, say, the outer half of Louisiana to the British, with the idea that the outer half would absorb them while the inner half would present a heavy wall of Indian resistance. Many Indian tribes lived between the Mississippi River and Santa Fe, and those tribes could be a defense in depth against Anglo-American intrusions. The problem, of course, was one of keeping the Indians attached to Spain. Thus was nurtured that policy new to Spanish officialdom: the alliance-fort-trader-gift system—of which the crux was the annual present, for without presents the Indians were rarely co-operative; they went somewhere else for presents. But presents required money, and money was always a Spanish problem.

Manuel Pérez,[102] the commandant at St. Louis, throws an interesting sidelight on the involvements of the distribution of presents, in his letter of 1788 to Miró, when he says that "for a long time English, and especially the Americans of some [document torn] district have been looking for the means to penetrate the Missouri [country]." According to Pérez, the Spaniards were "exposed to . . . the barbariousness of the one [Americans] and regarded with jealousy and envy by the others [English]." He says that he cannot hold the loyalty of the Indians because he has no substantial quantity of goods for them, and he asks how he can properly distribute gifts to forty or fifty men, "without counting the women," when he has "only seven and one half pieces of cloth, seventy blankets, seventy-two guns, eighty-eight striped shirts, eighteen white shirts, five hundred pounds of powder, and six barrels of *aguardiente* (these last after having suffered the ordinary leakage of the trip and remaining for a year hardly come to four)."[103]

Carondelet as governor of Louisiana, and Pedro de Nava[104] as

[102] Manuel Pérez, born in Spain in 1735, served in the army in Spain and Portugal and went to Louisiana with O'Reilly in 1770. He succeeded Cruzat in 1787 and was followed by Trudeau in 1792. He served thirty-nine years in the army and retired as lieutenant colonel of the Louisiana Regiment; he died in New Orleans in 1819.

[103] Pérez to Miró, No. 58, St. Louis, December 1, 1788, Papeles de Cuba, leg. 2361; published in Nasatir, *Before Lewis and Clark,* I, 128–29. The skeptical might wonder if certain undeclared charges were levied against the aguardiente.

[104] Pedro de Nava, a brigadier general of long service with the king, became commandant-general of the Western Division of the Interior Provinces in 1790; then Ugalde resigned, and Nava became ad interim commander of the Eastern Division but was soon replaced there by Ramón de Castro. Nava's salary was $10,000, and he retired in 1802 because of illness, being succeeded by Nemesio Salcedo by November 4.

commandant-general of the Interior Provinces, warned the higher powers of the importance of presents. Carondelet told Trudeau to use every effort to induce all tribes hostile to Spain to accept peace, and he warned Trudeau not to give firearms to Indians who did not know about them, and to give them sparingly to those Indians who did know about them.[105] The reasoning of Carondelet was that the security of New Mexico depended upon Indian allegiance to Spanish power, and that such allegiance was based on peace. Firearms were not conducive to peace, thus none would be given—unless the Indians demanded them.

Inasmuch as the Comanches were the most numerous and their tribes the most powerful of the Indian nations on the Plains, special emphasis was always placed on Comanche allegiance, and any foreign effort to win Comanche friendship was construed as a direct threat to New Mexico. And Spanish efforts to keep the Comanches from forming alliances with other nationalities were in general successful.[105a]

The Osage Indians were a different matter, for they were unceasingly warlike and apparently more treacherous. The Spaniards wanted to cut them off from Spanish aid and reduce them thoroughly. At one time Spain planned a war against them, intending to attack from various directions—even from Natchitoches—but the duplicity of the Osages, the differences between Spanish officials and traders of various posts, and Spanish fear that the Osages would go to the Americans to get their goods[106] kept the Spaniards from following this plan. The far-roaming Osages even preyed on Santa Fe in 1790,[107] and the Spaniards had little success as controlling them until Auguste Chouteau and his relatives were awarded exclusive trading privileges and built a post among them.

Even the women of Illinois became alarmed over the failure of the Spanish ministers to establish forts in the upper country to stop

[105] Carondelet to Trudeau, New Orleans, May 22, 1795, printed in Nasatir, *Before Lewis and Clark*, I, 325.

[105a] *Loyalty* is not a word ordinarily to be associated with the early Plains Indians.

[106] As noted, the Indians—primarily Osages—kept the English out of Spanish Illinois until 1765. The Spaniards previously had tried withholding traders from the Osages (in 1772–73) but found that the vacuum thus created drew traders from British Illinois.

[107] Peyroux to Miró, New Orleans, April 7, 1790 Papeles de Cuba, leg. 203. Miró to Las Casas, New Orleans, October 6, 1790: "The said nation [Osage] is . . . the one that is committing various incursions against the establishments of Santa Fe."

the English, and in 1790 they addressed an eloquent appeal, presumably to the governor, which was intended to stir some response in the council hall of the Indies:

"Remarque"[108]

In our petition, we regard the Illinois as the key to Mexico. No one is ignorant of the fact that one can penetrate there with ease via the Missouri, the Des Moines, and the River of St. Peter, rivers where it would be necessary to establish forts in order to favor our commerce and stop that of the English, who daily not only introduce themselves by these rivers with merchandise which they are in a position to sell at better prices than we, and who, upon leaving, carry off the best of the greatest part of the peltries produced in these countries, but who even engage the savages to attack the caravans, a thing that has already been done by the Big Osages and before long will again be repeated by that nation or others, accompanied by some English brigands who procure from their compatriots the sure means of penetrating there and perhaps of maintaining themselves there. Several have already introduced themselves there, have made use of the savages and of interpreters to obtain a perfect knowledge of the vast continent, and have returned only after having made exact maps.

We claim that the Illinois could become one of the most flourishing districts of the colony; in fact, with a little support [encouragement?] from [?], there could be taken out with great abundance furs, flax, wheat, cotton, tobacco of the finest [quality], and the best hemp, which would exempt Spain from exporting to foreign lands countless sums for rope that it needs for its navy, construction timber that would be easy to send down, abundant lead mines in a thousand diverse places, copper mines, and even silver mines. It would be a question then only of a little encouragement. . . .

. . . We ask these *Messieurs* who wish to force Heaven to favor them alone, if Spain, by taking possession of New Orleans, did not also oblige herself to spread her wings over all its [New Orleans'] dependencies. If this mother country has broken in their favor the bonds [ties] that should be attached to all their children with the same equality? New Orleans, soon conducted and directed by the most tender father, will

[108] Women of Illinois, undated (but about 1790, according to Hill.) This copy in French was found in the Papeles de Cuba, leg. 2362, and apparently is not the petition itself but "Remarks" that accompanied the petition. Often referred to but never printed, as far as we can determine. About one-half of the "Remarks" has been omitted here.

forget its disgraces; forced by his virtues and his goodness, it will no longer be agitated except by a perfect equality that will make [for] its happiness; that by a desire for fighting for their rights and to defend their soil and to fortify it by the sweat of their brow, persuaded of his love for his people; knowing, moreover, the bounty of his heart; we hope to claim the advantages of our brothers, desiring to illustrate them among the Indians themselves who do not know me,[109] that he will deign to listen to our complaints to do away with the dangers that menace us; to grant us his favors and to receive the most sincere of those who will not cease to be, with all respect and the most perfect gratitude,

Your very humble servants,

THE WOMEN OF ILLINOIS

Lower Louisiana also came into conflict with the British over wheat, most of which came to New Orleans from the Kentucky area. In 1796 Carondelet said: "The delay that we experience about the flour that is accustomed to begin to descend in the month of February, etc., all counsels us not to rest so much on the [Pinckney Treaty of 1795 between Spain and the United States]."[110] And again, eight days later, Carondelet noted the scarcity of wheat flour in Louisiana, remarking upon the foolishness of being forced to surrender because of hunger instead of force of arms. He requested that the viceroy "remit to us three thousand barrels of fresh flour, and of the best quality, since we hardly have enough for a month and a half"; he then discusses the certainty that England will attack Upper Louisiana through Canada, and will be assisted by the United States.[111]

It was about that time that France began to seek to regain Louisiana. In a letter to Godoy, the Spanish Secretary of State, on January

[109] This causes one to ponder the identity of the author. The "Remarks" are written in the inflammatory style of Manuel Lisa, and the references to exclusive trade and the attention to the word *justice* are distinctly Lisa-like.

[110] Carondelet to Las Casas, New Orleans, April 15, 1796, Papeles de Cuba, leg. 153A.

[111] Carondelet (unsigned) to Marquis of Branciforte, April 23, 1796, Papeles de Cuba, leg. 2364. The baron may seem unduly concerned, but it is a fact that the hunger for wheat bread is one of the strongest known to civilized Man. The scarcity of 1796 was also of concern in St. Louis—but it was not the first such occasion, for in 1792 Miró had complained that a barrel of flour worth 3 pesos *fuertes* (silver dollars) in Monongahela at the head of the Ohio River, brought 8 pesos *fuertes* in New Orleans. (From the Miró *informe*.)

1, 1797, Perignon said that William Pitt ruled America,[111a] and listed Pitt's objectives: possession of Nootka Sound, navigation of the Mississippi, and control of the Spanish provinces. He said the English were cultivating the Indians, and "England will declare war against Spain in the future, so face facts now: England is advancing toward Mexico from Canada, from the United States, and from California," and he goes on to say that if Spain will cede Louisiana and Florida to France, she will never have to concede anything to the United States and will never have anything to fear from England.[112]

Six and one-half months later, the long-dreaded English invasion seemed about to get under way, for the commandant-general of the Interior Provinces wrote the governor of New Mexico that the English planned an invasion with nine or ten thousand men from Halifax, Canada;[113] other Spanish documents say that six frigates and eight vessels were being loaded with supplies in Baltimore, that they would come via Santo Domingo,[114] and then presumably up the Mississippi to the Missouri or other tributaries, which would be followed to a point from which that very strong force could attack New Mexico.

Godoy wrote to Talleyrand in September, and the letter, filled with evasive and contradictory statements, seems to say that Spain would not consider ceding Louisiana to France, but it also said that she would, and that the matter now rested in the hands of the king.[115]

111a William Pitt was a British statesman and a great orator—the only one who dared to stand up to the parliamentary giants of England. He was opposed to the Revolution no matter how it might turn out. He became prime minister in 1783, negotiated the peace treaty with the United States, and resigned in 1801.

112 Perignon to Prince of Peace, Madrid, January 1, 1797, A.H.N., Estado, leg. 3891, apartado 3. General Dominique-Catherine de Perignon was French ambassador to Spain.

113 De Nava to governor of New Mexico, Chihuahua, July 14, 1797, New Mexican Archives, doc. 1390.

114 Noticias de Filadelphia, August 1, 1797, A.G.I. Estado Mexico, leg. 18, enclosure no. 1 with letter no. 1.

115 Godoy to Talleyrand, San Ildefonso, September 29, 1797, A.H.N., Estado, leg. 3958, carpeta 114. Arthur Preston Whitaker, "The Retrocession of Louisiana in Spanish Policy," *American Historical Review*, Vol. XXXIX, No. 3 (April, 1934). France's determination to regain Louisiana and Godoy's determination to avoid it without giving offense to France may explain the double-talk. Charles Maurice Talleyrand de Périgord was a French diplomat who became foreign minister of France in 1797 under the Directory. He was said to be a "man living in falsehood and on falsehood, yet not what you might call a false man."

The large-scale invasion from Halifax did not materialize, but in the summer of 1799 a group of Englishmen and Frenchmen went together and with allies drawn from the Arkansas, Cherokee, and Chickasaw tribes, turned up at Bexar (through the Taovaya villages) with a considerable quantity of merchandise. A force of twenty-two men sent against the Frenchmen and Englishmen at Bexar by José Miguel del Moral, commandant at Nacogdoches, was faced not only by the *contrabandistas* but also by two hundred Indians, and retired from the field.[116] This is a very startling development whether *ingleses* in this letter means Englishmen or, as it sometimes did, Americans, for it indicates that the Anglo-American contrabandists had grown so bold they took their goods from the Mississippi all the way to Bexar. Félix Trudeau, commandant at Natchitoches, is the one who notified Moral, and so there is no certainty of the route of the contrabandists; however, the letter or a copy of it was sent to the commandant of Arkansas Post the following March.

In October of the same year (1799), Félix Trudeau again got into the act and wrote to Nicholas Mª. Vidal, acting governor of Louisiana, to say that the English had penetrated as far as the Pani villages, then to the Caddoes. This is the same party that had defeated Moral and his men.[117]

Casa Calvo, the governor of Louisiana, wrote to the captain-general at Havana to say that the "Americans are not negligent. But on the western side we are open, and the English may penetrate the interior by the upper river, as already are doing the commercial companies of Hudson's Bay, Montreal, and Michilimackinac, penetrating via St. Peter's River, 40 leagues above our last establishment on this river or 540 leagues from this capital [New Orleans], as far as the nations of the interior of New Spain."[118] It is obvious that Casa Calvo was not

[116] Moral to governor general of Louisiana, Nacogdoches, August 19, 1799, Papeles de Cuba, leg. 135.

[117] Félix Trudeau to Nicolas Mª Vidal, Natchitoches, October 6, 1799, Papeles de Cuba, leg. 134A. Nicolas María Vidal was one of the principal judges of the province of Louisiana, and for a time he was acting governor after Gayoso's death. His reputation was rather poor, for it was said he sold his decisions to the highest bidder. Arthur Preston Whitaker, *The Mississippi Question, 1795–1803*, 32, 150. Laussat said the same to Du Terrage (Robertson, *Louisiana Under Spain*, I, 207).

[118] Casa Calvo to Someruelos, New Orleans, May 20, 1800, Papeles de Cuba, leg. 154C. Sebastián Calvo de la Puerta y O'Farrill, Marquis of Casa Calvo, was acting

apprehensive of the Americans but was strongly concerned over the British—not a very good guess in the light of subsequent developments.

In March of the next year (1800), in a letter from (probably) Caso Calvo to the governor of Texas, the writer promised to try to find out who were the English and French "of the Post of Arkansas" who had been in Texas, but, he said, "I fear they might be Americans."[119]

There is much evidence to indicate, first, that the Spaniards feared the English, and, second, that these fears were justified. The English were better traders than the French, and while they were alongside Spanish territory (until 1783), they penetrated Louisiana from the north, east, and southeast and went into Texas at will. In all the vast area of Louisiana, English trade was profitable. English traders became familiar with the country and acquainted with the Indians, and experienced Englishmen were left in the country to guide the next invaders—the Anglo-Americans—ever deeper into Spanish territory.

In the meantime, the Revolutionary War indirectly had pushed the Spaniards into the upper Missouri country, for Spain was well aware of the British traders' moving west and then south (and also of the Russians' coming down from the north), and began to look for a direct route to the Pacific Ocean, with the idea of establishing a chain of posts from St. Louis to the Pacific. After the conclusion of the war in 1783, however, the Spaniards began to move toward the Mandans. In 1787 Joseph Garreau went to hunt and trap on the upper Missouri, and in 1789 Juan Munier discovered the Poncas on the Niobrara River. Then in 1790 Jacques d'Eglise became the first Spanish subject to reach the Mandans; in March, 1793, D'Eglise and Garreau went

---

military governor of Louisiana from Gayoso's death in 1799 to Manuel Salcedo's arrival in 1801, while Nicolas María Vidal was acting civil governor. Casa Calvo had been with O'Reilly in 1769; he was an elegant gentleman, typical bureaucrat, unoriginal, unenergetic, but adorning; he did not like business, but preferred company and amusement. He was, however, a counter to Morales, the intendant, who squabbled endlessly, whose personal conduct was odious, and who disliked everything that he did not think of first. Casa Calvo was appointed to the U.S.-Spanish boundary commission after the transfer of Louisiana, but was looked on by the Americans as a spy, and finally was asked to leave New Orleans, and led American soldiers a merry chase into Texas. See Whitaker, *The Mississippi Question*, 159–60, 244–45.

[119] Letter or draft of a letter to Juan Bautista Elguezábal, March 10, 1800, Papeles de Cuba, leg. 135.

back up river but were stopped by the Sioux and the Arikaras; Garreau remained among the Indians.

Carondelet opened up the trade in 1792, and Jacques d'Eglise, who had already been upriver, returned in October, 1792; he seems to have reached the Mandans on the first trip, but when he made a second attempt in 1793, he was stopped by the Sioux and Arikaras.

British competition was hurting the trade on the lower Missouri, and by 1793 profits had been reduced from 100-300 per cent to 25 per cent. This decline became a matter of concern to the Consejo, which in 1796 recognized the necessity of ascending the Missouri, establishing trade with more tribes, and wresting the trade away from the British. Carondelet had already taken steps in that direction; in 1792 he had opened the trade to all Spanish subjects, and in 1793 he set up regulations that to a large extent gave control of the trade to the merchants of St. Louis, and in late 1793 the merchants themselves adopted regulations authorizing them to confiscate the goods of foreign traders. That organization of St. Louis merchants led Jacques Clamorgan to organize the Company of Explorers of the Upper Missouri (the Missouri Company) in 1794, and Carondelet was so pleased over that action that he offered $2,000 (later raised to $3,000) to the first Spanish subject who should reach the Pacific Ocean via the Missouri River.

The Missouri Company wasted no time and on June 7, 1794, sent Jean Baptiste Truteau with a small party up the river toward the Mandans. In August Truteau was overtaken by Jacques d'Eglise, who seems to have been making his third trip. D'Eglise passed Truteau and spent the winter among the Arikaras, then set out for St. Louis in May, 1795. Truteau had been stopped by the Sioux and had cached his goods and gone overland to the Arikaras. Later he returned to his cache and proceeded downriver to a wintering place in what is now Charles Mix County, South Dakota. In March he again ascended the Missouri, and apparently in January, 1796, he was still among the Arikaras or the Mandans.

In April, 1795, the Missouri Company sent a second expedition—this time under a man named Lécuyer, one of whose assistants was Tabeau, under orders to reach the Pacific Ocean. That expedition, however, got in trouble with the Ponca Indians, and another expedition under Antonio Breda was sent to its relief.

During the 1790's British activity continued: Menard lived with the Mandans, as did René Jusseaume; and among those who made trips from the Hudson's Bay posts or the North West posts were Hugh McCracken, David Monin, Morgan, Cardin, Joncquard, and David Thompson. And, strangely enough, the next man to ascend the Missouri for the Spaniards was James Mackay, who had visited the Mandans in 1787 for the British. In 1795, holding a passport good for six years, he took four pirogues and thirty-three men up the Missouri. That was in August, and he was to open trade, to go through to the Pacific Ocean, and to build forts for protection against the British. He spent the winter near present Omaha, Nebraska, and sent John Evans overland to visit the Arikaras. Evans was captured by the Sioux but escaped, and in January Mackay prepared to send him upriver again to attempt to find a passage to the Pacific Ocean. Evans left sometime between January 28 and June 8, 1796; he was at the Mandan villages on September 23 and took possession of the British fort, thus closing the upper Missouri to the British and giving the Spaniards control of it. The British apparently did not protest the Spaniards' taking control, and they began to close out their business affairs among the Mandans; some British traders continued to arrive, but Evans was forced to leave. In February, 1797, a Hudson's Bay employee, James Sutherland, wrote Evans, saying: "You need be under no apprehension of any more of our men visiting the Missourie." On the other hand, John MacDonell of the North West Company challenged Evans to show his authority.

Mackay's further movements on the upper Missouri are not well defined. He says he explored up to the area occupied by the Mandans, but he was back in St. Louis in May, 1797; Evans apparently returned later.

However, the British were working west from Prairie du Chien through Iowa and Minnesota and inciting the Poncas and Omahas to pillage the Missouri Company's expeditions, until in 1800 Jacques Clamorgan asked permission to build forts on the Kansas and Platte rivers. In 1800, also, François Régis Loisel went up the Missouri on a short trip for Clamorgan, accompanied by Pierre Antoine Tabeau. In 1800 Hugh Heney conducted an expedition upriver for Clamorgan, which was destroyed by the British, and in that year Heney also entered into partnership with Loisel. Loisel traveled upriver with Tabeau in 1802 and 1804.

In 1802 François Marie Perrin du Lac went up the Missouri to the White River, and Jean Vallé spent the winter of 1803–1804 on the Cheyenne River in the Black Hills of South Dakota.

D'Eglise made more trips up the Missouri, and there is fragmentary evidence of other trips for other merchants. In 1804 Jean Baptiste Lalande led several traders to Santa Fe via the Missouri for William Morrison, a merchant of Kaskaskia. Also in 1804 (or possibly 1803), Laurenzo Durocher and Jacques D'Eglise left St. Louis for New Mexico. Lalande, Durocher, and D'Eglise all reached Santa Fe, as shown by many documents from Santa Fe and Chihuahua and by Zebulon Pike's unpleasant comments on Lalande.

But in 1804 the efforts of the Spaniards came to a halt, for Louisiana, ceded back to France by Spain, had been in turn sold to the United States, which had already, in early 1803, begun to prepare for the Lewis and Clark expedition.

Thomas Jefferson had obtained from Congress an appropriation of $2,500 to further the cultural and scientific knowledge of the Missouri. Jefferson had not even thought of such a concept as the purchase of Louisiana when he engaged Meriwether Lewis for the Lewis and Clark expedition. Jefferson knew that American territory stopped at the Mississippi, and he realized that the expedition might be traveling (inadvertently, of course) in Spanish territory. The Spaniards were also aware of the planned trespass, and one of the great concerns of the Spanish officials from 1804 to 1807 was the invasion of their territory by the American party of Lewis and Clark. By the time Lewis and Clark began their travels, of course, Upper Louisiana belonged to the United States, but there remained at least a technical reason for concern, because the expedition would travel through Spanish Oregon.

From correspondence of Spanish officials, it is apparent that one of their great objectives in those years was to stop "Captain Meri."[120] It seems too that they might well have done so, but, although everybody talked about it, nobody had the courage to pull the string.

[120] In his excellent book, *Letters of the Lewis and Clark Expedition, With Related Documents, 1783–1854,* Donald Jackson calls attention to the Spanish reaction to the explorations of Lewis and Clark but leaves the documentation to us.

# V

## *The French Threat, 1790–97*

While Spaniards were combating —not very effectively—the British intrusion, and worrying about the incipient invasion of the Anglos, France also got back into the act—without, it would seem, any physical result to the glory of France, but certainly with enough menace to keep the Spaniards on their toes.

The French Revolution in 1789 resulted in turmoil in France and a scramble for power among the revolutionaries, and these unsettled conditions had ramifications in North America. There had been an early and continuous French interest in regaining Louisiana from Spain, and French intentions became clear in 1793 when Citizen Genêt conspired with George Rogers Clark to march on New Orleans and regain Louisiana for France.

The French policy concerning Louisiana as a whole was rather simple: to make the United States subservient to France in this area and to rebuild French power in the interior. To accomplish these two principal objectives, it was necessary, first, to obtain Louisiana; second, to bar the advance of the British (with whom France was at war); third, to get supplies from the French West Indies (especially tobacco and wheat); and, fourth, to use Louisiana to compel the United States to serve the interests of France. France wanted to hold the United States east of the Alleghenies, and to keep the United States weak.

There were three important French ministers during this period: Edmond Charles Genêt,[1] who tried to attain those various objectives

[1] Genêt, born in Versailles in 1763, was a French diplomat and minister to the United States in 1792, when the French Revolution was well under way. He tried to influence public opinion for France and against England, and in spite of Wash-

by intrigue, by conspiring with the Indians, and by using French sympathy in western and southern United States, and who accepted Clark's plan to take New Orleans; Pierre-Antoine-Joseph Fauchet, who took Genêt's place when the conspiracy was uncovered, who fought the Jay Treaty but without success, and who finally was relieved of his post at the instance of the United States (it is he who revived the idea of acquiring Louisiana by retrocession); and Pierre Augustus Adet,[2] who sent Collot to survey the Mississippi River, and who uncovered the Blount conspiracy.

The question during these hectic years was rather clear: who was to control the Mississippi Valley and the Gulf of Mexico in the face of Spain's decline?

Some consideration should be given to a would-be conspirator who might technically have been charged with treason to the United States but who seems to have been guilty primarily of a good many unflattering personal characteristics. If he had been made of sterner stuff, or if chance had turned up a different card or two—but *if*'s do not count.

He started as Doctor Fallon and served in the Revolutionary War; he became agent for the South Carolina Yazoo Company, and in 1790 tried—with complicated manipulations—to get the Spaniards to give him an immense tract of land for colonization by Americans on the west side of the Mississippi River, up- and down-river from Walnut Hills (Nogales), north and south from the mouth of the Yazoo River in present Mississippi; and when the Spaniards refused, he threatened to take the land by armed force.[3] He told the Spaniards that he had no more use

ington's proclamation of neutrality, Genêt armed and equipped privateers and raised recruits in American ports. These activities and his imprudent criticisms of the American government caused Washington to request his recall in 1794, and Fauchet, the new French minister to the United States, cancelled Genêt's plans. Genêt was warned not to return to France because of danger from the revolution there, and when Washington refused to extradite him, he settled in New York City, eventually becoming an American citizen.

[2] Adet was the author of several books on chemistry, served many years in the French foreign service, and was minister to the United States, 1795–97, during which time he tried to get Americans to declare for France, against England. He was suspected of violations of neutrality, and the United States set up a special fund of five hundred dollars to discover his accomplices.

[3] On O'Fallon, see John Carl Parish, "The Intrigues of Doctor James O'Fallon," *Mississippi Valley Historical Review*, Vol. XVII, No. 2 (September, 1930).

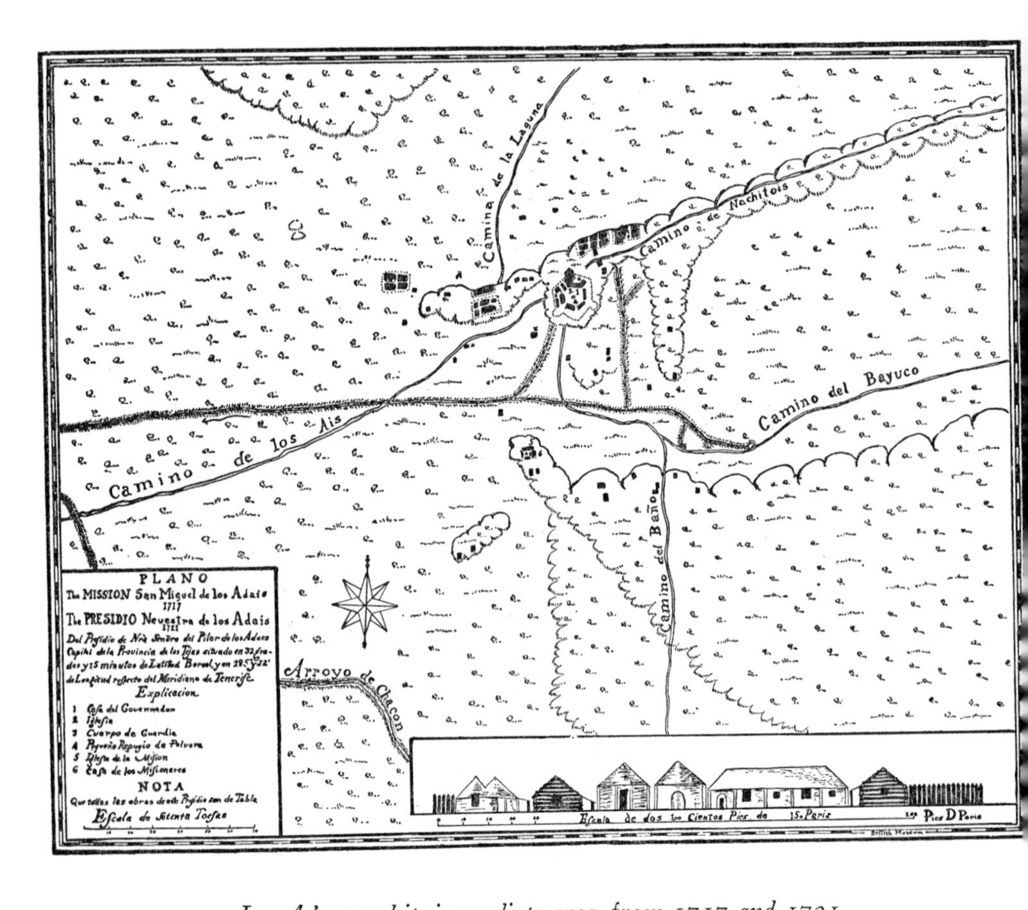


*Los Adaes and its immediate area, from 1717 and 1721*

Courtesy Katherine M. Bridges, Northwestern State College, Natchitoches, Louisiana

for the United States—but at the same time that he was castigating the United States to the Spaniards he was asking the U.S. Congress for concessions. He jumped from one project to another with considerable agility; he was called "insinuating and dangerous" and "a restless and turbulent adventurer." He was in jail more than once but was such a troublemaker that he could not be imprisoned in an ordinary guardhouse. He persuaded George Rogers Clark to command the troops he proposed to use in the Yazoo venture,[4] married a sister of Clark, and entered the Kentucky intrigues with him.

Up to the point of his operations in Kentucky, O'Fallon was doing well—but he made the mistake of allying himself with the nefarious General James Wilkinson.

When Governor Miró of Louisiana delayed an answer to O'Fallon's colonization scheme in the Walnut Hills region, O'Fallon threatened him with words that well illustrate his writing: They had "three to five thousand well-armed men," he said, and if they are led by someone unsympathetic to Spain, it "may well bring a *Firebrand* to your Door, which however effectually you may be enabled to circumscribe its blaze for a time, may at length throw such a spark into the combustibles which daily accumulate within the Bowells of these States, as would eventually plunge this empire and your's into a general combustion."

Miró was not entirely beguiled by O'Fallon's volatility. He organized the Indians against O'Fallon, and he played Wilkinson against him. Gayoso established a post on the east side of the river at Walnut Hills, near the mouth of the Yazoo, and Miró continued to let O'Fallon think that he could hardly wait to see him.

Shortly afterward, O'Fallon found that he had talked too loudly, for the United States issued a proclamation against him, and the United States attorney for the District of Kentucky was ordered to proceed against him, presumably for trying to make war from American territory. Wilkinson was working hard to discredit him, and since some of the incriminating material against O'Fallon comes from copies of letters written by Wilkinson, it may be that Wilkinson deliberately twisted O'Fallon's words or put words into his mouth. O'Fallon was so busy that he would not have known the difference, perhaps, and

[4] Parish, *ibid.*, 249.

obviously he was annoying Wilkinson, for in 1791 Wilkinson wrote Miró that it was his purpose "to hang up this son of Lucifer on the tenterhooks of apprehension & dismay."

O'Fallon was through. Wilkinson had betrayed him, and he had betrayed Wilkinson, but Gayoso had put the finishing touch on O'Fallon by building a fort at the place where O'Fallon had planned to put a settlement. Gayoso said later that O'Fallon had taken flight, but that since he was a turbulent busybody, no doubt he was concocting some new intrigue.

O'Fallon was indeed involved in other activities. According to his word, he had recently made his brother-in-law a temperate man—which implies that George Rogers Clark, besides being a chronic filibusterer, had been addicted to the bottle.

O'Fallon laid low for a while, perhaps because the district attorney was a friend of James Wilkinson, and Wilkinson certainly did not want O'Fallon placed in a position where he would have to testify under oath. But in the latter part of 1792, O'Fallon concocted a new scheme with George Rogers Clark—participating in the Genêt plan to take over Louisiana—perhaps the high point in all the intrigues in Kentucky during that period. As it happened on that occasion, O'Fallon did have some chance of success, for the French had been quietly working for some time upon a plan to regain Louisiana.[5]

The overthrow of the Bourbons in France by the Republicans had caused considerable alarm among members of the French aristocracy—especially Frenchmen such as Carondelet, who had been in Spanish service. Carondelet was fearful of the many factions—especially the Jacobins—that might try to spread the revolution to Louisiana, for New Orleans was filled with agitators. In 1793 petitions were signed asking the French government to annex Louisiana, and there was talk of having the governor-general (Carondelet) removed. Carondelet was even threatened with the guillotine.

[5] Obviously O'Fallon was a man who made good first impressions, but he was not solid of character, and he was too flighty to function as a leader. He had some qualities that lent themselves to intrigue, but he was not clever enough for it—and he was pitted against a man who was astute, clever, and unscrupulous—James Wilkinson. O'Fallon became discredited with the land company, deserted by his friends, and left with very little of the world's goods; he had betrayed and been betrayed; he came to blows with Clark; his wife left him; and he died at the age of forty-four.

In the spring of 1793, France and Spain declared war upon each other; Carondelet for a while had extra troops in New Orleans, and he banished sixty-eight persons accused of sympathy with the French Revolution. Then he began to investigate and counter the activities of a large number of conspirators. Edmond Charles Genêt, André Michaux, Charles de Pauw, Auguste de la Chaise, Citizen Pelletier, Michel Ange Bernard de Mangourit, Thomas Power, Jean Pierre Pisgignoux, Thomas Medad Mitchell, Benjamin Sebastian, Thomas Portell, George Rogers Clark,[6] General James Wilkinson, and a carpenter named Mathurin were involved in one way or another. The Genêt affair itself lasted less than one year, but it caused Carondelet a great deal of trouble, and just possibly it came close to success.[7]

Clark, inspired—or abetted—by O'Fallon, in February, 1793, wrote a letter to "the French minister," encouraging the French government to take Louisiana; he said he *knew the route to Santa Fe* and would be pleased to lead an expedition for its conquest; he also suggested that £3,000 would be needed to finance such an expedition.[8]

Genêt landed in Charleston and began raising troops before proceeding to Philadelphia, and in June, 1793, Charles de Pauw,[9] one of the

[6] George Rogers Clark, older brother of William Clark, of the Lewis and Clark Expedition, was born in Virginia in 1752 and became a surveyor, farmer, and major of militia in 1776 in Virginia. As lieutenant colonel, he took Kaskaskia, made an arduous cross-country march in the winter to take Vincennes from Hamilton. He fought at Cahokia, against the Shawnees, and in many other actions. Clark was involved in many schemes to march Kentuckians against New Orleans. He was a tall man, of commanding demeanor, and he was brave, resourceful, and a natural leader. He began drinking heavily in later years and died in poverty in 1818. James Alton James, *George Rogers Clark.*

[7] For this affair, see Frederick Jackson Turner, American Historical Association *Annual Report for 1896* (also in 1897 and Vol. II for 1903); and "Correspondence of Clark and Genêt," *American Historical Review,* Vol. III (July, 1898).

[8] Clark to French minister, Louisville, February 2, 1793; American Historical Association *Annual Report for 1896,* I, 967–71. Since the publication of that letter, Louise Kellogg Phelps, in the *American Historical Review* (Vol. XXIX [1923–24], 504), has shown that Clark's offer to lead an expedition against Louisiana reached Paris before Genêt left Paris, and must have been written in late 1792.

[9] Charles de Pauw was born in Ghent in 1756, educated in Paris. Several years before 1793 he was trading in New Orleans, later settling in the Blue Grass region of Kentucky. He had come to America with Lafayette and had married a Virginia girl; his wife and children were with him in New Orleans when the Genêt affair began. His grandson endowed DePauw University.

New Orleans revolutionaries, went to the United States to propose to Genêt that he organize and promote a campaign to take Louisiana from Spain. De Pauw assured him that the spirit of rebellion was militant in Louisiana, that the inhabitants actually groaned under the "yoke of Spanish tyranny."

Genêt was a militant revolutionary, and he immediately began to organize and propagandize. One of his first moves was to address an inflammatory pamphlet to the people of Louisiana, espousing the French Republican cause and urging the Frenchmen of Louisiana to join the "republicans" of the United States:

> The moment has arrived when despotism must disappear from the earth. . . . The French people can and will avenge your wrongs. A perjured king, prevaricating ministers, vile and insolent courtiers, who fattened on the labor of the people whose blood they sucked, have suffered the punishment due to the crimes. . . . The hour has struck, Frenchmen of Louisiana; . . . now is the time to cease being the slaves of government to which you were shamefully sold. . . . The Spanish despotism has surpassed in atrocity and stupidity all the other despotisms that have ever been known. . . . Your brethren the French, who have attacked with success the Spanish government in Europe, will in a short time present themselves on your coasts with naval forces; . . . the republicans of the western portion of the United States are ready to come down the Ohio and Mississippi.[9a]

A native of Louisiana, Auguste de la Chaise,[10] schemed with Genêt while Citizen Pelletier[10a] and the French consul at Charleston (Mangourit[11]) conspired to choose agents, make charts of the river, and stir

[9a] *A.H.A. Annual Report for 1903*, 265–68. With letter of October 7, 1793.

[10] Auguste de la Chaise, zealous, indefatigable, intrepid, a native of Louisiana who had fought in the French army in Santo Domingo before going to Louisiana in 1793, was a member of one of Louisiana's most powerful families and is said to have been the most feared by Carondelet of all Genêt's agents (Gayarré, *History of Louisiana*, III, 342). Physically, De la Chaise was 5 feet, 9½ inches tall, wore his hair short, and was a big, pleasant man. See Liljegren, "Jacobinism in Spanish Louisiana, 1792–1797," *Louisiana Historical Quarterly*, Vol. XXI, No. 1 (January, 1939), 9.

[10a] Pelletier was a New Orleans merchant who conspired with Mangourit at Charleston. He was to select trustworthy agents in New Orleans, make charts of the river channels, and prepare the people to cooperate with the French forces that would come to deliver them.

[11] Mangourit was consul in Charleston in 1792. He aided Genêt but left after Genêt's downfall, later holding various positions in the French foreign service.

up the people with inflammatory meetings, placards, martial dances, and revolutionary songs. Jacobin clubs were organized,[11a] and altogether the temper of the populace rose to such a dangerous point that Carondelet obtained three hundred soldiers from the District of Natchez (present Mississippi) to police the capital. Revolutionaries were arrested and deported to Havana; martial dances were prohibited, and the cocked hats and liberty poles of the Jacobins went under cover, while Carondelet persuaded many persons to sign oaths of loyalty to Spain.

In July, 1793, Genêt, having had time to check on Clark, and having been urged on by De Pauw and De la Chaise and others, wrote a warm letter to Clark and sent André Michaux[12] to Kentucky as agent for the French Republic, bearing a provisional commission for George Rogers Clark as commander-in-chief of the proposed army.

Genêt said there would be a strong French naval attack against New Orleans (the left flank), while in the Ohio Valley (the right flank), plans for an expedition under Clark were being made.

Carondelet knew about the impending invasion and worked hard to organize the turbulent populace against it. He made considerable use of the Negro theme: because there had recently been a violent and tragic uprising of slaves in Santo Domingo, Carondelet argued that if the French revolutionaries should take over Louisiana, they would immediately emancipate the slaves and chaos would result. By threats, punishment, and the spreading of fear, Carondelet brought about a measure of tranquility in New Orleans by January, 1794—but his troubles were not over. He was advised that Genêt's expedition had attracted a large number of recruits, and he anticipated that the expedition would descend the river on the spring floods in March, April, or May.

New Orleans, even in the 1760's against Ulloa, had been a hotbed of conspiracy and intrigue—and the hot-blooded young creoles were still at it. Sedition and propaganda were on every hand; freedom was a shining

[11a] Jacobinism: unreasonable or violent opposition to legitimate government; popular turbulence.

[12] André Michaux was a French botanist who had been in the United States sporadically from 1785, traveling much in the interior and forming good connections with the Indians. Jefferson made arrangements for him to explore the Missouri when Genêt's plans for insurrection in Kentucky interfered. After the cancellation of the Kentucky affair, Michaux lost his nurseries in France and 60,000 plants. He died in Madagascar in 1800.

grail, and the thought of liberty and equality was enough to inflame an excitable populace; books and pamphlets came from the United States; every sailor and every passenger on a ship was a potential revolutionary apostle.

Meantime, Carondelet was ordered by Spain to ease the servitude of the 25,000 Negro slaves in Louisiana, and did so—without going far enough to satisfy the Negroes, but going far enough to incur the enmity of the Creole slave owners who had been his main supporters.

In 1793 and 1794, Indian slaves in Louisiana also, but unsuccessfully, demanded freedom because it was guaranteed under Spanish law. French secret agents were at work in many directions. During that time, too, a shortage of wheat flour began to harass the residents of New Orleans.

In April, 1794, Luis de las Casas[13] passed on to Spain some of Carondelet's uneasiness when he credited Carondelet with the prediction that if the invasion from Kentucky should be carried into effect, "all Upper Louisiana should be considered indefectibly lost at the beginning of next May, and the consequences will be noticed as far as Santa Fe, where the enemies propose to penetrate, informing that there are no more than twenty-two days' march from Saint Louis of Illinois to that internal province (that of New Spain)."

In this letter, Ezekiel Dwet and Thomas Medad Mitchell are revealed as agents for the Spaniards. The letter contains a discussion of the Pisgignoux party and of plans to stop it, and finally Las Casas, considering the danger, mentions the belief that Santa Fe is only twenty-two days' march from St. Louis; Las Casas calls that an "enormous error" and says that sixty days are not enough to ascend the river from St. Louis to the area occupied by the Kansas Indians. Las Casas makes several statements about the time needed to travel to Santa Fe and seems positive about his data—offering little proof, however. At any rate, it seems obvious that Las Casas laid the groundwork for a decision by the Consejo in Spain that Carondelet's figures were in error.[14]

[13] Las Casas was from a family prominent in colonial affairs since the 1500's. His sister was married to Carondelet, and that probably influenced Carondelet's appointment. Luis de las Casas was governor of Havana and captain-general of Louisiana and the Floridas from 1791 to 1796. See Whitaker, *The Spanish-American Frontier*, 154, 162, 167.

[14] Las Casas to [Campo Alange], No. 374, confidential, Havana, Feb. 21, 1794;

Intrigue piled upon intrigue. Clark was working in Kentucky, Genêt was working in Philadelphia, and Wilkinson, as usual, was working both sides of the fence. Prospects for a full-blown invasion seemed promising. But the Spaniards were protesting in Philadelphia, and the United States, still attempting to maintain its neutrality, agreed to take action against the filibusterers. Finally the French Republic, pressed by the United States, withdrew its financial support from the Kentucky project. Genêt and Michaux[14a] both found themselves in bad standing with the United States, and in March, 1794, the new French minister, Fauchet,[15] publicly renounced the French Republic's sponsorship. Clark was called to Philadelphia for a reprimand, and another threat to Louisiana was under control.

It is interesting to note, now that the Genêt affair was over, that the Consejo finally got around to consideration of Carondelet's warning that if Spain should not grant navigational rights on the Mississippi, Kentucky and her sister states would attack Louisiana with five hundred men (which would have been an ample force to take over Upper Louisiana, at least) or they would place themselves under England's wing, "forming a power more terrible to Spain than that of the United States."[16]

About that time also the Consejo reviewed Carondelet's statement that, from Louisiana, the French could easily reach Santa Fe; the Consejo thought that at least sixty days would be required for the trip—a monumentally bad guess, for Pedro Vial had just made it in thirty-two days, and in 1795 would travel from Santa Fe to the Pawnees in ten days, as will appear later; from the Pawnees to St. Louis, it was eight days.[17]

Under pressure, France backed away from the intrigues in Kentucky, but there was still great unrest among the Creoles in New Orleans, and

Archivo General de Simancas, Guerra Moderna, leg. 7235; the same material is in summary of letters to minister, dated Apr. 20, 1794.

[14a] Michaux was just one of the several who turned down a chance to engrave their names forever in the pages of American history—a chance that ten years later was taken advantage of by Meriwether Lewis and William Clark, younger brother of George Rogers Clark.

[15] Jean-Antoine-Joseph Fauchet served as minister to the United States from February, 1794, to June, 1795. He repudiated Genêt's plans upon his arrival in Philadelphia but strongly advocated the retrocession of Louisiana.

[16] Nasatir and Liljegren, "Minutas," *Louisiana Historical Quarterly*, Vol. XXI No. 1 (January, 1938), 43.

[17] *Ibid.*, 36.

Jacobinism (rebelliousness) spread to Natchitoches, where tempers were thin because of the arbitrary action against that area's principal industry on the part of the Consejo; in 1790 it had reduced government purchases of tobacco from about 2,000,000 pounds to 40,000 pounds, demoralizing the market. The quota was raised to 120,000 pounds in 1794, but by that time Natchitoches had already become a hotbed of unrest, and the revolutionary partisans found a ready field, led by Louis Mongino, a disgruntled surgeon, Louis Badins, a trouble-making trader, and Jean Delvaux, an acting priest.

Respectable citizens did not dare leave their homes for fear of attack. Drunken meetings lasted for days; the revolutionaries yelled like savage Indians, hurled insults, sang inflammatory songs, and fired their muskets. Carondelet had to send a commissioner to restore order, but before the disturbance was quelled, the commandant at Nacogdoches became alarmed and requested the commandant at Natchitoches to cancel all passports to Nacogdoches. The ruffians had taken over, and were in control of Natchitoches for some time—until January, 1796, when thirty-five soldiers were sent to restore order. The insurrection had been going on for seven months.

Another name that occurs in connection with this particular period is that of Louis de Vilemont, who in 1795 presented to the Consejo a comprehensive plan for colonizing Louisiana with European settlers. Vilemont went so far as to propose religious freedom for a considerable portion of Louisiana.[18] His plan, however, was not carried out.

During the two or three years of extreme unrest in New Orleans, Carondelet had shown up rather well. He had not run, even from the threat of personal danger, but had used his resources to keep Louisiana under the Spanish flag. Gayoso de Lemos, governor at Natchez, had emerged as an active and forceful official who supported Carondelet but at the same time kept him from actions that would have weakened his position.[19]

[18] See *ibid.*, 63.

[19] Educated in England, Gayoso was well liked and apparently honest despite his friendship with Wilkinson. (But see our comment on him later.) He achieved the rank of brigadier general and was serving as governor of Louisiana at his death in 1799 at the age of forty-eight. He was gentlemanly, suave, and tactful, and a good judge of human nature. Gayarré says (405) that he was a "spendthrift" and died poor; perhaps his death was a result of an extremely convivial night with Wilkinson.

Gayoso established a gunboat patrol on the Mississippi near Arkansas Post and later transferred the patrol to the mouth of the Ohio River (in the 1790's the Spaniards had patrols all the way up and down the Mississippi). In 1795 Gayoso was sent by Carondelet to investigate Spanish Illinois and ascertain, among other things, the degree of loyalty of the people, and to treat with the Kentuckians. His report on November 24, 1795, must have been reassuring to Carondelet: "... after having visited all the establishments that we have with the exception of Fort Carondelet ... I do not wish to delay assuring you of the good disposition and loyalty of all the inhabitants of those most remote establishments. ..."[20]

He gave information about each post (Cape Girardeau, Ste. Geneviève, New Bourbon, La Salina, the pueblo of Carondelet, St. Louis, San Fernando, Marais des Liards, San Carlos, and New Madrid); he described each place physically and named its assets, mentioned the prominent citizens and characterized them, and commented on the loyalty of the populace:

> [As to St. Louis,] I myself have had the concept that the generality of the inhabitants of St. Louis were disaffected to our government, but I cannot do less than to declare the contrary now that I have carefully tried to investigate their opinion. There is not an individual with whom I have not spoken. I have been in their houses and at their meetings, and not even remotely have I recognized a thing that may be reprehensible; on the contrary, they manifest the greatest affection to the king. I have noticed the apparel of the women in a very brilliant assembly that I attended in the house of Mr. Chouteau, and I have seen neither a tri-colored ribbon nor adornment that may be able to give suspicion of the manner of thinking of their families. Only the wife of Mr. [Joseph] Robidoux had a dress of three colors, but I attribute this to the bad taste of the married lady; moreover, it was older than the French Revolution, and her husband and she herself are persons of good character. . . . There is only one wayward person in this pueblo, and he is Mr. Papin,[21] but his relatives and a large family

[20] Gayoso to Carondelet, New Madrid, November 24, 1795, Papeles de Cuba, leg. 2364. See Frances Ellen Coughlin, "Spanish Galleys on the Mississippi, 1792–1797," unpublished master's thesis, Claremont Graduate School, 1945, for thorough documentation.

[21] Jean Marie Papin, a mason and a well-known troublemaker who at one time

restrain him, and alone he is not capable of causing fear. Likewise, it is not possible for me to forget the popular industry of Mr. Chouteau, his enterprising character, and disposal to all that is of interest to the royal service. . . . Neither can I omit the name of Mr. Cerré,[22] of whom baselessly there was some suspicion, but it has surely been some bad intelligence, since he is a peaceful resident who only occupies himself with this commerce and his labor; rather, he must be considered as a useful and trustworthy vassal.

The Directors of the Company of New Discoveries [Missouri Fur Company] are animated by the most laudable ambitions and are worthy of the favor of the government. Mr. Soulard[23] has corroborated me in the first good opinion which I formed of him, and his conduct has dispelled the doubt in which he was left by the note which was found by Mr. Bohevie . . .

Lieutenant-Governor Don Zenon Trudeau[24] has the affection of all the inhabitants. They have all assured me that their happiness consisted in the permanence of this chief, whose character, because of being so well known, does not need eulogy.

San Carlos de Misuri is . . . only eight leagues distant from St. Louis. . . . A great part of the residents are employed in voyages to the Upper Missouri. It causes pleasure to hear the king's name pronounced by these people; they pronounce it with veneration and live in the hope that with his protection they will be the most happy men in the world. . . .

All the country of Illinois is delightful, good piece of ground, well wooded, with frequent springs which will be augmented in proportion as the country is opened. . . .

---

was banished from Cahokia for disturbing the peace. Not the same man as Joseph Marie Papin, a fur-trader who married a daughter of Madame Chouteau.

[22] Gabriel Cerré, who had come from Kaskaskia and was a leading merchant and citizen of St. Louis. Cerré, the Chouteaus, and Charles Gratiot were all wealthy (or at least very substantial citizens), and for many years were the leading fur merchants of St. Louis.

[23] Antoine Soulard, former army captain and special land surveyor for Upper Louisiana, was adjutant to the lieutenant governor at St. Louis for the last eight years of Spanish rule. He is the author of Carondelet's map of 1794, prepared for Truteau's expedition up the Missouri—a map that is important cartographically, for it shows the Platte and Kansas rivers with fair accuracy and indicates advancement in knowledge of the Missouri.

[24] Zenon Trudeau, born in New Orleans in 1748, was a lieutenant in the army, served as commandant at St. Louis from 1792 to 1799, and died in Louisiana. He was commandant at St. Louis when Pedro Vial went there from Santa Fe.

Back of San Carlos begin immense prairies which extend as far as the hunters have reached in all directions . . . The climate is most benign, favoring the production of all kinds of European fruits except oranges and lemons; it produces good wheat, maize, and all seeds known in Europe, cotton and hemp. All kinds of cattle would prosper if the population were more considerable in order to prevent the robberies which the Indians casually are apt to make . . .

It would be very important to foment emigration of a good quality of people to Illinois, since I consider it the most direct passageway to the kingdom of Mexico, and if this interesting object is not heeded, the English traders will not delay many years in introducing themselves there, and forces will follow them. It would be best to form a cordon of small posts from the Missouri, following from San Carlos, Carondelet, and continuing until uniting ourselves with the Interior Provinces. In this way we could command greater respect from the Indians, we would conserve their commerce, and we would efficaciously protect the kingdom of Mexico. . . .

It is with the greatest [pleasure] that I assure you of the good disposition of our people of Illinois. . . . You are not ignorant of the zeal which there always is among commercial people, and that by necessity they have connections in foreign countries. From this they have taken pretext for promoting suspicious ideas against those of St. Louis, but I flatter myself with knowing men, and I affirm that those of Illinois are good vassals. . . .

I forgot to tell you that in all the country of Illinois fifteen hundred armed men of good quality can be assembled.

. . . of New Madrid. . . . Waters, who is a subject of principles and who can be trusted. I assure you that I consider Portell[25] of infinite merit because of his managing them as he is managing them [the inhabitants? ]. . . .

[He discusses the problem of milling, and believes that mills will be established; wheat can be bought from Kaskaskia, on the American side of the river.] My opinion is that it [the mill at New Madrid] has been a speculation lightly conceived by Don Pedro Tardiveau,[26]

[25] Thomas Portell was commandant at New Madrid, 1791–96. When he surrendered a post in Florida to William Bowles in 1800, he was court-martialed and dismissed from Spanish service.

[26] Probably Juan Bautista Tardiveau, who was known also as Bartolomé Tardiveau; he contracted to build flour mills at New Madrid but discovered, too late, that not enough wheat was raised in the area to keep them busy.

accepted with sane enthusiasm by the Chevalier de Luzière[27] and by the other associates, and facilitated by the extraordinary ability of Mr. Vanden[28] without considering where the wheat was to come from. Vanden is a diamond in the rough, severe in his behavior, rude and inconsiderate upon first sight, but [on one's] knowing his character, he does not have a bad disposition, and even [in] allowing him to follow his nature, which he cannot suppress, he can be very useful and even accommodating. Dervino[29] is docile and young and looks upon Vanden because of his interests of his father-in-law[?], but he is a poor boy without malice.

It is impossible that there is evil in the heart of Mr. Luzière, but because of kindness he can be deceived. I am sure that he will never again give recommendations [?] to anyone. Madame de Luzière is not of such a fortunate character. She would be likable in a city, but she cannot conform to the conduct of country people. Therefore she is alone. The children are good boys, but, not having been destined for a hard life, do not find recourse in themselves in a manner which can alleviate their parents in spite of the poor fellows' doing what they can.

It is now 4 o'clock in the afternoon of the twenty-fifth. Power[30] has just arrived, but as it is impossible for me to decipher his letter in order to send it by this occasion, I shall send it by an extraordinary

[27] Pierre Charles du Hault Delassus de Luzière, the first commandant at New Bourbon, had been a landed aristocrat in Flanders. He and his wife were forced to leave France because he was a royalist, and had to relinquish an annual income of 45,000 crowns. Luzière, Pierre Audrain, and Bartolomé Tardiveau were instrumental in the establishment of New Bourbon.

[28] Joseph Vandenbemden was a native of Flanders and probably a civil engineer, as was his brother Louis, who was charged by Carondelet with the defense of St. Louis in 1796 and who went to New Madrid in 1797. Joseph is the one who built the mill on pilework, "with solidity and intelligence," according to Collot.

[29] There was a Pierre Derbigny—but hardly the same one, it seems. Pedro Derbigny received a large grant of land in Missouri, 1799, for services; he was better known as interpreter and captain of militia at New Madrid, and he was a partner of Pedro Antonio Laforge in trading.

[30] Thomas Power was born a British subject but was naturalized under the Spanish king; he was the chief agent for Carondelet, and his name appears in many documents. He was intelligent, cautious, and good at intrigue, according to Gayarré, *History of Louisiana*, III, 345–46. Indefatigable Power contacted Wilkinson, acting as emissary between New Orleans and Kentucky, and did his best to promote rebellion in the western states (that is, those between the Mississippi River and the Allegheny Mountains), and urged them either to set up a republic or to seek annexation to Louisiana. Power was later a member of the Spanish Boundary Commission.

occasion. However, you will know what he says by this letter, which I am remitting, and another for Gilberto.

Power assures me that Sebastian[31] and another who is not yet determined will come to treat with me between the tenth and twentieth of December, approximately. I do not have time to speak of Perchet or of anyone who resembles him.

Open defiance of Spanish rule was confined to New Orleans and Natchitoches. Order along the river seemed adequately maintained by Gayoso's gunboats, whose commanders had instructions to intercept Genêt's pamphlets and to arrest De la Chaise, De Pauw, Jean Pierre Pisgignoux, and anybody else who might have tri-colors or other suspicious objects in his luggage. Pisgignoux was arrested in early 1794, and two more galleys were stationed at New Madrid. Pisgignoux evidently was on the way to Lower Louisiana to prepare the people for Genêt's invasion, and his subsequent testimony put suspicion on many trusted officials.[32]

Conditions in Upper Louisiana were somewhat better than those that fostered sedition in New Orleans and Lower Louisiana. The towns in Upper Louisiana were few, and their population small. Upper Louisiana's only export product was furs, and although the market was poor in the middle 1790's, the people lived under frontier conditions and were largely self-sustaining; items that could not be manufactured or for which substitutes could not be found were obtained from Canada or the United States. The region had some surplus corn and lead, both of which commodities could be sold readily in Lower Louisiana. If Louisiana had been brought under conquest, the people of Upper Louisiana probably would have gone along, but in the meantime they were satisfied with conditions as they were.

Lower Louisiana, however, was struck by a series of calamities.

[31] Benjamin Sebastian was a soldier, clergymen, and lawyer, more inclined to intrigue than adapted to it. He was used by Carondelet to promote trouble in Kentucky in 1795 and received a "pension" from the Spaniards in 1797, but in 1804 his many intrigues were exposed, ruining him politically.

[32] Much of Pisgignoux' testimony was unfounded, according to Ernest R. Liljegren, whose article, "Jacobinism in Spanish Louisiana, 1792–1797," *Louisiana Historical Quarterly*, Vol. XXI, No. 1 [January, 1939]), was used freely in this chapter. Thumbnail biographies are copiously presented in that article and in Nasatir and Liljegren, "Minutas."

The cultivation of sugar cane had been largely abandoned since 1766 because of the difficulty of extracting the sugar; rice and corn were produced for domestic needs only; cotton was not profitable because of the difficulty of separating the seeds from the fiber. Tobacco was subject to arbitrary regulation by officers or bodies in Spain. Indigo had been introduced and had done well, but in 1793 and 1794 disaster struck when the indigo plant was attacked by an insect that devoured the plant down to the stem; thus planter after planter found himself on the verge of ruin[33]—and in addition to the insect plague, Lower Louisiana was stricken by hurricanes.

Besides those inimical manifestations of Nature, the colony found itself almost barren of hard money, and foreign ships seldom came to New Orleans because of the ban on exportation of silver. Naturally, too, there was contrabanding—illegal shipment of silver out of the colony (in one case as much as 40,000 pesos.)

In December, 1794, New Orleans for the third time was destroyed by fire, and in April, 1795, a mass conspiracy for an uprising of slaves was uncovered; the Negro leaders were hanged, the whites banished. Wild talk, whisperings, discontentment, suspicion, and anarchy were in the air. The Spanish soldiers preyed on the citizenry, and some persons predicted that Carondelet would be among the first to lose his head under the triangular blade.

Carondelet, as a member of the aristocracy, was very sensitive to mention of the guillotine, as may be seen in a letter that he wrote in April, 1795, to the viceroy, the Marquis of Branciforte:

> Our situation becomes each day more critical; each day arrive new songs, anonymous incendiary papers, etc., directed to make the officials odious [to the people] and to familiarize the vulgar [people] with the idea of guillotining us, to hang [us], and to commit the other atrocities that have afflicted France. We discover a conspiracy among the Negroes to kill their masters, and since then the others appear restless. Among the whites, many are partial to the new republic and are looking for no more than a pretext to shake off the Spanish domination.
>
> Distrust has reigned for the last two months, and many indications have been observed that denote an insurrection; in spite of our vigilance,

[33] Gayarré, *History of Louisiana,* III, 346–47. It was in 1795 that Étienne de Boré produced his first sugar from cane in a process that was to revolutionize agriculture in Lower Louisiana.

the houses whose roofs are of wood have been purposefully set afire various times at night, so that if we do not soon receive troops and money, we shall become victims perhaps of our own troops, in which there are many Frenchmen and other traitors; finally, we are reduced to not knowing whom we may trust, I say, [because] we Spaniards are so few.

A company of dragoons would be of great use for the night patrols, to restrain the common hordes in a riot, or during a fire—in which [cases] the officials do not risk themselves to give aid because of the justified fear of being assassinated during the confusion—much more so as the end of these vicious persons who set the fires, cannot be other than robbery or insurrection.

I am well persuaded that your Excellency will deign to attend to our situation, the most restless and critical, perhaps, which any governor in America has.[34]

Branciforte did send some dragoons, but they did not reach New Orleans until September. Meanwhile, Carondelet had taken an intelligent move to try to restore order: he had passed a regulation requiring the selection of officials from among the planters, and those officials were made responsible for the maintenance of order.

In October, 1795, Spain signed the Pinckney Treaty[35] with the United States, guaranteeing the free use of the Mississippi and the right to deposit goods at New Orleans, and setting the thirty-first parallel as a tentative boundary between the Spaniards in Florida and the Americans in Mississippi. The first two provisions took the steam out of the Kentucky insurrectionist aims.[36] But, even though France

[34] Carondelet to Branciforte, No. 7, New Orleans, April 28, 1795, A.H.N., Estado, leg. 4177, carpeta 7, cuaderno no. 12, f. 55 *passim.*

[35] The Treaty of San Lorenzo el Real. See Samuel F. Bemis, *Pinckney's Treaty* (New Haven, Yale University Press, 1960).

[36] Though the Pinckney Treaty may have been considered in Madrid the answer to the Anglo-American threat, it was not so considered in Louisiana, for Carondelet told Morales it had presented him with the major and highly important problem of reenforcing west Louisiana because of the propensity of Americans for frontier life and the curious inquietude with which they investigated everything and made themselves at home in foreign lands. Carondelet to Juan Ventura Morales, New Orleans June 11, 1797, Papeles de Cuba, leg. 2580 and leg. 179A. Morales was the intendant of Louisiana from 1796 until the Americans took over (with an interlude by Ramón Angulo López). Morales, though ever contentious and personally obnoxious, was said to be the only Louisiana official not suspected of venality. (Whitaker, *The Mississippi Question*, 31–32, 158–60).

and Spain had just signed a treaty, in December, 1795, Revillagigedo, the viceroy of Mexico, sent out warnings that the French might approach the coast of Texas, and he alerted officials for an attack in that area.[37]

Revillagigedo's apprehensions were not inconsistent with French ideas, for in the same month, the French minister at Madrid urged that one reason for the acquisition of Louisiana by France was exploitation of the riches of Santa Fe.[38]

The Genêt attack (the rumors of which undoubtedly had prompted Revillagigedo's warning) did not materialize, however, either by river or by sea. Then, in October, 1796, Spain declared war on England, and the French threat became a British threat, for it was rumored that an army was assembled on the southern border of Canada to invade Spanish Illinois. At about that time, the situation was further complicated by the actions of Brigadier General George Victor Collot, who was sent by the French government to make a military report on the Ohio Valley; he made that reconnaissance and then ascended the Mississippi to St. Louis, and finally descended the Mississippi to New Orleans. News of his activities had preceded him, inasmuch as he had told several prominent persons that arrangements for the retrocession of Louisiana to France were practically complete. Carondelet had him arrested when he reached New Orleans, listened to his rather contradictory statements, and sent him by sea to the United States. The extent of Collot's activities is shown in Carondelet's report to Godoy, which Carondelet copied in a letter to Las Casas:

> The minister of his Majesty [who was then Joseph Jáudenes] having notified by triplicate reports, regarding the United States, that the general of brigade, George Victor Collot of the French Republic, to whom he gave a passport at the request of Minister Adet to go by way of the Ohio down to this town from whence he was to sail for the northern part of America, was a very suspicious character, I decided to detain him with all his papers upon his arrival here, due to our

[37] Revillagigedo to governors of the colony of Nuevo Santander and the New Kingdom of León, No. 7, Mexico, December 18, 1795; A.H.N., leg. 4177, carpeta 7.

[38] Reflection by Roume, Madrid, 29 Frimaire, au IV (December 20, 1795); Archives du Ministère des Affaires Étrangères, Etats Unis, Supplément, Vol. 7, f. 28; see N. M. Miller Surrey, *Calendar of Manuscripts of Paris Archives and Libraries Relating to the History of the Mississippi Valley to 1803*, 3, II, 1680–81.

reasons for fearing his conduct having been confirmed. First: because, having changed his route, and instead of coming down the Ohio to New Orleans as stated on the passport, he went up the Mississippi, and from the Missouri to St. Louis of Illinois, he surveyed the whole province and its posts up to Natchez, bringing with him an adjutant-general of the French troops, a very able engineer named Carlos Joseph Warin, who made a reconnaissance of the Ohio River with the most minute details, and without doubt he must have done the same along the Mississippi although I found only three plans of Upper Louisiana on his person. Second: because he confided to various subjects that the cession of the province was a matter which was already effected, and that France would take measures to reassure the inhabitants of possession of the Negroes, etc., causing many subjects consternation and worry.

General Collot, upon being detained and the objective of his trip partially discovered, confessed in several very interesting and confidential conversations, being a man of great ability, that it all amounted to a military survey of the western country, that is, from the Allegheny Mountains, following the course of the Ohio to the Mississippi, and from there to the Missouri up to this capital and Balize,[39] having been commissioned for this purpose by the minister of France, Adet, who gave him a letter of recommendation to me, which is enclosed in the dispatch which I am sending separately as it seemed to me very urgent to notify your excellency without delay of what has been discovered and is being conspired by the said Adet, that is, if Collot is not deceiving us.

It seems that as a result of the treaty made between the United States of America and England, Adet, General Collot, de Autun, ex-minister of France, and several other French subjects of intelligence and influence, represented to the legislature the great influence that the English had already acquired in those states by means of an unjust and dangerous guarantee of the navigation of the Mississippi River, having made same to England, placing her in a position of being able to extend her position from the Saint Lawrence River up to Nootka Sound on the ocean, the South Seas, and the Gulf of Mexico through Balize, which exposes Spain to the certain loss

[39] Balize was an island in the mouth of one current of the Mississippi as it flowed through the delta. All incoming ships anchored at Balize, for which a pilot was necessary. They could go on to Fort Plaquemines, where they declared their cargoes, without a pilot. It was twenty-six miles on to Fort Plaquemines and sixty miles from there to New Orleans.

of Louisiana and, in time, of the kingdom of Mexico; that the French party had been annihilated in the United States because the republic did not have worthwhile possessions in this continent, therefore it is advisable to obtain the return of Louisiana from Spain or for her to declare herself in favor of France in order to force England to grant peace to Canada. The copy reproduced from memory, enclosed under No. 1, which I have found among Collot's papers, will better inform your excellency of what I have just related. After having addressed themselves thus to the legislature, the said subjects decided that Collot and the adjutant-general, Warin, must come to the western states to test the spirit of the inhabitants as to the side they would take in the event that the republic should succeed in obtaining the acquisition of Louisiana or Canada, and at the same time they were commissioned to survey and draw up plans of the entire course of the Ohio and Mississippi rivers. They have, in effect, all the maps and plans of Canada, and the banks of the Ohio, in the most minute details, its posts and forts, etc., with memoranda of everything pertaining to each place passed. There is a plan of Spanish and American Illinois which I took away from him,[40] also another small one of St. Louis,[41] which he considers a point of utmost importance for the overthrow and domination of Canada and the defense of Louisiana.

By the various conversations that I have had with him, I have learned that the United States of the West would declare themselves independent immediately after they see and know that Spain or France have respectable forces sufficient to give them powerful support. On my part, I do not doubt that if the republic obtains Louisiana, the separation of Kentucky and the rest of the western states will become effective immediately, which will put the kingdom of Mexico in a much greater danger than before and will expose it to a revolution which is inevitable in my judgment, because of the proximity of these two turbulent and enterprising nations, lovers of adventure and equally enthusiastic of republican principles. In summarizing, it appears that the purpose of this project is for Spain to cede to the republic all the west bank of the Mississippi, and that the boundary limits of each side should be its banks. Nevertheless, I believe that it

[40] This apparently is the map that eventually appeared in print in 1826. See Wheat, *The Spanish Entrada*, 160. While this map was not based on any explorations by Collot, it nevertheless represents, Wheat points out, a transition between the fanciful cartography of Soulard and the maps of Mackay and Evans on the upper Missouri.

[41] This little map appears in Houck, *Spanish Régime*, II, 238.

will be difficult for them [?] to renounce the possession of St. Louis of Illinois, in the event that Canada should remain in the possession of England.

Collot added that the last treaty upon the boundaries was of no importance and that the republic would know how to destroy it before it could become effective. The truth is the American commissioners have not opined as yet. If we are to believe his claims, Archbishop Autun will have already gone to treat upon this subject with your excellency.

Lastly, his opinion being in complete accordance with mine, which is that Spain cannot abandon the forts of San Fernando de las Barrancas, Nogales, and Natchez without exposing all of Louisiana and the united provinces to an immediate loss.

If all the efforts of the republic are aimed toward acquiring possessions in this continent in the vicinity of the United States, which might give to it the means of conserving an influence among them capable of counterbalancing that of the English, perhaps the republic would be satisfied with the cession of West Florida, next to that of Georgia, and much less dangerous for Spain than Louisiana if ceded, but if his Majesty resolves to keep the said upper posts, situated on the west [east?] bank of the Mississippi, under the various pretexts that I have represented confidentially in Nos. 79 and 81, it is obvious that with decorum we could stave off the imminent danger that threatens the kingdom because of the Americans or French, which can be done only by the sacrifice of an increase of two hundred thousand pesos which is needed for this allowance, with half of the ninety thousand produced by the customs, which duties should be reduced to one-third per cent of the importation and exportation in order to put the commerce in a position to sustain the concurrence of the Americans, who, not paying anything at all, will have contraband which will be impossible to prevent, together with a disbursement of two million pesos which is needed to put this frontier upon a respectable footing of war, his Majesty can be confident that within a few years Louisiana will have sufficient population to oppose the United States and to contravene its projects.

I hope to send, by the first opportunity, a plan which has been proposed to me by the most important subjects of the United States of the West who are endeavoring to establish in a space of three years a population of thirty-two thousand good laborers, enemies to the federal government, on the west bank of the Mississippi between New Madrid and Arkansas, without disbursement from the royal treasury. If this is effective, which I do not doubt, Spain can count upon a trebled immigration to this province from Europe, as well as from North America, in the three following years.

General Collot will leave for New York within eight days. I am holding him under arrest until his departure because I do not wish him to make a reconnaissance of the rest of Louisiana, remaining always with the scruples that Don Joseph Jáudenes, not having the slightest inkling of the purpose of his voyage, advised me that he was a suspicious character; the other being that it is not advisable, in the event that it is true, for his Majesty to be informed of this negotiation, nor for the English and the Americans to learn the reasons for Collot's trip, although he has told me that General Wayne intercepted his correspondence with Adet last August. He replied to my first objection to the secret that was confided to Don Joseph Jáudenes[42] that this minister being married to a daughter of a member of the federal government [page torn] Adet, to divulge the secret of the [page torn] No. 3 is a copy of one of the [page torn].

I shall send, in smaller copies, all the proceedings practiced by them before the arrest of General Collot. Through them your Excellency will realize that I have proceeded with thoroughness and in a manner to avoid compromising Spain in any way with the republic. With the same purpose I have answered Adet's letter, which is enclosed under No. 2, and I have reasons to believe that General Collot, a very intelligent and amiable person, will leave here satisfied with my procedures, even after having been held under arrest for eight days, which no doubt must be offensive to a general.

I am transcribing this to your Excellency for your proper information.[43]

In the following February (1797), Yrujo, Spanish minister at Philadelphia, wrote to Godoy with additional information concerning Collot's objectives:

General Collot, who is a general of the French Republic, has recently

[42] Joseph Jáudenes was an assistant to Diego de Gardoqui when Gardoqui was minister to the United States. (Gardoqui's father's firm was the chief secret supplier of goods to the Americans during the Revolutionary War.)

[43] This important document, containing a great deal of information on the problems of Louisiana in connection with Collot, was written by Carondelet to Las Casas, No. 163, confidential, New Orleans, November 1, 1796, Papeles de Cuba, leg. 1447. Carondelet's letter to Godoy, quoted by Carondelet, is No. 83.

been employed by this minister of France in the important commission of reconnoitering the course and surroundings of the Ohio and Mississippi, drawing plans of all the American forts on those frontiers, and examining the course of the Missouri, the Allegheny River, and the waters by which the English would be able to descend to the Mississippi from the lakes. . . . [He then] approached our frontiers, where he also continued the same observations.[44]

. . . In my previous letters I have manifested to your excellency the importance for France of establishing here a certain political influence and vigorously combating the efforts of the English party. As one of the principal means, in my opinion, they intend to have a point of contact with the United States, from which they can obtain with their threats what they cannot obtain by intrigues and stratagems, always slow when they find themselves counter-arrested by a powerful party. This makes me believe that the true object of the mission of the said Collot has been to reconnoiter the weak part of the United States and to calculate up to what point it could be useful to France to propose some exchange with Spain so that Louisiana, which it ceded to us in the peace of 1762, might be restored to it [France]. The discourses I have heard both from the cited general and from the minister of France, confirm me more and more in this idea.

Can this cession be useful to the interests of Spain? And can placing a new, powerful barrier to American ambition in that part contribute to the security of our possessions of New Mexico? . . .

I gather one indispensable consequence . . . that your Excellency try . . . to stipulate . . . the demarcation of limits between the English possessions of Canada and ours in this continent . . .

General Collot and the minister of France, in proof of the candor and good faith with which they are proceeding in these steps, which they believe as useful to Spain as to France itself, have offered me a copy of all the memoirs and annotations made by the cited general on this interesting voyage. Likewise, a copy of the plan and soundings of the Ohio which he navigated in sixty-seven days, the plans of all the American forts on those frontiers, state of the country and other notices which will be profitable to Spain, either keeping Louisiana or in case of making an exchange with France.

As the number of plans is very considerable and the nature of this work must be so secret and confidential, not finding anyone here of [sufficient] confidence and ability to make copies, I have written to

[44] Yrujo to Godoy, April 17, 1797, A.H.N., leg. 3889 *bis*, no. 34.

the commandant-general of the island of Cuba to send me immediately an officer of engineers in whom are united these qualities.[45]

Added to the letter was a memorandum from Godoy to Yrujo, acknowledging receipt of Yrujo's letter and adding:

> Although news was already had here of the voyage of this subject and the true object of his commission, I have read with pleasure all that your Excellency says in your cited letter and I am forewarning you to try to acquire and remit to me with the greatest possible haste, copies of all the memoirs and annotations made by the said Collot on his trip, especially of all the maps and plans that can serve for the demarcation of limits between the English possessions of Canada and ours in that continent. . .

An incomplete and unsigned letter that may also be from Yrujo to Godoy discusses the degrees of Collot's guilt and suggests that Collot and Warin, the engineer who had been with him, might not be offenders of state, and perhaps should be sent to Cádiz. Thus it appears, if this letter follows the preceding one, that Yrujo did not really learn much from Collot in spite of Collot's apparent frankness. What Yrujo wanted very much to know was the nationality of whoever was paying Collot for the reconnaissance. Yrujo speculates concerning whether Collot's commission from the French republic is false, and he suggests the diplomatic turns that may result from either eventuality. Yrujo says that if the commission is false, Collot is an offender against France; if true, Spain has a complaint against France; in any event, Collot is a criminal by reason of having violated the territorial sovereignty of Spain.[46]

He suggests that Collot may actually have been reconnoitering the province to determine its usefulness to France in anticipation of retrocession, and he believes that France, if she obtains Louisiana, will then extend her trade through Natchitoches to the Interior Provinces, using as a club the potential threat of invasion along the vast Louisiana–Texas–New Mexico boundary. Finally, Yrujo suggests that Collot is in bad standing with the French but is a confidant of the English, and since the war with England appears inevitable, Collot and Warin therefore

[45] Yrujo to Godoy, Philadelphia, February 18, 1797, A.H.N., leg. 3889 *bis*.

[46] However, Collot held both French and Spanish passports.

are enemies of the state of Spain. All these conclusions, says Yrujo, he has reached after following the trail of the two men. Yrujo learned much from Collot, and from that information disclosed Blount's conspiracy.

It gets complicated.

As a matter of fact, Collot had very definite designs on Louisiana, though those designs were not immediately apparent to the Spaniards. He wanted to expand Louisiana to include all the land to the Allegheny Mountains, with Fort Pitt (Pittsburgh) a strong point, and western America under the French government. He met George Rogers Clark, drunk, at Louisville, and undoubtedly discussed those ambitions, for they both knew that Pittsburgh and St. Louis would control the interior of North America. Collot thought that two thousand or three thousand frontiersmen or United States or British troops could take everything along the Mississippi to New Orleans without serious resistance—and he was undoubtedly right. Collot drew the best chart of the Ohio River up to that time, and altogether he seems to have been a more serious threat than even the Spaniards believed.[47]

Partly as a result of Collot's activities, in the following December (1796) Don Carlos Howard set out from New Orleans to New Madrid to lead a military expedition to Illinois and to fortify St. Louis—supposedly to counter British influence and especially to drive British traders out of the Missouri Valley in accordance with orders from Spain. On the surface, Howard's duties seem to be primarily concerned with investigating the problem of sedition in Upper Louisiana, and although he did find some wine-drinking and girl-kissing and wild-statement-making, he used good judgment and decided that there was nothing more than exuberance stimulated by a certain degree of inebriation. After a minimum display of authority, Carondelet granted full pardons, and everybody promised to behave.[48]

[47] See George W. Kyte, "A Spy on the Western Waters: the Military Intelligence Mission of General Collot in 1796," *Mississippi Valley Historical Review*, Vol. XXIV, No. 3 (December, 1947).

[48] Carondelet, though often characterized as effeminate, is described by Gayarré as a "short-sized, plump gentleman, somewhat choleric but not without a good nature." Gayarré says he was firm, prudent, business-like. Allowing for Gayarré's possible leaning in this matter, and for that of Whitaker, who does not like Carondelet, one might come close to the truth.

Howard's purposes were actually more serious than might appear from this report, however, for from St. Louis he sent one expedition up the Mississippi and another up the Missouri with orders to destroy British influence and forestall a British attack from Canada; he also sent spies to Canada and the United States and fortified St. Louis.

For Louisiana's survival through the threats of insurrection at home, and against the schemes of O'Fallon, Genêt, and Collot, one might be tempted to say the rulers were lucky, but one should also be willing to note that the rulers somehow handled the various situations so as to come out ahead. It is hard to resist, however, pointing out that the Supremo Consejo took one action that was in complete accord with Spanish ruling principles: on August 14, 1795, it decided that Louisiana should be made into a captaincy-general to resist the Americans.[49]

As if a political reshuffling would solve everything.

[49] Nasatir and Liljegren, eds., "Materials Relating to the History of the Mississippi Valley," *Louisiana Historical Quarterly*, Vol. XXI, No. 1 (January, 1938), 52. It was never carried out.

# VI

# *The Anglo-American Threat from Kentucky*

No Anglo-American threat developed until the United States became a nation, in 1783. Once the United States gained its independence, however, and the Americans were no longer busy fighting a war with England, Spain took cognizance of the Americans' inherent dislike for subordination to a higher authority and their propensity for finding out what lay over the next mountain. The American threat became real, and Americans began thrusting at Santa Fe from all directions.

American threats can be divided into six periods: the American threat from Kentucky in the 1790's; the American threat from the the Missouri, 1800–1807; the Lewis and Clark expedition, 1804–1807; the American threat from Lower Louisiana, which started with Philip Nolan in 1785 and ended about the time of the Lewis and Clark expedition with a flurry of governmental or quasi-governmental explorations; the Pike era, which started in 1806, and set off a series of expeditions that lasted into the 1820's; and the Santa Fe Trail era, which started in 1821 and lasted until 1846—at which time the Mexican War broke out, and Kearny took his Army of the West to conquer New Mexico and California.

The Kentucky threat was the most active, perhaps, when measured by the multiplicity of its plans, the seriousness of the intentions of various men involved, and the turmoil it created in Spanish governmental circles. In 1794 Carondelet predicted that the western states might give themselves into the control of England, that Louisiana would be lost to Spain, and that the Americans would promptly attempt to capture Santa Fe—but Spanish officials had been apprehensive over Anglo-

American aggression before that year. In fact, as early as 1785 Governor Miró of Louisiana had recognized the danger involved in allowing free travel to Americans over Spanish territory when he sent the following order for arrest to the commandant at St. Louis:

> You will be vigilant and will take the most efficacious steps and measures to prevent the Americans from introducing themselves in order to trade in the Missouri [area, since] there are strong reasons of state in which the particular well-being of the nation is interested for prohibiting foreign commerce in our America. . . .
>
> . . . you must judge the American who may introduce himself in the Missouri as a contrabandist and guilty of the crime of illicit commerce, and as such you must procure his apprehension, confiscate his effects, selling them in your post in public auction or remitting them to this post if they are peltries or if they cannot be sold well in your post, sending at the same time the criminals by special occasion in case the product of the confiscation can defray the expenses . . .[1]

Cruzat answered that "the news that I had communicated to your Excellency in my official letter No. 26 relative to what a subject of these establishments had secretly communicated to me concerning the intention which the American merchants had projected to introduce themselves to engage in commerce with the nations of the Missouri" have turned out false, but he adds that every day boats descend the Ohio and go to the "villages of Oca and Okao."[2]

But again, in 1788, Manuel Pérez wrote to Miró on the subject. This is the letter in which he speaks of the "barbariousness of the one [Americans]" and the "jealousy and envy" of the others (English). "For a long time the English," he says, "and especially the Americans of some [document torn] district have been looking for the means to penetrate the Missouri." If the country falls into the hands of one or the other, the loss "can be regarded as the epoch of vagabonds[2a] who will go into the province of New Mexico . . . they will assemble troops

[1] Miró to Cruzat, New Orleans, March 8, 1785, Papeles de Cuba, leg. 117A.

[2] Cruzat to Miró, St. Louis, August 16, 1785, probably attached to the letter of March 8. These villages are Cahokia and Kaskaskia.

[2a] The word *vagabond* did not then carry the strong connotation of worthlessness that it carries today. It meant a person without ties, a transient—hence a reckless person.

of vagabonds and will unite to go to pillage these mines [of New Mexico]." He speaks of the lack of goods for the Indians and of the six barrels of *aguardiente* that shrank to four. He tries to explain that his lack of goods is partly due to the fact that the city has been burned and Mr. Sarpy's bateau has been lost. He calls the governor's attention also to the fact that his predecessor had three times as much goods for distribution.[3]

A little over two years later (in 1791), Pérez wrote suggesting forts on the Des Moines and St. Peter's rivers, and said, "It is evident that the English and especially the Americans speak of nothing else than the kingdom of Mexico, and strive to learn about it and to find a way that will give them some loophole for approaching it."[4]

Pérez does not indicate in this letter that the Americans are already in Louisiana, but only that he considers them the greater threat.

However, Americans were already in Texas, and two years later the captain-general at Havana wrote to the governor of Louisiana in complaint against the *contrabandistas* from Arkansas Post:

> By the enclosed copy of the letter of the viceroy of New Spain and the enclosed document, your Excellency will be informed of the damages and injuries which the province of Texas is experiencing from the merchants of that province by [traders from] the U.S. who, crossing the Natchitoches River [the Red], penetrate the interior to trade with the barbaric Nations of the North [the Norteños]. To stop this traffic from taking hold, which has such lamentable consequences, I hope from the zeal of your Excellency that you will take the most rigid measures to repress it, taking for that purpose all the measures which your prudence may dictate and the local knowledge of the principal points where this practice is taking place, which can serve you to act in accord with the governor of Texas.[5]

The letter from Revillagigedo, enclosed by Las Casas, is brief but encloses a long one from Ramón Castro,[6] commandant at Bahía del

[3] Pérez to Miró, No. 58, St. Louis, December 1, 1788, Papeles de Cuba, leg. 2361.

[4] Pérez to Miró, St. Louis, April 5, 1791, Papeles de Cuba, leg. 1442.

[5] Las Casas to Carondelet, Havana, February 26, 1793, Papeles de Cuba, leg. 152A.

[6] Ramón Castro later became commandant-general of the Eastern Interior Provinces.

Espíritu Santo, dated July 31, 1792, that says the Apaches are getting too much ammunition (two muskets apiece), and are getting their arms and ammunition through the Attakapa Indians, via the posts of Attakapas[7] and Opelousas,[8] and he thinks a couple of raids against them when they barter with the Attakapas would make them ask for peace. He points out that vermilion, glass beads, and looking glasses are not items with which the Indians can make war, but he does not suggest that all trade in powder be prohibited. He points out that there are trade goods in Nacogdoches for the Indians but suggests that gifts be distributed in the Indians' villages, even though the Indians will receive much less. He gives quite an argument on this point, saying that it is a great advantage to the Indians to have their goods delivered—but one suspects that he is more concerned with keeping the Indians away from San Antonio.

From these letters, it seems obvious that Revillagigedo is suggesting that Louisiana officials go into Texas to trade—a noteworthy reversal in policy—but it is equally obvious that he does not comment on the letter from Castro.

Spain also feared the Indians in the Floridas, and a letter from Carondelet to Las Casas shows particularly the Spanish fear of American influence among those Indians. This letter was written in March, 1793, not long after O'Fallon had renewed his filibustering attempts by persuading George Rogers Clark to write Genêt, and in it Carondelet refers to the death of McGillivray, chief of the Creek nation,[9] who had

[7] The post of the Attakapas was in about south-central Louisiana, on the Vermillion River and the Bayou Teche, according to Jedidiah Morse, and near the sea, about fifty-five miles west and a little south of Baton Rouge; twenty-five miles north and a little west was Opelousas; and north of that was Avoyelles. These three posts, then, formed something of a cordon about fifty miles west of the Mississippi River.

[8] Opelousas, as indicated *supra,* was a post about fifty-five miles due west of Baton Rouge and some forty-five miles south of Avoyelles.

[9] Alexander McGillivray, the son of a Scot trader and a Creek-French woman, was well educated, lived as a wealthy planter, and became chief of the Wind Clan of the Upper Creeks and a strong friend of William Panton. During the Revolution he was a British agent among the Indians and later became a Spanish agent, inciting the Indians to raid the Americans. In 1790 he signed the Treaty of New York, but Panton and the Spaniards protested, and Spain paid him $3,500 to repudiate it. He died of pneumonia and a "gout of the stomach" on February 17, 1793. Nasatir and Lil-

been friendly to Spain, and the hostility of Payemingo,[10] who had succeeded McGillivray and who was friendly to the Americans. According to Carondelet:

> . . . It is necessary to take steps, or let the United States verify its intentions of separating Spain from the nations that are its allies and that surround this province. This would indispensably bring its [Spain's] devastation and loss, as well as that of the kingdom of Mexico.[11]

He recommends two rendezvous or "reunions" with the Indians, at which presents to the value of 14,000 pesos will be required. He says the death of McGillivray

> . . . could not have been more untimely, and will possibly be the cause of the separation of the Creek nation from the alliance with Spain, resulting in a war between it and the Chickasaw nation. The Americans will take advantage of such turmoil to realize their plans for settlements at Los Ecores de Margot, and on the Yazoo, because, as it is impossible for the Chickasaws to resist the Creeks, they will be forced to call upon the Americans of the settlement of Cumberland for assistance, as Payemingo the chief of same has already stated, and these [the Americans] will not lose such an opportune occasion to settle on the Mississippi.

Carondelet's outline of the situation calls attention to the fact that there was constant maneuvering on both sides—and, in fact, on the part of the French and British also—to swing the southeastern Indians, principally the Cherokees, Creeks, Chickasaws, and Choctaws, away from the Spaniards.

One important aspect of the Indian question in the Southeast was

jegren, "Materials Relating to the History of the Mississippi Valley," *Louisiana Historical Quarterly*, Vol. XXI, No. 1 (January, 1938), 16.

[10] Payemingo, or Piomingo, was a great chief of the Chickasaws and could read and write. He was friendly to the Americans and for years kept the Chickasaws at peace with the whites. Spain, on the other hand, paid a pension of five hundred dollars to one Ugulayacabé, the Wolf's Friend (the Americans called him Ugly Cub), who led a faction opposed to Piomingo. In 1794 Piomingo was murdered by a Chickamauga. Houck, *Spanish Régime*, II, 27.

[11] Carondelet to Las Casas, No. 69, Confidential, New Orleans, March 9, 1793, Papeles de Cuba, leg. 2353.

the fact that men such as McGillivray, Bowles,[11a] and McIntosh,[11b] were white or part white, and they knew enough about white ways to demand and get somewhat more than did most of the full-blood Indians. Carondelet's letter continued:

> To counteract the designs of Seagrove, the American commissary,[12] who has already sent a commissioner to the Upper Creeks to find out if he will be well received in case he goes there to see them regarding a treaty of commerce between that nation and the United States, which would ruin that of the House of Panton,[13] it has been necessary to

[11a] William Augustus Bowles, who called himself "General and Director of the Creek and Cherokee Nations," was born in Baltimore; was in the British army during the Revolution, but was dismissed for insubordination. Working for a British firm, Miller, Bonnamy & Company, he sought for years to defeat Panton, Leslie & Company, and was a great nuisance to the Spaniards. He tried to win Alexander McGillivray away from Panton, and argued to protect the Creeks from oppression by Spain, aggression by the United States, and exploitation by Panton. The Spaniards captured him and held him seven years. He was jailed in the Philippine Islands but made himself unbearable; they deported him, and he escaped to London, where he appeared as a very learned man. In 1799 he was back in the southeastern United States, pretending to succeed McGillivray. He captured Panton's store at St. Marks, Florida, and captured the Spanish fort from Thomas Portell (formerly at New Madrid) in an action that Portell never was able to explain to anybody's satisfaction. After five weeks, the Spaniards retook the fort, and Bowles turned to freebooting; the Spaniards put $4,500 on his head. In May, 1803, he was captured from among the Seminoles, and, in the prime of life, died a prisoner at Morro Castle at Havana. See Whitaker, *The Mississippi Question,* 162–75.

[11b] William McIntosh, son of a British officer and a Creek mother, was well educated and became a principal chief of the Creeks. In 1825 he agreed to sell the Creek lands to the United States, saying: "The white man wants our lands. He will buy them now. By and by he will take them, and our people will be left to wander without homes, poor and despised, and be beaten like dogs. We will go to a new home and learn to till the earth, grow cattle, and depend on these for food." He was opposed, however, by the Creek Hopothlayohola, and that chief conspired with fifty warriors to assassinate him. McIntosh heard them, opened the door, and was murdered, pierced by twenty rifle-balls.

[12] James Seagrove, aggressive U.S. agent among the Creek Indians.

[13] William Panton, a Scotsman, operated a chain of stores and had agents in southeast Indian country, with headquarters in Pensacola, Florida. He had great influence with the Creeks, and the Spaniards generally backed him to counteract American traders. He had agents in Havana, Nassau, New Orleans, and Chickasaw Bluffs (among other places), and when he died in 1801 he had exerted perhaps more influence than any other one man on the relations of the Spaniards and the Indians in that area. Nasatir and Liljegren, "Materials Relating to the History of the Mississippi Valley," *Louisiana Historical Quarterly,* Vol. XXI, No. 1 (January, 1938), 11.

immediately convoke the principal chiefs of the Upper and Lower Creeks to Pensacola, and Panton has taken this matter in hand himself, as there is no time to lose, because Seagrove is ready to pass to the Upper Creeks.

From the letter which the same Panton writes me, a translation of which I am enclosing, No. 2, your Excellency will be informed of the means he proposes in order that Spain may be assured of the influence she had when McGillivray lived, by separating it from a commerce that would ruin that of Panton, and [of the means he proposes that] would make those Indians devoted to Spain instead of being dependent upon the United States.[14]

While Carondelet was trying to deal with practical matters, other minds in the higher Spanish echelons had other sentiments about Louisiana. Revillagigedo, the viceroy of Mexico, expressed himself in a letter written to Alange:

Since the day in which by voluntary cession by the king of France, the province of Louisiana was incorporated in the dominions of our august sovereign, it has occasioned great care and expenses. . . .

They [the people of Louisiana] tenaciously resisted his gentle domination, and it was necessary to make it secure by torture, banishment, and other more or less severe punishments, of which they retain lively and very fresh memories. . . . their claims for aid, and [their] fomentations, always costly to the royal treasury, have been incessant. I therefore judge, in order to put it briefly, that Louisiana in the present system is a colony to be suspected because of the class of its inhabitants, because of its constitution, and because of its immediate proximity to the United States of America.[15]

Obviously the viceroy felt that Louisiana was a bad bargain at any price. The rest of his letter is largely a discussion of the responsibility of the viceroy as compared to that of the commandant-general of the Interior Provinces, and one might gather that he is not pleased over the independence of the Interior Provinces from the viceroy's authority.

But Carondelet kept at his own problems, and the following De-

[14] Carondelet to Las Casas, No. 69, Confidential, New Orleans, March 9, 1793, Papeles de Cuba, leg. 2353.

[15] Revillagigedo to Alange, No. 859, Confidential, Mexico, April 30, 1793, Simancas, Archivo General, Guerra Moderna, leg. 6921; photostat in Library of Congress.

cember he wrote a letter to Las Casas in which he summed up the Mississippi Valley situation in a not uncharacteristic manner:

> . . . preparations . . . are being made on the Ohio by a Colonel Clark, Doctor O'Fallon, a certain Paw (or DePaux), and various French officers, to attack this province at the first opportunity. The author of the said report is the same Mitchell mentioned in the dispatch from the envoys of his Majesty to the United States, sent to your Excellency under date of October 8 of this year.
>
> I have many reasons to distrust his intentions and to closely scrutinize his conduct, because of what I explain in the accompanying dispatch, No. 2, as I have already sent to the ministry of Spain in Philadelphia the account that agrees with the news I recently received from the commandant of New Madrid concerning the arrival of the French officials at Louisville, and of having won Colonel Clark and two other important Americans in favor of the convention.
>
> I do not have the forces to resist such an enterprise, at least for the settlements of Illinois and New Madrid, which are at a distance of 500 leagues from this capital. They will be able to assemble for their defense only about 90 soldiers and 200 militiamen upon whom they can depend. Even if the three galleys that I intend to send up to the place where the Ohio River empties into the Mississippi River, should be successful in intercepting the enemy there, nothing will prevent them from going by land to Kaskaskias, an American town across from Saint Louis of Illinois, where, crossing the river without any difficulty, they could take possession of that settlement, afterwards coming down by land to New Madrid, which is at a distance of more than 40 leagues from Saint Louis. It will attack that fort by land, as the possession of same will make them owners of the west bank of the river as far up [down] as Arkansas [Post], a distance of 250 leagues, which will consequently force the galleys to retreat to Nogales, which is 340 leagues below New Madrid and 130 leagues from Arkansas.
>
> Although the fort of Nogales is at a distance of 120 leagues from this capital and 40 from Natchez, and although it may take a month to sail up the river from this town to the said fort, it must still be the first and principal point of our defenses. Its situation upon the banks of this river being entirely advantageous, it provides many reliable means of retarding the enemy, in attention of which I have sent the governor of Natchez orders to transfer immediately to that fort, and to add to it all the means of defense that he possibly can during these winter months,

due to Nogales' being hardly able to make any resistance from there to Natchez. Therefore, the whole province up to this capital is liable to fall into the hands of the enemy without [our] being able to check them.

If the plan proposed by the enemies is effective, the whole upper part of Louisiana can be considered completely lost by the beginning of this coming May, and the consequences will extend as far as Santa Fe, where the enemies propose to penetrate, realizing that there are only twenty-two days' march from Saint Louis of Illinois up to that interior province. These reflections had, a little over a year ago, caused me to solicit that New Madrid be fortified in a respectable manner, adding one fourth of a battalion to the provinces as garrison in that post, from which there could be stationed garrisons at Saint Louis of Illinois, Saint Geneviève, etc., but, this plan not having been adopted by the court, there is nothing left for me to do but try in every possible way to prevent the loss of the greater part of Louisiana.

I intend to write to the English commandant of the post of Michelmakina [Michilimackinac], which is about 300 leagues distant from Saint Louis of Illinois, requesting him to help that settlement, the inhabitants of which have at all times, had friendly relations with them, as during the last war with England they never disturbed the good harmony existing between them; however, I have not much faith in this step.

I hope your Excellency will deign to forward everything through the Minister of War to his royal authority, informing me in the meantime of what you judge to be best.[16]

Carondelet must have known it was a desperation step to appeal to the English commandant at Michilimackinac, and it would seem his pride would have restrained him, for he was well aware that the chances of help from that direction were remote.

The report mentioned by Carondelet had been made by Thomas Mitchell, who had just traveled from New York to New Orleans via the Ohio River, and now we discover that Carondelet did not trust

[16] Carondelet to Las Casas, No. 99, confidenial, New Orleans, December 30, 1793, Papeles de Cuba, leg. 1447; draft in leg. 152B. See Nasatir, "The Anglo-Spanish Frontier in the Illinois Country During the American Revolution, 1779–1783," *Journal* of the Illinois State Historical Society, Vol. XXI, No. 3 (October, 1928), 181 ff., 178–80. Miss Coughlin has dealt with this problem at length; for description of this letter in the Consejo, see Nasatir and Liljegren, "Minutas," 26–31.

Mitchell. "I have many reasons to suspect his intentions," he said, "and to scrutinize very carefully his conduct . . . but his report agrees with the news that I received previously from the commander of New Madrid about the arrival of the three French officials at Louisville, and Colonel Clark and two other important Americans were in favor of the Convention."[17] Carondelet thinks they will take New Madrid and force the Spaniards to withdraw to Nogales, as he has already indicated; he picks Nogales as the Spanish base of defense, and has ordered Gayoso to go there; if the enemy takes Nogales, Carondelet says, they will turn toward New Orleans. Carondelet repeats a number of things he has said already and adds a document signed "M. M.,"[18] which gives a more detailed report on the American and French plans:

> The expedition planned against this province must be commanded or directed by George Clark, major general appointed by the French republic, which has conceded him the power to name officials for 5,000 men. The engineers and artillerymen must be natives of France. The infantry will be composed of all classes of people who want to take part in this cause. Doctor O. Fallon, an incendiary writer, has been the schemer of this undertaking. Mr. de Paw is named contractor and leader with a commission of captain, and every day new office-hunters present themselves.
>
> Three French officers had already arrived in Louisville, openly using the uniforms, and in the public papers they had asked for workers or mechanics, some of whom had already enlisted. Hardtack was being prepared in Fort Pitt,[19] and, in short, everything appeared to be ready for a determined invasion. O'Fallon told me in confidence that it would be unquestionable to offer recompenses and gratifications to the Americans to induce them to take part in this undertaking, adding that the pillage on the Spanish vassals who resist would be divided among the soldiers. The slaves and estates which they plan to seize, they believe will make the fortune of those adventurers,[20] and that the opening of

[17] Carondelet to Las Casas, December 30, 1793, Papeles de Cuba, leg. 152B.

[18] Thomas Mitchell was also known as Medad Mitchell. He was employed by Jáudenes and Viar to carry messages to Carondelet, but Carondelet, as he indicates, did not trust him. See Nasatir and Liljegren, "Materials Relating to the History of the Mississippi Valley," *Louisiana Historical Quarterly*, Vol. XXI, No. 1 (January, 1938), 32.

[19] Modern Pittsburgh, head of navigation on the Ohio.

[20] This is not filibustering but piracy. See Houck, *Spanish Régime*, II, 26, for Clark's generous offer of pay, bounty lands, and booty.

this river will increase by 50 per cent the worth of the Kentuckians. The inflammatory writings of O'Fallon have much weight with the people of Kentucky; to which should be added his extensive correspondence in the United States, and some friends in Congress. Such is then the prospectus of the enemies of the peace and tranquillity of these provinces. Nevertheless, they have some obstacles to overcome before fulfilling their wishes— (1) the bills of exchange of the chargé d'affaires of France have been protested, which should prolong considerably its warlike preparation; (2) the directors of this exploit, Clark and O'Fallon, have quarreled and (3) it can be expected that Congress will interpose its authority to avoid war with Spain. Independent of all this, it is not to the interests of the United States that this province should belong to France, because in that case there is no doubt that Kentucky would withdraw from the Union.

The artillery of this faction will be scarce and without much extra [ammunition?], since [although?] it is for this that they count upon the conquest of Ylinueses.

The defenseless situation of New Madrid is well known to de Pauw, who supposes that forces cannot arrive there in time to oppose him, and on that ground they consider it equally conquered.

. . . Through the reliable reports I have, the French in Ylinueses cannot be counted upon, but the Americans and vassals of Spain, if they have a prospect of a good success in case of a vigorous resistance, will act as good subjects.

M. M.[21]

Carondelet's judgment of men must have failed him here—for where could one find as accurate and reliable an appraisal of the entire situation?

There is another copy of Carondelet's letter of December 30 (without the Mitchell report) in legajo 1447, but the text is the same except for small details. However, with it there is a letter No. 2, dated December 28, written by Carondelet, addressed to Jáudenes and José de Viar, the Spanish agents in Philadelphia, which offers additional information:

. . . we do not know anything about what has become of the French

[21] Carondelet to Jáudenes and Viar, New Orleans, December 28, 1793, Papeles de Cuba, leg. 1447; enclosure No. 2 in Carondelet to Las Casas, No. 99, Confidential, December 30, 1793. Jáudenes and Viar, it will be remembered, were assistants of Gardoqui in Philadelphia. They were also agents of the Spanish government.

expedition, for which reason, and considering that the season does not allow a squadron to be kept along this coast, I have ordered withdrawn part of the forces that defended the mouth of the river, there remaining to us only the regret that the enemy did not present himself, considering that we were in very good order to receive him.

Through the copy of the report which Mr. M. has given me as a result of his voyage, you will be informed of the attempts of our enemies and of their preparations on the Ohio. I believe that, O'Fallon being the author of this project, and the same subject already outlawed by the Congress at the insistence of our court, for having planned to raise a body of troops against these domains of his Majesty for two years, I would agree that you should insist that the decree of Congress against him should be carried out to due effect and that he should leave the mentioned states.

You are also authorized to solicit the arrest and punishment of Colonel George Clark, an official and a close subject of the United States, who should neither be able to receive nor should have received a dispatch from another power without the consent of Congress, against an ally.

It is evident that if you win these two points, that project will be taken care of by itself.

The person who gave me these notices [Mitchell] received from you 500 pesos upon his departure on his voyage. He is an ambitious, intelligent, active youth, but capable of taking sides indifferently with us or with the enemy, [self-]interest being his first motive. I have many reasons to distrust his integrity, [he] having been found a year ago drawing the plan of New Madrid, and sent to this capital by the same as a prisoner. Nevertheless, having recognized in him much talent, and not having sufficient proof to verify his intentions, I treated him pleasantly, permitting him to return to the United States. Now he asks that he be employed in his Majesty's service, and, not having that power, I am in quite a bit of embarrassment, for it is not suitable to allow him to return before our suspicions have been satisfied, so I will try to put him off with hopes, and in the meantime I will give him whatever is necessary for his subsistence. I hope this will meet with your approval.

. . . If you find it suitable to make an offer to the President of the Congress that hostilities against the Cherokee nation should be suspended and that its boundaries should be dealt with in Madrid, I bind myself on my part to attract the same nation to laying down its arms from the first of next April, which will be observed with the greatest rigor by the Indians; I offer the same in regard to the Creek nation. I have decided to receive pleasantly the delegate from Congress, Mr. Seagrove . . .[22]

Now we have some characterization of Mitchell—and perhaps some of Carondelet. Two days later, the governor wrote his familiar song to Alcudia (Godoy):

The enemy extends its hopes much further than the conquest of Louisiana, and hopes to reach Santa Fe within a short time, knowing that not more than twenty-two days of march is needed from St. Louis to that city of the Interior Provinces [Santa Fe]. I do not doubt that it [the enemy] will be assisted by the inhabitants of Upper Louisiana and the Indians of that area, who have great affection for the French.[23]

Many Spanish officials in the New World were justifiably apprehensive, even though the fact was that the United States had no ambition toward Santa Fe, and was so beset with internal weaknesses and dissensions that it would have been unable to undertake such a venture; and the fact is that the Indians between St. Louis and Santa Fe would not have permitted it. However, the apprehension of the Spanish officials was not shared by the Consejo; the first indication of its line of thought was in the session of May 2, 1794, when the secretary read a summary of a letter from Las Casas dated February 24, 1794, and of several enclosures within it. An opinion apparently was given by somebody else —perhaps Godoy or the Minister of War:

Carondelet's concept of such a short distance [twenty-two days' marching time] from Illinois to Santa Fe in the Interior Provinces of New Spain, has its origin in the journey made from Santa Fe to Illinois by arrangement of the viceroy, the Count of Revillagigedo, and the consent of the governor of that province, Don Fernando de la Concha, by Pedro Vial and two other companions who left Santa Fe on May 21, 1792, as far as the town or settlement of the Kances Indians, where they embarked on the Missouri River which empties into the Mississippi,

[22] Also Carondelet to Jáudenes and Viar, New Orleans, December 28, 1793, Papeles de Cuba, leg,. 1447, enclosure No. 2 in Carondelet's letter cited in note 15.

[23] Carondelet to Alcudia, No. 23, confidential, New Orleans, January 1, 1794; A.H.N., Estado, leg. 3893, printed in A.H.N. *Annual Report for 1896*, I, 1027.

they walked 190 leagues, for which distance (according to the same Carondelet) are needed at least 40 days of march.

From the habitation of the Cances to San Luis of Illinois, said travelers dallied always down-river and carried by the current, exactly the same 22 days that Carondelet says are sufficient for going from Illinois to Santa Fe, and it is to be presumed that on this information is founded the enormous error that said governor has suffered, since 60 days will perhaps not be enough for merely ascending the river from Illinois to the Cances, without taking into account the throng of obstacles that are presented spontaneously in navigating against the current the large number of pirogues which are needed for the transport of two or three thousand men, their provisions and munitions.[24]

Others besides Carondelet, however, expressed alarm. Louis de Vilemont sent a letter with his colonization plan in 1795, in which he predicted grave consequences:

The conquest of Louisiana would cause inevitably the loss of Mexico. . . . The states of Kentucky and Cumberland to the north are able to arm at any moment thirty to thirty-five thousand combatants who within ten days could go down to Louisiana, and in less than forty can direct themselves by way of Arkansas to New Mexico. At the same time, in the south, Georgia and North Carolina could arm another corps of 25,000 men, who, crossing by way of Atacapas and Opelousas, could meet at an agreed place, forming one body of troops with the intention of marching with more safety against this same Mexico.[25]

Vilemont, of course, was trying to prove that the only defense was population of the colony. The plan is endorsed as follows (obviously by Godoy):

[24] Simancas, Archivo General, Guerra Moderna, leg. 7235. In contrast to the Consejo's rather flimsy reasoning, the Consejo did consider the testimony of Mitchell and of one Ezekiel Dwet, a Dutch farmer, undercover man for Gayoso, whose observations were in agreement with those of Mitchell. Mitchell is revealed in this report as an engineer and surveyor. It may be worth noting that the exact reasoning of this letter, and some of the wording, was used in the Consejo's decision, given in Nasatir and Liljegren, "Materials Relating to the History of the Mississippi Valley," *Louisiana Historical Quarterly*, Vol. XXI, No. 1 (January, 1938), 36–37.

[25] This series of documents on Vilemont is from A.H.N., Estado, leg. 3890, expediente no. 34. The plan is a lengthy one and rather eloquent; a good deal of it is printed in the minutes of the Consejo: Nasatir and Liljegren, *ibid.*, 57–63.

November 6, 1795—This subject wishes to credit himself as applied, and it seems that he has not lost time in traveling, but his project is one of absolute impossibility. Take notice of the progress of the United States, and see on what bases it is founded: vice, murder, theft, and, in short, all the many weaknesses of character that make a man suspicious. These are the testimonies with which those inhabitants are credited. A Catholic king cannot be indulgent in the observation of the law of God. There is no country that would not declare itself an enemy immediately after understanding its project which would then complain of immigration, but I do not want the author to be offended if I dislike his plan. Thus you place this together with the map before the Council of State so that the king, our monarch, fully instructed of everything, may decide whatever may be to his sovereign liking.[26]

That opinion was dated November 12, and the Consejo, meeting on November 13, made the decision:

In view of all this and of the mistake of Vilemont in believing Louisiana to be the key to the whole empire of Mexico, and more important than the island of Cuba [!], his Majesty was in conformity with the *dictamen* [formal opinion] of said Señor Príncipe de la Paz, which was followed by the eulogies of the entire Consejo, disregarding the project in the midst of the zeal of the author.[27]

Perhaps the Consejo was not aware of Pedro de Nava's letter to Godoy of the previous August 6. De Nava, commandant-general of the Interior Provinces,[28] raised Vilemont's 35,000 men to 50,000 "vigorous men, experienced on the plains, hills and forests. The guerrilla parties would have no difficulty in advancing toward our possessions."

On November 14, the Count of Montarco made an official report to Godoy, further identifying him as the author of the endorsement; and on the same day Vilemont was notified (probably by Godoy) that his plan had been rejected.[29]

[26] *Ibid.* Although it is unsigned, it seems to have been endorsed by Godoy, for Carondelet sent the transmittal letter to Godoy on July 30, and the endorsement was made on November 6. The opinion utters a loud protest.

[27] Nasatir and Liljegren, *ibid.*, 63. Señor Godoy had his way in the midst of more bad guesses than seems possible. It is nice that the Consejo extended eulogies to Vilemont—or were they for Señor Godoy, who had exposed all those incredible fallacies of Vilemont?

[28] De Nava to Alcudia, Chihuahua, August 6, 1795, A.G.I., Estado, leg. 37.

[29] There are a few more documents concerning Vilemont's later career, from

There was, however, considerable disagreement with the Consejo's judgment that Louisiana was not the gateway to Mexico, and one of the important declarations was made by Gayoso on November 24—eleven days after the Consejo had made its decision but before Gayoso could have known about it:

> It will be most important to encourage emigration of a good quality of people to Illinois because I consider it the most direct route to the kingdom of Mexico, and if this interesting objective is not taken cognizance of, it will not be many years before the English traders will introduce themselves there—and armed forces will follow them.
>
> It would be suitable to form a cordon of small posts from the Missouri to San Carlos, Carondelet, and continuing until they unite us with those of the Interior Provinces.
>
> In this way we shall cause greater respect from the Indians, we shall retain their trade, and we shall protect the kingdom of Mexico with effectiveness.[30]

And in the same year (1795), Auguste Chouteau had said of Fort Carondelet among the Osages, "In the future, according to my slight knowledge [it] will become perhaps one of the most safe ramparts of New Mexico."[31]

In February of the following year (1796), a council of war (*junta de generales*) took under consideration Carondelet's plea for adequate funds to police the area of Louisiana, and that council also put its collective head in the sand and came up with some strange reasoning. (Actually, it seems that the council made its decision on November 28, shortly after Vilemont's plan was rejected by the Consejo, but Las Casas in Havana did not write to Carondelet until February 12.) The decision was typical; "The Minister of War by royal order," says Las Casas, "under date of November 28 tells me the following":

---

which it appears that, indeed, the eulogies were for Godoy—not for Vilemont. For later ones, see Nasatir, *Before Lewis and Clark;* and Lyons, *Louisiana in French Diplomacy.*

[30] Gayoso to Carondelet, New Madrid, November 24, 1795, Papeles de Cuba, leg. 2364.

[31] Chouteau to Monseigneur, St. Louis, April 17, 1795, Papeles de Cuba, leg. 212B. See also Gayoso to Prince of Peace, No. 8, Confidential, New Orleans, Nov. 30, 1797, A.H.N., Estado, leg. 3900; and Gayoso to Santa Clara, No. 6, Confidential, Papeles de Cuba, leg. 1502B.

[They have considered Carondelet's statement, and believe that there are three avenues of attack: by sea, by land, and by the river. If by sea, they seem to think that a fleet will somehow materialize to protect the colony; if by land, it will be made by the Anglo-Americans, and] if it should be the American colonists who undertake it, aided by the Indians, they would find extremely difficult the kind of territory they would have to travel, and the different rivers that intervene, which obstacles would forcibly delay passage of a large corps of troops with a corresponding train of artillery, munitions, provisions, and other necessaries, for which reason it cannot only be considered risky for the invaders but impractical. To the same difficulties is subject the attack which they might plan by the Mississippi River, by its extensive course, rapidity of its currents, infinite number of turns, and many other difficulties which would present themselves by the descent through it of the light coast-guard fleet, troops, and considerable accouterments which they would necessarily take for the subsistence of the army and attack of the fortified posts, whose duration it would not be easy for them to pre-determine, the besieged persons having the opportunity of receiving aid, as has been stated. That to this be added that a short time ago the United States obtained their independence, that its constitution and government, however happy and well united it be considered, it is not possible that it be so consolidated that it would be capable of undertaking arduous expeditions, expensive and distant from its establishments; that they occupy a great extension of territory toward the coast, with the opportunity of increasing it by entering the interior of the continent; that the territory in their possession is very fertile, and that by good cultivation they will be able to import its fruits easily by the forts which they already have, creating thus a rich and constant (permanent) commerce, and preferable to the gold and silver of New Spain.

That the same United States have suffered repeated bloody attacks by the bordering Indians because they are brave and belligerent, and, it being probable that the latter will continue hostilities, they will keep them occupied forcibly, so that they will impede them from contemplation of conquests of greater importance and recognized uncertainty, which thoughts seem powerful enough so that we need not fear that they will try to seize Louisiana for many years, and much less the kingdom of New Spain.

That, nevertheless, the board recognize as well established any fear for the future, and with consummate prudence to guard from this hour against all events, with a plan of defense which will leave protected the province of Louisiana and other possessions of the Gulf of Mexico.

That in order to effect it with economy to the royal treasury and following the constant maxim of reducing in America all fortifications to only those essential posts which defend provinces, shelter important posts, or from whose occupation there results the advantage of keeping those on the borders in obedience, [and the council (*junta*) goes ahead to suggest a need for more information on the forts and their state of effectiveness; they want information also on distances, rivers, and Indians; the council is opposed to forts close to American territory, for such forts and troops would be lost immediately if attacked;[32] the council discusses some forts of Florida and the ordnance there; and the board wants complete information on troops already in Louisiana. The council also has enjoyed the benevolent condescension of his Majesty in approval of this decision.][33]

This is quite an astonishing document to be drawn up by a group of men who did not know the area or its people—but perhaps it can be explained by the thought that they did not want to be bothered under any circumstances. And, as usual, only a few days later there was evidence to indicate the wishful thinking of the council in Spain; this is recorded in a letter from Luis de Blanc, commandant at Natchitoches, on February 22:

Blanch says that M. la Mothe, returning from a trip among the Indians, heard from the Yamparica Comanches, whose usual camping ground was between the Red River and the Arkansas (and not, as a rule, east of the Texas Panhandle), found an American party in a blockhouse, and De Blanc supposed that the Americans had passed from the west bank of the Mississippi into Spanish Illinois, and had crossed the Missouri between the village of the Osages and others, which, Blanc says, would be very possible since the road from Santa Fe to the Illinois had been shown by Pedro Vial. De Blanc said La Mothe had offered to run them out, and De Blanc recommended it, but nothing in the way of a decision is at hand.[34]

[32] The council does not sound much like a military body.

[33] Las Casas to Carondelet, Havana, February 12, 1796, Papeles de Cuba, leg. 153A.

[34] DeBlanc to Carondelet, Natchitoches, February 22, 1796, Papeles de Cuba, leg. 2364; printed in Nasatir, *Before Lewis and Clark*, I, 365, and also in Houck, *Spanish Régime*, II, 192, where *Ambaricas* is mistakenly translated *Rikaras*.

Carondelet did not abandon his campaign. On May 1 he sent to Godoy a letter from Wilkinson that pointed out the unrest in Kentucky, the danger of opening the Mississippi to free travel, the weakness of Spanish defenses, the possibility of revolt in Louisiana in favor of the English, and the advice that New Orleans should be made a free port.[35]

And in June, one month later, when Gayoso wrote to Carondelet to discuss the consequences of the Pinckney Treaty, he foresaw troubles for Mexico as well as Louisiana:

> The discord that now reigns in the American states could bring about the separation of many of them, which would particularly alter the political status of that country, and subsequently the causes upon which our court based its decision to complete the treaty. [He considers the proper course in regard to the Pinckney Treaty in case the British should not relinquish Detroit and other posts to the United States, and he mentions the Indians.]
>
> The principal objective of the Anglo-Americans being the nagivation of the Mississippi in the manner that has been conceded, and, in order to keep it, they will surely cede their rights to these lands so as to avoid contentions with the Indians in such a remote place. . . .
>
> Besides this, there is added that perhaps the Atlantic states would be glad to find a well-founded cause to stop the increase that is so rapidly taking place in the western country, for if the case should arise where there is no hindrance for the delivery of this country, your Excellency can assure his Majesty that it would not be five years before a sufficient number of people would unite here, giving them the right to form an independent state, in which case the preponderance of the western states would be such that they would absorb all the power of the Union because of the advantages which the navigation of this river would offer them, . . .
>
> The purpose of the Anglo-Americans is well known, and, being guided accordingly, there is no doubt that once the first step across the river has been facilitated, they would penetrate as far as Mexico. And the least evil, although great, would be the illicit commerce that they would attempt; and settlements and towns of the Anglo-Americans, which would be very difficult to destroy, would continue to be seen in that vast and rich country.
>
> However, the foregoing is not the greatest danger that I foresee in

[35] Carondelet to Alcudia, No. 34, confidential, New Orleans, May 1, 1796, A.H.N., Estado, leg. 3899.

the cession of this country. The most noxious to this province is that the result might be a fiery civil war on this same territory, inasmuch as I have well-founded reasons to believe that these inhabitants, seeing that necessity separates them from his Majesty's dominion, which they prefer to any other, will oppose the force that would place them under the jurisdiction of the state of Georgia. It has come to my attention that after the delivery has taken place, they plan to force the retreat of the commissaries who might come there in the event they do not assure them of the ownership of their land, which most assuredly will not be done by the state of Georgia because of the system it follows at present, . . .

Although I am advising your Excellency generally, I have not concealed from you all that of which I have informed you, as I have thought it advantageous to dwell upon all these matters in order to add, wherever necessary, the knowledge that I have in regard to the individuals who pray to God for some favorable event to keep them under the dominion of his Majesty.

Due to this paper's not being long enough, I am refraining from stating any of my reflections, as also because I am sure that your Excellency does not need them in order to express to his Majesty that which is most suitable to his royal service at the present time.[36]

Also on June 7, Carondelet wrote to Branciforte,[37] the viceroy of Mexico, giving his opinion of the Anglo-Americans and taking note of De Blanc's news about the blockhouse, another alleged American post on the Bay of Saint Bernard, and the irrepressibility of the American frontiersmen:

I have had bad news that seems to merit complete confidence that the English companies of Canada that trade with the savage nations situated to the north of the Missouri River are beginning to form establishments on that [river], whose dominion belongs incontestably to his Majesty, and that lately, crossing this same river at some 300 leagues from its mouth on the Mississippi, they penetrated with 12 horses loaded with merchandise to the river that these colonists call

[36] Gayoso to Carondelet, No. 2, Natchez, June 7, 1796, Papales de Cuba, leg. 2354.

[37] Miguel de la Grúa Talamanca y Branciforte, Marquis of Branciforte, was a distinct contrast to Revillagigedo, whom he succeeded. A creature of Godoy and Queen María Louisa, he was vain, proud, selfish, and unpopular, and was accused of dishonesty. He was followed by Azanza. See Priestley, *Mexican Nation,* 189.

the Plete [Platte] River or Chato River to trade with the Panis, Abenaquis, and other nations, I was later informed by another party from the post of Natchitoches, that not far from the Santa Fee Mountains and the vicinity of the savage Yamparicas, who live between the sources of the Colorado and Arkansas Rivers, the English or Americans have formed a fortified establishment with a fortress. Lastly, various travelers of these provinces assure me that in the Bay of Saint Louis or San Bernardo on the Gulf of Mexico there exists another American establishment of considerable consequence that, if allowed to grow, will cause the Interior Provinces and our court a great deal of anxiety.

I have prognosticated with much feeling the prompt invasion of the Interior Provinces that will immediately follow the concession to the United States of the posts that we had on the eastern bank of the Mississippi; this must be carried out immediately in conformity with the treaty of friendship, boundaries, and navigation that the United States ratified in the month of March, it not being in my power any longer to restrain the eruption of the people from the western American states, who are approaching and are going to establish themselves on the eastern bank of the Mississippi on an expanse of 400 leagues, opposite which we have nothing but deserts. This is from the Ohio River to degree 31, or 60 leagues from this capital; it follows that your Excellency will see himself obliged to take beforehand the most active measures to oppose the introduction of those restless people, who are a sort of determined bandit, armed with carbines, who frequently cross the Mississippi in numbers with the intention of reconnoitering, hunting, and, if they like the country, establishing themselves in the Interior Provinces, whose Indians they will arm both to make the Spaniards uneasy and to further their fur trade; five or six thousand of those ferocious men who know no law nor any subjections, are those who are starting the American establishments and are attracting in their footsteps the prodigious emigration both from the Atlantic states and from Europe, which menaces the Interior Provinces that the Americans believe are very abundant in mines. A bit of corn, gunpowder, and balls suffices them; a house formed from the trunks of trees serves them as shelter; their corn crop finished, they raise camp and go further inland, always fleeing from any subordination and law.[38]

In short, those provinces being exposed to the hostile incursions

[38] The total effect of Carondelet's estimate of the Americans is somewhat different from that created by Godoy's scornful evaluation.

of the Americans by the side of the Mississippi and to those of the English from the Missouri side, I consider that they will need for their conservation all the zeal, the activity, and the talent that your Excellency has always manifested, and to the success of which you will be able to contribute, if you consider that I can for my part contribute to the peace of the same provinces and of the kingdom that his Majesty has confided to your vigilance.[39]

Such pleas as this, however, could be little more than alerts, and since Branciforte definitely was Godoy's man, such an epistle was wasted paper. Carondelet's letter writing was never dependent on the reasonable prospects of results, it seems.

Seriously, however, Carondelet's apprehensions were soundly based. As a matter of fact, the Blount conspiracy had been under way for some time—and there are indications that it, like many others, might have succeeded but for a careless act on the part of its prime mover, William Blount.[40] Documentation is by no means complete on the Blount affair, but, from what is available, it seems to have been connected with the turmoil at Natchez in 1797 and with the notorious Yazoo land speculations (such speculation being the only form of big business on the frontier, and certainly the favorite pastime).

Blount seems to have used his various governmental positions to improve his speculations in western lands, but in 1796 he seems to have been convinced that a filibuster was the key to a real coup. Perhaps his ideas were not quite as grandiose as those of Aaron Burr,

[39] Carondelet to Branciforte, New Orleans, June 7, 1796; A.G.I., Estado Mexico, leg. 6; printed in Nasatir, *Before Lewis and Clark*, II, 439–40; also in Papeles de Cuba, leg. 2364, with the notation: "He reflects on the dangerous situation, etc."

[40] Blount, of a respectable North Carolina family and member of that state's constitutional convention, was appointed in 1790 governor of the Southwest Territory, but by 1795 he was an enemy of the administration. He had always been a land speculator, and he and other Yazoo speculators (some years after Dr. O'Fallon) received a large grant at Muscle Shoals—but the Spaniards blocked his settlement there. He was one of the first two United States senators from Tennessee, and during his term in office he became involved in the conspiracy which now bears his name. He was expelled from the Senate, and impeachment proceedings were initiated, but the frontiersmen of Tennessee made it so difficult for the Senate to command his presence that those proceedings were dropped. Casa Yrujo was credited with uncovering this plot. Blount was later elected to the Tennessee legislature. See Whitaker, *The Mississippi Question*, 104–15; see the *Mississippi Valley Historical Review*, XXXIV (1934), 439–40, for bibliography.

of whom apparently he was a friend, but they were big enough. And in 1796 it seemed that France was about to recover Louisiana and the Floridas; therefore, quick action was called for. Spain was not respected as a military power, and she further weakened herself by going to war with England in October. On top of everything else, the bottom fell out of western lands and Blount was in bad shape financially, so he tried to play international politics to win a king-size gamble.

It appears that Blount enlisted the aid of the British, which complicated things for Timothy Pickering, the Secretary of State, who was an Anglophile and also a sworn enemy of Blount.

Documents now available seem to indicate that three expeditions were to attack Spanish possessions simultaneously: one column was to take New Madrid, another (headed by Blount) to take New Orleans, and a third to take Pensacola. The British were to blockade Pensacola and the Mississippi; the filibusters were to receive one-half of the public funds and private property, and 1,000 acres of land for each private soldier. The four Spanish posts on the east side of the Mississippi (Natchez, Walnut Hills, Confederation, and Chickasaw Bluffs) were not to be bothered.

The plan was nearing the working stage when Congress was convened in a special session, and Blount, a Senator, had to go to Philadelphia. He therefore wrote instructions to one of his chief subordinates—who immediately got drunk and talked. The letter fell into other hands and was sent to the President, who communicated to the Senate on July 3, 1797. Blount was immediately expelled from the Senate, and lost no time returning to Tennessee. In that country, so far from Washington, apparently the principal regret was that he had been caught.

Also in 1797 there was another alarm that for a while seemed real. News came from that area of New Spain that Carondelet and many others had long said was the object of every nation that threatened Louisiana—the Interior Provinces. A letter was written by De Nava, the commandant-general of the Interior Provinces, and was a copy of a letter De Nava had received from Ensign Joseph Guardiana, lieutenant-governor of the pueblo of Nacogdoches, which reported rumors of the United States's having declared war on Spain.[41]

[41] Annex No. 1 to Guardiana to De Nava, No. 18, Nacogdoches, by July 17, 1797, A.G.I., Estado Mexico, leg. 34.

Guardiana also enclosed a copy of a proclamation by Carondelet:

PROCLAMATION

The government, having been informed by his Majesty's minister plenipotentiary to the United States of America, that an expedition formed in the lakes is to attack the Illinois this winter, has believed it best for the security and tranquillity of Lower Louisiana to suspend the evacuation already begun of the posts of Natchez and Nogales [which actually had already been conceded to the United States], which, being the only ones that may defend it [Lower Louisiana], would place the English in a position to disquiet it and destroy it, once masters of Upper Louisiana, with even greater facility than by an article of the treaty [Jay's Treaty] previously concluded with Great Britain [in which] The United States concedes to the English the power to navigate freely and to frequent the posts belonging to the said states situated on the rivers in general, lakes, etc., a manifest contradiction to the treaty concluded with Spain [the Pinckney Treaty], which they appear to annul, since by the latter the United States agree that no other nation will be able to navigate on the Mississippi without the consent of Spain.

Notwithstanding the legitimacy of these motives of suspension [of the Pinckney Treaty], it [Carondelet's objections to U. S. actions] has been represented to the Congress of the United States with all possible truth, and intimated by my orders to the commissioner of limits and also to the commandant of the detachment of American troops now in Natchez. I have just learned that a detachment of the United States quartered on the Ohio is en route via the Hobstein [Holston] River toward Natchez, at the same time as the militia of Cumberland[42] have been alerted to be ready to march at the first warning.

. . . All this indicates to us that we must be alert and ready to defend our lands with that valor and energy which the inhabitants of these provinces have shown on all occasions, with that advantage and superiority supplied by the knowledge of the locale, and with that confidence that good law and justice inspire. . . .[43]

In September, De Nava wrote to Godoy, advising him that he was

[42] An area along the Cumberland River, west of the Cumberland Mountains, said F. A. Michaux in 1802. See F. A. Michaux, *Travels to the West of the Allegheny Mountains*, 165. F. A. Michaux was the son of André, who had been associated with Genêt.

[43] Also in A.G.I., Estado Mexico, leg. 34.

going at once to Texas,[44] and also that he was sending copies of the documents to the viceroy and to the king. And Yrujo, in Philadelphia, at about the same time also wrote to Godoy to add his estimate of the aggressive Americans and of the present defenselessness of Louisiana:

> [This letter] treats, although very generally, of the interests of Spain in relation to this country; it treats *of the conservation of many and very precious possessions of the king, our master, in this part of the world, which I see threatened within a few years.*
>
> . . . The nature of the products of this country so necessary in our colonies and the fruits of the latter so necessary in this present country necessitates reciprocal means of satisfying them. This can be the basis of a close connection between Spain and the United States. For this it is necessary to adopt a method entirely different from the present one concerning the manner of providing for our colonies. . . .
>
> Those interested in disorder and monopoly will try to oppose the reform of the abuses from which they obtain so many benefits; . . .
>
> This territory . . . has prospered extraordinarily in spite of the oppression in which England held its natives. . . . All the powers must carefully examine this progress, but our vigilance must be redoubled because of our most precious possessions in America being co-terminous with those of this colossus, which is growing and invigorating itself on this side of the Atlantic. The true *política* is that of foreseeing events, and truly no one is more interested than ourselves in trying to read in the book of the future. . . .
>
> From this land speculation [in America] has originated to a great degree the expedition[s] projected against the Floridas and Louisiana. . . . This restless greed for land makes the attention of all the private individuals and even the government turn toward our possessions on both sides of the Mississippi; and the prospect that by that road they can some day reach the rich mines which produce the metal that dazzles them, fixes all their attention on that part. . . .
>
> Within thirty-six years it [the number of inhabitants] will be twenty millions, of which at least ten million will be on the banks of the Ohio, the Mississippi, and other rivers contiguous to our possessions—possessions which they already regard with greed and anticipatory desires of snatching them from us.
>
> . . . All our defense consists of miserable forts scattered at a distance

[44] De Nava to the Prince of Peace, No. 18, Chihuahua, September 5, 1797, A.G.I., Estado Mexico, leg. 37.

of 100 or more leagues one from the other, in which it is usual to have regularly a picket of 20 or 30 men. . . . This perspective not only threatens us with the loss of the Floridas and Louisiana, but then the spirit of enterprise and the effects of greed may carry these wandering colonists to the very entrails of New Mexico. I have heard it said that via the Arkansas and San Francisco[45] rivers they can approach very near, and that from their upper reaches to the royal mines at Santa Fe, the land is level, covered with natural pasturage, and consequently very easy to traverse with artillery.

. . . It is absolutely necessary that we make of New Orleans a second Gibraltar [because New Orleans is the key to the entire region. He insists that] equally respectable works be built in St. Louis [which controls the mouth of the Missouri]. . . .

[The people of] Kentucky and Tennessee hate the federal government and detest England supported by it, and with these favorable dispositions it would not be difficult for us to contribute in the future to their total separation. What is certain, most excellent señor, is that we must throttle Hercules in the cradle.

. . . I do not doubt that your prudence and sagacity will indicate to the king, our master, the most opportune steps for saving in time one of the best jewels of the crown.[46]

Godoy[47] had been subjected to considerable persuasive power, but

[45] The San Francisco River runs north and south in eastern Arkansas and into the Mississippi at about Helena.

[46] Yrujo to the Prince of Peace, No. 73, Philadelphia, August 5, 1797, A.H.N., leg. 3891, expediente 23. In the crisis of 1797, there were many other letters; see Carondelet to Gayoso, April 24, 1797, and letters in Houck, *Spanish Régime*, II, 225–31 (at the bottom of 231 is Carondelet's prediction that the British may become even the masters of California).

[47] Manuel de Godoy, Duke of Alcudia, the Prince of Peace, was born of a noble family of Estremadura in 1767. He became one of the great triumvirate of Spanish ministers of the last third of the eighteenth century, according to Campillo: Aranda, who was Secretary of State and ambassador to France; Floridablanca, *fiscal* to the Consejo; and Godoy. Godoy became a minister in 1792, and replaced Aranda as first minister the following year. He became involved in intrigues with the French, and enjoyed great personal unpopularity—partly because of the fact that he used the queen openly as his mistress. Godoy is said to have had good intentions, but it is not always clear that his intentions were good for the nation or the people, or even for himself; he changed opinions at will. He was succeeded as minister by Saavedra in 1798, but did not relinquish his hold on Spanish affairs. He returned to office, and his disastrous policies until 1807 were largely responsible for the rapid decadence of the Spanish Empire. He was notoriously vain, grasping, and pretentious; intelligent and

he refused to be stampeded: "Informed of everything, I thank your Excellency for the zeal that you manifest, but I must tell you that, it not being possible to place competent defenses in such distant places, reciprocity and skill will assure [secure] them."[48]

Three months later, however, Gayoso, having succeeded Carondelet and now speaking as the governor-general of Louisiana, wrote a letter to Santa Clara,[49] the captain-general at Havana, to protest a reduction of troops at Fort Carondelet, and tried to show that such a reduction was not in good faith with the contract made by the Spaniards with Auguste Chouteau, and that such a reduction would actually cost more than it was costing the crown under the Chouteau contract.[50]

All in all, 1797 was a year of crisis between Spain and the United States—in fact, a more serious crisis than was known to anybody except Carondelet and the commandants at Nogales. Those two understood the threat, for Carondelet ordered the commandant to resist American occupation with force.

Under the terms of the Treaty of San Lorenzo in 1795, Spain was to evacuate four military posts east of the Mississippi: at Natchez (Fort Panmure), at Nogales (just south of the mouth of the Yazoo River), at Confederation (on the Tombigbee River), and at San Fernando (at Chickasaw Bluffs)—all forts north of the thirty-first parallel. The evacuation was ordered in 1796, but the order was later suspended by Godoy following the outbreak of war between Spain and England and the consequent fear of invasion from Canada. Another important factor

pertinacious, and had courage of a sort. Later he became pudgy and self-important, and died in 1851. Nasatir and Liljegren, "Materials Relating to the History of the Missississippi Valley," *Louisiana Historical Quarterly*, Vol. XXI, No. 1 (January, 1938), 21; Campillo, *Relaciones Diplomáticas, lxxxii–cv;* Whitaker, "The Retrocession of Louisiana in Spanish Policy," *American Historical Review*, Vol. XXXIX, No. 3 (April, 1934), 456–57.

[48] Unsigned letter to Yrujo, San Lorenzo, November 19, 1797, enclosed with Yrujo to Godoy, No. 73, *loc. cit.*

[49] The Conde de Santa Clara was born Juan Procopio Bassecourt in Barcelona, April 22, 1740; he became a lieutenant general of the Spanish royal army and succeeded Las Casas as captain-general, December 6, 1796; he relinquished the captain-generalcy in 1799, and died April 12, 1820.

[50] Gayoso to Santa Clara, No. 6, New Orleans, November 30, 1797, Papeles de Cuba, leg. 153B. Gayoso had one great fault: he did not always accept the decisions from Spain. Furthermore, he insisted on compounding the situation with logic and common sense.

was the extensiveness of the Choctaw incursions west of the Mississippi, and the fact that Nogales and Confederation were the principal controls over the Choctaws.

In November, 1796, Collot reported to Carondelet the possibility of a British attack on Upper Louisiana, and a conspiracy among the Tennesseeans. At that critical time, Carondelet received orders to defend Upper Louisiana against attacks from Canada, and he sent Howard to destroy English commerce on the Missouri and Mississippi, to send a force to the St. Peter's in Minnesota, to capture the British fort at St. Joseph, and to take the British fort among the Mandans.

At the same time, it was necessary to restrain the Choctaws from terrorizing the tribes west of the Mississippi, and it was to solve that perennial problem that Carondelet had approved the colonization projects of the Marquis de Maison Rouge and the Baron de Bastrop. At about the same time, Avoyelles was chosen as a center of defense for western Louisiana, and plans were made to lay out a road from Avoyelles to Ouachita Post.

In early 1797 Carondelet was notified that American troops were ready to take over the four Spanish posts—but Carondelet delayed his answer. In March, under Howard's orders, Fort San Fernando was evacuated, and the troops moved across river to Campo de la Esperanza; Fort Confederation was evacuated, and the troops moved down the Tombigbee to Fort St. Stephen. That left Nogales and Natchez.

Andrew Ellicott had reached Natchez in late February; Gayoso had not received the orders to resist, and cannon were being removed from Fort Panmure. But on March 22 Ellicott saw the cannon taken back to the fort; the order to resist had been received; Gayoso, of course, assured Ellicott that the treaty would be honored. Then Gayoso tried to prevent Lieutenant Pope and a small detachment of American troops from coming to Natchez, but Pope joined Ellicott anyway.

It was not a pleasant situation for Gayoso, for he knew that there were former British loyalists in Natchez, and he was aware also that American immigrants by that time were predominant in the area. Ellicott and Pope were demanding possession of the two forts, while both Carondelet and Gayoso were determined to hold them, and Carondelet sent an engineer to fortify Nogales. In May, 1797, six hundred muskets were sent to Upper Louisiana, and Carondelet arranged to buy one thousand more from William Panton; a military camp was laid out at Baton Rouge. In that month, Carondelet learned of the Blount conspiracy, and he also discovered (from Collot's papers) that May was the month in which the invasion from Canada and Tennessee was likely to come. Therefore, in that month he sent a company of grenadiers under Lieutenant Colonel José Corail to Nogales; then he discovered that Wilkinson was about to send troops to Natchez and Nogales.

On May 26 Carondelet sent Thomas Power to urge Wilkinson not to send troops, and to revive the idea of separating the West from the Union.

Nogales was the only fort between St. Louis and New Orleans able to resist an attack from the north, and on May 28, 1797, Carondelet wrote "very confidential orders" to Corail, in which he instructed Corail that if the Americans arrived in such numbers that Corail could not defend the post for one month, he was to parley, and especially to demand that the Choctaws and the British be restrained. However, if Corail should find himself able to defend Nogales for a month, he was to decline to evacuate, and to hold his troops "ready to open fire," knowing that the governor would march to his relief at the head of 1,200 men, then under orders to assemble in Baton Rouge.[51] Howard had already been ordered to descend the river with 250 men in the galleys, and Carondelet was preparing three gunboats to go upriver. It does not appear that Carondelet was fooling.

Unrest in Natchez forced Gayoso to retire to Fort Panmure. The inhabitants, encouraged by Ellicott, formed a Committee of Public Safety, and Gayoso was forced to let Natchez District remain neutral in the controversy. Shortly thereafter, Gayoso was appointed governor of Louisiana, and Stephen Minor was chosen acting governor of Natchez.

The "neutrality" at Natchez ended the crisis there, but the situation at Nogales was critical; the orders were unchanged: to fight if there was any hope of holding out. But, by a quirk of circumstance, perhaps, the outbreak was avoided, because the American troops were ordered to go to Natchez. The commandant at Nogales fired a salute as they went by on the river—and the situation was so tense that the

[51] Carondelet to José Corail, very confidential, New Orleans, May 28, 1797.

salute started a rumor that a battle had been fought, that the Americans had been taken prisoners.

Presently Howard reported that there appeared to be no danger of an invasion of Upper Louisiana, and in January Governor Gayoso received an order to evacuate Natchez and Nogales; the order had been written in September.

The year 1800 was approaching, and still neither England nor the United States had attacked Louisiana, but there were more alarms. On December 29, 1798, a letter was written from the royal palace to Juan Manuel Álvarez, Secretary of War, saying that the United States had sent one thousand men to the frontier, and two days later Álvarez (presumably) wrote to the Spanish minister in the United States, saying that they had no means to send one or two more regiments, and ordering the minister to give warning "with haste" of what "might be occurring to our governors and chiefs of that frontier." Madrid was sticking to its guns.[52]

During those hectic years, there had been activity on the lower levels also. In 1797 Spaniards arrested English traders in Iowa; in 1798 the war vessel *La Flecha* was sent up the Mississippi; in 1880 and 1802 St. Vrain de Lassus took *La Flecha* up the Mississippi River; in 1799–1800 they had agents in Canada and a spy in Detroit.

And Yrujo must have had time to receive that letter from Álvarez when he wrote to Saavedra, Secretary of State,[53] reaffirming the danger from the aggressive Americans and offering a plan to counteract them —a plan in which Yrujo would play a big part:

> The official letters that are in the enclosed parcel, I do not doubt, will convince our government of the necessity of adopting, and *without loss of time*, a plan capable of counter-arresting the ambitious intentions of the Americans [who are] not only trying to form a barrier of population on the right bank of the Mississippi against the one [that is, the population] that is so rapidly extending into the western possessions of the United States, but in order to leave likewise the state of absolute dependence in which the American government intends to hold all the

[52] [From the Palace] to Álvarez, December 29, 1798. A.H.N., Estado, leg. 3897. From an unsigned letter to Yrujo, Madrid, December 31, 1798, A.H.N., Estado, leg. 3897.

[53] Francisco de Saavedra, who opposed Godoy, had succeeded him as the king's minister in 1798 but did not remain long, being followed by Pedro Cevallos.

European islands in this part of the world in respect to articles of primary necessity. Unfortunately, this dependence is at present very real and true, and if measures are not immediately adopted in order to supply us from our own possessions with certain articles, the threat that they are doing us now by Mr. Otis' bill, a copy of which I am sending, they will be able to do so some day with very bad consequences to our islands.

The Americans, in general, are persuaded that they can eject us from Louisiana any time they wish, and they likewise believe that they will starve out the Spanish colonists, and they will cut the wings that agriculture is happily taking on in the island of Cuba, suspending for some time our commerce with them. From this results their insolence and their tone of superiority toward Spain, and I can not nor must I conceal that while efficacious [means] on our part are not taken to destroy these ideas (unfortunately too well founded at present), the influence of our powerful monarchy in the United States will be as small as that of the Republic of Lisca. . . .

Among the measures that must contribute most essentially to the end that has been proposed by his Majesty, is that of facilitating to these new vessels of the *right bank* of the *Mississippi* the exportation of their products, *and the combination of circumstances is so fortunate that the principal articles of their harvests are of prime necessity to the Spanish islands*, and that in order to obtain them, they depend now to a certain extent upon the caprice or will of the American government.[54]

. . . The Baron de Bastrop, a Hollander, has obtained from the king, our master, a concession of 150,000 acres of land on the banks of the Ouachita upon the condition of introducing and establishing some 100 families within a certain number of years. Mr. de Maison Rouge[55] has also obtained a very large extent of territory for the

[54] While other officials have pointed out the danger of allowing the navigation of the Mississippi, Yrujo points out the practical necessity of it.

[55] Carondelet was a firm believer in colonization. In 1795 the Marquis of Maison Rouge entered into an extensive contract to establish a colony and was granted 30,000 acres and many concessions. Bastrop in 1796 was granted 144 square leagues on the Ouachita in present Morehouse Parish, around the town of Bastrop, and Jacques Céran de Lassus de St. Vrain was granted 10,000 square *arpens.* Bastrop actually brought in one hundred persons and seems to have been active in the colony, but he ran afoul of Morales, and Gayoso suspended the contract in 1797. Maison Rouge and St. Vrain were not suited to life in the wilderness, and apparently they made no serious attempts to fulfill their contracts. An *arpent* was .84 acre in Spain; a square league was 4,633 acres; Bastrop's grant is often said to be twelve square leagues,

establishments of this nature which, at the same time that they contribute to consolidation of the wise intentions of the government and the welfare of the monarchy in general, offer likewise the perspective of considerable advantages for the empresarios; it has seemed to me, as a good vassal of the king, our master, that I can make no better use of my wife's dowry than dedication of it to an object that contributes so immediately to his royal service; and to this effect I am taking the liberty of asking his Majesty by means of a minister who, like your Excellency, knows the utility of my request.

First—Please concede to me between the Arkansas and White Rivers in the district where lands may not have been granted and can best suit me, 40,000 acres of land under condition that within the term of three years, counting from my notice of the concession, I shall establish on the said land forty families.[56]

Second—[He will erect a mill, and his flour will be admitted as Spanish flour and thus subject to lighter duty, to Cuba, Porto Rico, and Caracas and dependencies.]

Third—[To obviate his bringing in Anglo flour and selling it as his own, he sets up a system of certification.]

Fourth— [He requests a system of orders to avoid] the arbitrariness with which in many cases some intendants behave, aided by distance and slowness in investigations [which cause] a ruinous stagnation.

Fifth— [He will use Spanish vessels.]

To further his suit, Yrujo reminded Saavedra that he had discovered the Blount conspiracy and had aborted it. Saavedra approved his request, and it went through several hands and finally was approved by Miguel Cayetano Soler, Secretary of the Treasury, but on July 17, 1799, a marginal note says: "The king does not accede to this solicitation." Thus ended an attempt to obtain land by one of the most vigorous supporters of Spain. Strange are the ways of royalty—or perhaps it is merely that royal personages themselves are only human beings and subject to whim and caprice in the ordinary manner.

One year later, the Baron de Bastrop proposed to reinforce the Spanish military position in the Ouachita area in return for a trading

but the royal surveyor called it 144. See R. Woods Moore, "The Role of the Baron de Bastrop in the Anglo-American Settlement of the Spanish Southwest," *Louisiana Historical Quarterly*, Vol. XXXI, No. 3 (July, 1948).

[56] About one hundred miles north of the Bastrop grant.

grant for ten years, and the governor of Louisiana, Casa Calvo, granted the trading privilege and sent the papers on to Someruelos,[57] the captain-general at Havana, in June, 1801, for final approval. Someruelos considered Bastrop's proposition a good one, and approved the agreement on March 20.[58]

The date is now very close to the time of the cession. This chapter has dealt with fairly large movements or attempts at movement, and has omitted the adventures of individuals such as Solomon Colly (with Philip Nolan, who will be treated later) and James Pursley, whose activities actually preceded 1803 but were more in the nature of private ventures than they were symptoms of significant movements. Likewise, most of the movements of Anglo-Americans followed the Lewis and Clark Expedition.

It rather seems that there were a number of strong plans made to invade Louisiana from Kentucky, and that the French were implicated in many ways. They connived many times, but never came through. The officials of Louisiana, and Yrujo in Philadelphia, appear to have had a grasp of the situation and to have been fairly capable, on the whole, but their advice was not heeded in the high councils of Spain. It would seem that wisdom would have suggested some display of force to back up the diplomatic maneuverings by Spain. However, it all worked out for the best, inasmuch as Louisiana was about to be lost to Spain anyway.

Even the retrocession and sale of Louisiana, however, would not relieve Spanish officials of their fear of the Anglo-Americans, for as soon as Americans were in charge of St. Louis they began to plan trading trips to Santa Fe. Most of the early travelers to New Mexico's adobe-hutted metropolis were men with French names but with American citizenship by virtue of United States acquisition of Louisiana. Some were backed by men with French names (D'Eglise) or men with Spanish names (Lisa), or men from Kaskaskia (across the river from

[57] Salvador Muro y Salazar, Marqués de Someruelos, was born in Madrid in 1754. He served in campaigns against France and earned the rank of mariscal de campo and was captain-general of Cuba and the Floridas, 1799–1813. Louisiana was delivered to the United States under his command. He was a successful governor and was well liked. He died in Madrid in 1813.

[58] With the letter from Casa Calvo.

St. Louis) or elsewhere, but all were Americans, and all of them, to the Spaniards, were American aggressors.

Bourgmont in 1724; the Mallet brothers in 1739; Pierre Mallet in 1751; Chapuis and Feuilli in 1752; Pedro Vial in 1792 and 1793—all those had shown that Santa Fe could be reached from the Missouri River, and as soon as Americans owned Louisiana, the restless merchants of St. Louis and vicinity began to send goods toward Santa Fe with the hope of bringing the pack mules back to St. Louis laden with silver specie and gold bullion.

# VII

# *The Anglo-American Threat from the Missouri River, 1804–1807*

There must have been considerable activity along the Osage, the Kansas, the Republican, and the Platte rivers through all the years, for, as we have seen, many were the reports of Frenchmen and traders among the Indians. The Frenchmen usually are nameless, but seldom were they reported without evidence in the form of clothing, rifles, brass pots, and flags. There was not, however, much documentable activity except for that of Pedro Vial. He had been in Illinois in the early 1770's and had gone to Bexar by an unknown route, and eventually to Santa Fe; then he had made the monumental round trip, Santa Fe to St. Louis to Santa Fe, in 1792–93.

The only other man who undeniably made the trip from Illinois to Santa Fe is another Frenchman who went into Spanish service, and one who would be associated with Vial after 1800: Juan Chalvert. This man, in spite of his Hispanicized French name, probably was not a Frenchman at all, for he had been born in Philadelphia and was a Presbyterian; he had come down the Ohio River, and he may have visited St. Louis; he did go to Natchez and New Orleans, and later via Natchitoches to the Taovaya villages on the Red River (where there were Pani Piqués as well as Taovayas). De Nava, the commandant-general at Chihuahua, then took charge of Chalvert's life, as he says in a letter to Godoy dated November 3, 1795:

> I have had Juan Calbert[1] brought [from Texas] to the province of Coahuila and disposed that he be permitted to work at his trade to acquire his sustenance, but preventing him from fleeing and again

[1] His name was spelled several different ways: Chalvert, Calbert, Jarvet, Tarbet, and so on.

penetrating to the Indians, as he might attempt to do, since this class of wandering men love greatly the opportunity which facilitates their living among the barbarians in order to give free reign to their passions.[2]

De Nava's letter reveals that Chalvert had left Pittsburgh in 1794, and we know that he reached Santa Fe by 1803, whatever the route. His story of his troubles as told to De Nava was later supported by Lieutenant Melgares, who reported that on his expedition down the Red River in 1806 he found a ten-year-old son of Chalvert among the Panis.[3]

Actually there was not as much movement of the Anglos toward Santa Fe before the Lewis and Clark expedition as might be expected. The Americans were infiltrating Texas and the Arkansas River area and the Osage country, but the first serious movement toward New Mexico was made by William Morrison of Kaskaskia, Illinois, who in 1804 sent Lalande and Metoyer with goods for trading, in what was to create an episode and give Zebulon Pike a sounding board against Lalande. Metoyer would not stay in the Santa Fe area; Lalande would settle there and be a great success with the ladies. Chalvert would be hired by the governor as an interpreter (or had been already); Laurenzo Durocher would be in and out of Santa Fe and Chihuahua many times; and Santiago (Jacques) d'Eglise would go there to become a resident, accumulate a substantial estate, and be heinously murdered.

In July, 1804, not long after Lewis and Clark had left St. Louis, two traders, Baptiste Lalande and Jeannot Metoyer, went to meet one José Gervais[4] among the Panis and all three were equipped and supplied by William Morrison of Kaskaskia.[5] Gervais, "who knows the road well," was to guide them to New Mexico; in 1803 Gervais had

[2] De Nava to Alcudia, Chihuahua, November 3, 1795, A.G.I., Estado, Audiencia de Santo Domingo, leg. 37. Obviously the motivations for that type of life seemed simple—and slightly base—to De Nava.

[3] Probably at the Taovaya villages.

[4] Nuttall, "The American Threat to New Mexico, 1804–1822," 54, thinks that Joseph Gervais is Juan Chalvert, pointing out that a José Gervais lived in Kaskaskia, but now it seems likely, in face of Chalvert's Philadelphia birth—and since we lack, at this point, evidence that Juan Chalbert conducted the Panis to Santa Fe either in 1803 or in 1804—that they were two different men.

[5] Casa Calvo to Godoy, New Orleans, September 30, 1804, Papeles de Cuba, leg. 2368; printed in Nasatir, *Before Lewis and Clark*, II, 755–56.

taken the Panis to Santa Fe to make peace with the governor there; he had repeated the voyage in the spring of 1804, and Lalande and Metoyer were to meet him on his return from Santa Fe to the Pani home ground.[6] As usual, details are lacking, but certainly by May 22, 1804, they were in Santa Fe—but instead of Metoyer we find Laurenzo Durocher, whose appearance is mysterious, though he seems to have come from St. Louis.

Laurenzo Durocher had gone up the Missouri River, probably in 1804, with Jacques d'Eglise to find the shortest route to New Mexico; D'Eglise had been up the Missouri before that, and on this trip was still (or again) in the employ of the Missouri Fur Company. He did not return to St. Louis that year, and was presumed to have gone to New Mexico.[7] Whether Durocher and D'Eglise went to New Mexico together is not known, but in November, 1806, Jacques d'Eglise was murdered in New Mexico, and he may have been there all the time.[8]

On May 22, 1805, Durocher was petitioning for money to go to Chihuahua to get permission and money to return to his own country.[9] On September 9 Salcedo, the commandant-general, reported that Durocher and Lalande had arrived in Chihuahua as he had ordered (in a secret order of June?), and he was sending them back to Alencaster for a decision; he suggested Alencaster keep them there under observation.[10] A few days later, Salcedo advised the governor that he was

[6] Probably not the same Panis as those Chalvert had lived with on the Red River; they were several sub-tribes—and Metoyer ascended the Missouri into what later became known as Pawnee Country (in southern Nebraska and northwestern Kansas). Metoyer does not appear again; perhaps he was one of the countless victims of the frontier.

[7] Nasatir, "Jacques D'Eglise on the Upper Missouri, 1791–1795," *Mississippi Valley Historical Review*, Vol. XIV, No. 1 (June, 1927), 47–71.

[8] Lansing B. Bloom, "The Death of Jacques D'Eglise," *New Mexico Historical Review*, Vol. II, No. 4 (October, 1927), 369–79.

[9] Alencaster to Salcedo, Santa Fe, May 12, 1805, New Mexican Archives, doc. 1834; printed in Bloom, *ibid.*, 374–75. The memorial of Durocher is doc. 1834 also. From the time lapse, it is obvious that Durocher and his associate or associates had wintered with the Panis and had reached Santa Fe before Metoyer and Lalande. The usual course for the Spanish officials was to confiscate a prisoner's goods and property and apply the proceeds to the care of the prisoner: therefore Durocher and Lalande, who both had presumably arrived in Santa Fe with goods, would have got official permission to use the proceeds from the sale of the goods.

[10] Salcedo to Alencaster, Chihuahua, September 9, 1805, New Mexican Archives, doc. 1888; Bloom, *ibid.*, 375.

sending a sergeant with gifts for the Indians, and that he had furnished fifty pesos to Durocher and Lalande.[11]

A month later, they apparently had returned to Santa Fe, had been given a decision by Alencaster, and were preparing to return to the United States, along with "the other two Frenchmen also," and each, Alencaster says, with the idea of returning (to New Mexico).[12] But in November they must have changed their minds, for Alencaster reported that they had presented themselves (to him) and that "they solicit to continue as subjects of Spain in this province."[13]

By January, however, Alencaster was suspicious of the first two men, apparently for good reason, for he wrote the following report to Salcedo:

> Notwithstanding the good reports which I have given you regarding the good conduct of the Frenchmen Durocher and Lalanda, it seems to me proper to inform you of what has been reported to me by the Carbineer Juan Lucero,[14] Don Pedro Vial,[15] and Josef Jarbet [Chalvert] to have occurred on the journey to the Pawnees which they undertook in October.[16]

It seems that the Frenchmen had argued that New Mexico could not make as good gifts as could the Americans, and that the Indians would prefer to deal with the Americans for that reason; that the pay of ten pesos a month (which obviously Lalande and Durocher were getting as interpreters, following their petition to remain in Spanish service) was very small, that the Americans were paying twenty-five pesos a month and sometimes one peso a day; and Alencaster now asks Salcedo whether these two men should be permitted to return to

[11] Salcedo to Alencaster, Chihuahua, September 12, 1805, New Mexican Archives, doc. 1889; Bloom, *ibid.*, 376.

[12] The other two Frenchmen must have been Dionicio le Croix and Andrés Terién, who had reached Santa Fe on or shortly before October 2.

[13] Alencaster to Salcedo, No. 118, Santa Fe, November 20, 1805, New Mexican Archives, doc. 1925.

[14] Lucero was associated with Vial for a long time.

[15] Note that of the three men, only Vial's name is preceded by the honorary title *Don*—and it is used this way four times in one letter.

[16] Alencaster to Salcedo, January 4, 1806, New Mexican Archives, doc. 1942; printed in Bloom, "The Death of Jacques D'Eglise," *New Mexico Historical Review*, Vol. II, No. 4 (October, 1927), 376–77.

their own country, and also whether the "two Frenchmen and one American" should be permitted to return.[17]

Durocher's next move was to go to Chihuahua to ask for horses, presumably to return home; at any rate, Alencaster gave him a passport addressed to Joseph Manrrique, commandant at San Elecearío, twenty miles southeast of El Paso.[18] And on August 31 there was other business afoot, for Isidro Rey, lieutenant-governor at El Paso, wrote to Alencaster:

> I received your letter of August 16 and I am informed by it that Dimas Prosul [possibly James Purcell] must work at his trade of carpenter in this village and must not go to any other place but to Chihuahua, assuming that the commandant-general does not order otherwise. The said Anglo-American showed me his passport, and so did Lorenzo Duroret [or Durorel—Durocher], who [alone] will go to Chihuahua at the first opportunity, going via the presidio of Tiburcios with your passport and my endorsement to the commandant of said presidio.[19]

We shall hear more of Lalande when Pike reaches Santa Fe in the early part of 1807. In the meantime, there arises a question as to how the "two Frenchmen and one American" had reached Santa Fe. The two Frenchmen were Juan Bautista la Croix and Andrés Terién, who had gone up the Missouri in June, 1804, with Régis Loisel. The American was James Purcell (or Pursley), who was from Baird's Town, Kentucky.[20] In 1802, with two companions, he had gone from St. Louis west on the Osage River, had crossed to the White River, got into a fight with Kansas Indians; they had lost their horses to other Indians, had lost their pelts in the Osage River. Then Purcell had left his companions and gone upriver with Régis Loisel. La Croix and Terién were with Loisel, and apparently they had gone as far as the Mandans.

[17] *Ibid.*

[18] Alencaster to Manrrique, August 16, 1806, New Mexican Archives, doc. 2004. San Elizario was established in 1772 on the Mexican side of the Río Grande, twenty miles below El Paso. It has been said that the town or the presidio was moved before 1814, as much as thirty-five miles. Rex Strickland says the town was not moved but that the river changed and put the town on the Texas side.

[19] Isidro Rey to Alencaster, El Paso, August 31, 1806, New Mexican Archives, doc. 2009.

[20] For notes on Purcell, or Pursley, see Pike, *Exploratory Travels*, 314ff.; also in Coues, *Expeditions*, II, 756–58.

Then the three—Purcell, La Croix, and Terién—started out to trade with the Comanches and Kiowas, but tangled with the Sioux, reached the headwaters of the Platte, were captured twice by the Kiowas, but eventually made their way to Taos, from where they were accompanied to Santa Fe by Pedro Vial under orders, and two Indians.[21] Alencaster reported it to the commandant-general:

> The said Frenchmen do not carry a passport because they say that their master did not give them the one that he had when he sent them for the beaver trading, and they, though finding themselves well treated as captives, poor and without the means of returning directly to their country contiguous to this province, they did their best in telling the Cuampes about the good treatment of the Spaniards, . . . [The Cuampes, the Sayenas, and the Aas, says Alencaster, all ask for peace and trade, and Alencaster has obtained their permission to send Spaniards into their country:] the interpreter Vial, together with a resident of Taos to accompany them, and the Indian war chiefs who in similar cases have been in the habit of accompanying them in order to obtain for me certain interesting news concerning the condition and locations of said nations, their number, and other important things, . . .
>
> [The Indians asked him to give them clothes, which he did; and he also gave them tobacco and cartridges], which expense, that of the maintenance, and supply of provisions for their trip, which I believe I must charge to the Fund of the Allies if your Excellency does not order otherwise.
>
> The said Cuampes . . . carry a paper from the year '94 from the commandant of St. Louis, Luis Trudeau, which reduces itself to exhort peace to the allied nations, and one of the said chiefs carries a silver medal with the bust of Charles III and on the reverse side the inscription of excellent merit, a bas-relief, given by the said chief [Zenon Trudeau]. . . .
>
> The interpreter Vial and the said persons who accompany him will be here before the first, and if the news that the latter gives me requires a special express [courier], I shall send him [Vial] to give it to your Excellency. . . .

[21] Nuttall, ("The American Threat to New Mexico, 1804–1822") has a rather detailed account of the Anglo-American peregrinations of this period. Purcell obtained permission from Alencaster to trade with the Indians, but Purcell seems to have stayed in Santa Fe as a carpenter and practically as a prisoner; Chittenden, (*American Fur Trade*, II, 508) says he stayed in Santa Fe nineteen years, returning to the United States in 1824.

> The poor Frenchmen, for purposes of reconnaissance, have gone with the Cuampes to return to the place of departure with Vial. I have slightly helped the latter and the American who have been introduced to me, ill-clothed, with food and a little clothing, deciding to bear this small expense in honor of the good name of the nation until they are able to support themselves by their work, but if your Excellency believes it just that the public treasury bear this expense, you will inform me of it, which will spare a determined governor from giving alms which he will not be able to fail to repeat [which he cannot fail to have to repeat] on similar occasions.[22]

Salcedo answered the governor on July 19, approving everything Alencaster had done in the matter; it appears that in a later letter Alencaster had reported that the two Cuampe[23] chiefs had contracted measles, and that Vial had left them in Taos. Salcedo forewarned Alencaster that "the expense of clothing, food, tobacco, and powder which they [the three tribes] caused should be charged to the Account of Peace and War of this province."[24]

In October Alencaster wrote to advise Salcedo that the American had been incapacitated for two months, but now (in October) "his intention is to work until he has paid in full what he has spent for tools and the expense from September 1 for his support and subsistence, and to have some money together in order to take his resolution and the direction that suits him, . . . the expenditures that he has caused are 18 pesos and [?] *reales* for a costume of jacket, waistcoat, long trousers, hat, shoes, and two shirts, and maintenance and assistance in illness are 9 pesos." He continues to discuss the expenses of the prisoners and the fund to which they should be charged, indicating that a total of seventy-five pesos was spent for the purpose.[25]

It rather seems that the seventy-five pesos and their proper allo-

[22] Alencaster to Salcedo, Santa Fe, July 1, 1805; A.G.M., Guerra y Marina, 1787–1805, exp. 15; copy in Library of Congress.

[23] Sometimes spoken of as Comanches, but Hodge says a division of the Faraon Apaches *(Handbook of American Indians)*; Bloom, ("The Death of Jacques D'Eglise," *New Mexico Historical Review*, Vol. II, No. 4 [October, 1927], 372n.) says they were between the Pecos and the Río Grande.

[24] Salcedo to governor, No. 2, Chihuahua, July 19, 1805, New Mexican Archives, doc. 1859, no. 2.

[25] Alencaster to Salcedo, No. 87, Santa Fe, October 2, 1805, A.G.M., Guerra y Marina, 1787–1807, exp. 15; copy in the Library of Congress.

cation were more important than any other aspect of the affair, for in November Salcedo wrote to Alencaster, saying:

> As only in the case of their being treated as prisoners would there be a just foundation for the public treasury to bear the expenses which . . . your Excellency states have arisen, I do not agree to their being charged to the War and Peace Account of your province, and under this concept it is advisable that the said foreigners repay said expenses as fast as they acquire the means to do it. . . .

The next reference to the two Frenchmen and the one American seems to be in a letter of April 1, 1806, in which Alencaster acknowledges Salcedo's letter.[26]

Sometime prior to July 24, one Juan Bautista la Casa arrived in New Mexico under escort of El Ronco, the Kiowa chief. His origin and route are hazy, but he joined the others in trying to get out of Santa Fe. While Lalande had accepted his fate and settled down in the town (and would die there), his place in the ranks of the unrepatriated was taken by La Casa, and that fall (1806) Durocher and Purcell in one party were on the way to Chihuahua, and La Croix, Terién, and La Casa in another party were on their way to the same town. At that point, they seem to have disappeared.

On September 1 Alencaster advised Manrrique that "the Frenchmen who were from Louisiana, Juan Bautista la Casa, Dionicio, La Croix, and Andrés Terién," were going to Chihuahua after having been subsisted for thirty-two days at two reales each. Then on October 12 Alencaster gave another passport to Andrés Sulier and Henrique Visonot [Bissonet?], both of St. Louis.[27] Also, probably in that year, a man named Nicholas Coe and companion, Louis Baudouin, reached Santa Fe.

On October 8, 1806, Lt. Facundo Melgares, sent to reconnoiter the Red River and the Kansas area because of the Freeman party coming from Lower Louisiana and the reports of Lieutenant Pike's advance from St. Louis, took as prisoners two young "Frenchmen" (Coe and Baudouin) who lived among the Panis, and the governor sent them

[26] Alencaster to Salcedo, Santa Fe, April 1, 1806, New Mexican Archives, doc. 1979.

[27] The first passport is found in the New Mexican Archives, doc. 2010; the second, *loc. cit.*, doc. 2023.

on to the commandant-general.[28] In Melgares' letter, he says that Nicholas Cole showed him a passport and said that in Chihuahua he and his companions had received two reales daily (from which it appears that Coe, or Cole, and Baudouin had been in Chihuahua earlier[29]). Melgares also had taken the child of Chalvert from the Indians and was bringing him to Santa Fe.

The year 1806 pretty well ended the era of the stray Frenchmen—but not entirely, for in 1812 four unnamed French deserters to the Comanches were sent to Santa Fe,[30] their declarations were taken,[31] and they were sent on to Chihuahua and then to Arispe, Sonora, as prisoners—in which latter place they were as late as 1815.[32]

Whether those are the same four who were at Santa Fe in November, 1814, is unknown,[33] but as late as 1816 the New Mexican governor spoke of "nine Frenchmen" at Taos,[34] and it seems that in Spanish official language, the term "Frenchman" was reserved for a particular categorical use in official documents.

The Anglo-Americans, it is plain, wasted no time making tracks with the toes pointing toward Santa Fe—for although in 1803 and until the time of Pike, most of the travelers bore French names, they were United States citizens and were financed by Anglos: Morrison, Loisel, Lisa, Clamorgan, and the other fur traders who operated out of St. Louis and who were all United States citizens after 1803.

Others—perhaps many others—were aware of Santa Fe's allure, for on at least one occasion Anglo merchants tried to establish relations through diplomatic channels, when A. and R. Steel, of Shelbyville,

[28] Alencaster to Salcedo, Santa Fe, Oct. 8, 1806; New Mexican Archives, doc. 2022, no. 4.

[29] Coe, or Cole, probably was with Philip Nolan's ill-fated party in 1801, and, if so, had been prisoner for a long time; Lt. Pike would meet him in Santa Fe a few months later. He was a tailor from Connecticut.

[30] Garcia de la Mora to ad interim governor, Manrrique, Río Arriba, July 30, 1812; New Mexican Archives, doc. 2449.

[31] Manrrique to Second Lieutenant Elías Gonsales, Santa Fe, April 11, 1813, New Mexican Archives, doc. 2484.

[32] Bolton, "New Light on Manuel Lisa and the Southwestern Fur Trade," *Southwestern Historical Quarterly*, Vol. XVII, No. 1 (July, 1913), 61–66.

[33] Maynez to Bonavía, Santa Fe, November 20, 1814, New Mexican Archives, doc. 2565.

[34] Bonavía to Maynez, February 13, 1816, New Mexican Archives, doc. 2646.

Kentucky, requested their senator to speak to the Spanish minister in their behalf, as they wanted to extend their business to Santa Fe.[35] It was a novel approach, to say the least.

In 1803 the westward movement was about to receive its greatest impetus: the Lewis and Clark expedition, which would, in September, 1806, bring back the men who had been there and who would become our first mountain men; which would bring back information of the Missouri River and its source—the first such information available except for Pedro Vial's map of 1786 (which was unknown at that time); and which would inflame the highly inflammable Anglo imagination and inspire a new wave of popularity for that peculiarly American pastime of getting rich quickly and easily.

[35] A. and R. Steel to John Breckenridge, December 10, 1804; MS, Breckenridge Papers, Library of Congress.

# VIII

## *The Lewis and Clark Expedition*

The great news of the 1803–1806 period was of the Lewis and Clark expedition. The Spanish reaction to it was varied, as usual, and it is not apparent that the king's minister in Madrid ever reached any great pitch of apprehension. On the American continent, in Philadelphia, in Mexico City, and in Chihuahua, Spanish officials were somewhat more concerned, but both the commandant-general of the Interior Provinces and the viceroy of Mexico were inclined to throw the problem back to Casa Calvo in Louisiana. In all fairness, however, one must say that Casa Calvo's hands were tied, since Lewis and Clark did not reach St. Louis until December 7, 1803, only two weeks before Louisiana was to be transferred to the United States, and Casa Calvo, the boundary commissioner, had only dubious authority in Louisiana, for Manuel Salcedo was still the governor-general. Casa Calvo had been appointed to the commission for the settlement of the thirty-first parallel boundary question but soon found himself *persona non grata* as far as the United States was concerned, and he was actually requested to leave New Orleans because the United States suspected him of spying. He left New Orleans and went into Texas, complaining all the way, and also playing hide-and-seek with the United States Army.

Meanwhile, it seems that perhaps the ultimate responsibility for dealing with Lewis and Clark fell on Nemesio Salcedo y Salcedo,[1] com-

[1] Nemesio Salcedo y Salcedo, a general of the royal army, succeeded Pedro Grimarest about 1804 as commandant-general of the Interior Provinces. He was said by some to be cruel; he accumulated a considerable private fortune as commandant-general. Hidalgo and others were executed in Chihuahua under him in 1811, and Salcedo was succeeded in 1813 by Bonavía; the exact occupancy of the office is hazy during

mandant-general of the Interior Provinces, but he was never issued clear-cut orders to do anything about the expedition, and consequently he did not order the governor of New Mexico to do anything decisive until it was too late.

To tell the truth, as far as Salcedo was concerned—and he pointed it out to Godoy—he was under a severe handicap because of the lack of definition of the Louisiana boundary, and it may well seem that Lewis and Clark could hardly be accused of violating Spanish territory until they crossed the Rocky Mountains and got into the Oregon country. When Salcedo finally did take a step in the matter, he assumed a very broad jurisdiction, but it is hard to know what that signifies.

One of the most interesting aspects of the entire situation is that the responsibility was passed from one official to another, from high level to low level, until finally it rested on the shoulders of Pedro Vial, who for eight years had been listed as a deserter from New Mexico, but who apparently lost none of his standing and none of the respect held for him in official circles.

In 1802, the Spaniards at New Orleans, alarmed at the aggressiveness of the Kentuckians, had made it difficult for western growers (that is, growers west of the Allegheny Mountains) to float their goods down river to market, by withdrawing from them the right to unload their goods on the docks at New Orleans. It was not a surprise to anybody—not even to the Spaniards—that the Kentuckians immediately got up on their hind legs and howled. Everybody knew that Napoleon had maneuvered the retrocession of Louisiana two years before, and the Kentuckians assumed that Bonaparte was now bringing pressure on them.

Then, in 1803, before the huge territory was delivered to France, Napoleon sold it to the United States. What had been Spanish land for forty years suddenly became the property of the United States, and the Spaniards in New Mexico and Texas abruptly found themselves back

---

Salcedo's time. Nemesio's brother, Juan Manuel, was the inept governor of Louisiana from 1801 to December, 1803, when he and Casa Calvo turned it over to Amos Stoddard as agent for the French republic. Juan's son, Manuel María de Salcedo, was with his father in Louisiana, and became governor of Texas in 1807 in time to deal with the problem of American squatters in the Neutral Zone (without success); with the Mexican Revolution in 1810 and 1811, when he was captured; and with the Gutiérrez-Magee Expedition of 1813. He and his staff surrendered to the filibusters in 1913 and were executed. Manuel previously had been excommunicated by the church.

to their own borders; their Indian buffer state had vanished overnight. In the Texas area, the United States claimed as far as the Río Grande—not very positively, but perhaps with the idea of forcing a compromise and getting Florida. To the north and west, the boundary, after following the Red River of Natchitoches an undetermined distance, somehow reached the Rocky Mountains and went north to Canada. In the Spanish view, the Calcasieu and Mermento, the Red River, and the Arkansas River figured prominently. But one thing was certain: where Santa Fe had been some 800 miles from United States territory, now the little town was only 150 miles or less from it, depending on how one might draw the boundary—and if the Río Grande River should be the western boundary, then Santa Fe itself would be in United States territory![2]

On the Atlantic side of the Louisiana Territory, President Jefferson went ahead with great enthusiasm for a long-cherished scheme: exploration of the northwestern area and discovery of a waterway to the Pacific Ocean—the same objective that had occupied the Spaniards for a number of years. Minor but not negligible objectives of Jefferson's project were notification to the Indians of the change of government; uprooting of British and other foreigners from the territory; establishment of good will among the Indians along the Missouri, and preparation for American traders to go among them; and a long-range objective, the settlement of the land by United States citizens.

Exploration of the Northwest was not a new aim for Jefferson, for he had previously, even before his presidency, tried at various times to persuade different persons to explore the Missouri: he had suggested it to George Rogers Clark as early as 1783; he had persuaded and supported John Ledyard[3] in 1786, when Jefferson was ambassador to France; and he had made plans with André Michaux in 1793, before Michaux had become embroiled in Genêt's machinations. And aside

[2] Santa Fe is fourteen miles east of the Río Grande.

[3] John Ledyard, born in Connecticut in 1751, was engaged in a number of different activities. He accompanied Captain James Cooke on his third voyage, and in 1785, at Jefferson's urging, he undertook to approach America's Northwest through Siberia, and walked from Stockholm to St. Petersburg, 1,400 miles, in seven weeks in winter. He was arrested in Irkutsk, Siberia, and deported to Poland. He then engaged to go on an expedition to explore Africa, but he died in Cairo, Egypt, in 1789. He was said to be of fearless courage and enterprise, of great endurance, resolution, and physical vigor.

from Jefferson's attempts, in 1790 Captain John Armstrong had traveled the Missouri alone in a canoe under secret orders of the Secretary of War but had turned back supposedly because of Indian hostility.[4] But finally, in 1800, Jefferson became President, and at about the same time Spain returned Louisiana to France. In July, 1802, Jefferson asked Meriwether Lewis to lead the expedition, and in January, 1803, he asked Congress secretly for an appropriation of $2,500, believing that the Spaniards, who still ruled but no longer owned Louisiana, would not bother an expedition organized "as a literary pursuit." Jefferson was given secret authority to make the exploration,[4a] and the appropriation was granted later.[5]

The Spaniards were watching all these events with care and concern, but Casa Yrujo, the Spanish minister in Washington, though he knew about the secret message, did not think the exploration would be approved by the Senate, for on January 31, 1803, he wrote to Ceballos, the Minister of State, to reassure him:

> In my letter No. 313 [of December 2, in which he said that Jefferson had asked him directly about Spain's attitude toward such an exploration] I notified your Excellency that the President of the United States had [under consideration] a project to send travelers to explore the course of the Missouri, who, continuing their expedition to the northwest coast, were to examine the possibility or impossibility of communication by water between the Atlantic Ocean and the South Sea, and to contribute to the advancement of the geography of North America. I also told your Excellency of the conversation that the President had with me about that project, he desiring to know if our court would refuse to grant the necessary passports to the travelers, and all that I judged proper to answer him upon the subject. I thought that in consequence he would desist from this purpose, and thus I hinted to your Excellency; but since, I have learned that he has communicated his intention to the Senate, which has already taken a step toward execution. Notwithstanding I have learned that the good judg-

[4] Thwaites gives a brief summary of the early attempts in *Original Journals*, I, *xx–xxii;* there is documentation in *ibid.*, VII, 193–205.

[4a] Much has been made of the secrecy—but it does not seem to have been used for international reasons but rather to avoid pressure from the political infighters at home; the Federalists were always after Jefferson's scalp.

[5] A fine collection of documents on Lewis and Clark is Donald Jackson's recent *Letters of the Lewis and Clark Expedition, With Related Documents, 1783–1854.*

> ment of the Senate does not see the advantages that the President puts forth for this expedition, and that, on the contrary, they feared it might offend one of the European nations; and in consequence it is very likely that the project will not go any further. But as I promised to give your Excellency news of any latest occurrence, I thought I should advise you this for your information.[6]

In the meantime, however, the Senate did give Jefferson authority to make the exploration, and he went ahead actively. Meriwether Lewis took charge of the preparations and began to enroll men, build boats, and seek an assistant. Jefferson wrote many persons about various medical and scientific matters; passports were obtained from the French and British legations.

Then the furore arose over the interdiction of the deposits in New Orleans, and Jefferson instructed Livingstone to try to buy the Isle of Orleans to settle the question and quiet the Kentuckians, and he sent James Monroe to assist him. Then in June, 1803, came the astonishing news that by an unexpected turn of fate, the explorers probably would be in their own country along the Missouri River as far as the Rocky Mountains, for Napoleon had needed money more than he had needed Louisiana, and he had sold the entire enormous territory.[7]

Meriwether Lewis set out from Pittsburgh in his boats in August, 1803, picked up William Clark, and went into winter camp on the Dubois River, across the Mississippi from St. Louis; the expedition left St. Louis the following May, spent the first winter with the Mandans and the second winter on the Pacific Coast, and returned to St. Louis in September, 1806.

The French passport, issued by the French legation in Washington to Meriwether Lewis, was dated February 28, 1803,[8] and the British passport, issued by the British chargé d'affaires, was issued March 1, 1803.[9] It would seem that they would have gotten a passport also from the Spaniards, and there is indirect but definite evidence that they did

[6] Casa Yrujo to Ceballos, No. 320, Washington, January 31, 1803, A.H.N., Estado, leg. 5630, apartado 3.

[7] For a brief background, see Thwaites, *Original Journals*, I, *xvii–xxxii*.

[8] Signed by L. A. Pichon, March 1, 1803, in Papeles de Cuba, leg. 2368.

[9] Signed by Edwd. Thornton, Papeles de Cuba, leg. 2368. Both these passports are certified French copies; Donald Jackson in his research has been unable to turn up an English-language version of Meriwether Lewis' passport.

get one,[10] even though Jefferson at one time said the French and Spanish ministers had agreed that a French passport would be sufficient.[11]

The Spaniards were not at all pleased over the Lewis and Clark expedition,[12] and Casa Calvo, no longer governor of Louisiana[13] but now a boundary commissioner, started the Spanish campaign (which was to be rather feeble) against Lewis and Clark in a letter to Salcedo, commandant-general of the Interior Provinces, in March, 1804. He says that Colonel de Lassus[14] of Illinois has advised him under date of December 9, 1803, of the appearance on December 7 of Captain Merry Wether Lewis, "Captain of the Army of the United States, . . . who at the behest of their President intend to traverse the Missouri River to fulfill their mission of discovery and observation, and I advised the commandant to oppose their entry until he receives necessary permission from the general government," and continues:

> This move of the United States in the very act of taking possession of the province of Louisiana: their haste to inform themselves and to explore the course of the Missouri, whose source, they claim, belongs to them; setting their eyes on the Sea of the South, forces us of necessity to become active and to hasten to cut short the great steps of our neighbors if we wish, as is our duty, to maintain unharmed the dominions of the king and to prevent the ruin and destruction of the Interior Provinces and the kingdom of New Spain.
>
> The only course is to arrest Captain Merry Wheather and his party,

10 Inasmuch as they planned to follow the Columbia, it is hard to understand why they did not apply for a Spanish passport—and it will appear later that Casa Calvo did grant a Spanish passport, though with considerable reluctance. An interesting but not necessarily conclusive bit of evidence occurs in "The Missouri Journal by F. A. Larocque, Clerk of the North-West Co., 1804–1805," *Les Bourgeois de la Compagnie du Nord-Ouest* (L. R. Mason, ed.; Quebec, 1889), I, 299ff.; on p. 303 Larocque tells of meeting Captain Lewis, with Jussaume and Charbonneau, and presently he says: "They showed me their passports, and letters of recommendation from the French, Spanish and British Ministers at the city of Washington."

11 Nasatir, *Before Lewis and Clark,* II, 712.

12 Spanish officials warned Cevallos that the Americans were after the riches of Sonora and Sinaloa. See Nasatir, *Before Lewis and Clark,* II, 719n.

13 Succeeded in 1801 by Salcedo.

14 Carlos du Hault de Lassus de Luzière, an army officer, reached New Orleans in 1794; in 1796 he was appointed commandant at New Madrid; in 1799 he became lieutenant-governor of Upper Louisiana, which post he held until the transfer to the United States.

which can hardly avoid passing among the neighboring [Indian] nations to New Mexico, through their forts or villages.

A decisive and vigorous blow will prevent great costs and countless disagreements that must originate among the respective governments; and at this time we are impelled by the necessity of the moment, dictated by the public pretensions that they have made upon the extent of the province of Louisiana, which the French republic has sold to them. They claim nothing less for their western limits than from the mouth of the Río Bravo to the 30th parallel of north latitude; leaving undetermined the line of demarcation from this place [the junction—or closest proximity—of the Río Grande and the thirtieth parallel] from this place to the northwest as well as that toward the north, which is lost in the vast forests of the Soledades [the wilderness] even though [they are] not inhabited by Europeans.

What other object can there be in the repeated intentions and incursions of the Americans, *aun antes de la desgraciada para ellos* of Philip Nolan?

We should not lose a moment, and the least omission may be of great consequence, [which I know] because of the orders and the confidential instructions that I have; there would be charged upon us a grave responsibility if we should not take, without losing a moment, measures to remove these forces and allow time for measures to be taken to adjust the boundaries of Louisiana without compromising the interests of Spain or hazarding her vast and rich possessions.

In view of the risk, no doubt your Excellency will take the most efficacious measures to arrest the said Captain Merry and his retinue —which according to the news is composed of 25 men; impounding the papers or instruments that may be found, on the principle that they [the men] are in the territory of the Spanish government without its permission; there being no boundary line, it cannot be argued that it belongs already to the United States; *bien que combiene tanto para las intenciones reservadas del Ministerio; de que me allo instruido el de tener los progresos de estas investigaciones*, which, although there are no motives or any pretext whatever, will be forced when the arrest of the captain is verified; and to the end of exonerating you of all responsibility, I am giving immediately to the Court a full account, including a copy of this official letter.[15]

[15] Casa Calvo to Salcedo, New Orleans, March 5, 1804; Provincias Internas, leg. 200; printed in Nasatir, *Before Lewis and Clark*, 731–32.

A short time later, De Lassus, commandant of Upper Louisiana, wrote to both Salcedo, the former governor-general of Louisiana and now an official of Florida, and to Casa Calvo, the boundary commissioner, saying that the Americans maintained that the boundary of Louisiana approached to within thirteen or fourteen leagues of Santa Fe [the Río Grande?], and warning them that the Americans might begin setting up trading posts for contraband and start making trips into Mexico.[16]

Two days later, Casa Calvo wrote to Cevallos with considerable eloquence, begging for more attention to the American incursions:

> The duty of a vassal zealous for the glory of the king and the nation with irresistible force impels my pen to write and to assure that the moment is critical and it is best to take advantage of it, since, otherwise, the rich possessions of the kingdom of New Spain remain exposed. Thus I earnestly beg your Excellency to call the attention of his Majesty toward these dominions, if he does not wish to be witness to their proximate ruin and destruction.[17]

Salcedo, in Chihuahua, saw himself getting into a position where he might be blamed for a great many things, and in May he talked back to Casa Calvo—and not without justification:

> Today [May 3] I have received your official letter of March 5 last in which you notify me that the lieutenant governor of Illinois has advised me that on December 7 of last year Captain Merry presented himself . . .
>
> With this motive your Excellency reflects upon the ambitious plans of the said states [the United States] in justification of your ideas upon that which is convenient [*lo interesante*] to impede Merry's realization of his commission; but [since] the news of the [boundary] demarcation situation that you include in your Excellency's official letter, with the only maps of the territories to which they relate, and which I have before me, and noting among other things that five months have elapsed since the date of the dispatch [to you] by the lieutenant-

[16] De Lassus to Salcedo and Casa Calvo, St. Louis, March 28, 1804, Papeles de Cuba, leg. 140. At the time of De Lassus' letter, Upper Louisiana also had been turned over to the Americans; it was transferred to the French on March 9, to the Americans on March 10.

[17] Caso Calvo to Cevallos, No. 5, Confidential, March 30, 1804. A.H.N., Estado, leg. 5542; draft in Papeles de Cuba, leg. 2356.

governor of Illinois, I observe with regret that this combination of circumstances makes it difficult for me to take measures whose outcome would be as happy as I would desire.

It is eight months since I have communicated to the governors of the provinces bordering yours [New Mexico and Texas], the orders that I judged suitable, . . .[18]

On the same day, although Salcedo complained of Casa Calvo's delay, he also took a step toward doing something about the expedition by ordering that no American should be permitted to approach the Texas frontier or to mark the boundaries of Louisiana.[19] It appears that he might have had some trouble enforcing the latter part of that order.

He then wrote to the governor of New Mexico, suggesting Pedro Vial as a good man to reconnoiter the country, and wishfully speculating on the arrest of Lewis and Clark:

[As the Lewis and Clark Expedition may have objectives as stated by Casa Calvo, it is imperative that it be impeded. . . . Let us at least keep informed. It is imperative to punish the barbarous Navahos, and it is important to come to an agreement with the Comanches, and to send a reconnaissance party as far as the right (south) bank of the Missouri.]

If you deem it suitable to send with the Indians that your Excellency may designate to such an interesting service [reconnaissance of the country toward the Missouri], one or two soldier-interpreters, [you may do so]. I leave it to your judgment to arrange it, and also that you inform Don Pedro Vial of the object of this trip, in case he should wish to include himself in it as he is most experienced in those territories, and in this case he can outfit himself with what is necessary for his sustenance, advising him to keep an exact journal which he will present to you on his return.

Nothing would be more useful than the arrest of Merry, and although I know it is not an easy undertaking, it might be a thing that would give to us the means of success [in the matter of keeping Americans out of Spanish territory]. It will not be needless to make inquiries upon the matter among the Indians, enlisting their friendship and

[18] Salcedo to Casa Calvo, Chihuahua, May 3, 1804, Papeles de Cuba, leg. 2368; printed in Nasatir, *Before Lewis and Clark*, II, 732–33 (a different copy).

[19] Cox *(Early Explorations,* 45) says this order is in the Bexar Archives.

valor, offering them good compensation [for interference with the expedition of Lewis and Clark].[20]

Salcedo also on that day wrote to Ceballos in Spain, hoping to bring some diplomatic pressure to bear:

> Notwithstanding my insinuation to the Marquis of Casa Calvo, I judge that through the governor of Louisiana the attention of the President of the United States may have been called to this suspicious conduct, I am sending an official letter to the king's minister in Philadelphia, advising him in the present case where he can perform the best service, and thus I hope that you will pass this information on to his Majesty for his royal knowledge.[21]

Meanwhile, Casa Calvo, although he said he had advised De Lassus to oppose Lewis' entry, must have been asked for a passport and must have been unable gracefully to refuse, for Governor Chacón[22] of New Mexico wrote this startling news to Salcedo in May:

> By two Apache warriors who arrived here May 14 [1804], I received . . . [from you] copy of a letter from Casa Calvo, a commission for the delivery of Louisiana, by which [letter from Casa Calvo] he notifies you of the passports given for Mr. Merry, Captain of U. S. A., from last December 7 to explore the Missouri with the view of acquainting themselves with the limits of the territory belonging to their nation. . . . And inasmuch as the said Gentiles [Indian tribes] cannot find out anything [illegible] from the project of Bernard Castro [illegible] the Hill of Gold,[23] I shall dispatch a party [to reconnoiter?]

[20] Salcedo to governor, No. 3, May 3, 1804, A.H.N., Estado, leg. 5542, exp. 2; printed in Nasatir, *Before Lewis and Clark*, II, 734–35.

[21] Salcedo to Ceballos, Chihuahua, May 8, 1804, A.H.N., Estado, leg. 5422, exp. 2; also in A.G.M., Historia, vol. 200; printed in Nasatir, *Before Lewis and Clark*, II, 730–31.

[22] Fernando Chacón succeeded Concha as governor of New Mexico in July, 1794, though he had been appointed in August, 1793. He asked for a salary advance but apparently did not get it; he turned the office over to Alencaster in March, 1805. See: documents in Provincias Internas, leg. 204; appointment, f. 288–89; petition for salary advance, f. 294–95; petition of 1806, f. 313–14.

[23] The fabulous Hill of Gold probably came into imaginative existence about the time of De Niza; stories of it run like an undercurrent through Spanish records of the Southwest; Coronado and Oñate hunted for it, and so did many, many others; at the time of this letter, 260-some years after Coronado, they were still searching. For a lengthy treatment, see J. M. Espinosa, "The Legend of Sierra Azul," *New Mexico*

the country between this province and the said Missouri River, in this manner avoiding suspicion on the part of Merry or of the savage nations that could help him.[24]

It appears that at that very moment Bernard Castro was looking for the Hill of Gold (a last-minute attempt), and the governor would use that as an excuse to avoid offending Lewis and Clark. However, the American threat was a spectre that would not go away, and in June Casa Calvo did his best to stir up Salcedo by advising him of threats closer to home:

> . . . The President of the United States is going to send, immediately, an expedition comprised of one official, 12 soldiers, and a surgeon to each of the Rivers Colorado,[25] San Francisco,[26] and the Arkansas in order to examine and inspect them from their mouths in the Mississippi to their sources, with various instructions to make maps, explore the mine-sites, and acquaint themselves with the Indian nations.
>
> The mere reading of this actual information will make you understand how important and how urgent it is to employ immediately upon the receipt of this letter all precautionary measures, and orders that may combine and negate and even destroy similar expeditions if the integrity of these vast and rich possessions is to be maintained, at least following the strict rules of international law. . . . if we are on the lookout and as soon as they enter the interior of the well-known jurisdiction of those provinces,[27] it will be endeavored to arrest them, take their papers and instruments, and, treating them in the most humane and generous manner, they will be sent to their government while we complain of the infraction of the royal rights and privileges of his Majesty as well as the attempt to disturb the peace and good harmony that fortunately exists between both nations. I inform your Excellency

*Historical Review,* Vol. IX, No. 2 (April, 1934), 113–58, which has an extensive bibliography.

[24] Chacón to Salcedo, No. 82, Santa Fe, May 16, 1804, New Mexican Archives, doc. 1730. It now appears that Casa Calvo may have granted a passport on December 7, but he certainly was cagey about admitting it.

[25] The Red River of Natchitoches.

[26] The St. Francis River in northeast Arkansas.

[27] As long as Lewis and Clark should stay within the area bounded by the Missouri, they were in fair territory, but they were planning to go to the Pacific Ocean, and that almost certainly would involve land claimed by Spain. Likewise, note that Casa Calvo speaks of three rivers, one of which—the Red—was known to lead to New Mexico.

in fulfillment of my responsibility, animated by a zeal for the better service of the king, with the object that the measures that seem advisable be taken opportunely. With the understanding that on this date I am giving similar news to the governor of San Antonio de Bexar and to the commandant of the presidios of Nuestra Señora del Pilar de Nacogdoches.[28]

In due course of time, some of this news reached the viceroy of Mexico, Yturrigaray,[29] but he was not receptive to all that "Why don't you and him fight?" talk from the boundary commissioner without a few reservations—which he pointed out to Salcedo in September:

> . . . I have not been able to refrain from observing that your Excellency has with [proper] anticipation taken [all] possible measures to impede the plans of the United States government, but I have not been able [also] to refrain from observing that Señor the Marquis of Casa Calvo does not speak to your Excellency of having revealed these occurrences to our minister in Philadelphia, which was the best means for him to negotiate with the President or with the Congress in order to cut off in their inception those procedures that may have [such] regrettable effects, especially if events should occur as they may occur, following out the idea proposed of arresting the explorers, taking their papers and instruments.

It rather seems that the viceroy was somewhat peevish over Casa Calvo's protestations of innocence.

Then, on September 9, 1805, Salcedo finally got on the ball and issued definite instructions to Alencaster,[30] governor of New Mexico, telling him, in effect, to get the Indians to do the job. He was to infuse the Indians with horrors of the English and the Americans:

> Regarding the indicated ideas [Salcedo went on to tell the governor],

[28] Casa Calvo to Salcedo, June 27, 1804; Provincias Internas, leg. 200, ff. 346–47. By that time, Casa Calvo was the boundary commissioner, he having returned to Louisiana in January, 1803, in that capacity.

[29] José de Yturrigaray succeeded Berenguer as viceroy in 1803, and was succeeded by Garibay in 1808. He was a favorite of Godoy, and was ambitious. See Priestley, *Mexican Nation*, 198.

[30] Joaquín del Real Alencaster, a lieutenant colonel of infantry, whose early life is elusive, was appointed governor of New Mexico to succeed Chacón, who was being removed, in 1803, but he did not reach Santa Fe until March, 1805. He also got in trouble and was replaced in 1808 by Alberto Maynez. His pay was probably four thousand pesos a year, by decree of 1772.

it is necessary forcibly to oppose as far as reason and prudence dictate, and I do not doubt that your Excellency will meditate over them, because of your zeal and the responsibility with which you find yourself entrusted but, being in the position of being able to lose any time [since time is short], I warn your Excellency to take the most efficient measures to improve the frendship of the Pawnee Nation and likewise acquire that of the Otos and Lobos, as well as that of any other in the environs of the Missouri, Cance, [Kansas], Chato [Platte], Napeste, or Arkansas Rivers, . . . with the understanding that from all of them there must result for us the greatest usefulness in the present circumstances. For this [purpose], it is advisable as the most powerful sort of persuasion to present them with gifts on our part, to influence their chiefs so they may frequently go to your capital [Santa Fe], and order that our interpreters carry out the same in their camps, your Excellency advising them of the good faith that they must observe in order that there be no resentment or reasons to stop their cultivating friendship for us.[30a]

[The commandant-general suggests sending José Chalvert to the Pawnees] . . . taking some small presents for the chiefs, and that he make them understand that since there have occurred important matters to discuss, your Excellency desires that they present themselves in your village, where, through the medium of his able assistance and the gifts that you will have decided to give them, you will give them a new proof of the affection you have for them, and in case their meeting should take place there [in Santa Fe], your Excellency will proceed not only to install in them extreme dislike for the English and the Americans but also to . . . persuade them [the Indians] to openly refuse their [the Americans'] communications with the understanding [argument] that they [the Americans] have no other intention than to throw them [the Indians] from their lands in order to occupy them [the lands]—which idea, embellished with suitable vehemence, would be very useful to persuade them that, upon the return of the expedition of Captain Merri, which has as its object the reconnaissance of the Missouri up to its source and to give presents to the nations in the name of the American government, that they intercept it [the expedition], seizing its individuals—which, if it becomes difficult to attain [but if that becomes difficult of accomplishment], your Excellency will be able to induce them, at least under the assurance that they will be recompensed to their liking, to do everything possible to take away any boxes or

[30a] There is some involved syntax here.

papers that the same expedition carries, because if we acquire them, there would result considerable advantages without our being forced to place troops in the places where it is indicated, inasmuch as that perhaps would induce suspicion and tumult among the Indians.[30b] [He has ordered that emigrants from Louisiana be admitted to the Interior Provinces without duty on their goods if they are for their own use. He discusses the royal decree of April 14, 1789, that provides that Negro slaves who come to New Spain shall be free; he recalls that commerce with Louisiana is prohibited.]

I likewise warn your Excellency that if in doubt as to whether one must or must not carry to a pure and due effect the observance of the royal decree of April 14, '89, which declared that all the Negro slaves of foreign colonies who should present themselves in his Majesty's dominion should be free consistent with international law, it is ordered that until a new royal [decree]—to which [*which* end?], I realize, they will be detained in any part of the provinces of my command—the Negro slaves of Louisiana who present themselves with the object of that grace [freedom], notwithstanding any supplication that comes from their owners or on the part of the American government; and this your Excellency must bear in mind with the understanding that if any Negroes should meet you, imploring their liberty, you must assign them a place where they may remain confined until their fate is decided, remembering that they must be able to subsist by their labor or industry in the place you assign them.[30c]

. . . all direct commerce is prohibited between these provinces and that of Louisiana, and the indirect one that may be made by its [their?] inhabitants with the Indian nations; with this understanding, there must not be allowed, whenever it is practical to impede it, the traffic and commerce that the American individuals who navigate the Missouri River with this objective, practice among the same Indians; this should serve your Excellency as a guide and do away with all impediments in proceeding to the capture of those who are there, when there should be an opportunity to accomplish it.

[He encloses a map "drawn up to the minute" to] instruct your Excellency of the territory that your province encompasses: of its distance to the establishments at Illinois and to the English possessions

[30b] If this is not the finest example in any language of ambiguity in antecedents, it surely is among the finest.

[30c] Perhaps also the commandant-general should be awarded honorable mention for his use of dangling phrases and clauses, fragmentary sentences, and run-on sentences.

> on the course of the Mississippi and Missouri Rivers, those that bear the name Colorado, Arkansas, or Napestle, that enter the first, and those known as Caos, or Cancer [Kansas], Chato, Osages, and the others that enter the said Missouri. . . .[31]

In this very comprehensive and important letter of September 9, 1805, perhaps the most astonishing section is the designation of the area of Alencaster's authority, which seems to take in all the drainage system of the Missouri, and possibly all the drainage system of the rivers that flow eastward into the Mississippi.

It does not appear that Salcedo was on solid ground. He might have claimed to the Missouri River, but even that is open to question. As a matter of fact, in August, 1804, Salcedo's brother Juan, governor of Louisiana, had said very distinctly in a letter to Cevallos:

> It is then clear and evident that all the right bank of the Mississippi from its source to the sea, by the last treaty that France made with England, belonged to the province of Louisiana and the copious Missouri emptying into the Mississippi on the same right or west bank.[31a]

There does not seem, then, to be any basis for assuming that Nemesio Salcedo did not know that he was suggesting an invasion of territory that did not belong to Spain.

The phrase, "to the English possessions from the course of the Missouri and Mississippi River" cannot very well fail to cross what by that time was American territory. Therefore, in the light of his previous caution, why did he order Alencaster to send gifts to the Pawnees in central Nebraska and in northwestern Kansas along the Platte; and to the Otos and Missouris, who were east of the Pawnees?

Another phrase, " to the establishments of Illinois," is hard to recconcile, for even if he was unaware of the fact that was clear to his brother, and was referring to St. Geneviéve, Cape Giradeau, New Madrid, and other settlements below St. Louis (and not St. Louis itself), he could hardly argue that New Mexico extended to the Mississippi, for Louisiana certainly included New Orleans, and Lower Louisiana would have to have a land connection with Upper Louisiana.

[31] Salcedo to Alencaster, September 9, 1805, Mexico, Guerra y Marina, 1787–1807, cuaderno 15.

[31a] Salcedo to Cevallos, New Orleans, Aug. 20, 1804; Papeles de Cuba, leg. 2368; printed in Nasatir, *Before Lewis and Clark,* II, 747.

Salcedo could hardly have been ignorant of all these facts, and the puzzle persists. Is it likely that he felt the area between the Arkansas, say, and the Missouri to be more or less free country for the most vigorous claimant?

Surely Salcedo was not so naïve as to believe that the Anglos, who were known to be unbearably aggressive, would submit to such an intrusion; it seems doubtful that any Spaniard in the New World would have believed that. Was Salcedo, then, actually subject for the time being to a lapse of memory?

A few days later (in September), Casa Calvo wrote to Cevallos, taking exception to Salcedo's letter of May 3:

> I am enclosing to your Excellency a copy of the answer dated May 3, which is a reply by the commandant-general of the Interior Provinces to my letter of March 5. With it I also enclose my intention to record that my message's only object was the reconnaissance that the American Captain Merry Weather was going to make of the origin and course of the Misury. . . .
>
> In these parallel documents your Excellency will surely observe the indifference with which so important a message has been treated, and therefore, since . . . prompt measures might have to be taken following receipt of my letter, to compensate for the time and the distance. . . . Consequently, I think that before writing the second paragraph of his answer, he should have examined and inquired in every way possible concerning the immediate routes [surrounding passageways] to see if he could acquire news . . . because the expedition was en route to the Upper Missouri. This having been done, there would have been left no object for the delay of another message as long as five months.
>
> . . . the origin of that river [the Upper Missouri] is to the northwest. This in the general plan of the maps should bring it very near to the capital of the aforementioned kingdom of New Mexico.
>
> I cannot understand the idea of the commandant-general, nor on what basis he can uphold himself, nor to what expression of my letter he is making allusion when he says that the news of the boundary demarcation, which I include in my official letter, are the only maps of the territory in my possession [to which they relate], but are not satisfactory. I have tormented my spirit, but have not been able to find a single phrase in all my letter that gives rise to such a slighting

statement as announced. What limits are outlined in it? If the prefect himself, of whose propositions I made literal use when treating of the pretensions of France, speaks only indeterminately—who fixed them—how can it be imputed that I have pointed them out?

Therefore I find it extraordinary, as I have already mentioned, that the commandant-general has not taken more active measures because of an erroneous confidence, and I fear that this same confidence will injure the promptness of the dispositions that should be taken to stop the progress of Merry.[32]

Thus Casa Calvo, who took his own whimsical time advising Salcedo of Lewis' appearance in St. Louis, squealed with fervor when put on the spot by Salcedo. Five days after that letter, Casa Calvo wrote Salcedo that on June 23 "Captain Merry Wether" had been at a point ninety-one leagues from the Mississippi without having encountered any trouble with the Indian nations. Casa Calvo believed Lewis had, by the time of his letter, gone more than three hundred leagues up the river, and consequently was inside the Interior Provinces—and thus the ball was tossed back to Salcedo.[33]

Salcedo told Alencaster, on September 9 and again on September 12, to persuade the Indians to seize the Americans' boxes and papers, and Pedro Vial was sent on an expedition to the Pawnees to influence the Indians to intercept Lewis and Clark. The results of that expedition are told in a letter from Salcedo to the viceroy in January, 1805:

Since I was informed last May by the Marquis of Casa Calvo that the captain of the United States Army, Mr. Merri, had presented himself in the establishment of Illinois with a request to go into the interior of the Missouri River country, I ordered the governor of New Mexico to supply an expedition composed of a guide, two soldier-interpreters, and some loyal Indians, to reconnoiter as far as the said river and through the barbaric nations situated in those territories, obtain information regarding the operations and destination of the said Merri; and upon fulfilling his order, when the Marquis of Casa Calvo informed me subsequently [June 27] of the different expedition[s] decided upon by the President of the United States to the Colorado,

[32] Casa Calvo to Ceballos, No. 41, September 15, 1804, Papeles de Cuba, leg. 2368; printed in Nasatir, *Before Lewis and Clark*, II, 751.

[33] Unsigned letter to Salcedo, September 20, 1804, Papeles de Cuba, leg. 2368; printed in Nasatir, *Before Lewis and Clark*, 750, 752, 753.

San Francisco, and Arkansas rivers in order to inspect them in their entire courses and to become friendly with the Indian nations, I had no other new steps to take, as I informed your Excellency in the official letter of August 14 of that year [1804].

The governor of New Mexico [Chacón] has just notified me of the results of the expedition that I [had] arranged and that I put in charge of Don Pedro Vial, and both by the official letter with which he enclosed the respective diary[34] and a report from Vial himself, it is evident that through some Frenchmen who were in the pueblos of the Panana Nation and, it appears, presented themselves in Santa Fe, it has been learned, first, that the Anglo-Americans had sent another expedition to inspect the Missouri River [as opposed to the Red, the Arkansas, and the St. Francis] with the order to attract to their side all the Gentile factions, and, second, that from the nearest and best known of those nations they [the Anglo-Americans] took away the medals and patents that they had been given by Spanish officials, giving them others from the American republic, with flags of the same nation, and that only the Pananas had not agreed to receive them or recognize the republic as an ally. For this reason, and to assure the Gentiles [Pananas?] further in their manner of thinking, the governor of New Mexico presented their leaders with a fine gift.

In these circumstances, whose importance your Excellency will understand, because it is to be inferred that such expeditions have on the part of the United States the important object, among others, of seeking a harbor on the South Sea between the 40°–45° latitude, which is at the height where the Missouri River has its headwaters. . . .

Should conditions in Texas become aggravated, or if Señor Grimarest's[35] ascent to power should be delayed, and consequently the new establishments,—[and] I judge that his affairs are progressing satisfactorily,—it will be necessary for me to address myself to your Excellency for funds to strengthen that province, notwithstanding the fact that from the scant garrison of the neighboring province of Coahuila I have ordered as many as 50 men, which is the portion made possible to me, to march quietly and with apparent casualness.[36]

[34] Salcedo to Alencaster, Chihuahua, October 2, 1805, Mexico, Guerra y Marina, 1787–1807, cuaderno 15.

[35] Colonel Pedro Grimarest seems to have served as commandant-general for a short time in 1804.

[36] Salcedo to Yturrigaray, Chihuahua, January 23, 1805, Provincias Internas, leg. 200, ff. 308–10.

From this letter comes information that was hardly anticipated: in the latter part of the year 1804, Pedro Vial made a trip to the Pawnees to check on Lewis and Clark; and, of all the Indian tribes, only the Pawnees had remained loyal to Spain.

In the light of all the facts that are now known, it seems that Yturrigaray had a point in his letter of September 1: that the boundary commissioner had indeed passed the responsibility of stopping Lewis and Clark to his associates and subordinates when he himself might have done something about it.

In 1805 ( a little over a year later), Casa Calvo was confronted with the same proposition: Governor Claiborne of Louisiana asked him for a passport for William Dunbar to explore the three rivers mentioned. Casa Calvo then wrote a long letter to Ceballos in which he expressed his reluctance to issue the passport but agreed to do so providing Claiborne would send two Spanish observers along with Dunbar.

Casa Calvo's official letters indicate that he was not happy over the various expeditions proposed by the United States, but that he was not prepared to deny passage in view of the poorly defined boundaries of the Louisiana Territory.

With Lewis and Clark making steady progress up the Missouri, and Salcedo uneasy, Salcedo had passed the torch to the governor of New Mexico in his letter of September 9, 1805, in which he spoke of "the methods that are advisable to adopt with the object of preventing all risk as soon as the circumstances of the country permit it, and [which] is required by our indisputable rights over those lands." He pointed out that the American government was supplying gifts and goods, and especially firearms and munitions, so that the Indians might fight the Spanish, which, he said, "is the same as said government's exercising power within its [Spain's] ancient limits with regard to the cited province of Louisiana when it belonged to the king."[37]

This particular statement appears to be double-talk on the part of the commandant-general, for there is little doubt that Louisiana by that time (September, 1805) belonged to the United States, and Salcedo had seen the commission from Casa Calvo. Understandably, the Spaniards were resentful, but it would seem that the legal right of the United States to exercise its power within the limits of Louisiana was

[37] Salcedo to governor, Chihuahua, September 9, 1805; cited in note 31, *supra*.

hardly in dispute. If Spain had felt that the United States did not have the legal right, then Spain should have protested vigorously at high levels. However, the responsibility continued to be by-passed, and perhaps that obvious evasion caused Salcedo to urge the governor to make friends with the Pawnees—who, it will be remembered, had been listed previously as the only nation to remain faithful to Spain.

In Salcedo's letter to Alencaster on September 12, Salcedo said he realized that the goods in New Mexico were not sufficient for "this new kindness" to the Indians, and that he was sending Sergeant Tomás Ortiz with merchandise to the amount of 460 pesos, 7 reales, including 50 pesos supplied to Laurenzo Durocher and Baptiste Lalande.

Salcedo's customary avoidance of definite action changed the following month, when he sent Alencaster a "very confidential" official letter, saying that the Minister of State and of the Department of War had communicated to him the royal decree of May 22. Salcedo went on to say that Alencaster should arrest Americans among the Indian nations named in his letter of September 9, but he avoided any mention of Lewis and Clark:

> I insert it [the royal decree] to your Excellency in order that you may be informed of the extraordinary news it contains and may therefore take the precautionary measures which the security of that province requires, with which object I gave your Excellency in an order of September 9, last, all the warnings that are important in the present state of affairs, and they are the reliable news that said order refers to.
>
> In addition to the measures that I told your Excellency should be taken in order to bind and strengthen the friendship of the nations that inhabit the banks of the Missouri River and others, luring them with maxims contrary to those they acquire from the Anglo-Americans and presenting them with gifts in proportion to the affection that they affirm, I cautioned your Excellency, basing my opinions on royal orders, not only that you impede all traffic and commerce of the former with said villages but [also] that you proceed to the seizure of any subjects of the government of the United States who are in them,[38] and I repeat the same to your Excellency now in order that you may carry it out, availing yourself of all the means possible by virtue of

[38] This is not exactly what he said in the letter of September 9; he suggested that the Indians should be persuaded to detain them.

the fact that this measure is now not only advantageous but also absolutely necessary to remove to a distance from that *Indiada* [Indian land] all the persuasion that is harmful to us.

Likewise, it is of forceful necessity that your Excellency try through the individuals of the Indian bands from there [New Mexico] who introduce themselves by means of their interpreters and their traders, to get information of any news that may take place in the country that is interposed between that province [New Mexico] and Upper Louisiana, since it must serve as a warning for preparation of the advantageous measures. Your Excellency will give me prompt information by special courier of those steps that might occur to you.[39]

He uses this letter to reaffirm his letter of September 9, and assumes or pretends to assume that he was more definite on September 9 than he actually was; however, he finally issues an order that Americans in those Indian nations be arrested—and still it is noticeable that he avoids any mention of Lewis and Clark.

On October 2 he also wrote to the viceroy, complaining that of the two hundred soldiers sought for the presidio at Bexar, fewer than seventy had arrived, and advising his Excellency the viceroy that he should be guaranteed one or two officers of engineers and an officer and fifteen or twenty artillerymen, with as many flying cannon troops as possible; he points out that in Chihuahua he has only seven cannon, and he requests from eight hundred to one thousand guns or rifles, since he has no body of militia and would have to arm the inhabitants in case of need. He speaks of the Lewis and Clark expedition and the proposed Dunbar expedition, and, as might be expected, the influence of the Americans on the Indians is to him the most threatening aspect of the explorations.[40] And of course it was true that one of the principal objectives of the Lewis and Clark expedition was to make friends with the Indians.

On October 8, 1805 (six days after Salcedo wrote to Alencaster and to the viceroy), he wrote to Casa Calvo, reiterating well-known facts but adding that the governors of the bounding provinces of the

[39] Salcedo to the governor, Chihuahua, October 2, 1805, Mexico, Guerra y Marina, 1787–1807; cuaderno 15; copy in the Library of Congress.

[40] Salcedo to Yturrigaray, San Diego, October 6, 1805, Provincias Internas, leg. 200.

Interior Provinces (probably New Mexico and Texas) had been forewarned to stop the expeditions.[41]

Three days after that (on October 11), Alencaster wrote a brief note to Salcedo, acknowledging the letters of September 9 and September 24, and enclosing a map that he did not identify, but which he said corresponded with an old one and with information he had acquired from Pedro Vial.[42] By that time, Lewis and Clark were descending the Columbia River, at the mouth of which they were to spend nearly four months.

Then, at long last, on February 11, 1806, a little over one month before Lewis and Clark would start their return trip, Salcedo wrote to Alencaster, advising him that he had received a letter dated October 12, 1805,[43] which quoted a letter dated September 4 from the Secretary of State, telling him that Casa Calvo had sent a warning about Lewis and Clark, that the king had ordered his minister to make a protest, and that Casa Yrujo in Philadelphia had already made such a protest on March 12, 1805. Perhaps Yturrigaray's pointed observations concerning the matter had produced results, or perhaps the cumbersome Spanish bureaucray had managed to move of its own accord—two years and two months after Meriwether Lewis' appearance in St. Louis.

Salcedo observed to Alencaster that Yrujo had said the American Secretary of State had complained that the Spaniards were fortifying frontier posts, and now Salcedo points out to Alencaster that it is finally evident that they are authorized to stop Lewis if he should enter Spanish territory:

> Although it is not clear nor does Yrujo mention what the Secretary of State has answered him concerning the matter of the commission of Captain Merry [to explore the Missouri and the Columbia], it is evident that after having made representations in due time, our government is sufficiently authorized to stop Captain Merry in the progress of his commission if he attempts to carry it forward within the dominions of the king, which is what his Majesty has ordered me to inform your

41 Salcedo to Casa Calvo, Chihuahua, October 8, 1805, New Mexican Archives, doc. 1856, no. 4.

42 Alencaster to Salcedo, Santa Fe, October 11, 1805, Mexico, Guerra y Marina, 1787–1807, cuaderno 15; copy in the Library of Congress.

43 Since it had come from Spain, there might have been a legitimate reason for the long delay.

Excellency, so that through the ministry of your charge the commandant-general of the Interior Provinces may be informed of what is best, although always charging him to use proper moderation.[44]

At that time, Lewis and Clark were in Spanish territory, and before they should again cross the Rocky Mountains they would have been in Spanish territory for almost one year. At any rate, something had finally been decided—but seldom has an order (if it is one) been issued in more circumlocutory fashion. Once again, nothing definite was likely to be done, because nobody had really issued an order; Salcedo's ambiguous relaying of the king's order might well be interpreted to mean that the king had ordered that they had authority, but Salcedo himself does not say that it means that, nor does he tell Alencaster to stop the expedition. In the last paragraph he says: "And I am enclosing it to you so that you may be informed of the sovereign resolution that is included in it for your intelligence and fulfillment in the part that concerns you." And along with the lack of an order for actions that might very well precipitate a serious affair, nobody bothered to define or even suggest the boundaries of Spanish territory except Salcedo in his letter of September 9. Even though it had been known from the beginning that Lewis might go as far as the Pacific Ocean, apparently no move had been made along the coast. Any move in the interior should have been made by the governor of New Mexico, for even as late as 1819 (the Yellowstone expedition), Spanish officials considered the Yellowstone area within the jurisdiction of Santa Fe.

Meanwhile, Lewis and Clark and their men (along with Sacajawea and her papoose, Ba'tiste) were making free use of Spanish territory; by mid-summer of 1806 they were back across the Continental Divide into American territory, and on September 23 they reached St. Louis.

They had been on the road a long time when Salcedo wrote his letter of February 11. A skeptic might think the Spaniards had waited long enough to be thoroughly safe, but it rather looks as if there were too much caution, too much red tape, and too much of that venerable pastime sometimes spoken of as passing the buck.

The damage had been done: Lewis and Clark had made the incredible journey with the loss of but one man; they had made observa-

[44] Salcedo to the governor, No. 167, Chihuahua, February 11, 1806, New Mexican Archives, doc. 1967.

tions of flora and fauna and had collected specimens; they had kept minutely detailed records and had drawn maps. The expedition had established relations with many Indian tribes, as the Spaniards had foreseen; it produced the first generation of mountain men, who were essential to the subsequent opening of the West; it did everything necessary to open the way to American traders and American settlers. It failed in only one respect: it lost eight years before the journals were published (in 1814). In the meantime, there were Pike and all those who came after him, and in Lower Louisiana there were Philip Nolan and Sibley and Freeman and Dunbar. They were all on the road to Santa Fe—but Philip Nolan gave the Spaniards more sleepless nights than did all the others put together.

# IX

# *The Anglo-American Entrada from Lower Louisiana, 1791–1806*

Starting about 1791—or, according to one authority, as early as 1785—Americans looking for king-size land grants began to cross Lower Louisiana to make their way into Texas. Sometimes they went through Arkansas Post, sometimes through Natchez and Concordia,[1] sometimes through Manchac[2] and Baton Rouge, sometimes through New Orleans, and sometimes through the bayous and swamps and prairies where they left no permanent trace. Whatever the route, they aimed first at Texas and its vast herds of wild mustangs, secondarily at Indian trade, eventually at the gold and silver from the rich interior mines of Mexico. Naturally every such threat was a threat to Santa Fe, either directly by an advance against the little town, or indirectly by severance of the line of communications.

A man named John Rozée Peyton appears to have been, perhaps, the first Anglo-American to enter Santa Fe from the east. His story has been questioned because there is no corroboration from other documents, but a thoughtful reading will suggest that credence be given to it. He was on a ship in the Gulf of Mexico in 1773, which was captured by a Spanish ship; he and his companions were marched, under the usual harassing conditions of that time and place, up the Río Grande to Santa Fe. With the help of the jailer's daughter, Annetta, who was in love with Peyton's Jamaican servant, Peyton escaped in February, 1774, accompanied by Annetta and his servant, and they made their way, under difficult conditions, to St. Louis.[3]

[1] Concordia was a Spanish post across the river from Natchez—on the west side.

[2] Manchac was a post a short distance below Baton Rouge on the Mississippi. River.

[3] John Lewis Peyton, *The Adventures of My Grandfather*. Reprinted in *New*

Many men went to Texas—some to stay—and in 1795 Barr, Davenport & Murphy, traders at Nacogdoches, were granted 207,000 acres of land. Such grants were intended for use as ranches but those grants did not stop contrabanding, and many Americans engaged in it. They caused a great deal of trouble for Spanish authorities, but most of them left no record unless they were unfortunate enough to find lodging in a Spanish jail—and it seems that most of them were too clever to be caught.

There was one, however, who left a mass of documentary evidence. It appears also that he had indisputably hostile designs on Texas, and that he might have succeeded in them but for a series of mistakes that would not have been made by a person of sound judgment. That man is Philip Nolan.

In spite of all the documents, his origin seems vague beyond the fact that he was born in Belfast, Ireland, in 1771 and was reared by James Wilkinson. He was an associate of Wilkinson, for a while a friend of Gayoso, on good terms with Miró and Carondelet, an adviser to Thomas Jefferson, a friend of Thomas Ellicott, and a corresponder with Pedro de Nava. He was a mustanger and a good one, but he got too big for his breeches: he thought he could fight off the Spanish army.

For years he had a mistress in Nacogdoches, who followed him to Mexico and who sometimes lived in his house at San Antonio. At one time he apparently was about to go into contrabanding with Gayoso, but something happened and Gayoso turned against him and eventually brought about his downfall at a time when he had a wife of a few months pregnant in Natchez while he was sending intimate notes to his mistress in Nacogdoches—and perhaps the immediate cause of his downfall was a jealous husband.

He was a dashing, handsome young man, a prodigious adventurer —daring, ambitious, and seemingly without deep loyalty to anybody but himself. He was, perhaps, the apotheosis of the mustangers of the 1790's

He is said by Yoakum to have been in Texas as early as 1785—but it seems doubtful from Nolan's own words. He was in New Orleans, however, by 1780, for in that year he handled business there for Wilkinson.

---

*Mexico Historical Review*, Vol. IV, No. 3 (July, 1929) (edited by F. W. Hodge), 239–72; John Rosée Peyton, *Three Letters From St. Louis* (1958).

Sometime in 1791 Nolan got a passport from Miró and made his first documented trip to Texas—where they suspected him of being a spy and took his goods. He wandered among the Indians between San Antonio and the Illinois for two years, and was a favorite with the Taovayas and Comanches. He went back to civilization, made another trip to Texas, and captured wild mustangs. He formed a friendship with Antonio Leal,[3a] and considerably more than a friendship with Leal's wife, Gertrudes de los Santos. Gertrude came to handle his business in Texas, and she went on trips and lived with him in San Antonio.

He returned to New Orleans from his second trip in 1794 with 50 horses, and Carondelet gave him a passport for a third trip to Texas, although Carondelet certainly knew it was contrabanding.

Nolan made trips to Chihuahua, Laredo, San Antonio, Nacogdoches, and along the coast. In 1796 he wrote Wilkinson that he had returned from his "third trip to the *unknown land*." He had brought 250 horses to Natchez, and had hidden them in the canebrake while he paid his respects to Carondelet. He finally drove some of the horses to Kentucky. Apparently, however, he did not deliver to Carondelet a certain horse that he had promised, for Carondelet in May, 1796, wrote to Gayoso:

> The damage that Nolan has done to me is worthy of an Irishman. I do not want the horse that he has sent me for nothing, and so I have told [Daniel] Clark. I am told by reliable persons that the one [horse] that he took to Kentucky was magnificent and well trained and worth the 150 pesos that I owed for it [or that I had agreed to pay for it]—and he agreed, so he could not break the agreement in honesty.[3b]

[3a] Leal was born in San Antonio in 1750.

[3b] Carondelet to Gayoso, New Orleans, May 30, 1796, Papeles de Cuba, leg. 23. Daniel Clark, Jr., went to New Orleans to go into business with his uncle, Daniel Clark, Sr., in 1786. He was Irish by birth, and of uncommon perspicacity and with a talent for intrigue. He was associated with Wilkinson and, although apparently not in the conspiracy, knew a great deal about it. Though not a rascal, Whitaker says, he would hardly characterize him with the words *honor*, *probity* and *fidelity*. He burrowed his way through life in the Southwest, leaving many indications of activity but seldom revealing its full extent. He became U. S. consul in 1801, though he said he had become a Spanish subject; he went to France to get concessions on navigation, but failed. He had unusual energy, intelligence and adaptability, and much ambition, and it is hard to probe New Orleans history of this period without running into him. See Whitaker, *The Missisippi Question.*

It was a tactical error, and in January, 1797, Nolan committed another: he gave Andrew Ellicott[3c] information about Louisiana and especially about the inhabitants of Natchez. Ellicott was on his way to Natchez to settle problems in connection with the treaty of 1795, and he was appreciative. But Gayoso, the Spanish governor of Natchez, was not. Wilkinson tried to reassure him of Nolan's trustworthiness.

In September, 1797, Wilkinson wrote to Carondelet: "Philip Nolan will deliver this. It is to claim a grant of land within the limits of Louisiana, to which I may resort in case of necessity. Nolan will make the survey, and I pray that the grant *may issue* in his name."[3d]

In 1797 Nolan hired Jesse Cook, who had been a merchant at Islas Negras[3e] and who was to stay with Nolan to the end. Then in March, 1797, Nolan proposed to Gayoso a scheme to make a great deal of money for them both:

> When last at San Antonio, I got acquainted with the governor of *La Colonia* and had some conversation with him on the practicability of introducing a cargo of merchandise by *sea* to his capital, St. Anter [San Antonio].
>
> He [Muñoz] is a rich commercial man and did not discourage the idea.
>
> Dry goods, *there*, would command a profit *in cash* of one hundred

[3c] Ellicott has been referred to a number of times—but the U.S. surveyor was Major Andrew Ellicott. He finished running Mason and Dixon's line, surveyed the District of Columbia, and was appointed by Washington as commissioner and surveyor to establish the 31° boundary provided by Pinckney's Treaty. He went to Natchez in 1796 and was on the job some five years, but nowhere do we find any references to a James Ellicott. However, second- and third-hand names often got twisted by Spanish correspondents. See Catherine Van Cortlandt Mathews, *Andrew Ellicott, His Life and Letters.*

[3d] Wilkinson to Baron, Fort Washington, Sept. 22, 1796; Papeles de Cuba, leg. 2375. It appears that Nolan was a surveyor. We have found no evidence that such a grant was made.

[3e] Islas Negras, or Black Islands, has not been easy to pinpoint. In Pichardo, *Limits of Louisiana and Texas,* III, 334, it is said to be an Indian pueblo on the road from Canada to New Mexico; in *ibid.*, III, 301, it is said to be on the banks of the Mississippi (in 1689); in Mattie Austin Hatcher, *The Opening of Texas to Foreign Settlement, 1801–1821,* 167, it is said that Girardeau lay within its boundary while St. Louis did not (De Nava to Alcudia, Nov. 3, 1795; A.G.I., México, leg. 18, No. 5); we have just seen that Samuel P. Moore said that, from Texas, Nolan was going to the Black Islands and then to Kentucky.

pr. cent, and a large batteau (calculated for coasting), would carry 100 thousand dollars worth of such goods as are suitable for that country.

Properly recommended by yr. Excellency and the Baron [Carondelet], I have not a doubt but I can make an arrangement with him that at *one stroke* will make our fortune. I can command merchandise. I require nothing but your Excellency's protection, counsel, and advice, and will consider you entitled to *half the profits.*

If this plan should meet your Excellency's approbation, I would set out immediately and return in time to perform the voyage next winter.

Yr. Excell. most devoted servant,

PHILIP NOLAN[3f]

Nolan must have been fairly sure of his ground, but it seems a brash thing to do, for in June, 1796, Nolan had spoken to Wilkinson of "suspicions that were nearly fatal to me." Since Spain and England were at war in 1797, and Louisiana officials expected the British to come down from Canada, it seems that Spanish officials may have suspected Nolan of being a spy for the British. Certainly there is no question that this letter from Nolan proposes a four-way conspiracy—or perhaps a two-way conspiracy, since he offered Gayoso half the profit—perhaps relying on Gayoso to persuade Carondelet. It is noticeable that Nolan indicates that Muñoz is a wealthy merchant, and the whole proposition does not provide a very flattering atmosphere for Muñoz and Gayoso.

The next move was from Gayoso, in a letter also written in March and dated at Natchez. The date is hard to decipher, but it may have been the 13th:

Mr. Philip Nolan, I require that you will explicitly answer the following question: What political interest do you embrace? And what

[3f] Nolan to Gayoso, Natchez, Mar. 13 or 14, 1787; photostats in University of Texas Archives. It appears that Gayoso accepted the proposition; see his letter to Wilkinson, Natchez, Apr. 1, 1797, printed in Grace King, "The Real Philip Nolan," in Louisiana Historical Society *Publications*, Vol. X (1917), 99. It is hardly necessary to point out that Nolan, in writing the letter, must have had reason to believe that Gayoso would be receptive—though this does not, of course, convict Gayoso. An interesting question could be asked as to Nolan's reason for writing Gayoso in a letter dated at Natchez. A copy of this letter in Papeles de Cuba, leg. 213, dated Mar. 14, 1797, bears no place name.

interest do you regard with indifference or for which you would take an active part?[3g]

Such a peremptory letter may not have sat well with Nolan. It was a very tricky game being played among Nolan, Carondelet, and Gayoso, but Carondelet granted a passport for the fourth trip, and Nolan wrote Wilkinson in April, 1797:

> I have got such a passport that I apprehend neither risk nor detention. I have instruments to enable me to make a more correct map than the one you saw [which he had given to Carondelet—or a copy thereof]. Ellicott assisted me in acquiring a more perfect knowledge of astronomy and glasses; and Gayoso himself made me a present of a portable sextant. My timepiece is good. I shall pay every attention, and take an assistant with me who is a tolerable mathematician.[3h]

Apparently Carondelet was still on Nolan's side, and perhaps Carondelet's motivation is revealed by Nolan's letter to Samuel P. Moore: he said the Baron expected him to make discoveries, and give him plans and information of the country—but Nolan added, "I shall take good care to give him no information, unless such as may be calculated to mislead him."[3i] Nolan was devious.

The United States and France were fighting then on the sea, and there was some fear that Spain would be drawn in against the United States—so strong a fear that President Adams organized a "New Army" on the Ohio, destined to invade Spanish Louisiana under the command of Alexander Hamilton. Under these explosive conditions, Nolan again wrote to Wilkinson (according to Wilkinson), and said that Gayoso was "a vile man and my implacable enemy. . . . I may yet be obliged to shoot the monster with a poisoned arrow. . . . The baron has given me every credential. . . . Gayoso is appointed governor-general."[3j]

[3g] Gayoso to Nolan, Natchez, Mar. [13?], 1797; Papeles de Cuba, leg. 213. It is regrettable that the date is not clear, for the implications if written after Nolan's letter are quite different from the implications if written before. Perhaps, in the light of what is to come, a good guess is that the 13th is the correct date.

[3h] Nolan to Wilkinson, Apr. 24, 1797; in Wilkinson, *Memoirs,* II, Appendix II. The passport, issued June 17, 1797 (supposedly after his letter to Wilkinson), is in Historia, vol. 413. It will be observed that Nolan was rather well educated, and apparently always willing to commit his thoughts to paper.

[3i] Deposition of Samuel P. Moore, in Wilkinson, *Memoirs,* II, Appendix III.

[3j] Nolan to Wilkinson, Natchez, July 21, 1797; Wilkinson, *Memoirs,* II, appen-

The day after Nolan wrote that letter (in July, 1797), he left on his fourth trip to Texas. He went to Nacogdoches and renewed his friendship with Antonio Leal and Gertrudes. Then from San Antonio he made another move in the dangerous game: he wrote Gayoso a letter that itself should have reminded him there were basic differences between the two men:

> From your Excellency's desire *(just as we parted)* [Italic in this letter indicates underscoring by Nolan] to *communicate everything* I may hear, I find that I was not understood. When I said that I would be employed as a *warrior* and not a *negotiator*, I meant that I would do what is honourable and detest everything mean. He that is capable to betray, *even the confidence of an enemy*, is unworthy your protection or esteem, and I lament that yr. Excellency has misunderstood me.
>
> I will take the first opportunity to inform Mr. Ellicott that *I am a Spaniard* and that the part I have already acted was with a view to promote the interest of both countries.
>
> If your Excellency thinks proper to employ me against the British on the Missouri, or any other enterprize that may be honourable, I flatter myself you will find your confidence not misplaced—with sentiment of attachment and esteem I have the honor to be
>
> Yr. Excelly. obt. servant,
>
> PHILIP NOLAN[3k]

Nolan is giving Gayoso some high-level double-talk.

In November, 1797, Nolan asked Nava, the commandant-general of the Interior Provinces, for permission to stay in Texas ten more months. He was still in San Antonio next spring—but he pushed his luck too far. In the spring of 1798 he asked permission to go to Nueva Santander; Nava referred the request to the viceroy—and it happened that the Baron of Carondelet was in Mexico City on his way to Quito. Carondelet's evidence was in Nolan's favor but not very reassuring, and Nava told the Texas governor to get rid of Nolan—who set out in July with horses and burros.

dix, doc 2. Had Gayoso rejected Nolan's conspiracy in contemptuous terms? If so, why did Gayoso not write the news to Carondelet?

[3k] Nolan to Gayoso, Monday 13th [Nov. 13, 1797]; Papeles de Cuba, leg. 188–2. The year is not given, but the only Mondays that fall on the thirteenth between Nolan's departure and Gayoso's death are in November, 1797, August, 1798, and May, 1799—and it appears that 1797 is a good guess.

The period of 1798–1800 is not clear; perhaps Nolan stayed at Nacogdoches to help Gertrudes watch his horses. Nevertheless, in a series of letters written by Gayoso in January, October, and November, 1798, while Gayoso was governor-general of Louisiana, Gayoso proposed to go into partnership with Wilkinson, Minor, Joseph Collins, and Nolan, to bring livestock across the Mississippi from Texas and split the profits four ways. So apparently in November, 1798, in spite of their differences, Gayoso had not yet taken steps to bar Nolan from Texas.[4]

However, when Nolan finally reached Natchez in mid-1799, he learned from Daniel Clark that Gayoso by that time had sent a letter to the viceroy (or to the governor, or both) advising Nolan's arrest,[4a] and that Nolan would have been arrested in San Antonio but that Muñoz, the governor, had died July 27, 1799, and that his mail had not been opened.

Nolan apparently had driven one thousand horses to Natchez and left fifteen hundred in Nacogdoches. Then, immediately upon hearing about Gayoso's letter, he sent Jesse Cook to drive the remaining horses from Nacogdoches—and also gave him a letter for Gertrudes:

> My very esteemed and beloved Gertrudis:
>
> I owe to Davenport $20, which do me the favor to pay and ask him for some papers of my arbitration with Murdock [a man with whom Nolan had been in partnership]. If by chance, alas, you are embarrassed by the going of the horses, do not pay the debt, keep the money for your own use.
>
> That little girl Shabus wrote me.
>
> Arocha has come from St. Antonio and alas there is much trouble. It appears to me it will be necessary to freight a house to Nacogdoches for the time until I send a carpenter to make one.[4b] In all the

[4] This incriminating series of letters from Gayoso to Estevan Minor, Jan. 10, Oct. 23, and Nov. 29, 1798, is in the Gayoso papers in the Department of Archives, Library of Louisiana State University; there is also a letter from Ellicott to Timothy Pickering on the subject, dated at Pensacola June 18, 1799, in the Southern Boundary mss. in the National Archives.

[4a] Apparently he had been moved by the unfriendliness of the officials to change his headquarters from San Antonio to Nacogdoches. We can only speculate on the reason for this turnabout on the part of Gayoso. Gayoso had previously expressed his doubts of Nolan—and when strong, wilful men are engaged in illegal activities . . . Perhaps it is a good guess that Nolan, for some reason, backed out of the deal or tried to leave Gayoso out of it—which would leave Gayoso in the very tender position of having agreed to a conspiracy but having later been spurned.

months between I will send more goods and money if I am able to get them.

Have no anxiety. When I have a dollar I will give the half to thee.

The little Negress can expect the flowered silk.

In thee I have much confidence and thou mayst send to me with all liberty. I hope in the course of the year to come by to Natchez on return from the colonies.[4b] By the coming year I shall have a house and shall have the greatest pleasure in seeing thee. I am enough embarrassed now in paying my debts and hope that the horses that will be brought from the colony the coming year will help me.

If thou dost command me or if thou desirest I will go to Nacogdoches to see thee in these colds though this composition is the cause of not having gone now.

Write me all thou thinkest and desirest and believe me with all thine heart.

Many memories to the little girl. When thou goest lead the horse sent the little girl by me to Natchez.

Farewell my dear Gertrudis. Write me all and send to Nacogdoches, and write my scrivener also.

Thy most constant, NOLAN.

If thou dost not, alas, trust to write of secret things, thou canst say them to Mr. Cook.[5]

It is one of the most eloquent love letters of the times.

Gayoso himself had written a rather eloquent letter to the governor of Texas to advise Nolan's arrest. He said that Nolan's knowledge of the country might be injurious to the Spanish Empire; that Nolan was "a consummate hypocrite who made fun of the religion when he lived in the territory of the United States while, on the other hand, he professed the Catholic religion when he found himself amongst us" (the ultimate crime, of course, that no good Spaniard could overlook). Gayoso also said that he believed Nolan had "a commission from General Wilkinson to make an expert reconnaissance of the country, since he is as skilful in the forest as the most skilful Indians."[6]

[4b] That is, from Kentucky and his conference in Philadelphia, probably, with Jefferson.

[5] *Publications* of the Mississippi Historical Society, IV, 318–19. Who was the "little girl Shabus"? A daughter of Gertrudes? And how unusual it was that a "little girl" in that primitive area could write a letter! To whom does "my scrivener" refer?

[6] Nava to Berenguer, Nov. 25, 1800; Historia, vol. 413. At this point, it is fitting

The wheels had been set in motion, and Nolan knew it—but there occurred another incident that nobody might have foreseen. Gayoso went on an all-night drinking bout with Wilkinson and was drunk under the table; in fact, he died from it, in the same month that Governor Muñoz died in Texas. Gayoso was succeeded by Casa Calvo, and Nolan paid his respects to the new governor and made a good impression.[7]

At Natchez, however, another strange thing occurred: Nolan began to pay court to Frances Lintot, a sister-in-law of Steven Minor—and that promised trouble, for Frances Lintot's family was very high society in Natchez. Therefore, the family frowned on Nolan, even though—judging from his letters—he was not uncouth. The family forbade Frances' seeing him, but the usual thing happened: they were married in late 1799.[8]

In the following May, Nolan prepared to go East to tell what he knew of Texas to Thomas Jefferson, and Wilkinson wrote a recommendation to the President, saying:

> In the Bearer of this Letter—Mr. P. Nolan, you will behold the Mexican traveller, a specimen of whose discoveries, I had the Honor to submit to you in the Winter 1797, Mr. N—s subsequent excursions have been more extensive, & his observations more accurate. He feels pride in offering Himself to your investigation, and I am persuaded you will find pleasure, in his details of a Country, the Soil, clime, population, improvements & productions of which are so little known to us.[9]

---

to point out that the letter from Nolan to Wilkinson, July 21, 1797, which spoke of "shooting the monster with a poisoned arrow," does not altogether ring true with Nolan's other letters; the phrase "vile and implacable man" does not at all sound like Nolan, who spoke in more circumspect terms. Inasmuch as the letter of July 21 is on the strength of Wilkinson, it may be that Wilkinson wrote it for purposes of his own. The true story of Philip Nolan remains difficult to work out because of such doubts on material presented only by Wilkinson.

[7] Casa Calvo said he was young, Irish, friendly, capable, benevolent, and persuasive: Casa Calvo to ————, New Orleans, Nov. 18, 1800; A. H. N., Estado, leg. 3901.

[8] For more details on this episode, see King, "The Real Philip Nolan," in *Publications* of the Louisiana Historical Society, Vol. X (1917).

[9] Wilkinson to Jefferson, "Head Quarters on the Mississippi, Fort Adams," May 22, 1800. Fort Adams had been set up near Natchez to await the occupation of Natchez by Americans. It is noticeable that Wilkinson speaks of more than "droves of wild horses." In this connection, an interesting sentence appears in a letter from William

The details of Nolan's meeting with the President are not known, but the meeting probably took place in June, 1799, and then Nolan returned to Natchez, courted and married Frances Lintot, and then began to prepare for his fifth trip to Texas, organizing men and equipment. But José Vidal, commandant at Concordia, the Spanish fort across the Mississippi from Natchez, learned of the preparations and complained about Nolan to the American authorities, who called Nolan to account on a charge of filibustering. Nolan appeared before Winthrop Sargent, governor[10] of Mississippi Territory, and Col. Peter Bryan Bruin,[10a] judge of the superior court, in a proceeding that was reported by Vidal to Casa Calvo:

> The principal judge commenced by charging Nolan with the damage that I had alleged; to which he [Nolan] answered that it was true that he was preparing with some people to go to the other side of the river, and that he considered himself authorized to do so in view of a letter from Don Pedro de Nava written in 1798, which he presented, which contained a paragraph that I have seen [which] said in substance "that he would be pleased to see a map from Nolan that would show the communications between the provinces of Mexico and that of Louisiana; that because he was concerned with mustangs, he [Nava] had already given an order to Muñoz, the governor of San Antonio, that he should let him catch them."
>
> When I finished reading, I represented to the judges the following:
>
> That the permission that Philip Nolan produced, I considered of no force, because it should comprehend only the time during which Nolan

Dunbar to Jefferson, Natchez, Aug. 22, 1801, in which he says: "I have received some imperfect account from Mr. Nolan and his man who instructed us in the signs [i.e., Indian sign language], of an uncommon Animal having been seen by the Natives in a considerable lake in a sequestered situation in New Mexico." It is perhaps one of the few sea-serpent stories of the Southwest—but why was Nolan in New Mexico, or why did he say he had been there? A moment later, Dunbar says: "Mr. Nolan informed me that he was once very near that lake." Both these letters were printed in *Southwestern Historical Quarterly*, Vol. VII, No. 4 (April, 1904).

[10] Sargent, born in Massachusetts, served through the Revolution and later became governor of Missisippi Territory; said to be a sour and unpleasant man who was a friend of Nolan, according to Claiborne (who is extremely biased against Ellicott), in *Mississippi as a Province, Territory, and State*, 161. Sargent died in New Orleans in 1820.

[10a] Colonel Peter Bryan Bruin also was friendly to both Nolan and Ellicott. See Kinnaird, "American Penetration Into Spanish Louisiana," in *New Spain*, 348. Vidal called Bruin judge of the supreme court and Sargent the *promotor fiscal*.

was in those places the last time; that it was indisputable that Nolan had been forced to leave those countries as a fugitive, and that [alone] was enough to imply that Nolan's trip would be very disagreeable to my government—particularly [Nolan's] taking armed men—and foreigners—to places where it was prohibited—which could well indictate hostilities rather than the peaceful pursuit which he pretended to say was the object of his trip. Nolan answered that the armed men whom he was taking were for defense against the outlaws and to hunt for their maintenance and that of his party; that his intentions were solely to recover the animals that he had left behind, and to return without molesting anybody.

In view of these and other exchanges that passed between Nolan and me, the principal judges said, addressing the following to me: "Señor, the American government wishes to do all justice to the Spanish government, and nothing would satisfy me better than that this occasion should offer that of showing my good inclinations in fulfillment of this important obligation. You have discharged your duty in showing us what has come to your attention, [but] what is expressed in your representations is outside our power and contrary to the Constitution of the United States—to hinder its citizens who go forth from the territory when it cannot be proved under oath that their intentions are hostile." I observed then that this could never be verified because it would be easy for whoever might intend to violate his Majesty's territory to guard it [the intention] with the greatest secrecy, and in this way to keep himself safe from all prosecution. He answered to this that if there were a hundred or two hundred armed men in that territory, then the number would afford sufficient suspicion so that measures could be taken with them. I could not do less than answer him that I could not understand why [there was] no existing law to hinder thirty or forty, when he had already advised me that he could detain a greater number.

He replied that in such a case as he had indicated, it [his action] would be governed only by the circumstances, and he continued speaking. Mr. Nolan assured him that his aims were not hostile, that he was going to those countries, considering himself authorized to do so; but if such a confession was not truth, he ought to know that if he should commit hostilities in that country, he was subject to suffer the punishment that the Spanish government might consider suitable, and that if, fleeing from it [the punishment], he should enter the territory of the United States, he would still be at the requisition of the Spanish government. The *promotor fiscal* added that if it should be proved that Nolan was going to disturb the peace among those Indians, breaking an article of the treaty between his Majesty and the United States, the most lamentable consequences would result. The said judge concluded by assuring me that the cause remained open and that if at any time I could produce proof of the hostile intentions of Nolan's trip or of any other impropriety, he would with the greatest resolution administer the most rigorous justice that the matter might require, and that my complaint in time should produce the necessary results.

On the following day I received the answer of the governor, which original I enclose to you under No. 2, and under No. 3 a copy of the protest that Philip Nolan made.

Also it appeared appropriate to me to communicate with the commandant of Nakedoch [Natchitoches or Nacogdoches? ], which you will please see in the confidential copy included under No. 4, which original I sent by the forest guard of this post to the commandant of Rapides, to whom I wrote that I was directing it to the commandant of Natchitoches, and to that one [the commandant of Natchitoches] that I remitted it to that [the commandant] of Nagedoch [Nacogdoches], who without doubt will receive it in seven days from this post.

In spite of all these affairs, and in spite of the particular conversations that I have had with Nolan to keep him from carrying out his project, I have not obtained it [the cancellation of the project], notwithstanding that for some days he pretended to make me believe that he did not think he would go; but on the contrary he enlisted men, and I know some of them [are] determined and capable of following danger.

The propositions that Nolan made to his people are that he will give each one five horses if they are caught, and if not, they will have nothing to reclaim from him.[11]

Vidal had put the wheels in motion, and a few days after the trial Nolan wrote to Jesse Cook at Nacogdoches—a letter that was to prove Nolan's undoing:

I saw Santos this morning. He was in a hurry. He promised to stay until tomorrow, but I believe he has been employed to carry some intelligence of an intended voyage of mine to the westward, very much to my injury.

I intended to go to River Grand, leaving *a little* Nacogdoches to

[11] Joseph Vidal to Casa Calvo, Concordia, October 11, 1800, Papeles de Cuba, leg. 71-A.

the north, but the intelligence has gone before me—I must keep down near the sea to avoid the soldiers of Nacogdoches, who no doubt will set out in search of me. Keep this to yourself as you esteem my friendship.

I am taking a large quantity of goods. Everyone thinks that I go to catch wild horses, but you know that I have long been tired of wild horses. I expect to return by January.

From the best information I am well convinced that if you do not immediately on rect. of this set out for this place with your horses and as many of mine as you can collect, you and I will both lose all. Take my advice, my friend. Don't lose one moment in setting out—say everything to keep Gertrude in spirits; tell her that so soon as I will return, I will send by you everything she may want.

I find Vidal has some idea of the route I intend to take, and I know he has sent information to Nacogdoches, but fear nothing. I have good men and never will be taken. Come in, my friend, if you value your own safety.

I know the coast so well between Opelousas and River Grand[12] that it will be difficult to overtake or attack me. I have my matters so well arranged at Revilla[13] that I won't be detained two days. Burn this letter as soon as you read it. If Santos was not in such a hurry, I should send something to Gertrude, but I must defer it until another opportunity.

Your friend,

PHILIP NOLAN[14]

This is a damning letter, for he admits that he is not interested in wild horses. What, then, is left? Conquest.

Surely he did not expect to conquer Texas with a handful of men—though his later actions make one wonder. Did he expect the United States to invade Texas, and was he obtaining horses for a conquest? No,

[12] Apparently the Río Grande, and presumably he is speaking of the mouth of it; this means that he planned to go to Nuevo Santander if he should find it desirable.

[13] Revilla has not been identified, but it is spoken of more than once and appears to have been a port of entry either up- or downriver from Laredo. Apparently Nolan had bribed the commandant there.

[14] Nolan to Jesse Cook at Nacogdoches, Natchez, October 21, 1800, Papeles de Cuba, leg. 71-A (the original); also a copy certified by Félix Trudeau at Natchitoches; one certified by Layssard at Rapides; and one by Duralde at Opelousas, in Papeles de Cuba, leg. 217.

he said he was not interested in horses. Was he interested in robbing gold trains, as later alleged by Hannah Glasscock? It hardly seems consistent with Nolan's character. Whatever his motivation, so far his political aims are somewhat more obscure than his romantic objective.

And then the plot began to thicken, for one José de los Santos took a hand (could he have been a son of Gertrudes?), as Vidal advised the commandant at "Nakedoch" (probably Nacogdoches) on October 20:

> I have advised you by an express under date of the 6th of the current month that Philip Nolan of the United States was preparing with 30 or 40 Americans armed with rifles to go to those countries, and to take from them with force all the mustangs that he could find, and drive them to the territory of Natchez. . . .
>
> . . . Yesterday there arrived here José de los Santos from that post [Nakedoch], but without a passport from you, and by the confidential information that I had, I knew that he had come as an express to carry letters to Nolan from an American there called Cook, who without the least doubt will communicate to Nolan the state of things in that country, and he will not forget to tell him as a principal point that the garrison of the post under your command has been augmented to 70 men—which news the very same Santos confided to his friends here. This morning he presented himself to me, asking for a certificate that he has been married in the Territory of Natchez; and with this motive I took the occasion to learn from himself that it was true that he had carried letters from Cook to Nolan, but that his trip had reduced itself to seeking a certificate of marriage. As I did not trust his veracity, I did not dare to entrust him with this letter, and therefore I am sending it by an express with all diligence.
>
> I am informed that the said Cook several months ago transported a great quantity of merchandise from Natchez to that country, that he expects shortly to take from those countries and to drive to American territory a considerable number of horses, and that furthermore he is a great friend of Nolan, it being the opinion of some that he is a partner in business with Nolan; through which circumstances it very strongly appears that Cook or somebody—whoever it may be—is ignoring the precautions that you have taken. I understand there are some other foreigners in that post who cannot be trusted, whose aims are none other than to deceive our government while pretending the greatest modesty and hiding their duplicity, until they arrive at another abode,

where, relating their adventures and travels, they would revile the government that they leave, and unjustly lay before the public, blame upon the same officials. This is the case with all these people, . . .

At this instant I have just learned that Nolan carries with him a great quantity of merchandise to buy his way in Camargo and on the Río Grande, and that he will go to those places, following the coast along the Gulf of Mexico. This news I relate to you as I have acquired it, but what you can count on with assurance is that within three days without fail Nolan should leave for those countries with 30 determined Americans, armed with carbines and munitions, besides the Spaniards whom I have indicated to you and that the object of his voyage is difficult for me to find out, it being nevertheless presumable that a party of armed men with hostile aims cannot be led [without] acting in defiance of the rights of nations and of the right that is owed to the dominions of his Majesty.

I fear that the Louisianan does not deceive me when he assures me that he was going to return to his country, but I believe that Santos will verify it, and from him you can learn the names of the Spanish who go with Nolan, because to me he pretended to be ignorant of all, to the extent that he passed this day in their company, and without doubt will carry Nolan's answer to Cook.

[Vidal sends a copy of this letter to the governor of Louisiana, and requests that the commandant of Nacogdoches send a copy to the governor at San Antonio.][15]

On the same day (October 20), Vidal sent a letter to Luis De Blanc, the commandant at Attakapas, advising him that Nolan would pass near that post.[16]

As of October 25, Gertrudes de los Santos comes to life for the first and only time in a letter written by Valentin Layssard, commandant at Rapides, to Martin Duralde, commandant at Opelousas:

By an official letter from Don Joseph Vidal, captain and commandant of the post of Concordia across from Natchez, under date of the 22nd of the current month, he informs me that the man named Philip Nolan set out to introduce himself into the Interior Provinces without a passport but with a company of brigands. As

[15] Vidal to the commandant of Nakedoch [Natchitoches], Concordia, October 20, 1800, Papeles de Cuba, leg. 71-A.

[16] Vidal to commandant at Atakapas, Concordia, October 20, 1800, Papeles de Cuba, leg. 217.

I received this letter, there arrived a Spaniard who bore a packet of mail from Madame Leal, a resident of Nacogdoches, to the man Philip Nolan at Natchez; presuming that he [the Spaniard] was bearing papers relating to the enterprises of Nolan, I took steps to stop him and indeed found the various letters. . . .[16a]

On November 1 Vidal wrote to Casa Calvo with news that portended ominous things for Nolan. Hannah Glasscock had returned from Natchitoches with a copy of the letter from Nolan to Cook; Glasscock said that Nolan planned to rob trains of gold between San Antonio and Camargo. There is also a hint in Vidal's letter that Nolan is to be killed on sight.[17]

The net was beginning to draw tight, and it rather seems that Nolan was rushing headlong to disaster. Seemingly he had not yet left Natchez, and there was time for reconsideration. However, he had already sent a man down the river with merchandise, as Vidal advised the commandant at Nacogdoches on November 3.[18] Vidal apparently had an efficient spy system—and one wonders if Nolan ever gave that fact any thought. Somebody was reporting events in Natchez as fast as they happened.

In the letter of November 3, Vidal also revealed some information about the one ignored but important factor in the situation—the husband of Gertrudes—when he said that one of Nolan's confidantes was "one Leal of advanced age, a native of those countries, who came with Nolan the last time to Natchez; and both intend to come with a great drove of horses for the American territory, and that particularly the old man should bring those of Nolan, driving them in his name."

At any rate, Nolan proceeded with his expedition, whether or not he was aware of the official excitement. The exact date of his departure from Natchez is not known, but we can guess rather accurately, for on November 10 Vicente Fernández Tejeiro, the commandant at the post of Ouachita,[19] about one hundred miles north and a little west of

[16a] Layssard to Duralde, Rapides, Oct. 26, 1800; Papeles de Cuba, leg. 207 (a copy in French).

[17] Vidal to Casa Calvo, Concordia, November 1, 1800, Papeles de Cuba, leg. 71-A.

[18] Vidal to commandant of Nakedoch, Concordia, November 3, 1800, Papeles de Cuba, leg. 71-A.

[19] Ouachita Post, once known as Fort Miró, was on the Ouachita River at about present Bastrop in northeast Louisiana, some eighty miles north of Concordia; west and a little north of Nogales.

Concordia, wrote to Casa Calvo, saying that, "On the morning of the fifth . . . some neighbors had seen two Americans pass on horseback . . ." And later, at eight that morning, one of Tejeiro's men reported seeing thirty Americans on horseback, "all armed with pistols, saber, and carbine, [and] commanded by Philip Nolan, who was armed with saber, four pistols, and two carbines."

Nolan and his party passed to the north of the post of Ouachita, not molesting the Spaniards or any of their property or stock.

Tejeiro believed it to be "of the greatest importance to prevent . . . Nolan's return with the horses to the United States, as much to avoid this robbery and those that will follow if it turns out well, as because with this opportunity the Americans will acquire knowledge of all the entrances to and exits from the kingdom of Mexico, . . . ."[20]

Tejeiro's letter also reveals other bits of information. It establishes within a day or so the date of Nolan's crossing of the Mississippi. From Natchez to Nogales is about fifty miles, and from Nogales to Ouachita is roughly fifty miles; it may fairly be presumed that the Nolan party left Natchez or its vicinity on October 31 or November 1, took two days to Nogales, crossing the river on about November 2 or 3, then went on to Ouachita, where they were discovered on November 4.

An important part of that letter, also, relates to the equipment and arms carried by the men: they had pack animals, and all were armed with pistols, sabers, and carbines; Nolan had a saber, four pistols, and two carbines. To the practical Spaniards, such armament could mean but one thing: Nolan's men intended to attempt to conquer Texas.

In Tejeiro's letter, we find also an unpleasant side to Nolan's character, for Tejeiro quotes two letters from Nolan—one to Tejeiro and the other to the commandant:

> Sir
>
> As you have been misinformed with respect to my intentions, I take the liberty to solicit your attention for a few moments.
>
> I am destined for the province of Texas and not expecting to touch at any of the posts of your government. I have not provided myself with a passport, and knowing that you cannot with propriety

[20] Tejeiro to Casa Calvo, Ouachita, November 10, 1800, Papeles de Cuba, leg. 71-A.

permit me to go through your settlement, I have determined to pass to the north.

With profound respect . . . Novr 6th, half past 6.

The second letter is addressed to "The Commandant of Washetaw":

> Nolan presents his respectful compliments to Father Brady and requests on the score of their former friendship that he may in future keep his sexton employed in holy functions of the church, and not again as today alarm a party of defenseless and harmless travellers [!] with a cannon (not of the church) supposed to be loaded with *chain shott.*

Tejeiro says:

> I believe it is of the greatest importance to prevent, at all risk, Nolan's return with the horses to the United States, as much to avoid this robbery and those that will follow if it turns out well, as because with this opportunity the Americans will acquire a knowledge of all the entrances to and exits from the kingdom of Mexico, . . .

Another letter written by Vidal[21] provides some information that previously has been lacking: a definite reason for the Spanish government's determination to stop Nolan. We have already had indications that the Spaniards feared Nolan would turn his talents to the British cause, but now Spain has another reason for stopping him: to avoid the depredations by the Americans that must inevitably follow a successful outcome of Nolan's enterprise, and the implied aggression of the American nation—a chronic and thoroughly justified fear on the part of the Spaniards.

It is a very unpleasant picture we have of Nolan from the episode at Ouachita. Up to now we have excused his rash actions, because he has written courteous, respectful letters—but now he has cast discretion aside and revealed an unpleasant aspect of his character. What happened? Was he so put out with Gayoso that he recklessly decided to taunt the Spanish army? It does not seem likely. It may be more fruitful to speculate on his private life. He had married a girl in Natchez when he really was in love with Gertrudes; perhaps that marriage had not turned out very well; his continued thoughts of Gertrudes suggest it. He had left

[21] Vidal to Casa Calvo, Concordia, November 20, 1800, Papeles de Cuba, leg. 71-A.

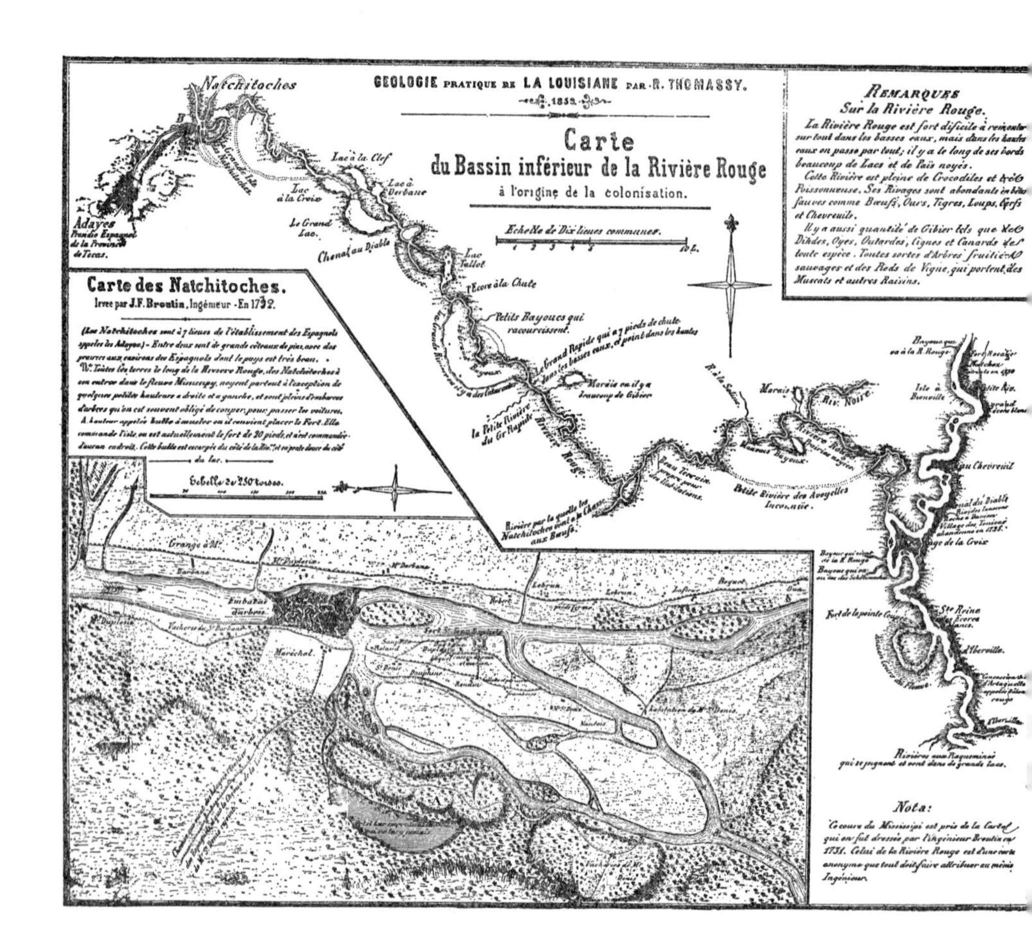


Natchitoches in 1732

Natchez without even a passport. Was he that fretful to rejoin Gertrudes? Was Antonio Leal putting up a barrier?

He was a young man, strong, virile, and healthy, and he was in love. He was not a man of iron will power, but rather of a dynamic will; he wanted what he wanted—and that was Gertrudes.

The matter of Nolan's entry was considered so important that on November 18 Casa Calvo advised Someruelos, the captain-general at Havana, of the dispositions that had been made to stop Nolan.[21a] He said also that he had known before Vidal of Nolan's departure, and that that information had come from the mouth of José de los Santos, a Spaniard.

On August 8, 1800, Nava had ordered Elguezábal to have Nolan arrested, and presently Elguezábal gave specific instructions to Lieutenant Miguel Francisco Músquiz, commandant at Nacogdoches, to intercept Nolan. (On December 22, Casa Calvo ordered Nolan's hostilities arrested, and sent fifty rifles and two hundred pounds of powder to Natchitoches.) Músquiz set out from Nacogdoches on March 4 with seventy regulars and fifty militiamen, guided by Tawakoni scouts, who located Nolan's camp on March 21. Nolan and his men were ragged, bearded, and hungry; they had been camped in this location some five months.

Músquiz and his men surrounded the camp on three sides and demanded surrender. When Nolan refused, two of his men deserted: Vicente Lara and Juan José Martínez. Four men were captured by the Spaniards: Refugio de la Garza, Francisco Berbán, Thomas House, and Stephen Richards. The siege, which had begun early in the morning, continued until nine o'clock, when Nolan was killed by a chance shot in the forehead. The other men fled from the camp; three were captured. Músquiz opened up with a small cannon, and another surrendered. Finally the rest of the party asked for terms, but when nothing was offered except unconditional surrender, they accepted. Nolan's body was buried by his two Negro slaves, but both ears were cut off and sent to Elguezábal in the care of William Barr.

Músquiz' report shows the names of twenty-four persons who accompanied Nolan: Spaniards: Luciano Garcia, Vicente Lara, Refugio

[21a] Casa Calvo to Someruelos, New Orleans, Nov. 18, 1800, No. 26, reservada; Papeles de Cuba, leg. 1573.

de la Garza, Juan Joseph Martínez, Lorenzo Ynojosa, Joseph Berban, and Joseph de Jesús de los Santos; Anglo-Americans: Simon Macoy, Jonas Walters, Salomon Cole, Elías Bin (Ellis P. Bean), Joseph Rid (Reed), William Doneley, Charles Yuin (King), Steven Rechar (Richards?), Joseph Pierce, Thomas Taus (House?), Ephraim Blackburn, David Fero, Juan Bautista (Nolan's Negro slave known as Caesar); escaped: Robert Ashley, John Taus, Michael Moore, and Robert (another Negro slave of Nolan).

The survivors of the Nolan party were sent to San Antonio in irons, then to San Luis Potosí (where they were in jail for sixteen months), and finally to Chihuahua, where they were put on trial five years after their capture. After the men were found guilty as charged, the penalty was left up to the king, who decreed that every fifth man be hanged. By that time there were only nine survivors, and they threw dice, blindfolded, on a drumhead, and it has been said, without authority, that Ephraim Blackburn threw the lowest number—a four—and was executed. At least two members of the party may be accounted for: Solomon Colly, or Nicholas Cole, was in Santa Fe when Pike got there in 1807; Ellis P. Bean eventually returned to Texas.

Who was the spy who kept Vidal so well informed of Nolan's affairs? His name came to light in August, 1802, when Vidal wrote to Manuel de Salcedo:

> Luis Eavans [Louis Evans?] has been *alguacil mayor* in the Territory of Mississippi, and I can do no less than advise you that when the defunct Nolan undertook that trip to the possessions of the kingdom of Mexico, the said Eavans gave me all the news that he could acquire under cover.[21b]

[21b] Vidal to Salcedo, Concordia, Aug. 9, 1802; Papeles de Cuba, leg. 77. E. E. Hale makes good use of these documents in "The Real Philip Nolan," in *Publications* of the Mississippi Historical Society, IV, 288–328. See also Kinnaird, "American Penetration Into Spanish Louisiana," in *New Spain,* 337–67, for material on Nolan; Historia, vol. 413, for several hundred pages on various Nolan affairs; Maurine Wilson, "Philip Nolan and His Activities," unpublished master's thesis, University of Texas, 1932; and many other sources. The affair was reviewed by the Consejo, and there was the inevitable Spanish checking-up on costs—which means many documents. According to the *Handbook of Texas,* after Nolan's death Leal and Gertrudes were arrested as Nolan's accomplices and were the defendants in one of the most famous trials in Texas history. Jesse Cook, Peter Longueville (long-time steward for Nolan), the commandant at Nacogdoches, the priest, and many others were required to testify. After

An important reason for sending such an impressive expedition after Nolan in March, 1801, was given by Casa Calvo to Berenguer, October 21, 1800. The long-standing fear of invasion from Canada, coupled with the trouble with Bowles in Florida, was enough to give real stature to the officials' fear of the British. A second factor, of course, was fear of the Americans, for the Spaniards knew that if a passage should be opened up, the Americans would pour in from Kentucky.

The fear of the Americans grew stronger. If one man and thirty armed followers could cause such turmoil in five provinces, reaching the commandant-general in Chihuahua, the viceroy in Mexico, the captain-general in Havana, the audiencia in Santo Domingo, the Council of the Indies in Seville, and even the king himself, it is possible to imagine the effects of a concerted effort to establish a trail between Kentucky and Texas. The northern frontier of New Spain was thoroughly aroused, and all subsequent activities of the Americans were met with suspicion: Wilkinson's advance to the Sabine River, Pike's expedition to Santa Fe, and the incursion of any other Americans into Spanish territory.

The Nolan affair had some important effects: it confirmed, for the Spaniards, the fears of American penetration; it aroused the Spanish frontier to frantic defensive action; and it sowed suspicions that would exist for a long time. It had also shown the hazy nature of Spanish thinking, the great desire to delay action as long as possible.

U. S. citizens, perhaps delayed by the Spanish reaction to Nolan, did not really start the penetration of Spanish territory until after the delivery of Louisiana to the United States on December 20, 1803 (in New Orleans) and March 10, 1804 (in St. Louis).

In May, 1803, the governor of Louisiana, Juan Manuel de Salcedo,[22] issued an order prohibiting the importation of cattle and horses

the trial, Leal and Gertrudes were ordered to move from Nacogdoches to Béxar. Leal died there about 1802, whereas Gertrudes married the commandant of Béxar—whom she survived. Inasmuch as Nolan was killed March 4, 1801, while many of the depositions of these witnesses are dated from January to April, 1801, it appears that this "trial" started as an investigation before Nolan was killed.

[22] Juan Manuel de Salcedo, governor of Louisiana, and Nemesio Salcedo y Salcedo, commandant-general of the Interior Provinces, were brothers; Manuel María de Salcedo was a son of Juan Manuel and was governor of Texas from 1808 until he was executed in 1813 by members of the Gutiérrez-Magee expedition.

into Louisiana from Texas.[23] A few months later, when Nolan's name arose in connection with the Ashley-House expedition to the Comanches, Nemesio Salcedo asked reinforcements from Nuevo León and Nuevo Santander.[24] It is a reflection of the changing Spanish attitude that some of those reinforcements arrived promptly; there was not, however any occasion to use them against the Ashley-House party.

In December, 1803, the United States took possession of New Orleans and Lower Louisiana and immediately, because of the vagueness of the treaty, claimed all territory as far west as the Río Grande and north to the source of the Mississippi River. Spain maintained silence for the moment, but finally in January took a definite stand concerning the boundary line. She said the Missouri River was the boundary, and orders were issued that Spanish commandants were not to give up any posts on the Missouri. It may be, however, that the order never reached Salcedo in Chihuahua; we have found no record of it.

In January, 1804, Casa Calvo wrote a rather surprising letter to Cevallos in which he urged that Cevallos take the measures that he deemed advisable "in order to avoid having the west side of the Mississippi from its mouth up past the river St. Pierre remain in other hands than those of our government."[25]

Casa Calvo also arranged for a French clergyman and traveler, Claude C. Robin, to make a trip up the Mississippi, the Red, and the Washita Rivers to the post of Ouachita, to furnish information for the use of Casa Calvo.[26] The clergyman reported that American immigrants did not represent a real threat, and that he felt that it was an appropriate time for Spain to show resistance to any such penetration.

Spanish commandants were ordered to hold their posts on the Missouri River, and a royal order was issued in March, 1804, from the Council for Fortification and Defense of the Indies, to the effect that the line between Texas and Louisiana should begin at the gulf between Caricut, or Carcasen, and the Armentu, or Mermento, River,

[23] Manuel de Salcedo to Félix Trudeau, New Orleans, May 18, 1803, Papeles de Cuba, leg. 76.

[24] Salcedo to Yturrigaray, October 13, 1803, A.G.M., Sección California, Vol. 22.

[25] Casa Calvo to Cevallos, New Orleans, January 13, 1804, Papeles de Cuba, Estados de Misisipi; printed in Robertson, *Louisiana, Under the Rule of Spain, France, and the United States, 1785–1807*, II, 162–67.

[26] Cox, *Early Explorations*, 62.

and run north to the Red near Natchitoches; from there, it says, the limits of both Texas and New Mexico extend much farther than the Missouri River; it appears also that the *junta* had decided on January 19 that the confluence of the Missouri and the Mississippi rightfully belonged to Spain, as well as did both banks of the Missouri, and that American navigation should be stopped.[27] Although it was believed then that the Missouri rose in the Southwest, it nevertheless seems that the *junta* was taking in a considerable piece of territory.

In July, 1804, Casa Calvo wrote to Pedro Cevallos, the first secretary of state, saying that no time should be lost in reinforcing the Interior Provinces, and commenting further:

> . . . It is not true, as supposed, that the system of administration of the United States does not lend itself to collecting great contributions in order to establish an army and a considerable navy for greater undertakings. For three months after taking possession of this province the American Governor (Guillermo) C. C. Claiborne, assured that the collection of customs duties will be sufficient to cover the expenses of the government which already maintains in the province a corps of eight hundred to one thousand troops and the employees for the administration of justice and the collection of revenues [*rentas*] at much greater salaries than those our government paid. Thus the customs collectors alone, who are also more numerous [than ours were], have a monthly pay of 60 pesos without other gratifications.
>
> [He points out the facility with which the American troops move, and] the frugality with which these people travel a hundred or two hundred leagues with no other aids than a sack of cornmeal and flask of powder. . . .[28]

He then—perhaps to justify his position as boundary commissioner—goes into a discussion of historical limits, not neglecting to point out that France always intentionally left boundary descriptions vague, and that she profited by doing so. He thinks the United States will have a post on the Pacific Ocean within five years.

[27] Junta de Fortificationes y Defensa de Indias, Madrid, March 17, 1804, copied at New Orleans, September 30, 1804, and at Chihuahua, April 22, 1805, in New Mexican Archives, doc. 1816.

[28] Casa Calvo to Ceballos, New Orleans, July 25, 1804, Papeles de Cuba, leg. 2368; also cited by Cox, *Early Explorations*, 157. At that time, of course, Casa Calvo was no longer governor.

Also in July, Elguezábal, governor of Texas, wrote to Casa Calvo about President Jefferson's three proposed expeditions along the Red, Arkansas, and San Francisco rivers and urged that Casa Calvo stop the proposed exploration of the Red, even though part of it, he concedes, belongs to the United States; he thinks that the other two rivers are within American territory.[29]

Also in July, 1804, Captain Turner, the American commander by that time at Natchitoches, informed Governor W. C. C. Claiborne, of Louisiana, that an American named Sanders had gone five hundred miles up the Red River to the Pani (and Taovaya?) Indians and had found them eager to trade with Americans. Sanders was chased by the Spaniards, but he evaded them and reached Natchitoches in safety.[30] In October, three American traders were killed by Indians near Natchitoches[31]—very likely, it seems, at Spanish instigation.

Jefferson had for many years gathered information about Louisiana Territory, but he had begun making more active efforts in July, 1803, soon after the territory was acquired by the United States. In August he felt that Louisiana included the principal streams of the Mississippi and the Missouri,[32] and three months later he wrote to Meriwether Lewis and mentioned some of the projects he had in mind: exploration of the Red and the Arkansas; exploration of the Pani [Platte] and the Padouca [Kansas]; exploration of the Moingona [Des Moines] and the St. Peters [Minnesota]. All those, he emphasized, were distinct from the mission of Lewis and Clark. In March, 1804, Jefferson wrote to William Dunbar in Mississippi, a scientist, about the Red–Washita expedition. Jefferson appointed Dr. George Hunter, of Philadelphia (a chemist), to accompany the expedition, but Hunter caused delay, and nobody did anything in Louisiana pending Hunter's arrival; then the expedition was postponed because of threatened hostility from the Osage Indians and because Salcedo had, the preceding May, issued an order that no American should be permitted to mark the boundaries of Lou-

29 Elguezábal to Casa Calvo, San Antonio, August 3, 1804, Papeles de Cuba, leg. 141.

30 Turner to Claiborne, July 16, 1804, in W. C. C. Claiborne, *Official Letter Books of* ——, *1801–1816*. Cited by Isaac Joslin Cox, "The Louisiana-Texas Frontier, II," *Southwestern Historical Quarterly*, Vol. XVII, No. 2 (October, 1913), 156.

31 Claiborne to Madison, October 5, 1804; cited by Cox, *Early Explorations*, 157.

32 Cox, *ibid.*, 42–43.

isiana or even to approach the frontier of Texas.[33] Dunbar then proposed that he and Hunter explore the Washita River and the Hot Springs at its head. They made the start in October, 1804, completed the trip without incident, and returned in February, 1805.[34]

During the winter of 1804, President Jefferson received information about the Red River from another man: Dr. John Sibley, who had left the East because of marital difficulties. Sibley was prone to exaggeration, and he was very effective at publicizing himself—but he attracted the President's attention, and gave him a rather complete report of settlements and rivers in Lower Louisiana (not in Texas) as seen through the eyes of an untrained observer. He was appointed surgeon for the army post at Natchitoches and was acting Indian agent. He served in these capacities for a number of years, and he gained the reputation, among the Spaniards, of being a revolutionary. His reports were important because they stirred Jefferson to go ahead with the exploration of the Red River.

In May, 1805, Jefferson began to organize such an expedition—to go up the Red River and to descend it rather than cross to the Arkansas. Claiborne obtained a passport from Casa Calvo, but the expedition was not to get under way for some time.

Casa Calvo left New Orleans early in 1806; Jefferson was already working on the Red River expedition. Sibley had traveled on the Red River within American territory, but Jefferson wanted to know something about the upper reaches, and the leadership of the party fell to Lieutenant Freeman. In April, with thirty-seven men, he went upriver and passed Natchitoches. Sibley notified him that Spanish soldiers from Natchitoches would intercept him, but Freeman and his men continued upstream, detouring the Great Raft in their boats—possibly the first time it had been done by boat. Somewhere past the mouth of Little

[33] Salcedo to governor of Texas, May 3, 1804, Bexar Archives; cited by Cox, *ibid.*, 45.

[34] Cox, *ibid.*, 47–51. Caso Calvo describes Dunbar as a Scotsman of Natchez, formerly of Baton Rouge, "very much in sympathy with our government"; "a great mathematician and very interested in natural Philosophy, gentle, and consequently respected by all"; an intimate friend of Gayoso de Lemos, governor of Natchez; a friend of Thomas Power, employed on the boundary commission. He describes Power as having a vast local knowledge of the interior provinces; as possessing energy and sagacity, and speaking several languages, especially English (though he was a native of the Canary Islands). Casa Calvo has appointed Power to accompany Dunbar.

River, some two hundred miles above Natchitoches, he met a Spanish force under Francisco Viana; since the Americans were outnumbered five to one, they withdrew and went back down the river to avoid a conflict. Freeman had gone up the Red about six hundred miles, not much farther than the French had occupied it.

Freeman had failed by two hundred miles to reach the Pani Piqués, and by several hundred miles to reach the headwaters of the Red, but he had had no orders to fight, and it rather seems, from the determined opposition of the veteran Viana, that it would have been disastrous if he had tried to force his way past them.

Sibley, from time to time acting as Indian agent, eventually had become something of a factotum at Natchitoches. He had already been characterized by Salcedo as "a revolutionary, a friend of new [ideas?], and an enemy *a cerrimo* [to the greatest extreme?] of the public peace."[35]

All in all, in the early part of 1806 the events along the Louisiana-Texas border, aside from Freeman's expedition, created a tense situation. The Spaniards were ordered to keep the Americans east of the Arroyo Hondo; the Americans claimed the land all the way to the Sabine River and ordered the Spaniards not to cross that river; the Spaniards established a post to hold the Arroyo Hondo; both sides were suspicious and alert.

General Wilkinson, meanwhile, in his capacity of commander-in-chief of the United States Army, had made the Neutral Ground Agreement with Colonel Herrera (after the Spaniards had mobilized some 1,200 men), creating a Neutral Zone (sometimes called the Twilight Zone) between the Sabine River and the Arroyo Hondo,[36] so that Spaniards and Americans would be less likely to come into conflict in such ways as those mentioned by Salcedo in his letter of February 23. Such a neutral zone pretty well precluded any expedition up the Red River, even though Jefferson later contemplated sending Freeman up the river again (but did not do so primarily because of the lack of funds).

As to the reason or reasons for Nolan's building a fort in the middle of Spanish territory, we have not yet given a complete answer. An ex-

[35] Salcedo to Yturrigaray, Chihuahua, July 16, 1805, Provincias Internas, Vol. 239, ff. 126–36.

[36] Marshall, *A History of the Western Boundary*, 30.

planation cannot hold up on the ground of Nolan's stupidity, for Nolan was well acquainted with Spanish laws, and it can hardly be imagined that he believed the Spaniards would complacently allow him to establish a strong point of armed men for any purpose whatsoever. As to Gertrudes: she must have been quite a women (to Nolan, at least), but—even assuming Nolan to have been thoroughly in love—that explanation has flaws, the principal flaw being that he could have had her without building a fort; he could have taken her with him on the trip. No, these speculations are pretty thin. There is one, however, still unspoken. Nolan said he was not interested in horses, that he had his sights on bigger things. And since he himself made no move to effect an active conquest of Texas, is it reasonable to suppose that James Wilkinson was in the background, that Nolan's mission was to go into central Texas and establish a fortified point from which Nolan's men could threaten the entire state while Wilkinson's column came down from Kentucky? Perhaps we shall never know, but it would not be inconsistent with James Wilkinson's multifarious ambitions.

If so, why didn't Wilkinson follow through? Perhaps from lack of resolution. More than once Wilkinson sent out a man to open the way and then failed to support him. Aaron Burr is the best-known example: Wilkinson sent him out as advance agent, and then, when circumstances changed, Wilkinson denounced Burr to clear himself.

It would be thirteen years before another United States expedition would travel in Louisiana Territory. Somebody did, however, have designs on Santa Fe: that same man of many parts, James Wilkinson, who on his own, without higher authorization, sent Zebulon Montgomery Pike to Santa Fe. A number of Pike's men were imprisoned in Chihuahua, and their treatment stirred that righteous resentment that Americans have always been quick to muster.

Pike's expedition would be important because it would open the way for many others, including that of Jacques Clamorgan, the first man to take trade goods to Santa Fe and make a profit.

The United States never forgot Santa Fe. When George C. Sibley wrote to Samuel H. Sibley in January, 1809, he said: "Should we go to war with England, and Spain should also declare against us, it is likely that this [Fort Osage] will be a rallying post from whence to attack Santa Fee, we could march there and Seize their rich mines in less than 20 days. And I have no doubt if we have a war, but seize them we shall. To those who look upon Wealth as a chief good, here is a field worth their attention. 20 days or a month at farthest would place them within the very lap of fortune."[37]

Whenever men began to dream, Santa Fe was very much in their minds.

[37] George C. Sibley to Samuel H. Sibley, Fort Osage, January 18, 1809; Sibley MSS in Missouri Historical Society, quoted in *Missouri Historical Review,* Vol. XXXIV, No. 4 (July, 1940), 446.

# X

# *The Pike Period of Exploration, 1806–21*

The Pike expedition to Santa Fe, in 1807, was one prong of James Wilkinson's multiple machinations, and was closely connected with the Burr conspiracy.[1] But although there are many evidences that Wilkinson contemplated an attack on Mexico, most historians are agreed that there is no evidence that points to Zebulon Montgomery Pike as a conspirator with him.[2] It seems to most that Pike's actions were prompted by selfishness and vanity and carried out in stupidity—on which last count, certainly, it would not be hard to sustain a conviction.

Wilkinson became governor-general of Louisiana Territory (which by that time was Upper Louisiana only) in June, 1805, and was visited near St. Louis by Burr in September. Wilkinson long before had reached the conclusion that there were two important keys to Mexico: St. Louis for the approach via Santa Fe, and New Orleans for the left-flank approach through Texas. In 1805, then, Wilkinson was in St. Louis, and Aaron Burr went to New Orleans—but Wilkinson had started work on his New Mexican projects six weeks before Burr had visited him in St. Louis.

[1] I. J. Cox offers a brief but illuminating treatment of the origin of the Pike expedition in an article, "Opening of the Santa Fé Trail," *Missouri Historical Review*, Vol. XXV, No. 1 (October, 1930), 30–66, with particular attention to Wilkinson's motivations.

[2] Walter F. McCaleb, *The Aaron Burr Conspiracy*, proves Pike innocent; Stephen Harding Hart and Archer Butler Hulbert, *Zebulon Pike's Arkansaw Journal*, spend thirty-three pages explaining the integrity of Pike's actions; while Kyle S. Crichton, "Zeb Pike," *Scribner's Magazine*, (Vol. LXXXII, No. 4 [October, 1927], 462–67), finds no defense for him; and Thomas P. Abernethy, *The Burr Conspiracy*, seems to agree that Pike has much for which to answer.

Wilkinson, as usual, had many strings to his bow—one of the important ones being his personal interest in the fur trade on the upper Missouri. With that area in mind, he had taken with him to St. Louis an army captain named John McClallen, who brought a ton of trade goods supplied on credit by a merchant in Baltimore (for a piece of the enterprise), and shipped part way under the official frank of James Wilkinson to save freight charges. Those goods technically were the property of Wilkinson, but were in charge of McClallen; two of the officers in physical control of the shipment were Lieutenant George Peter, who seems to have had the strange impression that the whole affair was an honest piece of business (and who did not thereby make himself popular with the general), and Lieutenant Moses Hook, who replaced Peter. Lieutenant Hook had been asked by Meriwether Lewis to go with the Lewis and Clark expedition at a time when Lewis thought Clark was not going, but Hook had declined, making one of the worst guesses in history.

Within about thirty days after Wilkinson's arrival in St. Louis, he sent Lieutenant Peter and a military escort to the Osage country with Auguste Chouteau to investigate the water route to Santa Fe via the Osage River. Wilkinson's plan was to cross over to the Arkansas River and follow it to the mountains within one hundred miles of Santa Fe; and in September Wilkinson sent plans to the Secretary of War for a movement against New Mexico, and said, "If I do not [should not] reduce New Mexico at least in our campaign, I will forfeit my head."[3]

At about the same time (July 30, 1805), Wilkinson sent Pike to find the source of the Mississippi River, to reconnoiter the country with fur-trading in mind and to make friends with the Indian tribes; and he sent his son, Lieutenant James B. Wilkinson, to establish a fort at the mouth of the Platte River.[4] All this was accomplished by the end of October, 1805. Pike was back in St. Louis by the following April, and he immediately began to prepare for the Santa Fe trip, which was to be a military reconnaissance of the country between St. Louis and Santa Fe, with the secondary objective (or perhaps a primary objective) of open-

[3] Cox, "Opening of the Santa Fé Trail," *Missouri Historical Review*, Vol. XXV, No. 1 (October, 1930); Clarence E. Carter, "Burr-Wilkinson Intrigues in St. Louis," Missouri Historical Society *Bulletin*, Vol. X, No. 4, part I (July, 1954).

[4] Cox, *ibid.*, 43.

ing the Santa Fe Trail to commerce. At that time (mid–1806), Herrera and Wilkinson were having trouble along the Sabine, and obviously the gathering of information about the country between St. Louis and New Mexico was a legitimate military project. Also obviously Wilkinson could be expected to give himself whatever commercial advantages he could devise.

Pike left St. Louis on the Santa Fe trip on July 15, 1806, with Lieutenant Wilkinson, the general's son; Dr. John H. Robinson, who seems to have been Wilkinson's man, who joined the party as surgeon and who in New Mexico was entrusted with the rather informal claim of William Morrison against Baptiste Lalande for the goods Lalande had taken to Santa Fe in 1804. In addition to these three, there were one sergeant, two corporals, sixteen privates, an interpreter, and fifty-one Osage Indians who were returning home. The expedition was without any official sanction save that of Wilkinson himself.

Pike had hardly gotten started when Manuel Lisa came on the scene by having the sheriff arrest Pike's interpreter, a man named Vasquez, for a debt of three or four hundred dollars. Lisa was never a man to leave a stone unturned, and probably the arrest of Vasquez had as its purpose the delay of Pike's party. However, Vasquez managed to obtain his release (with Wilkinson's assistance?), and rejoined Pike a few days later. They were soon launched on a trip that came to resemble, for wildness, unpredictability, irresponsibility, and general haphazardness, the similar one made by that other stalwart self-promoter, John Charles Frémont, forty-two years later in almost exactly the same region—the San Juan Mountains of southern Colorado.

As with the Lewis and Clark expedition, however, the Pike exploration was to set off a series of other movements, and some of those on the expedition would be connected with later parties, until the spreading roads to Santa Fe began to resemble a hugely complex network wherein many of the men were involved with many of the others.

With Pike on the way, Spanish officials made vigorous efforts to intercept him. In April, 1806, Lieutenant Facundo Melgares[5] with

[5] Facundo Melgares was born in Europe, and his uncle was a royal judge in New Spain; he had distinguished himself against the Apaches and other Indians. A man of immense fortune, he was generous, had a liberal education, a high sense of honor, and a good military sense according to Pike (*Exploratory Travels,* 182–83 note.)

sixty soldiers was sent to reinforce the frontiers, but when he reached Santa Fe he had 105 men, and to that number were added 400 militia and 100 Indians. With 2,000 horses and mules and sufficient supplies to last six months, Melgares marched down the Red River for 233 leagues (Freeman had been stopped and sent back by Viana). He met some Pani-Mahas who stole many of his horses, and he took half his force to the Republican River to meet the Pawnees, with whom he made a treaty. Then he returned, with his entire force, in October, bringing back Chalvert's son and the two traders, Andrés Sulier and Henrique Visonot.[6]

It was the greatest expedition the Spaniards had ever sent out from New Mexico for any purpose, but it had not accomplished very much. It had not met Freeman because Freeman had been sent back by Viana, and it had missed Pike entirely because Melgares had reached the Republican River one month ahead of Pike. And even though Melgares made a deal with the Pawnees to stop Pike on his arrival, Pike bluffed the Indians and went on through, following from time to time the trail of Melgares' army into New Mexico.[7]

While Pike was still among the Osages, however, he met three Frenchmen led by Jean Baptiste Duchouquette, who were waiting for a man named Labbadie, who was supposed to have some trade goods. That was on August 19, and it has been suggested that Labbadie may have been Lisa; however, there was a Sylvester Labbadie in St. Louis, as noted by Quaife,[8] and Thomas James says there was an M. Labbadie who was a partner of Lisa in the fur trade.

Pike's party split on October 28, 1806; young Wilkinson, complaining bitterly, took one group down the Arkansas River; Pike left part of his men near what is now Larned, Kansas, and took the rest to build

[6] Nuttall suggests that Melgares brought back Chalvert's son and Sulier and Visonot, all from the Panis on Red River (Nuttall, "The American Threat to New Mexico, 1804–1822," unpublished master's thesis, San Diego State College, 1959); New Mexican Archives docs. 2022, 2023. Perhaps the two men had come from St. Louis; they might have been arrested anywhere on Melgares' trip, which covered a large territory, and during which he came in contact with at least three different tribes of Pawnees.

[7] Nuttall has a good brief summary of Melgares' movements in his thesis, *ibid.*, 79–83.

[8] Thomas James, *Three Years Among the Indians and Mexicans,* 8; see Nasatir's edition of Manuel Lisa.

a fort at what is now Pueblo, Colorado, where he left some men, while he took others and crossed the Sangre de Cristo Mountains to build a fort near the mouth of Conejos Creek in February, 1807. During those months they experienced the full rigors and the deadly horrors of cold and starvation—of winter in an area where the mountains are said to stand on end, where the wind blows a constant gale, the snow falls incessantly and the drifts grow forty feet deep, and where the thermometer demonstrates unbelievably recessive tendencies. Unfortunately, too, a major characteristic of the country—unforeseen or ignored by men like Pike and Frémont—is an almost complete absence of game in the winter because of the great cold.

In the meantime, Wilkinson had not relied on Pike alone. He had sent John McClallen to the Platte with trade goods very soon after Pike's departure; William Clark met him one week before the Lewis and Clark expedition's return to St. Louis. The outcome of John McClallen's trip, however, has not come to light, and there is no evidence that he reached Santa Fe with Wilkinson's goods.

Pike's building of the two forts had not been accomplished without a great expense of energy and suffering. On January 6, his party was divided into eight straggling groups; men and animals were scattered all over the country. Some men suffered frozen feet; all were near starvation. Pike's journal for February 17 says:

> They [Dougherty and Sparks] had hailed them [the relief party] with tears of joy, and were in despair when they again left them, with the chance of never seeing them more. They sent on to me some of the bones taken out of their [frozen] feet, and conjured me, by all that was sacred, not to leave them to perish so far from the civilized world. Ah! little did they know my heart, if they could suspect me of conduct so ungenerous.[9]

Dr. Robinson went to Santa Fe alone, but as a spy rather than for relief, though Cox believes that his mission was to stir up the Spaniards so they would send out soldiers to take Pike into Santa Fe, where he wanted to go on his reconnaissance. Relief parties came and went among the various small detachments left here and there among the mountains.

[9] Elliott Coues, *The Expeditions of Zebulon Montgomery Pike*, II, 505.

Presently, indeed, Spanish soldiers came to Pike's fort, and Pike professed innocence, and says in his diary, "thinking we were on Red River, and of course in the territory claimed by the United States."[10] Eventually another party of Spaniards arrested Pike and his men and took them to Santa Fe, where he found Solomon Colly from Nolan's party, and Baptiste Lalande, who apparently was sent by the Spaniards to spy on Pike. This latter action caused Pike great indignation:

> I told them that I believed him to be an emissary sent on purpose by the governor, or some person, to endeavor to betray me; that all men of that description were scoundrels, and never should escape punishment, whilst I possessed the power to chastise them—[Lalande was frightened, and said] that he had been ordered by the governor to meet me, and endeavor to trace out what and who I was, and what were my designs, by endeavoring to produce a confidence in him, . . . After this confession [obtained at the point of Pike's saber], I ordered my men to release him, and told him that I looked upon him as too contemptible for further notice.[11]

On April 1, Alencaster reported Pike's arrest to the viceroy. He said that on February 15 a young American prisoner (Dr. Robinson) had been captured; Alencaster had sent out troops and found "Lt. Mongo-Miri-Payke" with six soldiers near the main stream of the Río del Norte, well within the boundaries of New Mexico, for they were on the west side of the del Norte, on Conejos Creek near La Jara, Colorado, some sixty-five or seventy miles north of Taos. Of the thirteen men in the party, two had frozen feet and most of their fingers were gone. They presented themselves in Santa Fe March 2 and showed orders of Wilkinson, the diary of Pike, and other papers. The American government believed all rivers emptying into the Missouri

[10] Elliott Coues, in editing the journal, becomes disgusted at Pike's multiple and clumsy fabrications.

[11] Coues, *Expeditions of Pike,* I, 602. One is rather hard put to understand why Lalande's action was any more contemptible than that of Pike, who was also a spy in Santa Fe under false pretenses. It is interesting to speculate on the real reason for Pike's hostility toward Lalande. Small men often have small reasons. Could it be, for instance, Pike's fright over the possibility of being caught in his deception? A nitpicker might observe that this "confession" was obtained from Lalande at the point of Pike's sword while Pike's men held Lalande.

were within their boundaries, and Alencaster emphasized the need for more Spanish forts.[12]

On April 7 Salcedo wrote to Wilkinson, reporting that Robinson had come to New Mexico,[13] and also that the Spaniards had found Pike and eight Americans (and eventually six more); Salcedo reported that Pike said he had mistaken the Río Grande for the Colorado. The Americans had been sent to Chihuahua, where they had arrived April 2, and Pike had turned over his papers to Salcedo:

> By the constancy of these documents, which to your Excellency are notorious, by the repeated representations with which the king's minister near to the U. S., and the Marqués de Casa Calvo when he was in Louisiana, have solicited from the American government [its assurance] that it not put into effect the project of making expeditions over territories which indisputably belong to his Majesty, your Excellency will recognize without the necessity of any more reflections or references, the grave offense that has been inferred, and that at the same place where it was found, all the members of the company should have considered themselves under arrest; but in spite of such solid reasons for this just procedure [for conduct which] stretches to the limit the system of good harmony, and over all firmly persuaded that your Excellency would take the steps required in order to avoid consequences, I have resolved that, retaining in this captaincy-general until the decision of the king, my sovereign, the papers all presented by the First Lieutenant Pike, [I] shall return him and his own, after having treated them with attention and provided them with as much help as they have needed, to present them to your Excellency in entire liberty.[14]

In the meantime, Alencaster had not been idle. Anticipating that when the danger of snow should be over, other American troops might try to come in, he sent out several small parties to reconnoiter, as well as two parties of about forty men each. The larger parties were sent

[12] Alencaster to Yturrigaray, Santa Fe, April 1, 1807; Provincias Internas, Vol. 200. Interestingly enough, Robinson was captured by two Ute Indians, who were paid, on February 19, 1807, twenty-one pesos for bringing him in; New Mexican Archives, doc. 2084.

[13] For a biography of Robinson, see Harold A. Bierck, Jr., "Dr. John Hamilton Robinson," *Louisiana Historical Quarterly,* Vol. XXV, No. 3 (July, 1942), 644–69.

[14] Salcedo to James Wilkinson, Chihuahua, April 7, 1807; Provincias Internas, Vol. 200.

to points where they could watch the passes, and act as liaison for the the smaller parties. In a letter to Salcedo, Alencaster said:

> The Anglo-American soldier-patient, companion of Juan Pakes [Sparks],[15] informed that said parties were going to leave in charge of the aforementioned officials [for Chihuahua],[16] spoke to the interpreter of the Pawnees, José Tanvert [Chalvert], and told him that he wanted to show me that they [the Spaniards] were in danger. Regarding this, when they went out to their expedition, the Gral. Paike proposed that if he [Pike] did not appear [in St. Louis soon] after Christmas Eve, he [Wilkinson] would believe him prisoner of the Spaniards and would order a search for him, that he [Pike] would not care if he were held prisoner even if it should be for three months; that he [Dougherty] was Paike's orderly; that he heard him talk to Rovinson about this same thing at different times, and [heard him say] that the parties that would go in search of him would be four, composed of three or four thousand men, each one going via a principal river, and that he believed unfailingly that these parties might already be near. As soon as the said interpreter gave me [Alencaster] this news yesterday morning, I ordered the aforementioned Anglo-American soldier to appear before me, and he confirmed what I have said; and to assure myself further I later called the tailor, Nicolas Colee, as he has a command of the same language, and upon [Dougherty's] being questioned, he again repeated the same.[17]

The significance of this letter, which shows Pike's knowledge of Wilkinson's plans, cannot be overlooked.[17a]

[15] Apparently Dougherty; he and Sparkes were left behind on January 22 with frozen feet, and Pike said one was his "waiter," a young man of twenty. The crippled men arrived in Santa Fe on March 18.

[16] Those who had not gone in with Pike had arrived March 18; by that time, Pike had left Santa Fe (on March 4).

[17] Alencaster to Salcedo, No. 396, Santa Fe, April 15, 1807; A.G.M., Guerra y Mariana, Vol. 1787–1807, cuaderno 15; a copy is in the Library of Congress.

[17a] The editor of the American Historical *Review* refers to it very briefly in Vol. XIII, page 804, but it now seems, some fifty-five years later, that this letter is an important piece of evidence. There seems nothing on its face or in connection with it to impeach it, for the man was Pike's orderly, and, in spite of his ordeal, there is not suggested even by Pike that there was anything but friendship on Dougherty's part (and Pike surely would suggest it if he suspected it). Nor is coercion by the Spaniards anywhere indicated.

Dougherty told the story to Chalvert and again to Cole or Colly (Philip Nolan's Salomon Cole), and Salcedo notes no discrepancies. It might well have been an attempt to gain the good will of the governor—but that would not impeach the testimony.

Daugherty said that Pike spoke of the matter several times to Robinson, so there is no indication that Pike got the information from Robinson. If Pike said the rescue parties might already be near, it seems sure that he was aware of Wilkinson's plan to send troops to rescue Pike and his party in the event of their capture. It does seem to be an addition, however, that might easily be said on the spur of the moment to give urgency to the information.

Wilkinson's many and devious duplicities and his known feeling toward New Mexico make the entire structure quite believable. As far as Pike is concerned, some writers mention his "high reputation for veracity"—which does not seem to call for comment.

One writer scorns the thought that four columns of men, ascending four different rivers, would go to Santa Fe, pointing out that 3,000 or 4,000 men would be a far-fetched figure, since the entire United States army then consisted of only 3,200 men. However, there are volunteers, and Wilkinson the preceding September had written to Senator John Smith to propose 5,000 men to sweep the country to the Río Grande, 5,000 more to Monterey, and 20,000 to 30,000 to California and Panama.[18] Dougherty's figure begins to seem modest.

An interesting bit of supporting evidence is in Pike's speech to the Pawnees on September 29, 1806: "after next year we will not permit Spanish officers or soldiers, to come into this country."[19] He seems pretty sure.

It does not take a military strategist to know that one does not send three thousand men to rescue sixteen. Pike was an army officer and a graduate of West Point, and we must be naïve indeed to think that he was not aware that such a force would be sent for invasion.

Following Dougherty's warning, Alencaster says, he sent out a party of two hundred men to reinforce the advance parties, and ar-

[18] "Letters in Relation to Burr's Conspiracy, 1806–1808."

[19] It is not given this way in Coues, *Expeditions of Pike,* (II, 414, 415), but Abernethy, on page 509, cites A.H.N., Estado, leg. 5548, exp. 20, no. 17.

ranged for the people to take up arms, and he added, "I shall present myself where I am most needed, without my illness's serving as the least obstacle." And he offers some observations:

> With just sentiment it appears necessary to me to state to your Excellency a sad observance which I have made especially since the arrival of Paike. The citizens of this province have accepted both the residents of Louisiana who have come here and the Anglo-Americans with extreme fondness and hospitality, the first being the soldier Basquez, and even the tailor, Nicolas Colee, an American. With great secrecy I have had information of their ambition, hardness, and the many taxes and charges that they impose upon the residents. Apart from this, I have instructed myself from the conversations of the town that the Anglo-Americans will come, and of the facility with which they will make themselves owners of this province without observing displeasure in the people or hearing expressions of animosity from them or willingness to risk their lives to guard their homes, but speaking with the greatest coolness and timidity.

A few days later Salcedo wrote to the viceroy, enclosing a copy of his letter to Wilkinson. Pike, he said, would be conducted via the frontier of Texas to Louisiana, but Salcedo would retain his papers, diaries, and other written items until "His Majesty may determine . . . the matter . . . to his royal pleasure."[19a]

On the same day, Salcedo revealed his estimate of Pike's and Robinson's veracity:

> Although prudence demands not to neglect absolutely the rumors spread by Rovinson, the Lt. Pike, and the soldier Paker, we should recognize that the first two, having spoken untruthfully in those things where it is possible to ascertain the truth, they probably have not said anything without some definite intention, as the correspondence that has been found on them, their memoranda, and their own behavior testify that they possess all the credentials that their government considered necessary to accredit their expedition, and this makes doubtful all that they report.[20]

Pike reached Natchitoches on July 1, but he left some of his men

[19a] Salcedo to Yturrigaray, Chihuahau, April 20, 1807, Provincias Internas, Vol. 200.

[20] Salcedo to Governor, Chihuahua, Apr. 25, 1807; Provincias Internas, vol. 200.

in Chihuahua. Most of his papers had been retained by the Spaniards but his journal was rolled up and hidden in the rifle barrels of his men, and as soon as he reached the United States he went to work to reproduce the confiscated documents.[20a] His report on Mexico was highly colored, especially with anecdotes to demonstrate Pike's great bravery and uprightness; he turned in a map partially plagiarized from Baron von Humboldt. But all the circumstances, romanticized by Pike's righteous protestations as he came back to face accusations of complicity with Burr, combined to excite the flood of adventurers waiting at St. Louis. Wilkinson was busy with other things, for he was about to break faith with Burr and denounce him to the President, and the country was already up in arms over the Burr machinations and their implications. Pike's star would not go very high, for Lewis and Clark had returned; with no flamboyancy, they had made a real expedition of discovery, and the information they brought back was first-hand. Meriwether Lewis would be killed in Kentucky two years later, but William Clark would be a man to reckon with in Louisiana for a long time.

In August, 1807, Alencaster recapitulated his military situation in New Mexico:

> [He needs some troops and officers to form military units from the country people, and] Your Excellency knows . . . that their firearms will be scarcely a thousand, and that two thirds are of little or no use and the other third is bad and in unskilled hands, although there are now more than three thousand archers, who at the cost of infinite trouble can be moderately equipped. Some of the janizary[21] and few of the Spaniards will be found to be skilful in handling the bow and arrow; the others are very clumsy, and the total of the Indians is extremely cowardly, and although there are some skilled ones among them, they are only used to *jarear* [steal or chouse?] cattle.[22]
>
> Your excellency has probably observed my efficiency in stating the necessity for assistance and in soliciting it, . . . I have the advantage that providence gave me the help of being of the opinion since my

[20a] Hulbert suggests that their rifles were regulation flintlocks, U. S. Model 1795, of 70-caliber—which makes this concealment not as impossible as it might seem. They were not really rifles but smoothbore muskets. Hart-Hulbert, *Arkansas Journal*, 110.

[21] Prisoners trained to use arms and employed as soldiers.

[22] It should be noted that this is not the opinion expressed by most previous governors of New Mexico concerning the Indians' ability.

first years in the service that the true military man's last happiness is to die honorably in old age with the sword in his hand, and that the battlefield is his most appropriate tomb.[23]

Pike had left nine men behind him in Chihuahua. Sergeant Meek was detained in Mexico until 1820. The other men, however, were detained only two and one-half years, for in October, 1809, Salcedo wrote to Wilkinson:

> You should have received from Captain Daniel Hughes my letter of July 23 last and with it verified evidence of my defense to the requests of the President, by virtue of the delivery, made to the said captain, of the rest of the expedition of Lt. Montgomeri Pike who were detained here.[24]

However, Pike's papers did not find their way back as promptly; they were not brought to the United States until 1925.[25]

While Pike was eulogizing himself on his cleverness in fooling the Spanish officials, another man, also Spanish, was trying to establish trade with Santa Fe. His name was Manuel Lisa, and he was one of the most dynamic men in the Missouri country in its early days; he was trapper, trader, outfitter, financier, organizer, and politician. He once testified that the reason he got most of the trade from the Indians was that, while somebody else was sitting around talking about an arduous trip, he was making it.[26] And indeed he was—and was often cordially disliked by those whom he bested. With or against Auguste Chouteau, Jacques Clamorgan, Régis Loisel, and all the great names of the early Missouri fur trade, he made the wild Missouri River his highway, and the savages along its shores were his suppliers and his

[23] Alencaster to Salcedo, No. 482, Santa Fe, August 31, 1807, Provincias Internas, Vol. 200. This is an interesting reference to Alencaster's age; we have been unable to find any biographical data about him, but this letter indicates that he is elderly; later reference will be made to this item.

[24] Salcedo to Wilkinson, Chihuahua, October 9, 1809, Provincias Internas, Vol. 239, f. 63–64.

[25] Pike had been given an inventory and certificate of the papers taken from him on April 8, 1807; this list appears in Coues, *Expeditions*, 817–20. There was no further knowledge of those papers until Bolton found them in the Mexican archives, nearly one hundred years later, and reported it in the *American Historical Review*, Vol. XIII (July, 1908), 810–27. Even then it took seventeen years more to get them back.

[26] See Nasatir's edition of Manuel Lisa.

customers. He was a schemer and a driver, and there is some evidence that he had designs on Santa Fe and possibly reached that town very early in the race. Lisa was never a man to wait while somebody else took the cream of the trade.

The first documentary reference available is a letter from Wilkinson himself to Pike, dated at Cantonment, Missouri, August 6, 1806:

> It is reduced to a certainty that ——— [Manuel Lisa] and a society of which he is the ostensible leader have determined on a project to open some commercial intercourse with Santa Fe, and as this may lead to a connection injurious to the United States, and will, I understand, be attempted without the sanction of law or the permission of the executive, you must do what, consistently, you can to defeat the plan. No good can be derived to the United States from such a project, because the prosecution of it will depend entirely on the Spaniards, and they will not permit it, unless to serve their political as well as their personal interests. I am informed that the ensuing autumn and winter [of 1806] will be employed in reconnoitering and opening a connection with the Tetaus, Pawnees, &c.; that this fall, or the next winter, a grand magazine is to be established at the Osage towns, where these operations will commence; that ——— is to be the active agent, having formed a connection with the Tetaus. This will carry forward their merchandize within three or four days' travel of the Spanish settlements, where they will deposit it, under a guard of three hundred Tetaus. ——— will then go forward with four or five attendants, taking with him some jewelry and fine goods. With these he will visit the Governor, to whom he will make presents, and implore his pity by a fine tale of sufferings which have been endured by the change of government; that they are left here, with goods to be sure, but not a dollar's worth of bullion, and therefore they have adventured to see him, for the purpose of praying his leave for the introduction of the whole of the goods will be carried forward; if he refuses, then ——— will invite some of his countrymen to accompany him to his deposit, and having therefore exposed to them his merchandize, he will endeavour to open a forced or clandestine trade; for he observes the Spaniards will not dare to attack his camp. Here you have the plan, and you must take all prudent and lawful means to blow it up.[27]

[27] Printed in Coues, *Expeditions,* II, 573–76.

The plan sounds like one that Lisa would have thought of, and it also sounds a little like one of Wilkinson's fabrications; he sometimes wrote a letter, signed it with somebody else's name, and then pretended to find it. The one certain thing about this letter is that it was not a military communication; therefore, Wilkinson, as a private citizen, was using the army to hold Lisa away from Santa Fe. That was not necessary, of course, for Wilkinson was commander-in-chief of the U. S. Army, but it is the way Wilkinson dealt.

There is also an interesting letter from Onís, the Spanish minister at Philadelphia, that hints that Lisa had established communication with Santa Fe, or at least had come close:

> It is not strange that besides these expeditions there is one by Don Manuel Lisa by land along the rivers Norte, Grande, Colorado, and Missouri, and that this chieftain or spy should try to surprise us in the kingdom of New Mexico, for he has much knowledge of that country by his previous expeditions, and he has assured everyone that in them he has reached within two days' journey of Santa Fe.[28]

With these various indirect or second-hand references to expeditions by Lisa in 1806 and 1807, Jacques Clamorgan,[29] another power in St. Louis fur-trade circles, became restless over the prospect of profits to be made in Santa Fe and decided to see for himself. Lisa furnished money for goods, but Clamorgan, although he was seventy-four years old, made the trip in person with three Frenchmen, a Negro slave, and four mule loads of goods. He went up the Platte to the Pawnees, then cut across to Santa Fe, arriving in that town on December 12, 1807. He was sent to Chihuahua and was allowed to sell his goods there, and he returned to the United States through Texas and Natchitoches in 1808 with the distinction of being the first American trader to earn profits on a trip to Santa Fe.[30]

The next recorded (and discovered) American to reach Santa Fe was one María Raphael Henderson, who traveled from Kentucky to

[28] Onís to viceroy, Philadelphia, November 3, 1810, A.G.M., Notas Diplomáticas, vol. III, f. 13–14.

[29] For a brief article on Clamorgan, see Nasatir, "Jacques Clamorgan: Colonial Promoter of the Northern Border of New Spain," *New Mexico Historical Review*, Vol. XVII, No. 2 (April, 1942).

[30] New Mexican Archives, doc. 2249.

the Río Grande in 1809, alone.[31] But no more information is at hand on Henderson.

Following Henderson was a party destined to be gone for two years: Joseph McLanahan, Reuben Smith, James Patterson, Manuel Blanco, and three slaves. They left St. Geneviève on November 20, 1809, and reached Santa Fe in the latter part of February, 1810. The governor, Manrrique,[32] did not believe their story that they were simply sizing up the country with the purpose of settling there, and his distrust was intensified when he intercepted a letter from McLanahan to José Pablo Maese, to be delivered to Manuel Botas. Eventually the two Mexicans were released, but Manrrique was worried over New Mexico's vulnerability, and he obtained permission to call out the militia if necessary, while at the same time he encouraged New Mexicans to take out trading licenses so he could have a constant source of information from the Indians.

McLanahan and his men were placed in jail, and their imprisonment created a flurry of publicity. A Philadelphia newspaper claimed the men were spies or emissaries of Napoleon, saying that they were in jail in Chihuahua, and the story continued:

". . . in a case of this nature justice should not be delayed in order to purge the Spanish soil of such vermin."

The Louisiana *Gazette* also picked it up:

> Mark the pretended ignorance of these bloodhounds, they knew these gentlemen were from St. Genevieve in the Territory of Louisiana, . . .
>
> *Vermin!* what a prostitution of language! Messrs. Smith, M'Clanahan and Patterson strangers to the policy of Mexico and the monkish barbarism of the natives, they conceived they would visit white men clothed with the Christian name; unhappy incredulity! They would have found more generosity in the breast of an Arab, more hospitality in the den of a Hiena.—*The assassins of Mexico have ere this butchered three respectable inhabitants of Louisiana!!* Men whose virtues were

[31] James, *op. cit.*, 287–88; cited by Nuttall, whose thesis, "The American Threat to New Mexico, 1804–1822," contains a good account of this period.

[32] Lieutenant Colonel José Manrrique was ad interim governor of New Mexico, 1808–14. Otherwise, information about him is scarce, except that in 1799 he had been "enrolled" by Chacón in the Santa Fe [Presidial?] Company, and by 1800 he was "western commandant."

admired by all who knew them. Men who never dreamt of coalescing with any hostile party, who would not resign the name of American citizen for all the honors in the gift of a Joseph Bonaparte, or the blood stained gold of Mexican Inquisitors. Yet a little while and a day of terrible retribution will arrive.[33]

General Andrew Jackson wrote to the Department of State and was assured that steps were being taken:

> Your letter respecting James Patterson, Reuben Smith & others who you apprehend have been arrested in the Spanish Dominions, has been received & no time was lost in taking such steps for their release as seemed to be most likely to prove successful.[34]

In fact, some unauthorized steps were being taken, for in March, 1811, one Captain Walker and a Mr. Scott, with six companions, were stopped by the Osage Indians and held for American authorities. Walker, a former officer in the U. S. Army, said they were to be joined at the junction of the Canadian and the Arkansas by three hundred well equipped men from Kentucky country, and from that point they would march on Mexico to release the McLanahan party and seize what gold they could find.[35]

The confinement of the McLanahan men was not too harassing; they were kept in prison for one year before their return in June, 1812, to Natchitoches, where they promptly sullied the hysterical eulogy of the *Gazette* when they joined the Gutiérrez-Magee filibustering party, an all-fated venture that actually held San Antonio for a while.[36]

While the men were in Natchitoches, McLanahan wrote a letter to the governor of Louisiana to assert the intention of himself and Smith and Patterson to go into Texas, for on September 3, 1812, James Monroe, Secretary of State, wrote to Governor Howard to say:

> It appears by this communication that its authors intend to visit

[33] Nuttall, "The American Threat to New Mexico, 1804–1822," 125–26.

[34] R. Smith to Andrew Jackson, November 10, 1810, National Archives, Washington, State Dept., Domestic Letters, Vol. XV, 460.

[35] The objectives of Walker are told in Onís to the viceroy, Philadelphia, April 24, 1811, A.G.M., Notas Diplomáticas, f. 49–50. Onís also announced, in this letter, the departure of Wilson P. Hunt for the Columbia River country. See also Nasatir's edition of Douglas' Manuel Lisa.

[36] See Julia Kathryn Garrett, *Green Flag Over Texas.*

> some of the provinces of Spain, and as may be inferred from the recital, it gives of the circumstances attending a former journey there, and the motives assigned for the proposed one, that their object may be and probably is, of an unfriendly nature. . . .
>
> If the projected visit contemplates any measure of hostility to Spain it is repugnant to the policy of the United States. It is also positively prohibited by law.[37]

The Spaniards, evidently, were less concerned over McLanahan's party than were U. S. officials. Manrrique, when he captured the party, was alarmed but not excited. He impounded everything but personal clothing and money.

Six weeks later, Salcedo advised Manrrique that he had warnings from the viceroy, arising from newspaper articles, and that they were being communicated to the captain-general at Havana, to the commandant-general of the Interior Provinces, and to the governor of Texas. He urged care in watching for any papers that the Americans might leave around, and in observing their conversations—in compliance with both of which items it appears that Manrrique was extremely diligent.

Then began a series of rumors. Americans or other traders were reported in the area; beaver hunters and otter hunters were said to be in the mountains, especially near Taos. The governor sent parties to search—as many as one hundred men in each party—but found nobody. They were advised, though, that American traders came and went, and that many of the Indians had American rifles and goods, so it rather seems that there must have been a certain amount of traffic. Perhaps Lisa and the men working for him, and perhaps others now unknown, realized they could trade with the Indians and return safely if they would stay out of reach of Santa Fe.

In August, 1810, Rafael Luna said that two Comanche captains reported 876 Americans on the Arkansas, building a fort at the junction with the Almagre, but a party of soldiers sent to reconnoiter found nothing.[38]

There has long been current a book purporting to relate the adven-

[37] Monroe to Howard, September 3, 1812, National Archives, State Dept., Domestic Letters, Vol. XVI, 199.

[38] Letter to Manrrique, Santa Fe, August 2, 1810, in answer to letter of August 1, which had transmitted diary of Ygnacio Elías Gonzales, New Mexican Archives, doc. 2346.

tures of three men—Ezekiel Williams, James Workman, and David Spencer, who are said to have been at the Mandan villages and then to have gone south to the Arkansas River, from which point Williams went back to St. Louis, while Workman and Spencer by mistake descended the Colorado River and wound up in northern California, but returned and reached Santa Fe in the summer of 1810. This is the story in David H. Coyner's book, *The Lost Trappers*. Ezekiel Williams was with Lisa in 1810, but he did not write the book, and it has since been found to be "an apocryphal book, never materializing out of fable-land into historical environment,"[39] "one of the completest fabrications that was ever published under the guise of history,"[40] and "worthless as a source of authentic and true history."[41] Therefore, it seems that the Workman-Spencer-Williams adventures do not at this time merit further serious consideration.[42]

The year 1811 was a year of several explorations: it was the year Wilson Price Hunt raced Manuel Lisa up the Missouri, crossed the Rockies, and went on to Astoria; it was the year Henry Marie Brackenridge went up the river with Lisa to join his friend, John Bradbury, who had gone up the river with Hunt. It was the year Gabriel Franchère went to Astoria in the *Tonquin* around Cape Horn; it was also the year Thomas Nuttall went up the Missouri with Hunt and Bradbury. All in all, it was quite a collection of naturalists and journalists that descended on the Mandan villages that year, while there were even more exciting doings at Astoria at the mouth of the Columbia River.

The year before, Lisa had sent twenty-three men from the Mandan country to trade with the Arapahos on the South Platte, and he had learned that the Spaniards made annual trips to trade with the Arapahos. By 1811 Lisa was set to capitalize on that information, and in August, 1811, he sent out another party headed by Juan Bautista Champlain

[39] Elliott Coues, *The Journal of Jacob Fowler, xix–xx.*

[40] H. M. Chittenden, *History of the American Fur Trade,* II, 651.

[41] A. P. Nasatir, "A Critical Examination and Evaluation of Coyner's *Lost Trappers*," unpublished manuscript, 20.

[42] See Frederic E. Voelker, "Ezekiel Williams of Boone's Lick," Missouri Historical Society *Bulletin,* Vol. VIII, No. 1 (October, 1952), 17–51. See also Nasatir's edition of Douglas' Manuel Lisa.

and Juan Bautista Lafarge, with Ezekiel Williams (on whose letter in the Missouri *Gazette* was based Coyner's *Lost Trappers*), a man named Porteau, and several others. The fate of the various members is unknown, but they spent the winter on the Arkansas, were on the Platte in June, and split up a number of times. Some crossed the Rockies: Williams went back to St. Louis; in the latter part of 1812, four of them set out for the Spanish settlements and no doubt were one of the parties that gave so many alarms to the Spaniards in Santa Fe.[43]

We cannot be positive about Lisa's first few ventures toward Santa Fe, but by 1812 he was in full swing. In that year he again went up the Missouri to the Mandan country (accompanied by John Luttig, who left a famous journal), and in September he sent Carlos Sanguinet with Charles Latour and Cadet Chevalier and a letter "To the Spaniards of New Mexico":

> [He begins by describing previous years' efforts with the Arapahos, and it is not positive that he means that twenty-three men were in the previous year's party; he may mean over several years. He had given goods to the party of 1811, and since he has not heard from that party, he is sending Sanguinet with two *engagés* to tell them where to deliver their pelts.] . . .
>
> . . . some Spaniard who may be desirous of communicating with me on those honorable principles [that is, with deference to Spanish laws], and in no other manner, my desire being to engage in business and open up a new commerce, which might easily be done. [He suggests that he can fill any bill of goods and deliver them to a rendezvous that may be agreed upon; he invites them to visit him in company with Sanguinet, and he promises an escort for their return to New Mexico.][44]

Sanguinet sent Lisa a letter in December, saying, in summary, that three men had been killed by the Blackfeet, Lafargue and five others had gone to the Spanish, eight had gone to the Crows and were with Reuben Lewis (brother of Meriwether Lewis and Lisa's employee on the Little Big Horn), and three or four could not be ac-

[43] See Bolton, "New Light on Manuel Lisa and the Fur Trade," *Southwestern Historical Quarterly*, Vol. XVII, No. 1 (July, 1913), 61–66.

[44] Bolton, *ibid.*

counted for.[45] Thus it appears that the original party might have been twenty-three men after all.

Sanguinet never reached Santa Fe, although the letter from Lisa finally was put away in the archives in Chihuahua. And so Lisa, probably without ever seeing Santa Fe, made no more efforts from the Mandan country. (The War of 1812 interrupted the Missouri Company's operations, and the company did not make money.) It would seem that Lisa expected Sanguinet to go on to Santa Fe, because Lisa had invited the Spaniards to accompany Sanguinet back to Fort Mandan, but Sanguinet bought some horses from the Arapahos and returned to Fort Mandan in January, 1813.

Before Lisa had sent his letter to New Mexico, another party had left St. Louis—one that was to become more famous than the Smith-Patterson-McLanahan party of 1809. This was the party led by Robert McKnight, Samuel Chambers, and James Baird, which in April used Pike's journal to find its way to Santa Fe with six mule loads of goods.[46]

Spanish officials not only refused permission to trade but also confiscated the goods and sent the members of the party to Chihuahua, where they were imprisoned. Some of them were not released for ten years, and during all this time their keep, at 18¾ cents a man per day, was taken from their goods, which originally had been valued at $10,000.

They were tried for complicity in the Hidalgo uprising of 1810, and apparently found guilty and sentenced. Baird was sold as a slave to work in the silver mines of Durango, but escaped, was recaptured, and confined in a dark dungeon for nine months. The governor's wife, observing the traditional compassion of Spanish women for the *pobrecitos*,[46a] smuggled to him some thread, a piece of linen, and a bone that he made into a needle, and he did a few stitches of needlework a day to keep from losing his mind; his hair was snow white when he was released.[47]

Apparently none of those prisoners was released until May, 1820,

[45] See John C. Luttig, *Journal of a Fur-Trading Expedition on the Upper Missouri, 1812–1813*, Stella M. Drum, ed., 35.

[46] See Frank B. Golley, "James Baird, Early Santa Fé Trader," Missouri Historical Society *Bulletin*, Vol. XV, No. 3 (April, 1959).

[46a] A word later made famous by George Wilkins Kendall in his classic story of the Texan–Santa Fé Expedition of 1841: *Narrative of the Texan Santa Fé Expedition.*

and Golley cites a newspaper article with a number of interesting items of that period: Sergeant William Meeks, who had been left in Chihuahua by Pike in 1807, arrived at Fort Smith; ten men, most of whom were from the McKnight expedition, had been permitted to leave Mexico; Simon McCoy and C. King, who had been captured with the Nolan party in 1800, were permitted to leave at the same time; William Mines decided to stay in Mexico; McKnight had a store two hundred miles west of Durango, and Allen had a small store there, but had gone toward California; Thomas Cook had died; and Michael McDonough had become a monk in a convent at Zacatecas.[48]

Shortly after the McKnight party arrived in Santa Fe in 1812, four Frenchmen, unnamed, appeared in Taos, were sent to Chihuahua, and finally to Arispe, where they were imprisoned. As it turned out, Salcedo became suspicious of the Mexican who had first reported the four Frenchmen, and he warned against giving aid or information to foreigners and told Manrrique that any person who was a poor risk in that respect should not be allowed to make a trip to the plains.[49]

At about the same time, McLanahan, Patterson, and Smith were entering Texas on the Gutiérrez-Magee expedition.[50]

During the year 1813, the Santa Fe cross-plains traffic was either light or non-existent, and that situation continued through most of the following year, but in November, 1814, four Frenchmen (probably not the same four of 1812) who said they had been on the Platte for six years and that three of their party had been killed, reached Taos and were sent on to Chihuahua.[51]

Up to that point, two parties had been imprisoned with enough se-

[47] For a sketch of Baird, see Golley, *ibid.*

[48] Pittsburgh *Statesman*, April 28, 1821, from St. Louis *Enquirer*, July 12, 1820.

[49] Bolton says these are not the men of Lisa's letter, but Nuttall points out that they may have been from Lisa's party of 1811.

[50] Some authors have suggested that George Drouillard, who contributed information to William Clark for his monumental map of 1814, had made a trip to Santa Fe for Manuel Lisa in 1812. Drouillard had been a valuable man with Lewis and Clark, and was one of the great mountain men of the very early years, but he could not have gone to Santa Fe in 1812, as Wheat points out *(Mapping the Transmississippi West, 1540–1861*, II, 53), for he was killed by Blackfeet in 1810.

[51] Cited by Nuttall, "The American Threat to New Mexico, 1804–1822," 145; Maynez [?] to Bonavía, Santa Fe, November 20, 1814, New Mexican Archives, doc. 2565.

verity to become each a *cause célèbre*—and then, in 1815, there was a third, which became known as the Chouteau-De Mun party, which left St. Louis in September, 1815, and included Auguste Pierre Chouteau, Jules de Mun, and Joseph Philibert.[52] The first two had a license to trade with the Comanches and Arapahos; Philibert had a license to trade on the Platte and Arkansas rivers, and he had men in the territory from the year before. On the trip west, however, Philibert sold out to Chouteau and De Mun. Those two men did not find Philibert's men in Pawnee country, and so in January, 1816, De Mun went on to New Mexico, apparently in ignorance of the possible consequences; he found Philibert's men in Taos, and went on to Santa Fe to ask permission to trap. Fortunately, a new acting governor was in charge—Alberto Maynez[53]—and he was friendly toward Americans and said he would write the commandant-general. Then began a series of extraordinary trips on the part of Chouteau and De Mun, among Santa Fe, Taos, and their various camps in northern New Mexico. Surely no innocent men could have extended their necks so many times. One count shows that De Mun made ten such trips besides one trip to and from St. Louis. They were ordered to leave, but they were there to make money and they kept trying.

They trapped all winter, and then De Mun went back to Taos to see if the decision had been reversed. There, however, he heard that Anglos had built a fort at the fork of the Arkansas and the Río de las Ánimas, and would station 20,000 men there. De Mun offered to remain as a hostage, with his life as surety for the behavior of his own party while the report was being investigated, but finally Chouteau remained in custody while De Mun went with a Spanish officer to look for the fort. They found nothing, but De Mun and Chouteau delayed their own departure from Spanish territory until they were arrested and taken to Santa Fe on June 1, 1817. By that time, Maynez had been

[52] For the Chouteau-De Mun affair, see De Mun's letter to William Clark, November 25, 1817, in *Annals of Congress,* 15 Cong., 1 sess, II, 1960–66; *American State Papers, Foreign Relations,* IV, 211–13; and Thomas M. Marshall (ed.), "The Journals of Jules de Mun," Missouri Historical Society *Collections,* V, 172–82.

[53] Alberto Maynez, ad interim governor of New Mexico, 1814–16, is another of the early New Mexican governors who seem not to have left much record of themselves. Maynez seems to have acted as governor without appointment, 1807–1808.

replaced by Allande,[54] who was hostile to Americans; Chouteau and De Mun were imprisoned (in chains until June 7).[55] The other members of their party were imprisoned also, and finally, after forty-four days, the leaders were brought before a court-martial. The trial was a farce; Allande confiscated their goods and allowed them to leave—on the two worst horses they had. Subsequently the others of the party, twenty-one in all, were allowed to leave also. By that time, Chouteau and De Mun were claiming damages from the Spaniards; it took a long time to get a decision, but eventually they were awarded more than $75,000.

In 1818 De Mun's brother Louis, a lieutenant colonel in the U. S. Army, after a trip to the Arkansas River prepared a detailed report entitled "Notes Concerning the Province of New Mexico Collected on My Mission to the West," in which he used Pike's journal and some information from his brother Jules. Pike's journal was found inaccurate in many respects, for much of his implied first hand information was actually hearsay.[56]

On August 30, 1818, the Yellowstone Expedition got under way in a cloud of heated argument and congressional inquiries. It was a fair-sized contingent of 350 men—preceded by Manuel Lisa, naturally—which was to establish a fort at the Mandan villages, and possibly one at Council Bluffs, and eventually to go on to the Yellowstone area to negate British influence. There was considerable alarm in certain areas of New Mexico when news of the expedition reached there, but eventually the Spaniards realized that the Yellowstone area was not within striking distance of Santa Fe. Nevertheless, José Chalvert with fifteen men reconnoitered and discovered that there was no expedition-

[54] Pedro María de Allande succeeded Maynez in 1816 and was followed by Melgares in 1818.

[55] Nuttall, "The American Threat to New Mexico, 1804–1822," 149–53.

[56] A copy of the report, in French and unsigned, is in the Archivo General de Mexico, Sección de Notas Diplomáticas, Vol. I, f. 192–97, and a Spanish copy also is here, Vol. IV, f. 166–67. Alfred B. Thomas used the French copy in his "An Anonymous Description of New Mexico, 1818," *Southwestern Historical Quarterly*, Vol. XXXIII, No. 1 (July, 1929), 50–74. Since that time, Nasatir has found the "Notes" in the original French, with an accompanying map, enclosure No. 7, in De Neuville to Le Duc de Richelieu, Washington, June 3, 1818; France, Ministry of Foreign Affairs, Paris Series, Correspondance Politique, Fond, Etats Unis, Vol. 75, f. 188–91. This copy is signed by Louis de Mun.

ary force in the Yellowstone area; Congress had limited the expedition's funds, and it had had to stop at Council Bluffs.[57]

One year later (in 1819), David Meriwether was given the familiar treatment in Santa Fe: arrest, imprisonment, and confiscation of goods; finally he was released and given a broken-down horse. Thirty-four years later (in 1853), he returned to Santa Fe as territorial governor of New Mexico.[58]

In 1821, however, a man named Thomas James began to stir Santa Fe affairs with considerable virtuosity and no little acerbity. James had had a taste of the Western country in 1809 in an expedition motivated indirectly by the Mandan chief, Shehaka, whose only fault was that he wanted to go home to his people. He had come down the river with Lewis and Clark on promise of safe return to his village; the Americans had tried to return him in 1807 but had been repulsed by the Arikaras. His return then became an affair of honor—a refutation to those who imply that the government is devoid of that attribute—and the War Department made a contract with the Missouri Fur Company to escort Shehaka to his native village. The fur company's party consisted of some 125 armed men under Pierre Chouteau (for the return of Shehaka), plus 225 men who went along on fur-company business. One member of the party was Thomas James, a frontiersman, outspoken and critical—perhaps with some reason, although it appears that he had a sharp tongue and a penchant for exaggeration. James and others were not very concerned over Shehaka, but went because the fur company's party, once Shehaka should be safely delivered,

[57] Edgar B. Wesley, "A Still Larger View of the Yellowstone Expedition," *North Dakota Historical Quarterly*, Vol. V, No. 4 (July, 1931), 220; Cardinal Goodwin, "A Larger View of the Yellowstone Expedition," *Mississippi Valley Historical Review*, Vol. IV, No. 3 (December, 1917), 299–313; Chittenden, *Fur Trade*, II, Chap. II; Wesley, *Guarding the Frontier;* Alfred B. Thomas, "Documents Bearing Upon the Northern Frontier of New Mexico, 1818–1819," *New Mexico Historical Review*, Vol. IV, No. 2 (April, 1929). The story of the reaction to the Yellowstone affair has yet to be written; we have a good deal of documentary material. Thomas has printed "An Anonymous Description of New Mexico, 1818," *Southwestern Historical Quarterly*, Vol. XXXIII, No. 1 (July, 1929); and "The Yellowstone River, James Long, and Spanish Reaction to American Intrusion Into Spanish Dominions, 1818–1819," *New Mexico Historical Review*, Vol. IV, No. 2 (April, 1929).

[58] He was, says Nuttall, the last Anglo-American to be so imprisoned in Santa Fe. See David Meriwether, *My Life in the Mountains and on the Plains: The Newly Discovered Autobiography* (Norman, 1965).

was to start for the Rocky Mountains to hunt and trade, with supplies to be furnished by the fur company. James later was highly critical of the contract that he signed for the trip, and said he had been "deceived" by it. Also, he disliked Lisa extremely, and his troubles became intensified when Lisa took charge of the party after Shehaka's delivery.

James bitterly criticized the fur company,[58a] but later prospered, for in 1818 he had $17,000 worth of goods—and it was that fall that Samuel Chambers, James Baird, and Peter Baum of the Robert McKnight party returned to St. Louis after nine years in Chihuahua's prison. Robert McKnight himself was still in Mexico in 1818, and Robert's brother in St. Louis, John McKnight, who wanted to go after him, proposed that they take James's goods to Santa Fe. It happened that James had heavily over-bought and was facing possible bankruptcy, so he agreed. They loaded a keelboat in May, 1821, with $10,000 worth of trade goods, and started down the Mississippi. With a party of eleven men they ascended the Arkansas River, and at the Osage villages on the Verdigris River in present-day Oklahoma they met the Fowler-Glenn party, which also had some trade goods but appeared to be on a trapping venture, with no designs on Santa Fe. James and his party went on through Oklahoma until they ran into Comanches. When they were about to be massacred (at least, so James says) by the Comanches, they were saved by Mexican soldiers, who explained that Mexico was free and independent of Spain and that the Americans were their brothers. Guided by the Spaniards, James went on to Santa Fe, and began to sell what goods he had left.

Meanwhile, Hugh Glenn and Jacob Fowler had gone into southeastern Colorado, and they also were approached by Mexican troops and advised of the new regime. Glenn went to Taos, while Fowler built a fort in the area of Pueblo. Mexican soldiers returned, and Fowler joined Glenn in Taos, and they separated to trap beaver in that area.

By June the McKnight brothers returned from Chihuahua. James met Glenn, and they went to Taos and met Fowler, then started back

[58a] An interesting example of James's many biases is his comparison of the Spaniards, for whom he expresses great contempt, with the Navajos, whom he regards as regal and noble. It would be hard to find another account that supports this evaluation of the Navajos of those times.

to St. Louis. They were attacked by Indians, and Glenn, says James (who dictated his memoirs in 1846—twenty-five years later), pushed on ahead in fright. Thereafter the two parties traveled separately, more than once coming within sight of each other, but not hailing each other. It sounds characteristic of James.

The most significant trip ever made in the West was that made by William Becknell in 1821. Attracted by news of Mexico's independence, he left Boone's Lick transporting his goods by pack mules, reached Santa Fe ahead of James, sold his goods at a profit, and returned to St. Louis in January, 1822. Later in 1822 he took three wagons and struck out across the present Panhandle of Oklahoma on what became known as the Cimarron or desert route. It was on that trip that the men almost perished for lack of water; Becknell, wandering alone, saved himself with water from the stomach of a dead buffalo, and eventually saved the caravan.

James Baird got back into the traffic in the last part of 1822 when he took pack mules with $9,000 worth of goods into raging blizzards and snow, and lost most of his animals. Then when spring came, he cached his goods and went into Taos for pack mules. He reached Santa Fe and sold his goods at a profit, stayed in Mexico and applied for citizenship in 1824 and trapped the Mogollon Mountain area. In 1826 he became ill on a trip and returned to El Paso and died; his wife thought he had been murdered. His body has disappeared, for there is no record of his death at El Paso, and his burial place is unknown. Strangely enough, his former partners also returned to Mexico. Chambers died in Taos; Robert McKnight became a citizen, made a fortune in Santa Rita copper mines in the Gila Mountains, and died in March, 1846.[59]

William Becknell was closely followed by Colonel Benjamin Cooper and his nephews, Braxton and Stephen, and twelve other men. James, Glenn, and Fowler all met the Cooper party as they themselves returned to St. Louis.

The great rush was on. The big wagons pulled over the buffalo grass by plodding oxen would cut great furrows in the sod, and the trail would be half a mile wide in a few years. Hundreds of sun-hardened men would ramrod the oxen and mules through Indian country, across the

[59] Golley, "James Baird, Early Santa Fe Trader," Missouri Historical Society *Bulletin*, Vol. XV, No. 3 (April, 1959).

"desert" of the western plains, and over the mountains to Santa Fe. Many men would return to Franklin or Independence and dump their rawhide bags of silver pesos on the wooden sidewalks, cut them open with an ax, and let the money spill out and roll into the dust.[60] Some of the men would lose their hair to Indians; many would go on down the trail to Chihuahua and would establish themselves there. Some of those Chihuahua Americans would become important to the history of New Mexico: James Wiley Magoffin, who in 1846 maneuvered the surrender of New Mexico to Kearny without a shot's being fired by Armijo, the Mexican governor; Dr. Henry Connelly, who later became territorial governor of New Mexico.

Before 1821 traveling to Santa Fe was an adventure, a challenge with only a few winners; from 1821 to 1846 it was still an adventure, a fight with the elements and with Indians, a contest with Mexican officials, honest and dishonest. But after 1846 the trip was a business. The Stars and Stripes waved over the Governor's Palace along the west side of the Plaza in Santa Fe; Kearny went on to California. The element of chance was largely removed. More men undertook the trading venture to Santa Fe, and competition forced prices and profits down.

From a plane today, the great furrows cut by the four-inch iron tires can still be seen. It was a magnificent era—one that will not come again.

[60] Perhaps not "untie the thongs," as James suggests, of a rawhide bag—for the virtue of a rawhide bag was that it would harden like iron and could not be opened by ordinary methods, or carried off easily by Indians. No thongs would be needed—and there would be two ways to open it: soak it in water or cut it with a heavy, sharp blade.

# XI

# *Pedro Vial's Expedition from Bexar to Santa Fe in 1786 and 1787*

No official correspondence seems to have turned up concerning the immediate motivation for opening a road between Santa Fe and Bexar. Each province considered its problems pretty much its own, and dispositions for defense of the frontier were usually carried out on a local or regional basis. At higher levels, however, there was an awareness of the need for protection of the northern frontier and of the value of consolidating communications between Santa Fe and Bexar and thus establishing a front with an anchor at each end, for in 1751 the Marquis of Altamira, adviser to the viceroy of Mexico, urged that direct communication be established between the two posts to hold back the French intrusion.[1] Communication between them in the eighteenth century, up to that time, had been impossible because of Indian hostility, except by a very roundabout route: from Bexar south to Saltillo, west and north to Chihuahua and El Paso, and north to Santa Fe—a distance of approximately 1,700 miles. By muleback or ox cart, it was a long and time-consuming route. (The distance today between Santa Fe and San Antonio via Lubbock is about 730 miles.)

Perhaps as a result of Altamira's urging, San Saba was founded in 1757 as a link between the two towns. Only one year after its establishment, however, the Comanches made a determined attack and massacred all but three of the residents, and thus that potential link in the chain between San Antonio and Santa Fe was seriously damaged before it had a chance to become firmly established.

In 1762, perhaps again from Altamira's suggestions, the governor of

[1] See Bolton, *Texas in the Middle Eighteenth Century*, 128.

New Mexico sent a band of Indians from Pecos to San Saba, but they failed to reach the Texas post.[2]

In 1766–67 the Marqués de Rubí made his famous inspection, and in 1772 his recommendations were substantially adopted, leaving both San Antonio and Santa Fe far outside the cordon of posts on the northern frontier, and it may well be that this strategic isolation of Santa Fe and San Antonio suggested to the commandant-general of the Interior Provinces that those two towns should have a connection. As we approach 1786, the year of Pedro Vial's first trip, we know that there had been but one approach by road to Santa Fe: through Chihuahua—but we find singularly little documentary material relating to the immediate motivation for Vial's trip. It seems likely that Ugarte, commandant-general of the Interior Provinces, or Rengel, commandant-inspector for New Mexico and Nueva Vizcaya, instructed Cabello, governor of Texas, to carry out the expedition, and it is not at all unlikely that those instructions came originally from the viceroy's office. It was the kind of expedition which appealed to the upper echelons, for it was to be undertaken by Pedro Vial in company with only one other person, and therefore the expense would be small.

Where Altamira had envisioned the line of communication as a protection against the French, most likely the commandant-general faced reality and saw the need for protection from citizens of the United States, for in 1783 (only three years earlier) the United States had won its independence, and every Spanish official in northern Mexico was concerned about traditional aggressive American instincts. No American thrusts had yet been made; it was several years before Philip Nolan would enter Texas for mustangs (and possibly soundings in the bays); it was nineteen years before James Purcell would make his way to the village of the Holy Faith; but Juan Gasiot, a French agent among the Indians, in 1783 warned Neve, the commandant-general, against the Americans: "We will see the citizens of the United States of America . . . make frequent incursions to establish trade with the natives. [They will] continue to advance in this manner until they reach the limits of our borders, where they will have to be stopped. But by that time they will have become irresistible." And Gasiot recommended immediate

[2] *Ibid.*, 128.

and strong steps to win the support of the Indians.[3] Certainly by 1783 the Spaniards had seen enough of American drive to know that the restless men would never be satisfied to stop at the Mississippi River.

Into this situation stepped Pedro Vial. He had been born in Lyons, France,[4] and though his birthdate has not been exactly determined, examination of the data indicates that he must have been born between 1746 and 1755. He was probably at least thirty-one years of age when he was sent to establish the first overland trail between Bexar and Santa Fe, and there are some indications that he was much older.

In this connection, Alencaster, whom we have already established as probably elderly in 1805, spoke of Vial as "the elder Vial" compared to Chalvert, and again in 1806 Alencaster spoke of him as "the old man Vial." Since Alencaster himself was elderly, Vial must have been at least sixty; this line of reasoning (if it is that) would put Vial's birth date in 1746 or earlier.

We may note also that Vial is invariably referred to as "Don Pedro Vial," and since he was of ordinary birth and held no position beyond that of interpreter, it seems again that he must have been of more than ordinary age for one in his occupation. This conclusion is supported by his mileage on a trip, which averages substantially less than that of other diarists.

One indication of age comes from a set of three letters written by Cesaire Bormé at Natchitoches to the governor of Louisiana in 1779, and one letter written by the governor to Bormé at about the same time. The first, written by Bormé on May 31, finds Bormé in temporary command at the post of Natchitoches while De Mézières is on an expedition, and Bormé reports an Indian attack on a convoy of La Mathe at the Brazos; Ensign Jean de Mora fell, presumably dead.

The second letter, written June 3, concerns settlement of the estate of St. Denis (whose widow was not satisfied). Then Bormé says that a Spanish woman was going to New Orleans, whose husband had been robbed and enslaved by Indians, and that one Pierre Vial (who also was going to New Orleans) had redeemed him from captivity.

[3] Juan Gasiot to Felipe de Neve, October 9, 1783, San Francisco el Grande Archives, XXXIII, 151–62; cited in Castañeda, *Our Catholic Heritage*, V, 149–50.

[4] See the first page of Fragoso's journal, *infra.*

The third letter apparently was written by the governor to Bormé on July 3, 1779, and adds more information on Vial:

> I have learned that this Vial professes the trade of gunsmith and that he usually lives among the savage nations, our enemies, for whom he repairs their arms, and even that he taught his trade to one of them. As this is very harmful to the king and his subjects, I beg you to check this Vial's doings and to stop him from returning among the enemy nations under any pretext whatsoever.[4a]

Since the Taovaya villages on the Red River near present Ringgold, Texas, were for a number of years a trading center for *contrabandistas* from Arkansas Post, and since at various times it has been said that Frenchmen lived in those villages and supplied the Indians with rifles and ammunition, and since Vial will turn out later to be well acquainted with the Comanches to the west of the villages, the Wichitas in the villages, and the Wacos and Tawakonis southeast of the villages, it may be that Vial made his headquarters in those villages at least as early as 1779.

At any rate, by 1786, Vial had left the Indians—among whom he lived and practiced his trade as a gunsmith—and was chosen to open an overland trail from San Antonio to Santa Fe. Some confusion exists concerning the date of that first trip; the copy of the journal in Historia 62, which is a certified copy made at Chihuahua in 1793, puts the beginning date as October 4, 1787, but at the end it spells out the final date as July 5, 1787. Ugarte's letter to Anza, which is No. 944 in the New Mexican archives at Santa Fe, announcing the departure of Vial, is dated October 26, 1786, and the instructions to José Mares, who left in July, 1787, are to find a "more direct route," so there seems little doubt that Vial's initial, trail-breaking trip began in 1786. And inasmuch as the documents leading up to the departure have not appeared, it is appropriate to refer first to Ugarte's letter that advised Anza, the governor of New Mexico, that Vial was on the way.

Ugarte was commandant-general of the Interior Provinces at that time,[5] Anza was governor of New Mexico, and Domingo Cabello

[4a] Bormé to [Governor], Natchitoches, May 31, 1779, signature and rubric; Bormé to [Governor], Natchitoches, June 3, 1779, signature and rubric; [Governor] to Bormé, New Orleans, July 3, 1779—all in Papeles de Cuba, leg. 192.

[5] At that period, it seems the Interior Provinces were divided into three sections: one section was under Juan de Ugalde as *commandante de armas;* another under José

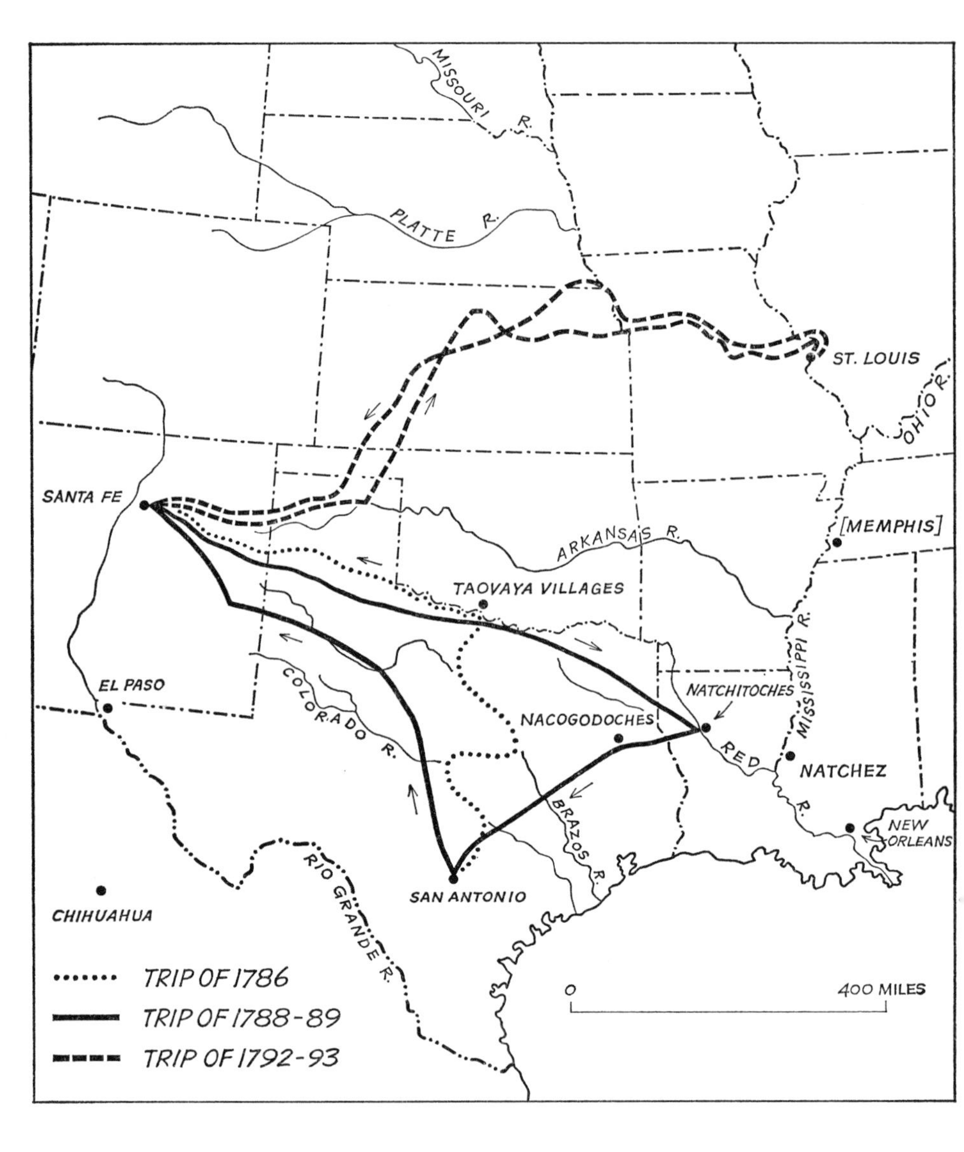


*Pedro Vial's three principal trips, 1786–87, 1788–89, and 1792–93*

was governor of Texas. Ugarte told Anza that Vial, living in Texas, had offered to go alone, without escort, on a trip from Bexar to the village of Santa Fe, going by the hamlets of friendly Indians to the north and also by villages of the Comanches.[6] This letter was to verify the trip and add Ugarte's approval.[7]

Vial had promised to make the trip in the most direct route and to make an exact itinerary that would be an adequate guide for anyone who might go in the future. "And I do not doubt," said Ugarte, "that the peace [which we now observe] with the Comanches and the knowledge that Pedro Vial has of that nation will guarantee his safe passage through their country."

That apparently referred to the fact that, not long before the letter was written, Vial had had a great deal to do with bringing about peace between the Spaniards and some of the Indians, for, not long before Vial started his journey, a band of Indians had attacked a Spanish force under José Menchaca and had been repulsed, and there had been subsequent meetings in Bexar. Vial in his diary tells of discussions with both the Tawakonis and the Comanches concerning the recent trouble; the Indians had lost a number of warriors and were for the moment concerned about the official Spanish attitude, as appears in Vial's diary for January 11: "They [the Comanche chiefs in Zoquiné's lodge] told me that the chief who was with me at San Antonio when I made the peace had been killed by the Spaniards."

Ugarte instructed Anza to aid Vial when he should arrive in Santa Fe and to make a copy of his itinerary:

> You will have an opportunity to inform yourself of the state of the eastern settlements of Cuchanees [Kotsoteka Comanches] and also of the passage of the said Vial, to form with greater knowledge your convictions [*convinaciones*] about the conclusion of peace and arrangement of the various terms.
>
> And if it should appear opportune to you for other persons of that province to have equal knowledge of the road blazed by Vial, for

---

Rengel as *commandante-inspector;* and the third (Sonora, Sinaloa, and California) under Ugarte as commandant-general with limited authority over the other two.

[6] He distinguishes between friendly Indians and Comanches.

[7] Jacobo Ugarte y Loyola to J. B. de Anza, Chihuahua, October 26, 1786, New Mexican Archives, doc. 944.

purposes which may develop in the future, you will arrange [affairs so] that, returning by the same route, he will be accompanied by those whom you judge suitable to serve as guides to the parties which you [will] wish to dispatch in the future from that village, availing yourself of this good opportunity at extremely small cost [to carry out] reciprocal communication between the two provinces.

Vial was an able and experienced frontiersman. He was familiar with the tribes of central Texas, and he knew the locations of their villages, and he could determine the tribal affiliation of a dead Indian. He was intimately acquainted with many Indian chiefs, but apparently had no knowledge of Athanase de Mézières, the commandant at Natchitoches who had traveled much among Texas Indians from 1772 to 1779. Vial left Bexar with only one companion, Cristóbal de los Santos, and one packhorse with provisions.

### *Diary of Pedro Vial, Bexar to Santa Fe, October 4, 1786, to May 26, 1787*[8]

Diary which, by the grace of God, I (Pedro Vial) am starting to make from this Presidio of San Antonio de Bejar until I arrive at that capital village of Santa Fe, by appointment of my governor, Don Domingo Cavello,[9] governor of the Province of Texas, with an account of the daily travel from this day, October 4, 1787.

October

4 We departed from this presidio [and] arrived at the Comales[10] without mishap.[11]

[8] Our translation is made from the copy in Archivo General in Mexico City, Sección de Historia, leg. 62, no. 2. Other copies are in Historia 43, no. 14 (the Talamantes-Pichardo copy, with which we have compared), and in Historia 52, no. 17.

[9] Domingo Cabello was governor of Texas, 1778–86.

[10] There is a Comal Creek northeast of San Antonio, and if Vial reached it the first day, he should credit himself with eight more leagues of travel. However, we are not going to make out the itinerary, for the late H. Bailey Carroll, of Austin, Texas, worked on the routes of Vial and his contemporaries for several years; he traveled over them on horseback and examined them in connection with all available journals, and it is to be hoped that his book will be published. In the meantime, we shall content ourselves with very general comments on the itineraries.

[11] Herbert E. Bolton, in his map in *Athanase de Mézières*, indicates that Vial started northeast, but that direction does not seem to work out. Bolton also traveled

5 We left this place and crossed the Rio de Guadeloupe, where, upon crossing the stream, a horse was drowned [and] we lost the provisions. 8[12]

6 We set out to the north from this place and traveled until we reached a rivulet with water. 5[13]

7 We set out from this place in the same direction and went to the Rio de los Chanes[14] without mishap. 7

*From this point on, we shall have trouble following Vial's route. Quite obviously he forgets to mention many of the rivers he crosses, and sometimes he uses his own names for them. Also, his recorded distances are inaccurate. It must be remembered that Vial wrote in French, and it may be assumed, from his composition, that writing was not easy for him—which may explain why "north" seems to mean "in a northerly direction" or anywhere from northeast to northwest, and sometimes not even those. Undoubtedly, too, errors occurred in translating and transcribing the journal and in making copies.*

8 We left this place, heading in the same direction, and went to the Colorado River,[15] where I arrived ill. 8

9 I departed from this place, going upstream on a western route, until I arrived at the same river [again].

10 I set out from this place to the north, going up the river to a region of low hills. 7

11 I departed from this place in the same direction [and went] to a river which unites with the Colorado. 6

12 I set out from this place in the same direction, [and traveled] until I reached a small stream which joins the same river.[16]

13 I set out from this place [and traveled] until I came upon

the entire route on foot and horseback. Carlos E. Castañeda, *Our Catholic Heritage in Texas, 1519–1936*, V, 150–55, presents the route in some detail but with unexplained discrepancies. Again, we shall await Carroll's log.

[12] In his journal, Vial adds figures in the margin after each entry for the distance traveled.

[13] Probably the Blanco River.

[14] This may have been the Pedernales.

[15] At the moment, Vial seems to be moving north and west.

[16] The San Saba.

a trail which I later determined was that of the Taguayaces[17] and Guichitas[18] who had gone to Sant Antonio to steal horses.[19] 6

14 I set out from this place in the same direction, [going] until I reached an arroyo where, fainting by reason of sickness, I fell from my horse and was unconscious for two hours before my senses returned [*hasta que volvi en acuerdo*]. [As soon as] I regained my senses, my companion [De los Santos][19a] asked me for a paper so that if I should die, it would not be thought that he had killed me. To which I responded that I trusted God that I should not die, and that we should go to the pueblos of the Tahuacanes[20] where it might be that some Indian would have some remedy. 4

15 We set out to the north on the way to the Tahuacanes, [going] until we reached a lagoon [pond?]. 6

*From this point on, we cannot reconcile the itinerary with the geography. We should be lost indeed if it were not for the fact that later he mentions the village of Quiscat, a Tawakoni chief, and positively identifies it, as will be seen. Quiscat's village was rather well known in the late eighteenth century, and we now have to assume that by some route—probably devious—Vial traveled until he arrived at a point eighty miles due east of present-day Priddy. His movements to the east must be assumed, in spite of the fact that he says he is going north all the time.*

16 I set out from this place in the same direction, [traveling] until I reached a plain where I found two springs. 8

17 I remained in this place because I was very unwell. 4

18 I set out from this place in the same direction, [going] until I arrived at a stream which unites with a river called los Brazos de Dios.[21] 5

19 I set out from this place in the same direction, [going] until

[17] Taovayas.

[18] Wichitas.

[19] This obviously refers to the trouble at Bexar, already mentioned.

[19a] It is interesting to observe that this is the name of Philip Nolan's *inamorata* only ten years or so later.

[20] Tawakonis.

[21] This might be the Leon River or the North Bosque.

I reached a trail of some Indians who had been hunting; here I remained until the 21st, when I set out. 4

21 I set out from this place on the same route to the north, and reached a stream of water. 7

22 I set out from this place in the same direction, and reached a stream which is on the edge of a large plain. 5

23 I set out from this place to the north, seeking the village of the Tawakonis until I slept on the same plain. 3

24 I set out from this place in the same direction, [traveling] until I reached the village [of the Tawakonis] about 4 in the afternoon, but I found it deserted because they had gone to another place [deeper in the interior.] 3

*The evidence of Vial's wandering route is now complete. Castañeda suggests this was a village on the Bosque—which would be seventy-five or eighty miles east of Priddy, where he had become ill and had fallen from his horse, according to Castañeda. But Vial records 45 leagues, or 125 miles. From this fact—as well as from the length of his stay at the Tawakoni village when he arrived there—it may be concluded that Pedro Vial was extremely ill and probably delirious a large part of the time.*

25 I set out from this place to the north, searching for the Tawakonis until I arrived at the Brazos River [*los Brazos de Dios*]. 6

26 I set out from this place in the same direction and slept by the same river. 5

27 I set out from this place [and traveled] in the same direction until I stopped at a place on the edge of the same river. 5

28 Leaving the river, I went north until I reached a place where the Indians had camped. 4

29 I set out from this place in the same direction, [going] until I arrived at a stream which joins the Brazos River, where I found the Tawakonis at about 2 in the afternoon. Having arrived at the lodge of Captain Quisquaie's [Chief Quiscat] home, I [found the people] seemed very much surprised to see me, and they asked me where I was going, to which I replied that I was going to the Cumanches [Comanches], and from the Comanches [I expected] to discover [get information about] the road to Santa Fe.

*Vial has finally reached the village that provides an orientation point: the village of El Quiscat, on the Brazos River near Waco. It seems that it had been moved since the time of Vial's last visit, and since the time of De Mézière's visits (of which he made three—one in 1772, one in 1778, and one in 1779).*[22]

Many chiefs having come together, they asked me if there was a certain Tahuaayase [Taovaya] in San Antonio who had gone there to steal horses, and I responded that I already knew what they had to say to me, and I told them that the Taovayas and Guichitas [Wichitas] had gone to San Antonio, and one night had stolen several horses; and [I said] that the captain at San Antonio had thought they were Apaches, and the following night he ordered the sentinels to be on guard, and, when they returned that night, the sentinels killed one. To this the said Chief Quiscat answered that, on their return from San Antonio, the Taovayas and Wichitas had been in his village, and that he had chided them because of the theft, and had taken some horses from them, telling them that they were fools to injure the Spaniards, [and] that the Tawakonis were brothers with the latter. And they [the Tawakonis] told me that because of these various facts [*por esto*] I should not think that the chiefs had sent them, and [Quiscat said] that I could now see how he restrained his people from doing injury; he said that it was true that before knowing the Spaniards he had made war on them, and that then there had come to his village a French captain called Don Atanasio de Mecier,[23] Knight of the Cross of St. Louis,[24] who had persuaded him to stop making trouble, and that he [Quiscat] had been taken to San Antonio [and placed] before the Baron de Riperdá,[25] who was a *tomes* [?] governor, and to him he [Quiscat]

[22] Bolton, *Athanase de Mezieres*, I, 144ff.

[23] Athanase de Mézières, to whom we have previously referred. He was a well-born Frenchman who went to Natchitoches in the 1740's, when the post belonged to France. He continued in the Spanish service and was appointed lieutenant-governor of Natchitoches in 1769. De Mézières had a particular interest in Indian relations, and he traveled over Texas several times; apparently he enjoyed the confidence of his superiors, for in 1779 he was appointed governor of Texas; but he died in San Antonio following a severe fall on his last trip. See Bolton's *Athanase de Mézières.*

[24] This decoration was received by De Mézières on his trip to Europe in 1773 and 1774.

[25] Colonel Juan María, Baron de Riperdá, was another non-Spaniard in the

had given his word neither to do injury nor to make war, and he [Quiscat] said that he had been rewarded with a complete suit, a horse, a medal, and a flag,[26] and that for that reason [thus] he always kept his people quiet, as one could see; that he could watch his villages without danger, and that it was for this reason that he had so much merchandise from the Spaniards which he had not had previously when he had acted like a frightened man. I advised him not to lose the friendship of the Spaniards and [thus] always to keep his people clothed.

I told him [then] I was ill and [asked] if anyone would try to cure me; he said yes, they would call someone to heal me; he promptly commanded his people to look after me, and he kept me in his lodge until the 15th of December, when I set out well [again].[27] 3

15 I set out to the north, going right along the Brazos River until I stopped for the night on the same river. 5

16 I set out from this place in the same direction, and slept without any mishap by the same river. 5

17 I went in the same direction from this place until I arrived at an arroyo[28] with water. 8

18 I set out from this place in the same direction until I came to a lagoon [*laguna*[29]] with water. 7

19 I set out from this place in the same direction, [traveling] until I returned to the same river for the night. 5

20 I set out from this place in the same direction [and traveled] until I came to a forest, where I found water. 5

21 I set out from this place in the same direction and along the

Spanish service, like Oreilli, O'Conor, and Odonojú. Riperdá, descendant of a Flemish family and a native of Madrid, was governor of Texas from 1770 to 1778; an outstanding feature of his governorship was the work of De Mézières in winning the Indians over to the Spaniards.

[26] De Mézières does not mention taking Quiscat to Bexar, although he speaks twice of Quirotaches, a Taovaya chief.

[27] He had spent almost two months in Quiscat's village, which indicates a severe illness, but he does not give any indication of its nature.

[28] Vial often refers to an "arroyo" and to "an arroyo with water." An arroyo is nominally a small stream, and a stream bed or water course is an arroyada, and in the Southwest, that usually means a dry stream bed; Vial probably means it to be dry unless he says "with water."

[29] *Laguna:* pond, lake, stagnant water, or marsh. When he refers to a "laguna," he probably means a marsh with water as contrasted to one without water.

same river; about 4 in the afternoon I saw a smoke [signal], which I answered, and presently men were made out, and as I began to shout, I was answered. After we had crossed the river and stopped, two men came up—a Wichita and a Spaniard of this kingdom [but] now a captive—who were coming from San Antonio, where they had been stealing horses; they wanted to camp with us for the night. The Spaniard was called Juan de le Cruz, [and] on the following day we traveled together.[30] 6

22 We set out from this place in the same direction until we arrived, without event, at a back water bay. 4

23 I set out from this place along the same river until I came to a stream. 6

24 I set out from this place in the same direction through a region of low hills, crossing the river near a village of the Taovayas; [I traveled] until I stopped for the night in another low, hilly region where I found water. 5

*It has become difficult again to follow him; it would seem reasonable that, having met a Wichita, who is traveling with them, they should go on along the Brazos to the Wichita village of Ovedsita, south of present-day Wichita Falls. He continues to speak of traveling west, but that must be discounted. Castañeda suggests that he cut north from Dennis, but Bolton indicates that he followed the Brazos much farther, and then went northeast to the Taovaya villages on the Red River.*

25 I set out from this place and crossed the same river, [going] until I stopped at a stream where there was good water. 6

26 We set out from this place, following the river to the west, and traveled until we stopped for the night with the Wichitas; we slept in an arroyo, going until I stopped in it to sleep.[31] 5

27 I set out from this place by the same arroyo, [going] until I stopped to sleep in it. 8

28 I went west from this place until I reached the village of the Taoyavas and Wichitas, where I spent the night. The chiefs, being assembled as soon as I arrived , at the lodge of Chief Corichi, began to

[30] Castañeda places this in the vicinity of Dennis. *Our Catholic Heritage*, V, 153.

[31] From the context, it is now apparent that he means a dry stream bed.

say (in the same [place]) that even if some had gone to injure the Spaniards, they knew that the Spaniards had fired a shot at them, and they asked me if the Taovayas whom the Spaniards had killed, had been seized or killed. To them I replied that because they saw me alone—with only one companion—they should not think that I was afraid to tell the truth, and that they knew already that I was not a liar. [I told them] that their companion was dead, that I had seen him with my own eyes, and that I had heard the shots, and, carrying my weapon in my hand, I had gone to see who was fighting against the Spaniards. [I told them that] when I had arrived where the Spaniards were, they had said to me: "Here is a dead man; you know all the nations; you can tell us to which nation this one belongs." [I told the Indians that,] having gone where he was, I found him in the grass, still alive but dying, and that I knew at once that he was a Taovaya, and that among us we had carried him to the guardhouse. [I told them] that when the governor came, he asked me if I recognized him [the Indian], and I replied that he was a petty Taovaya chief from among the five who had come recently to San Antonio; [I told them] that his Excellency had said to me that it was a good thing that he was dead, and that these [people] were fools for trying to injure the Spaniards; that he [the governor] did not want to believe that the Taovayas were making trouble, and that he had thought [the guilty ones] were Apaches [but] that now he knew that [the Taovayas'] peace was feigned, and that they were bad people; [I told them] that he admonished them not to do evil, because all the Indians who roamed about the presidio would follow and kill them [if they should do evil], and that [even] if [the Spaniards] should see any Spaniard who was going to do them [the Indians who roamed about the presidio] harm, they [the Spaniards] would kill him also, [and certainly] the Indian who would harm the Spaniards would not be recognized as a friend. [I told them] that if they were angry on account of this death [of the petty chief], they already knew where San Antonio was, and his Excellency knew where the Taovayas and Wichitas were located.

At that point, I held a parley for the purpose of speaking to them as follows: "If you Taovayas and Wichitas are among those who send their people to make trouble at San Antonio, there will be no one to save you from those who may harm you. What you [must] wish is to see your villages destroyed and your families enslaved by other nations. Do you want to be equal with the Spaniards, who know how to make guns, powder, shot, axes, grubbing hoes [*azadones*], and other weapons that are necessary, while you know how to make none of these? The captain at San Antonio sends to you traders who bring you all that is necessary for you to keep your strength against your foes, and now it appears that you wish to rise up against the Spaniards, and the captain at San Antonio knows that you do make trouble, as is shown by the death of the Taovaya whom they [the Spaniards] killed. Do you not think that it will be easy for them [i.e., for the Spaniards] if no one brings goods to your village? Then you will find yourself very poor, and you will have many difficulties; then the other Indians, your enemies, who learn that you do not have powder and balls, will come to make war on you, and they will steal your sons and your women, and you will not be able to go out to hunt to support your families, or to sleep in peace, and then the other nations that are friends of the Spaniards will hate you. And if the captain at San Antonio is vexed, he has only to speak a word to the other nations, and you will be very much humbled, and thus you will be able to see that all the [other] nations are friendly and very quiet, hunting in peace, while every day traders come and go to their villages without causing them any difficulty. If you do not feel any shame for not fulfilling the word which you have given to the captain, if you wish to make war on the Spaniards, it is not necessary for the men to go; send the women—which will be the same. You regard as enemies the Guachases[32] and also the Apaches, who every day are killing and driving off your horses while no one of you has the heart to go bring in a band of horses. You chiefs, be on your guard; free yourselves from those fools who cause trouble.

"Now I am going to open this road to Santa Fe in order that the Spaniards of San Antonio may cross through the Comanche country and that those from Santa Fe may pass from there to San Antonio, since they are all friends. And if on my return I see that you Taovayas are quiet, I will take you to San Antonio before the Spanish captain, and you will see that he is a kind-hearted man to you as soon as you promise him not to do harm."[32a]

[32] Probably he means Guagages (Osages).

They replied that all that I had said to them was true; that I should see them act thus [as he impliedly suggested they should act] in the future; that they were not the ones who had advised the youths to make trouble; that they who had gone to do wrong were four fools, setting out at night and saying they were going on a campaign against the Apaches, [and] that they had given them advice to which they would not listen. They promised [then] to wait for me until I should return in order to go to San Antonio, because they were afraid to go alone. They told me that they were waiting for a chief who had gone to give assurance [to the Comanches] that they were going to the Comanches to dance [*bailar la pipa*], and that as soon as they should trade,[33] they would return.

I was here until the sixth of January, when I departed. 12

January

6 This Chief arrived with 6 Comanches, saying that all the Comanches were fools for letting the Taovayas and Wichitas go to dance in their country. 3

8 [?] I set out from this place to the west with many of those people, [going] until I reached the vicinity of the road. 4

9 I reached [the place] where the Comanches were [camped], and, having arrived at the lodge of the head chief, who is called Zoquiné, I did not find him there because he had gone to a settlement to get some animals that the Comanches had stolen from the Taovayas in order to return them to their owners. 2

11 [?] This chief, who was glad to see me, arrived with the animals, and many chiefs assembled in his lodge to smoke the pipe. They began to ask me where I was traveling and why I was going to Santa Fe—to which I replied that their father the captain at San Antonio, was sending me to open the road from San Antonio to Santa Fe; that I carried a letter which I was to deliver to the captain at Santa Fe so that the Spaniards and the Comanches might be able to travel from one part [of the country] to another. [I said] that the Spaniards

[32a] Surely one of the most impassioned, moving, and effective speeches on the frontier. Vial out-Indianed the Indians.

[33] The Taovayas were long-time intermediaries between the Comanches on the west side and the legal traders from Natchitoches on the east, or the *contrabandistas* from the Arkansas country on the northeast.

looked upon the Comanches as brothers and that the captain regarded them as sons. To this, they replied that they were very pleased, but that now it was not possible to travel because of the extreme cold and heavy snows in Santa Fe. [They said] that now I could pass the winter with them, and at the coming of spring they would accompany me until they should place me in Santa Fe.

They asked me if I knew of the recent occurrences of which they had heard, [and] I replied no, that I did not. They told me that the chief who was with me at San Antonio when I made the peace[34] had been killed by the Spaniards. [They said] that all the Comanches, having gone on a campaign against the Apaches, were traveling on a large plain and had come upon the tracks of many persons, and having followed the trail, they reached the place where the people were; they knew they were Spaniards because of the commotion that they made in camp, but at the same time they [the Comanches] made their escape [*fuga*] in another direction to search for the Apaches and to send two youths as spies. [The youths] returned in the night and said they had heard the people talk, but they did not know what [nationality] they were, and then they began to prepare to give [battle] to them, thinking they were Apaches. At daybreak, about 4 o'clock, they set out at full speed, and the youths, who had good horses, went ahead of the chiefs, until, arriving [at the place] where the people were, they saw that they were Spaniards. [Then] the Spaniards, having seen them, began to shout to the Comanches, treating them like friends [as] on many [previous] occasions; and the Comanche youths began to say that it would be a good thing to steal the horses of the Spaniards, but a chief called Patuarus [Paruarus?] [, recently] arrived, told them that the Spaniards were good friends of theirs, [and] asked why they [the Comanches] wished to hurt them [the Spaniards]. But the foolish boys said that they [the older ones] were afraid, and thus [that if he—Patuarus—was determined to be friendly with the Spaniards] he would not be recognized as chief. Then the said chief was angry, and said that *all* the Comanches were *not* fit to face danger before the Spaniards,[35] and immediately the Comanches fired at the people [who opposed them?]. Then the chief himself and another chief fell dead

[34] Referring to the trouble he had discussed at Quiscat's village.

[35] Underscoring is in the copy.

from the shots, and the Comanches, seeing the heavy shots that the Spaniards fired, fled in retreat. The chiefs, having reached the place [of safety] where the [Comanches] were located who had been sent back during the fight, began to reprove the youths for having fought. Then they raised the flag, and a chief named Tanicón, brother of the Chief Zoquiné and the chief Guaquangas, surrendered to the Spaniards, and, having come up to them, the Spanish captain, [who was] Don Josef Menchaca,[36] embraced them. Then the other Spaniards and the Comanches arrived, and they buried the two dead Comanches and set up the flag at the head of the principal chief.

Then the Comanches traded with the Spaniards, and they returned to their country well satisfied.

They told me that I should not think that they would do anything to me, although here [around me] were all the relatives of the dead men, for they [the dead men] were guilty. To which I responded that they were not guilty, [for] the Spaniards regarded them as brothers [even though] they were not like them. [I said] that when they [the Spaniards] regarded a nation as friendly, they did not try to commit treason as they [had done]. They then replied that it was true. 3[37]

17 Many chiefs gathered in the lodge of Chief Zoquiné to smoke, and they told me that they had no tobacco [and asked] that I promise to send to the captain at San Antonio for some. [I wrote and] they dispatched a minor chief with another—a strapping youth—to carry it and to find out what nation had killed a brother of the captain named Taraquiqui, for they [that is, some nation] had killed this man along with another.

They told me that San Antonio was very far distant for them, and that there was [as] much danger from the Apaches as from the Tancaguas [Tonkawas]. [They said] that if the Spaniards wished to establish the presidio of San Saba as it had been formerly,[37a] it would

[36] José Menchaca was a lieutenant of cavalry, stationed at Bexar in 1778, and he accompanied De Mézières on his expedition of that year. In Texas thirty years, he became captain of the presidio at Bexar; he was in command of a Mexican division and was killed at the battle of Medina in 1813. Bolton, *Athanase de Mézières,* II, 35n.

[37] It is a matter of curiosity as to why Vial includes figures when he does not seem to have traveled.

[37a] San Sabá presidio was established about 60 miles northwest of Béxar in 1757; the infamous massacre occurred there in 1758, and certainly the Comanches took part

be much better [than San Antonio] because it was much closer to them, or to place a settlement on the Pedernales River[37b] so that they could trade, and the young men would be able to hunt where they lived [on the Red River], and they would not have cause to do any harm. Afterward, the Chief of the Shirt of Mail, who is called Guaquangas, told me that he was waiting to go to San Antonio with me, and [that he would] take along many persons to see the great captain.

*Guaquangas, or Cota de Malla, was the great Cuchanec (Kotsoteka) Comanche chief known to the Spaniards as Ecueracapa (Leather Cape), or Cota de Malla, presumably because of his wearing either a heavy leather vest or a chain-mail vest taken from some early Spanish explorer. Anza refers to him as El Huérfano in war, Contatanacapara, and Grulla de Cruz; he had a son called Ozmaquea. Ecueracapa succeeded the great chief Cuerno Verde, or Green Horn, who had been killed in battle by the Spaniards, and went to Santa Fe to seek peace in July, 1786, at which time Anza, the governor, noted that Ecueracapa was universally respected by the Comanches.*[38] *On November 19, 1793, Concha, governor of New Mexico, wrote to Nava to say that the Comanches were going to hold a council on the Colorado River to name a general to replace the defunct Ecueracapa—who turned out to be Chief Encaguañé.*[39] *There were later Comanches with similar names: Iron Jacket (Pohebits Quasho), a Kotsoteka Comanche killed in 1588; Iron Shirt, a Tanima Comanche, living in 1865.*

*Pedro Vial must have been astonished to find the great Ecueracapa in his audience, but he takes it in stride. He minces no words with any of them but he lays down the law, holding out hope, however, in the*

in that; from 1762 until 1769 the Comanches, along with Apaches and Taovayas and perhaps others, waged almost continuous warfare against the presidio and forced its abandonment. It had been planned originally as a link in the Béxar-Santa Fe line of communication.

[37b] The Pedernales flows east, about 25 miles north of Béxar, to join the Llano River. The Comanches were indulging in their usual double-talk, for the Pedernales was about 290 airline miles from the villages on the Red River, while San Sabá was only 255 miles. Perhaps the Comanches had in mind that if the presidio should not be so near the trail to Mexico and should not be in the canyon they had used for decades as a rendezvous, they would not be tempted quite so much.

[38] Thomas, *Forgotten Frontiers*, 325–26.

[39] Nava to Concha, Chihuahua, December 31, 1793, New Mexican Archives, doc. 1272, no. 2.

*event of their good behavior. It is the kind of talk the Indians would understand and respect.*

18 We set out to the east [!] and halted on an arroyo of water, where we stayed. 3

19 We set out in the same direction and stopped on the same arroyo, [remaining here] until the 4th of March.[40]

March

4 We set out to the west from this place,[41] and halted in another arroyo of water, to which place came a Taovaya chief to ask the Comanches if they had seen any of his people who had gone to rob the Spaniards; and the Comanches, who had that day arrived from San Antonio, told them that sixteen had been imprisoned. Then I brought up the previous conversation, and the Taovaya replied to me that he was ashamed of this, and that when they should return to their village, they would make them stop all the meanness. 2

15 We set out from this place in the same direction, [going] until we arrived at the Río de Mermellon. 3

16 We went west from this place until we stopped for the night in another arroyo that joins the same river. 5

17 We went in the same direction from this place until we reached the same arroyo which joins the same river. 3

18 We set out from this place in the same direction, looking for buffaloes, until we arrived at an arroyo that joined a river that passes Naquitochi and which the Frenchmen call the Río Colorado River.[42] 6

19 We traveled from this place in the same direction until we stopped for the night at another arroyo which joins the same river. 5

[40] The place where they established a winter camp for six weeks, says Castañeda, is in the region of Clara or Burkburnett. Undoubtedly Vial had traveled west from the Taovayas, rather than east.

[41] No explanation is given for the ten-day lapse. It sounds as if the name of the river was garbled in translation; it may have started out as Vermejo, Spanish for Red. Castañeda says it was the Pease; in early spring it might have been full and roily and easily mistakable for the Red.

[42] It is obvious now that he did not mean the Red River when he spoke of the Mermellon, nor it is likely that in 1786 he would have been speaking of the Prairie Dog Town Fork as a separate stream from the Red. As noted, perhaps the translator made an error.

20 We set out from this place in the same direction [and went] until we stopped at another arroyo, where we remained until the 24th. 2

24 We marched in the same direction until we made camp for the night on an arroyo with water. 3

26 [*sic*] We went in the same direction until we stopped for the night at a lagoon.

27 We marched from this place in the same direction and again passed the night on the same [branch of] the Colorado River.[43] 3

28 We traveled in the same direction until we stopped for the night at another arroyo, where we remained until April 6. 3

April

6 We set out from this place in the same direction, [traveling] until we returned to the same arroyo. 6

7 We set out from this place in the same direction [and marched] until we made camp for the night at another arroyo, at which place there arrived two Comanches from another settlement. They told [me] that three Comanches had come from San Antonio and had said that I had come to deceive them, that the Spanish captain of Santa Fe had written a letter to the captain at San Antonio de Bexar, saying that if the Comanches were going to San Antonio de Bexar to barter [*rescatar*], and were many in number, they were going so that the Spaniards might kill them, and that I was going to take the Comanches to Santa Fe in order to kill them [also]. Then I defended myself insofar as I was able, saying that they should not believe that the Spaniards would do any treasonable act, that because those men [the ones who came to warn] always have a bad heart, they believed that the Spaniards were the same [as themselves]. Chief Zoquiné replied that he would not leave me until he should see me in Santa Fe, and, concerning what they had said, they knew afterward that they had told a lie. 3

*For the third time, Pedro Vial has demonstrated his resourcefulness, his knowledge of Indian psychology, and his ready tongue. He threw the lie back at them and accused them of being bad, and obviously Chief Zoquiné admired and approved his stand. A moment of hesitation or weakness would have been fatal in this spot, for the Comanches respected nothing as much as strength. On March 4 Vial said*

[43] This can hardly be other than the Pease, it seems.

*the Taovaya chief came to ask a question of the Comanches, but not until now has Vial told us that the Comanches were traveling with him—when we find indirectly that Chief Zoquiné is going with him as a guide to Santa Fe, as Zoquiné has promised to do previously.*

8 We set out in the same direction, [traveling] until we reached an arroyo of water, where we remained four days. 5

12 We set out from this place in the same direction along the same arroyo, and we slept in it. 3

13 We went north from this place until we reached the Colorado River, where we remained six days.[44] 3

19 We set out to the west from this place, and we stopped until the 27th on a little stream [*ri(a)chuela*] which joins the Colorado River. 5

27 We set out from this place in the same direction, and we stopped on another arroyo which joins the same river; we were [here] a day. 3

29 We marched from this place in the same direction until we stopped on the same Colorado River; I was here 3 days.[45] 5

May

2 From this place we set out in the same direction toward Santa Fe with four chiefs and two braves—all with their squaws—and we slept on another arroyo. 6

3 We went in a northern direction until we stopped for the night on another arroyo.[46] 7

4 We proceeded in the same direction to a canyon with a spring of water, where we slept. 6

[44] At this point, they must have reached the South Canadian River, somewhere north of present Amarillo; they seem to have avoided the precipitous Caprock. Vial does not mention the Caprock, and if he approached the river by a northern route, he might have avoided it altogether. Castañeda suggests that he mistook the South Canadian for the Red, because he called it Colorado—but that is not necessarily true, for the South Canadian was called the Colorado in New Mexico long before Vial reached it—and it still is.

[45] He does not say so, but he must have suffered from his recurrent illness, for he has traveled only seven days in April.

[46] They were "heading the breaks"—keeping far enough away from the main stream to avoid the rough terrain, but close enough to find water in the intermittent tributaries.

5 We went in the same direction until we reached another canyon with water. 5

6 We marched in the same direction to some other springs of water, where we slept. 4

7 We set out to the west and made camp for the night at some other springs of water. 3 [5]

8 We went in the same direction until we reached another canyon, where we remained until the 11th. 8

11 We set out in the same direction, entered a large plain, and stopped for the night without water. 5

12 We went up-grade in the same direction until we reached a spring of water. 8

13 We traveled in the same direction until we stopped in a canyon with water. 6

14 We set out from this place in the same direction, [going] until we stopped on an arm of the Colorado River,[47] where we found the villages of the Tupis,[48] and immediately the chief called Paranuarimuco[49] brought out the Spanish flag and took us to his lodge. There we were well received, and he talked to us [very] much about the captain at Santa Fe, saying that he was well pleased with him. I was here a day. 5 leagues

16 I set out from this place in the same direction, [going] until we slept on the same river, where I found a village of Yamparicas who also spoke with us, also very friendly. 2

18 We set out from this place in the same direction, and we slept by the same river. 5

19 We set out from this place in the afternoon, [traveling] until we stopped for the night in a plain without water. 12

20 We set out from this place to the north, and stopped at a spring of water. 8

21 We went west until we reached an arroyo which joins this Colorado River. 13

22 We set out from this place in the same direction and we slept by the same arroyo. 9

[47] Castañeda places this camp near present Logan, New Mexico.

[48] The Tupis, says Hodge, were Distakana (Yamparica) Comanches.

[49] Paranuarimuco was a famous Yamparica chief who succeeded Toroblanco, who was killed in 1785.

23 We went from this place in the same direction until we stopped for the night on a plain without water. 8

24 We traveled west from this place until we stopped for the night in an arroyo which joins the Pecos River. 12

25 We set out from this place, [traveling] until we reached a village of Pecos, where we arrived with the flag unfurled. 10

26 We marched from this village until we arrived at Santa Fe, where the troops came out to receive me; I went along with them until I delivered the banner to Señor Captain Don Manuel Delgado. 8

And in order that what this itinerary mentions may be manifest and certain, I offer in proof the accompanying map upon which I indicate the territory that I know (as he will see who may go search out the same road from this kingdom by the governor's commission), in order that he may go by the route on which the settlements and villages of the gentiles [Indians] are located.

Santa Fe. July 5, 1787.

PEDRO VIAL

This is a copy. Chihuahua, September 12, 1793.
MANUEL MERINO [*rubric*]

[Total 459 leagues]

[Marginal note from Historia 43: "*Yo no le* [*he?*] *visto este mapa y deseará verlo por las muchas mas que da especialmente del Río de Natchitoches.*" Obviously neither Talamantes nor Pichardo saw the map.]

Thus casually does Pedro Vial, the first man in recorded history to travel from Bexar to Santa Fe across the Panhandle of Texas, end his epic voyage, having traveled some 1,157 miles through an uncharted wilderness. The country through which he traveled was not unexplored, because Vial had been in many parts of it before. On this trip he had left Bexar on October 4 and had been seven and one-half months en route—two months of which had been spent in recuperation with Quiscat, and six weeks in winter camp, leaving four months of traveling time. He had not hesitated to go through the country of the Apaches, the Tonkawas, the Wichita tribes, and two or more Comanche tribes, and apparently the Indians respected him, for at least six Comanches and their squaws accompanied him to Santa Fe; presumably Chief Zoquiné was among them.

He had been ill, had fallen from his horse, had traveled a hundred and fifty miles to find an Indian medicine man to doctor him, and had recovered; he had faced the Tawakonis in the village of Quiscat when confronted with the trouble at San Antonio, and had talked them down; he had spoken straight to the Taovayas and Wichitas in their own village, and had made believers out of them; he had faced the implacable Comanches and had backed them into a corner; he had talked aggressively to them when a group of Comanches had come after him and had urged the others not to go on to Santa Fe with him because he was leading them into a trap. On any one of those occasions, if he had failed to back down the Comanches, his life would have been the forfeit.

Vial reached Santa Fe on May 26, 1787, but he did not sign the translation of his diary until July 5—probably because it took some time to get it translated. But the map that would show where he had traveled and the territory that he knew, has not been found. It appears that that map would have been concerned with Texas and eastern New Mexico, and it is not the same map that he made in October of that year, some months later. In his diary he says, "the enclosed map," but its whereabouts, if it exists, is unknown, as is the whereabouts of Vial's original journal in French—both of which appear to have dropped from sight as soon as the translations were made—as has also the original signed copy of this diary.

When he spoke of "the enclosed map," the date was July 5, 1787. On July 31, José Mares left on the return trip, and Vial, undoubtedly prompted by the governor, then drew another map showing all the territory that he had traversed in the trans-Mississippi West. It is a very remarkable map, and gives rise to some interesting questions that will be discussed later. One rather obvious problem, however, is the whereabouts of the original. The Historical Society of New Mexico has a photostat of the original, and Castañeda has used the map twice, but Carl I. Wheat was unable to find the original for his monumental atlas, *Mapping the Transmississippi West.*[50]

Pedro Vial must have had thorough knowledge of the Indians, great confidence, complete resourcefulness, and a large portion of guts. He

[50] Carl I. Wheat, *The Spanish Entrada to the Louisiana Purchase, 1540–1804* (Vol. I of the series, *Mapping the Transmississippi West, 1540–1861* [5 vols.]), I, 238.

was hardly out of Bexar when he lost his provisions; he was closer to Bexar than to Quiscat's village when he became ill, but he chose to go ahead, even on a roundabout route; it really was quite a path that he blazed through Texas, and it is no wonder that the governor of New Mexico immediately sent Mares with instructions to find a more direct route.

Vial had taken his time, but he had shown the way. He had opened the first road to Santa Fe since the Chihuahua Trail had been established almost two hundred years before. He was to establish three new routes to Santa Fe: from the southeast, from the east, and from the northeast. The one from the southeast was now a matter of history, and even before Vial had drawn his second map, José Mares was on the way to the Taovaya villages on the Red River of Natchitoches.

# XII

# *José Mares, Santa Fe to Bexar, July 31 to October 8, 1787, and Return, in 1788*

José de Calahorra, a missionary at Nacogdoches, had learned in the 1760's that the Taovaya villages on the Red River were only fifteen days' travel from New Mexico, and that French traders from a post on the Arkansas had established that French traders from a post on the Arkansas had established five posts between the Taovayas and New Mexico.[1] Apparently there had been more than a little travel along that route, and undoubtedly Governor Concha was aware of it, and, realizing also his isolated position with respect to the northern provinces of Mexico, was greatly interested in finding a shorter and more direct route between Santa Fe and Bexar. It was Mares who was commissioned to find it.

Pedro Vial reached Santa Fe on May 26, 1787, and by the early part of July his journal, translated from Vial's French into Spanish, and examined by Governor Anza, who had replaced Concha, may have suggested that Vial had not come by the shortest route. It seems likely also that the map (now lost) may have given a more graphic demonstration. Probably Vial was drawing the map while the translator was working on his diary; at any rate, there does not appear to be any preliminary correspondence between the governor and the commandant-general to plan Mares' trips, and the time element suggests that it was Anza who ordered the second trip largely on his own initiative, for Vial signed his diary on July 5, and Mares left Santa Fe on July 31. The interval was not too short for correspondence with Ugarte, but it would have been unusual for such a decision to be made so promptly unless Ugarte had already laid the groundwork for Mares' trip.

[1] Castañeda, *Our Catholic Heritage*, V, 146–47.

At any rate, less than four weeks after Vial signed his diary, José Mares left Santa Fe, accompanied by Cristóbal de los Santos (who had made the trail-breaking trip with Vial, as we shall learn later), and Alejandro Martin or Martín, an Indian interpreter who is mentioned a number of times in New Mexican documents.

### *Journal of José Mares, Santa Fe to Bexar* *July 31 to October 8, 1787*[2]

Year of 1787

Journey of discovery en route from the capital of New Mexico to that of the Province of Texas, made by the retired corporal, José Mares.

In the name of Almighty God and of the Most Holy Virgin Mary of the Immaculate Conception, My Lady of the Rosary, conqueror of the kingdom and province of New Mexico, conceived in grace, amen:

I, the Corporal José Mares, retired,[3] of the royal presidio of the capital town of Santa Fe, make this itinerary for the information and knowledge [of all] of the trip which I am starting to make to the presidio of San Antonio de Bexar, today, the 31st of July of the present year, 1787, placing in the margin [of the paper] the indication of the number of leagues of each day's journey, and at the said presidio of Santa Fe there is being solemnized the celebration of the exaltation of the Holy Cross with the motto, guidance, and company of this royal standard, I left the presidio of Santa Fe on the expressed day, month, and year, heading southeasterly, and I arrived at the village of Pecos.[4]

Indication of leagues

I left Pecos August 1, heading south, and came to the ford of the Río de Pecos, where I rested; and at 3 o'clock I marched to the east, leaving the river, which flows to the south, on the right. Heading east, I spent the night in the little canyon of Bernal, where I slept among some very small rivulets and some coarse grass [*en unos ojitos*[5] *muy cortos con unos carrizalitos*]. 6

From here I set out southeasterly on the 2nd [of August], and

[2] Our copy is a certified copy in Historia, Vol. 62, No. 3. There are other copies: in Historia, Vol. 43, No. 13; and in Historia, Vol. 52, exp. 17. We have compared them.

[3] In this connection, *retirado* means pensioned (probably at half-pay), and it would seem to indicate that Mares was just past the age of active duty.

[4] Accompanied by Cristóbal de los Santos and Alejandro Martín.

[5] Ojito does not seem to mean "spring" in this sentence.

camped for the night at the Gallinas River, much below the last cottonwoods.[6] 8

From here I set out on a straight road on the 3rd, heading south, and entered into the midst of some broken table lands; the soil and rocks are red. I took a siesta in an arroyo[7] of cottonwoods which flows to the west. The water is not constant [, but] I named it Nombre de Dios. 7

*Castañeda suggests that he camped the night of August 1 near present-day Bernal, and the night of the second near Chaparito. That gets us into trouble in a hurry, for Chaparito is almost due east of Bernal, with some very rough country between; the natural route would have taken him east southeast to the Gallinas, from where he would have had to go north to Chaparito. An unnamed creek that flows into the Pecos River just below Esteros Creek is the only one that flows west in this general area.*

From this place I set out toward the east, and camped for the night on an arroyo that is close to a mesa and a mountain. There was much water [in the arroyo], but it was only rain water [as opposed to flowing water]. 13

From here I set out toward the west on the 4th, always staying close to a chain of broken table lands, which I kept on my right and to the south. I named it Santa Cruz. I left Santa Cruz on the fifth, heading east, [and] after going a short distance, I turned to the south, still keeping close to the same mesas. I stopped for the night on an arroyo of cottonwoods, where there was running water. I asked the Comanches if it was permanent, and they told me that it was not. It contains many cottonwoods [, and] I named it Mi Señora de la Luz. From this place I set out towards the east, and camped for the night at another arroyo with water which was not permanent. I named it San Cristóbal. 16

I left this place on the 5th, and having followed the mesas all the

[6] The word *álamo* is strictly translated "poplar," but in the Southwest, it means "cottonwood." The cottonwood botanically is a poplar, but in the Southwest the word "poplar" means the Lombardy poplar. All the poplars, including the cottonwoods and the aspens, are well known for the tremulous and continuous movement of the leaves in the slightest movement of air.

[7] Unlike Vial, Mares uses *arroyo* to indicate a running stream.

*Estevan Miró, governor of Louisiana, 1785–91.*

From Louis Houck, *The Spanish Régime in Missouri*

*François L. Hector, the Baron of Carondelet, governor of Louisiana, 1791–97.*

From Louis Houck, *The Spanish Régime in Missouri*

*Juan Vicente de Güemes Pacheco de Padilla, Conde de Revillagigedo, viceroy of Mexico, 1789–94.*

From Ralph Twitchell, *The Spanish Archives of New Mexico*

*Miguel de la Grúa Talamanca y Branciforte, Marqués de Branciforte, viceroy of Mexico, 1794–99.*

From Ralph Twitchell, *The Spanish Archives of New Mexico*

Num.º 50

Mui Señor mio: El 7. del q.e
Govierno, llegó á esta Capital Chris-
tobal de los Santos vezino de ella,
con dos Cumanches, el que fue á-
compañando á Pedro Vial para
descubrir el Camino de esta a la
del Nuevo Mexico desde el
tiempo de mi antesesor Don
Domingo Cavello haviendose
quedado en Santa fee dho Vial.

Al dia siguiente
llegaron quatro Capitanes Cumanches Orientales, y diez Indios
principales, con treinta y ocho
de Armas veinte y tres Mu-
geres y seis niños. Acompañan-

*First page of a letter from Governor Raphael María Pacheco of Texas to Juan de Ugalde, commandant-general, to advise the commandant-general that Cristobal de los Santos, who had gone with Vial in 1786, has returned to San Antonio. This letter is important because it is proof of the trip of 1786.*

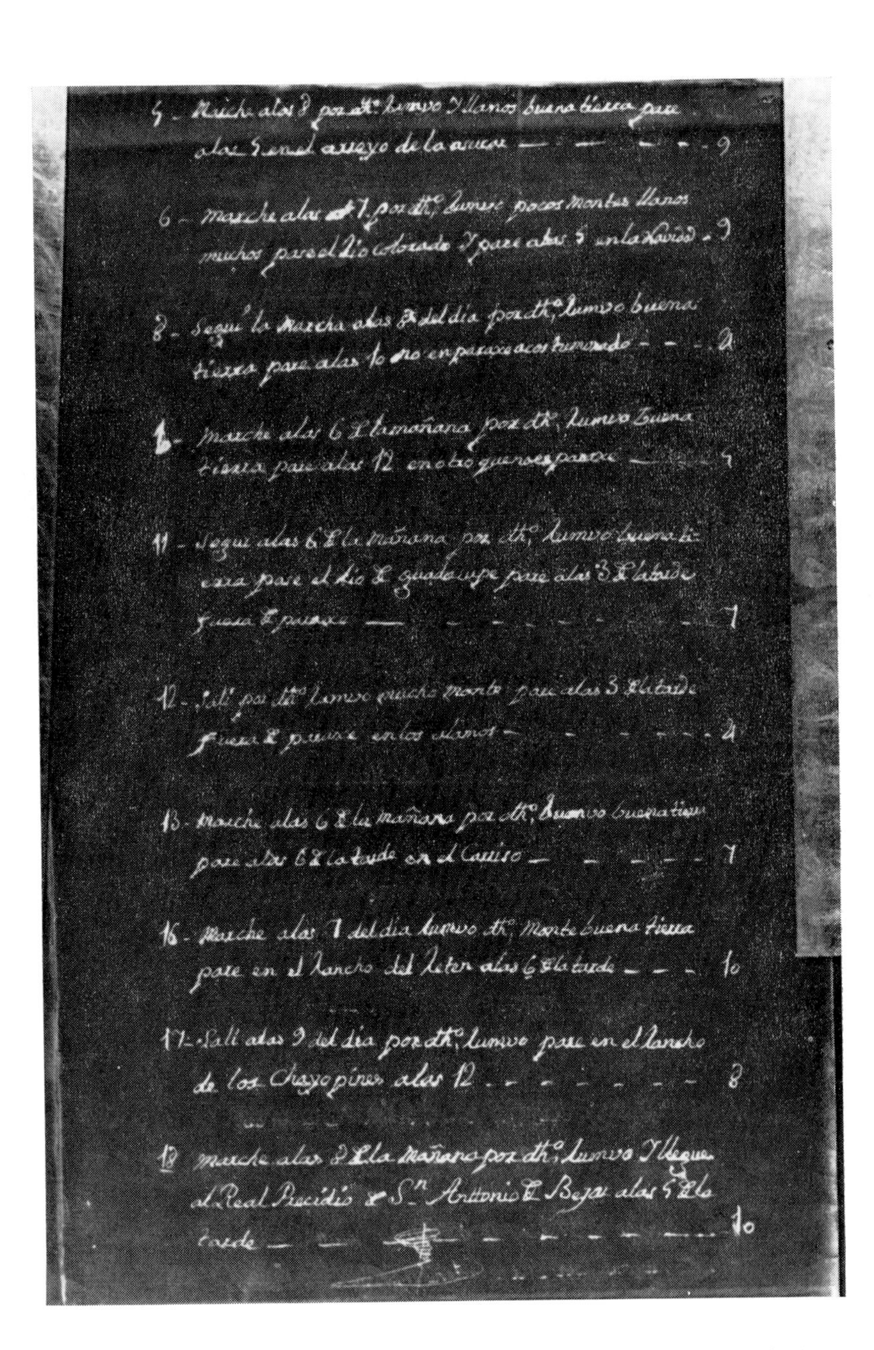

*A page from the journal of Francisco Xavier Fragoso on the trip from Natchitoches to Santa Fe; this is the last page, and bears the rubric but not the signature of Fragoso. Original in the Public Land Office of Texas.*

*The last page of Pedro Vial's will, with his signature, clearly identifiable with that of 1793, written over the text near the bottom. Original in the archives of the Museum of New Mexico (now in the State Records Center).*

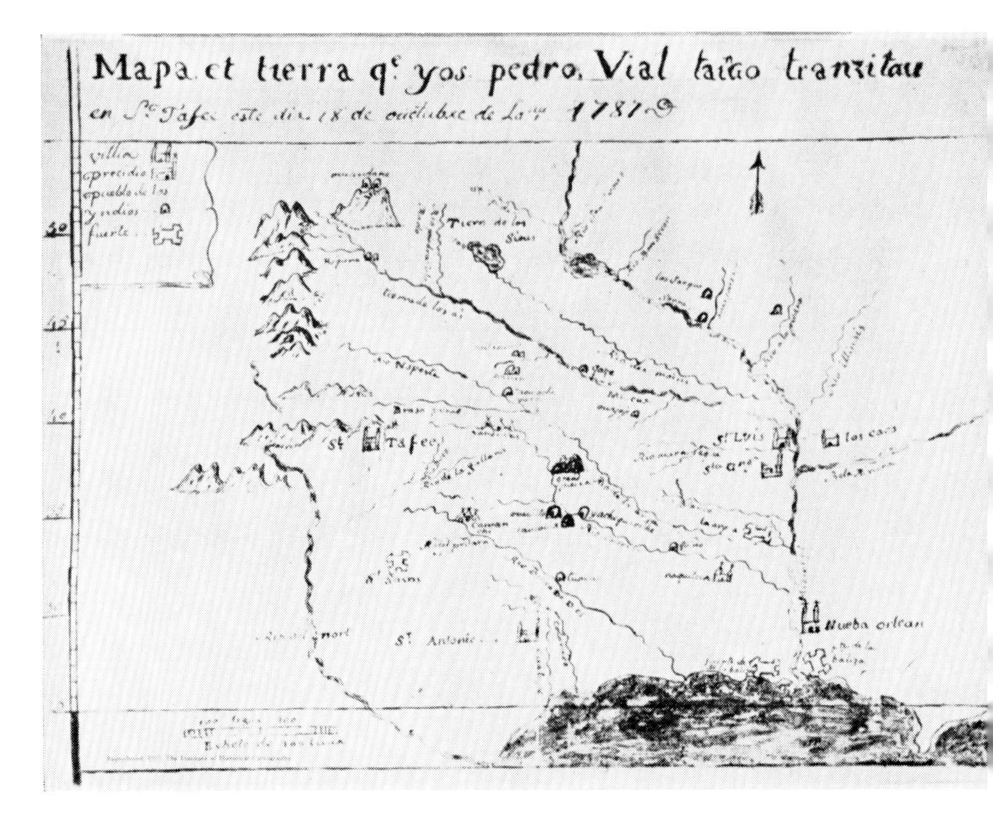


*The strange map of Pedro Vial, that seems to indicate that Vial had covered a great deal of territory. From Carl Wheat,* Mapping the Transmississippi West. *The original map has disappeared, although reproduced a number of times. Wheat's copy was a photostat of a photostat in the Historical Society of New Mexico.*

way, a famous landmark, came to an arroyo with temporary water, where I took my siesta. On this day I met two Comanches, who told me that they were coming from a raid, and that in May they had killed five Apaches and captured thirty. I named the place Mi Señora del Rosario [, and continued] my course toward the east. 5 [Total in margin at this point is 55.]

I set out from Mi Señora del Rosario on the 6th, going toward the east; and, continually skirting the chain of mesas, came to some watering places, where I slept. I called the place Mi Señora del Tránsito because there I crossed the mesa. 4

On the 7th I set out toward the south across a plain, leaving now the chain of mesas. I traveled very rapidly this day across a very wide plain which contains no landmarks[8] other than an arroyo which runs to the east and which has two clumps of chinaberry trees. The cliffs [here] are white, [and] below this arroyo there is a very large pond; I took my siesta at another pond, which I called Señor San Miguel. 5

From this place I set out very rapidly to the south at 3 o'clock [A.M.] and came upon a valley with two water holes, some chinaberry trees, and a trail which I followed to the east. At 8 o'clock at night I came to the source of the Blanco River,[9] where I slept. 10

On the 7th[10] I set out from the source of the river, going east right along the river. I took my siesta by the same river, [which] is permanent.[11] 4

From here I set out at 3 o'clock in the afternoon, heading south across a very large plain. As a landmark, there is only one pond. At vesper time I descended into an arroyo with much water and a regular

[8] In *The Texan-Santa Fé Pioneers,* 14, I said the Llano Estacado had not been crossed since the journey of Martin and Castillo in 1650. I was mistaken, for Mares is definitely crossing it now. Vial went along the Canadian River, but Mares is striking out across the plains.

[9] Tierra Blanca Creek, which flows into the Palo Duro Canyon, and joins the Prairie Dog Town Fork of the Red. In Bolton's map, he shows the Prairie Dog Town Fork, or Upper Red, and the Blanco River. It seems likely that Mares hit García Lake in Deaf Smith Country (perhaps the area of Mucho Que, the rendezvous of the *comancheros* a few years later).

[10] Obviously an error. See second paragraph above.

[11] Apparently near Hereford, for only there does the Tierra Blanca become a permanent stream. He is in the middle of the arid Llano in August—a good time to tell whether a stream is permanent.

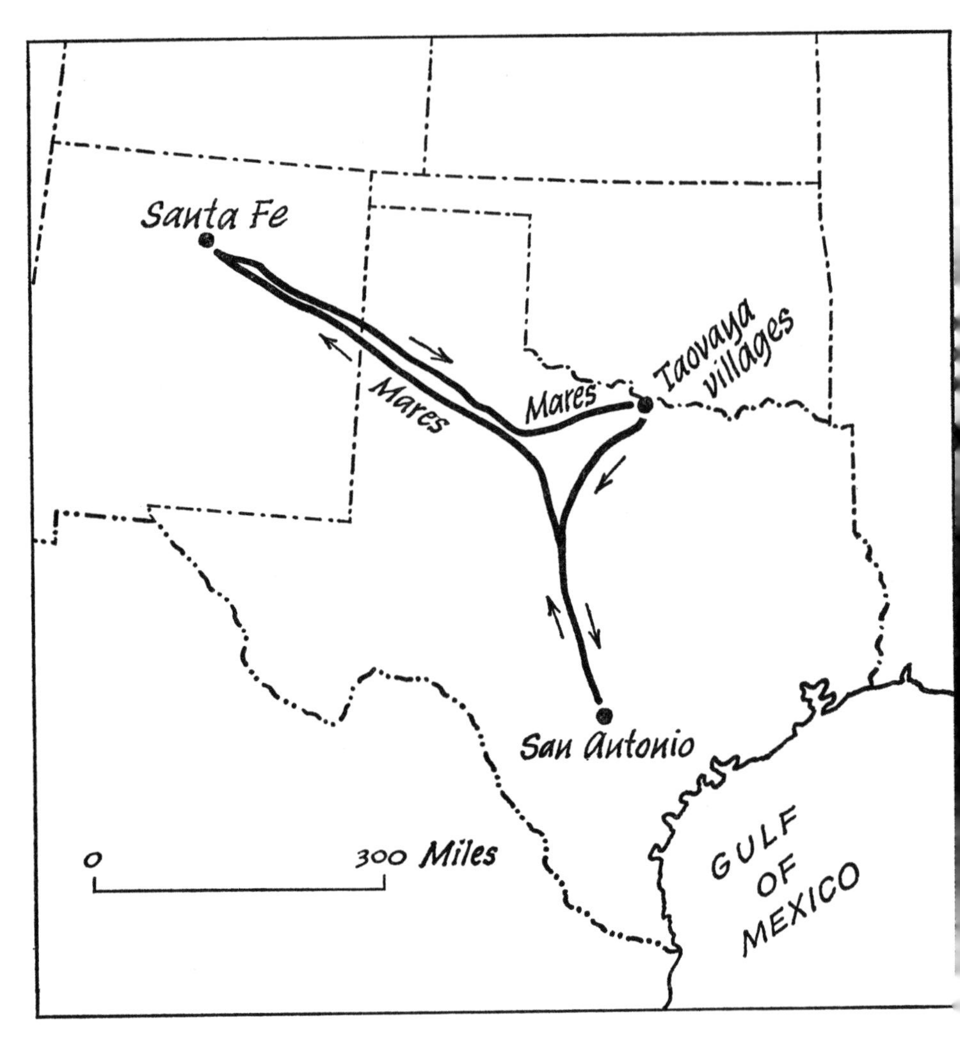


*José Mares' trips from Santa Fe to Bexar and return in 1787–88*

trail, along which I traveled until 8 o'clock in the evening, when I camped. I named it the Arroyo de Cíbolo.[12]

On the 8th I set out to the south from Cíbolo across some very broad plains, and traveled very rapidly from sunrise until 1 in the afternoon. I took my siesta in the Río del Tule;[13] it is permanent, and has cottonwood trees and many reeds [much marsh grass]. 11

I left the Río del Tule at 3 in the afternoon, heading east, and made camp for the night on a plain without water or any landmark. I named it San Geronimo. 7

*Apparently he left the Tule before he got down into Palo Duro Canyon, and found himself on the Llano again.*

On the 9th I set out from San Geronimo across the same plain, heading southeasterly, and arrived at the edge of a precipitous mesa.[14] Down this [cliff] runs a path by which I descended. There is much timber, and below there are two rivers. I named one Señor San José, and the other Sangre de Cristo. The timber of these mesas is juniper. 6

I set out southeasterly from Sangre de Cristo at 3 in the afternoon,[15] and came to a settlement [of Comanches] in another arroyo with cottonwoods and permanent water, where I slept. Here I found Chief Zoquinatya and El Taraquipe and Anagana and the Chief Sogayes.[16] I named it San Juan Baptista. 5

On the 10th I set out to the east, skirting the same arroyo, through mesquite land. After going a short distance, I crossed another arroyo with permanent water, which I skirted until I stopped on it. It contains many cottonwoods, and I named it Santa Rosa. 5

On the 11th I set out to the east across an isolated plain, [which had] the south side much broken with ravines and woods of junipers,

[12] It appears that he found buffalo in this area, for *cíbolo* is the Spanish word for bison. From this fact, we may deduce that the summer had up to that time been less dry than usual, for, in the normal course of things, there was not much game, especially buffalo, on the Llano in August.

[13] In the vicinity of present Tulia, Texas.

[14] The Caprock, which at this point is some eight hundred feet high—two hundred of it vertical; the Mexicans later called it the Ceja (Eyebrow).

[15] His repeated starting of the day's march in the middle of the afternoon indicates that the weather was very hot, as is usual on the Llano in summer.

[16] Castañeda reports them as Zoquinatoya and Tazaquipi. In another place he reports "Sofias" as a Penateka Comanche.

which are called Tascau. Here I found two villages [of Comanches] and arrived at the dwelling of Chief Nocay. I named the place Mi Señora de Guadalupe. 4

On the 12th of the current month I set out to the east from Guadalupe across a plain from which woodland could be seen only on the north [or "only on the north could be seen woodland"]. I came with the [people] of the two bands who had joined me [so he now has a retinue], and I slept in an arroyo of willows, [where] the water is permanent. I named it Mi Señora de los Dolores. 5

I set out to the east from Mi Señora de los Dolores on the 15th, heading east, and came to a canyon with much permanent water and many willow-trees, and slept there. There are many catfish [*bagre*] here, and I named it San Francisco. 6

I set out from San Francisco to the east on the 18th, and traveled across a plain heading east, leaving the said arroyo to the right. I stopped at another arroyo with water, although it is not permanent, where there are many trees of white wood, and here I slept. I named it the Arroyo de la Mula [, and] on the north are some small red ravines. 4

On the 20th I set out to the east from the Arroyo de la Mula, and traveled across a plain, keeping the arroyo in sight on the left until I halted on the same arroyo; there was much permanent water and many groves of different [kinds of] trees, cottonwoods, and some mesquite. I named it San Bartolo. 6

I set out from San Bartolo on the 22nd, following the same river, which I crossed as soon as I set out and left to the south, going to the left. I followed the crest of the table land, but with the river in sight, and halted on the same river. The water is very red, and there are many groves. Here I joined two other bands, for we [all?] arrived at the same place, and two chiefs, one Tociniquinta, and the other Ychape. I called the place La Ranchería. 6

*From the time of his descent from the Caprock, he has now recorded forty-seven leagues, and the use of Haggard's conversion factor*[17] *gives a figure that would put him on Beaver Creek, which flows*

[17] The figure is 2.6 miles to a league. J. Villasana Haggard, *Handbook for Translators of Spanish Historical Documents*, 78. Pichardo, Coues, and others work out this factor, but all come between 2.6 and 2.65.

*into the Wichita River; he might well be on the Wichita itself, for he says the water is very red. A considerable discrepancy occurs during this stretch between Castañeda's account and that given here. Bolton's account agrees with the apparent itinerary of this journal, by which Mares appears to have headed the breaks along the Pease River for a distance, and then cut across to the Wichita. By our account, he will now go across to the Little Wichita, and will follow that river to the Taovaya villages on Red River where Vial had talked turkey the preceding winter.*

I set out to the east from La Ranchería on the 23rd, along a ridge following the same river. There is some mesquite here. I crossed the river and immediately stopped on the southern side. The river runs through a gorge,[18] and the water is very red. There is much timber. I called it, together with all the settlements, the Río de San Marcos.[19] 4

On the 27th I set out to the south of the Río de San Marcos across a plain; after going a short distance, I crossed an arroyo with many groves of trees, and I called it El Paraje del Cavallo Pinto. 3

On the 28th I set out from El Cavallo Pinto, heading between east and south, and crossed many arroyos, all having many trees, and came to the Río de los Taguayazes,[20] where I slept. The water is very red and very muddy [*atascoso*], and flows to the east. 6

On the 30th I set out from El Río de los Taguayazes, heading between east and south across a plain where there are some scattered mesquite trees. I made camp for the night in a valley and an arroyo with many trees, and about three of them are cottonwoods. It is called La Cañada, and it flows toward the east. The country is flat, as is true of all other places; there is no bad surface; all are level. I stopped here on the last day of August. 5

[September]

Going eastward on the 3rd day of the month I went in toward the Taovayas, across a plain, and arrived at a pond which is found in a little river which has much timber. I slept on the near bank be-

[18] *Hocinado:* cut up in ravines.

[19] Perhaps the Pease.

[20] The River of the Taovayas is the Little Wichita.

cause the stream was swollen by the heavy rains, and named it La Laguna del Tule. 6

On the 4th I set out to the east across another plain, always following the river, however, which I kept on my left. I made camp at night on another arroyo, also swollen, which has many trees, among them liveoaks. I named it El Enzinal. 6

On the 5th I crossed the arroyo to the east. After going a short distance, I took a trail, always following the river, however, which now had joined the arroyo, until I arrived at the Taovayas, where I was well received. I went through the villages. The first contains 23 lodges, the next 40, and the other, which is on the other side of the river, has 27. I was accompanied by all the bands [*rancherías*] of Comanches, who went to the fair, leaving the rest of the people in the Cañada Seca, and I returned through the same place. 8

*Mares has reached the Taovaya villages, with no untoward event. It seems to appear later that he was ordered to find a more direct route, and one may wonder why he has returned to the Taovayas, whose villages are considerably east of San Antonio. The governor of Texas will have some sour comments on that detour, but there may be more than one explanation for it. For example, the Taovaya villages were well situated in the center of the Texas-Louisiana-New Mexico region and for some twenty years had been well known, and it is possible that Mares considers them a necessary stop. A second reason is that he has been traveling with Comanches who have come to trade with the Taovayas, and it is not always easy to part company with Comanches at one's own initiative.*

*We now have another check on Mares' figures. He has recorded 85 leagues from the Caprock; Haggard's factor of 2.6 gives us 220 miles, and a ruler laid across the United States Geological Survey map shows almost exactly 220 miles.*

*Mares' last sentence is explainable: the governor of Texas will note his picking up Indian traveling companions; and the Taovayas were traditionally the tradesmen for a very large area, much as were the Mandans on the upper Missouri; at this time (1787) they are rather hard hit by the withdrawal of the French in 1769 and the loss of white trade goods, rifles, and ammunition, and are trying to devise ways to retain their position.*[21]

On the 9th I set out to the south from the Cañada Seca, across a plain containing some mesquite, and at the end, when I stopped, I was on a high point between two very small mesas near some temporary water holes which are to the north. The place is called El Comercio de los Franceses because there some of the foreigners[22] traded with the Comanches. The latter were at the Taovaya village when I arrived there. 3

On the 10th I set out to the south of El Comercio de los Franceses across a plain with some very scattered mesquite, leaving to the left some gorges and folds.[23] We made camp for the night at some water holes where there are some chinaberry trees and where there is a good plain. I named it San Diego. 7

On the 11th we left San Diego along the crest of a ridge [*llano*] and camped for the night. We went to sleep at a settlement of the same Comanches, which is [in] a valley with many trees. I named it La Cañada de los Simarones.[24] The water is permanent. [Total in margin at this point is 202.]

On the 12th we set out to the west over the crest of a plain from Cañada de los Simarrones. After traveling a short distance, the two

[21] Elizabeth Ann Harper, "The Taovayas Indians in Frontier Trade and Diplomacy, 1719 to 1768," *The Chronicles of Oklahoma,* Vol. XXXI, No. 3 (Autumn, 1953), 279.

[22] Undoubtedly French *contrabandistas.* The French had long used the Taovaya villages as a trading post, and many continued to trade there after the French officially withdrew from Louisiana, coming up the river from Natchitoches, and from Arkansas Post overland through Osage country (Oklahoma). The Natchitoches trade was usually illegal, and the Arkansas trade was always illegal, but legal status seemingly made no great difference. A number of British *contrabandistas* were involved, but traditionally the traders were French, and on at least one occasion several Frenchmen lived with the Taovayas.

[23] Illegible: *cargas* or *arrugas.*

[24] It would be interesting to know what animals he saw in the valley, for *cimarrón,* meaning wild or unruly, also was used in New Mexico to denote a male bighorn sheep.

bands [of Comanches] separated [from us], and we continued with two others to the Río del Brazos de Dios.[25] It is permanent. 5

On the 13th I set out southeast from the Brazos de Dios across a plain, without coming upon a single valley; in the midst of the plain, I turned west and south, [but] in the middle of the plain I headed south, and ended by stopping at a valley and an arroyo with water holes, which I named La Cañada de San Julian. It is permanent. 8

On the 14th I set out to the south from San Julian from a woods [interspersed] with some water holes, where I slept. I named it Mi Señora del Pilar. 5

On the 17th, heading south, I left Mi Señora del Pilar through a clearing in the woods, and went until I arrived at a valley with many trees and reddish arroyos. The water is not permanent. I named it La Cañada del Yndio Triste.[26] 7

On the 18th I set out to the west from La Cañada del Yndio Triste over an elevation in an open forest. After half a league, I turned north to avoid a valley with many gorges, and after an eighth of a league more, I again changed my course and went south. I camped for the night on an elevation with some small reddish ravines. I named the place El Paraje Buenavista.[27] 9

On the 20th I set out to the south from El Paraje de Buenavista through a very dense forest. I traveled on this day over ground broken by many arroyos, all of which contain water, and through much timber. I came to a valley with much water, where I slept. The plain is very beautiful [, and] I named it Santiago. 8

On the 21st I set out to the south from La Cañada del Señor Santiago through a very dense forest. The surface was good, only the timber causing fatigue. I came to the Río de San Rafael y Pedernal; it has much forest and woodland, and the terrain is rough. It flows to the east. 9

[25] He was moving south and somewhat west, and Castañeda says he had reached the West Fork of the Trinity, somewhere near Jacksboro, rather than the Brazos, which is another ten leagues away.

[26] The Valley of the Sad Indian. Presumably the Brazos, but we do not know to what event he has reference. Considering the distance he has traveled he must have crossed the Brazos considerably below the Wichita village which Vial had visited some months before.

[27] The Historia 43 copy says 9; our copy says 3.

*Forty leagues, his estimate of the distance from the Brazos, would place him at the Colorado, but Castañeda puts him on one of the branches of the Leon, pointing out that this can certainly not be the Pedernales. It is true that his figures from the Taovayas to Bexar come to 172 leagues, or 447 miles, whereas the map measures about 340 miles. It is rough country and difficult traveling, which justifies a deduction of almost one-fourth from his recorded mileage.*

*Haggard's conversion factor seems to come from Pichardo, who says that a league is three miles or less, and that one should deduct about one sixth of the estimated distance—or more—to get the airline distance.*[27a] *That would give 2.5—very close to Haggard's figure. Pichardo says the number of leagues traveled was customarily determined by the time, probably at about one league per hour.*[27b]

*Mares' present distance estimates indicate that he measured according to the time spent traveling—and it is well to note that from this point Mares will be in much broken and heavily wooded country, and his actual distance traveled will be further reduced. He is now, by his journal, 110 leagues from San Antonio, and an airline measurement shows 205 miles. From this point, then, the conversion factor will be 1.8, but even this figure will have to be adjusted for the terrain.*

On the 23rd I left San Rafael over a rocky elevation, and went through a very dense forest. After a short distance, it opened up so that I came upon some small plains, over which I traveled with great pleasure. I made camp for the night in a canyon whose arroyo runs to the north, but it was without water. I named it El Arroyo de San Marcial. 10

On the 24th I set out southeasterly over a high pass [*por el alto de un puerto*] in these mountains, until I was confronted with a mesa, which was the first I had seen in these hills. I left it at my right and turned south through a forest very dense but not very long. I came out at another small plain, where I slept by some water holes that were not permanent. I named it San Estevan. 6

On the 25th I set out to the south from San Esteban and came upon a valley with much rock, and went into a ravine, since these Gentiles

[27a] *Pichardo's Treatise,* I, 305 ff.

[27b] *Ibid,* 312.

[Indians] know the clearings of these hills as [well as] I know the corners of my house. And so I came along, skirting some mesas that are seen to the west; those I left to my right, and descended a very deep valley that looks [as if it contains] a river well covered with trees. It has large tributaries, and is known to be permanent. The plains of the bottomland have much timber, and I named it El Arroyo de Mi Señora del Socorro. 7

On the 26th I set out to the south from Mi Señora del Socorro. As soon as I ascended from the arroyo, I gained the heights by another clearing. There is no landmark to point out, other than the clearing in these mountains. I made camp for the night on another arroyo with a good bottom and with many walnut and other kinds of tree. I named it La Cañada y Arroyo de San Ysidro. It runs to the east. 6

On the 27th I set out from San Ysidro, heading south through a clearing like the others, sometimes a prairie and sometimes forest but not very dense. The paths that are sometimes found in these valleys are made by the buffalo herds. If you follow [one of] them and take care not to leave it, it sometimes lasts for a long time, as happened to me today, for I descended into a valley, and the path lasted until I left the valley. As soon as I descended from a high knoll, I came to another valley with timber and permanent watering-places, where I slept. I named it El Parage de San Carlos. 9

On the 28th I set out to the south for San Carlos through another clearing, but within four leagues I got into a very dense forest. I did not cross a single valley—it has been entirely wooded [country]. I came to a river [of red water], where I slept, [and] I named it El Río de San Felipe y Colorado. It carries much water, and flows to the east.[28] 8

On the 29th, going to the south, I traveled through a forest that was not very dense, and after a short distance I came upon a small plain with scattered timber and much rock. I came to a stop in a valley with a very level plain. The water, which runs to the north, is not permanent. I named it La Cañada y Paraje de Señor San Miguel. 10

On the 30th and last day of September, I traveled to the south from Señor San Miguel through a pass in a chain of mesas which runs from east to west. I traveled on this day through more plains than

[28] Bolton shows the course generally south with a slight drift to the west. Mares' distance now is considerably more than the distance shown on the outward trip.

forest, and camped for the night on a Río de los Llanos, which flows to the east.[29] 5

October

On the 1st day of October, I traveled to the south through a forest of very dense liveoak until I arrived at the slope of a valley; this slope is a bad one—it is not high but it is very broken and very rocky. On this day I crossed the Río de San Sabá.[30] It is a very beautiful river with much water, and well grown with cottonwoods, [and] flows to the east. I came to a valley with a very level bottom, where I slept. I named it San Buenaventura. I am told the water is permanent. 7

On the 2nd I set out from San Buenaventura, heading between east and south through a pass and [along] a path with low hills on the left and on the right. We [traveled] this [path] through the whole length of the canyon, which had much timber, but it was big [*alto*] timber and [hence] not fatiguing. In the same valley I came upon a pond from whence sprang a very fine spring. Here I turned to the south and camped for the night on a small plain at a little arroyo with water that was not permanent. I named the place Paraje San Antonio. 7

On the 3rd, going to the south along the same path and through the same forest, I also arrived at a river well grown with trees and with much water which came above the shoulders of the horses. All these rivers are abundantly supplied with very palatable wild fruits and with water. Each small arroyo, however poor it may be, has its water spring. This river which I crossed is called El Río del Al-con.[31] I came to another smaller stream with a very good bottom. I named it El Río de San Francisco Solano. 6

On the 4th, heading south, I traveled through a forest like the others, not very dense. I was still on a trail, searching for the valleys in those forests which are well known to these Gentiles, and I went into some round hills, among them a large one to the west, the top of which is a flat rock; to the east there are other small ones, also of rock. Having arrived at these, I crossed. To the south I crossed another arroyo with water, still on the south which, perhaps, has been long in use

[29] The San Saba, says Castañeda.

[30] Castañeda says this is the Llano, and that Mares will cross the Guadalupe on October 7.

[31] The Pedernales.

among them [the Indians], although it is not very well opened. I ascended by a knoll of no great height, and entered a pass between two hills, and stopped for the night on an arroyo with much water. I named it Santa Theresa. It flows eastward over a level bottom. 9

On the 5th I traveled to the south, close to some high hills; I left them to the right and came to the Río de Nuestra Señor de Balbanera y de los Valcones,[32] where I took my siesta. I came to an arroyo with much water, where I slept. I traveled all day across a level plain, no longer woodland but [and] not bad. I called it San Leonardo. 8

On the 6th I set out to the south from San Leonardo, by a hill, and as soon as I descended into a valley, I turned eastward through a very hilly country [*lomería*] with slopes and grades and with very much bad timber. I crossed a large river and traveled along the hillside, for there was no more room between the river and the rocks than a vara in some parts, and in others a vara and a half,[33] and the river close by, which was deep and had a fast flow of water which was never seen in the world. I named it the Misericordia de Díos [, and] as soon as I ascended [the bank], I slept there. There will be only a short trip more. 4

On the 7th I traveled to the south through a very dense forest of about a league. Then the forest became less dense, and presented a good plain. I came to a very spacious canyon with a good bottom but without water, where I slept. I named it El Puerto Biejo. 14

On the 8th I set out to the south between some knolls and woods —not very thick, although [scattered over] with some rock. On this day I arrived at San Antonio de Bexar. 4 [Total in margin at this point is 373.]

San Antonio de Bexar, October 19, 1787.

JOSÉ MARES

This is a copy of the original, which remains in the archives of the government under my charge.

San Antonio de Bexar. October 22, 1787.

RAFAEL MRZ. PACHECO.

This is a copy: Valle de Santa Rosa, December 15, 1787.

JUAN UGALDE [*rubric*]

[32] The Guadalupe.

[33] A vara was about thirty-three inches in the Southwest. It is now evident that Castañeda's rivers are hard to reconcile with Mares' estimate of the distance he has traveled.

José Mares had, by his own count, covered 373 leagues, as compared to Vial's 454, but he certainly had wandered all over the country. Mares' journey had taken almost ten weeks, and he had actually traveled fifty-five days. Although he was a man old enough to be retired, his average was 17.6 miles a day. Vial, on the other hand, was on the road eighty-four days and traveled approximately one thousand miles by the map—an average daily march of 12 miles or 4.5 leagues; these figures do not include the days he stayed in camp. Could it be that Vial was considerably older even than we have already guessed? As to Mares' indirect route, perhaps the official correspondence will throw some light.

On October 12 Governor Pacheco reported to Ugalde, commandant-general of the Eastern Interior Provinces, that

> . . . there arrived at this capital [San Antonio] on the seventh of this month Cristóbal de los Santos, resident of it [San Antonio], with two Comanches; he is the one who accompanied Pedro Vial to open said road as far as New Mexico from the time of my predecessor, Don Domingo Cabello (which he verified immediately), said Vial remaining in Santa Fe. On the following day there arrived four Eastern Comanche chiefs and 10 principal Indians with 38 warriors [*de armas*], 23 women and 6 children. Accompanying them were Mares, an interpreter, and a servant.
>
> Mares has advised me that he has not opened the road immediately [because], although with this destination in mind, he was not successful because the Comanches arrived at the Taovaya villages.
>
> [One of the chiefs, Sofais, has promised to go to New Mexico at once so that the opening of the said road may be successful.] Mares will remain here until March because of the heavy snows of winter.
>
> I have not sent you Mares' journal for not having finished *sancar en limpio*.[34]

Then Ugalde wrote to the viceroy, enclosing Mares' diary and offering some further information:

> The Commandant General of the Interior Provinces of the East encloses the diary that has been entered by José Mares in his journey from New Mexico to Texas, saying what he has to offer upon it, and his subject.[35]

[34] Pacheco to Ugalde, No. 50, October 12, 1787, Spanish Archives of Texas; cited incorrectly by Castañeda, *Our Catholic Heritage in Texas*, V, 158.

[35] This is a marginal notation.

On October 8 last there entered the presidio of San Antonio de Bexar, the retired corporal of Santa Fe, José Mares, accompanied by four Comanche chiefs, 10 Indian sub-chiefs, 38 braves [*gandules*[36]], 23 women, 6 boys of the same nation.

That individual left the village of Pecos in the province of New Mexico the 1st of August of the current year with the object, it is said, of effecting the opening of the most convenient and direct road to the capital of Texas, but because the Comanches encumbered him excessively and guided him between the east and southeast in order to fall upon [visit] the important establishments of the Taovayas, the work that he especially undertook resulted in a failure.[36a]

The diary of his journey, a copy of which the governor of Texas has remitted to me and which I enclose for your Excellency, will inform you in detail in the matter; but as it is entirely defective and inconsistent in many parts, I believe that you will also realize that Mares is not the individual to accomplish such a useful undertaking.[37]

I am not informed of the orders that have been handed down on this matter; neither am I informed of the progress [toward establishment of a road] of the Colonel Don Domingo Cabello [who preceded Pacheco] through the [efforts of the] Frenchman, Pedro Vial, who is now in New Mexico;[38] [but] if the project of opening this road is as important to the government as it appears [to be], it must reassure your Excellency that the peace [between] the Comanches and Lipans facilitates it at present with many fewer difficulties than a similar objective would present if those nations were at war.

Finally, if your Excellency wishes me to give my opinion as to its success, I shall produce it for you when I inform myself as to the official communications which must be in Texas, separating myself always from [omission] of importance to individuals not capable of accomplishing

[36] The translation of *gandule* is tramp or vagabond, and undoubtedly the Spanish official class looked on all Indians as tramps unless they were chiefs of some sort, but the word is inaccurate. Perhaps *warrior* is a better word. Interestingly enough, Spanish documents often refer to French *voyageurs* as *gandules.*

[36a] Now at long last we learn what had held back Mares: a retinue of eighty-one Comanches! They must have had great fun, leading him all over West Texas.

[37] It appears that perhaps Pacheco, with the aid of his officers, who were natives of Bexar and knew the country, had as much trouble following Mares' route as did Casteñada.

[38] Five months after Mares had left Santa Fe, Chacón had not reported to Ugalde, commandant-general, about it; however, there had been several changes in the Interior Provinces in 1785, 1786, and 1787, and it is doubtful that anybody knew where to send his reports.

them with efficiency, both for lack of principles in the necessary power for it and because of the fact also of being little recommended by temperament; they lack also the characteristic of being frontiersmen [*campitas*], which is necessary to get used to such trips.[39]

The viceroy tried to smooth things over:

With your Excellency's letter No. 12 of December 15 last, I have received the copy of the diary of the march made by the retired soldier, Joseph Mares, from the village of Pecos in the province of New Mexico to the capital of Texas, accompanied by 4 Comanche chiefs, 10 Indian sub-chiefs, 38 braves, 23 women, and 6 children of the same nation.

The suggestions that your Excellency makes to me on the laying out of this road seem good to me, and right away I want you to tell me your opinion; but I judge that you will not be able to find in San Antonio de Bexar complete papers on the matter, because it [the affair], perhaps, will be [has been?] promoted by the governor of New Mexico in view of the orders of the Commandant-General Don Jacobo Ugarte y Loyola.[40]

Nevertheless, your Excellency, inform me at the proper time whatever you wish, and provide as usual for the retired Mares the help that he needs to return to his destination, since it is just to pay attention to the service that he has done for the sake of the king and [in] fulfillment of the orders of his superiors, exposing himself to the risks of an extensive trip and trusting himself to the good will of the Comanches.

These Indians have continued in good faith, and I am convinced

[39] Juan Ugalde to Manuel Antonio Flórez, Valle de Santa Rosa, December 15, 1787, Historia, Vol. 62.

[40] It now seems evident that Ugalde's opposite number, Ugarte, is the one who had ordered Anza to send Mares. Ugarte had been governor of Puebla but had succeeded Neve in the Interior Provinces in May, 1785; then the Interior Provinces was divided into three military commands, with Ugalde in the east (including Texas), and Ugarte in the west. There was trouble between Ugarte and Ugalde, and in December 1787, the three divisions were changed to two: the Eastern under Ugalde (including Texas), and the Western under Ugarte, whose authority moved all the way to the Pacific Ocean. These rapid changes would explain the confusion, but do they explain the letter listed by Bolton on page 113 of the *Guide* (Provincias Internas, Vol. 134), from the viceroy to Ugarte, December 12 (three days before Ugalde sent his letter to the viceroy, saying that the diary is incomplete, that Mares allowed the Comanches to lead him by the Taovayas, and that Mares is unfit for the task)? It is noticeable that in this present letter (written January 29, 1788) the viceroy does not take cognizance of his letter to Ugarte.

that your Excellency has taken wise measures to convince them of our friendship, to conserve the important peace of this nation [the Comanches] and others of the north [the Norteños]; on [all of] which matters your Excellency will inform me of what may occur.[41]

It is noticeable that Mares set out on the return trip in the middle of January—an extremely bad month for traveling in that area; ordinarily he would have waited until April. The reason for the early start is unknown; perhaps he wanted to get back to Santa Fe; perhaps the governor made him unhappy. At any rate, Mares left in January to find a shorter route:

### *Itinerary and Diary of José Mares, Bexar to Santa Fe, January 18 to April 27, 1788*[42]

Itinerary and diary that cover the number of leagues from the capital of San Antonio de Bexar, province of Texas, to that of Santa Fe, New Mexico, which I, José Mares, retired corporal of the company [of the latter place] am making across the country through which the Indians, friendly Comanches, conduct me in order to find a road by the most direct route.

January, 1788

On the 18th, I set out to the north from San Antonio de Bexar through some plains and scattered timber, and came to the arroyo del Novillo, where I made camp. 3

On the 19th, heading north, I left Novillo through a hilly country, and stopped at the Río del Cívolo, which runs permanently toward the east over a good plain. 4

I set out from Cívolo at 3 o'clock in the afternoon through a forest of oaks where there is much rock, but the ground was good. I reached the Río de Guadalupe, which flows toward the east, and slept there. 4

On the 20th, heading north, I set out through a forest with much rock; for about 2 leagues it was bad traveling, but from there on the plain was good. I went through a pass in the chain of knolls which runs

[41] Viceroy to Ugalde, Mexico, January 29, 1788, Historia, Vol. 62 (a draft, filed with No. 12).

[42] José Mares, Derrotero y Diario, Historia, Vol. 62, No. 6, f. 149 *et seq.;* ours is a certified copy. A certified copy is in Historia, Vol. 43, No. 16; and in Historia, Vol. 52, exp. 17. Our copy (from Vol. 62) is endorsed: "Ser. LII. Taken from papers pertaining to the Secretary's Office."

east to west with a little river [nearby],[43] on which I took my siesta. I named it Santo Domingo.[44] 6

At 3 [o'clock] I marched to the east to avoid a bad stretch that confronted me, and after a league I veered to the north across a good plain. I camped for the night on the Río del Alcon, [at a place] which I called Mi Señora del Belén. 4

Going to the north on the 21st, I ascended a slope through a forest that was not very dense, [then] I descended [through] an arroyo of water that runs to the east, and I headed up a canyon that had a good bottom; [there was] heavy timber [but] it did not obstruct [my passage]. I took my siesta at the Río de San Gabriel,[45] which runs to the east. 5

At 3 o'clock I marched through a thick forest [and] descended a river that flows to the east; I descended the entire [length] of the valley, with hills on both sides, until I reached an elevation, from which place on, there was a good plain. I stopped for the night at another cañada with permanent water, [at a place] which I called Mi Señora de Sapopa. 7

On the 22nd I marched to the north, close alongside a mesa, [going] through a small canyon with mesas on both sides; [there was] a dense forest [which caused] trouble for about a league; [then] there was a good plain until [I reached] the Río de los Chanas,[46] where I met Lieutenant Curbelo, who had come from San Antonio with soldiers to get the Comanches.[47] 8

On the 24th my course was to the north. This day I made an attempt (by order of Captain Don Rafael Martínez Pacheco) to purchase a female captive—one whom they [the Indians whom he has obviously just met] did not wish to sell, but after having marched, I ordered Chief Tociniquinta to return and [persuade them to] sell her, which command he presently obeyed, and [they] sold her for eight

[43] Over the hills to the Blanco.

[44] He will still be naming his camping places until he gets back on familiar ground.

[45] Castañeda identifies this as Sandy Creek, a tributary of the Llano.

[46] The Llano.

[47] Castañeda says the officer was on a private trading expedition, but the word is *sacar,* which can mean "to compel to bring forth," and might refer to the captive mentioned in the next paragraph.

horses. I marched through a very dense forest and stopped for the night at some suckholes [*chupaderos*] of permanent water, and I named [the place] Santa Clara. 3

*The references to the captive are Castañeda's translation, but the Spanish text presents some problems, for it could be translated as, "I ordered Chief Tociniquinta to return and sell her," and it might mean that the chief was ordered to return to Curbelo to sell the girl. Mares had met the chief at his village on the Little Wichita on August 22, and now it seems that Tociniquinta is one of those who accompanied Mares to Bexar. The Spanish text is:* "El día 24 rumbo al norte en dicho día se trato de comprar una cautiba por orden del Capitán Don Rafael Martínes Pacheco le que no quisieron bender y despues de haver marchado mande a el capitan Tosiniquente que volbiera y la vendiera lo que obedecio y la vendio por ocho caballos." *It would seem strange that, after trying to negotiate with strange Comanches and being turned down, an experienced frontiersman like Mares would set out on the march, and then suddenly "order" the chief to buy the girl. It seems more reasonable that the chief had the girl or woman all the time, that Curbelo had come with orders to buy her back but had failed, that when Mares resumed the march, he laid down the law to the chief.*

On the 25th I marched to the north through a forest until 8 o'clock at night. I ascended a mesa which was bad because of rocks. Beyond it were plains with many rocks, where the animals walked with the greatest difficulty. I camped for the night at the Río de San Saba, which runs to the east and is heavily wooded. leag. 14

On the 27th I went west through a forest with much rock, and stopped the night in a valley without water, there being nothing but a little snow. I named [the place] Santa Ysabel. leag. 3

On the 28th I set out to the north through a dense forest with a very bad surface; I came to an arroyo with no water, but some snow, and took my siesta. I named [the place] Mi Señora de las Nieves.[48] leagues 4

At 3 o'clock I again took up the march to the north, across a very

[48] He is moving northwest to get away from the breaks and the timber, but it appears that he hit some bad weather.

bad plain with arrollos and mesas on both sides, [running] from east to west. [I traveled thus] until I ascended an elevation, where I came upon a good plain without rocks, while to the west were some wooded mesas. I stopped for the night at another arroyo with water holes, not permanent. I named it the Arroyo de San Pedro. 3

On the 29th I went to the north through a forest and some small plains with a good surface. I did not go by the direct road, which is bad because of much rock and timber, the other [road] makes a deviation but is, on the whole, very favorable. I camped for the night on the Río Colorado de San Rafael,[49] to which [place] I gave the same name. It is heavily wooded. leagues 7

On the 30th, I went up the river to the west over a good surface, but there was timber. I slept on the same Colorado River.[50] leagues 4

On the 31st, my course was to the north through very dense and rock timber, which was hard work until I descended into a valley where I found a large lake of water. From there on, there was a good surface. I took my siesta in a valley with permanent water, [which place] I named El Agua del Venado. leagues 6

At 3 o'clock I set out from the Agua del Venado through timber and some small plains [*llañetes*] leading toward the north until I ascended an elevation. I came upon a plain [which lasted] until I reached an arroyo of water, where I slept in front of only one small mesa, [which] I named San Casimiro. It flows to the east. leagues 7

February

On the first of said month [I set out] to the north, [and after] a quarter of a league I entered a very dense forest, skirting a mesa to the east and knolls to the west. I took my siesta on an arrollo of permannent water that runs to the east [and has] a good plain. I named it San Dimas. leagues 4

From here I set out to the north at 2 o'clock in the afternoon through a wooded canyon with low hills on both sides but over a good surface and along a regular path of the buffalo herd. I came to another arrollo of permanent water, where I slept; it runs to the east and has many walnut [trees]. I named it Mi Señora de la Candelaria. leagues 5

[49] The Colorado River, says Castañeda.

[50] Now one wonders if he knows more about the rivers than his names indicate.

On the 2nd I marched to the north through a plain with some scattered hills and a chain of mesas and knolls. I came to stop at another arrollo (with water though not permanent), where I took my siesta. I named it La Quemada. [There is] a good plain. leag. 6

On the 3rd I marched to the north through scattered timber and came upon a pass in a chain of mesas which runs from east to west. There are two passes, which are separated by a mesa which is in the middle. I passed to the west and took my siesta at the opening. I named it La Cañada de la Gallina. There is permanent water and a good plain. leagues 6

I set out at 3 o'clock in the afternoon and traveled northwest across a good plain close to some mesas. I stopped for the night at a canyon without water, which I named San Dionicio. leag. 3

On the 4th I headed to the north through a forest and some small plains, always staying close to the mesa, which I kept on my left; I stopped for the night at the village of Chief Soxias [Sofais?] which was coming with him [who came with me?]. I named it Can Ygnacio de Loyola. The water is permanent. leag. 9

On the 6th I set out to the west through a canyon, wooded but with a good surface, with some arroyos having very precipitous sides but without stones. The mesas are some distance to the left. I stopped for the night in the same canyon with all the band [of Indians]. I named it the Cañada del Coyote. The water is permanent. 4

On the 7th I marched northwest across a high plain on which there is some timber. I came to another canyon with temporary water, where I slept. I named it Santa Catarina; the plain [is] good. leagues 3

On the 8th I marched northwest over a plain and through wooded canyons. I camped for the night in another canyon with very much timber, a good surface, and permanent water, the course of which is toward the east. I named it Santa María Egipciaca. leagues 3

On the 11th I marched north through a plain with a very good surface. At a short distance I came upon two small mesas, which I left to the west side. I came to another wooded canyon with permanent water, where I slept. I named it La Cañada de los Corales. leagues 6

On the 29th[51] I marched northeast through the entire canyon

[51] Mares apparently wintered on the Double Mountain Fork of the Brazos in southeast Stonewall County, some forty miles north and west of Abilene. It is noticeable

until I came upon the Río del Pedernal, on which there is much mesquite. I camped for the night on the same river, facing two hills. The plain is good. leagues 7

March

On the 6th I set out northeastward from the Río del Pedernal through a dense forest. I camped for the night in a canyon with a very good bottom and water permanent but brackish [*salobrega*]. I named it La Agua Salada. leagues 6

On the 9th I marched northeastward through a forest of high [timber], well scattered. I descended a wooded canyon; to the north [there were] two wooded mesas [with] blue rocks and red soil. I stopped for the night in the same canyon. The surface [is] good and the water [is] permanent. I named it La Matanza. leagues 6

On the 15th I marched to the north through a forest with a good surface and came to Arrollo del Taspe [Saspe], where I slept. The water is permanent and runs to the north.[52] leagues 3

On the 16th I set out to the north from the Arrollo del Saspe, leaving the band with which I had been marching, with two chiefs and another Comanche, the Chief Chojais [Sofais?] and Quenaracaro. After a half league, I crossed the Brazos de Dios[53] and entered a forest with a very good surface. I stopped for the night on another arroyo with a dense forest and with permanent water. I named it San Crisanto. leagues 6

On the 17th I set out to the north through a forest that was somewhat scattered; to the west a mesa with some timber, and at some distance another mesa, which I named Le Huerfana, separated itself. Having passed on from this, I entered a very dense forest and came to the Río Salado, where I slept. It was so salty that the animals could not drink it. Its course is to the north; the cliffs of red; the ground is sandy.[54] leagues 8

that he has foregone the pleasure of visiting the Taovaya villages on the Red River and has taken a much more direct route.

[52] Clear Fork in Haskell County?

[53] Probably Double Mountain Fork.

[54] The Salt Fork of the Brazos? Beginning about here, it is perhaps better to read "northwest" for Mares' "north."

On the 18th I marched to the north through a passageway with many low hills, mesas, and very sheer[55] arroyos which I was able to traverse with difficulty. I crossed another salty river in which the animals were not able to drink. I stopped on the same river, where there is a fine salt [deposit]. I named it Las Salinas de Mi Señora de la Luz; the plains [are] bad; the course [of the river] is to the east. leagues 5

On the 19th I marched northwest over an elevation [in a region] of many low hills and very deep and impassable arroyos, [there] being much work and also some very bad forests; it is without water. I camped for the night in an arroyo [with] sweet water, which I named San Fernando. leagues 6

On the 20th I traveled to the north by a road along an elevation with a good surface by a piece of good fortune which continued until I arrived at an arroyo with much water and a grove of poplar trees and some mesquite; the water is permanent and runs to the east, and I named [the place] Santa Casilda. leagues 3

On the 21st I set out to the north through a plain, and some hills and wide canyons. I stopped for the night in another canyon with permanent water. It runs toward the east and has a few cottonwoods on [its banks]. I named [the place] Santa Maria Magdalena. leagues 9

On the 23rd I traveled north across a plain with some hills to the west and one mesa, separated from some high ones at some distance. I made camp for the night at an arroyo where I had found the first [Indian] settlement when I was going to San Antonio,[56] and to the same canyon that is called San Juan Baptista, I gave the same name. The water is permanent; it has a good riverbed with three springs of fresh water, [and] runs to the east. leagues 5

On the 24th I set out to the north through a forest, and [after traveling] half a league, I descended a canyon and arrived at the mesa mentioned above, which runs from north to south. I proceeded through this canyon and met a band of Comanches of the Cuchuntica [Kotsoteka division] with the Chief Comguitanquesaran and Chief Paruamumpes [Paranuarimuco?] and Chief Tanchaguare. The river flows to the east, and I named it Mi Señora de Soterranea. leagues 3

[55] Sheer: *estinados,* a corruption of *hocinados.*

[56] Refers to August 9, 1787.

April

On the 6th[57] I set out to the north, leaving the settlement on the same river, where I [had] remained to strengthen my animals, which were becoming very run down. There were the chiefs who had accompanied me turned back, but Chief Tanqueoyaran gave me two of his sons in order that they might accompany me as far as Santa Fe. And thus I traveled close to some mesas, which I left to the west, on a small hill which these [people] call El Cerrito Puerco. I crossed the Río de La Sangre de Cristo and made camp for the night in the [Río] de Señor San José, which is at the foot of the mesa mentioned in the other itinerary; it runs to the east. leagues 9

Going to the west on the 7th, I ascended the rough mesas mentioned in the other diary,[58] and made camp for the night at El Tules.[59] leagues 13

On the 9th I marched to the north across a plain not very large. I stopped for the night at Cíbolo.[60] All this region is a plain. leagues 11

On the 11th I set out to the north from an arroyo del Cíbolo across a plain without landmarks.[61] I stopped for the night on the Río Blanco.[62] leagues 5

On the 13th I set out from the Río Blanco to the west, going upstream. [The river] runs to the east, and has many trees. I camped for the night on the same river at its source.

On the 16th I set out to the west from the source of said river, and arrived at La Cañada de Los Dos Aguajes, which has in it some chinaberry trees. Here I turned to the north and camped for the night at La Laguna del Señor San Miguel. leagues 10

On the 18th I marched northward toward a plain that had no landmarks other than a very large pond, which I left on my right. I stopped

[57] A line appears to have been missed by the copyist; Historia 43 and Historia 62 are the same.

[58] Both references to his previous diary are to the entries for August 9; he is getting close to the end of his second journey now.

[59] The Río del Tule, previously mentioned August 8.

[60] Previously noted August 7.

[61] He said the same thing about landmarks as he went east from the Río del Tule August 8.

[62] South Deaf Smith County?

for the night at Mi Señora del Tránsito.[63] This day I left the mesa.[64] leagues 6

On the 20th I traveled to the west, close to the mesas referred to in the other itinerary [which I made] when I was [going] to San Antonio.[65] I crossed from Mi Señora del Rosario and camped for the night in an arroyo with cottonwoods, which runs to the east. leagues 9

Going to the west on the 22nd, I passed through Mi Señora de la Luz. There I turned to the north, and at a distance of six leagues I again turned to the west, always [keeping] close to the mesas. I stopped for the night at Santa Cruz. The plain is good; there is much water but it is not permanent. leagues 16

Going northwest on the 23rd, I came to El Río de las Gallinas, where I slept; it runs to the south, and there is a good plain. leagues 13

On the 24th I set out northwestward across a plain of El Río de las Gallinas and [west] through the passage called La Mesa de los Lipanes. I slept in a little canyon of Bernal, which runs to the south. The plain is good. leagues 7

On the 25th I set out to the west from the little canyon of Bernal, [going] all the way through a canyon close to some hills which are seen to the south. I came to the ford of the Río de Pecos, which runs to the south, and took my siesta. At 11 o'clock in the morning I set out from the ford through a forest close to a mesa that extends from north to south. I stopped for the night at Nuestra Señora de Pecos. leagues 8

On the 27th I marched to the north across a plain, and on descending into a canyon, I turned to the west between this mesa and the ridge of hills; having ascended from the canyon, I directed my course to the north until I arrived at Santa Fe, the capital of New Mexico. leagues 6

JOSEPH MARES

This is a copy of the original, which remains in the archives of this government in my care, to which I certify.

Santa Fe, New Mexico, June 20, 1788.

FERNANDO DE LA CONCHA

leagues 325

[63] Near the Texas-New Mexico state line; see entry for August 5–6, 1787.

[64] Probably the Llano, which extends far into New Mexico.

[65] See entry for August 5, 1787.

This is a copy. Chihuagua, September 12, 1793.

MANUEL MERINO [*rubric*]

Mares took considerably longer for the return trip, but he made it in the winter and early spring. He spent forty-four days in travel and covered 325 leagues—845 miles—an average of 19.2 miles a day. While there was more time between towns, the distance is less than Vial's by 125 miles, the travel time is less by eleven days, and the average rate of travel has been increased by 1.6 miles per hour.

Pedro Vial's original figure has given way to competition, and Mares has made two trips between the towns of San Antonio and Santa Fe. Mares seems to have made an easy job of it, and possibly even the governor will forgive him for bringing to Santa Fe with him whole bands of Indians. (Those Indians did present a problem, however, because they expected presents.)

The road between the two towns has been fairly well established, and now Pedro Vial will be sent east from Santa Fe to bring in the third important point in the frontier triangle: Natchitoches, far to the east.

# XIII

# *Pedro Vial, Santa Fe to Natchitoches to San Antonio to Santa Fe, 1788–89*

When Mares returned without difficulty, the governor of New Mexico must have been greatly encouraged to learn more about the Indian tribes in northern Texas and to establish communication with Natchitoches. Apparently Vial himself had thought about it, according to the letters, for Ugarte wrote to Fernando Concha,[1] the governor, in January, 1788, saying that Concha's predecessor, Anza, had sent him the diary of Pedro Vial from Texas to Santa Fe, and also a "representation" of Vial's, in which Vial proposed to go directly from Santa Fe to Louisiana. That letter from Anza was dated July 14, 1787, and on October 20 Anza said he had ordered Mares to go to Texas by a route more direct than Vial's. In the letter of January 23, 1788, Ugarte approved the expenses allowed Vial by Anza, but he ordered that Vial make the trip to Natchitoches only, and return to San Antonio. He told Concha to thank Vial for his

[1] We have not found out anything about Concha's early life. He attained the rank of lieutenant colonel on January 1, 1783; became "employed in the government" of New Mexico December 10, 1786 (at that time he was forty-nine years old and had over thirty-four years' service); he took possession of the government of New Mexico August 25, 1787. Concha "made peace and began it" with the Comanches and continued peace with the Utes and Navahos. In 1788 he asked for the rank of colonel and was proposed by the Minister of War but did not receive the promotion. Enclosure in Concha to Revillagigedo, No. 2, Santa Fe, November 1, 1791; Provincias Internas, Vol. 102, f. 190. Concha to Flores [the viceroy], Santa Fe, November 10, 1787; Provincias Internal, Vol. 102, f. 174. Concha to Flores. Santa Fe, June 20, 1788; Provincias Internas, Vol. 102, f. 176. He left the governorship in autumn, 1792; and stayed in Chihuahua, Durango, or Mexico City for a long time to answer charges of the Inquisition and to take care of various money matters with the bishopric of Durango. In 1800 he received permission to marry Ramona de Santillana of Carriedo, Santander—his first marriage, at sixty-three.

zeal, and he promised to send an *informe* (information and recommendation) to the viceroy about Vial upon the latter's return. Ugarte had news of the arrival of Mares in Texas, and Pacheco had sent him Mares' diary.

Concha answered on June 20, saying that on the 23rd he had sent Vial to open a direct route to Natchitoches. Vial was accompanied by four countrymen (all young) who had volunteered: Fragoso, who could read and write and had an honorable reputation, having been for many years a soldier in the province; and by José María Romero, Gregorio Leyva, and Juan Lucero. There is no information about the last three. Vial had told Concha that he knew the location of the water holes as far as the country occupied by the Taovayas; Concha had sent with him a Comanche interpreter and two other persons (possibly Indians). The party expected to reach Natchitoches in about eighteen to twenty days and to use only fifteen days for the return trip. Concha had provided them with ten horses and two mules from the king's supply, as well as food, and tobacco and presents for the Indians. And, as Ugarte had ordered, Concha had praised Vial, who, said Concha, wanted to return to Santa Fe and establish himself. "I beg you to permit it," said Concha, for Vial was a man of good character and a valuable man to have; Concha wanted him in New Mexico, and inducements had been offered him.[2]

So it was less than a month after Mares reached Santa Fe that Pedro Vial left Santa Fe for his second monumental trail-blazing: the trip to Natchitoches. The project had been ordered by Ugarte in order to open routes from Texas and New Mexico to Louisiana, and with California and Sonora,[3] and Concha, the governor, reported to the commandant-general that Vial and his party had left on June 24, 1788.

The official letter from Concha to the commandant at Natchitoches was dated June 23, and the copy now at hand does not have an address, but the substance makes clear the approximate date:

> By superior order, Pedro Vial with four residents of this province under my command goes forth to discover a direct route from this

[2] Concha to Ugarte, June 26, 1788; cited in Woodbury Lowery, *A Descriptive List of Maps of the Spanish Possessions, . . . 1502–1820*, 420.

[3] Ugarte to Manuel Antonio Flores, the fiscal, No. 432, January 5, 1789, Provincias Internas, Vol. 183.

> post to that under your command. As soon as they do so, they will present themselves to you, at which time I ask you to supply them against the king's account with whatever they have used up or lost during this journey, so that they may undertake their return to the province of Texas as they have been ordered.[4]

Vial started with several companions. One party was a squad of three cavalrymen commanded by Santiago Fernández, to escort Vial as far as the country of the Taovayas; Fernández was to keep a diary and was to return to Santa Fe from the Taovayas. There were the New Mexicans: José María Romero, Gregorio Leiva, and Juan Lucero (who will henceforth appear many times in connection with Vial); and finally Francisco Xavier Fragoso, who was to keep a diary of the entire trip from Santa Fe to Natchitoches, back to San Antonio, and return to Santa Fe. With this considerable entourage, Vial set forth on the second of his epoch-making trips.

### *Diary of Santiago Fernández from Santa Fe to the Taovayas and Return to Santa Fe, June 24–July 21, 1788, and July 24–December (August?) 17, 1788*[5]

Itinerary, diary, and calculation of distance which I, the undersigned, make in a [journey of] exploration from this [village] of Santa Fe to the villages of the Humanes [Taovayas] by the superior order of the Governor Don Fernando de la Concha [and] under the leadership and guidance of Pedro Vial. It is as follows:

On Tuesday, June 24, 1788, I began the march from this capital at 2 o'clock in the afternoon, and, [going] to the southeast, reached the pueblo of Pecos, the distance being estimated at [eight] leagues. 8

On the 25th I set out to the south from this pueblo, keeping on my right a wooded mesa, and I stopped to take a siesta at the ford of a river from 9 until 2 in the afternoon. Then I took up the march and stopped at the Huevos [Huecos?] de Bernal. 12

[4] Concha to [Commandant at Natchitoches], Santa Fe, June 23, 1788, Papeles de Cuba, leg. 14.

[5] There is a copy of Fernández' diary in Historia, Vol. 43, No. 15; and a copy in Historia, Vol. 52, No. 17; our copy is a certified copy from Historia, Vol. 62, No. 5.

On the 26th I set out from this place at 6 in the morning in an easterly direction through good country until I stopped to take my siesta in the little canyon of the Siparines from 10 until 1. Then I arose, and, traveling through good country, arrived on this day at the Río de las Gallinas, [where] I stopped at 7 o'clock in the evening. 13

On the 27th I set out from this river about 10 o'clock in the morning because it had rained all last night; we traveled to the east through good country until we arrived about 7 o'clock at a place called Pajarito. 10

On the 28th we remained in this place because of the heavy rains.

At 8 o'clock in the morning of the 29th, we set out to the east across a plain, and at a short distance came upon three mesas on our right. At 11 we took our siesta in a canyon with cottonwoods. At 2 in the afternoon we took up the march in the same direction, and at 8 in the evening arrived at the end of the last mesa. 8

On the 30th, at 4 in the morning we set out from this place in the same direction, keeping on the left a dark mesa and on the right two small hills with many red slabs and a small mesa which is in a valley which we called El Valle de Santana; we reached a mesa that is called Tucumcari. 11

[July]

On the 1st of July at 7 in the morning I took up the march, keeping the same direction toward the east across a plain in which, at the distance of 3 leagues, we came upon a village of Comanches with 56 lodges over which Chief Naisaras was ruling. They received us with pleasure, and, having smoked and talked with them, we told them our destination, to which they replied that we were taking the right course. We were accompanied by some of these Comanches to a place where we found a river on which we took our siesta from 12 until 1 in the afternoon. Then we continued the march until we arrived at the end of a white mesa. 12

On the 2nd at 4 in the morning we set out from here, continuing in the same direction and keeping on the right the same mesa until we took our siesta from 11 until 2 in the afternoon at a spring on a plain; continuing our march, we arrived at a pass in this mesa at 8 o'clock at night, estimating [the leagues] this day at 14

On the 3rd we took up the march at 5 in the morning, and after a short distance we ascended some plains on which we found, in the course of the day, thirteen ponds [lakes] of water. At 6 in the evening we stopped on the same plains, and at the last pond. 13

At 3 in the morning of the 4th we set out, following the same eastwardly direction across all the plain, and at a short distance we came upon a canyon in which flows the Río Blanco, which goes to the Jumanos. We proceeded along this, having taken our siesta from 10 until 1 in the afternoon; we stopped at 7 o'clock. 8

On the 5th, at 6 o'clock in the morning we set out in the same direction along the same river, and took our siesta from 12 until 2 in the afternoon at the place where the canyon of this river begins. In that [canyon], we came upon some Comanches [women] and one Comanche [man], who conducted us to his village, where we slept; there were four lodges. We and our horses were well cared for. 9

On the 6th, at 8 in the morning, we departed, continuing in the same direction along the same river until we stopped on it at 6 o'clock. 10

On the 7th at 5 in the morning we set out in the same direction, traveling along the same river until we stopped on it at 5 in the afternoon. 10

On the 8th at 5 in the morning we set out along the same river in the direction mentioned, and came to a bend [where there were] cottonwoods; from this place the hills and [the] canyon of the river diminish. We stopped at 6 in the evening. 11

At 6 in the morning of the 9th we marched in the same direction [along] the river mentioned, and at about 10 o'clock we came upon a village of Comanches composed of fourteen lodges. They asked us to stop, which we did. Some and then others also came, walking, and having talked and smoked with them in a very agreeable manner, we all slept at that place. The chief, who was [called] Pochinaquina, told us that that river would lead us to the Jumanos [Taovayas].[6] 4

At 9 o'clock in the morning of the 10th we departed, taking the same course and river, going [turning] to the left at 12 o'clock; and at 5 in the afternoon we arrived at a rivulet [a small river] that is at the foot of a small mesa. 13

On the 11th, at 5 in the morning we marched in the direction men-

[6] Jumanos may be translated either as Jumanes or as Taovayas.

tioned, crossing hills and arroyos until we came back to the Río Blanco, on which we stopped at 6 in the evening. 9

At 3 in the morning of the 12th we set out from this place with the same course and along the same river. We stopped to take our siesta at a spring which is near this same river. [We were here] until 2 in the afternoon, when we again marched [and continued] until 8 o'clock at night, when we stopped on a bayou [*ancón*][7] of the said river. 14

At 4 o'clock in the morning of the 13th we set out, following the same river in the same direction, and took our siesta on the bank of a river that descends from the north and joins the one that we are following. At 3 o'clock in the afternoon we set out from this place and stopped near some high hills that are near the same river. 12

At 5 in the morning of the 14th we continued our march, following the same course and river, and at about 11 we came upon another large river which also descends from the north to join the one referred [to above]. There we took our siesta until 1 in the afternoon, when we continued until we stopped at 6 on the river mentioned. 10

At 4 in the morning of the 15th we set out, still following the same course and river, and having traveled about 6 leagues, we came upon a trail of Comanches. There I took my siesta until 2 o'clock in the afternoon, when three chiefs reached that point. With many importunities they took us to their villages, which are composed of 372 lodges and over which rule these three chiefs, namely: Zoquacante, Cochi, and Visimaxe [Pisimapo]. Those villages were situated on a larger river, near which we slept. 10

At 5 in the morning of the 16th we continued the march with our course to the north, having left with one of those chiefs the exhausted beasts and having replaced them with others. As a guide, we took along a Comanche of those villages, who accompanied us to the Jumanos. We stopped by this river. 4

At 9 [Historia 43 says 3] in the morning of the 17th we set out to the south with the aforesaid Comanche, who is called Zoja [Sofais?], and traveled until we arrived at the Río Blanco which we had left. We stopped by it at 5 in the afternoon. 12

At 5 in the morning of the 18th we continued our eastwardly course

[7] Perhaps *rincón*.

along the same river until we arrived at another river that descends from the north. On that [river] we took our siesta until 3 in the afternoon, when we proceeded, and at 6 o'clock we stopped on the same river beyond [above?] a hill. 10

On the 19th we set out, following the same course and river until we arrived at a hill that has some water holes.[8] 8

On the 20th, at 5 o'clock in the morning, we set out, taking the course and river aforementioned, traveling until we arrived at and crossed over to the pueblo of the Jumanos[9] at 11 in the morning. In it we were received with much pleasure and were given good lodgings. They asked us where we were going, and we replied [that we had come] for the purpose of becoming acquainted with them, and to act as escort to the explorer Vial, who was going to Naquitochi [Natchitoches].

This pueblo consists of 17 huts made of straw. The people raise maize, kidney-beans, watermelons, and pumpkins. The Río Blanco, to which reference has been made, flows through its environs.

There are two other pueblos immediately after this, within the short space of half a league; the other two contain, with slight difference, the same number of huts as this one, and [the people] raise the same crops. Here we remained on the 21st, 22nd, and 23rd.

*Fernández gives no distance for the last day, and no total distance. They have now reached the Taovaya villages on Red River—the great trading center for the Texas–New Mexico–Lower Louisiana area. The villages on the Brazos near Waco were visited also by Morfi in 1781—five years before Vial's arrival there. Traditionally, the Wichitas and the Taovayas were on the Red River from Spanish Fort to Wichita Falls, and on the upper Brazos south of Wichita Falls; from the villages on the Red, it was two hundred miles south and a little east, down the Brazos, to the traditional Tawakoni villages, chief of which were El Quiscat and El Flechazo, six leagues apart.*

*It is interesting to observe that three small villages of seventeen*

[8] *Artenejales.* Perhaps he means *tinajeros.*

[9] The villages of the Taovayas were centered around present-day Spanish Fort, near Ringgold, in north-central Texas, and on the Brazos.

*huts apiece (the Taovayas on the Red River) were so important for so many years in the Spanish Southwest.*

*Fernández now returns to Santa Fe.*

On the 24th, at 5 o'clock in the morning, I undertook my return [trip], taking a western course. We proceeded by a direct road, different from that which we had taken [before], by the advice of the Comanche who accompanied us [Zoja, or Sofais?], and he assured us that it was the shortest road by which we would reach his village, where we had to go in order to return his animals and to receive our own. Having parted from the aforesaid Vial, whom I left at a pueblo mentioned [above], we traveled until 6 o'clock in the afternoon, when we arrived at a plain.[10] 7

On the 25th we set out to the north at 2 o'clock in the morning, leaving the Río Blanco in order to go [to the place] where were situated the villages of the Comanches that we had left before. I stopped from 1 to 3 to take my siesta [and] then we continued our course until 8 o'clock that night, when we stopped on a river that I called El Nogal. 12

On the 26th we took up our march to the west at 4 o'clock in the morning, and at a short distance I came to the villages, where I stopped at 11 in the morning; we spent the night [there] also. 7

For this day [our] only [activity was] conversation with the Comanches, who asked me about my captain, whom they desired to know.

On the 27th, at 4 o'clock in the morning, we set out from this point, leaving the animals they had loaned us and taking our own. [We were] accompanied by a Jumano and his wife and a Comanche and his wife. We traveled very rapidly across some plains until 6 in the evening, when we stopped on the same plain. 13

On the 28th we set out to the west at 2 o'clock in the morning, [traveling] until we arrived at a little stream at 9, by which we took our siesta at 3 in the afternoon. I continued my march, and we stopped without water on a plain. 10

On the 29th, at 2 o'clock in the morning, we continued the march in the same direction [across] the plain, meeting many [wild] mustangs, buffalo herds, and antelopes, until we arrived at a river with little tim-

[10] The phrase "When we arrived at a plain" is not in Historia 43.

ber. On it we took our siesta until 3; then we continued [our course], following the same direction [until we stopped] on the high part of a plain. 12

On the 30th, at 3 in the morning, we took the same course across level country without pasture, and at a distance of 2 leagues we came upon a large river of salt water that runs to the south; it is called Las Conchas. Having passed this and still [going] rapidly, we ascended another plain with many herds of game and [bands of] horses. [We proceeded] until we arrived at another small stream of good water—[but] very narrow—which is called La Nutria.[11] By it we took our siesta until 3 in the afternoon, when we continued [our journey], and at 6 o'clock stopped on a wooded hilltop after having passed nine small mesas. 12

At 3 o'clock in the morning of the 31st we continued our march in the same direction and along the edge of the same ridge, without ceasing to encounter cattle [buffalo] and horses until 10 in the morning, when we descended to the Río Blanco;[12] on that [stream] we took our siesta until 3 in the afternoon, when we continued our course, traveling through bad country; leaving the said river to the right, we stopped at 6 o'clock on a hill. 10

[August]

On the 1st of August we continued the march to the west, continually in bad country until we again descended to the said Río Blanco. There we took our siesta until 3 o'clock in the afternoon, when, leaving it to the left, we stopped at 8 on a rocky hilltop. 13

On the 2nd, at 4 in the morning [we set out] in the same direction [and] traveled continuously across a plain until [we arrived at] some springs of water, where we took our siesta until 3 o'clock; then we proceeded to a thicket of mesquite, in which we stopped. 10

On the 3rd we set out from this place at 2 in the morning, following the same course through a wide canyon, keeping some hills on the right. We took our siesta at some springs of water that I named El Espíritu Santo. At 1 o'clock in the afternoon we continued until we

[11] The Otter.

[12] Castañeda says that Blanco refers to the Prairie Dog Town Fork of the Red River.

arrived at a river that is called El Capulin [and] on this I stopped at 6 o'clock. 12

On the 4th we continued our march, ascending by the end of a mesa [and] following the direction mentioned across a large plain. Having taken my siesta on it, I set out at 3 in the afternoon and slept at the end of another mesa. 12

On the 5th we tarried in this place until 3 in the afternoon, when we continued our journey in the direction indicated [across] a plain on which we came upon a large pond [buffalo wallow?], where we stopped at 6 o'clock. 3

On the 6th, at 1 in the morning, we continued the march in the same direction across a plain until we reached a river that appears white at the mouth of a canyon. There we took our siesta until 3, when we proceeded, leaving that canyon and entering a plain; we stopped on the Colorado River.[13]

With our course to the north on the 8th, we traveled through a bad country, and at 12 o'clock stopped to take our siesta at some water holes;[14] at 3 o'clock in the afternoon we continued to a large marsh, [which we reached] at 5 o'clock. 12

On the 9th, at 3 o'clock in the morning, we set out to the west through broken country, and took our siesta until 3 o'clock among some small white mesas, when we continued our course and slept by the same Río Colorado. 11

On the 10th we set out from that place in the same direction, and we took our siesta on the same river until 4 in the afternoon; then we continued [our course] until we stopped on a back-water [*ancón*] of the river [above] mentioned. 12

On the 11th at 4 in the morning we continued the march in the same western direction, and took our siesta at some small canyons; we slept at the edge of a large mesa that comes right down to the same river. 13

On the 12th we continued the march in the same direction along the river and took our siesta from 12 until 3; we stopped at 6 in the evening on the river. 14

On the 13th we set out at 2 in the morning [and] continued in the

[13] Probably the Canadian. See Thomas, *After Coronado*, 1.
[14] *Artenejales de agua.*

same direction named; and we slept by the same river at the end of a hill. 12

On the 14th we continued our march, ascending by the end of a mesa [and] following the direction mentioned across a large plain. Having taken my siesta on it, I set out at 3 in the afternoon, and we slept at the end of another mesa. 12

On the 15th we set out from this place, taking the direction named [and] leaving the said mesa behind. We went to the end of a wooded hill, where we took our siesta until 3 o'clock. From there we continued to the Río de las Gallinas, where we stopped. 9

On the 16th, keeping the same mesa on the right, we continued the march until we arrived at El Gusano.[15] 13

On the 17th we set out from that place in a northwesterly direction, and we continued the march as far as this capital village of Santa Fe, [which we reached] at 6 o'clock in the afternoon, where I presented myself before my governor, Señor Don Fernando de la Concha, by whom I had been appointed.

Santa Fe, December 17, 1788.[16]

SANTIAGO FERNANDEZ

This is a copy of the original, which remains in the archives of the government.

Santa Fe, June 20, 1789.

FERNANDO DE LA CONCHA

It is a copy. Chihuahua, September 12, 1793.

MANUEL MERINO [*rubric*]

*Very often when an Indian proposed a different route, he was serving some purpose of his own, but in this case the Comanche was honest, and Fernández' return trip was twelve leagues shorter than the trip out.*

*They had come out through Tucumcari, Glenrío, and south of Amarillo into the Palo Duro Canyon, where they followed the Prairie Dog Town Fork of the Red River (which Fernández called Blanco River). At about Vernon, Texas, they crossed the Red River to the north*

[15] *El Gusano* means "The Worm."

[16] His diary ends August 17, but he did not sign it until December 17. Since the diary is the original, there is no ready explanation for this delay.

*bank and continued to the Taovayas. They had traveled twenty-six days and had covered 255 leagues (663 miles).*

*The return trip, a little shorter, had followed approximately the same route, along the Prairie Dog Town Fork, up to the Llano at about Canyon, Texas, then across to Tucumcari as before. The return took twenty-three traveling days and covered 243 leagues (632 miles).*

*Now we flash back to the beginning of this expedition and follow the diary of Fragoso from Santa Fe. This is not as simple as it sounds, for there are four known copies of Fragoso's rather extensive journal of the Santa Fe–Natchitoches portion: one in the Archivo General de Indias in Seville; one in Volume 43, Sección de Historia, Archivo General y Público de la Nación, México City; one in Volume 62 of the same Historia; and one, in abbreviated form but signed by Fragoso and apparently in his handwriting, in the General Land Office at Austin, Texas—and they are quite different at times.*

## *Diary of Francisco Xavier Fragoso, Santa Fe to Natchitoches, June 20 to Aug. 20, 177*[17]

[Historia 43:]

### Diary of Francisco Xavier Fragoso, Santa Fe to Natchitoches to San Antonio to Santa Fe, June 24, 1788–August 20, 1789.[18]

Itinerary, diary, and calculation of distance in the exploration of a direct road from this province of New Mexico to the fort of Natchi-

[17] The documentation on the Natchitoches trip is rather complicated. Of the four known copies of the part from Santa Fe to Natchitoches, the Seville copy is in the Archivo General de Indias, Papeles de Cuba, leg. 1394 (and is signed by Fragoso), and it ends at Natchitoches. The copy in the Archivo General de Mexico, Sección Historia, Vol. 43, No. 17, is a copy made in Chihuahua, September 12, 1793, certified by Manuel Merino, and covers the entire trip; the copy in Historia, Vol. 62, No. 7, was made and certified at the same time and place and by the same person as the one in Historia 43, and it also covers the entire trip. The one in the General Land Office is in Fragoso's handwriting and is signed by him at beginning and end; the Land Office copy is short and does not contain a description of Natchitoches, Nacogdoches, or San Antonio. An attempt to determine which is the original presents problems, as will be seen. The commandant at Natchitoches sent the original diary to Miró, the governor of Louisiana, who in turn sent it to Havana, and it seems the original most likely is in the Papeles de Cuba, leg. 1394. We have compared them all.

[18] They reached Natchitoches on August 20, 1788, and Santa Fe exactly one year later.

toches and to that of Texas, which I, the undersigned, by superior order, go to perform in the company of Don Pedro Vial, commissioned for this purpose.

[Seville copy:] Town of Santa Fee, June 24, 1788.

Accompanied by Josef María Romero, Gregorio Leyva, and Juan Lucero.

FRANCISCO XAVIER FRAGOSO [*rubric*]

*Tuesday*, [*June*] *24*. This day, about 11 o'clock in the morning, having made ready all things necessary for this purpose, having received all the orders from the governor of this province, Señor Don Fernando de la Concha, and having been given the correspondence and dispatches for the governors and commandants of the said fort and [the] province of Texas, the following set out from the capital, Santa Fe:

Don Pedro Vial, a native of León [Lyons] of France.

Francisco Xavier Fragoso, of the City of Mexico.

Josef María Romero, José Gregorio Leyva, and Luis Lusiro [Juan Lucero], natives of this town. We directed our course to the south, toward the pueblo of Pecos. Upon leaving the forest, we penetrated a short canyon and [then] a mountainous plateau [wooded mesa] from which there is a view of the village. Stopped at 4 P.M. Leagues covered 8

[Historia 43 says they left at about 11 o'clock in the morning. All copies give Vial's nativity.]

[The following entry is from the Seville copy:]

*Wednesday 25* We set out at 9 A.M. in a southerly direction, heavily wooded, having on our right [to the south] a plateau [a mesa]. We went as far as the ford that is called Pecos. There I rested, and, [after] continuing the march, I came to stop at that of Bernal. Leagues covered[19] 10

[From this point on, we follow first the Seville copy:]

*Thursday, 26* Left the said district at 6 A.M. in an easterly course; good land [pasture], wood and water. Arrived at the Río de las Gallinas. Leagues covered 10

[19] Historia 43 and 62 both say he set out to the west; Land Office copy says to the south. In general, Historia 43 and 62 are the same; the Land Office copy is much shorter and contains different information.

[The copy in Historia 43 says: We stopped at 6 in the evening, having made 11 leagues.]

[Historia 62: We marched to the east.]

[Land Office: I marched at 6 A.M., going eastwardly; good land. I arrived at the Gallinas (River) at 6 P.M. It is a place. 11]

*Friday, 27* Set out on march at 6 A.M., same course in the aforementioned good land. Stopped at 6 P.M. at a steady [permanent] spring of water. There is a cottonwood, and it may be a red *serrito.* Leagues covered 10

[Historia 43 and 62: 4" 27—At 11 o'clock in the morning we set out in the same direction (through) a good, level country, and stopped at 6 in the afternoon at Pajarito, (where) there is a permanent spring; 8 leagues were made. 8]

[Land Office: 27. I got myself on the road at 11 A.M., traveling eastwardly; good land, pasture, firewood, and water. I stopped at Pajarito at 6 in the afternoon. It is a spring (and) there are cottonwoods. 8]

*Saturday, 28* I did not go out, due to the heavy rain.

[Historia 43: 5" 28—(We remained) here in the same place because we were not able to travel on account of a heavy rain (*aguada*) (that lasted) all day and night.]

[Historia 62: Same as Historia 43.]

[Land Office: No entry for this date.]

*Sunday, 29* Set out on march at 8 A.M., and in the same direction [,] and to the south there is a little red hill, and at a distance of about a league to the north [there is] another red mesa—but all plains until we arrived at a grove of cottonwood trees [;] and past that, I followed [skirted] a forest of savin [juniper or red cedar] and a black mesa; on the south, the water is not permanent. At 6:30 I stopped at San Pedro. Leagues covered 8

[Historia 43: 6" 29—We set out in the same direction at 8 o'clock in the morning; to the south there is a little red hill and a small red mesa, while to the north there is another red mesa and a canyon with cottonwoods. From there on continued a juniper forest for about two leagues, while to the south there was another black mesa; there was no water. The place is called Sn. Pedro. We stopped at half past four in the afternoon, having made 9 leagues. 9]

[Historia 62: Same as Historia 43.]

[Land Office: 29. I was on the march at 8 o'clock in said (direction) course, good land; there is a small red mesa to the south, and another to the north at a distance of 1 league. Presently we came to a forest of juniper which was 2 leagues long. I made a dry camp at Sn. Pedro, having traveled 8]

*Monday, 30* I set out on the march at 8 A.M., [traveling] easterly, cutting off a blackish plateau to the south, and to the north two small hills of red slabs and a small mesa; there is a large valley, without water, called Santana. Leagues covered 10

[Historia 43: 7″ 30—At 8 A.M. we marched in the same direction through a level country, keeping on the right the mesa of the preceding day; to the left were two small hills of red slabs; to the north was a small mesa. From there on is a very large valley without water which is called Santa Rosa; we stopped at 7 o'clock at night, having come 10 leagues. 10]

[Historia 62: Same as Historia 43.]

[Land Office: I was on the march at 8, (following) said course, keeping a dark-colored mesa on the right, and two small hills of red *sosos*, and a very great valley without water, which is called Sta. Ana. I stopped at 6 in the afternoon. 10]

## [July]

*July 1, Tuesday.* In the morning I set out on the march to the east, leaving at the south a white mesa, and at the north some small lakes, and coming on to a brushy wash, I found a village of Comanches in which the chief was commanding. He came out to meet us with great pleasure. The said chief is named Naisare. Shortly after we arrived, after having eaten and talked of our business, they told us that we were going well and very directly. Then we left, and were accompanied by many of them for there were other villages where we rested at the village of *maya*, which was near. Belarde left and went to where he said the Pawnee [would be] awaiting him at the time they had set; and [but] the said Pawnee not having come, he [Belarde] marched with me because he was alone and very far away [from home]. I stopped at the point of a black mesa which is called Santa Rosa, at 7 P.M. Leagues covered 12

[Historia 43: 8″ July 1—At 8 o'clock in the morning we set out in the same direction, leaving to the south a white mesa and to the north some small ponds. After going 3 or 4 leagues, we came upon a settlement of Comanches in a valley with permanent water, and, following it a distance of 3 leagues, we found three other settlements of Comanches; in these and in the former we were received with delight by the inhabitants. At 7 P.M. we stopped at the point of a black mesa which we called La Punta, having made 12 leagues. 12]

[Historia 62: Same as Historia 43.]

[Land Office: July 1. I was on the march at 7 A.M. by said course, keeping on the south a white mesa and on the north some small lakes. I stopped at the edge of a dark-colored mesa which I named Sta. Rosa; I stopped at 7 P.M. 12]

*Wednesday, 2* Set out on march at 8 in an easterly direction, with the same mesa to the right, and a very extensive plain to the left. There is a good spring of water [and] a cottonwood tree. Stopped at 9 P.M. at the edge of the said mesa. Leagues covered 10

[Historia 43: 9″ 2—We set out in the same direction at 8 o'clock in the morning, keeping the same mesa on the right, and a very extensive plain on the left. We stopped at 7 o'clock at night at a spring of water which we called El Puerto; we advanced 12 leagues. 12]

[Historia 62: Same as Historia 43.]

[Land Office: 2. I was on the march at 8, (following) said course; good land; keeping said mesa to the right and a very broad plain to the left; the said mesa *la regula* is 10 leagues long, and the plain is 20; there is a spring of good water and a cottonwood tree. I stopped in El Puerto at the edge of the mesa at 7 P.M. 12]

*Thursday, 3* Set out on march at 6 A.M. in an easterly direction. We left the plains, which are so extensive that one sees only sky and plain. I found thirteen ponds. I stopped at 7 P.M. Leagues covered 12

[Historia 43: 10″ 3—At 7 A.M. we set out in the same direction (across) a plain so extensive that neither a ridge nor knolls are to be found in any direction. This day we passed thirteen ponds with considerable water and stopped at 7 P.M. at the source of the Río Blanco; we made 12 leagues. 12]

[Historia 62: Same as Historia 43.]

[Land Office: I was on the march at 6 A.M. on an easterly course. Presently I left the plains which are so extensive that only sky and plain may be seen. There are on this day's march thirteen ponds. I stopped at 7 P.M. on the source of the Río Blanco. 12]

*Friday, 4* I set on the march in an easterly direction at 5:30 A.M., and shortly afterward I arrived at the headwaters of the Río Blanco which I followed. There are water, good land, plains, wood, and much pasturage. I stopped at 6:30 and gave it the name of St. Louis. Leagues covered 7

[Historia 43: 11″ 4—At 5 A.M. we set out in the same direction (along) the river (mentioned) above. There are pasturage, firewood, and a good country. We stopped at 6 o'clock in the evening on the same river or stream, having made 7 leagues. 7]

[Historia 62: Same as Historia 43.]

[Land Office: 4. I was on the march at 5:30, (following) said course along the said Río Blanco. Water, good land, plains, pasture land, [and] plenty of firewood. I stopped at 6. 6]

*Saturday, 5* Set out on march at 5:30 A.M. in an easterly direction and downstream, [where there is] land, wood, and much good pasturage, finding Comanches and unattached Comanches everywhere, their tents in the lagoons and sleeping on the said river. At a short distance from there I found another river named Del Tule, which joins with the said Río Blanco. A Comanche came there and with much graciousness took us to his village and put us in a house, where he entertained us and gave us supper, and joined my beasts of burden with his [put mine to pasture with his]. I arrived at 6 P.M. Leagues covered 6

[Historia 43: 12″ 5—About 5 o'clock in the morning we marched in the same direction, going down the river (through) good country. At a distance of 3 leagues it (the river) is joined by another which comes down from the north and which we called El Tule. We changed the course which we were pursuing, in order by so doing to oblige some Comanches who took us to their lodging about 4 o'clock in the afternoon. 6 leagues were made. 6]

[Historia 62: Same as Historia 43.]

[Land Office: 5. I set out at 5 A.M. by said course to the east and downstream; good land, and at a little distance, this river-course is seen, where it is joined by a river that comes from the north, called the Río del Tule. We stopped at 6 P.M. at that point. 6]

*Sunday, 6.* Set out on march at 9 A.M. in an easterly direction, always taking the [course along the] said Río Blanco and without resting, and because of the diversion of many Comanches and very hot weather, I covered, due to deviation from the course, 5 leagues. 5

[Historia 43: 13″ 6—we set out about 9 o'clock in the morning to search for (our) course and the river that we were following. We stopped at 6 o'clock in the evening in a good country with pasture, firewood, and water; 6 leagues were made. 6]

[Historia 62: Same as Historia 43.]

[Land Office: 6. I was on the march at 9 o'clock *de el día,* my course always following said Río Blanco, on which I stopped to sleep at 6 P.M., (where there was) firewood, pasture, and water. 6]

*Monday, 7* Set out on march at 5 on the said easterly direction, and rested at 11. Again set out at 3 P.M. I always stopped on the said river, which they call Castor [Beaver Creek?]. Leagues covered 10

[Historia 43: 14″ 7—At 5 A.M. we set out in the same direction (along) the same river, (through) a level country with pasture. We stopped at 6 o'clock at the place called El Castor (The Beaver), having made 9 leagues. 9]

[Historia 62: Same as Historia 43.]

[Land Office: I got myself on the march at 5 A.M., (following) said course and said river, which has become broader—more than a musket-shot. I stopped on said river—the Castor—at 6. 9]

*Tuesday, 8* I set out on the march at 8 A.M. by said [river] in the said direction, and without a siesta I stopped in a woods of cottonwood trees where the hills were diminishing and the river was growing bigger. I stopped at 6 P.M. Leagues covered 10

[Historia 43: 15″ 8—At 5 A.M. we set out in the same direction and (along) the same river, and stopped at a wood of cottonwood trees. From here on, the knolls and hills begin to get smaller; all this is a good country. We stopped at 6 o'clock in the evening on the same river, having made 10 leagues. 10]

[Historia 62: Same as Historia 43.]

[Land Office: 8. I was on the march at 5:30 A.M., (following) said course along said river, and stopped in a wood of cottonwood trees, where the hills are getting smaller. I stopped at 7 P.M. 10]

*Wednesday, 9* I departed at 6 A.M. in the same direction and by the said river, and at about 10 I came upon a settlement of Comanches, all traveling along, who very affectionately stopped us, and, giving us a lodge to protect [us] from the sun and water, bringing us food at about 11 A.M. Leagues traversed 4

[Historia 43: 16″ 9—At 5 o'clock in the morning we set out along the same river in the same direction, and presently, about 10 o'clock, stopped to kill for food some buffaloes which we came upon; 4 leagues were made. 4]

[Historia 62: Same as Historia 43.]

[Land Office: 9. I was on the march at 10 A.M., (following) said course (along) said river, and presently, without going farther, I stopped from necessity at 12 o'clock. 4]

*Thursday, 10* Because I bade the said Comanches goodbye and left at about 9 and because of having found a spring of sweet water (because the other one is brackish), I (did not leave until) 9 o'clock. This was right after our going out, because, taking the guide, Don Pedro Vial went on ahead of us, and he could not be overtaken, for they had told me the night before that he was going in search of the Yamparicas,[20] which is a separate nation. That was at about 4 P.M., and at the same time Santiago Fernández [got lost] looking for water. They could not find him. Leagues covered 5]

[Historia 43: 17″ 10—At 9 o'clock we set out in the same direction, and after walking about 3 leagues we found a spring of water and stopped because of the heavy rain; 3 leagues were made. 3]

[Historia 62: Same as Historia 43.]

[Land Office: 10. I was on the march at 9 A.M., (and) having found a spring of good water [the other being brackish], much pasturage and firewood, without losing the course of the river, I stopped at 3 in the afternoon. 7]

*Friday, 11* I set out on the march at 5 A.M. by our opinion in an easterly direction in search of the river which we had left, which was where the Comanches had told us. We followed the river [and found] much pasturage, wood, [and] good land. I stopped at 7 P.M. Leagues covered 10

[Historia 43: 18″ 11—We set out at 5 o'clock in the morning in the same direction and crossed bad country because of a turn made by the Río Blanco, which we were following. At 9 o'clock at night we

[20] Another division of the Comanche tribe.

stopped on the same river at a cottonwood, having made 13 leagues. 13]

[Historia 62: Same as Historia 43.]

[Land Office: 11. I was on the march at 5 A.M., (following) the same course and downstream, but the Comanches advised me not to follow the river, (so) that by it (the advice) I went right. I stopped at 7 at Sn. Diego; pasture, firewood, and no stones. 12]

*Saturday, 12* I set out on the march before dawn by the former direction; flat land. I came to the river and rested there at 11, and took up the march at 3 P.M., following the river until about 8 that night, when I stopped. Leagues covered 12

[Historia 43: 19" 12—At 3 A.M. we set out downstream in the same direction through a level country (with) pasture and firewood. At 8 o'clock at night we stopped at a place called Sn. Juan; 11 leagues were made. 11]

[Historia 62: Same as Historia 43.]

[Land Office: 12. I was on the march before daybreak, (following) said river and course; level land, and the river wider. I traveled until 8 o'clock at night. 13]

*Sunday, 13* I set out on the march by the said direction and river at 4 A.M. through good land, and at about 9 o'clock I found Santiago Fernández,[21] and, proceeding from the river on the north, we saw the low ranges that we had information were near the towns of Jumas (Jumanos), and at about 10 A.M. we arrived at another copious river coming from the north, which is named the Río Puerco. At this junction of the river, I rested at 11 A.M., and, continuing the march by the said river at 3 P.M., I stopped at 7 on the said river. Leagues covered 11]

[Historia 43: 20" 13—At 4 A.M. we set out (along) the river in the same direction, and, leaving it of necessity to the north, we got sight of some hills that are opposite the pueblos of the Jumanos. At the distance of 6 leagues from where we set out, we came upon another river with much water that comes down from the north and unites with the previous Río Blanco. At 7 o'clock at night we stopped on the bank of said river; we came 12 leagues. 12]

[Historia 62 here adds the total leagues: 161.]

[21] From the fact that almost never does Fragoso mention the other men on the trip, and that, when he does, it is usually of meeting or leaving them, one might infer that the expedition is divided into at least three separate parties, traveling independently.

[Land Office: 13. I got myself on the march at about 4 o'clock in the morning, on said course and (along) said river, and, setting out for the north side of the river, we saw the low ranges of hills that we had (been advised) were those of the Jumanos. There [the river] is joined by another river that comes from the north, bearing a great deal of water, which is called the Río de Plumas, less salty than the Blanco. I made a stop at about 7 P.M. at said river at Sn. Dimas, that I named at the stopping place. 12]

*Monday, 14* I set out on the march at 6 by the said river and direction, and at 11 arrived where this river joins another larger one, coming from the north; from here, all rivers and hills *exployer*, since one sees only one not very large mountain range on the north. At about 4:30 in the afternoon, it joined another river coming from the north, and, coming out into an open plain, I stopped on the bank of the said river at about 6:30 P.M. Leagues covered 10]

[Historia 43: 21" 14—We marched at 6 A.M. along the river in the same direction, and at 11 A.M. another river, larger than the first, which also descended from the north, joined ours. At 4 o'clock in the afternoon, another larger river, moving along at a good pace, which likewise came from the north, joined these. At 6 P.M. we stopped on its bank in a valley; 10 leagues were made.[22] 10]

[Historia 62: Same as Historia 43.]

[Land Office: 14: I got myself on the march at 6 A.M. on said course and along said river, (which) joins another river that comes from the north, greater and full of water, which extends the other river [*esplayando todo*]. Rivers and hills and a range are seen, not very large, in the north; but another river that also comes from the north joins the said Río Blanco; and, setting out from a very great plain, I stopped at about 6:30 in the afternoon. 10]

*Tuesday, 15* I took up the march via the said river and direction at 6 A.M., and, having gone about 6 leagues, I met a very large band of Comanches. I rested there on a large river that descends from the south, and shortly I left and crossed the river, which is very large, and stopped on the said river at 7 P.M. with the same band. Leagues covered 10

[22] It seems that the North Fork and the Salt Fork of the Red River are the two streams mentioned here.

[Historia 43: 22″ 15—We set out in the same direction along the same river through good country; at a distance of 6 leagues a little river descends from the south and unites with the former, with which it forms one that is very large. This made it necessary for us to stop on the far bank at 7 P.M.; we made 10 leagues. 10]

[Historia 62: Same as Historia 43.]

[Land Office: 15. I continued the march by said course and (along) said river at 6 A.M., and, traveling along said river across good land, well provided with pasturage and firewood and meat, I stopped at 7 o'clock at night (and) crossed the river, which is very large; on this day's trip I crossed an arroyo that descends from the south. 10]

*Wednesday, 16* I left at 5 A.M. in a northerly direction on the [trail of the] band, and overtook the camp. Then they came out to receive us and made us welcome into their tipis, and I stopped at 9 A.M. Leagues covered 4

[Historia 43: 23″ 16—We set out to the north at 5 o'clock in the morning, and at 10 o'clock stopped at the village of Chief Pisimanpit in accordance with the request that he made of us. We were cared for and entertained by him and the rest of his band; we came 4 leagues. 4]

[Historia 62: Same as Historia 43.]

[Land Office: 16. I marched out at 9 A.M., the course (the same) until (we came upon) a very large track of Comanches; and in order to find out whether it was going well or not, I overtook them; and I stopped with them at 6 in the afternoon. 6]

*Thursday, 17* I set out on the march at 9 A.M. in an easterly direction, the Comanche [Sofais] who led Don Pedro Vial to Santa Fe from San Antonio, leading us, and he led us across some very great plains and good land, and very directly there is steady water, wood, and good pasturage. In this camp there are three chiefs: one is Pisimanpit, the second Quibuniputimi, the other Chobacante. At about 5 leagues I came upon another very large band. I did not arrive [I did not go up to the village], but the said guide tells me that there are more than two hundred lodges. I stopped at a water hole of good water at 10:30 P.M. Leagues covered 11

[Historia 43 & 62: 24″ 17—We marched at 9 o'clock in the morning again in search of our route and river, guided through good country (large plains with permanent water) by a Comanche called El Soja and his wife. We stopped at 10 o'clock at night in a place called Sn. Antonio, having advanced 12 leagues. 12]

[Land Office: 17. I got myself on the march at 7 A.M. to take the easterly route, (being guided) by a Comanche, the same who guided Don Pedro Vial to Santa Fe; he guided me across some very wide plains with good land and very level, with pasturage, firewood, and sweet water; I stopped at 10 o'clock at night at Sn. Antonio. 2]

*Friday, 18* I set out on the march at 5 A.M. in a not very direct southerly direction. We stopped at a river that comes from the north to join the river that I have followed, which is the Río Blanco, and we passed across plains and through good land. I stopped at 6:30 P.M. Leagues covered 10

[Historia 43: 25″ 18—At 5:30 A.M. we set out to the southwest (southeast?) through good country in search of our course and river. We stopped on a river called Sn. Marcos, which descends from the north and incorporates itself with the same Río Blanco; we stopped at 6 in the evening, having come 10 leagues. 10]

[Historia 62: Same as Historia 43.]

[Land Office: 18. I set out at 9 A.M. (The rest is the same as Historia 43.)]

*Saturday, 19* I set out on the march at 5 A.M. in the said direction through land and across plains, good land; oddly the said river, very muddy, joins another large river that comes from the south; the Comanches say it is the Río del Mermelon. Then it immediately joins another river from the north; I don't know its name, [but] I called it the Río de Dolores. As soon as we crossed the said [river], there was a very extensive plain on which there is a forest of oak. There I slept, stopping at 3 P.M. in order not to arrive late at the towns of the Jumanos. Leagues covered. 8

[Historia 43 and 62: 19—At 5 o'clock in the morning we marched southwest (*sic*) through open plains and good country, and at 12 o'clock we found the Río Blanco, which we followed. We crossed to the opposite bank with much trouble, because it had mirey banks. At a short distance, another large river called Dolores, which descends from the north, joins this one. As soon as this was passed, a great plain was entered upon, in the center of which is a forest of very beautiful liveoaks, in which we stopped at 3 o'clock in the afternoon. We came 8 leagues. 8]

[Historia 62 also totals the number of leagues: 219.]

[Land Office: Similar to the Seville copy, except that the river from the south is called the Almagre by the Comanches, and the forest of liveoak is called the Sn. José.]

*Sunday, 20* I set out on the march at 5 A.M. in an easterly direction, and crossing the river that we have followed from the beginning. There was then a plain from which it will probably be two [or 3] leagues to the [first] villages [of Jumanos, or Taovayas]. I arrived at 9 [and] they received us very graciously. Leagues covered 4

These towns of Jumanos are two on one bank of the river and one on the other. The harmony [among them] is great, since the country is the most beautiful that I have seen.

Leagues that I traversed from Santa Fe to the said country 227

[Historia 43: 20—We set out to the east from this forest at 5 A.M., crossed the river and entered a plain that must extend about 3 leagues or as far as the first village of the Jumanos, where we were well received and well treated by its inhabitants; 4 leagues were made 4]

[Historia 62: . . . which extends about 3 leagues, to arrive at the first village of Jumanos, . . . Leagues covered 231]

[Land Office: 20. I marched out at 9 A.M., the course (being) easterly, and, passing the river, a plain offered itself of 2 or 3 leagues in length to reach the Taovaya villages, [where] I arrived at 9 A.M. 4]

[Historia 62: 21—In the first village of the Jumanos. 22—At the same place. 23—The same. 24—The same.]

*Fragoso seems to give us a good deal more information of Indians and of rivers than has anyone else, and he certainly gives more useful information than has anyone else on the important factors; terrain, pasturage, wood, and water.*

*Very puzzling, however, are the various versions of his journal. In many, many places, information occurs in one that occurs nowhere else. On the whole, the Historia 43 version seems to present the most information of names and places; it resembles the Land Office version—and Historia 62 is very similar to 43. We are almost compelled to believe that Fragoso had a hand in them all; otherwise, the copiers took wholly unwarranted liberties. Perhaps a short version was expanded after the journalist reached his destination, but he may have curtailed a longer version.*

*A letter dated December 8, 1961, from Virginia T. Houston, translater of the General Land Office, says: "There is nothing to indicate that the copy here was carried in the field. Fragoso's rubric appears after his signature in the heading of this document and also at the end. That would indicate to me that he himself wrote this account. How are the others signed?"*

*The Historia 62 copy, made in Chihuahua, has no signature of Fragoso and no rubric; the Seville copy has both signature and rubric at beginning and end.*

*It might be that at Natchitoches Fragoso, knowing that his original diary was to be sent on to Spain, made a shortened copy for the governor of Texas, perhaps putting in from memory the local items that would be important to anyone following the route.*

*Fernández started back for Santa Fe on July 24, but Vial and Fragoso stayed with the Taovayas until July 26, at which time they resumed their journey to the east.*

[Historia 43: 25—At 11 o'clock we departed from this place, leaving the second village and arriving at the third and last. The country is level and there is ample pasturage. We stopped at 11 o'clock, having traveled a league and a half. 1½]

The Seville copy:

*Saturday, 26* I set out from the last town at 6 A.M. in a southeast direction, crossed the river; then a forest of heavy oak presented itself on the good plain land [in the middle of the prairie]. This forest is probably four leagues long,[23] then there was a very beautiful and extensive plain. I stopped at 3 P.M. at a spring of steady water that is called *Santana*. Leagues covered 7½

[Historia 43: 29" 26—At 6 A.M. we set out to the east, crossing the Río Blanco. Presently we entered a forest of very tall liveoaks; all this is good, level country with pasturage and water; its length must be about four leagues, and from there extends a very beautiful plain.

[23] It seems that this should be the Western Cross Timbers, but later developments make it doubtful.

At 3 in the afternoon we stopped at a spring of water called Santa Ana; 7 leagues were made. 7]

[Historia 62: Substantially the same as Historia 43.]

[Land Office: Substantially the same, except that he says he marched at 6 A.M., bearing south; and stopped at 5 o'clock. 7]

*Sunday, 27* I set out on the march at 6 A.M. in an easterly direction over unwooded prairie, abundant water, many pastures near to one another. At 11 I rested and again took up the march at 3 P.M. from a river of good water named San Juan. I stopped at 6:30 P.M. Leagues covered 9

[Historia 43: 31″ 27—We set out to the east at 6 o'clock in the morning; the country is good and there is much water. At 4 o'clock in the afternoon we stopped at Sn. Juan on a little stream that descends from the south. This day our first guide left us, and a Jumano called Bautista accompanied and guided us; 9 leagues were made. 9]

[Historia 62: To "much water," adds "firewood and pasturage."]

[Land Office: Adds little.]

*Monday, 28* I set out at 6 A.M. in an easterly direction, and at a distance of 4 leagues there is a very beautiful forest of oak which they say is more than 200 leagues long and only 3 wide. It is called *Monte Grande.*[24] Leagues covered 4½

I stopped in the said forest three days because of the beasts of burden.

[Historia 43: 32″ 28—We set out at 6 A.M. in the same direction and reached the Monte Grande, as it is called. According to those natives, it must have a length of more than 600 leagues. We stopped in it in the company of a Catalan called Dr. Cristóval *y el Colorado enter ellos*. We came 4½ leagues. 4½]

[Historia 43: 33″ 29—In the same place. 30—The same.]

[Historia 62: Makes it "200 leagues according to those natives." It also totals the distance: 253 leagues.]

[Land Office: About the same.]

*Thursday, 13* I set out on the march at 6 A.M. in an easterly direction, and at the departure from the said forest a river, not very small, runs from north to south. They say it is the Trinity, and from there it goes onto the plains, which are immense. I stopped at 5 P.M. at a spring called El Venado. Leagues covered 7

[24] Again a reference to the Cross Timbers.

[Historia 43: 34″ 31— . . . after about 3 leagues we came to the Trinity River.]

[Historia 62: Same as Historia 43.]

[Land Office: . . . at the exit of the said forest I passed a steady *richuelo*, not very small, that runs from north to south; they say it is the Trinity. . . . 7]

[August]

*Friday, August 1* I set out[25] on the march at 7 A.M. in a southeast direction. Then at 2 leagues I stopped on account of heavy rain. Leagues 2

[Historia 43: . . . across prairie.]

[Historia 62 and Land Office: Same as Historia 43.]

*Saturday, 2* I did not leave.

[Historia 43: 36″ 2— . . . the rain did not cease until after midnight.]

[Historia 62: Same as Historia 43.]

[Land Office: No entry.]

*Sunday, 3* I set out on the march at 6 A.M. in the same direction across some plains with many scattered [*a saltos*] woods, pastures, and firewood [*lena*], two steady rivers that flow from north to south; the first is the Río Negro and the second Azul. I stopped at 1 P.M. because of the rain. Leagues covered 5

[Historia 43: 37″ 3—At 6 o'clock in the morning we set out in the same direction (across) plains and stopped at 3 o'clock in the afternoon. We passed two small permanent streams; one runs to the north and the other to the southwest;[26] 5 leagues were made. 5]

[Historia 62 says "two permanent streams."]

[Land Office: . . . across heavily wooded plains with much water, pasturage, and firewood—and no rocks. I stopped at 2 o'clock . . . 4]

*Monday, 4* I set out on the march at 7 A.M. in the said direction across plains and rivulets [and through many] plum thickets.[27] I stopped at 11 A.M. on the bank of a stream. Leagues covered 3

[25] The Seville copy says: *Me puse en marcha;* Historia 43 and 62: *Salimos;* Land Office: *Marché*—often *Salí.*

[26] They seem to be on the watershed between the Red and the Trinity.

[27] It was August, and the sand plums would have been ripe.

[Historia 43 says they stopped "because of the heavy rain."]

[Land Office the same, except that it indicates they were forced to stop at an arroyo because it was running full of water.]

*Tuesday, 5* I set out on the march at 6 A.M. in the said direction, now across plains without woods, and only arroyos with small trees. I rested at 11 at a water hole called Los Ormos, and left at 3 P.M. across the said plains, on which in no direction does one see highlands or hills. I stopped at 6 P.M. at the exit of another wide forest of oak, which is probably ¼ league wide by 1½ leagues long. I stopped at 6 P.M. Covered 8 leagues. 8

[Historia 43: 39″ 5—We marched at 6 o'clock in the morning in the same direction (across) plains, (with) pasture, firewood, and water in abundance. We stopped at 6 in the afternoon at the beginning of a forest of liveoaks called El Largo because it is larger than that of the 28th of last month; that is (in) its width, because we crossed it only transversely, of all its length going little more than ¼ league; we advanced 8 leagues. 8]

[Historia 62 says they stopped "at the exit" of the forest.]

[Land Office: Similar to Historia 62.]

*Wednesday, 6* I set out on the march at 7 A.M. in the same direction across plains of good land with some small stream of very little water, and at about 12 leagues from the forest of Natchitoches I rested at a spring. At 3 o'clock I set out on the march, bearing more to the south, and at about 6 P.M. I stopped at steady water. Leagues covered 8

[Historia 43: 40″ 6—At 7 o'clock in the morning we set out to the south through good country, and at 12 o'clock arrived at the great forest of Natchitoches;[28] we stopped at 6 o'clock in the evening. This forest is composed of a multitude of cedars, walnuts, royal junipers, liveoaks, and brambles. We stopped on the bank of an arroyo at this place, which we called Sn. Diego. We made 8]

[Historia 62: Same as Historia 43.]

[Land Office: About the same.]

*Thursday, 7* I set out on the march in a southerly direction

[28] Judging from the distance he has traveled, this should have been the Eastern Cross Timbers—but it isn't. This seems to be the long strip of postoak from Paris to Corsicana, for a note in the margin says: Forest of Natchitoches to the north before the Río de Sabinas.

through the said forest, very dense and craggy, on a path so narrow that at times it was lost and it was necessary to stop to hunt for it. There is much steady water. I stopped at 5 P.M. on a river. Leagues covered 5

[Historia 43: 41″ 7—At 6 o'clock in the morning we marched in the same southerly direction through a forest, along a path that is very narrow and in part entirely obliterated; there is much permanent water. We stopped on the edge of a steep, rocky slope that is close to a small arroyo. We made 4½]

[Historia 62 gives the total distance: 209½ leagues.]

[Land Office: About the same.]

*Friday, 8* I marched at 9 in the said southerly direction and by the said forest. I rested at a marsh that is called De Namosa, and at 3 I set out again. I stopped at 6 P.M. on an estuary of good, steady water, which is called La Piedra de Amor.[29] Leagues covered 3

[Historia 43: 42″ 8—We set out at 9 o'clock in the same southerly direction, and at 11 o'clock passed a marsh called De Ramos; it is large and well grassed. At 6 o'clock, having advanced, we stopped on a bayou that we called La Piedra de Amolar.[30] 4]

[Historia 62 says they stopped at 3 o'clock.]

[Land Office: The same as the Seville copy, but he says the estuary is called La Piedra de Amolar, and says: *La Piedra de Amolar por esta una muy esquisita* on the branch of said estuary.]

*Saturday, 9* I set out on the march at 8 A.M. in the said direction in the forest, in which are found two very large bayous. I rested at 12 on the Savinas [Sabine] River, and stayed there. Leagues covered 4

[Historia 43: 43″ 9—At 9 o'clock in the morning we set out in the same direction through the same forest and passed by the bayous where there are many alligators; at 12 o'clock we reached the Sabine River; it is large and deep. Today we lost the path and stopped, (but) we advanced 4½]

[Historia 62: Same as Historia 43.]

[Land Office: The same.]

*Sunday, 10* I left at 8 A.M. in said direction and forest. I found two steady rivers that flow from south to north. I rested on the second, which is named San Josef; the former is the De Ánimas. The forest

[29] The Rock of Love.

[30] The Whetstone—somewhat different.

is so high and so dense that one does not distinguish *rintiro* from stone. I stopped at 6 P.M. at an uncertain water hole. Leagues covered 8

[Historia 43 says that the two arroyos ("rivers" in the Seville copy) are 3 leagues apart. They stopped in a canyon.]

[Land Office: says it was "a canyon of cottonwoods."]

*Monday, 11* I left at 8:30 A.M. in a southeast direction in the said forest, heavily wooded land. I rested on a large, steady river that is called the Río de Lobo, and I went about 2 leagues through a valley called El Carrizo, and stopped at 6 P.M. on a steady stream called De la Casa. Leagues covered 9½

[Historia 43 and 62: the same.]

[Land Office: The same except it says, "There are no rocks."]

*Tuesday, 12* I got myself on the march at 6 o'clock on said course and [through] said forest, and at about 2 leagues there runs a small river that is called San Pedro, and at about 2 more leagues there runs another that is called San Carlos; they run to the north. At a distance of 1 league is a beautiful spring of water that is called El Lucero.[31] I took my siesta on an arroyo of intermittent water, and continued the march at 3 o'clock in the afternoon, and at about 5 leagues I arrived at the village of the Nadaco. Leagues covered 8

[Historia 43: . . . At 5 o'clock in the afternoon we arrived at the pueblo of Nadaco,[32] where we were well received by the natives, who are gentiles. They have grass houses sufficiently large and to the number of 14 or 15 lodges. We made 8]

[Land Office: About the same.]

*Wednesday, 13* I reconnoitered said pueblo [and found it] composed of 13 lodges, [but] in all the village I did not encounter more than three men. The lodges [are] very *dispesas* [well spaced?], one from the other; the village very *toscoso* but good people. I set out at 3 in the afternoon, and stopped at 7 at night on an *estero*[33] with steady water. Leagues covered 3

[Historia 43: 47" 13—We set out in the same direction at 3 o'clock in the afternoon, (going) to a small stream and to a bayou where there

[31] The Morning Star.

[32] Note in margin: Nadacos Indians to the west of the Río de Sabinas.

[33] *Estero* may mean a creek or slough up which the tidewater flows.

are alligators—as well as in the former. We stopped at 7 o'clock at night, having traveled 2½ leagues. 2½]

[Historia 62 says they set out at 3 A.M.]

[Land Office: 13. I set out at 6 in the morning on an easterly course (through) said forest, and stopped presently on an *estero* of steady water. 2½]

*Thursday, 14* I set out from said place on said course and [through] said forest, and having been on the road about 3 leagues, I arrived at a bayou very large, where were seen alligators, and at a short distance I crossed for the second time the Sabine River; there is good land but it is very heavily grown up in cane and other kinds of tree. I came to stop at 4 o'clock in the afternoon at the ranch of an Adai[34] Indian. Leagues covered 6

[Historia 43: 48″ 14—At 5 o'clock in the morning we set out in the same direction and crossed to the edge of a bayou or large lake. We crossed the Sabine River, which is large and deep, by a good ford. Then follows good country with much timber. We came to a *rancho* of the Vidai[35] nation, where we stopped at 4 o'clock in the afternoon, having traveled 6 leagues. 6]

[Historia 62 says they came to a *rancho* of an Indian of the Vidai nation.]

[Land Office also says an Indian of the Bidai nation.]

*Friday, 15* I set out on the march at 6 A.M. in the said direction and [through] said forest, and stopped at 10 o'clock due to rain. Leagues covered as far as the ranch of [the Frenchman called] Atanasio[36] 5

[Historia 43: Note in margin: Rancho of the Frenchman to the east of the Río de Sabinas. 6]

[Land Office also says 6 leagues.]

*Saturday, 16* I set out on the march at 5 A.M. by the same direc-

[34] A Caddo tribe, says Hodge, closely related to the Kadohadacho, Hainai, or Anadarko tribes.

[35] Members of the Vidai or Bidai tribe in the late eighteenth century were the chief intermediaries in the French firearms trade with the Apaches; the tribe is now extinct.

[36] Our friend, Athanase de Mézières (dead before 1788)—for they are now near Natchitoches.

tion and [through] the said forest. I arrived at the house and ranch of Cadelafita at 11 A.M. Leagues covered 3 or 7

[Historia 43 says they stopped at 5 or a little before, having traveled 5]

[Historia 62: The same as Historia 43.]

[Land Office says they stopped at 9 o'clock in the morning at the *rancho* of Pablo de Cadelafita. Leagues 4]

There is no entry in the Seville copy for August 17 or 18.

[Historia 43: 51″ 17—Here. 18—The same.]

[Historia 62: Same as Historia 43.]

[Land Office: No entry for August 17 or 18.]

*Tuesday, 19* I set out on the march at 10 o'clock by the said direction and (through) said forest. I rested at the ranch of Lavina and stopped at 6 P.M. at the house of an Englishman who says he is Mr. Chacón. Leagues covered 7

[Historia 43: 52″ 19—About 10 o'clock in the morning we set out (through) the forest in the same direction and (passed) by four other ranches of Frenchmen, and at 6 o'clock in the evening stopped at (the ranch) of an Englishman; we did not understand his speech nor he ours, (but) he treated us splendidly. 7]

[Historia 62: Same as Historia 43.]

*Wednesday, 20* I set out on the march at 6 A.M. in the same direction and [through] the same forest. I arrived at the Fort of Natchitoches at 5:30 P.M. Leagues covered 10

Leagues covered from Jumanos to Natchitoches 127½

I inform that from the ford called De Pecos there is an abundance of buffalo, deer, *astadas* [crawfish?], sheep, partridges, quail, and turkeys, and many horses as far as the Great Forest.

Natchitoches, Aug. 23, 1788.

FRANCISCO XAVIER FRAGOSO [*rubric*]

[Historia 43: 53″ 20—At 6 o'clock in the morning we set out in the same direction (through) the same forest; this (forest) is on high ground, and on the slope one discovers the large fort of Natchitoches situated in a medium-sized valley at a (distance) of a little more than a quarter of a league. It is a large settlement; its dwellings, which are of wood, are large and splendid. A river, large and deep, flows through it, the houses being situated on either bank. On this river was a great number of large and small canoes in which the natives make their voyages and trading expeditions to the village of New Orleans. Its population numbers some 2,700 to 3,000 persons of both sexes of the French and English nations, with some Negroes, although (the latter have) little wealth, and part of them—with whom this population abounds—are reduced to servitude and slavery. At 6 o'clock in the evening we arrived at the house of Don Luis Blanco [Louis de Blanc], commandant at this place to whom we made the customary salute. He showed us much kindness. He sent us with a soldier with whom we should rest, and, handing over the official dispatches of our mission, we went to our lodging, where we were well treated and entertained. We made 10½ leagues. 10½

[Calculation of leagues from Santa Fe, New Mexico, to the Fort of Natchitoches is 361.]

[Historia 62: Same as Historia 43.]

[Land Office: No different—only three lines.]

*So ended another monumental trail-breaking—some 938 miles through the north Texas wilderness—and we may imagine that "well treated and entertained" is a polite way of saying that the soldiers of Natchitoches threw a party to end all parties. And why shouldn't they? These two outposts—one of Louisiana and one of northern Mexico—had at last been linked.*

*If St. Denis had been in Natchitoches in 1788, the trail to Santa Fe would soon have been hot with mule caravans. But alas, both St. Denis and De Mézières were gone, and their descendants, while plentiful around Natchitoches, were not of the same caliber.*

*The signed copy of the Fragoso diary to Natchitoches in the Papeles de Cuba is said by Roscoe R. Hill to be the original, and apparently it is the one transmitted by De Blanc to Miró. The Land Office copy, it still seems, was made in Natchitoches from the original, but shortened and changed. The Historia copies, made four years later, must have been greatly enlarged on by Fragoso, perhaps from the Land Office copy.*

Concha's letter to De Blanc was as follows:

By superior order Pedro Vial goes with four residents of this province of my command to discover [open] the most direct road to your post. As soon as they do it, they will present themselves to you, whom I ask to equip them for the account of the king of what they used up or lost during their trek in order that they may again undertake their venture to the province of Texas, as they have been ordered.[37]

That letter was sent by De Blanc to Miró, the governor of Louisiana, in the transmittal letter for the diary, which said:

> I am enclosing to your Excellency a copy of the official letter of the governor of Santa Fe, New Mexico, so that, instructed of its contents, you may be informed that I supplied to Pedro Vial for the account of the king the quantity of 491 pesos and 2 *reales*, which was indispensably necessary for his undertaking the [return] trip to the province of Texas, as he was ordered. This sum is verified in his receipt which I am withholding in order to present it to your Excellency personally with the original letter, and in view of these documents, your Excellency will please order that I be reimbursed the said amount by the royal treasury.
>
> I am also enclosing to your Excellency the diary and itinerary of Francisco Xavier Fragoso, who accompanied the said Don Pedro Vial, so that if your Excellency desires it, you may be informed of the distance from Santa Fe to this post, with a road very passable in all seasons and with no risk other than that from the Osages, since the Comanches are already very peaceful and are our friends.[38]

The transmittal letter from Miró to Ezpeleta, the captain-general at Havana, was dated almost two months later:

> Enclosed your Excellency will find a diary which the commandant of the post of Natchitoches, Don Luis de Blanc, sent to me of a voyage undertaken by superior order from Santa Fe, the capital of the New Kingdom of Mexico, to the said post of Natchitoches. It being best that the Court have information of this with all possible haste, I am remitting the original to your Excellency that you may be pleased to send it by the first occasion which presents itself.[39]

It is noteworthy that the governor sent the original diary, contrary to the practice in the case of Vial's diaries, which had to be translated.

[37] Concha, Santa Fe, June 23, 1788, enclosed in Luis de Blanc to Miró, No. 37, Natchitoches, September 1, 1788, Papeles de Cuba, leg. 14.

[38] De Blanc to Miró, No. 37, Natchitoches, September 1, 1788, Papeles de Cuba, leg. 14.

[39] Miró to Ezpeleta, New Orleans, October 23, 1788, Papeles de Cuba, leg. 1394.

It is appropriate here to mention Vial's third map (his second map of which we have a copy). This shows the road from Santa Fe to Natchitoches, and Wheat suggests that it was drawn (or copied) at Natchitoches. It is untitled and unsigned, but the original is in the Archives of the Indies at Seville,[40] in company with the diary and itinerary of Fragoso, together with a statement that the documents were transmitted by the governor of Havana with a letter dated January 2, 1789.

Not long after Vial arrived at Natchitoches, De Blanc sent a letter to the commandant of the Interior Provinces, saying:

> By my knowledge of [the road from] here to the Jumanos and from the diary of Vial, I advise you that [the journey from] Santa Fe to Natchitoches is easy to make in 40 days with loads, in spring and autumn.[41]
>
> But from here to the Taovayas, the savage nations can cause some damage, but with an escort of twenty-five men, the trip can be made without any trouble or risk.
>
> If for the royal service it should be desirable to send aid from here to New Mexico, it is indispensable to establish a post in the Taovaya villages with a good garrison and an experienced commandant to protect the road and to stop contrabanding from the Arkansas and White rivers to those villages, because, [he said, there were many Englishmen in Arkansas, and they traded rifles, powder, balls, and other arms to the Indians. He also noted that the Taovayas raised corn, beans, squashes, melons, and *sandillas* (little melons); in the country, he said, were buffaloes, *venados* and *ciervos* (both words mean deer), bears, and *puercos montes* (wild boars). It was a fine country, he said, with rivers, fish, and lots of water, and beaver and *nutrias* (otter or sea-otter).][42]

[40] A.G.I., estante 86, cajón 6, leg. 9, according to Wheat *(Mapping the Transmississippi West,* Vol. I, 239).

[41] It is interesting to note that a few years later the governor of Louisiana, Casa Calvo, advised the captain-general at Havana, in discussing the menace of the Americans, that the open forests and the prairies would permit wagons to make the trip from Natchitoches to Santa Fe in fifteen days. Governor to Someruelos, New Orleans, confidential, May 21, 1800, Papeles de Cuba, leg. 2355.

[42] De Blanc to Commandant of Provincias Internas, Natchitoches, August 26, 1788, Provincias Internas, Vol. 183. De Blanc was a nephew of Saint Denis. Nutria meant beaver in New Mexico, but probably not to De Blanc, who was a Frenchman.

De Blanc's letter was sent by Ugarte to Concha on January 26, 1789,[43] and Concha answered on June 15, 1789.[44]

Finally, De Blanc wrote to the commandant-general of "New Spain" and said that Vial had arrived there in accordance with Concha's letter of June 23, that De Blanc had given them 491 pesos, 2 reales from the king's fund, and that Vial had been ordered to go from Natchitoches to Bexar.[45]

On a higher level, Ugarte, the commandant-general of the Interior Provinces, sent the request for payment on to Manuel Antonio Flores, the *fiscal* of the royal exchequer, and asked if the governor of Texas should not be required to reimburse De Blanc for Vial's expenses.[46] The *fiscal*[47] in his report said expenses for the trip from Bexar to Santa Fe and from Santa Fe to Natchitoches were included in those granted to New Mexico, and he asked for the 491 pesos, 2 reales, as cost of the return trip. It seems that again matters got bogged down as soon as they started talking money.[48]

Ugarte said he had ordered the governor to send Vial to Natchitoches to open routes from Texas and New Mexico to Louisiana, and with Sonora and California.

In the following April (of 1789), Concha wrote to Ugarte about the payment, and about the new discovery made by Vial to the *rietto* of St. Louis of the Illinois in Louisiana,[49] and he says, "This interpreter [Vial] was for many years a captive of the Comanches and lived part of them [those years] among the Jumanos; is accustomed to the roads [skilled at getting along in the wilderness] and knows perfectly the

[43] Ugarte to Concha, January 26, 1789, New Mexican Archives, No. 1033.

[44] Concha to Ugarte, Santa Fe, June 15, 1789, New Mexican Archives, No. 1049.

[45] De Blanc to Commandant General of New Spain, Natchitoches, August 30, 1788, Provincias Internas, Vol. 183.

[46] Ugarte to Flores, Valle de San Bartolomé, January 5, 1789, Provincias Internas, Vol. 183.

[47] The *fiscal* was a sort of district attorney, among other things, and gave advice on legal matters, protocol, matters of state, and especially affairs connected with money. He was an officer of the king, and his recommendations were usually followed. See Bolton, *Athanase de Mézières,* I, 277n.; and Haring, *Spanish Empire in America.*

[48] *Consulta* of January 5, 1789 (?), Provincias Internas, Vol. 183.

[49] A slip of the pen, apparently.

shortest road to those settlements." Concha had started him out with ten horses and two mules, tobacco, *cigarros*, and other presents.[50]

The difficulty of keeping the separate diaries begins to lessen when Vial and Fragoso leave Natchitoches, for the Seville copy ends at Natchitoches.

### *Diary of Francisco Xavier Fragoso from Natchitoches to Nacogdoches to San Antonio, August 30, 1788, to September 18, 1788*[51]

[We follow the Historia 43 copy, and note only the differences or changes that appear in the Historia 62 or in the Land Office copy.]

[August]

Historia 43: From the twentieth above (mentioned), the day of our entrance, until the thirtieth of the present [month of] August, we continued in the said fort. And, being dispatched on the latter day by the aforesaid commandant, at about 10 o'clock in the morning we directed our course to the west, toward the province of Texas, through broken and wooded country. At 6 o'clock in the afternoon we stopped at Buenavista.[52] 9

[The march was to the south according to the Land Office copy.]

Historia 43: 31—We set out about 9 o'clock in the morning, leaving to the rear and to the east the said fort of Natchitoches. In order to take our course to the province of Texas, we had to bear to the west, ¼ south, because of information that we received that there is a well known road[53] that goes to [Texas]; it follows the timber nevertheless. We stopped at 3:30 in the afternoon at Señor San José, having made 6 leagues. 6

[September]

September 1—At 8 o'clock in the morning we marched in the same direction and [through] the same forest. We took our siesta on the

[50] Concha to Ugarte, April, 1789, Provincias Internas, Vol. 183, No. 7.

[51] The Seville copy has ended; for the trip to San Antonio, we shall use the copy in Historia 43, that in Historia 62, and that in the Texas Land Office.

[52] From this point on, Historia 62 and the Land Office copy will not be used unless they differ from Historia 43.

[53] He speaks of the Camino Real.

Sabine River, which we had crossed on the fourteenth of the preceding month. The country is good. At 6 o'clock in the afternoon we stopped at El Patrón, a place well known. We made 10

[Land Office says he crossed the Sabine River.]

2—We set out at 6 o'clock in the morning to the west, [a direction] that we have taken since yesterday. About 2 leagues before we stopped in a good country, we passed a ranch that is called Lobanillo,[54] a dwelling [place] of Spaniards from the pueblo of Nacogdoches. We crossed a river that is called Los Aes,[55] and stopped at 7 o'clock at night, having advanced 13 leagues, at the ranch of Atoyaque, a well-known place. 13

[Historia 62 makes the river Saez.]

3—At 7 o'clock in the morning we set out in the same direction [through the same] forest, which [was] not very dense. We passed a ranch called El Atascoso, a dwelling [place] of Spaniards of Nacogdoches, and reached this village at 6 o'clock in the afternoon; we made 13 leagues. 13

[Land Office says they arrived at Nacogdoches at 6 o'clock in the afternoon.]

4—At dawn we arrived at this village of Nacogdoches, which is situated in the midst of a forest of different kinds of tree [and has] dwellings made of wood. The lieutenant of the governor of San Antonio de Bexar, Gilibarbo[56] by name, lives here. The number of the houses must be 80 or 90, and [the number] of inhabitants from 200 to 250 Spaniards and Frenchmen. Here all of us except Dn. Pedro Vial were attacked by chills and fever, from which we suffered until the twenty-third of October, when, partially recuperated, we arranged to undertake our journey the [next] morning.

October 24—We set out to the southwest from this pueblo at 11 o'clock in the morning through a good wooded country, and at 3

[54] The ranch of Gil Ybarbo.

[55] Or Los Adaes, on which, in the town of the same name, the capital of Texas was located from 1721 to 1772.

[56] Antonio Gil Ybarbo of Los Adaes was owner of the large ranch, El Lobanillo, at the time Spanish settlers were removed from the eastern frontier of Texas in 1773, and was one of the leaders in the re-occupation of East Texas, which almost amounted to a revolt. See Bolton, "Spanish Abandonment and Re-occupation of East Texas," *Southwestern Historical Quarterly*, Vol. IX, No. 2 (October, 1905), 67–137.

o'clock in the afternoon stopped at El Loco, a well-known place; we made 4 leagues. 4

25—At 8 o'clock in the morning we set out in the same direction through much larger timber, and at 5 o'clock in the afternoon stopped at a place called Los Charcos del Alazán;[57] 10 were made. 10

26—At 7 o'clock in the morning we proceeded in the same southwesterly direction, [still] through timber. At 5 o'clock in the afternoon we stopped on the near bank of the Neches River; we made 10 leagues. 10

[Land Office: I continued the march on said course and (through) said forest; good land. I stopped at Sn. Pedro at 5 o'clock in the afternoon. I crossed the Neches River. 10]

27—We set out at 8 o'clock in the morning and crossed the said river with ease, because at this time it was low in water. We proceeded in the same direction [through] the forest, and stopped at 5 o'clock in the afternoon at El Carrizo, having made 9

28—We set out at 9 o'clock in the morning in the same direction [through] the same forest, and stopped on the Trinity River on this bank, on which was the settlement of Nacogdoches;[58] we came 4 leagues. 4

29—At 1 o'clock in the afternoon we proceeded in the same direction [through] the same forest [and] stopped at 5 o'clock on the same [day] at La Laguna de los Nisperos;[59] we made 2½

30—At 6 o'clock in the morning we set out to the south [through] small wooded sections in a level country. At 2 o'clock in the afternoon we stopped at the stopping place of La Leona, having traveled 7½ leagues. 7½

31—We set out in the same direction at 6 o'clock in the morning; the country is inhabited and wooded. We stopped at Corpus Christi at 5 o'clock in the afternoon, having made 10

[November]

September [*sic*] 1—We set out at 7 o'clock in the morning in the

[57] The Ponds of the Sorrel.

[58] Does he mean Bucareli? On Rubí's recommendations, the East Texans were moved to San Antonio in 1773; they were allowed to move back as far as Bucareli in 1774, and they abandoned it for Nacogdoches in 1779.

[59] The Lake of Persimmons.

same direction; the whole country is a plain. At 5 o'clock in the afternoon we halted on the Río de los Brazos de Dios, having made 8 leagues. 8

[Historia 62 makes it November, and adds the total number of leagues: 116.]

2—We stopped here.

3—At 8 o'clock in the morning we took up the march in the same direction and crossed the river mentioned [that is, the Brazos]. We proceeded through good country, and at 5 o'clock in the afternoon stopped at Las Cruzes. 9

4—We set out in the same direction at 8 o'clock in the morning. There are knolls and timber, but the [lands] are good. At 4 o'clock in the afternoon we stopped on a small plain which we called El Azúcar; we made 9 leagues. 9

[Land Office says it was not a usual stopping place.]

5—At 6 o'clock in the morning we marched in the same direction, [through] good country, and stopped at 5 o'clock in the afternoon at an arroyo of the same place that we called Azúcar. [9]

6—At 7 o'clock in the morning we set out in the same direction [over plains]. We crossed the Río Colorado, which is very large, and stopped at La Navidad. Here there is a small rivulet; we made 8 leagues. 8

7—We stopped here.

8—At 9 o'clock in the morning we took up [the march] in the same direction [through] good country. At 1 o'clock in the afternoon we stopped at a small watering place, having come 4 leagues. 4

[Historia 62 says they started at 8, stopped at 10.]

9—We stayed here.

10—We set out in the same direction at 6 o'clock in the morning; the country is good. We stopped at 12 o'clock in the morning, having made 5

11—At 6 o'clock in the morning we set out in the same direction [through] good country. We crossed the Río de Guadalupe, and at 3 o'clock in the afternoon stopped on the bend [*remesa*] of this; we made 7 leagues. 7

12—At 9 o'clock in the morning we marched in the same direction [through] much timber. At 3 o'clock in the afternoon we stopped at some cottonwoods, having made 4

13—At 6 o'clock in the morning we took up the march in the same direction; [there is] timber, but the country is good. We stopped at 5 o'clock in the afternoon at El Carrizo, having made 7 leagues. 7

14—We remained here. 15—The same.

16—We set out at 6 o'clock in the morning in the same direction; the country is good but wooded. At 6 o'clock in the evening we stopped at El Rancho del Reten, a dwelling place of Spaniards from Sn. Antonio. We made 10

17—At 6 o'clock in the morning we marched in the same direction [through] wooded country; here there is a small river. At 12 o'clock in the morning we stopped at El Rancho Chayopines, a dwelling place of Spaniards. 7

18—At 8 o'clock in the morning we set out in the same direction [through] timber, and at 5 o'clock in the afternoon arrived at the royal presidio of Sn. Antonio de Bexar. 10

[*rubric only in Land Office copy*]

*It now becomes apparent that if Fragoso made the Land Office version in Natchitoches, he must have carried it with him to San Antonio, and there copied the Natchitoches-to-San Antonio part. As a matter of fact, there is some indication that this was done, for there is an ornamental line across the middle of the page at the end of the Santa Fe-Natchitoches journal; and the Natchitoches-San Antonio journal starts immediately below the line.*

*This ends the Land Office copy.*

*They traveled twenty-seven days, were ill in Nacogdoches (except for Vial) forty-eight days, and laid over five other days. They covered 205 leagues (533 miles), an average of almost twenty miles a day.*

*Historia 43 and Historia 62 continue:*

This [presidio] is situated in the center of the village of San Fernando, division of the province of Texas. It contains about 700 Spanish persons. Some of its dwellings are of rubble work, but more are of wood of moderate structure. Inside the wall there is the metropolitan church or parish in which lives a clergyman who is the priest. Outside this presidio there are five missions[60] which the Fernandine religious administer. These are situated on the opposite bank of a large river which surrounds this village and takes its source half a league to the north, where there is a spring of water. There is a moderate amount of trade among the citizens in food and clothing. The principal official is Don Rafael Pacheco, governor and commandant, to whom we delivered the dispatches in our care. We were well received and lodged in quarters which he arranged and ordered furnished for our subsistence while our return was being determined [upon].

[Historia 62 totals the leagues: 205.]

From the eighteenth day of November, on which we made our entrance into the presidio of Sn. Antonio, we remained sick, occasionally recuperating, however, until the last of February, '89, and through all the months of March, April, May, and until the twenty-fourth of June, the evening of our return. Now we were well, and, having made ready the things for the morning, we took leave of the said governor and received his orders; he told me that on the twenty-sixth he would forward the dispatches.

*From November 18, 1788, to June 24, 1789, all those on the expedition were ill or were recuperating from that illness except Pedro Vial—who had also escaped it in Nacogdoches. From the description of chills and fever, it seems that the disease may have been malaria—and Vial's immunity is something of a mystery. Fragoso does not say that Vial was not ill, but on June 17, 1789, the governor of Texas reported a list of presents that Vial and Francisco Xavier Chaves had taken to the Comanches, so we assume that Vial, if he was stricken at all, must have recovered more rapidly than the others.*

### *Vial's Expedition to the Comanches, 1789*[61]

### Number 25

Notice [or list] of the goods and supplies which have been provided for Pedro Vial and Franco. Xavier Chabes, who have gone as emissaries to the villages of the Comanche Indians to treat for the estab-

[60] San José y San Miguel de Aguayo, San Antonio de Valero, Purísima Concepción de Acuña, San Juan Capistrano, and San Francisco de la Espada.

[61] Domingo Cabello to [?], San Antonio de Bexar, June 17, 1789; originally in the Bexar Archives, but our copy was obtained from J. H. Richardson at Hardin-Simmons University. The year could have been 1788, but 1789 seems more likely.

lishment of a stable and legal peace with this government; also showing the price and value of goods which have been supplied to them, in the following form and manner:

| | Pesos Rs. Gs.* |
|---|---|
| To Make Presents to the Comanche Chiefs | |
| o/o 70 twists of tobacco from Louisiana | 039.00† |
| o/o 21 *varas*‡ of colored Limbourg cloth for petticoats | 031.40 |
| o/o 2 pounds of vermillion at 3 ps. | 006.00 |
| o/o 10 pounds of blue and white beads, at 6 rrs. | 007.40 |
| o/o 2 dozen knives at 10 for a peso. | 002.40 |
| o/o 7 flags of the ten which have come from New Orleans | 007.00 |
| To Equip the Emissaries—Charged to Their Expense | |
| Firstly, 6 horses, 5 of which are for their supply, and on which no price is put; only one that was bought | 006.00 |
| 4 Mules at 20 pesos each | 080.00 |
| 2 Packsaddles with all appurtenances | 009.20 |
| 2 Chairs with all their *apenos* [trappings?] | 026.40 |
| 2 Pairs of *Coginillos*§ at 15 reales per pair | 003.60 |
| 2 Pairs of spurs at 12 reales | 003.00 |
| 2 Bridles at 14 reales each | 003.40 |
| 4 Dozen awls at 3 reales a dozen | 001.40 |
| 6 Pounds of powder at 4½ reales | 003.30 |
| 12 Pounds of balls at 9 granos‖ | 001.10 |
| 1 Pound of vermillion | 002.20 |
| 2 Hats at 1 peso each | 002.00# |
| 2 Black silk handkerchiefs at 22½ reales | 09.90 |
| 2 Jackets of Queretaran cloth with their trimmings and *echuras* | 016.26 |
| 2 *Chupines* of colored cloth with all their trimmings and *echuras* | 008.34½ |

* Pesos (worth about $1.58), reales (eight to the peso, worth about twenty-one cents); *granos* (worth about two cents); see J. Villasana Haggard, *Handbook for Translators of Spanish Historical Documents.*

† Although the heading reads, "Pesos, Reales, Granos," most of the extensions are given in pesos and reales; thus, two bridles at fourteen reales each are valued at "003.40"—three pesos and four reales.

‡ About thirty-three inches to the *vara.*

§ A small leather pocket or carrying case (see Coues, *Expeditions of Zebulon M. Pike,* II, 613).

‖ This figures out at 12 *granos* to the *real.*

# This figure does not come out right.

| | | |
|---|---|---|
| 2 | Pairs of drawers of Queretaran cloth with their trimmings and *echuras* | 008.97½** |
| 4 | Shirts made of *pontivi* | 017.10 |
| 6 | Pairs of white drawers made of *pontivi* | 008.96 |
| 6 | Pairs of shoes *de baqueta* at 3 reales, 8 granos | 002.60†† |
| 2 | Pesos of brown sugar | 002.00 |
| 4 | *Pynes* at 3 granos each | 000.70‡‡ |
| 1 | Peso of soap | 001.00 |
| 6 | *Varas* of wide ribbon | 001.20 |
| 2 | Worms§§ at 2½ reales‖‖ | 000.90 |
| ⅔ | [*Vara*] of Queretaran cloth for [horses'] tails | 001.28 |
| 6 | *Varas* of woolen ribbon to tie the hair | 000.60 |
| 1 | Lance with its point [metal tip?] | 002.266¶¶ |
| 1 | Fanega*** of corn as *pinole*, and bread | 007.30 |
| 2 | Pairs of scisssors at 1½ reales | 000.30 |
| 1 | Quire of paper for the diaries | 000.60 |
| 2 | Nabaja folding-knives at 3 reales | 000.60 |
| 4 | Leather chests for their clothing and provisions | 003.96 |
| | To repair the arms they carry | 003.20 |
| 2 | Mirrors at 2½ reales | 000.90 |
| 2 | Pesos of cigars | 002.00 |
| 1 | Jar of bell-copper | 003.06 |

For 74 pesos supplied to the two servants whom they take for the care of the cargoes, mules, and horses, which has been given them on account of the salary which they have been earning from this day until their return, at the rate of 6 reales daily††† 074.00

For 10 pesos which have been given in money to said Vial and Chaves 010.00

| | |
|---|---|
| o/o 1 axe to cut firewood | 003.00 |
| o/o 4 Dozen steels for striking fire on rifle | 002.00 |
| o/o 4 Pounds of blue and white glass beads | 003.00 |

** It seems to mean eight pesos, nine reales, seven and one-half *granos*—but why nine reales?

†† This figures out at twelve *granos* to the real.

‡‡ It does not make sense.

§§ Sacatrapos: a worm to draw the wad of a firelock rifle.

‖‖ We are in trouble every time we run into a half real.

¶¶ Two pesos, two reales—and what?

*** About two and one-half bushels.

††† This item contemplates an absence of forty-one days.

| | |
|---|---|
| o/o 2 Dozen knives | 002.40 |
| o/o 1 twists of tobacco from Louisiana | 009.00 |
| Total sum | 430.72 |

Accordingly, it appears from the items in the preceding account that it totals four hundred thirty pesos, 1 real, and 2 granos, in full.[62]

First Note

Of the 430 pesos, 1 real, and 2 granos, the total of the preceding account, 329 pesos, 1 real, and 2 granos have been spent on the goods that have been supplied to the emissaries in the presidio, and the 109 pesos remaining[63] is the value established according to the statement arrived from New Orleans, adding the goods and supplies that had to be provided in the village of Nacogdoches, and which came from that town.

Second Note

The parties who march, carry the details of their account that it may be understood clearly [what] are the goods that the emissaries must take from the village of Nacogdoches, and [which have] come from New Orleans, which provision has been taken because of the total lack of them in this province, and the others are the properties with which they have been provided in their business.

The royal presidio of San Antonio de Bexar, June 17, 1789.

Domo. Cabello

It seems likely that Vial did not keep a diary on the trip to the Comanches. However, Governor Cabello's correspondence turns up a further letter to add some information:

> Dear Sir:
>
> Having seen how much is contained in your letter of last August 25 in which you approve all that I have done in ordering the commission that I have sent to the Comanche tribe in charge of Pedro Vial and Francisco Xavier de Chabes, together with the other information that is contained in it, I find myself under the obligation of rendering to you the most grateful thanks for the honor that you have been kind enough to grant me, and that divine providence has seen fit to favor my

62 His written-out total is not the same as his total in figures.

63 His subtraction is not accurate.

heartfelt intentions with such good results. I take this opportunity to inform you that on the afternoon of the 29th day of last month there appeared in this presidio my said emissaries, advising me of their return from the commission that was entrusted to them, and for proof of its happy outcome, they brought with them three of the principal chiefs of the Comanche tribe, who alone have come with their wives with my emissaries to comply with the principal object contained in paragraphs 23, 24, 25, and 26 of the instructions that I gave them (which are [included in] document No. 26 which I included to you in my letter No. 89), in consequence of which they were dismounted in the first lodges at the entrance to these settlements, not having permitted [part omitted].

Bexar, Oct. 3, 1789.

DOMO. CABELLO

Señor Don José Antonio Rengel.[64]

The letter, endorsed "Peace. No. 120:" seems to indicate that Vial and Chaves had returned from the Comanches on September 29; if they left San Antonio about the time of the governor's expense report, the seventy-four-day estimate was not far off. But we know that Vial joined his own expedition party on July 1. It seems likely that he introduced Chaves to the Comanches and then left. The trip turned out to be quite an extended one for Chaves.

Fragoso's diary on the return to Santa Fe was resumed on June 25:

### *Diary of Francisco Xavier Fragoso from San Antonio to Santa Fe, June 25 to August 20, 1789*[65]

[Historia 43:]

June 25—As has been said, [we set out] to the north with four Comanches as guides. We turned back at 5 o'clock in the afternoon and stopped at 6 o'clock on the spring of water that was mentioned before. We made 0½

26—We set out about 1 o'clock in the afternoon after having received the dispatches which the general and commandant [at San Antonio] delayed to send yesterday, which were brought by a corporal

[64] Cabello to Rengel, Bexar, October 3, 1789; also obtained from Richardson and apparently a part of the same file.

[65] From this point on, only the two diaries from Historia are available. These are continuations of the previous journals.

and a soldier. [We set out] to the north through good country and stopped at El Paredón; we made 4 leagues. 4

27—We proceeded in the same direction at 6 o'clock in the morning, now we began to penetrate a forest which was very rocky and broken. We stopped at 6 o'clock in the evening after having passed the Río de Guadalupe mentioned above; we advanced 9

28, 29, and 30—we stopped here on the bank of the aforesaid river, expecting that Dn. Pedro Vial would join us—which he had proposed to do in the morning [tomorrow morning.]

[July]

July 1—At 3 o'clock in the afternoon, Vial, a corporal, and eight soldiers armed with orders for the latter to accompany us to the Colorado River.

2—[Our party] now assembled, we took up the march at 6 o'clock in the morning, going in the same northerly direction through very broken country. At 7 o'clock in the evening we stopped at the spring Sn. Juan; we made 10

3—We set out in the same direction at 6 o'clock in the morning; the country is good, with stretches of timber. We crossed the arroyo of the Pedernales; it is permanent and [now] swollen. Here there are many herds of cattle and bands of mustangs. We stopped at 5 o'clock in the afternoon at the water hole of La Carrera; we made 8 leagues. 8

4—At the usual hour we marched to the north [through] good country containing a little timber. We stopped on the far bank of the Colorado River; it is fairly wide and somewhat deep. We made 5 leagues. 5

5—At 7 o'clock in the morning the corporal and soldiers returned, as was indicated [would happen] in the first entry for this month, while we retained in our company the four Comanches to whom reference was likewise made on the twenty-fifth of June. We continued in the same direction, going up to the Colorado River, and stopped on its bank at 5 o'clock in the afternoon. 8

6—At 8 o'clock in the morning we set out [along] the same river and in the same direction [through] much timber and broken land. We stopped at some pools at 4 o'clock in the afternoon. 6

7—We proceeded in the same direction at the usual hour, leaving the said Colorado River; the country is rocky and bad. We stopped at a water hole of rain water, having made 10

8 and 9—We marched at the regular hour in the same direction [through] good country. At 12 o'clock noon we stopped at El Agua Vieja. 5

[Historia 62: (We stayed) here because it was raining hard.]

[Historia 43: No entry for the tenth.]

[Historia 62: We marched at the common hour, our course (over) good land. We stopped at 12 o'clock noon at the water hole of La Vieja.] 5

11—At 7 o'clock in the morning we set out to the north through level country. At 10 o'clock we stopped at some permanent springs, having come 4

12—We took up [the march] in the same direction at the regular hour; the country is good. We stopped at 2 o'clock in the afternoon at a rain-filled water hole. 7

13—We set out at the same hour in the aforesaid direction through a wooded and broken country; after a march of 4 leagues we came upon 17 Comanches—strapping youths without a chief, who were going on a campaign against the Lipan Apaches; here one of the four who came with us left us and went with those mentioned above, to whom we gave some tobacco and food. After eating, we continued through the same forest, and at 2 o'clock in the afternoon we stopped on a plain, having traveled 7

14—At the appointed hour we marched in the same direction [across] country that is good and level but wooded. We stopped at 8 o'clock at night on the brow of a hill, having made 9 leagues. 9

15—At the same hour we set out in the aforesaid direction [through] much timber, and stopped at 7 o'clock at night among the Jumanos,[66] [where there were] holes filled with rain water. 9

16—We proceeded at 8 o'clock in the morning in the same direction [through] bad wooded country with much rock. We stopped with water at La Cañada at 5 o'clock in the afternoon; we traveled 8 leagues. 8

17—At 9 o'clock in the morning we set out in the same direction [through] the same kind of country. We stopped at 2 o'clock in the

[66] Note in margin: "Jumanos at more than a hundred leagues from Bexar toward the northwest." This distance is according to Fragoso.

afternoon at La Culebra, a rain-filled water hole, having made 10 leagues. 10

18—At 6 o'clock in the morning we marched in the same direction [through] good, level country. At 5 o'clock in the afternoon we stopped on the Río Brazos de Dios, mentioned above. We made 9

19—At 9 o'clock we set out in the same direction, up the river [through] good country. We stopped at 4 o'clock in the afternoon on the bank of the same Río de Brazos de Dios, having made 7 leagues. 7

20—We took up our march at 6 o'clock in the morning, in the same direction up the river [through] good country. We stopped at 3 o'clock in the afternoon on the same river, having come 6

21—At 8 o'clock in the morning we set out in the same direction along the aforesaid river; the country is good. We stopped on the same stream, having advanced 6

22—At 6 o'clock in the morning we marched in the same direction, and, leaving the river, at a distance of 4 leagues made a dry camp on a plain, having made 7 leagues. 7

23—At 8 o'clock in the morning we proceeded in the same northerly direction, and at a distance of 4½ leagues came to the Río del Mermellón.[67] We stopped on its bank at 5 o'clock in the afternoon, having made 9 leagues. 9

24—We took up the march in the same northerly direction at the usual hour. We entered a very large plain and stopped at the edge of the river that is called La Sal, at a spring of fresh water called El Toro. We made 8

25—We left at 8 o'clock in the morning, in the same direction, depriv , good land. We stopped on the bank of a river at 5 o'clock in the afternoon. 9

26—At 7 o'clock in the morning we marched in the same direction, still north, [along] the same river, [over] level country. Leaving the former [river] a distance of 3 leagues, we stopped at 3 P.M. on the bank of a river that descends from the south. 9

27—[We set out] in the same direction at the same hour, and,

[67] The Marmellón, or Mermellón, is usually considered to be the Pease. On Vial's initial trip from San Antonio to Santa Fe, he reached the Mermellón very soon after leaving the Taovaya villages, and it may have been the Red River or the Wichita. Now, he has traveled 163.5 leagues (424 miles), and could well be at the Red River—except that they keep traveling north. They are now 73 miles north of the Brazos.

again following the Salt River, we stopped at 5 o'clock in the afternoon in a canyon with water that enters the river. 8

28—At the regular hour we set out in the same direction along the same river [over] good country, [and] at 5 o'clock in the afternoon stopped on its bank. 7

29—We proceeded as indicated above [over] good land, and stopped at 6 o'clock in the afternoon—still on the same stream. 9

30—At 8 o'clock in the morning [we set out] just as before, but now along fresh water. At 3 o'clock in the afternoon we stopped on the bank of the stream named [above], which, because of the salines that it had previously [or higher up?] is salty. 8

31—We continued in the same northerly direction at 9 o'clock. We left this river, and at 3 o'clock in the afternoon we stopped on an open plain that is at the foot of a white cliff;[68] we made 7 leagues. 7

August

August 1—We took up the march at 6 A.M. in the indicated northerly direction, [but] at 12 o'clock it was necessary to stop on a plain because it was raining heavily. 4

2—We continued in the same direction at the usual hour, and at 6 o'clock in the evening stopped at the foot of a mesa on the edge of a stream that descends from the south. Here we met a Comanche who told us of a lake that is in the middle of the Llano,[69] and that in that place there was one lodge of Comanches—toward which we directed our course. 9

3—At 7 o'clock in the morning we set out in the same direction, and, with the guidance of the Comanche, advanced until after an hour's journey we stopped in a white canyon containing water that descends from the south. 9

4—We marched at the regular hour, and, going to the west across

[68] A well-known landmark.

[69] *Llano* is not capitalized in the text, as often proper names are not capitalized in Fragoso's journal. However, he has used a number of different words for "plain," though not this one before. Their geographical situation—or at least the distance covered—indicates that they are near or on the Llano Estacado; therefore we may assume that this information refers to the all-important knowledge of water on the Llano—for this is August, and the Llano is hazardous. For a fuller description, see Loomis, *The Texan-Santa Fé Pioneers,* 13–19.

flat plains, arrived at 3 o'clock in the afternoon at the lake and lodge of the Comanche mentioned previously, where we provided ourselves with sufficient meat—which was given us by the owner [of the lodge]. We made 8 leagues. 8

5—Having passed the night with our Comanche benefactor, and the regular hour having arrived, we proceeded in the same westwardly direction. We crossed another white canyon, also with water that comes from the south; we stopped at the White River at a stopping place indicated in this journal under the date of July 3, '88.[70] From here we took a straight course to Santa Fe, having arrived at a village of Chief Malla, or Ecueracapa; here we slept, giving orders that the chief should immediately send his people to detain thirteen of their people who were going to the pueblos of Pecos and Taos to barter, in order that we might overtake them, and [then] they should go in our company; he extended us much honor, which we received with great satisfaction. On this day we made 10 leagues. 10

It does not appear to me to be necessary to go over the stopping places and the number of leagues again from here to the capital of Santa Fe, for in this respect one can see both in the cited entry for July 3, when I show the distance to be 80 leagues, and [since] I have to go through the same journey [each day], it is necessary only to put in the margin the named places through which we shall pass through August 6 until August 20, when we entered the said village at 3 o'clock in the afternoon. 80

Total 348½

Note. In order that I may be able to advance the royal service of his Majesty, I [will] say that the country of this entire trip is filled with many herds of buffaloes, wild cattle, mustangs, *bacuno, alzado,* deers of various kinds, prairie chickens and other fowls, as well as nuts and wild fruits that are very convenient for travelers.

[70] This should be the headwaters of Prairie Dog Town Fork of the Red River, in southern Deaf Smith County. They are now, by Fragoso's count, eighty leagues (208 miles) east of Santa Fe. This distance agrees with modern geography. This remark seems to indicate that Vial still had a copy of the outgoing journal with him, perhaps the Land Office copy.

General Summary of Leagues

| | |
|---|---|
| From Santa Fe, New Mexico, to the Fort of Natchitoches | 361 |
| From Natchitoches to Nacogdoches | 51 |
| From Nacogdoches to Sn. Antonio de Bexar | 154 |
| Total | 566 |
| From Santa Fe to San Antonio by direct road | 348½ |

Second Note. [I say] that from the date of June 25 of the present [year] of '89, on which we undertook our return to this capital town, I have calculated 348½ leagues, as is seen from the sum above, which are those [the number of leagues] from San Antonio de Bexar to the town named, excluding the trips which we made to the villages of Natchitoches and Nacogdoches, from which it may be seen that the corrected route from here to said San Antonio de Bexar [is in length] 348½ leagues.

Villa of Santa Fe, August 20, 1789.

PEDRO VIAL
FRANCO. XAVIER FRAGOSO

It is a copy. Chihuahua, Sept. 12, 1793.

MANUEL MERINO [*rubric*]

It was a monumental trip, and would not be duplicated for quite a while. From the Spanish viewpoint, the sad part is that it should have opened up great possibilities of trade. A straight run from Santa Fe to Natchitoches, by boat from Natchitoches to New Orleans, and by ship from New Orleans to Havana or Vera Cruz—what a wonderful opportunity! It would have provided an outlet in Santa Fe and Chihuahua.

As a matter of fact, it appears that De Blanc did make an attempt to open trade, for he wrote a letter to Ugarte on January 26, 1789, mentioning Vial's diary and proposing the opening of commercial relations between Louisiana and New Mexico.[71] But they failed to carry it out. They were too busy trying to control the penetration by the Americans. So, as a result, they neither controlled the Americans nor

[71] Ugarte to Concha, January 26, 1789; cited in Woodbury Lowery, *A Descriptive List of Maps of the Spanish Possessions, . . . 1502–1820*, 420. Concha answered. the letter on June 15.

developed their own obvious potentiality. It is possible that if the Spaniards had built up a commercial empire in Santa Fe, an alert viceregal government would have levied against that business and might well have obtained enough money to protect the New Mexican frontier. Here is still another *if* that might have kept New Mexico in Spanish hands.

However, speculations on what might have been are easy. The hard fact is that the road from Natchitoches to Santa Fe was now open, but nobody took advantage of it in any substantial way.

The next important trail to be opened would be that from Santa Fe to St. Louis, and the Anglo-Americans—not the Spaniards—would pour down it with their endless goods.

# XIV

# *Pedro Vial, Santa Fe to St. Louis, May 21 to October 3, 1792, and Return, in 1793*

In the early 1790's the Spaniards were concerned over the Anglo-American thrusts toward Santa Fe, and over the involved and rather strong French machinations following the French revolution, toward New Orleans and Mexico—and both these factors may have been important in the Spanish objective of opening the trail to St. Louis and making friends with the Indians between Santa Fe and St. Louis.

It rather seems that the commandant-general of the Interior Provinces may have been planning a St. Louis expedition in 1789, for in Provincias Internas, Vol. 183, are "documents concerning the expedition of Vial and concerning a new one to St. Louis." That one, however, did not materialize immediately, for Vial returned to Santa Fe in 1789 and did not set out on his first transit of the Santa Fe Trail until 1792. When the actual trip came, it seems to have been at the instigation of Revillagigedo, the viceroy, for a letter of Las Casas, the governor-general at Havana, to the Minister of War in 1794 says: "Perhaps Carondelet's concept of such a short distance [twenty-two days of marching] from Illinois to Santa Fe . . . has its origin in the journey made from Santa Fe to Illinois by arrangement of the viceroy, . . ."[1]

Fernando de la Concha, governor of New Mexico, gave Vial a letter to the commandant at St. Louis:

> Pedro Vial, who by order of his Excellency, the viceroy of New Spain, is chosen to open communication from this province under my

[1] Las Casas to Alange, No. 374, Confidential, April 20, 1794, Archivo General de Simancas, Guerra Moderna, leg. 7235.

charge to the other settlements of the king in this America, is leaving this very day to explore the communications to Illinois, [which is] a dependency of the government of Louisiana. He goes with only two persons of this country, and according to the knowledge that he has of the barbaric nations that lie between [the two points], and the distance that we suppose [it is] to the said point, it [seems] likely that he will be in the Fort of Saint Louis, under the charge of your Excellency, sometime during the coming month of June. I hope that, in deference to the best service of the king, your Excellency will inform him when he arrives all that appears proper for the completion of his commission, and that when he returns, you will supply him with what is absolutely necessary for his trip, which should be by a different route from the one by which he comes, as your Excellency will know by the instruction that I have given him, which he should present [to you].

Whatever small expense he may incur during his stay, and for his return, your Excellency may, if it appears best to you, apply it to the extraordinary expenses of the province of Louisiana, or send me a voucher [*documento justificativo*] so that I may draw from the extraordinary fund of this province, to the amount that you indicate. Since this [expense] is charged to his Majesty's account under any circumstances, I judge the first method less complicated.[2]

Concha also issued specific instructions to Vial:

Instructions to be followed by Pedro Vial, appointed to open direct communication with our settlements in Illinois, located on the shore of the Missouri River, and dependencies of the government of the province of Louisiana.[3]

1. He will leave this town May 22 for the village of Pecos, accompanied by two young men of the same town, José Vicente Villanueva

[2] Concha to Commandant at St. Louis, Santa Fe, May 21, 1792, A.G.I., Audiencia of Santo Domingo, Louisiana, and Florida (Duplicates of Governors and Intendants for the Year 1793), estante 86, cajón 6, leg. 26. Certified copy by Trudeau, October 7, 1792, A.G.I., Audencia de Santo Domingo 86-6-26; A.G.M., Historia, Vol. 43; A.G.M., Provincias Internas, Vol. 183, f. 269-70. Enclosed in Trudeau to Carondelet, No. 267, St. Louis, January 10, 1793. Printed in Houck, *Spanish Régime,* I, 352.

[3] Instructions are in A.G.I., *ibid.* Another copy is in Papeles de Cuba, leg. 2362; another is in A.G.M., Historia, Vol. 43, No. 18; and another is in A.G.M., Provincias Internas, Vol. 183, f. 269-70. The Seville copy was made by Trudeau and sent to Carondelet, by him to Las Casas, and by him to Alange, the Minister of War. Printed in Houck, *Spanish Régime,* I, 352.

and Vicente Espinosa, who will obey the said Vial in all things, and who will each be paid thirty pesos of silver immediately on their return. Vial will assign to them four horses from those that he takes belonging to the king, so that they may make the trip, and [he will give them] necessary supplies.

2. From Pecos he will march to the east as far as the villages of the Huagages,[4] from which point he will continue east northeast, which is where runs the Missouri River in the district closest to Illinois. By means of the compass that he carries, and of the explanations that I have made to him, it will be easy not to make a mistake in the directions cited.

3. From Pecos to the villages of the Osages, it is expected that he will meet no other tribes than our allies, the Comanches, on whose assistance and knowledge he can depend with assurance.

4. According to all information I have acquired, he ought not to encounter other tribes from the Osages to the Missouri, but if on the contrary it should be learned from the Osages that others intervene, he should try to take two or three of the former with him to serve as interpreters and guides, rewarding them with goods that he carries for that purpose.[5]

5. Both in this first journey, as well as in the return trip, until he arrives at his destination[6] he will try to keep a diary as accurately as possible, marking in it the courses and the daily distances, the rivers that he encounters, their flow and the volume of their water, the mountains and tablelands that he comes across, explaining their configuration, and giving names appropriate to it [the configuration]; the tribes that he encounters, the customs they have, and whatever he can learn from them, with all the other [information] that may seem to him can serve as new knowledge [to make for] better understanding.

6. When he arrives in Illinois, he will rest as long as he considers it necessary, presenting himself to the commandant whom he finds in charge of that detachment and giving him the official letters that he carries from me, and these instructions, and asking him for what is very necessary for his return, which ought to be in the coming month of September.

[4] Interlined by a different hand in the Historia 43 copy, in quotes: "*Parese que son los Osages.*" We have translated "Huagages" as "Osages" throughout.

[5] Point 4 omitted from the copies in Seville and in Houck. It is taken from Historia 43 and from Provincias Internas 183.

[6] Historia 43 and Provincias Internas 183: "During all the trip that he makes until he arrives at his destination."

7. He shall undertake his return by taking a course to the west and west northwest, passing the settlements of the Pananas[7] [Pawnees], and [then] to the south to the Comanches, without the need of approaching the Ricaras, and, arriving at the Río Napestle [Arkansas River], he will come straight to this capital, trying always to explain in detail in his diary all the data referred to in Article 3 relative to his going.

8. Whatever unforeseen accident may occur during his march, he will overcome it, and remove it as best he can from his knowledge, but in the light of prudence, in whatever manner may to him appear most useful to the service of the king and the honor of this province.

9. As the said Vial does not possess enough [knowledge of] Castilian to enable him to make a diary sufficiently clear in that language, it will be satisfactory for him to keep his own in French, so that, I translating it in his presence as soon as he returns, it may be signed [by him and by me] in order to send it on to higher authority.

Santa Fe, May 21, 1792.

FERNANDO DE LA CONCHA

St. Louis, Illinois, Oct. 7, 1792.

ZENON TRUDEAU [*rubric*]

Note on the margin: "Taken from the original letter—which I certify."

## *Diary of Pedro Vial from Santa Fe to St. Louis, May 21 to October 3, 1792.*[8]

Diary of the journey undertaken by me, Pedro Vial, under the order

[7] Both Historia 43 and Provincias Internas 183 say "Pananas y As." (The A's were Caddos, who lived much farther north at that time.)

[8] Documentation of this diary is more complicated than it was for Fragoso's diary. There is a copy in Historia, Vol. 43, No. 19, used by Alfred B. Thomas in *Chronicles of Oklahoma*, Vol. IX, No. 2 (June, 1931), for the return trip only, though the diary covers both (this is the Talamantes copy, document LV, No. 19 f. 1–12; correspondence and instructions are in No. 18); there is one in Historia, Vol. 62, No. 9, copied at Chihuahua, ink badly faded, the same as the one in Historia 43. There is also a copy in Provincias Internas, Vol. 183, f. 272ff., including copies of the correspondence; this copy, enclosed in Las Casas to Revillagigedo, Havana, February 1, 1793 (Carondelet to Las Casas, transmitting Vial's journal); there is one in the Archivo General de Indias at Seville, Audiencia of Santo Domingo, Louisiana, and Florida, estante 86, cajón 6, leg. 26, in which the diary is almost identical with that in Historia 43, and in which the entire is almost identical with that in Provincias Internas 183 (the Seville copy, which covers only the first half of the trip, was used by Houck in *The Spanish Régime*, I, 354–58); there is also a copy of the outward

of Señor Don Fernando de la Concha, colonel of the royal army and governor of the province of New Mexico, commissioned to open communication with Saint Louis of Illinois, province of Louisiana; accompanying me [are] the two young men, Vicente Villanueba and Vicente Espinosa.

May, 1792

[Days]

21—We set out from the town of Santa Fe, and slept at the village of Pecos, distant 9

[The Seville copy says 7 leagues and continues to be 2 leagues less all the way; the Seville copy writes out the number of leagues and also gives figures in the margin.]

22—We stayed in said village, arranging our packs.

23—We set out from said village, the course to the east, and made camp at night in the mountains, having traveled 5

24—We slept at the Pecos River, distant 4

25—We left in the morning about 7 o'clock, and after traveling a league to the east, we met seven Comanches with their wives, and with them a Spanish interpreter named Francisco Xavier Chavez,[9] who, having been for some years a captive of the Comanches and Taovayas, was coming to the province of New Mexico from San Antonio de Bexar to see his parents, and they made us return to the Pecos River in joy of having met me, for it was a long time since they had seen me. Consequently that day's march was lost.

[Seville copy does not offer this much information.]

26—We set out in the morning on the same easterly course, and reached the Gallinas River, having traveled 10

27—We set out in the morning at 7 o'clock, course to the northeast. We traveled across a plain and tablelands and made 6

trip in Papeles de Cuba, de Cuba, leg. 1442, and another in leg. 2362. The copy we shall follow primarily, with notations of variance from other copies, is in Provincias Internas, Vol. 102; it is an original, with Vial's signature, and was transmitted by Concha to Revillagigedo, December 4, 1793. It is No. 2, f. 214–24, and is a copy of the original that was given to Vial to be carried with him, dated at Santa Fe, July 20, 1792, and signed by Concha.

[9] Chaves must have been Vial's old buddy from the Comanche expedition of 1789. Inasmuch as they both had been captives of the Comanches also, we may imagine it was quite a gathering.

[Seville copy invariably says, "We traveled *about* six leagues."]

28—We set out at 7 o'clock in the morning on the same course, northeasterly, and stopped at an arroyo that joins the Colorado River,[10] having traveled 6

29—We traveled to the east across plains, and slept at the Colorado River, having traveled 6

30—We followed the same course easterly, always across plains, along the bank of the Colorado River itself, and camped on it, having traveled 6

31—We set out on the same course along the river, and slept a short distance from it, having lost a horse and having traveled 6

June

1—We followed the same course along the same river and across flat plains,[11] and stopped, having made 3

2—Upon the same river and the same easterly course, we traveled across flat plains [llanuras] but stopped until noon because of the bad weather. We traveled 6

——— We followed the same course along the river, always across flat plains until we encountered a river whose current and volume impeded our crossing it. We traveled 2

4—In the morning we crossed the said river, and on the same course we traveled across plains and tablelands. 8

5—At 6:30 we undertook the march on the same easterly course, and traveled across flat plains and tablelands. 8

6—Because I was seriously ill, I delayed in this stopping place until the 17th.

———

085

17—Feeling better, we undertook the march on the same course to the east, and traveled 3

[Houck omits this entry.]

18—At 7 o'clock in the morning the march was continued on the same course and along the same river. We encountered plenty of arroyos, and traveled 5

[10] Houck thought it was the Río Grande, but the Canadian in eastern New Mexico was from early times called the Colorado—and still is.

[11] Again he is on the Llano Estacado.

19—At mid-day we continued the march on the same course, and traveled 3

20—At mid-day we continued the march by the same course, and traveled 6

21—Bad weather and roads across a broad land forced us not to leave before mid-day, and we traveled only 3

*It is appropriate to point out that Pedro Vial's use of language has improved considerably since his diary of 1786; part of this may be from the difference in interpreters, but probably much of it is from Vial himself. It may be that in 1786 he had not long been rescued from the Comanches, and that therefore he had considerable difficulty, because it is a fact that white persons captured by Indians lost the knowledge of their own language in a remarkably short time. Now he shows more variety in his use of language; his entries are longer for ordinary days; he gives more than primitive facts; "we" now predominates where "I" predominated previously; his syntax becomes more sophisticated.*

22—At 7 o'clock in the morning we undertook the march [or "the march began"], course to the northeast, leaving the Colorado River in search of the Napestle, which is called in French the Arkansas River, and we encountered another that flows into the Colorado, and we named it the San Acacio; its shores are heavily wooded and it carries a great volume of water. We traveled 6

23—In the morning we continued the march northeast in search for the Arkansas River. We found another that flows into the Colorado, which we named the San Juan. We traveled 5

24—On the same course northeast, looking for the said Arkansas River, we continued the march at 7 o'clock in the morning across flat plains, and at a distance of 3 leagues we came to a river with plenty of water, which entered the Colorado. This day we traveled 6

25—The march was begun early in the morning, course to the north in search of the said Arkansas River; but another river was encountered with a heavy flow of water that disembogues into the Colorado, and we named it San Guillermo. We traveled this day 8

26—The bad weather that we had the night before did not permit us to march until mid-day, when, traveling on the same course, we made 4

27—In the morning early we continued the march to the north across spacious lands to the Arkansas River, where we made camp for the night, having traveled 8

*It is risky to draw up a route from a diary and a map, but a guess may be made here. He had traveled 103 leagues when he turned north; that would put him about at present Borger, Texas, but he could well have gone as far as the present town of Canadian to hit open country and also to reach the point nearest the Arkansas—for at that point the Canadian River is at the top of its bend to the north, and opposite that point, about 120 miles away, near present Bucklin, the Arkansas is at the bottom of its bend to the south. Bear in mind that he had been in a good deal of bad weather—rain, at that time of year—and that rivers and creeks ordinarily low or even dry might have been heavy with water.*

*After he left the Canadian, then, he might have hit, in succession, Wolf Creek, the North Canadian River, the Cimarron River, and Bluff Creek, and finally the Arkansas. They fit the distances fairly well; they all flow into the Canadian; the total distance is not far off.*

*His distance to the point of turning north is 268 miles; Canadian, Texas, is about 300. His distance from the Canadian River to the Arkansas is 96 miles; the actual distance is around 120.*

28—We kept quiet all day in order to rest our horses. [This entry is not in the Seville copy but is in the others.]

29[12]—At the break of day we continued the march along said river, which runs east northeast, and, traveling, we found some buffaloes killed by the Indians, who, we think, are of the Osage tribe, hunting in this area. We wanted to find them because I knew that they were well disposed toward the government of the province of Louisiana. And at about 4 o'clock in the afternoon we found them in their hunting-camp on the shore of the same Arkansas River. They approached us, and with the river between us, we fired some shots into the wind so that they would hear and see us. They immediately began to move, and came across to us. The first who met us, greeted us affectionately, shaking hands. I asked them what tribe they were, and they told me they were Kansas. At the same moment they took possession of our horses and

[12] The date is 28 in Provincias Internas 102, 29 in all others.

equipment, cutting our clothes with knives, leaving us entirely naked. They wanted to kill us, at which one of them cried to the others [Seville copy: some of them shouted to those who were going to do it], telling them they should not do it with rifles or arrows but with hatchet-blows or lances, because they had us surrounded and they might cause some unfortunate accident to themselves. In this conflict, one of them took our part, begging and supplicating the others not to take our lives. At that time I was approached by another whom I had known among the Frenchmen, and, taking me by the hand, he made me mount his own horse with him. Then another one came up behind and hurled a spear at me, but my good friend guarded me, dismounting from the horse, leaving me on it, and grabbed the evil-intentioned one. When they saw that, many of them rushed up and tried to kill me from behind, but a brother of the one who had just protected me, seated himself on the croup of the horse with the same intention [of protecting me]. That had hardly happened when I was approached by another Indian who had been a servant [*criado*] in the village of St. Louis of Illinois,[13] who spoke very good French, and he, recognizing me, began to shout, "Don't kill him! Don't kill him! We shall find out from where he comes, because I know him." And, taking the reins of the horse, he took me to his lodge and said, "Friend, how your Excellency must hurry if you want to save your life, because among us it is the custom and the law that, after having eaten, no one can be killed." I did it with the promptness that the case required, after which they left me alone. After a moment, some of the chiefs came to me and asked me from where I came, to which I answered that I had come from Santa Fe, sent by the great chief, their Spanish father, to open a road from Illinois—to which Spanish chief [in Illinois] I carried letters. Thereupon they left me alone until the following day, when they reunited me with my two companions, who had suffered violence equal to mine and had been freed by other Indians of good heart, although Vicente Villanueba came out with his head cut and a daggerthrust in the belly that would have been fatal if, at the moment of receiving it, he had not pulled away, and had [he not had] the good

[13] The information that the Indian had lived among the French is not in the Seville copy. Otherwise, the two copies are substantially the same, though they vary in small details.

services of another Indian who saved him, receiving the force of the blow on one arm, which left him seriously wounded. They kept us naked in that encampment until the 16th of August, we having traveled that day 4

*If anyone now doubts Pedro Vial's ability with the language, let him look at the above account and compare it with Vial's account of his argument with the Indians in the Taovaya village in Texas, six years previously. Note phrases like these:* "con igual intención, me preguntaron de donde venía, que habían sufrido igual tormenta." *The choice of words and the greatly improved syntax now indicate a man of some learning.*

*On the other hand, one may speculate as to the reason for Vial's easy capture. He says they fired "some shots" in the air—which might indicate they had pretty well emptied their rifles. No American frontiersman of experience would have done that, and certainly Vial knew, if anybody did, that the best negotiations with Indians were conducted from a position of strength. Perhaps he depended too heavily on his ability to understand them—or there may have been other circumstances not now apparent to us. At any rate, the Kansas (if they* were *Kansas) deceived him.*

*The matter of language also presents some difficulty. He seems to have understood their language without, somehow, being positive of their tribal designation. This may be accounted for by the fact that Kansas and Osages are members of the Siouan tribal stock.*

16—With that settlement [that is, with that band of Indians] I traveled ten days on a northeasterly course across broad plains all the way to their village. 50

25—We arrived at their village which is situated on the banks of the Kansas River which discharges into the river called Missouri, where we remained until September 11, at which time there came a Frenchman with a pirogue loaded with various kinds of merchandise, with permission of the government to trade with that tribe. He supplied both me and my companions with clothing to dress ourselves, a pound of vermilion [worth] five pesos of silver, four pesos worth of tobacco, four blankets and one ell of cloth, which will be settled for with the commandant on his return, as well as two pounds of powder, four pounds of balls, and a musket worth ten pesos.

September

16—We set out from the village of the Kansas in search of the Missouri River, embarking in a pirogue belonging to the traders from St. Louis, traveling by the Kansas River to its junction with the Missouri, which distance is 120 leagues [312 miles], uninhabited on either shore.[14] After eight days of navigation, we entered the Missouri. On this river the masters of the pirogue frequently stopped to hunt deers and bears, which abound on the shores—for which reason we did not arrive at St. Louis, Illinois, until October 3, at night, notwithstanding the fact that that place is not more than 140 leagues from the confluence of the Kansas and the Missouri.[15] On the shores of the latter, I had formerly [*antiguamente*] been acquainted with two villages [of Indians], one of Osages and the other of Missouris, but now they are deserted because of [the inhabitants'] having been driven away by the Sioux [or Sacs] and Iowas.

As soon as I arrived at the town of St. Louis, I presented myself to the commandant and delivered to him the letter and the instructions that I was carrying from the governor of New Mexico, and also the diary of my trip.

I made my residence in St. Louis from the said third day of October, 1792, to June 14 following, 1793, which delay was unavoidable, as much because of the season as from fear of the Osages, who frequently interrupt navigation and travel on the Missouri River.

[Provincias Internas 102 copy ends without certification or rubric,

[14] From somewhere near Bucklin he traveled fifty leagues to the Kansas village on the Kansas River; if he was on the Republican River, that would put him near Alma, Nebraska; if on the Solomon River, near Glade, Kansas. Alma is about 170 miles north of the Arkansas River—not far from his estimate of 130 miles (plus, actually, four more leagues they traveled the first day, making, in all, 140 miles). He says they traveled overland north and northeast, but Alma is almost due north from Bucklin. Then he gives 120 leagues down the river to the Missouri; it seems likely that he overestimated the distance traveled in the pirogue.

[15] He overstates the distance from the mouth of the Kansas to St. Louis about 30 per cent; if we apply this figure to his journey from the Kansas village, we find that he perhaps left from about Superior, Nebraska, or Beloit, Kansas—more in accord with his "north and northeast" report.

and picks up with June, 1793, which makes it seem that Vial carried his copy back to Santa Fe with him. Considerable information in the last three paragraphs is not in the Seville copy used by Houck, which, however, gives October 6 as the date of arrival in St. Louis.

[The Seville copy is signed and bears a rubric. Provincias Internas 183 ends with the rubric only. Historia 43 says: "1792—Pedro Vial—Baron de Carondelet. (No certification)."]

For the record, Vial's route measures about 1,100 miles; he records 456 leagues, or 1,185.6 miles. He traveled eighty-two days, for an average of 14.1 miles per day traveled.

Those few extra lines in the copy from Provincias Internas, volume 102, for September 16 give us a great deal to speculate about. We have already seen that Vial, in 1786, drew a map of the Missouri country that he should not have been able to draw, and now we have concrete evidence that he was in Illinois a long time before 1792.

Let us return to the first map mentioned in Chapter XI, which Vial prepared for the governor. Vial had reached Santa Fe on May 26, 1787, and signed the translation of his diary on July 5—probably because it took some time to get it translated. That first map has not turned up. It rather seems, from his diary, that it was of Texas and eastern New Mexico. He speaks of "the enclosed map," but perhaps it was carried by Mares on his trip back over the route, or maybe it has gone the way of Vial's original French journals, which appear to have dropped from sight immediately after the translations were made.

Vial spoke of the "enclosed map" on July 5, 1787. Shortly thereafter, Mares left on the return trip (Santa Fe to San Antonio), and Vial, undoubtedly prompted by the governor, then drew another map, in it showing all the territory that he had traversed in the trans-Mississippi West. This is the map that we have. It is a very remarkable map, and gives rise to some interesting questions.[16]

To appreciate this map, it is necessary to know the state of geographical knowledge of the upper Missouri at the time Vial drew the map. Vérendrye probably had visited the Mandans in 1738, and he

[16] The original seems to have disappeared, but the Historical Society of New Mexico has a photostat of it; Castañeda has used it twice, but Carl I. Wheat was unable to find the original. See *The Spanish Entrada*, 238.

guessed that they were on the upper Missouri, but the information on Vérendrye's map is extremely vague: the river itself is not identifiable with the Missouri except that Vérendrye named it the "River of the Mantans, which is believed to be the Missouri"—and Wheat points out that it is hardly credible that accurate information of the Mandans' position would have filtered through Europe and back to Vial in Texas.[17]

D'Anville in 1746 and Vaugondy in 1750 and others had shown the Missouri, but much shorter than it really was, and sometimes it cut the Rocky Mountains and turned southwest and headed toward New Mexico. In 1758, Governor Kérlerec of Louisiana said that even the savages maintained that it never had been possible to find the sources of the Missouri River,[18] and again in 1766 Aubry, a commandant at New Orleans, said the Missouri was unknown.[19] A little later, in 1785, Governor Miró drew up a rather comprehensive report on Louisiana at the request of Neve, commandant-general of the Interior Provinces, and he said that no one ever had gone higher on the Missouri than the River of the Sioux, two hundred leagues from the mouth of the Missouri.[20]

Under the British flag, Jonathan Carver explored the Minnesota area, 1766–68, but he did not, apparently, go as far as the Missouri; his farthest point west seems to be a wintering place on the Minnesota River.

In 1785 Peter Pond made a map of Canada with a notation to the effect that on the banks of the Missouri lived the Mandans—but that information does not account for Vial's map, as Wheat indicates. And in that year, Governor Miró, who obviously made a considerable effort to gather information, said among other things that the Missouri River "cuts this chain of mountains [the Rockies] to the north of the aforesaid River Brabo."[21] When he said it "cut" the mountains, he was subscribing to the old theory that the Missouri (often confused with the Platte) headed somewhere west of the Rocky Mountains."

[17] *Ibid.*, I, 173.

[18] Nasatir, *Before Lewis and Clark*, I, 51.

[19] *Ibid.*, 65.

[20] *Ibid.*, 77–78; the River of the Sioux was the Platte.

[21] Nasatir, "An Account of Spanish Louisiana, 1785," *Missouri Historical Review*, Vol. XXIV, No. 4 (July, 1930), 528.

Three years later (1788), in Ruggles' map, shown in Wheat, the notation is: "The head of this river is unknown."

Vial made his map in 1787, *in Santa Fe;* five years later (in 1792) Jacques d'Eglise ascended the Missouri to the Mandans and brought back the first direct information the Spaniards received from the Mandan country.[22] In 1794 Carondelet wrote to Aranda, saying that the Missouri arose in the mountains forty leagues from the ocean.[23] On the same day in 1794 Carondelet made a "Military Report on Louisiana and West Florida," in which he said: "All the maps printed both in England and in the United States and in France, are absolutely false, especially in regard to the course of the Mississippi and Missouri Rivers"; two pages later he said: "The kingdom of Mégico, which the Mississippi and the Missouri Rivers encircle from the gulf almost to the South Sea, . . ."[24] In that year also, Carondelet encouraged the exploration of the river and the discovery of a waterway to the South Sea, and sent a copy of an important map with his military report to Las Casas in Havana (which copy has not been found), indicating that he then, as had Miró nine years earlier, believed the Missouri "cut" the Rocky Mountains.[25]

James Mackay had furnished information for that map,[26] and Mackay was one man who might have known about the upper Missouri, for he had visited the Mandans from the north in 1787[27]—but the map that he gave Truteau shows but a single source for the Missouri

[22] Nasatir, "Jacques D'Eglise on the Upper Missouri, 1791–1795," *Mississippi Valley Historical Review*, Vol. XIV, No. 1 (June, 1927), 47–71.

[23] Carondelet to Aranda, No. 129, confidential, November 24, 1794; A.H.N., Estado, leg. 3897; printed in Houck, *Spanish Régime*, II, 9–17. See extracts printed, and notes and citations in Nasatir, *Before Lewis and Clark*, I, 253–54.

[24] Carondelet to Las Casas, "Military Report on Louisiana and West Florida," November 24, 1794, A.H.N., Estado, leg. 3897. Robertson has printed in full the military report from Papeles de Cuba, leg. 2354, in *Louisiana Under the Rule of Spain, France, and the United States*, I, 293–354; he says the map is not with the document in the archives. See various citations in Nasatir, *Before Lewis and Clark*, I, 253–57.

[25] Carondelet's letter is printed in Nasatir, *ibid.*, I, 253–54; this is from Robertson. Carondelet in his dispatch No. 48, *reservada*, dated New Orleans, December 1, 1794, says he is remitting a map to accompany a copy of his military report, Papeles de Cuba, leg. 2354.

[26] Aubrey Diller, "Maps of the Missouri River Before Lewis and Clark," *Studies and Essays in the History of Science and Learning*, 1946), 512.

[27] *Ibid.*

River. One of Truteau's missions was to obtain information on the distance to the Rocky Mountains, which Carondelet said then were located to the west of the Missouri's source. Truteau learned about the Columbia and the Yellowstone from the Cheyennes in 1795, and he gathered information about the Missouri from its mouth to the Yellowstone,[28] but he himself did not go far above the Arikaras, and he learned nothing about the Missouri above the Yellowstone.

In 1795 Arrowsmith published the earliest map with details of the upper Missouri, but he did not show the river all the way to the Mississippi;[29] as a matter of fact, Arrowsmith's map of 1802 still exhibited considerable white space.[30]

In 1795, however, the engineer Soulard made a copy of Carondelet's map of 1794, and this time we know it was made in St. Louis[31] with Mackay's help[32]—and it shows the South Platte encircling New Mexico, the Missouri with the Great Bend and Grand Detour in one, and with a single source of the Missouri River.

Wheat says:

> When this [Soulard's] map was first produced no one yet knew the location of the Mississippi's source, much less where the Missouri took its rise, the true nature of the Rocky Mountains or the complexities that they encompassed. . . . West of the Mandan villages all was conjecture. . . . Until Lewis and Clark's own map appeared in print in 1814, the Soulard map, in the version offered to the public by Arrowsmith and Lewis [not Meriwether Lewis] in 1804, constitutes . . . the most informative published attempt to portray the West and Northwest of what is now the United States.[33]

In 1796 Winterbotham's map also shows a single source.[34] In that year too, Victor Collot, getting information from Mackay and Chouteau, drew a map of the Missouri showing two forks at the head.

In 1797 John Evans, who had been associated with Mackay in his

[28] Nasatir, *Before Lewis and Clark*, I, 91.

[29] Wheat, *The Spanish Entrada*, 176.

[30] *Ibid.*, 181.

[31] *Ibid.*, 157. The Soulard map was published in large size in Nasatir, *Before Lewis and Clark*, I, 46.

[32] Wheat, *From Lewis and Clarke to Fremont, 1804–1845*, 158.

[33] *Ibid.*, 6–7.

[34] *Pacific Railroad Surveys*, XI (Part A), p. 16.

trip up the Missouri in 1795 and his effort to find the South Sea, drew a series of eight maps, which are, says Wheat, nos. 5, 6, 7, 8, 9, 10, 11, and 13 of the Lewis and Clark maps in Thwaites' *Original Journals.* No. 13 shows a single source, so obviously John Evans, who had been sent ahead by Mackay but had not gone the distance, did not know much about the source. A single source also is shown by Wheat's No. 243 (from Mackay and Evans) and his No. 244 (Jedediah Morse)—both about 1797.

It rather appears that the first map after Vial's to show the Three Forks at the head of the Missouri may be Wheat's No. 255 (author unidentified), dated 1802; the next would be Clark's map of 1806, drawn with the help of Drouillard, one of Lewis and Clark's guides (Wheat, No. 280); then would be Lewis and Clark (the King version, No. 284), 1806; and Robert Frazer's map of 1807. As for publication, however, Diller says the Three Forks were added to the Arrowsmith and Lewis maps of 1804, and first appeared in the *Travels of Captains Lewis and Clarke* in 1809. The *Travels,* of course, was a spurious edition, and the official version did not appear until 1814, but the Tardieu map, printed with the journal of Patrick Gass, a sergeant with Lewis and Clark, was published in 1810 and showed the Three Forks.[35]

But the inescapable fact is that for fifteen years (from 1787 to 1802) Pedro Vial appears to have been the only white man with an accurate knowledge of the upper Missouri River.

The legend on Vial's map is: "*Mapa et tierra qu*$^{e}$. *yos. pedro Vial taingo tranzitau*"—an interesting combination of Spanish and French that seems to say: "Sketch [or geographical picture] and [of?] land that I, Pedro Vial, have traveled over." A second and smaller line reads: "*en S*$^{t}$. *Tafee este dia 18 de ouctubre de La*$^{nn}$. 1787."

The word *tranzitau,* whether French or Spanish, means literally to cross over, to transit, and so we may expect to examine the map for something other than the Three Forks. It shows the Río Grande heading in Colorado; the Texas rivers are well placed, especially the Brazos and the Red, with the proper Indian settlements; Natchitoches is properly shown, as is the Arkansas River (and the map was drawn before the Natchitoches trip), with a settlement of "Taouiache" Indians on the Arkansas above the mouth of the Cimarron.

[35] Wheat, *From Lewis and Clark to Fremont,* 3.

Vial might be expected to have a good knowledge of the rivers in Texas and surrounding territory, but his knowledge seems to go further afield. Running into the Mississippi from the east side, he shows the White, the Ohio, the Maramec; the Illinois, the Rock, the Wisconsin, the Chippewa, and the St. Croix; Lake Pepin in the middle of the upper Mississippi. On the west side, at the north, he shows the St. Pedro (the Minnesota, then called St. Peter's); the Des Moines, heading in a lake in the "land of the Sioux" (the Des Moines River does not actually arise from a lake, but within a few miles of its source it passes very close to Lake Heron in southwestern Minnesota). Below the mouth of the Des Moines is the mouth of the Missouri, and the map shows the Osages, the Pawnees, and the Aes; the Mandans and Arikaras. He has the Río Piedra Colorado (Red River of the North?) flowing into the Missouri; this seems to be the only important error he makes in this map.

He does not show the Great Bend or the Grand Detour of the Missouri, but he shows the Three Forks and he shows them rising in the mountains.

His map is scaled, and the lengths of the rivers, compared with the lengths of the same rivers as given in *Nelson's Perpetual Looseleaf Encyclopædia,* are interesting:

| | Nelson | Vial |
|---|---|---|
| Río Grande | 1800 | 1800 |
| Red River | 1550 | 1540 |
| Arkansas | 1500 | 1800 |
| Des Moines | 550 | 1290 |
| Missouri | 2945 | 1800 |
| Mississippi | 2500 | 2060 |

Likewise, Vial's map has indications of latitude, and a comparison of these with the actual figures is not without interest:

| | Actual | Vial |
|---|---|---|
| Mandan villages | 48°–50° | 50° |
| St. Louis | 39° | 40° |
| Santa Fe | 35°–36° | 39° |
| San Antonio | 29° | 28° |
| New Orleans | 30° | 30° |

Perhaps Vial was not as unlettered as we may have assumed.

We now know, from the new information from the copy of Vial's journal in Provincias Internas, Vol. 102, that Vial had been in Illinois before 1792. He speaks of the villages of Osages and Missouris, formerly known to him to be inhabited, but now deserted because of attack by the "Siux and Ayohuay" (or Saux and Ayohuay), and the implication is that those villages were destroyed after Vial was there. The map by D'Anville of 1746 shows two villages, one of Osages (they were Little Osages) on the north side of the Missouri, just east of the Grand River, which enters the Missouri about eighty miles east of Kansas City; the Missouris are shown south of the river and almost opposite the mouth of the Grand.

William Clark mentions them in his journal of June 13, 1804, when he says: ". . . behind a small willow island in the bend is a prarie in which the Missouries Indians once lived and the Spot where 300 of them fell a sacrifise to the fury of the *Saukees*."[36] The Coues edition says:

". . . the ancient village of the Missouris. Of this village there remains no vestige, nor is there anything to recall this great and numerous nation, except a feeble remnant of about 30 families. They were driven from their original seats by the Invasions of the Sauks and other Indians from the Mississippi, who destroyed at this village 200 of them in one contest, and sought refuge near the Little Osage, on the other side of the river. The encroachment of the same enemies forced, about 30 years hence, both these nations from the banks of the Missouri.[37]

Clark says on June 15:

Camped on the S. S. [south side][38] nearly opposite the *antient*

[36] Reuben Gold Thwaites, *Original Journals of the Lewis and Clark Expedition, 1804–1806*, I, 47.

[37] Elliott Coues, *History of the Expedition Under the Command of Lewis and Clark*, I, 22–23. Biddle, who prepared this edition originally, did some writing on his own account, but he also had the help of one man (George Shannon) who had been on the expedition, and of consultations with Clark.

[38] Carl H. Chapman, in a letter dated June 23, 1961, points out that Thwaites erred in believing that "S.S." means "starboard side" (which would be the right side, going upstream), but that Clark customarily spoke of the south side or the north side of the river; therefore, "S.S." means "south side"—and that is the side the villages are on.

*Village* of the *Little Osarges* and below the ant[t]. *Village* of the *Missouries* both Situations in view and within three M[s]. of each other, the Osage were Settled at the foot a hill in a butifull Plain which extends back quite to the Osage River, in front of the Vilg: next to the river is an ellegent bottom Plain which extends several miles in length on the river in this low Prarie the *Missouries* lived after they were reduced by the *Saukees* at their Town Some Dist[e]. below. The little osage finding themselves much oppressed by the Saukees & other nations, left this place & built a village 5 M[s]. from the Grand *Osarge Town*, about years ago a fiew of the Missouris accompanied them, the remainder of that Nation went to the Otteaus on the River Platt.[39]

It seems that the Missouris were first massacred by the Sacs, and moved close to the Little Osages; that both villages were then harassed by the Sacs until they moved from the area about 1774, according to Clark.

Carl H. Chapman says: "I think that the Coues edition of Lewis and Clark, where Clark says that the Missouris and Osages were still living in these villages about thirty years, hence is approximately correct . . . about 1777." Vial says, "I had known them formerly," and this seems to place him in Illinois in 1777 or before. And Vial, when he was saved from the Kansas, said one Indian who saved him was a man who had formerly been a servant in St. Louis, and who spoke the French language well, and Vial says of him: "recognizing me."[39a]

An interesting question arises concerning the "yos." in the title of

[39] Thwaites, *Original Journals of Lewis and Clark*, I, 49.

[39a] It appears that Vial had a knowledge of the Upper Missouri, but apparently none of the middle stretches, for he was not aware of the Grand Detour or the Great Bend; therefore it seems that he may have gone into the Mandan country from Canada, and have gone back to Canada and then to Illinois. In spite of diligence on the part of Nasatir, Wm. Kaye Lamb at the Dominion Archives, Mrs. W. C. Heidenreich at the University of Toronto, and myself, no documentary evidence has been turned up to connect Vial with the North West Company or the Hudson's Bay Company—but there are other possibilities. When Jacques d'Eglise went up the river in 1792 he found one Menard, who had been living with the Mandans for fourteen years. And there was Joseph Garreau, who lived with the Arikaras. May not Vial have done the same? It might be noted that on May 13, 1794, Trudeau wrote to Carondelet to say: ". . . an old man who has just come from the Panís tribe where he has been for ten consecutive years . . . has gone overland with the Paducahs to the source of the Missouri," beyond which lay a large river whose current flowed to the west, he said. Trudeau to Carondelet, No. 185, St. Louis, May 31, 1794; Papales de Cuba, leg. 2363; printed in Nasatir, *Before Lewis and Clark*, I, 228–29.

Vial's map. The *s* is not a flourish but is quite plain, and some have suggested that *yos.* means, "I, Señor"—but Pedro Vial, in all his journals, never once refers to himself as "señor," nor is he ever so referred to by those who write about him; often he is called "Don Pedro Vial," but never "señor." Carmen Romero James at the Library of Congress, Eleanor B. Adams at the University of New Mexico have lent a hand without anything concrete except "señor"; can it mean *yo se mismo* for *yo me mismo?* Carmen Edmondson of San Diego suggests it is an abbreviation of *ellos,* referring to the lands.

At any rate, Vial must have spent considerable time in Canada and on the headwaters of the Missouri, and then gone to Spanish Illinois. He then lived in St. Louis for some time before he finally drifted into Texas—probably down the Mississippi and up the Red or the Arkansas, and then into the villages of the Taovayas. There were many unnamed *contrabandistas* in Texas in those days.

Whatever Vial's age and whatever the exact route of his moves from Lyons, France, to San Antonio, in 1792 he was deceived by the Kansas, captured, almost killed, and held naked for six weeks. Then he and his two companions went downriver in a pirogue, reaching St. Louis after a leisurely jaunt during which the men who owned the pirogue hunted deers and bears. In the meantime, Governor Concha, back in Santa Fe, had communicated the news of Vial's departure to Nava at Chihuahua, and had added some comments on Vial himself:

> I resolved to send him to Illinois [says Concha], and he left May 22. [Concha enclosed a copy of the letter he had written to the commandant at St. Louis, and a copy of the instructions he had given Vial. And then he went into another matter:] In letters of Jan. 23, 1788, and 26 instant of 1789, Ugarte [says Concha] tells me he has recommended Vial to the viceroy for his merit, [but nothing has happened, says Concha. Vial has] contributed to the pacification of Comanches in this province and in the Interior Provinces of the East. He has been successful in opening roads from here to Natchitoches and to Texas. [But] despite all this, there is no result to Vial as yet. [Concha believes Vial's service useful, and, besides, it keeps Vial occupied. He ends by saying:] News that I have received from the Comanches, Taovayas, Aes, and Pananas has persuaded me that the expedition will be carried out without any obstacle and with great happiness.[40]

On the same day Concha wrote to the viceroy: "Ugarte recommended to your predecessors the merits of Pedro Vial; my predecessors and I have recommended him [, but] nothing has happened in his favor."[41]

An obvious question here is: what is this all about?

It is this letter that gives us information on Pedro Vial's ability or lack of ability to write Spanish: "As the said Vial does not have sufficient command of the Castillian language to keep a diary sufficiently clear in that language, it has been provided that he keep one in French, and that [later], when it is translated in his presence, presently when he returns he can sign it for passing on to higher authority."

Nava answered Concha on August 6, approving the governor's commissioning Vial to explore a route to Illinois—which plainly indicates that Concha had taken that step on his own initiative, even though he may have discussed it with Nava's predecessor—though that would extend pretty far back, for Nava had assumed office in 1790. Nava now assured Concha that he was sending an account to the viceroy, and promised that he would recommend Vial as his predecessor, Ugarte, had done. He noted the added merit of Vial, which, he implied, was already high because of Vial's pacification of the Comanches and his trips to San Antonio and Natchitoches.[42] On August 9 he wrote to the viceroy, sending Concha's letters and copies of Concha's enclosures, but it rather seems that he crawfished on helping Concha to get whatever he was after for Vial, because he said, "When I receive the diary, I will send it to you and at that time make my recommendations."[43]

Revillagigedo wrote to Nava on September 4, saying: "As soon as you send me the diary and your recommendations, I will pay attention to it as you recommend."[44] On the same day, however, he wrote

[40] Concha to Nava, No. 328, Santa Fe, July 20, 1792, Provincias Internas, Vol. 183, f. 253–54.

[41] Concha to Revillagigedo, No. 14, Santa Fe, July 20, 1792, enclosing the letter of May 21 to the commandant at St. Louis, and a copy of Vial's instructions, Provincias Internas, Vol. 183, f. 260–61 *et vo.*

[42] Nava to Governor, Chihuahua, August 6, 1792, New Mexican Archives, doc. 1205.

[43] Nava to Revillagigedo, No. 485, Chihuahua, August 9, 1792, Provincias Internas, Vol. 183, f. 258 *et vo.*

[44] Revillagigedo to Nava, September 4, 1792, Provincias Internas, Vol. 183, f. 259.

also to Concha, asking for documents on Vial;[45] it sounds as if Revillagigedo was serious.

While everybody but Nava was trying to see that Vial should get whatever it was he wanted, Vial was a guest of the Kansas Indians, but he arrived at St. Louis in due course of time, as shown by the letter of Zenon Trudeau, commandant at St. Louis, to the governor of Louisiana, written on October 7:

> Last night there arrived from the town of Santa Fe, in the kingdom of New Mexico, Pedro Vial and two young men who accompanied him. He was commissioned by the governor of that province, Fernando de la Concha, to open a road from that town to these establishments, and he delivered to me an official letter addressed to me and his instructions for the conduct of his trip—a copy of which I am enclosing to your Excellency. I am also enclosing the diary that he has kept on this trip. All this will instruct your Excellency as to the object of this trip, and of everything that has occurred on it. It appears that he will remain all winter in this place because it is not the season to undertake a return to Santa Fe—a thing that would not have occurred had he not encountered difficulty, for he says that he could have arrived here in a good twenty-five-day march.
>
> I find myself obliged to supply them with the provisions and clothing that they will need during their sojourn [here], as well as the equipment necessary when they begin their [return] trip—all of which I shall do with due economy.[46]

Carondelet sent the news of Vial's journey to Las Casas, the captain-general at Havana, on January 10, 1793, enclosing a copy of the letter from Trudeau as lieutenant-governor of the post of Illinois; Concha's instructions; Vial's "recommendations" to Trudeau; and the relation of the voyage.[47]

Las Casas completed the chain a few days later when he sent all the

[45] Draft, Revillagigedo to Concha, answering No. 14, September 4, 1792, Provincias Internas, Vol. 183, f. 259.

[46] Trudeau to Carondelet, St. Louis, October 7, 1792; original in Papeles de Cuba, leg. 25-A; copy in A.G.I., Audiencia of Santo Domingo, Louisiana, and Florida, estante 86, cajón 6, leg. 26; also in Provincias Internas, Vol. 183, f. 269 *vo.*

[47] Carondelet to Las Casas, New Orleans, January 10, 1793; enclosed with Trudeau letter above; printed in Houck, *Spanish Régime*, I, 351. There is another copy in Papeles de Cuba, leg. 1442, and also in Provincias Internas, Vol. 183, f. 269.

documents and a copy of Carondelet's letter to Alange, the Minister of War in Spain; and he said a curious thing: "I have informed the viceroy of New Spain of its [the trip's] outcome, in order that, together with the information concerning this voyage communicated to him by Governor Fernando de la Concha, he may form his ideas better"; and he added that perhaps Alange would determine whether it was worth while to inform the king.[48] Vial's name was getting into very high levels.

It was not getting to Concha, however, for in November he had written to Nava, saying:

> Notwithstanding that I admonished Pedro Vial when he undertook his expedition to Illinois, that he should try to return to this capital during last October, he has not done so—from which I infer that he must have deviated perhaps from the route he was supposed to follow. This suspicion does not lack substantiation, for some Eastern Comanches have informed me that they met him and talked to him as well as to the two young men who went in his company in the neighborhood of San Antonio de Bexar, at which place he might have arrived to start anew to continue his enterprise; and thus I do not expect him [now], and the return is not likely until next May, which is when the weather will permit.[49]

Apparently the Comanches were up to their old trick of telling the great white father what they thought he would like to hear.

Nava dutifully informed the viceroy of the news from Concha.[50]

In January, Carondelet okayed Trudeau's payment of Vial's immediate expenses:

> In conformity with what you request in your official letter No. 45, there has been given a warrant against the general account of the army to Gabriel Cerré in the sum of 412 pesos, 7 *reales,* and 17 *maravedís* for the goods and money supplied Pedro Vial and his men accord-

[48] Las Casas to Alange, Havana, No. 254, February 5, 1793; covering letter for the enclosures; printed in Houck, *Spanish Regime,* I, 350. Also in A.G.I., Audencia of Santo Domingo, 86–2–26; drafts in Papeles de Cuba, leg. 1484 and leg. 2262.

[49] Concha to Nava, New Mexico, November 9, 1792, Provincias Internas, Vol. 183, f. 268.

[50] Nava to Revillagigedo, Chihuahua, December 27, 1792, Provincias Internas, Vol. 183, f. 279 *et vo.*

ing to the official letter directed to you by Colonel Fernando de la Concha, governor of New Mexico.

As soon as Vial sets out [to return to] his destination, you will send me a detailed account of the costs, signed by him and by you, which you will send me in due time to obtain reimbursement from the treasury of the new kingdom of [New] Mexico, to which it should be charged.[51]

On February 1, Las Casas wrote to the viceroy as he had said, and he also transmitted some documents—presumably the same copies he sent to Alange.[52] On March 27 the viceroy answered, acknowledging receipt of the letter of February 1, enclosing the letter of the governor of Louisiana to Las Casas, and Vial's instructions and diary. He also said:

When your letter reached my hands, there had [just] resulted by [action of] his Majesty the independence of this viceroyalty from the commandancy general, and naming as chief of the commandancy-general the Brigadier Pedro de Nava, to whom I have sent the documents mentioned for his government, and that he may order the *succesivas de terminaciones* that appear suitable to him. I am advising you in answer.[53]

And on the same day Revillagigedo wrote to Nava, "enclosing copies of the letter and diary" of the trip made by Vial, sent to him by the governor at Havana, las Casas.[54]

The viceroy followed it up, for one month later he wrote again to Nava, and commented:

This exploration, that made in 1787 from said province of New Mexico to Texas by the retired corporal, Interpreter Mares, and others that have been carried out in previous years across the same lands and over those [traversed by] the opposite course from the west to open the roads from the first-mentioned province [New Mexico] to those of Sonora and California, have been and can be very important and conducive to counteract the dangerous designs of foreign powers.

[51] Draft, [Carondelet] to Trudeau, New Orleans, January 30, 1793; Papeles de Cuba, leg. 25.

[52] Las Casas to Revillagigedo, Havana, February 1, 1793; Provincias Internas, Vol. 183, f. 279 *et vo.*

[53] Draft [Viceroy] to Las Casas, March 27, 1793, Provincias Internas, Vol. 183, f. 281.

[54] [Revillagigedo] to Nava, March 27, 1793, Provincias Internas, Vol. 183, f. f. 282.

Under these suppositions, and in light of what might happen, it will be necessary to repeat some of the indicated explorations. If his Majesty might deign to forewarn and will advise me how it can be done, or if urgent reasons come up for immediately executing them, I hope that your Excellency will please advise me of the results of the last trip of Pedro Vial, and of whatever other [trip] of similar nature that may have been undertaken or is being undertaken in your provinces, so that I can make the decisions that come up in conformity with the judgment of what is ordered by his Majesty in Article 2 of the royal order of August 22, 1776, issued for the establishment of that [your] commandancy-general independent of this viceroyalty.[55]

Shortly thereafter, Nava replied:

When Pedro Vial returns to Santa Fe, I shall send to your Excellency a copy of the diary that he has kept on his return to that province from the fort of St. Louis, Illinois, in accordance with what your Excellency was kind enough to tell me in your official letter of the 30th ultimate.

I have ordered brought together the itineraries of the trips made by Vial himself, Josef Mares, and others from the province of New Mexico to that of Texas and the fort of Natchitoches, in order to send copies of them to your Excellency.

Vial had not arrived on May 6 at Santa Fe, because I have just received correspondence from the governor, Fernando de la Concha, which extends to that date, and he tells me nothing of the matter.[56]

Now it appears that Vial started the return trip on June 14, 1793, and Trudeau reported the fact to Carondelet on the sixteenth, after which Trudeau addressed himself to the most tender subject in New Spain: expenses:

Pedro Vial has left for his voyage to Santa Fe in a pirogue which for that purpose is going to conduct him and his people as far as the Paní nation, who [Vial] was commissioned to attract them [the Panís] to peace with the Comanches, whom here we call the Laytanes. I gave

[55] [Revillagigedo] to Nava, April 30, 1793, Provincias Internas, Vol. 183, f. 280 *et vo.*

[56] Nava to Revillagigedo, No. 54 (?), Chihuahua, May 22, 1793, Provincias Internas, Vol. 183, f. 283 *et vo.*

him all that he asked for. . . . I shall remit to your Excellency the general account of his expenses.[57]

The account itself went in later:

I am remitting to your Excellency the general account of the expenses (as your Excellency has ordered me) that have been incurred in this post by Pedro Vial, Vicente Villanueva, and Vincente Espinosa, who left for their destination the sixteenth of last month.[58]

General account of what has been supplied by various merchants of St. Louis to Pedro Vial, Vicente Villanueva, and Vincente Espinosa, commissioned by order of the governor of the province of Santa Fe, Fernando de la Concha; in this district of Illinois during all the time of their sojourn in it, and for their return to the said province, both for their maintenance, lodgings, and laundry as well as for the necessities of their voyage in the purchase of horses for the same, pirogue loaded for their trip to the Paní nation, and merchandise to regale the Indian chiefs through whose territories they have to pass.

To wit:

| October 8, 1792 | Pesos | Reales | Maravedis[59] |
|---|---|---|---|
| 12 ells of cloth at 5 pesos | 60 | 2 | |
| 18 Shirts at 3 pesos | 54 | | |
| 1 Hat | 8 | | |
| 2 Hats at 5 pesos | 10 | | |
| 18 Handkerchiefs at 3 pesos each | 54 | | |
| 4½ Ells of calico at 2 pesos 4 | 11 | 2 | |
| 3 Pairs trousers at 4 pesos | 12 | | |
| 8 Pounds of soap at 5 pesos | 5 | | |
| 1½ Dozen large metal buttons | 3 | | |
| 2 Same—small at 1 peso | 2 | | |
| 3 Pairs Shoes at 3 pesos | 9 | | |
| For thread | 1 | | |
| 3 Blankets of 3 points[60] at 4 pesos each | 12 | | |

[57] Trudeau to Carondelet, No. 84, St. Louis, June 16, 1793, Papeles de Cuba, leg. 26, and draft of reply, July 16, 1793.

[58] Trudeau to Carondelet, No. 90, St. Louis, July 10, 1793, Papeles de Cuba, leg. 26.

[59] Nominally worth ½c to ¾c.

[60] At a somewhat later date, Hudson's Bay Company blankets were marked diagonally across one corner, the parallel bars or "points" each indicating one pound

| | | | |
|---|---|---|---|
| 3 Buffalo skins *pasado* at 3 pesos each | 9 | | |
| To redeem a receipt given by the said Vial to Basilio Vasseur[61] of 106 *libras*, 10 *sueldos*[62] in skins, which value he received in the Kansas nation—the said skins at the current price of 40 sueldos in money | 42 | 5 | 17 |
| Money in hard silver | 120 | | |
| June 10, 1793 | | | |
| 9 Ells of cloth at 6 pesos | 54 | | |
| 9 Pairs of shoes at 3 pesos | 27 | | |
| 9 Pairs of trousers at 4 pesos | 36 | | |
| 9 Shirts at 4 pesos | 36 | | |
| 9 Handkerchiefs at 2 pesos | 18 | | |
| 2 Razors at 2 pesos | 4 | | |
| 3 Hats at 4 pesos | 12 | | |
| A Pair of pistols | 15 | | |
| 1 Saber | 10 | | |
| 1 Carbine | 45 | | |
| 2 Muskets at 20 pesos | 20 | | |
| 3 Saddles for horses at 25 pesos each | 75 | | |
| 3 Bridles for horses at 4 pesos each | 12 | | |
| 10 Pounds powder at 1 peso, 2 reales each | 12 | 4 | |
| 20 Pounds bullets at 1 real each | 2 | 4 | |
| 3 Pairs of spurs at 2 pesos | 6 | | |
| 3 Mosquito nets at 8 pesos | 24 | | |
| 1 Large axe | 4 | | |
| 1 Small axe | 2 | | |
| 50 Pounds tobacco at 20 sueldos | 10 | | |
| 200 Gun flints | 2 | | |
| 1 Copper boiler for cooking | 6 | | |
| 20 Pounds of soap at 4 reales | 10 | | |
| 4 Quires of paper at 4 reales | 2 | | |
| 1 Mariner's compass | 12 | | |
| For making of various clothes | 43 | 5 | |
| 3 Blankets at 3 pesos | 19 | | |

of weight of the blanket. Larpenteur, *Forty Years a Fur Trader* (Milo M. Quaife, ed.), 55n.

[61] Undoubtedly the owner of the pirogue or at least the Frenchman who brought clothing and goods to Vial and his men on the Kansas River.

[62] As usual in Louisiana, the coinage system is confused.

| | | | | |
|---|---|---|---|---|
| | For making of various clothes | 43 | 4 | |
| 6 | Pieces of Limburg cloth at 40 pesos | 240 | | |
| 30 | Blankets at 3 pesos | 90 | | |
| 10 | Pounds of vermilion at 2 pesos, 4 reales | 25 | | |
| 30 | Pounds of powder at 1 peso, 2 reales | 37 | 4 | |
| 80 | Pounds of bullets at 1 real | 10 | | |
| 10,000 | grains of *porcelana*[63] at 6 pesos | 6 | | |
| 6 | Dozen large knives at 2 pesos | 12 | | |
| 24 | Mirrors at 4 reales | 12 | | |
| 6 | Muskets at 8 pesos | 48 | | |
| | For equipment [for crew] of pirogue—provisions and rowers: | | | |
| | For the pay of 4 rowers at 60 pesos | 240 | | |
| 7 | Quintals of biscuit [*galleta*] at 10 pesos | 70 | | |
| 4 | Quintals of bacon at 2 pesos | 125 | | |
| 1 | Barrel corn *pilado* | 6 | | |
| 6 | Oars at 1 peso | 6 | | |
| 1 | Oil cloth | 20 | | |
| 1 | Pirogue | 20 | | |
| | For food, lodging, and laundry which have been supplied to Pedro Vial and his young men, Vicente Villanueva and Vicente Espinosa, from October 7 last year until the 15th instant: | | | |
| | For 8 months and 8 days of maintenance, lodging, and laundry of Pedro Vial at 30 pesos per month. For same time for the said items supplied to Vicente Villaneuva and Vicente Espinosa at 15 pesos per month for each | 248 | | |
| | Total | 2460 | 17 | 0 |

I, Pedro Vial, have received through the medium of Señor Don Zenon Trudeau, commandant of this post of St. Louis, all that this present account shows, the sum amounting to 2,460 pesos, 17 *maravedís*, for my maintenance and that of the two young men who have accompanied me in the commission given me by Señor Don Fernando de la Concha, governor of the province of Santa Fe, to open a road from that town to St. Louis, and for the expenses necessary for my return to the said province, and in order that it be verified and so

[63] This may refer to a white and blue coloring material for porcelain, which presumably would have been used in trade the same as vermilion.

that the corresponding charge be entered, I am attesting this in St. Louis, Illinois, June 15, 1793.

PEDRO VIAL [*rubric*]

With my intervention
ZENON TRUDEAU[64] [*rubric*]

It is worth while to note some of the supplies that each man took for himself: three pairs of shoes, three pairs of trousers, three shirts, three handkerchiefs, three hats; a pair of pistols, a saber, a carbine, and two muskets (note that their personal muskets were valued at twenty pesos each, while trade muskets were only eight pesos each). For the three of them, they had two razors; does this not imply that one man wore a beard? And, if so, was that not Vial, since the other two were young men?

The prices charged for goods are also interesting. For a pair of spurs in St. Louis they paid two pesos, whereas in San Antonio in 1789 they had paid one and one-half pesos; for bridles they paid in St. Louis four pesos, in San Antonio one and three-fourths pesos; for powder in St. Louis ten reales, in San Antonio four and one-half reales; for balls in St. Louis 1 real per pound, in San Antonio slightly less; mirrors in St. Louis four reales, in San Antonio two and one-half reales. Other items are difficult to compare. Also, one may note that the four rowers of the pirogue were to receive sixty pesos each, whereas Vial's young men, for making the entire trip, both ways, were to receive thirty pesos.

One may possibly be justified in thinking that there was considerable inflation in Illinois; on the other hand, it must be recalled that there was a long distance between St. Louis and Santa Fe, and perhaps M. Trudeau was indulging in the ancient sport of hanging it on a stranger. Costs may have been higher in St. Louis.

Whatever the reason for the unusually high charges on certain items, Vial was well equipped for the return voyage, and with a pirogue and four rowers to take him upriver, he left St. Louis on June 14, 1793:

### *Pedro Vial from St. Louis to Santa Fe, June 14—November 16, 1793*[65]

[64] Trudeau to Carondelet, St. Louis, July 10, 1793, Papeles de Cuba, leg. 26.

[65] Alfred B. Thomas printed this portion of the journey in the *Chronicles of Okla-*

June, 1793

14—I set out from St. Louis in a pirogue with four young men whom the commandant gave me,[65a] and [with] my two companions came from this place to sleep at San Carlos [St. Charles], a new establishment of about one hundred inhabitants. We made about 15 leagues. 15

15—I set out in the morning about 9 o'clock, accompanied by five traders with their pirogue, who were going to trade with our Indian friends. We traveled west. 3

16—We set out at 7 o'clock in the morning, and stopped to sleep at the stopping place that the Spaniards call the Ysla de Buen Hombre; and in the entire day we could not travel more than two leagues because of the strong currents that resulted from the rise of the river. 2

17—We again undertook the journey, and continued on a constant western course, and [the progress in this direction] lasted until August 24, during which time we suffered the same difficulties with the current, which did not permit us to make more than two or three leagues a day. In addition to these difficulties, there was also the necessary precaution that had to be taken to prevent discovery by the Osages. That nation is at war with most of those around it, and particularly with the Europeans of the settlements of Illinois, for which reason I could not cross the river immediately, and to make my way by land as I have been forewarned to do in my instructions. Instead, I found it necessary to ascend 160 leagues against the strong current of the Missouri River[66] from St. Louis to the Little Nemaha, where I arrived August 24. This is the general disembarkation point [rendezvous] for all the traders

*homa*, Vol. IX, No. 2 (June, 1931), using a copy in Historia, Vol. 43; our copy is from Provincias Internas, Vol. 102—a continuation of the one used on the outward trip. There is another copy in Historia, Vol. 62, and another in Provincias Internas, Vol. 183.

[65a] They were on the road 71 days, for an average daily journey of 2.3 leagues (6 miles); it is noteworthy that on the first day they seem to have made 15 leagues. Another question arises: Vial did not intend to go all the way in the boats; he wanted to turn off but did not do so for fear of the Osages; therefore, if the oarsmen were hired for only a couple of weeks (or, at most, a month), it was perhaps the most highly paid occupation in Louisiana.

[66] Near Nemaha, Nebraska, says Thomas. Thus they passed up the Kansas River to go farther north. Nemaha is in the southeastern corner of Nebraska, just off the Missouri—and they probably went that high to avoid the Osages.

who have business with the Pawnee [he says, "Panana"] nation,[67] in which they consider themselves safe from invasion by the Osages.

In this place we stayed until September 11, awaiting the Indians of the Pawnee nation who were to guide us to their village; we dispatched two men to advise them [of our readiness]. As soon as they received the news, they set out on the march and came to meet us.

September

12—We set out from the said Little Nemaha, accompanied by the Pawnees, and taking the road across a great prairie [*llanura*], course to the southwest. Having traveled four leagues, we halted on the bank of a river that discharges into the Little Nemaha. 4

13—From that stopping place we went on to sleep on the waters that drain into the Nemaha River [*a los agotaderos de dicho Río Nemaha*]. 6

14—We continued at 7 o'clock in the morning on the same route, and marched 7

15—Course to the west, we marched this day across plains and good lands. 7

16—On the same course, we marched 5

17—Across good prairie land on the same course, taking our siesta on a little stream that flows into the Kansas River.[68] We traveled this day 6

18—By the same course and over similar land, taking our siesta on an arm of the Kansas River;[69] we marched 5

19—Following the course and continuing across good land, we saw a hill of great height which the Indians call Blue Hill,[69a] and we slept on the banks of a small stream that flows into the Kansas, having traveled 4

[67] Though not all agree, *Pananas* usually is translated Pawnees. See Carroll and Haggard, *Three New Mexico Chronicles*, 196; Thomas, "The Massacre of the Villasur Expedition," *Nebraska History*, Vol. VII (1924), 68–81.

[68] The Big Blue River, says Thomas.

[69] The Republican River.

[69a] A letter from Charlotte B. Ross says that in the southwest corner of Mitchell County, extending north and west, there is a line of hills called the Blue Hills that appears quite blue from a distance, and that there was once a post office called Blue Hill. That area is some sixty miles southwest of Concordia, and is rough country, still unbroken and largely used for grazing.

20—On the same course and across similar land, we started the march at 6 o'clock in the morning, sending in advance one of the Indians with us to notify the chief called Sarisere, who came to meet us with other Indians at about 12 o'clock, and when we saw him coming we raised the flag, and he came to us with manifestations of rejoicing. Alighting, he kissed the flag, saying that he was very happy, that that [the flag] was the mantle of his father's heart. Afterward, he embraced us all with great affection. Then he took us to his village, at which we arrived about 3 o'clock in the afternoon, having traveled 5

21—We stayed in this town and were greatly entertained. This is a nation of good character, and, according to what I observed, they like the Spaniards a great deal. They make war against the Osages, the Taovayas, and the Comanches. Their allies and neighbors are three other villages of Pawnees, the Maha nation, the Otos, and the Kansas. This village must have about 300 warriors, while the other villages of Pawnees have 1,000 men, so that the entire nation comprises 1,300 men; those of their allies have about 1,100 members, and that of their enemies, the Osages, 1,000; that of the Taovayas about 400; and that of the Comanches, countless.

The Pawnees have their towns at a distance of 20 leagues, a little more or less, from one another; the Kansas are about 30 leagues away from them, the Otos about 50, various ones situated on the banks of the Platte River, which flows into the Missouri. The Osages are about 60 leagues to the east, located on the banks of the river of their own name, which also flows into the Missouri.

Having held a council, all being seated in a circle in the lodge of the chief, he arose with his pipe in his hand, telling me that he was very happy, that his heart was open to us, that he understood that I had come to open a road between the Spaniards who live in the west and those who live in the east, and he expressed great happiness that the road should be opened. [He said] that his father in the east had sent him a medal and a flag by a trader named Baudauin,[70] and he exclaimed, "Some day I shall go to become acquainted with my father who lives in the west; every day I tell my people that the Spaniards are good people, that if it were not for my father who sends us guns, powder,

[70] Juan Beaudouin was given a license by Trudeau to trade on the Missouri, August 1, 1792; Nasatir, *Before Lewis and Clark,* I, 162.

and balls, and other goods, our enemies would destroy us, and we would be slaves of the other Indians. Let the road be opened, that I may see a Spaniard coming from the west! Now they can go and come when they please. I will send with you two chiefs and some boys to go to see my father and to hear the words that will come from his good heart, that from there they [the chiefs] will go on to the Comanches to make peace, that there will be no more war."

We were in said village until October 3, and there we bought ten horses.

October

4—Before setting out, I regaled them with various items from those that I carried, and I set out from said village with seven of them, who accompanied me, and we stopped on the same river where they live.[71] The course was to the southwest, and we traveled 3

5—I continued the march across the prairie, and followed the same course, traveling 6

6—We continued on the same course, and stopped on a small stream. 7

7—We set out at 5:30 in the morning, following the same course, and crossed several arroyos of the same river, traveling 7

8—Across the prairie we marched on the same course. 6

9—The march was continued on the said course until [we reached] a running spring. There were traveled 7

10—The course was to the west, and we traveled until we reached a small stream that flows into the Kansas River. 7

11—The course was to the southwest. We traveled 7

12—On the same course across the prairie, we traveled 7½

13—The march was continued until we reached a small stream that flowed into the Río de Napestle.[72] 6

14—On the same course, we traveled to the Arkansas River.[73] 3

15—On the same course, we crossed the Concha River and stopped to sleep at the *torcido*. 5

16—We marched across good land on the said course, and slept at the Río Claro. 7

[71] The Smoky Hill River.

[72] Arkansas River.

[73] This apparently was near present Dodge City.

17—We set out in the morning on the said course, [across] good land, and stopped on the Río Salado, having traveled 7

18—On the said course [we traveled] to the Río Arenoso,[74] having traveled 6

19—We set out at 6 o'clock in the morning on said course, and slept on the banks of the same river. At midnight we were attacked by 56 warriors armed with 22 muskets, a blunderbuss, and the rest of them [with] lances and arrows. They beat my boys with cudgels, thinking we were Comanches, and for a little while did not fire their rifles.[75] They recognized our horses and made an outcry, and we awoke and seized our arms. Then the Indians with me told me not to fire at them, that they were their own people. There were two chiefs who then joined us and shook hands with me. One of them was displeased with the blows they had given my boys, and took a cudgel and beat those who had done it. Then, seating himself at my side, he told me it was fortunate they had discovered our horses, for if they had not, they would have killed us, thinking we were Comanches. I then took out four twists of tobacco and gave them to the chiefs to distribute to their people. The whole night was spent smoking and talking. The two chiefs who had come with me were displeased with the others because those others were going on campaign against the Comanches while the chiefs with me were going to make peace with them and to see their Spanish father. But the new chiefs answered that the Comanches had already killed their relatives.

At 8 o'clock in the morning of the 20th, those who had come with me, without saying a word, returned to their village, and left me with the new chiefs with whom they were displeased. These latter told me that my life was safe, that they would not kill us, and they asked me for powder, balls, and other goods, and when they received those, they left, leaving me alone with my two young men and one [Indian] who remained because he was eager to see his Spanish father and the Comanches, and even though they would kill him, he had to come. We

[74] Probably the North Canadian, says Thomas, near Dombey, Oklahoma.

[75] Thomas says, "for a short while they shot at us," but Provincias Internas 102 says, "*por poco no hacen una descargo.*" It makes a considerable difference, whether it is *no* or *nos*. Indian attacks were almost always sneak attacks, to do as much damage as possible before awakening the victims. Obviously also Vial and his men would not have slept through a volley of musket shots, then have awakened at an outcry.

left on the 21st, hiding ourselves in the cañadas, camping without wood or water. We traveled 8

22—On the same course and same river, we traveled 7

23—Along the said river and course, we traveled 6

24—Our course to the southwest, we encountered a medium-sized river,[76] which we followed, and stopped on its bank, having made 6

At midnight, Vicente Villanueva awoke me, telling me, "Look, here is a horse saddled; perhaps it is a Comanche coming to attack." At once I took my arms and, going out, recognized that it was one of mine. I reprimanded him for not having unsaddled it, but the young man told me, "I think the Indian may have saddled it to steal it." The Indian, pretending to sleep, simulated fear on awakening, asking, "What has happened?" To which I answered that I had found a horse of mine saddled, and he told me that he did not think so, that we were camped in a stopping place [burial ground] of the Comanches; that some of the dead must have saddled the horse; that in his dreams he had heard their whistling. He asked me for tobacco, and, raising his arm, said he was going to bury it to quiet the dead. We passed the rest of the night without sleep, taking care that our horses should not be run off, and at daybreak I sent him [the Indian] back to his village, giving him some small presents.

25—On said course and river, we continued the march to the head of the river, taking a direct road from there to the south across prairies in search of the Canadian [Vial says Colorado] River, and stopping on a plain without food or water. We traveled 8

26—On said course, we reached a small river, where we found good water and plenty of wood. We traveled 6

27—Course to the west. We arrived at the Canadian River, and along its banks we traveled[77] 6

28—Along the same river and course, we traveled 4

29—On the same course and along the same river we continued the march, and at a little distance we made out a hill to the south of the river that appeared to be Toconcari, and because the animals were very footsore, we did not go more than 4

30—We continued the same course along the same river, and traveled 5

[76] Beaver Creek.

[77] Near Magenta, Texas, according to Thomas.

31—The march was continued on the same course and along the same river, and we traveled 3

Having traveled this short distance, we stayed over to kill some buffaloes for food, until the morning of November 2.

November

2—By the same river and course, we arrived at a spot where we had been on the way out, having now made 4

3—On the same course and river, we made 3

4—On the same course, we continued as far as a mesa which was one league from the river. We traveled 4

5—Course to the south, leaving the river on the right. I recognized Tunconcaro,[78] and stopped at a distance of 5 leagues [from it], having traveled 7

6—We continued the march opposite Tucumcari, having traveled 5

7—Course to the west. We traveled among mesas and arroyos which lead to the Canadian River. We traveled 3

8—On the same course. It snowed on us as we went past the slopes of a mesa, and at the foot of a hill we stopped, and a Comanche Indian arrived, naked, without shoes and without arms, dying from cold, hunger, and thirst. I dressed him and gave him something to eat, and he came along in my company. We traveled today 3

9—On the same route, we climbed a mesa and had a view of the mountains of New Mexico. We stopped to camp on the Gallinas River, having traveled 5

10—On the same course along the road that the Comanches take when they come to trade, we arrived at a canyon with water. We traveled this day 5

11—We followed the same course to the Pecos River, having traveled 5

12—On the same route to the Palo Flechado, making 4

13—On the course mentioned to the town of Pecos. 4

14—We rested at said town.

15—At daybreak I continued the march to the town of Santa Fe, which I reached at nightfall, and where I presented myself to the governor, in whose hand I put a letter from the commandant of the detach-

[78] Tucumcari Peak in New Mexico.

ment of Illinois, and I gave him an account of all that had happened, delivering to him at the same time the diary that I made on the outward trip, during my stay there [in St. Louis], and on my return, as his lordship had ordered me. 9

480½

Santa Fe, November 16, 1793.

PEDRO VIAL [*rubric*][79]

Again Vial had capably demonstrated his competence with the savage Indians. He had been captured, and detained naked for six weeks by the Kansas; he had made a liaison with the Pawnees; he had lived through an attack by Pawnees; he had saved a Comanche from death.

His average daily travel distance, as usual, was low. From the time he left the village on the Nemaha, he traveled forty-eight days and covered 427 miles—about nine miles a day, and that under good conditions. After five months on the road, he signed his diary in Santa Fe with a firm signature that leaves no doubt concerning his familiarity with writing materials.

On December 4, 1793 (two weeks after Vial signed the diary), Concha wrote to Revillagigedo, saying:

> On November 16 Vial returned from his expedition that your Excellency was pleased to approve September 4 last year. It has appeared to me proper, in accord with my responsibility, to include to your Excellency, as I am doing, the diary formed by Vial himself, which contains the routes followed in going and returning.[80]

On the same day, Concha wrote to Nava, transmitting Vial's diary and a copy of the letter from the commandant at St. Louis. And now at long last we find that Vial had been asking something for himself: the rank of second *alférez*—an officer in the army somewhat similar to a second lieutenant. Obviously, then, Vial was no ordinary man, or he, an Indian interpreter and guide, would not have aspired to a commission that had to come from the king. He asked for the rank and

[79] Both Historia 43 and Historia 62 have the following certification: "It is a copy. Chihuahua, January 9, 1794. Manuel Merino. (rubric)."

[80] Concha to Revillagigedo, No. 36, Santa Fe, December 4, 1793; Provincias Internas, Vol. 102, f. 212. The answer is dated January 15, 1794, and accompanies the letter, f. 213: he has received Vial's diary and thanks him; the diary is f. 214–24.

salary, says Concha, and adds: "With it [the rank] and with his supernumerary[81] addition to this presidial company [of Santa Fe], he will find himself always in position to undertake new expeditions and services dictated by higher authority."[82]

We must have admiration for Concha, for he wasted no time going after the appointment that Vial apparently had long wanted. It is interesting to note that never does Concha say that Vial wanted it, has asked for it, or has complained because of not receiving it (as far as we know).

Nava answered promptly:

> With your official letter of the fourth of the last month, I have received the diary formed by Pedro Vial on his trip outgoing and on his return, from Santa Fe to St. Louis [and back to Santa Fe]. I am advised of the news that it contains, as well as that in the two copies that accompany it, and I will give an account of it all to his Majesty, recommending [Vial also for] the merit that he [Vial] showed previously [for his trip] from San Antonio to Santa Fe, and from there to Natchitoches and from there to San Antonio—for which give thanks to him, as you deem worthy, and for which I judge him equally worthy [*para que le dispense las gracias a que contempla V. S. acrehedor y de que yo le juzgo digno igualmente.*][83]

Nava also sent a copy of the diary to the viceroy, saying:

> I am remitting to your Excellency a copy of the diary that Pedro Vial kept on his round trip from the town of Santa Fe, capital of the province of New Mexico, to St. Louis, Illinois, which Colonel Fernando de la Concha, governor of [New Mexico], has addressed to me; in order that your Excellency may inform yourself of the events that occurred, of the intermediary nations, of the distance from one to the other point; he gives no description whatsoever of the country he traveled, and it is desirable that similar explorations be performed by persons of greater intelligence and broader interests.[84]

[81] Referring to an officer attached to a unit in which no vacancy exists.

[82] [Concha] to Nava, Santa Fe, December 4, 1793, New Mexican Archives, doc. 1268.

[83] Nava to Concha, Chihuahua, December 31, 1793, New Mexican Archives, doc. 1272, no. 1. Acknowledgment was made on January 29, and a copy of that is in Historia, Vol. 43, f. 209.

[84] Nava to Revillagigedo, January 9, 1794, Historia, Vol. 43; also Historia,

Nobody can be smaller than a man in high position. It is now apparent that Nava never had any intention of recommending Vial's appointment. He talked sweetly to Concha, but used a sharp knife when he wrote to the viceroy. One wonders why.

It seems an extremely ungracious thing for the great commandant-general to do to a man who had served Spain as well as had Pedro Vial; to a man who had opened the Santa Fe Trail, destined to become one of the great highways of the world; to a man who had finally connected the Interior Provinces of New Spain with the Illinois country and the province of Louisiana.

Vol. 62, f. 208 *et vo.* Revillagigedo acknowledged receipt of the diary January 29, 1794; Historia 62, f. 209.

A note on the margin of the diary sent on January 9 says: "This diary same as the former but because the translations of the original French in which its author Vial made it are different and vary somewhat, and also because the return diary is added, it is repeated here." It thus seems that Nava sent Revillagigedo two copies of the first diary.

# XV

## *"Arrest All Frenchmen"*

Even while Pedro Vial was in St. Louis, events that would affect him were building up in Spain, for revolutionary Frenchmen were at work in Philadelphia, in Charleston, in Kentucky, and in New Orleans, and when finally their activities became a matter of official knowledge in Madrid, a royal step was taken that was to result in the arrest of Frenchmen all over the Interior Provinces. The viceregal order, dated January 6, 1794, reached Chacón in early 1795 from Nava, the commandant-general of the Interior Provinces, and said that "Just reasons have obliged Viceroy Branciforte to take the serious step of ordering the arrest and imprisonment of all Frenchmen in the viceroyalty."[1]

The order was to be put in force January 15 to assure tranquillity, because, said Nava, some scattered Frenchmen were trying to disturb the peace. Therefore, Nava was adopting similar rules for the entire commandancy-general, and in a rather long document he laid down nine rules for enforcement of the order. No. 1 provided that one arrested for a grave crime or for suspicious conduct should be deprived of all communication, and his funds seized and impounded, and his real property likewise. Rule No. 2 seems to provide for solitary imprisonment. Rule No. 3, however, provided that they should not seize the property of those married to Spanish women, Indian women, or women who were partly colored, whether or not there were children; however,

[1] Nava to Chacón, very confidential, Chihuahua, January 6, 1795, New Mexican Archives doc. 1304. This was preceded by a letter from the viceroy to Nava concerning steps to be taken with the Frenchmen, December 10, 1794, A.G.I., Estado, México, leg. 18, p. 402.

inventories were to be made of property, and such property would be used to pay for the prisoners' sustenance until a further order.

Rule No. 4 provided that the judges of the various jurisdictions should make their returns within two days, and that the prisoners be secured in jail in the capital until further orders.

Rule No. 5 provided that the goods seized and impounded would go into a common fund in each province to reimburse all costs of maintenance and other necessary costs incurred by the French prisoners—and that order included impoundage of money. Furniture, merchandise, and clothing were to be sold at public auction at fair prices, and the proceeds put into the common fund, but the real property was not to be sold or destroyed until an order should be received from the king, but was to be entrusted to persons of known probity and good conscience. Under Rule No. 6, the partially exempted Frenchmen under Rule No. 3 were to be maintained from the common fund. Rule No. 7 exempted from arrest those publicly known to be of irreprehensible conduct—and their money was not to be sequestered; they were to be notified to keep themselves in a state of house arrest, and they would have to give surety for their persons and their goods.

Rule No. 8 provided exemption for those who were natives of Louisiana or Mobile (Vial, of course, was a native of Lyons); they would be expected to take oaths of vassalage to the Spanish king. However, in case some of those very Frenchmen might be suspicious in their conduct, all governors and intendants (under Rule No. 9) were to make lists of them, each one's name, class or rank, trade or employment status, town of birth, French province to which he belonged, the length of his stay in Mexico, how and with whom he came, and how he was making a living. Then Nava thoughtfully wrote to Godoy to advise him of the measures he had taken against the Frenchmen who lived under his command,[2] in view of the viceroy's order of December 10, 1794, and a few days later he advised the viceroy that in New Mexico two men had been arrested: Domingo Labadia and Pedro Laborra.[3]

On January 31 Nava sent orders to Chacón to thwart the Frenchmen and Americans who were trying to introduce into Spanish colonies

[2] Nava to Duke of Alcudia, February 5, 1795, A.G.I., Estado Mexico, leg. 18.

[3] Nava to Branciforte, February 23, 1795, A.G.I., Estado Mexico, leg. 18. Laborra had been a cook for Viceroy Bucareli (see Rydjord, *Foreign Interest*, 137).

a Philadelphia book—*Desengaño del Hombre (The Undeceiving of Man,* or *The Enlightenment of Man),* which was considered revolutionary and highly subversive[4]—to thwart the Frenchmen and Americans in their schemes to secure free navigation of the Mississippi and to seduce the Indians. Pedro Vial is mentioned in the letter from Nava to Chacón.

The real report on Vial, however, was made by Chacón on May 12 (in reply to Nava's order of January 6), when he said that the two Frenchmen who lived in his province had been confined. One, Domingo Labadia, was married to a Spanish woman; therefore, Chacón had merely inventoried his goods and ordered him to stay in confinement; Labadia had lived there many years. The other, Pedro Vial, said he was a native of Louisiana, and took an oath of faithfulness to the king of Spain, and was allowed to stay in his place of residence with "some of his children"; it seems, however, that Chacón had some doubts of Vial, for he said he had not found sufficient evidence of Vial's trustworthiness, and so precautions would have to be taken, and it seems that Vial had some horses that would have to be incarcerated in the public corral and fed in the morning and afternoon. The governor did take notice of the good services that Vial had rendered to his Majesty in New Mexico and Texas; he was, said Chacón, of equally good conduct, and of a disposition and aptitude for whatever he might be employed at.[5] Nava acknowledged that report without comment; he was more concerned over the Anglo-Americans' attempts to influence the Indian tribes on the frontier of New Mexico.[6]

Soon afterward, the viceroy ordered Nava to stop all foreigners' or suspicious persons' entry into New Mexico, Coahuila, and Texas, according to the royal order of February 13, 1795.[7] Again, three weeks later, Nava wrote to the governor:

> . . . Watch with most scrupulous care all persons who have passed

[4] Nava to Chacón, Chihuahua-Coahuila, January 31, 1795, New Mexican Archives, doc. 1309.

[5] Chacón to Nava, May 12, 1795, New Mexican Archives, doc. 1324.

[6] Nava to Governor, Chihuahua, June 20, 1795, New Mexican Archives, doc. 1329.

[7] Historia, Vol. 430; see Bolton, *Guide,* 58, nos. 8–10. The royal order of February 13, 1795, to keep foreigners out of the realm, is in f. 134ff. Correspondence about it to the Prince of Peace, 1795.

or may pass from the United States of America to this kingdom, because the king has well detailed news that they are going to send emissaries to subvert the inhabitants.

Carondelet has had to act hostilely against the greedy inhabitants of the western states, because of whom there have already been some internal disturbances in the province under his charge, caused by the many Negroes who live there, and even by the Louisianans themselves.

I order you to use great care . . . to prevent the entry into your province by way of the neighboring nations of any foreigner or person whatever who may be suspected . . . apprehend those who do come in, and keep them secured . . . and send me their (1) state [marital], (2) country, (3) religion, (4) motives and purposes with which they come into our territories, if others have accompaned them or if they have been assisted by vassals of the king, [and you will] gather papers found on them.

Although the American colonies are at a distance from that frontier, it is not difficult to open a passageway. If their establishments were farther from ours, you might consider the risk remote [but, since that is not so, you will consider the risk immediate].[8]

This seems to be the order used against Pike in 1807.

On August 6, 1795, Nava made a report to Spain, listing Frenchmen in Nueva Vizcaya, Sonora, Coahuila, Texas, and New Mexico—but in this one document where we would have a chance to learn something more about Pedro Vial, Vial is not listed at all. Nor is José Chalvert, who is to become increasingly important in connection with Vial. A good many names are listed from the other provinces, but not from New Mexico.[9]

On September 30 Nava's orders were renewed when he asked all subordinates to report on foreigners in June and December. He wanted to know about their conduct, and he reminded Chacón that "foreigners" included Frenchmen. The governor was also to find out, secretly if possible, if each person, regardless of his origin, class, etc., manifested adherence to the pernicious maxims of the system of liberty, equality, and lack of respect for the king.[10]

[8] Nava to Governor, Chihuahua, July 30, 1795, New Mexican Archives, doc. 1337.

[9] Report of Nava to Branciforte, August 6, 1795, A.G.I., Estado Mexico, leg. 18.

[10] Nava to Chacón, very confidential, Chihuahua, September 30, 1795, New Mexican Archives, doc.. 1344.

Finally, in November, Nava gave Chacón a clean bill of health for the Frenchmen arrested in New Mexico (who obviously do not include Labadia and Vial, for they were merely confined), saying that there was no suspicion against them, but that Chacón must take new declarations of their inclinations, maxims, and conduct. Chacón was then to free them, but they could not leave the province without previous permission from Nava, and they would have to report to the governor every six months.[11]

There does not seem to be much evidence that these extensive measures uncovered any subversion, although one reckless Frenchman had been so rash as to suggest that the Spanish king was a drunkard. However, the general confusion must have turned up more than one interesting document on Frenchmen—as, for instance, Nava's report to Alcudia answering a request for information.[12]

From among the Indian nations (perhaps in Texas), said Nava, they had taken one Juan Calbert (who must be José Chalvert). This man was a Presbyterian, twenty-eight years old. He had left Philadelphia six years before (in 1789), and had gone to Fort Pitt on the branch of the River Xayo (Ohio), then to Natchez, New Orleans, Natchitoches, and the villages of the Taovayas and Tawakonis, where he had lived fourteen months, hunting buffaloes and mustangs, and in *componentes* [repairing?] firearms, inasmuch as he was by trade an armorer and silver worker. Chalvert said there was no other colonist with the Indians, and Nava sent him to Coahuila.

Before the order for arrest was made in 1795, Nava had written to Chacón in regard to using Vial with the Pawnees:

> [This is in answer to No. 43, dated November 18. Our allies are the Comanches, the Utahs, the Navahos, and the Jicarilla Apaches.] It appears a good idea to me that at the instance of the chief of the former [the Comanches], you send Pedro Vial to treat for reconciliation and friendship with the Pawnee Indians, giving them some items to please their chief. I await news of the results [and] the diary that naturally the said Vial will deliver to you on his return to explain

[11] Nava to Chacón, Nov. 3, 1795, New Mexican Archives, doc. 1345. This same letter reveals that Vial was not to leave New Mexico without permission.

[12] Nava to Alcudia, No. 5, Chihuahua, November 3, 1795, A.G.I., Estado, Mexico, leg. 18.

the happenings of his trip and the details of the lands that he may pass over.[13]

Even though Chacón did not trust Vial and Nava did not like him, and Vial was confined to his home as of May 12, nevertheless, by the first of June or so he was sent to make a peace treaty with the Pawnees. Strange thing, to send a man you suspect of sympathizing with the enemy to one point in North America where he can do the most harm—for Nava was already worrying about the Anglo-Americans' disaffecting the Indians on the frontier. Nevertheless, on July 4, 1795, Trudeau reported to the governor of Louisiana:

> The one named Pedro Vial, who two years ago was commissioned by the governor of Santa Fe[14] to come to these establishments of Illinois, arrived this year (with four young men who accompanied him) as far as the Pawnee nation (commonly called republic) which has its village on the bank of the Kansas River. There he met our traders [that is, traders from St. Louis], with whom he remained fifteen days. He said that he came in order that the said Pawnee nation might make peace with the Laytanes [Comanches]. He delivered a medal, a complete suit of clothes, and other things to the chief. He caused peace to be made as he desired, conducting our traders as far as the Comanche nation. In proof of the intentions of the government of both provinces that the said Indians live in friendship, he desires to take our traders to Santa Fe, very near to which vicinity they had [already] arrived, but the latter refused because they did not want to abandon their [own] interests.
>
> The mentioned Vial said that he traveled from Santa Fe to the Pawnees in eight days; from that nation to St. Louis, the traders regularly arrived by water in ten days, which [makes me] infer that we are very close.[15]

[13] Nava to Chacón, Chihuahua, December 31, 1794, New Mexican Archives, doc. 1303A. A first reading of these letters indicates that Vial made a trip in late 1794, but further examination suggests that it was in the spring of 1795, for Chacón seems to have written to Nava on May 12, 1795, transmitting Vial's diary.

[14] He must have his time confused, for Vial had been in St. Louis until the middle of June, 1793.

[15] Trudeau to Carondelet, No. 229, St. Louis, July 4, 1795, Papeles de Cuba, leg. 22; printed in Nasatir, *Before Lewis and Clark*, I, 329–30. Interestingly enough, less than one year before, Las Casas, the captain-general at Havana, said sixty days were not enough for the trip, and that Carondelet's lesser estimate was an "enormous error"; Liljegren and Nasatir, "Minutas," 36–38.

That information on the short time needed for the trip between the two towns caused Carondelet considerable anxiety, as has been seen;[16] he acknowledged Trudeau's information on December 10,[17] but he was not able to convince the proper levels in Spain that there was danger.

Once again Vial, however, had done the job he had been sent to do.

In the meantime, Spanish officials since 1788 (starting with Ugarte) had been dabbling with the idea of opening a road from Tucson across the Gila River northwest and north to the Indian village of Zuñi, west and a little south of Santa Fe, with the idea of establishing a road between Tucson and Santa Fe. After considerable Indian-chasing by various units, starting in 1788, that journey finally was made in 1795, but nothing much came of it. Perhaps if Captain José de Zúñiga had gone on to Santa Fe and dramatized his trip a little, it might have stirred Chacón to some movements of his own in the opposite direction. Captain Zúñiga, in fact, was urged to go on from Zuñi to Santa Fe by a Franciscan friar at Zuñi, but he went back to Tucson instead, and the road had not been opened.[18]

There is at hand no record of Vial's activities immediately after that treaty of peace with the Pawnees, but it must have been the knowledge that he had always done a good job for Spain, plus the impoundment of his property, plus the added annoyance of having been often recommended for the position and pay of second *alférez* but never having received the appointment that impelled him to his next move: he got out of Santa Fe and left New Mexico to its own resources.

The first news we have of his flight is from a letter written by Chacón to Nava on November 18, 1797:

> Don Pedro Vial of the French nation, domiciled in this province as interpreter, and who was paid for his services at the time of the *alsamiento* of the Comanches, a wage of 6 *reales* daily, which was paid to him from the *ramo de aliados*, having sought a license in May to go to trap beaver on the Río Arriba, deserted with a servant of that

[16] Carondelet's estimate of its importance is shown by his letter to Trudeau, May 22, 1795, Papeles de Cuba, leg. 22; printed in Nasatir, *Before Lewis and Clark*, I, 325.

[17] Carondelet to Trudeau, New Orleans, December 10, 1795, Papeles de Cuba, leg. 22.

[18] George P. Hammond, ed., "The Zúñiga Journal, Tucson to Santa Fé," *New Mexico Historical Review*, Vol. VI, No. 1 (January, 1931), 40–65.

jurisdiction to the Gentile nations, and on passing through the Comanche nation, bartered a musket and some burros that he had, for horses, according to the story of said Comanches; in view of which, I hope your Excellency will tell me, in case of his return: must his wages be continued, and [also] those that he may have lost?

Meanwhile, with respect to the debts that he has left, I have ordered that the house and various effects that he left in it be inventoried, without proceeding to the satisfaction of said debts, in the meantime, [because] the creditors have not presented documents to substantiate them, and I await [*saber*] your final judgment.[19]

There is one more possible mention of Vial in a letter of the same date, Chacón to Nava, when two Spaniards, one from Guadalajara and the other from Vera Cruz, reported that they had worked for a Frenchman trading among the Indian nations, that one band of Indians had attacked the company to rob it; the two Spaniards had fled to the Comanches. Vial is not named, nor is there any hint concerning his fate.[20]

Vial's name is not very prominent for the next few years, although he is mentioned by Commandant De Blanc at Natchitoches in a letter to Carondelet on February 22, 1796, when De Blanc speaks of him as "the one named Pierre Vial dit Manitou."[21]

In 1799 Vial was listed as a resident of Portage des Sioux,[22] and in 1801 a Pierre Vial was at Florissant.[23]

Concerning Vial's residence in Louisiana during these later years, an interesting series of letters has turned up in the Papeles de Cuba. The first is from François Vallée, the commandant at St. Geneviève, saying, "Send a request considering the seizure demanded by Joseph Robidoux

[19] Chacón to Nava, No. 219, Santa Fe, November 18, 1797, New Mexican Archives, doc. 1404.

[20] [Chacon] to Nava, No. 220, Santa Fe, November 18, 1797, New Mexican Archives, doc. 1404.

[21] De Blanc to Carondelet, Natchitoches, February 22, 1796; Papeles de Cuba, leg. 2364; printed in Nasatir, *Before Lewis and Clark*, I, 365. *Manitou* is a Chippewa Indian word rather widely used for a time in the West; it means devil, or great spirit—and again we have a mystery about Vial. Why was he called Manitou? Because of his age or appearance, or his uncanny way of getting along with the Indians? Or was it something we have not guessed?

[22] Houck, *History of Missouri*, II, 90; Portage des Sioux was established in 1799 between the Missouri and the Mississippi, north of St. Louis.

[23] *Ibid.*, II, 69.

against Sieur Pierre Vial dit Manitoux."[24] The second is from Vallée to Delassus at St. Louis, July 25, 1800, sending the declaration of Pierre Vial dit Manitoux and [one other] concerning discoveries they have made after several months of search for lead mines near La Côte de Cedres about six leagues from Mine à Breton and one and one-half leagues from the road to Mine à Breton. "The discovery," says Vallée, "will be fortunate for inhabitants of this post. You will grant them a quantity of land that you judge reasonable for the discovery and exploitation of lead."[25]

The others are from the second Vallée letterbook, and the first is from Vallée to Don Ramón de López y Angulo, the intendant at New Orleans, in January, 1800, concerning the request of Pierre Vial and La Breche concerning the discovery of new lead mines. "I have sent a copy of the request to the lieutenant-governor," said Vallée, "who returned it to me to be transmitted to you."[26] The routing of the request indicates that it probably was granted. Then on May 18, 1801, Vallée wrote to Camille Delassus (not the governor), saying that "Stone, an American, assassinated a man named O'Connor at the Mine à Manitou. If he is in your district, conduct him under guard."[27] On May 25 he wrote to Carlos Delassus, saying that in the murder committed at Mine aux Cedres by Stone, there are implications that Sieur Baker was involved. He asks for instructions in the case and requests that Moro, Angulo's warehouseman, act as clerk. This letter was followed the next day by a decree that Abraham Baker come immediately to St. Geneviève to testify at the trial over the deceased O'Connor.[28] On the same day (May 26), Vallée wrote to Pierre Vial, saying: "On account of the

[24] Francois Vallée to Louis Rancour, St. Geneviève, December 23, 1799, Letterbook of Francois Vallée, in Papeles de Cuba, leg. 217.

[25] Vallée to Delassus, St. Geneviève, No. 10, July 25, 1800, Papeles de Cuba, leg. 217.

[26] Vallée to Don Rámon López de Angulo, St. Geneviève, January 10, 1800, Second Vallée Letterbook, entitled "Suite du Carnet pr Enregistre les offices de l'année 1800," in Papeles de Cuba, leg. 217.

[27] Vallée to Camille Delassus, St. Geneviève, May 18, 1801, Second Vallée Letterbook, in Papeles de Cuba, leg. 217.

[28] Vallée to [Carlos] Delassus, St. Genevieve, No. 50, May 25, 1801, Second Vallée Letterbook, in Papeles de Cuba, leg. 217. Followed by a decree of May 26, 1801, relating to Abraham Baker.

murder of O'Connor, you will make an exact note of all belonging to O'Connor."[29]

From this series of letters it may be seen that Pedro Vial was in the St. Geneviève area for two years at least, that he found and operated a lead mine, and that he was a man of some standing in the eyes of the commandant, François Vallée.

In New Mexico during those years, they were still sending out men to the plains between Santa Fe and the Missouri River, and in 1800 Chacón reported such an expedition to Nava:

> On the eighth of the present month [June], Josef Miguel Zenguaras, the interpreter in three languages, left with a passport and corresponding instructions and with two Indians from Taos and four halfbreeds [*genízaros*] from the same jurisdiction, to examine the territory that is between this province and the Missouri River.
>
> The head genísaro, who claimed to have accomplished this expedition [previously], having become ill, and, not finding anyone who dared to make such a long and dangerous journey, I offered to reward those who dared to do it, with which stimulus the six individuals cited above enlisted and were given at the expense of the king, without responsibility [for their return], two horses each, a carbine, three packages of the same, a cartridge box, a hat, and the supply of provisions that two mules could carry, which, upon the conclusion of the journey, should also remain in possession of the six, assigning a similar ration to some of their wives.
>
> The interpreter was given full permission to give gifts to the Gentile nations that he might meet on his trip, and to pass through poor [line illegible] carmine, *azarcon* [red lead], and tobacco, a dagger and one [illegible] for the happening, and besides a flag, a cross of Burgundy painted blue because the color red is a sign of war among the Indian savages.[30]

The price of exploring parties had gone up; for some twenty-four days on that dangerous journey, the *genízaros* (and their wives) were handsomely paid. One wonders if Chacón gave a thought to Pedro Vial, who had always worked for six reales a day, and who had been denied a minor appointment in the army.

[29] Vallée to Pierre Vial, St. Geneviève, May 26, 1801, Second Vallée Letterbook, in Papeles de Cuba, leg. 217.

[30] Chacón to Nava, June 10, 1800, New Mexican Archives, doc. 1490.

(Actually, in 1795 the general situation of the Frenchmen in New Spain had already been reversed, for in 1795 Spain and France signed the Treaty of Basel and became allies; then in October, 1796, Spain and England went to war, and the pressure against Frenchmen underwent considerable easement.)

In April, 1802, Nava published the royal decree of indulgence to deserters from the army, following a royal decree of the previous year. Nava says that in accordance with the royal order of April 30, 1801,[31] one who has deserted from the army will be forgiven under certain conditions.

It does not seem likely that the decree had any direct effect on Pedro Vial, for he seems to have been a civilian employee of the government, and was under a cloud only because of his nationality. It seems, however, very likely that this decree may have, by implication, further softened the Spanish attitude toward Frenchman. At any rate, the word got back to St. Louis that Vial would not be unwelcome in Santa Fe, and he returned to the town that he knew so well. The first knowledge of that return comes from Nava:

> In view of the *instancia* of Don Pedro Vial, I have resolved that from July 4 of last year [1803], when he presented himself to you, according to the account you give in official letter No. 38 of November 18, *se la asuta* with the assigned daily wage of 6 *reales* which this superior authority has assigned in remuneration for his merit in having brought about the pacification of the Comanche nation and of that which he contacted on the trips from Bexar to your capital, from that capital to Natchitoches, St. Louis, Illinois, and to other distances through lands inhabited by that tribe, the Comanches, and other friendly Indians.
>
> Charging it to the account of costs that are occasioned by the Indian allies. . . .
>
> Nothing has been decided here [in regard to] Vial upon the application of his goods, of which you accompany an inventory [with your letters], to the payment of the creditors whom he left . . . but if anything occurs to you upon this point, you will do it, administering justice in whatever you do.[32]

[31] Royal decree, Aránjuez, April 27, 1801, New Mexican Archives, doc. 1595. This is the date of the royal order, but it was not published by Nava until the following year. The document itself is no longer in the New Mexican Archives.

Obviously Vial asked for his interpreter's pay from the day he returned—and got it; but it sounds as if he applied for release of his property to pay his debts (or at least with that excuse), but the commandant-general passed responsibility for the decision back to the governor.

In March, then, Chacón reported:

> In obedience to your Excellency's order of January 19, I am arranging to assist Don Pedro Vial with the assignment of 6 *reales* daily, which he had previously had assigned by your authority in consideration for the merits contracted in this province and that of Texas, charging the total to the expenses of war and peace, as was done before his last absence.[33]

As might be anticipated, it would not be that easy in official circles, for Chacón felt called on to explain it to Salcedo, who by that time was commandant-general:

> I am sending an account of expenses pertaining to the objects of war and peace in this province to the end of October (a short period of this year)—and to support the said expenses in the subsequent year, I am of the opinion that the sum of 4,000 pesos will be necessary because of the extraordinary expenses which my successor is bound to have on his entry upon his duties because of the Gentile nations that will gather at the capital on the pretext of meeting him; for which reason the fund is overdrawn, as a result of the excessive costs occasioned in the discovery of the Hill of Gold, a greater gathering of allied nations, gifts of the auxiliaries of this class after discontinuance of their campaigns, and the back pay of Don Pedro Vial.[34]

Certain activities of the Indians during July may offer a reason for the commandant-general's conceding back pay, for it seems very likely

[32] Nava to Governor, Chihuahua, January 19, 1804, New Mexican Archives, doc. 1705. Twitchell credits this document to Salcedo, but this is an original signed by Nava. Theoretically Nava's incumbency ended in September or soon thereafter, 1802; Salcedo followed him, then was recalled to Spain and succeeded by Pedro Grimarest; Salcedo was back in 1806. It is difficult to be sure.

[33] [Chacón] to Salcedo, No. 66, Santa Fe, March 28, 1804, New Mexican Archives, doc. 1714.

[34] [Chacón] to Salcedo, No. 135, Santa Fe, November 13, 1804, New Mexican Archives, doc. 1771.

that Vial was prominent in those activities. They are shown in an extract of news:

> July. The 7th, there entered this capital 8 chiefs, 2 warriors, and 5 women from the Comanche nation with news that on the 10th there would arrive the ransom [party?] at the pueblo of Taos to the number of 7 [or 10] lodges, and although they encountered the Pawnees, who are their mortal enemies, they conducted themselves with the best harmony in accord with the warning that had been given them upon the matter in regard [not only to the Pawnees but also] to all the different nations that frequent this capital.
>
> 8th—The alcalde of Taos informed [this office] of the arrival there of 40 persons, men and women of the Nations of the North, with goods for barter, soliciting *frenos*, axes, and tobacco [*tobacho-punche*].
>
> 14th—There arrived here a general of the Comanche nation, with 8 chiefs, 68 warriors, and 6 women. They came to make a campaign against the Kiowas and the Aas, in which they had been employed for 96 days without being able to meet their enemies.
>
> August 13—The alcalde of Taos informed this office of the arrival of interpreter Joseph Mirabel, who went to seek out the Pawnee Indians as far as the Arkansas River, [but] with nothing happening, he having enjoyed on his return a fine buffalo-hunt, with [the results of] which the entire escort supplied itself.
>
> 22—There arrived here the Comanche chief Cuernoverde,[35] alias El Caricortado, with 5 chiefs,—warriors, and 3 women from the Comanches, to explain what had occurred in the discovery of the Hill of Gold.[36]

And Vial was soon to go on another expedition.

[35] Not, of course, the original Cuerno Verde—who had been killed by Anza's forces.

[36] Santa Fe, August 29, 1803, New Mexican Archives, doc. 1673.

# XVI
## *Expeditions to the Pawnees, 1804, 1805, and 1806*

Carlos du Hault de Lassus had become the commandant at St. Louis, succeeding Trudeau, in 1799, and he was the last Spanish commander at St. Louis. During his commandancy (1799–1804) Spain was threatened in Louisiana by the British on the north, and by the Americans—who presented a constant threat to Santa Fe—from the east. It was generally believed that the Missouri arose in the mountains somewhere near Santa Fe, and naturally it was understood that, if so, the Missouri River constituted a highway from St. Louis to Santa Fe—one that the Americans were sure to discover sooner or later. That was De Lassus' biggest apprehension, and certainly it was not relieved by the activities of men such as Metoyer, Lalande, Durocher, and D'Eglise—all hunters and traders who wanted to get to Santa Fe with its traditional wealth of gold, silver, and furs, and its well-known desire for goods. Nor were the apprehensions of the Spaniards in the Interior Provinces relieved when the Americans took over Louisiana, for the Americans were attracted to New Mexico by the thought of commerce and profit just as, earlier, the Frenchmen had been.

On April 5, 1803, De Lassus asked Régis Loisel to give him the benefit of the knowledge he had gained on his last voyage on the upper Missouri, and in 1804 Loisel made the report, in which he said that it was possible to travel by water from Hudson's Bay to the mountains of Santa Fe, with the exception of a one-half-league portage between the James (or Dakota) River and the Cheyenne River. Loisel observed that the Platte River arose west of Santa Fe but that it was not navigable; however, he said, it was not needed because overland transportation was easy and the distance was short. He noted also that one might ascend the Missouri and the Yellowstone, which latter arose in the farthest west mountains of New Mexico, and thus impliedly reach Santa Fe. In all, then, Loisel, mentioned at least four different routes to Santa Fe—all of which, it seems from his words, offered feasible access to the wealth of New Mexico and northern Mexico.[1]

Such reports caused grave apprehension among the officials in New Spain—the commandant at St. Louis, the governor at New Orleans, the governor at Santa Fe, the commandant-general at Chihuahua, the captain-general at Havana, and the viceroy in Mexico City—and they dutifully informed one another of the threats. Reports went back to Spain, and each official in New Spain waited for higher authority to take cognizance of the problem and to issue orders to cope with it.

On August 10, 1804, De Lassus wrote the governor of Louisiana, Casa Calvo, saying that Baptiste Lalande and Jeanne Metoyer were to meet Gervais [Chalvert] at the Pawnee village, and that Laurenzo Durocher had left St. Louis to make the same trip—for the destination was Santa Fe, and Gervais, whom they were to meet in the Pawnee village, was to conduct them there. Durocher, said De Lassus, though somewhat old, knew a little about the route.[2] (Nuttall points out[3] that perhaps the man they were to meet was really Vial, because De Lassus said Gervais had conducted some Pawnees to Santa Fe to meet the governor in 1803 and again in the spring of 1804—and these activities are consistent with Vial's usual movements. Nuttall points out also that Durocher was in Santa Fe as early as May 22, 1804, whereas Chalvert did not arrive in Santa Fe until June 20, 1804.)

It is definite that Vial made a trip to the Pawnees in 1804, for Salcedo reported to the viceroy:

> Since last May [May, 1804] I was informed . . . I ordered the governor to supply an explanation. . . .
>
> [He] has just notified me of the effects of the expedition that I arranged for and that I put in charge of Don Pedro Vial, and both

[1] Loisel's report, dated at St. Louis, May 28, 1804, is in Papeles de Cuba, leg. 2368. It is printed in Nasatir, *Before Lewis and Clark*, II, 735–40.

[2] De Lassus to Casa Calvo, St. Louis, August 10, 1804, Papeles de Cuba, leg. 141; printed in Nasatir, *Before Lewis and Clark*, II, 742–45.

[3] Nuttall, "The American Threat to New Mexico, 1804–1822," 54.

by the official letter with which he enclosed the respective diary and a report from Vial himself, . . .[4]

In June of the following year (1805), Vial was sent to Taos to bring back two Frenchmen and an American carpenter.[5] These two Frenchmen might have been Lacroix and Terien, and the American surely was James Purcell.

On the same date, Alencaster told more about the Frenchmen, the Cuampe chiefs, and another Frenchman:

> On the fourth of last month, there were presented to me with the interpreter, Don Pedro Vial, whom I commissioned to conduct them from Taos, the two Cuampe chiefs, two Frenchmen from Louisiana, and an American. These latter said they left St. Louis, Illinois, June 8 of last year with their proprietor, Mr. Lauselle [Loisel],[6] as far as the establishment that he had among several nations, with the license of the governor, where they were until they left their proprietor with the effects that he furnished them so that they could infiltrate the country to barter for beaver skins in said nations, and they joined one who went out at the time as they from said house [or fort] called *de la cuente azul;* that three months and a half later they separated, going to trap furs on the Platte River, and, being at the head of said river, the Kiowas attacked and captured them, despoiling them of all they had under the pretext of leaving them empty handed [so that other tribes would not kill them]. With those [Kiowas] they were two months, and left, returning to sustain themselves by fishing in said river, and after ten days they were made prisoners a second time by the Kiowas, from whom they escaped after nine days, fearful that [the Kiowas] were going to kill them, and in the flight they were

[4] Salcedo to Yturrigaray, Chihuahua, January 23, 1805, Provincias Internas, Vol. 200, f. 308–10. Vial made the trip in 1804, but the diary and report have not turned up.

Vial also apparently made a trip to the Pawnees in 1794, according to document 1303a in the New Mexican Archives, Nava to Chacón, December 31, 1794, mentioning the trip; and document 1329 (1) in the New Mexican Archives, Nava to Chacón, June 20, 1795, Vial's diary transmitted. The diary itself is not in evidence.

[5] Alencaster to Salcedo, October 13, 1805 (enclosure in No. 156, Santa Fe, November 20, 1805), New Mexican Archives, doc. 1900.

[6] Régis Loisel of St. Louis (who made the report to De Lassus also) was a man prominent in the fur trade on the Upper Missouri, sometimes in partnership with Jacques Clamorgan. See Pierre-Antoine Tabeau, *Narrative of Loisel's Expedition* (Annie Heloise Abel, ed.), Introduction.

assisted by the Cuampes, with whom they have remained until now, being well treated by that band, which at various times wanted to go in search of the Kiowas to take vengeance for the Frenchmen, but they [the Frenchmen and the American] persuaded them not to do it.

Said Frenchmen did not have a passport because, they say, the one their proprietor had when he sent them to trade for beaver, he did not give to them, and that they [the two Frenchmen], finding themselves already well treated as captives, and being poor and without means to return directly to their country, and [finding themselves] close to this province, took great pains to show the Cuampes the good treatment of the Spaniards, their good faith and generosity, so much so that they resolved to bring them to Taos, assisting them with horses and whatever else was necessary with the object of seeing if they could relieve their poverty, and already, it may be, to establish themselves in this province, or to enjoy favorable *cuyuntura* to return to their country.

The Cuampe chiefs say that a short time ago they had an establishment in the vicinity of one branch of the Platte River, about 40 leagues from the Arkansas River and a little less from Taos; they say that the object of their coming is to ask for peace, alliance, and commerce with this province and the Spanish nation, as they have had it with Louisiana, and that they ask for said peace also in the name of the Sayenas [Cheyennes] and the Aas [Caddos], two tribes with whom they are allied; and that likewise they have come, wishing the Spaniards to treat and trade with them; to which I answered them that while awaiting your Excellency's opinion, there would be no difficulty in extending the peace that those three nations asked for, under the same conditions as that extended to others; but that for trade or commerce as the other allies had it, they would have to come to the villages assigned at the proper times to carry it out; and when they insisted that there should be some Spaniards sent to their country [to trade]. I told them, exaggerating a little, that it was a great favor granted them in [allowing] Pedro Vial to accompany them, along with a resident of Taos; and the Indian war chief, who in similar cases has gone out to accompany them so that he might obtain for me certain important information upon the condition and situation of said nations, their number, and other official [information], made known to them that to treat for peace it is necessary that the general or chiefs of each nation come [to Santa Fe] and comply with the customary procedure.

This tribe does not know this province nor has peace with it nor makes war on it, and its commerce seems confined to skins of buffalo, bear, beaver, elk, and antelope in some abundance.

Within twenty-four hours of having presented themselves to me, the Cuampes, on their second conference, asked me by signs to *los vistiese* [to dress them or give them clothing] as [we had] other tribes; and although I had not intended to do so, they were made to understand by the interpreter that it was a particular favor to do it on this occasion, and I ordered that they be clothed before setting out on their trip on the sixth, giving them tobacco which they had also requested, and a package of cartridges for the two; whose cost, and that of their maintenance and food for their trip, I believe ought to be charged to the [Indian] allies' fund if your Excellency does not order me otherwise.

The said Cuampes have shown joy and great satisfaction always when they have talked with me, especially when I have ordered them clothed. They brought a paper of the year 1794 from the commandant of St. Louis, Trudeau, which exhorted all the Indian allies to keep the peace, and one of the chiefs had a silver medal with the bust of Charles III, and on the reverse the inscription, "Of excellent merit," under a warrant given by the said commandant.

I have not sent you this by express; I believe you will approve my holding it until this [regular] mail, and it appears to me in any event to tell your Excellency that if I do not receive an extraordinary message with an order to the contrary, presently, when the leading men of said nations—the Cuampes, Cheyennes, and Aas—present themselves, I shall make peace with them on the same terms that are agreed on with the other Gentile nations, giving your approbation in consideration of that, according to the wishes that they imparted to me, I shall [be able to] persuade them that they should not wait until September to present themselves to me.

The interpreter Vial and the others who accompany him will be here before the tenth [or the first], and if the news that he gives me should indicate any extraordinary mail, I shall dispatch it to your Excellency, suspending the peace conference, even if they make difficulty, until [I receive] your decision.

The destitute Frenchmen, by way of gratitude, accompanied the Cuampes with Vial to re-establish themselves [to earn some of their keep?] Those and the American who presented themselves to me destitute, I have assisted meagerly with food and with a minimum of clothing, [and] I resolved to endure this small cost in honor of the good name of the nation, until with their work they can support themselves; but if your Excellency thinks it just to charge this cost to the royal treasury, you will so advise me, and it will turn out that a governor obliged to give alms will not find it necessary to repeat it under similar conditions.[7]

On September 9 the commandant-general answered:

. . . To avoid losing time, I advise you to take the most effective steps to strengthen the friendship with the Pawnee nation and to make friends with the Otos and Lobos, as well as any other nations located in the vicinity of the Rivers Missouri, Kansas, Platte, and Napeste or Arkansas; to do this, it is best—as a most powerful attraction—to court them on our part to incline the chiefs to concur frequently in your capital [Santa Fe], and have our interpreters do the same in their villages, imposing upon them the good faith that they have to observe so that there be no resentment or motive that may dissuade them from cultivating their inclination toward us.

If in the time that you have had [to observe] the new interpreter to the Pawnees, José Calvert, he has been of good conduct, truth, and desirous of giving proof of his usefulness, I consider it proper that, taking advantages of the present season, in which the Indians return from the hunt, you will advise him to go to the country of the Pawnees, carrying some small presents for the chiefs, and that he should make them understand that some matters of importance have occurred and should be treated, and you want them to present themselves in that town [Santa Fe], where by means of your assistance and the honor that you have resolved to do them, you will give them a new proof of the affection that they owe you, and that in case they do assemble in your town, you proceed only to implant in their minds a horror of the English and Americans, and also persuade them to openly rupture communication with them, in the view that they [the English and Americans] have no other views than to root them out of their lands in order to take possession of them.[8]

In the following month (October), Alencaster tried to straighten out his accounts:

[7] Alencaster to Commandant-General, No. 39, Santa Fe, July 1, 1805; Guerra y Marina, leg. 1787–1807, exp. 15 (Library of Congress copy).

[8] Salcedo to Governor, Chihuahua, September 9, 1805, Guerra y Marina, leg. 1787–1807, exp. 15 (Library of Congress copy).

. . . I am advised that in the case of the treating for peace with the Cuampes, Sayenas, and Aas, I ought to charge the cost of clothing the two Cuampe chiefs to the fund of peace and war.

The American and the two Frenchmen who accompanied the chiefs are living here; the first has not been able to work at his trade of carpentry until the first part of September, because of suffering from the measles and indisposition that attacked him, and his intention is to work until he can satisfy what I have spent on *erramientas* and costs since September 1 for his maintenance and subsistence, and to have some money together to take whatever direction suits him, which I do not find inconvenient if it meets your approval; the expenses that he has caused are 18 pesos and *reales* in an outfit of jacket, waistcoat, long pants, hat, shoes, and two shirts, and in his maintenance and assistance in illness, 9 pesos.

The two Frenchmen have incurred each one the same expense for clothing, and only 10 pesos in maintenance of both until the end of August. They have no other trade than fur-hunting and beaver-trapping—for which they lack traps, and wish therefore to leave this province with the Cuampes for their own country on the first occasion—which I am thinking of permitting.

The 75 pesos of expense indicated in helping the three men, which [expense] now has ceased, I shall not charge to the account of peace and war without obtaining your approval, unless the case should arise—which is possible—of forming [balancing?] the fund for this year, without having obtained it [your approval].[9]

Salcedo took up the matter of the charge in November:

As only in the case of treating them as criminals would there be a just reason for which the royal treasury should suffer the expenses that you tell me have originated in your official letter No. 87 of last October 2, I do not find it proper that you should charge them to the account of war and peace of that province, and under this concept, the said foreigners must reimburse [you for] the expenses, as fast as they acquire means of doing so, according to the occupations that they might take up in order to subsist.[10]

[9] Alencaster to Commandant-General, No. 87, Santa Fe, October 2, 1805, Guerra y Marina, leg. 1787–1807, exp. 15 (Library of Congress copy). We get only seventy-three pesos out of this.

[10] Salcedo to Governor, Chihuahua, November 14, 1805, Guerra y Marina, leg. 1787–1807, exp. 15 (Library of Congress copy).

On October 11 Alencaster mentioned Pedro Vial, though briefly:

. . . The attached map that I have received, exhibits the most useful information, and this conforms with an old one that we have here and the news that I have obtained from Don Pedro Vial.[11]

On the same date, Alencaster proposed an expedition to the Pawnees. It was by no means the first; it was not even the first for Vial—but it would be the first in force since, perhaps, that of Villasur in 1720:

In accordance with your letters, I shall always treat the Indian nations that inhabit the borders of the Missouri River from its confluence with the Platte to the west with the greatest respect whenever they present themselves in this capital, and I consider it advantageous to order Don Pedro Vial and the interpreter José Chalvet [Chalvert] with two carabineers and 50 armed men with a convoy to leave on the 14th next, and go to look for the Pawnees; and find them, they expect, at the head of the Kansas River between it and the Arkansas; to investigate, if they [the Pawnees] are not on the way to this capital, the cause or reason that they have for not coming this year and acquiring the interesting information, and informing me through the medium of the carabineers and men, who are to be returned in November; and Vial and Chalvert remain to spend the winter with the said Pawnees in order to inform themselves well of the progress of the Anglo-Americans in Missouri, especially in the spring, in which season they will work united or divided in attracting to our friendship the Lobos and others, and any other faction or tribe that seems amenable, and in good season to come with chiefs from all of them to this capital.

If, on the way, they encounter the Pawnees on the way to this capital, they will return [there] with them, and upon their return [the Pawnees' return to their own home], they will accompany them for the purposes expressed. If interesting news occurs in the winter, I shall have communications that Vial will send me through the medium of a party of Pawnees.

Vial goes forwarned that if he considers it necessary, after winter [is over], that he order Chalvert to come with the Pawnees and even with those from the other nation or nations, so that he can remain, going into the interior both to acquire the friendship of the others

[11] Alencaster to Commandant-General, No. 94, Santa Fe, October 11, 1805, Guerra y Marina, leg. 1787–1807, exp. 15 (Library of Congress copy).

and to approach those nearest the Missouri and inspect the condition and progress of Captain Merri's expedition [the expedition of Meriwether Lewis and William Clark], and also to see if he can influence in any way against them, and their conclusion, succeeding wholly or in part in the plan and undertaking that your Excellency suggests to me in the fourth paragraph, especially at its conclusion, of the official letter of the cited September 9, a point that I very much recommend to Vial and Chalvert.

I have also interested them in painstakingly convincing the Indians of the ideas that the Anglo-Americans have in acquiring their friendship, and that they [the Indians] will be immediately rejected from the Missouri within a short time after being entertained by them [the Americans].

Although Chalvert has a special influence over the Pawnees, and surely is the one who persuaded them not to accept the friendship of the Anglo-Americans to whom, although having been called, he [Chalvert] refused to present himself. He does not have all the talent and disposition, or the knowledge that the elder Vial [*el viejo Vial*] has to treat with and take advantage of the different nations that interest us; because of this, I considered it advisable that the two go, considering that at some time it will be very essential that we have a spy among the Pawnees or other nations.

The aforementioned carry a modest gift in order to make use of everything advantageously and usefully.

It appears to me that it would be advisable for your Excellency to ask Mexico for half a dozen seven- or eight-ounce silver medals with the busts of our sovereigns, similar to the plate of the Guide of the Strangers, and on the other side a border of laurel and some other adornment, with an inscription for merit; and two dozen similar medals, also of silver, with the weight of one and one-half ounces and proportionate size; and also a dozen walking canes with large silver heads, with stems of little worth, or an imitation of these, and good tips, similar to the medals and walking canes that the Americans have started to give them.

I shall take pains to see that the instructions they carry are complete.

On this occasion, Durocher and Lalande leave for their country, and the other two Frenchmen also go back, each with ideas of returning [here], and those who accomplish it will be able to give me interesting news.

I have received, through the retired sergeant, Tomás Ortíz, the merchandise that is comprised in the memorandum that your Excellency was kind enough to enclose, and I shall take into consideration in the expense account of peace and war the 460 pesos, 7 *reales* of its total amount, including the 50 pesos supplied to Durocher and Lalande, in order to reimburse that treasury.[12]

Salcedo acknowledged that letter within two weeks: "I believe that step good and opportune. I have sent the letter to the viceroy to obtain medals that you request for distribution among the nations."[13]

The expedition to the Pawnees left on October 20, and on October 24 Alencaster notified Salcedo that it had gone, that Vial and Chalvert were to winter with the Pawnees, to learn what they could about Lewis and Clark.[14] He had already issued instructions to Vial:

> Instructions to which Don Pedro Vial and the interpreter José Chalvert of the Pawnee Nation, Otos, Lobos, and any others of those located in the environs of the Rivers Missouri, Kansas, Platte, and Arkansas must conform to acquire news and knowledge of the state of Captain Merri's expedition on the Missouri River and the trade and commerce of the nations located on it with the Anglo-Americans.
>
> 1. Juan Lucero and Francisco García and fifty residents and half-breeds [*genízaros*] will leave this province through Taos with two carabineers from this presidial company, armed, supplied with ammunition, and provisioned, three animals each; also the former French residents from St. Louis, Illinois: Lorenzo Durocher, Juan Bautista Lalande, Dionisio Lacroix, and Andrés Terrien,[15] will accompany them; the necessary supply of provisions will be delivered and taken, and all will acknowledge him [Vial] as chief of the expedition, but in the case of an attack or danger of attack, he shall proceed in agreement with the two carabineers, and the action will be commanded by the oldest one as a man of known spirit and proven intelligence in war.
>
> 2. It will go past the Arkansas River toward Nogales and the upper part of the Kansas River in search of the Pawnees, continuing until he finds them, and he will gain the indicated lands, and as soon

[12] Alencaster to Commandant-General, No. 95, Santa Fe, October 11, 1805, Guerra y Marina, leg. 1787–1807, exp. 15. (Library of Congress copy).

[13] Salcedo to Alencaster, Chihuahua, October 24, 1805, New Mexican Archives, doc. 1906.

[14] Alencaster to Salcedo, No. 96, Santa Fe, October 24, 1805, Guerra y Marina, leg. 1787–1807, exp. 15 (Library of Congress copy).

[15] At last we have the four Frenchmen named all together.

as he meets them [the Indians], if they are not on the march toward this capital town, he will interest himself in examining the cause or reason for their failure to come this year, and in acquiring interesting news concerning whether or not they have made friends with the Anglo-Americans; if they have some trade or commerce with them, or if they have obtained it from other nations on the Missouri, and whatever news may be useful to me concerning the operations of these new inhabitants of Louisiana, and [he] will inform me by means of the carabineers and men of the convoy, who will have to return in November, while [he] will remain with his companion, Chalvert, to spend the winter with the aforementioned Pawnees in order to inform himself, as prearranged, of the progress of the Anglo-Americans in Missouri, especially in the spring, in which season they will work together or separately in attracting to our friendship the Lobos and Otos and any other nation which may offer itself, and in good time they will come with chiefs from all of them to this capital.

3. If on the way they meet the expedition to [from] the Pawnees on the march for this capital, they will go back with them [to the Pawnee country], and upon their return they will accompany them [repetition?] for the aforementioned purposes, and if during the winter interesting events occur, he will communicate them to me through the medium of a party of Pawnees whom he will generously bestow with gifts.

4. Upon the expedition's arrival at the Kansas River, the four Frenchmen will separate, building their canoes in order to continue their trip up to San Carlos and other cities.[16]

5. If he considers it proper to remain after the winter is over, he will order Chalvert to come with the Pawnees and even with the chiefs from other nations. He [himself] will live there and will go into the interior to obtain the friendship of others, and to approach the tribes nearest the Missouri, and examine the state and progress of the expedition of Captain Merry, in case it should be possible for him to have any influence against the aforementioned progress and expedition, at its conclusion managing to prejudice the minds of some Indians in order that they may not accept any friendship other than ours, assuring them that an agreement and commerce with the Spaniards presents no risks to them, and that the idea of the Anglo-Americans can

[16] Although the four Frenchmen were expected to return to Santa Fe, they were also going to St. Charles, a few miles from St. Louis. Possibly their travel there could be connected with Vial's special mission.

be no other than to destroy them a few years after obtaining their friendship in order to make themselves owners of said river and of the lands of both sides, which ideas they may not fear from the Spaniards, for in the many years that this province of New Mexico has had allied tribes, it has taken the lands of none, nor has it failed them in the slightest thing.

6. It will not be difficult through my mediation for the allied Comanches of this province as well as the Cuampes, who have requested peace, and other nations to make peace with the Pawnees in order that they may all have commerce with this province.

7. It is important to acquire news and give this to me opportunely, sending whatever is important without delay, of the ideas and operations of the Anglo-Americans toward these lands, also of any other event that merits it.

8. In order to attract and present gifts to the tribes whose friendship concerns us, as it has been explained before, he carries some merchandise, a suit, and an excellent horse, of which stock he will make use with the greatest economy, method, and utility.

9. Vial may acquire the information which is explained by remaining through the spring, not returning until summer has started; this is so necessary and useful that he should not come without it, for in the present circumstances it is likely that it may be necessary that Chalvert return when Vial leaves in order that one of them may always be among the Pawnees or any other nation nearest to the Missouri because of the news which may concern us and for the prompt information of all that occurs that should deserve my attention.

10. It will be a good precaution, after the expedition has passed the Colorado River, to march only at night in order to avoid fire and being attacked.

11. Vial will take special care in observing the best harmony with Chalvert, both doing their best in order that it [harmony] reign, likewise among those who comprise the expedition, to which end Corporal Lucero, as commandant of the troops, and his assistant García will contribute—among whom and the aforementioned Vial I advise a true friendship and interest be established for the best success.

12. Vial will bear in mind the interesting confidential charge that I have entrusted to him, for which accomplishment he will not omit any necessary step, being confident that the accomplishment and the success of this expedition which I entrust to him will furnish him a just reward and a real compensation.[17]

13. If the necessity for help should occur in the country where he finds himself, he will request it by sending, opportunely, a special express in order that we may supply him so that nothing is lacking for its accomplishment.

14. If all the commission has been carried out, arrangements shall be made to come with Pawnees and others from different tribes. Vial and Chalvert shall carry this out.

15. Vial shall watch carefully that no child of any age shall be purchased from the Gentiles, since it is forbidden by superior order, but the members of the convoy and those comprising the expedition may bring back all the merchandise and animals supplied them.

16. He will draw up a corresponding detailed diary.

Santa Fe, Oct. 13, 1805.

JOAQUIN DEL REAL ALENCASTER.[18]

### *Diary of Pedro Vial on Expedition to the Pawnees, October 14–November 19, 1805*[19]

Diary drawn up by Pedro Vial by order of the Governor of Santa Fe, Don Joaquín del Real Alencaster, destined to the Pawnee Nation.

[October, 1805]

14 The 14th of October I left this capital with 50 men, including the two carabineers, Juan Lucero and Franco. Garcia, besides five Frenchmen.[20] I traveled as far as the pueblo de Pouvoque [Pojoaque]. I traveled about 00.5[21] [leagues]

15 Left in the morning until we reached the above river, and traveled about 00.4

16 Left in the morning [and traveled] until I reached Cieneguilla[22] 00.7

17 Left in the morning, and arrived at the Plaza de Taos, where I made my camping place and remained until the 19th. I traveled 00.7

20 I started my march with 50 men from my expedition and 50

[17] It sounds as if perhaps he has suggested that Vial organize the Indians to stop Lewis and Clark.

[18] Guerra y Marina, leg. 1787–1807, exp. 15 (Library of Congress copy).

[19] *Ibid.*

[20] He means four Frenchmen and one Anglo-American.

[21] Obviously the period is not intended as a decimal mark.

[22] He is traveling north and a little east, to go through Taos.

men from the escort. I traveled as far as the Cieneguilla de la Sierra and stopped as usual. I traveled about 00.8

21 I left in the morning, and arrived at the Casa del Rayado. I traveled about 00.8

22 I left our place in the morning and arrived at the Río Vermejo,[23] stopping as usual. I traveled about 00.7

23 Arrived as usual at the Colorado River.[24] I traveled about 00.9

24 Left in the morning and arrived safely at the Rincón de la Uña del Gato. I traveled about 00.4 On this day we found many bison.

25 We stopped here until the 26th so that the people should get meat to provision themselves.

27 I left in the morning after having returned the 50 men from the escort who accompanied me. We went as far as the Río de la Trinchera, and saw a man. Believing him to be from some [Indian] tribe, I sent Carabineer Juan Lucero with four men to examine him, and it was one of our own men who had returned. Nothing unusual. We traveled about 00.6

28 We stopped the entire day.

29 We left in the morning; we traveled across plains in a northern direction until we arrived as usual at the Agua de la Cueva. We traveled 00.6

30 We stopped the entire day because of bad weather.

31 We left in the morning in said direction through said canyon. We traveled about two leagues, the bad weather making us stop in the Cueva del Chacuaco until the following day. No unusual occurence. 00.2

November

1 We left in the morning and made camp at the Casa Colorado. No unusual occurrence. We traveled about 00.7

2 We left in the morning in the same direction throughout the whole Canyon of the Casa Colorado until we arrived at the Río de Ánimas [the Purgatoire]; camped as usual. We traveled 00.5

[23] There is still a Vermejo River on the map northeast of Taos. Obviously he is skirting the mountains, or, rather, following a well-used trail that is quite familiar to him.

[24] Also still on the map as Red River. He was following the route of present Highway 64.

3 We left in the morning in the same direction along said river as usual, and traveled about 00.6

At night the *real de caballada* [the horse-guard] espied three men who gave indication of wanting to rob or [at least] to inspect us closely. Carabineer Juan Lucero with his cavalry garrison took all the precaution possible; consequently, they obtained nothing.

5 We left in the morning and soon discovered many signs of Indians, and, not knowing which tribe it could be, we traveled up the junction of the Río de las Ánimas with the Arkansas River. We traveled about 00.4

We stopped early in order to go and inspect, fearful of an enemy ambush. I immediately sent Carabineer Juan Lucero with five men, and they returned about dusk with the news that on the other bank of the Arkansas there were many footprints for a long period of time during which they had come and gone; they were cutting a path into the earth; with this news, I ordered all the men to arms and vigilance in order that we would not be surprised. About eight o'clock in the morning I saw six men on the other bank of the river, and immediately sent Interpreter José Jarvet [Chalvert] to take the flag and show it, calling them and telling them to come to us, that we were going to solicit them to make peace and to reward them, telling them who we were. But we not only failed to get them to come to us, but they also did not want to talk to us, and they withdrew up the river where they had their men. About midnight they attacked us in three bands, one the horses, and two the encampment. It was necessary to help the [men with the] horses, and most of the men went to help them. Only six men remained in the encampment, so it became necessary to leave the encampment because of the superiority of the enemy, and to join the others, when the enemy managed to get possession of our supply of *trastes* [kitchen utensils or utensils of some other type?], taking the greater part of them, both those belonging to the people [of the expedition] and those destined for presents. I had separated the presents into separate groups in order that in case we met tribes, we could, as we went along, give them each what was suitable; they took more than two of the three shares, leaving us only what was inside a trunk. The men who attacked us must have been about a hundred and some in number, because after having pillaged the encampment, they gathered to take horses to make their escape, but both our men citizens and carabineers and the Frenchmen proved themselves to be courageous, and recovered them [the horses]; until they took the horses from the enemy three times, and at the end of three hours, the enemy, seeing the payment or benefice they were getting, notwithstanding the fact that their force was three times the size of ours, started to withdraw from sight, taking with them only Interpreter Chalvert's horse, which had left the *caballada*, and we rushed on them until we threw them into the river, where they burst out in outcries, because of which it is considered some harm was done to them. Upon returning to our encampment, I found it as I have said, pillaged by the enemy; and considering the bad place where we found ourselves, I decided to load the few implements and provisions that remained, and leave in order to find better terrain. After we started our march, they again attacked us on foot and on horseback, and we fought with them for about three leagues, until they left of their own will, gaining nothing more in this attack than wounding one of our men in the leg with a bullet. At the end of it all, we were not able to recognize which tribe it was because they neither spoke nor cried out in any language; they only gave, while fighting, a very extraordinary shout; for them to have been Pawnees, there is the objection of the mounts, because this nation [the Pawnees] does not use them in war; as for being the Kiowas, [there is the objection of] the large amount of clothing with which they were dressed. They were all fully dressed in the colors of white, red, and blue, with a cloth tied on their heads. They had no arrows, but all had firearms.[25] Finding ourselves devoid of munitions for our defense, we all decided to return to Santa Fe. Because I feared another attack and that they should catch us unaware, I traveled all night, and we took a nap at dawn at Peñasco. By day, on the sixth, we started our march, and arrived at the Casa Colorada, where we stopped. We traveled about 0.20

[25] There are indeed some strange aspects of this attack. One is that the Indians used no language that could identify them; another is the clothing, and especially its colors and the cloth tied on the head. A third and important one is the fact that all were armed with firearms. A fourth is the persistence of their attack: after the initial go-round, they made three attacks on the *cavallada*, and later followed the Spaniards for seven or eight miles. It does indeed have all the earmarks of an American-instigated attack.

We left in the morning. We traveled through said canyon without trouble, and stopped at the Cueva. We traveled 00.7

8 We left in the morning; we traveled about 2 leagues through the heavy snow that fell. No new occurrence. 00.2

9 We left in the morning in order to arrive at the site of the Tinaxa [water hole]. We stopped about 3 in the afternoon in order that the men should provision themselves with bison meat, because we had lost all the provisions in the battle when the enemy attacked us. We traveled about 00.6

10 We left in the morning in order to arrive at the site of the Chicurica, where we found footprints of about 25 or 30 men. I presumed that they had come in search of us. We traveled about 00.5

11 We left in the morning and arrived at the Colorado River without any trouble. We traveled 00.8

12 We left in the morning and arrived at the Vermejo River, still traveling very carefully. We traveled 00.8

13 We left in the morning and arrived at the Cuesta. 00.8

14 We left here and I sent Carabineer Juan Lucero to ask the alcalde for pack animals. We traveled about 00.8

We slept on the Agua Fría, with nothing new.

15 We left in the morning and arrived at the Plaza de Don Fernando [Taos]. We stopped at the home of the alcalde.

16 We stopped the entire day to build up the cavallada.

17 We left in the morning and stopped to sleep at Embudo.

18 We left in the morning and stopped to sleep at San Juan.

19 We left in the morning and arrived at the town of Santa Fe in the presence of the governor, where I delivered the diary I had drawn up concerning my experiences.

I had this expedition in my charge in order to be able to reach all the nations that are included in my instructions, but the trip could not be carried out because of the enemies that we met. I know these tribes and all the directions and roads where they travel; one cannot travel on these roads with so few men nor with so few munitions. All these nations are very avaricious when they go out on a war raid or campaign; if they meet anyone, whoever it may be, if they have some goods, they take these away from them; and he runs the risk of being killed, as has happened on several occasions; but, by having many men go with good firearms and enough munitions, they will recognize the advantages which the Spaniards have, and they will be respected in all the places where they could travel among all these nations without any fear, and they will all come to peace with us.

And for the security of our province, it is advisable to construct a fort on the Arkansas River in order to subdue all the tribes, as well as to avoid the entrance of the Americans, because the Anglo-Americans place all their strength to attracting all the tribes to their side.[26]

By putting the said fort on the said river, it will not be difficult for me and Interpreter José Jarvet [Chalvert] to attract all these tribes in order to make peace with them.

Santa Fe, Nov. 20, 1805.

PEDRO VIAL

On the same day—November 20—Alencaster made his report:

In fulfillment of what I informed your Excellency in my official letter No. 95 of October 11, last, there left from Taos Vial and Jarbet, and the 26th they arrived at the place known as El Río de la Uña del Gato, from where, with an escort that Vial had for that purpose, he returned the convoy, leaving himself with one animal, and informed me of continuing without incident.

Last night the aforesaid Vial and Jarvet [Chalvert] and the four Frenchmen presented themselves to me. For what occurred, your Excellency will examine the enclosed diary[27] that I am sending to you, as well as the instructions that I gave him for the fulfillment of the objects toward which the expedition was directed.

It is not possible to find out what nation it is that received our men with fire, only that they are either well regaled by the Americans with presents furnished by the government or [are] in close commercial relations with the merchants of the same nation or with Frenchmen who are living among them. That they were not Pawnees is proved by the *sacos de cíbulo* [bags of buffalo hide?] that the latter never use, and the mounts, especially mules, whose tracks are recognized in the crossing and re-crossing of the Arkansas River. That they were not Kiowas, there is the fact of the negotiations that they [the Kiowas] have made for peace, and the statements of a Ute woman who was a prisoner among them, and two Comanches in the same case, who assure us that they, the Kiowas, wish to treat for

[26] This had been advocated by nearly everybody.

[27] This diary has not been found.

peace in order that many Spaniards [traders] may go to their lands, [and that the Kiowas may then] surprise them, rob them, and assassinate them. They may also be the Apaches of the Cuesta Azul or some other tribe of the Missouri located in that territory, waiting to make war on the Cuampes and Kiowas or upon the Pawnees, or [they may be] Comanches, or even, finally, some tribe incited by the Americans to impede our [making] peace, trade, and commerce with the referred-to [tribe] and with other tribes—which undoubtedly is the truth and must be believed, [because] the Americans have had more than enough time to regale and attract to their friendship various tribes, as is proved to us. They solicited the Pawnees, according to the information of Jarvet, who about a year and one half ago arrived in this country, and by him and the other Frenchmen, Durocher and Lalande, and the recent arrivals with the Cuampes this year, proved to this government the said solicitation of the Americans, and licenses conceded to merchants to trade with all the tribes whose friendship interests us, and who had considerable supplies of clothing and even quantities of firearms [to give] in consideration for that trade.

Only trade [that is, a trading venture] with some tribe of those mentioned can quit me of my doubt, [and] I am considering finding means to have the Cuampes come in order to acquire important news without exposing an expedition that may have to sustain the functions of arms [that is, fight] until we know who are the true enemies and whether it will be best or not to attack them. With the news that I may acquire, I shall consult and inform your Excellency of everything that may occur.

It also may happen that I shall acquire some news from some one of those in the four villages whose emissary, an Apache captain, was very well satisfied—concerning which I have informed your Excellency.

Of all that they carried [that is, the Vial expedition] for purposes of regaling, there has been brought back less than a third part, which remainder will have a proper disposition.

From all information, it is apparent that Corporal Lucero and Carabineer Garcia acquitted themselves with valor and intelligence, and that the forty men of the escort and the Frenchmen also acquitted themselves with valor.[28]

[28] Alencaster to Commandant-General, No. 156, Santa Fe, November 20, 1805, New Mexican Archives, doc. 1925, part 32; also in Guerra y Marina, leg. 1787–1807, exp. 15 (Library of Congress copy).

It is noticeable that Alencaster reserves his opinion of Vial and Chalvert. On the same date he sent his expense account for Indians for 1805, which he says will require $8,500. He explains the need for more money by saying that he expects four retired parties on the public rolls, and more parties of Comanches; also, as a result of Vial's and Chalvert's expedition, he is expecting delegations from the Pawnees, Lobos, Otos, and others from the vicinity of the Missouri, and also from the Cuampes (Comanches), Kiowas, Caddos, and Laytenes [another division of the Comanches?][29] It is easy to see that he would need some money for presents.

Meantime, Alencaster wasted no time sending Lucero out again—this time to the Kiowas. He reported it on Christmas Day, 1805; the first page appears to be missing, but a marginal note says:

> Giving news of the trip of Carbineer Juan Lucero to the Kiowas, and of his having presented in [Santa Fe] a chief of that tribe, sent by the principal chief of the tribe, upon peace for that tribe and others.

The Kiowas also, it seems, turned out to be as fussy about their medals as Alencaster had anticipated:

> Medals given them were less well liked. They want large and better engraved ones, as I asked your Excellency. Among these Gentiles whose friendship is important to us, there are certain well-known ideas and knowledge, and to regale them I need more and finer things. . . . I am sending this by an express, a corporal and eight men, who will wait at San Eleceario for your Excellency's order until the eleventh, when they will return if your Excellency does not need them for something.
>
> Lucero saw in the hands of the Kiowa two old Spanish flags of silk, and the same [the Kiowa] showed him two suits of fine cloth and two pairs of flaxen pants that he claimed were many years old.[30]

Alencaster believed in sending parties to the Indians, and early in January, 1806, he advised the commandant-general of another such trip:

[29] Alencaster to Salcedo, No. 142, November 20, 1805, New Mexican Archives, doc. 1926, part 26. This is undoubtedly an estimate for 1806.

[30] Alencaster to Commandant-General, No. 157, Santa Fe, December 25, 1805, New Mexican Archives, doc. 1937.

Consequently to what I stated to your Excellency in my official letter No. 151 on November 20, I am verifying the departure of Interpreter Alejandro Martin on December 6 last for the settlements of Somiguase or the new Yamparica General Carlos on the Colorado River,[31] and he returned, presenting himself to me on the twenty-sixth of the same month, saying that he had encountered said Comanches well supplied and with all the signs of having traded with those from this province, and that although commerce had been opened, all they had was small and negligible, for which reason they exchanged only some buffalo and fewer than twenty furs of little value; that they [Martin and his men] were not treated well, and were robbed by the Comanches without their being successful in getting the general to make the Indians return what was stolen. That in their conversations and affairs that he heard, he did not recognize the best affection toward us, and [heard] unfavorable opinions about our armed forces and courage, attributing it all to the continuous trade that they have always had and still have with the residents of the Río Arriba and jurisdiction of La Cañada, who [that is, the residents] continually, in spite of the restriction, live among them, and are the ones of worst conduct in all the province, and with some halfbreeds [*genízaros*] and Gentiles from El Bado who were baptized—as, in like manner, it is attributed to having abolished the ancient rule of there always existing among the Gentiles an interpreter to be on guard and to inform [the authorities] of whatever is significant, and [also to inform] if residents present themselves in the province to trade with them without the proper license.

He also learned that one of those chiefs had been among the Jumanos and had spoken with two Europeans who had given him a large amount of tobacco to give to his friends, and to advise them to come to that place for trade, and they would give them as much arms and munitions as they wanted.

The foregoing, plus the fact that neither the Pawnees nor the Cuampes have presented themselves here this year, and the skirmish that crippled and cut short the expedition of Vial and Chalvert; the Pawnees' thinking of the time lost by not having been extraordinarily rewarded in the past year 1804 and accompanied by Chalvert, who

[31] From the fact that these Yamparicas were northern Comanches and their habitat was normally along the Arkansas River, and that this tribe was in touch with the Jumanos, perhaps we may assume that this Colorado River means the Red River of Natchitoches.

was certain of the consideration and appreciation that they had for him, and contributed much toward their not accepting trade with the Americans, as he affirmed; and other data give well-founded suspicions that the said Pawnees are in complete agreement and commerce with the Americans, which prejudice [, however,] there is still hope of destroying if we exert great diligence; and bearing in mind what you stated in your official letters that I received on the 5th of October, dated September 9 and 12, and the confidential letter of the second of the same month, which includes royal order of the 5th of June, copying the confidential letter *en papel de* May 22, I have devoted myself to thinking over the present state of this province and the prejudices that threaten and that may be calculated, both because of the above mentioned letter and because of the ambitious ideas of the Anglo-Americans, and deducing that in order to assure my responsibility at all times, I must propose to you: will the following innovations, and measures, and help be advisable?[32]

In the first place, I shall consider it indispensable to show that there exist more forces in this province, both in order that our allies may appreciate our friendship more and so that they will not be so easily seduced, and that they will leave it [the province] alone, and even though they wage war on us, and in this case to inflict exemplary punishment on them if they dare—an object that cannot be carried out with those forces that exist here, because they are too small and because this was proved to be true in the last war with the Navaho tribe.

It is also necessary that in regaling said Gentiles it be looked upon with the same interest that the high economy, the splendor, noticed as innovation, considering that this one [nation] can furnish more goods than arms with singular economy, and that as soon as the Anglo-Americans took possession of the vast province of Louisiana, the Spanish government was obliged to incur more than double its expense in sustaining this province and avoid damage from the ambition of said possessors.

It will be advisable to send to each of the Comanche [tribes], the Navaho, Ute, and Jicarilla tribes, and to the Pawnees and others whose friendship is confirmed, an interpreter to live among them, alternating with another to relieve him opportunely at certain times, and that this practice be established in this year as it was originated in the time of Governor Codallos, who succeeded in obtaining information and in surprising in a meeting all the small governors, war chiefs,

[32] He gets impressive mileage out of dependent clauses.

*fiscales*, and *caciques* [chiefs] of all the Indian villages, so that it [the meeting] was cut short; and he punished with death the said head chief, and the others with imprisonment in San Juan de Ulloa, because of which it will always be necessary that the strict administration of justice be established in this province and that Indians and residents see examples, punishment, and large numbers of troops to maintain the authority of the government—which cannot easily be done without it [troops].

Also, through the expressed means the illicit trade with the Gentiles may be cut short at the cost of refusing pardon to the infractors of the old prohibition, and, what is more, making it impossible for them to do it by means of the zeal of the interpreters and vigilance in small, separated parties—the exact fulfillment of which can easily be endangered.

I believe there are precedents in that [your] commandancy-general of the project of a fort and settlement on the Arkansas River, which establishment the Interpreter Don Pedro Vial thinks would be advantageous, because the trade that might be carried on in it would be very useful to different nations that are far from the Missouri, such as the Pawnees, Otos, Lobos, and all those situated along the cordillera at the foot of the Sierra del Almagre, and friends of the Kiowas and Cuampes as far as the Sayenas, who are the most distant ones but who trade with them, on which point your Excellency will indicate to me what you consider advisable.

Upon the completion of the suggested expedition of Vial and Chalvert the following spring [the coming spring], depending upon its results, if it should be necessary, let me go out in command of another expedition for purposes that may interest the State; I am ready to carry it out in case your Excellency approves and orders it.[33]

On January 11, 1806, Salcedo answered Alencaster's letter of December 25 about Lucero:

By your official letter No. 157 of December 25 last, I have been informed of the fact that, taking advantage of the good disposition of the carabineer, Juan Lucero, you determined that with 25 men chosen to your satisfaction you would repeat the expedition that the ones named Vial and Chalbert were unable to conclude, and that, having left Taos November 27, last, after eleven days' march, he [Lucero]

[33] Alencaster to Salcedo, No. 162, January 4, 1806, New Mexican Archives, doc. 1942 (last sheet missing).

reached the villages of the Kiowa band, where he was well received, and [where he] informed himself of the ideas that the chiefs of them had of taking all the steps that were possible for them to maintain peace with the Spaniards, and through his mediation they requested the Comanches to make peace with them, offering also to induce ten other bands to present themselves with similar pretensions of peace with us.

I am likewise informed that, having been led to your village by the Carabineer Lucero, the Kiowa chief named El Ronco, asking for two flags and other articles as presents, proposed to your Excellency that you should dispatch an express to ask from the Comanches that both sides come together in your town and make their peace, and afterward should go to their respective villages for the purpose of confirming it, and taking with them the Spaniards who might be named for that purpose.

I approve that you deferred to the indicated requests and likewise that when, at the determined time, they may present themselves there, the said Kiowas, with their head chief, Bule, then you should try to keep them firmly in our friendship, and to require proof that they not carry on commerce with the Americans or English—which point, although it may be difficult to carry out, both because of the remote situation in which they are (which allows them to do whatever they may wish), and by the interest [profit] that results to them, which point you must recommend to them effectively, without, in so doing, compromising yourself to the contributions of continuous presents as long as it would be an expense totally useless on account of the doubt of its producing the ends to which it is directed.

Under similar consideration and the consideration that the best method of maintaining the dependence of the Indian tribes is the facilitation to them of commerce and exchange for the furs and other articles that they have, whenever for that purpose they might come to our establishments, I find no objection to your ordering the journey of Vial and Chalvert in the next spring to the country of the Pawnees, charging them very particularly that they try to acquire news of the tribe to which belonged the individuals who attacked them on the preceding expedition.

It is well, holding in mind the orders that are in force concerning the exchange of commerce of children with the Gentiles, that you propose to me the means that may occur to you to prevent the damages that you say spring from similar prohibition. And concerning the necessity that you have for medals in order to woo the Indian chiefs, this will serve you officially, that since the first occasion on which you told me of the subject, I asked his Excellency the viceroy for them —who up to today has not answered me.[34]

Around the first of March, Alencaster proposed to send Lucero to the Cuampes and Kiowas to find out what tribe had attacked Vial and Chalvert,[35] and a few days later he demonstrated that he had taken Alencaster's recommendations seriously, for he advised him that he was sending Lieutenant Facundo Melgares with sixty men to Santa Fe—but it turned out that Melgares' first job was to reconnoiter the Red River and stop the Freeman party if it should not be stopped by Viana at Nacogdoches. Melgares was then to go north to the junction of the Platte and the Missouri.

He reached Santa Fe with 105 men, and there added 400 New Mexican militiamen and 100 Indian auxiliaries, and started down the Red River with 2,000 animals. He held a council with Comanches, then struck out overland, ran into Pawnee-Mahas. He held a seemingly successful parley with the Pawnees—but that night they stole or stampeded a great number of his horses and mules. Melgares left about half his men on the Arkansas River, and went on to the Pawnee villages on the Republican River, made a nice treaty with them, and went home, blazing a path for Zebulon Pike's men, who would soon be crossing Kansas.[36]

Two weeks after Salcedo advised Alencaster of Melgares' departure for Santa Fe, he discussed the coming expedition of Vial and Chalvert to the Pawnees:

In official letter No. 214 of the first of the current month, your Honor discusses the expedition planned for this spring in charge of Vial and Chalvert; that without compromising yourself to dress the individuals of the tribes that present themselves once a year, [you

[34] Salcedo to Governor, No. 150, Chihuahua, January 16, 1806, New Mexican Archives, doc. 1953, part 3.

[35] Alencaster to Commandant-General, No. 214, Santa Fe, April 1, 1806, New Mexican Archives, doc. 1980.

[36] Salcedo to Alencaster, April 12, 1806, and Alencaster to Salcedo, May 30, 1806—both in Guerra y Marina, leg. 1787–1807, exp. 15 (Library of Congress copy); see Hart and Hulbert, *Zebulon Pike's Arkansaw Journal,* 79, and Coues, *Expeditions of Pike,* II, 413, 583–84.

say] it is not possible to obligate them to make the peace, that it would be advisable that the children which the Indians present for ransom should be bought at the expense of the public treasury or other funds, and lastly, that your Honor be permitted to arrange one or more cargoes per year with the friendly faction in order to facilitate the commerce of that province.

On the first of said matters, your Honor should be aware of the contents of my order of the twelfth; regarding the second matter, to proceed according to the communications in order to economize the expenses of war and peace, endeavoring to omit what is useless, and reducing to the absolutely necessary those which you deem desirable; with the idea as I told your Honor on January 16 that the best means of maintaining the dependency of the Indian nations is to facilitate their commerce; on the third, nothing can be determined regarding which, notwithstanding the advantages of thought, should occasion a considerable tax that the royal treasury cannot carry, nor is there another fund to which to charge it; and finally, covering the fourth point, I advise you to proceed according to past decisions of this commandancy-general and to the indication that I have made to you about its being advisable that our allied factions find in our establishments opportunity to sell their commodities and manufactures, and that they notice no alteration in the system that has been followed up to now and that has proved good.[37]

Vial started his next expedition on April 24, but it likewise ran into trouble, as Alencaster reported to Salcedo on May 24.[38]

Ten days later (May 30) Alencaster reported Vial's and Chalvert's return from the 1806 expedition, Melgares' arrival in Santa Fe, and the new expedition being planned under Melgares, with 605 men, to the Indian nations.[39]

Information on this expedition of Vial and Chalvert is singularly lacking. With no diary at hand, it appears from evidence after the fact that Vial's men deserted, and the expedition was another failure. And indirectly again—but obviously—Alencaster did not accept the desertions complacently. A letter from Salcedo gives the news:

[37] Salcedo to Governor, April 24, 1806, New Mexican Archives, doc. 1986.

[38] Alencaster to Salcedo, Santa Fe, May 20, 1805; Guerra y Marina, leg. 1787–1807, exp. 15, f. 146.

[39] Alencaster to Salcedo, Santa Fe, May 20, 1806, Guerra y Marina, leg. 1787–1807, exp. 15.

Informed by your letter No. 269 of May 20 last that *desovedesiendo* the sergeants and corporals in charge of the second expedition of Vial and Chalbert, they [Vial and Chalbert] abandoned it, the men and Indians named as their escort returning to their villages. I approve the step that you took in consequence, that one tenth of the number of said individuals should be conducted to your capital with the object of making a judicial record [*formar causa*] upon the matter, and a determination. I advise you to give me an account of it, to decide what is fitting.[40]

If Vial did keep a diary, it has not turned up, nor has any mention of it turned up, but almost one year later Alencaster reported to Salcedo on the deserters:

With your official letter of April 14 last, I have received the file [*expediente*] made against various persons of the jurisdictions of La Cañada and Taos for having abandoned voluntarily and without any cause the expedition in charge of Don Pedro Vial and Corporal José Antonio Alari, [which] set out from this town April 19 of last year to visit the Pawnee nation; and I have gone through it, carrying out what your Excellency had resolved. I will return it to your Excellency's hands in fulfillment of what your Excellency will be pleased to advise me.[41]

This seems to be the last available information on the punishment of the deserters, and, as usual, it is explicit in the details already known, but utterly silent concerning what happened. Further information is lacking.

However, the trend of events in these years is clear: The Americans were having considerable influence with the Indians. The Spaniards' long-time conservative policy of watching the treasury first in every matter, and perhaps especially of refusal to give firearms to the Indians, was not able to stand before the onslaught of the Americans, who were concerned with immediate results. Meriwether Lewis held at least one memorable conference with the Sioux, and made believers of them, as well as of many of the tribes with which he came into contact.

[40] Salcedo to Alencaster, No. 235, Chihuahua, July 18, 1806, New Mexican Archives, doc. 2001.

[41] Alencaster to Commandant-General, No. 445, Santa Fe, June 16, 1807, New Mexican Archives, doc. 2058.

The Spaniards were eminently correct in their prediction that the Americans would oust the Indians from their lands, but it rather seems the Indians were more impressed by foofurraw and firearms and sometimes whisky. Not many of the Indians looked beyond their noses.

And so Vial's later expeditions failed, and the Spaniards undoubtedly were disgruntled at the stupidity of the Indians, but there was nothing they could do about it. It would take a long, long time for the truth to penetrate to Madrid—and by that time the charging Americans would have possession.

# XVII
# *Vial's Cohorts*

With Vial probably not in very good standing at Chihuahua or Mexico City because of his two fiascos, Juan Lucero, nevertheless, continued to make trips to the Indian country. Lucero had been with Vial on his trip to Natchitoches, and was with him on the first attempted expedition to the Pawnees (in 1805), and undoubtedly many other times. He was sent out to make peace with the Kiowas in late 1805.[1] He was not with Vial on the expedition of 1806, but a few weeks later he was on another of his own; Alencaster reported this last trip on August 30, 1806:

> On July 24 the carabineer, Juan Lucero, presented himself, saying that on the second he arrived at the village of the Kiowas without anything unusual having occurred on his trip. That he was well received by them [the Kiowas], who told him they had not been able to join with five other nations because the latter were attacked by the Aa's despite their not being at war—which advice had been given them by an express, assuring them that at the end of August they would come to join with them [the Kiowas], but that on account of this new occurrence, the chief of the Kiowas, named Dientecito or Bole, decided not to come because he had arranged to come and had believed he was going to come with other chiefs of the five above-cited nations, [and Bole] added that if they should come before [the end of August?], he would let them know, and, if not, Lucero should go at the end of August to get them.
>
> That in the village there were thirteen lodges of the tribe known

[1] Alencaster to Salcedo, Santa Fe, January 4, 1806, New Mexican Archives, doc. 1942. See also docs. 1937, 1953, and 1956.

as Orejones[2] who inhabit [the country] near the Missouri, from whom two chiefs attended the council, where was distributed tobacco and a little powder that had been carried for regaling them, it having been necessary to increase the gift with what could be gathered from the members of the escort so that the Indians might be satisfied.

The said Orejones came to the council so that the chiefs might consider the matter of coming to this capital [Santa Fe], but six Frenchmen had caught up with them, and asked them where they were going and for what purpose, [and the Orejones], having answered them, were regaled with fifty guns, a quantity of copper and brass kettles, and long suits of finely woven cloth of the best quality, and [the Frenchmen said] that they would return with more gifts to the same villages of the Orejones, and that the latter, who were messengers of the [Orejones? ] tribe, advised the Kiowas that they should not fail to attend the council. The said Orejones asked about the Frenchmen and the American who accompanied the Cuampes, and about the last one who came with El Ronco, named Juan Bautista la Casa, manifesting great interest in order that they should go with them [the Orejones] when they [the Orejones] should return from having visited me.

Chief Roncon, a Kiowa, with his wife and a small daughter, came with Lucero to await an occasion for going to live with the Yamparica Comanches because of being married with a daughter of Somiquaso.

Lucero will leave September 6 next to meet with the Kiowas, well instructed to affirm them in the thought [*método*] that they should remain in Taos to make their [illegible], and that only the chiefs may come to the village in order to avoid [our] expenses, and in the future if they established [the practice of] coming to trade, it is regular to arrange that only one chief come to visit me. All of which I am informing your Excellency as I must.[3]

Lucero was to go to look for the Kiowas again on September 6, but he had bad luck:

On the second of this month Carabineer Juan Lucero arrived at this capital on his return from his last voyage to the Kiowas, but in spite

[2] A tribe whose original habitat was near the Texas coast. Probably this is a name applied to designate a stray band of Indians whose tribal affiliation was not known to Lucero.

[3] [Alencaster] to Commandant-General, No. 302, Santa Fe, August 30, 1806, New Mexican Archives, doc. 2006, part 1.

of his having gone in search of said tribe as far as the Río de la Ceja de la Blanca,[4] he was not able to find them in spite of having traveled many days on the mules; the Kiowas were going toward the Missouri River. He says that on the next to the last time he was with them, the said Kiowas had agreed to meet him in the valley of the Salada, but he, having arrived at that point, observed that in fact he knew they [had] come to await him but that perhaps they had felt the rumor or [had seen] the smoke of the expedition of Lieutenant Melgares, and they had fled the country, afraid of being attacked by it; and that, considering very *remos* [?] *el alcaimarlos,* he determined to return, fearful that they [the Kiowas] should encounter another, unknown tribe [and be tempted from their loyalty to the Spaniards—in which case Lucero wanted to be on hand to swing them back to the Spaniards].

Against this opinion of Lucero, there is something for your Excellency to take cognizance of in the diary of news revealed by a Jicarilla Indian recently arrived at Taos, a fugitive from the Kiowas.

In the light of everything we know, it appears to me advisable that Lucero should not again go out in search of the Kiowas, and that those will come when it suits them, since they have the *paso franco.*[5] All of which, I hope, merits your Excellency's approval.[6]

The next documentary reference to Lucero occurs on November 20, when a census report of the Presidial Company of Santa Fe was made:

Notice of the seniority and fitness of the sergeants, corporals, and carabineers of the said company. Carabineer Juan Lucero, a native of this province, of very good conduct, of spirit and demonstrated valor, of knowledge in the field and of a disposition suitable for command;

[4] Apparently the White River that rises on the Llano Estacado near the Texas–New Mexico boundary and flows east to join the Prairie Dog Town Fork of the Red River. Ceja means eyebrow—the Caprock. This is the first time we have had any definite information on the Kiowas' habitat.

[5] The right of passage.

[6] Alencaster to Commandant-General, No. 334, Santa Fe, November 20, 1806, New Mexican Archives, doc. 2030, part 4. Regarding Melgares, see Pike's report to Dearborn, Secretary of War, October 1, 1806; printed in Twitchell, *Spanish Archives of New Mexico,* II, 503–505, and in full in Coues, *The Expeditions of Zebulon Montgomery Pike,* II, 582–85. Incidentally, it appears that most or all the documents relating to the arrest of Robinson and Pike have been carried away from the New Mexican Archives, but copies of some of Alencaster's notes were in Twitchell's hands, and are reprinted in *Spanish Archives,* II, 509–11.

his height, 5 feet, 1 inch; 17 years, 20 days of service. He knows how to read.[7]

A few months later, Lucero was off to the Río del Almagre:[8]

On the fourteenth of this month, Lieut. Ignacio Sotelo with a party of 27 foot-soldiers, well armed with firearms, parleyed with the Cuampe and Flecha Rayada[9] tribes, which made a night camp with the advance guard and manifested that they were always faithful friends of ours and desired our friendship; they were coming from a hunt, to establish themselves some 500 [torn] on the headwater, of the Almagre, and they would already have come to see me, but they advised me that they expected there might be some [Spaniards] from the province [to visit them], because they needed some things and [they had] skins with which to barter. Consequently, to assure me where and how many would establish themselves, and to help prove their friendship, and to make it known also with other friends of theirs, in accordance with orders that I am bearing in mind, the Carabineer Lucero goes out this very day with twelve men of the jurisdictions of La Cañada and Taos, carrying a flag and moderate supplies to regale them—whose cost and that of the necessary food for said carabineer amounts to 104 pesos, 4 *reales*.

Said Carabineer Lucero is advised to make them see that they should come to present themselves to me and to parley formally for a peace with me, the chief of each one of the tribes that are together there, and in that case I will give them their *patentes*[10] and their walking canes and I will place a medal with the bust of the king [around their necks] in the name of his Majesty, and I will give them gifts. He is also to make them understand that he cannot return to hunt them,

[7] No. 336 (possibly included with Alencaster to Salcedo of the same date), November 20, 1806, New Mexican Archives, doc. 2030, part 6. It would be hard to get a better recommendation in the army. His height probably was not less than average, according to reports even as late as 1841 (see Loomis, *Texan–Santa Fé Pioneers*, Biographical Roster). He was said to be "young" when he went with Vial in 1788; "young" meant about fifteen or sixteen; now, eighteen years later, he has been in the army for seventeen years.

[8] The Fountain River near Colorado Springs, Colorado. Called by the mountain men Fontaine Qui Bouille.

[9] A division of the Tawehash or Wichita tribe, says Hodge; location probably in south-central Kansas.

[10] A patent or writ conferring an exclusive right or privilege; a certificate of chieftainship.

or put at their disposal an escort so that they may come. The said Indians have not had trade with the Anglo-Americans, but they had had trade with other Indians in order to supply themselves with arms and munitions.[11]

As usual, the Spaniards utterly failed to take cognizance of the fact that they were in competition with the aggressive Anglo-Americans. In spite of the fact that the Orejones had been given fifty rifles, and in face of the fact that the party of over one hundred that attacked Vial's expedition in 1805 had been equipped with firearms throughout, Alencaster instructed Lucero to advise the chiefs that only one chief was to go to Santa Fe at a time, because the gifts were too expensive. One can sympathize with the governor, for obviously the Indians were getting what they could out of him. What the Spanish officials from Madrid to Santa Fe failed to open their eyes to, is the fact that they were in competition with the Americans. To Alencaster's credit, he did seem to have, when he started, an idea as to what he should do, but Salcedo was forced to dampen his enthusiasm. When the Spaniards were allowed to move, they attained a creditable degree of success, but more often it was too little, too late.

Lucero continued to be busy for a number of years. From November to March, 1808–1809, he took an expedition to the Arkansas and kept a diary;[12] on February 16, 1809, he went to the Comanches; in that year also he was made first commandant of a troop of halfbloods *(genízaros)*;[13] from July 1 to August 1, 1809, he and Manuel Martin, an interpreter, traveled together;[14] and the new governor, Manrrique, reported it to Salcedo:

> [He refers to his letter No. 250 of the twenty-second, on which day, he says, he sent Lucero with two soldiers to El Bado to join Martin and some volunteers, to go to a Quegua (Comanche) village. The Indians appeared in El Bado, he says, with Cordero, Calles, Mugnir, and six boys (or six children), and received word from Manrrique. They were going to see Manrrique in Santa Fe to talk about a cam-

[11] Alencaster to Commandant-General, No. 416, Santa Fe, May 23, 1807, New Mexican Archives, doc. 2052.

[12] New Mexican Archives, doc. 2185.

[13] Manrrique to Salcedo, Santa Fe, June 20, 1809, New Mexican Archives, doc. 2234.

[14] New Mexican Archives, doc. 2237.

paign against the Apaches. Lucero seems to have canceled his trip for the time being, and perhaps accompanied the Indians to Santa Fe, where they arrived on the twenty-sixth. Manrrique warned them if they expected to give him their united support, they could not go against the Apaches, because the Apaches' support would be necessary if they all should have to fight the Americans.]

Lucero had also the duty of observing some of the six strangers that Manrrique had sent to Salcedo.[15]

In March, 1810, Lucero and Martin paid a visit to the Comanches, probably on the Arkansas and the Almagre rivers, and there they ran into news of the McLanahan party. Lucero sent a messenger to Santa Fe for reinforcements and began to hunt the Anglo-Americans—whom he found in the Comanche Chief Pasagogo's village: McLanahan, Smith, Patterson, Manuel Blanco, and two slaves, all of whom accompanied him back to Santa Fe. It appeared that Manrrique then sent Lucero and Martin back to the Comanches, for Salcedo wrote on May 2:

> Likewise I am informed of the steps that you took with respect to Corporal Lucero and Interpreter Martin, that they reside with the Comanches until the end of last month [April]. They will try to observe and to obtain news as to whether or not the six foreigners sent to this town brought others in their company, which could very well have happened, and [they could have] withdrawn in consequence of the warning that those latter might have given them when they saw our people.[16]

On August 6, 1816, Lucero made another trip to the Comanches, and in 1818 he visited them twice; in 1819 he made a trip to the "Indians," and on October 21, 1819, it appears that Lucero with some of his men was expected to be captured by "the enemy"; does this refer to rebellion? Thereafter, Juan Lucero seems to fade from sight. Perhaps he was displaced in the Mexican revolution.[17]

The origin of Juan Chalvert has been given; the first documentary

[15] [Manrrique] to Salcedo, Santa Fe, March 29, 1810, New Mexican Archives, doc. 2310. (Most of the references to interpreters or guides, unless otherwise cited, have come from the New Mexican Archives).

[16] Salcedo to Manrrique, Chihuahua, May 2, 1810, New Mexican Archives, doc. 2316.

[17] For documents on Lucero, see New Mexican Archives, docs. 1937, 1953, 1956, 2030, 2076, 2185, 2234, 2632, 2672, 2771, and 2854.

reference that has been found concerning him is in New Mexico, where, on May 28, 1805, he offered to interpret for one-half the price of the other interpreters. (At various times his name is given as Gervais, Tarvet, Jarvet, Charvet, and in other forms.) It is interesting to note that he later offered to serve on an annual basis; on June 12 his offer was approved by Salcedo.[18] In July a chief and 120 warriors of the Cuampe tribe appeared in Taos bearing a flag of a white cross on a red background, and on September 1 El Frances Chalvert was appointed interpreter to the Pawnees.

On September 9, 1805, the fear of Lewis and Clark was mounting, and Salcedo wrote to the governor:

> If in the time that you have had near you the new interpreter of the Pawnees, José Calvert, you have judged him to be of good behavior, truth, and desire to give proof of the usefulness of his services, I consider it opportune that by taking advantage of the favorableness of the present season in which the Indians withdraw from their hunts, . . . he can take some small presents for the chiefs and invite them to make an appearance in Santa Fe.[19]

One year later (1806), when Melgares returned from his excursion on the prairies with a *cavallada,* with invalids, very ill men, and others who arrived greatly in need of rest and recuperation, he brought a diary and some interesting news, for among the Pawnees he had found two Frenchmen, Andrés Sulier and Henrique Visonot, both of whom requested permission to go to the interior of Mexico, and a ten-year-old son of Chalvert, who also was taken from the Pawnees and was sent to Salcedo in Chihuahua.[20]

On December 19, 1810, Manrrique sent for Chalvert—for what purpose, does not appear. The last documentary reference that has turned up is a letter from Lieutenant Melgares in 1819. He had taken a force of men to meet—or at least to scout—the Yellowstone Expedition from the United States, and he says that he sent Interpreter

[18] [Alencaster] to Commandant-General, Santa Fe, May 28, 1805, and note on this letter, New Mexican Archives, doc. 1838.

[19] Salcedo to Governor, September 9, 1805, Guerra y Marina, leg. 1787–1807, exp. 15 (Library of Congress copy).

[20] Alencaster to Commandant-General, No. 315, Santa Fe, October 8, 1806, New Mexican Archives, doc. 2022, part 1.

Chalvert with fifteen men, well mounted, close to La Roche (Yellowstone) without his obtaining any information of the march of the ambitious Americans.[21]

More needs to be said about Durocher and Lalande. When Vial and Chalvert came back from their ill-fated expedition of 1805, there must have been some hard feeling between them and the two Frenchmen. As a matter of fact, Juan Lucero reported that he had noticed repeated conversations between said Frenchmen and Don Pedro Vial, and Chalvert, understanding something of the talk, questioned Don Pedro repeatedly; Vial explained to him that the Frenchmen were arguing that the province of New Mexico could never make gifts like those of the Americans, and the Indians would always like the Americans better—while Don Pedro maintained the opposite. The Frenchmen said to Chalvert that the pay of ten pesos that he was receiving was very small; that the Americans were paying interpreters twenty-five pesos a month, and that when they were traveling with the Indians they always received one peso a day, but Chalvert said he preferred to serve Spain at small pay, and that he hoped they would reward his merit by increasing his pay;[22] Durocher especially advanced opposing arguments.

Vial and Chalvert verified Lucero's report to the governor.[23]

Durocher was born probably between 1734 and 1749; in 1804 he was called an old man; he was a French-Canadian who went to St. Louis in 1778; he ascended the Missouri in 1804 to find a short route to the Mandans; he was in Santa Fe early in 1805; there he wanted to return to his own country, and asked for money. Alencaster told him he must see Salcedo and must go to Chihuahua. Alencaster asked permission to incur expenses for Durocher's travel to and maintenance in Chihuahua with Lalande. In Chihuahua, Durocher asked to be allowed to live in New Mexico as a Spanish subject. Salcedo sent him back to Santa Fe in September, 1805, and agreed to permit them to return

[21] Melgares to Alexo Garcia Conde, Santa Fe, July 9, 1819; certified copy in A.G.I., Papeles de Estado, leg. 33.

[22] It will be remembered that Chalvert had offered to work for half-pay, and had been accepted; Vial was getting six reales a day, which seems to make $22.50 a month.

[23] Alencaster to Salcedo, January 4, 1806, New Mexican Archives, doc. 1942; printed in *New Mexico Historical Review,* Vol. II, No. 4 (October, 1927), 376–77.

home; he granted them expenses and effects to hold the friendship of the Indians on the Missouri River from the mouth of the Platte westward.

In October, 1805, Durocher and Lalande accompanied Vial and Chalvert on the expedition to the Pawnees—and talked too much. In view of their attitude, Alencaster refused to permit them to go home without Salcedo's approval. Salcedo expressly ordered it, but on August 16, 1806, Durocher had a passport from Santa Fe to Chihuahua; on August 31 he was at El Paso with the Anglo-American carpenter, Purcell—both en route to Chihuahua.

Durocher was last heard from on the trip to Chihuahua, where he probably was going to argue his case before Salcedo for the second or third time. His compadre, Lalande, died in Santa Fe some years after Pike was there, leaving a large family and a large estate.

There was another man who was with Vial more than once: Alejandro Martin, a Comanche interpreter. He first appeared with Mares on the way from Santa Fe to San Antonio; he made a trip to the Comanches in 1804; he was with Vial and Lucero in 1805; he made a trip to the Comanches in December, 1805; he was sent to treat with Somiquaso, the Comanche chief, in January, 1806; and it is interesting to observe that when Vial died, in 1814, he left his property to a woman named Martin.[24]

Jacques d'Eglise reached New Mexico and was assassinated there in 1806; his murderers were executed in 1809, Juan Bautista la Casa and Dionisio la Croix and Andrés Ferien came from Louisiana (and Vial went to Taos to meet them in June, 1805); Visonot and Andrés Sulier came from St. Louis; Jacques Clamorgan and three others, with two more Frenchmen, came from Louisiana. Altogether, between 1804 and 1809 at least twelve Frenchmen besides Durocher, Lalande, and D'Eglise reached New Mexico.

Some names of men who appeared as interpreters and scouts (not often but interestingly) are: Josef Miguel Zenguaras, who spoke three languages (1800); Juan Cristóbal (1803); Josef Mirabel, interpreter to the Pawnees (1803); Josef María Gurule (1804); José Antonio Garcia, with Vial and Chalvert (1805); Martin, Mirabel, Josef

[24] These records of interpreters are fragmentary at their very best; one gets the impression that they were very active at times, and perhaps many were on a permanent basis on the payroll.

Campo, Cristóbal Tenorio, and Pedro Salar (all mentioned in 1805); José Campo Redondo, who was mentioned in 1805, but who, almost a year later, was separated from the service "for lack of intelligence"; Garcia to the Navahos (1818; he may have been with Vial in 1805); Manuel Mestas, who was said to be seventy years old in 1805, with fifty years' service as a Ute interpreter[25] (a man named Mestas was sent to the Comanches in 1825—but it does not seem that Manuel would have changed tribes at the age of ninety; perhaps the later one was his son).

All these men played their brief roles—some well, some badly, some haphazardly. Very few of them left enough record of themselves to warrant more than a small mention. It is too bad, for they too served in their small way.

[25] Joseph J. Hill, "Spanish and Mexican Exploration," *Utah Historical Quarterly*, Vol. III, No. 1 (January, 1930), 16–17. This seems to be a copy of Alencaster to Salcedo, September 1, 1805, in New Mexican Archives, doc. 1881.

# XVIII

## *Francisco Amangual, San Antonio to Santa Fe to San Elzeario to San Antonio, in 1808*

Lewis and Clark returned from their famous expedition; Zebulon Pike came to Santa Fe, went on to Chihuahua, was released, and started back through Texas; Dr. Sibley was at Natchitoches; and the Kiowas, Comanches, and Pawnees were still on the warpath. In June, 1807, as Pike neared Natchitoches, Alencaster wrote to the commandant-general:

> Many Kiowas, Cuampes, and other tribes were united in friendship in the vicinity of the headwaters of the Almagre River, and at various points as far as the Arkansas River, and appear to have the idea of joining the Comanches to attack the Pawnees and make war upon them.
>
> On the eighth, a Kiowa chief with a Yamparica Comanche presented themselves to me; they were going to treat with those of the said party [those on the Almagre?] about the peace that *hace tiempo*. The Kiowa assured me that he had not really wanted to come to this town, but, having spoken with Captain Vargas, at the slightest insinuation he came to see me, and was well received. He wanted to find out for himself.
>
> Today the said Gentiles began their march dressed and regaled as is customary, with a portion of tobacco and a very little powder. They could not (or did not) want to go on foot, so I sent them two horses as a gift of the king.
>
> The Kiowa chief said the principal chief of his village was named Bule, and he was thinking of coming to see me soon.[1]

[1] Draft of a letter from Alencaster to Commandant-General, No. 442, Santa Fe, June 3, 1807, New Mexican Archives, doc. 2056.

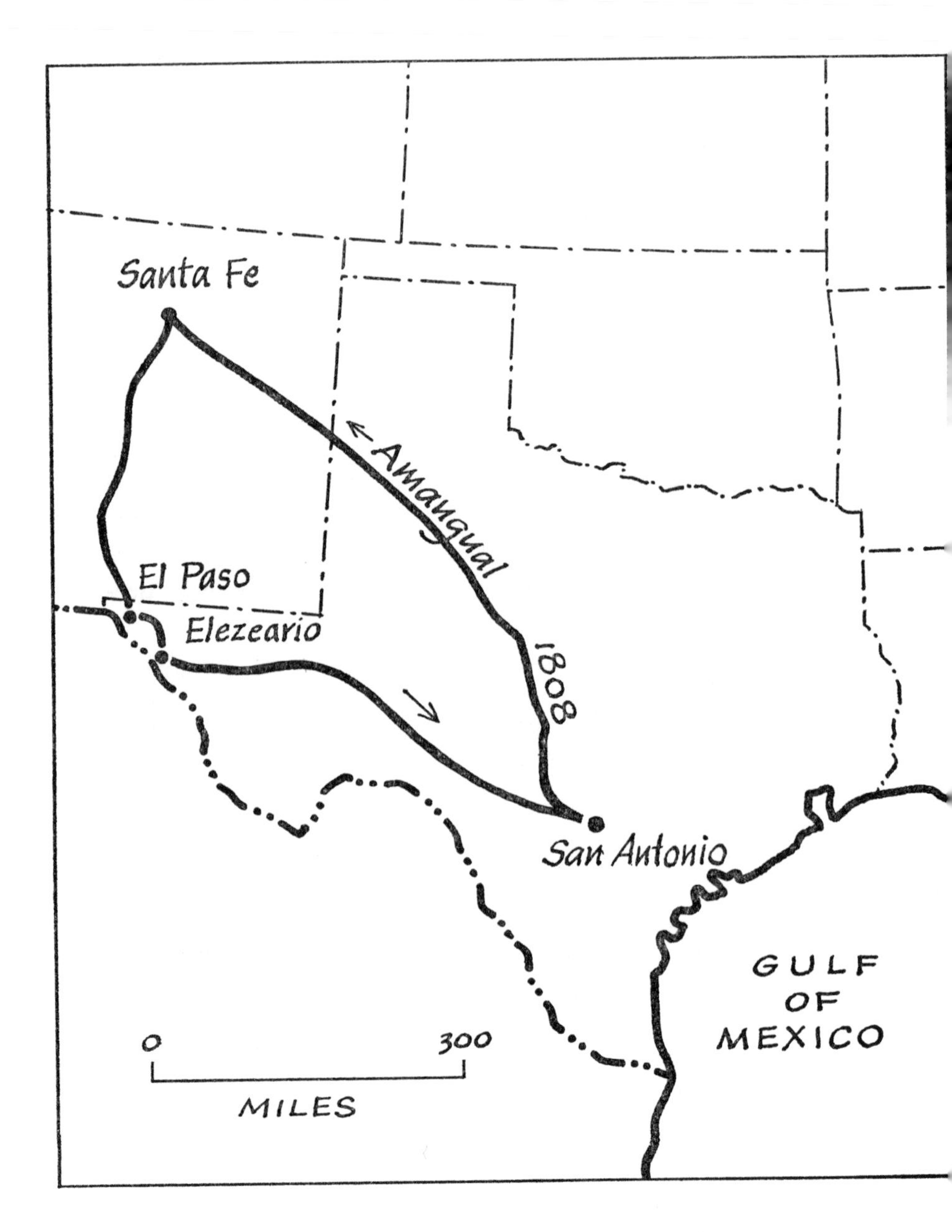


*Francisco Amangual's route in 1808*

### *Francisco Amangual, San Antonio to Santa Fe to San Elzeario*

On February 5, 1808, Governor Cordero of Texas wrote to the commandant-general, suggesting a reconnaissance of soldiers through the territory along the Texas-New Mexico boundary. There appeared to be a basis for the United States' claiming that Louisiana extended to the Río Grande;[2] Pike had already been in Santa Fe; Freeman had tried to ascend the Red River. American pressure was considerable from the north and east, and certainly in 1808 it was still as desirable as it had been in 1786, to have a road between Santa Fe and San Antonio.

Salcedo must have approved Cordero's suggestion, for on March 24 Cordero issued instructions for the expedition, putting it in charge of Captain Francisco Amangual, commandant at La Bahía.[3]

Amangual had been in Texas at least since 1779, had spent most of his time stationed at San Antonio, but had been in La Bahía many times, and had been on many campaigns and Indian expeditions; he had reconnoitered along the coast during the Philip Nolan excitement of 1800 and the concurrent fear of invasion, and in 1808, at the age of sixty-nine, he was waiting for promotion to lieutenant colonel.

On the expedition to Santa Fe, he was to find a northern route to Santa Fe (among other things), to locate water holes along the road, to visit the Indian tribes and make friends with them. Undoubtedly this was a counter to the mounting pressure from the Anglo-Americans.[4]

Amangual was on the way by the last of March, and he kept the most complete diary of all. He led a military expedition of two hundred men, and it would seem to be quite a feat to get such a body of men through the wilderness and across the Llano.

[2] Marshall, *History of the Western Boundary*, 10.

[3] Amangual was born at Majorca about 1739, entered military service in 1762, was assigned to the Company of San Antonio, and sent to watch the Comanches. He was *alférez* at San Antonio in 1779, on a Sonora expedition in 1767–71, was elected paymaster at San Antonio; in 1797 he was described as honest and of good conduct. He was captain before 1804, at which time he was at Bahía to intercept contraband goods. He was superintendent of the first hospital in Texas and was in charge at San Antonio de Valero in 1806. After his return from the expedition to Santa Fe, he married for the last time, and retired. From 1772 to 1812 there are many Amangual documents in the Béxar Archives.

[4] In Santa Fe he received supplementary orders for local reconnaissance, and for return via San Elzeario.

## *Diary of Francisco Amangual from San Antonio to Santa Fe, March 30–May 19, 1808*[5]

Daily record of events in the party under command of Captain Don Francisco Amangual.

### Year of 1808

Diary of the events and operations of the expedition that is being made from this province of Texas to that of New Mexico by superior order, the first in command being Franco. Amangual; second in command, Captain Don Agabo de Ayala; on March 30, 1808.

### 30th day of March

From the mission of San Antonio up to the Arroyo del Novilla, where we stopped, there was nothing new but the loss of one mule loaded with *piloncillos*[6] belonging to the Second Company of New Santander. 2 leagues

### 31

This day dawned without any change other than the loss of an unsaddled male mule of La Bahía Company. We undertook the march through rocky country with a few trees, generally black oaks, until we arrived at the Arroyo de Leon, where we encamped without any other incident. 8 leagues

### 1st of April

This day having dawned without change, we continued the march over a beautiful plain. The high ground on both sides of us was rocky but passable and covered with good grass although it is sterile.[7] We camped in the Arroyo del Cíbolo without having seen any buffaloes in the area. Nothing unusual happened during the day. 8 leagues

[5] A copy of Amangual's diary is listed by Bolton in the Mexican Archives, Relaciones Exteriores, second series, caja 1835–1838, but Professor Nasatir has looked for it three times without success; a copy is in Guerra y Marina, 1836, leg. 7, No. 2. A fuller but different copy is in the Bexar Archives, and is found in the Indexed Translations. There are entries in the Guerra copy that are not in the Bexar copy, and there is considerable material in the Bexar copy that is not found in the Guerra copy. There are extensive omissions from each. Our copy is the Guerra copy, collated with the Bexar copy.

[6] Two-pound cones of brown sugar.

[7] Not very nourishing.

April 2

This day dawned with a furious storm, accompanied by terrible thunder and lightning and constant rains, very cold. For this reason we stopped there, and no other unusual incident occurred except that the *cavallada* [horse band] of the New Kingdom of León and veterans stampeded; 87 animals were lost, and a party of 10 men and a corporal went out to look for them, and returned with them at 4 o'clock without one missing. It continued to rain and the weather stayed cold. Night fell with no other unusual incident.

April 3

This day dawned very rainy and we could not continue our trip. A severe norther, accompanied by rain, began to blow, but at nightfall the wind stopped, the sky cleared, and there was no other unusual incident except that the *cavallada* of the Colony stampeded, and a saddled horse belonging to one of the men who guarded the *cavallada* ran away and was lost. There were 9 animals missing, and some men went out to look for them. Night fell without any other unusual incident's occurring.

April 4

This day having dawned clear and calm, we continued our march over a good, level plain; at 10 o'clock in the morning we arrived at a small pass in the hills, where the width is about 50 *varas*. It is impassable; it goes half-way up the side of the left hill, but it is the only possible pass between this point and a point about half a league from the Río de Guadalupe. We traveled over low, hilly country with good pasture and some trees. At 2 o'clock we crossed the arroyo named Los Baleones, and we stopped as soon as we crossed the said Guadalupe River with no other event than the fact that we left a party of 10 men, a sergeant, and a corporal in search of the saddle and the lost horses. At sundown the party looking for the saddle returned. 9 leagues

April 5

Dawn came today without any unusual incident. There was no departure today because 7 men and a corporal were missing from the party that had been left to look for the 9 horses that had been missing the day before. At nightfall the corporal and 7 men arrived with the horses, with no other unusual incident than the loss of a package of cartridges.

April 6

We set out, traveling through a very hilly country with many hills and several high, rocky slopes. After traveling 2½ hours, we crossed a very extensive canyon called San Francisco, with a creek of clear running water that flows north and south, with many turns. It is a very pleasant place, a *figurosa* valley. There was no other unusual incident save that the soldiers driving the mules broke two rifles when their animals bolted. Six hours later we passed the Arroyo Blanco, which runs east and west across a very large plain; and after crossing a small section of hill country thickly covered with liveoak, we arrived at Pedernales Creek, which runs from east to west. We camped on a promontory on the north side with an excellent view and several clumps of liveoaks, whose arroyo runs east and west. We camped without further incident. 10½ leagues

April 7

Today we set out, following the arroyo [and traveling] across high and extensive country with broken ground and hills, much liveoak on both sides. This creek has many pools of considerable depth and width, with many clumps of trees around them. We crossed this creek five times, and at almost every crossing it was necessary to open up paths and descents because those found were impassable, especially for our party. To this end an officer and four men were detailed with axes, crowbars, and pickaxes [or grubbing hoes] to make ascents and descents. We continued on our way until we arrived at the headwaters of said arroyo,[8] where night came upon us suddenly without unusual incident. 9 leagues

April 8

We left the said area, continuing our course through a hilly country with very rocky plains overgrown with weeds and trees, with many up- and down-slopes but without any view whatever. In this situation we

[8] Amangual seems to use the word *arroyo* to mean the entire system of a cut in the earth and the creek at the bottom, or the creek itself, and possibly a dry cut.

traveled until 10 o'clock in the morning, when we came upon open country with high evergreen oaks and some dense forested hillocks [which we traveled over] until we arrived at an arroyo called El Chimal, where they killed a bear and where was sighted a herd of buffalo at a considerable distance. This arroyo is situated between two hills with red *barrancas*, and in order to get to it, we had to descend a very high slope and continue on the level until we crossed some *barrancas* in a *rivera que have*. We pitched our camp there, with no unusual incident having occurred on the way. 8 leagues

April 9

We set out from this place, continuing our march over a terrain almost impassable because of its dense woods. The plain was red sand without any grass whatever. We traveled over this country for three hours until we came into more open country with many high and barren elevations and stretches of level ground; on the west side, there were hills like little mesas, and on the east side there are plains. At 12 o'clock in the afternoon[9] we arrived at some very high hills with rocky cliffs, then we descended over a steep precipice to the river called Llanos, which runs through hills of solid rock, with much water flowing east and west. It is very wide; its bottom meadows, with few trees, are covered with very fragrant onions of the same taste as those we use in our food, and are very tasty, and we replenished [our supplies]. We camped in that place, no unusual incident having occurred other than that we left a party of four men to look for some horses that were missed when we left; at sundown they returned and said they had not found them. Night fell with no unusual incident. 9 leagues.

April 10

We continued our course through country with very high and rocky hills, and after an hour, the road emerged on high plains with level ground, and some red sand, many evergreen oaks, little grass. The earth is generally very poor and sterile; there is not found even grass of any kind. Until we approached the San Saba River, we traveled through hills; then we descended into a large, low flatland with many groves

[9] It is 1:30 in the Bexar copy.

of trees. We soon crossed the river and camped a short distance from it. On the way we saw several herds of buffalo. Night fell with no unusual incident. 11½ leagues

April 11

Today at daybreak two Comanche Indians presented themselves and said they came from the village of Cordero and were going to Bexar. We did not continue on our way because we needed to rest the *cavallada* and the mule herd, as they were thin and lame [run down] because of the travel over rocky terrain with little grass. This river has abundant water, a large grove of walnut trees and other trees; there are many fish in the river, many turkeys, bears, and all kinds of animals; it flows from east northeast and west southwest to west, and there is a distance of 4½ leagues from our encampment to the abandoned presidio.[10]

This morning I set out with a patrol of 10 men to examine the presidio, and upon my arrival, I found a small plaza, well enclosed by a wall on all sides; the wall is constructed of rock but is badly deteriorated. There are indications that there were bastions in each corner of the square, and on the north a two-story ruined house. It can be seen that there was also a covered road by which they went down to the river to get water. [The presidio] is north of the river, very close to the river, which flows east and west, is quite deep, and has a good view. The country is a level plain as far as the eye can see to the north; on the south, there are hills of the same shape, forming mesas, and there is a sort of stairway. There is a beautiful ditch of water [*saca de agua*] that runs from east to west, which, it can be seen, served to irrigate a very extensive plain which extends from the hills to the river on the south; the land is very pleasant and suitable for all kinds of seeds. I returned to the camp without any unusual incident.

April 12

Today having dawned without unusual incident, we continued our course through a country with a good view, good grass, and sparse

[10] Of San Saba, abandoned some fifty years before. Inasmuch as Amangual, until he leaves Santa Fe, seldom gives the direction of his march, we have been somewhat in the dark, but this definite point shows us that he had been veering considerably west. His camp would be a little west of present Hext, in Menard County.

woods, but before we had traveled 3½ leagues, we encountered low hills with some rocks, and, as the Indian guide told us that we were near the village of the Indian [Chief] Cordero, two soldiers and one Indian were sent to report our arrival. After a little while, a Comanche Indian came running to report that Cordero had moved his village to a place where there was good grass and plenty of water, and was waiting for us there. Therefore, we immediately changed our course, and traveled over some low hills with good grass. From the top of one, [Bexar copy: we sighted the village, which looked like a city, located on a beautiful plain; also] we saw a multitude of Indians on horseback, who accompanied Cordero and his chiefs. They were painted with red ochre and dressed in various costumes, and we received them with our troops in column formation, and with our drums beating a march. After the ceremonies of politeness and friendly relations, the companies filed by and continued on their way; we were accompanied by the most important Indians, the rest going along on one side until we reached [Bexar copy has missing pages and there are no entries for the rest of April 12, for April 13, 14, or 15.] the vicinity of the said village, forming a square when we stopped. We encamped, and, the [our] Indian having departed with the rest, their chiefs issued the proper orders. In the afternoon we went, with two chiefs and an assistant, to visit them at his [Cordero's] lodge, and he received us with much jubilation, having prepared seats by covering the floor with buffalo skins. After the caravans had passed by, we returned to our own camp with no unusual incident. 8

## April 13

This day dawned with no occurrence in the place named the Arroyo de Conchos. There was no departure [today], in order to have a discussion with the Indian Cordero[11] regarding our expedition, and also to rest the horses and mules, who are very thin, and because the land was

[11] Cordero, as we already know, was a principal Comanche chief. At this point in Amangual's narrative, Cordero was not far north of San Antonio, and probably was a Penateka or Southern Comanche. In 1818 he was at Natchitoches for two weeks with fifteen of his tribe, and conducted himself well. In 1821 he saved Thomas James and his party, on the way to Santa Fe, from annihilation by three hundred Comanches on the Canadian River in the Texas Panhandle; he was then, James said, tall, regal, and about seventy years old. See Thomas James, *Three Years Among the Indians and Mexicans*, 75–78, 133.

good for the purpose. At 4 o'clock in the afternoon I prepared to go with the two chiefs, an assistant, and an interpreter to the lodge of Cordero to make the delivery of his walking cane and rifle sent by our governor, Antonio Cordero, to govern and defend his [the Comanche Cordero's] village—which he received very cordially, and after this act there was a discussion of the information that we needed concerning our course of action, he answering everything that was asked with sufficient clearness and energy. Also there was discussion of the guides whom we would need from his tribe—who should be experienced, loyal, and of good conduct. He offered to supply them, and said he had information that there was a Spaniard who had served as cowherd to an Indian under his command, and that the latter, as soon as he heard of our arrival, had hidden himself; he [Cordero] was told to try to get his people to find him and to bring him to us, and that if he needed help, it would be given to him. Night fell; nothing new.

April 14

This day dawned without unusual incident, and I invited the captains of militia, Chief Cordero, and other Indian chiefs to come to eat at our table at noon—which nine chiefs did. We received the nine chiefs with honors, for they which were very grateful, and gave us many thanks and true affection. They retired to their lodges, the Indian Chief Cordero informing us that they had not found the Spaniard who was wanted, and that the search for and apprehension of the man remained in his care. Night fell with nothing unusual, but at 10 o'clock there arose a very strong and cold north wind which seemed the most rigorous of the winter.

April 15

This day dawned very cold, with a strong north wind, for which reason it was decided to move the encampment to a place where there would be shelter, in order to be able to endure it—which was done, through a country covered with evergreen oak, skirting the arroyo de Conchos until we arrived at a place with much water, much pasturage, and good shelter for the troops from the strong norther, which was almost impossible to endure. In this manner, night fell without any unusual incident. 4 leagues

April 16

Today the weather was rather calm, and we continued our march, accompanied by Cordero's band. We traveled over a very beautiful plain with good grass and some elevations with a splendid view, until we arrived at a spring called Los Nogales, where there were water holes, much grass, and some woods in the neighborhood. We camped in this place, and a short distance away Cordero encamped his band, it being his intention to accompany us until we should find a large herd of buffalo, so he could get meat for his band, and also for our troops. As soon as we passed [reached?] this point, four men went with the Indians to hunt and prepare meat. They returned at sundown with a large amount of meat and five calves on the hoof. Night fell without further incident. 6 leagues

April 17

This day we stayed in camp in order to cure the meat and let the *cavallada* rest. At 9 o'clock in the morning, the troops attending in the accustomed manner, and after hearing mass, the penal laws were read to them, and there was a review of arms and munitions. Afterward, five men went out in company [with other Indians] to hunt meat, taking pack-mules to bring back the meat. A short time later, there arrived a muleteer from the company of the New Kingdom of Leon with the news that he had injured a finger while pulling one of the mules. He was treated. And at sundown the hunters returned with a quantity of meat, three calves on the hoof among them—one a year old and very wild. Night fell with no further unusual incident.

April 18

This day having dawned with no change, we left through wooded country that made it necessary to cut passageway for the troops as far as some very rocky hills. There we came to a beautiful spring of clear water which the Indians said had no name, and we named it El Ojo de la Pascua. It is located in a ravine of rough rock and flows in abundance on the surface; the terrain [vegetation] is abundant, and there is a beautiful clump of trees nearby. In all directions, as far as the eye can reach, it is level. The purpose of traveling to the west was [to find] water and because some of the villages were in that direction. When we left, there remained a corporal and 6 men in search of six animals that were missed upon leaving. Night fell with no further incident 3½ leagues.

April 19

This day dawned with no unusual incident, and we set out. At sunrise there arrived the corporal and five [they started with six] soldiers, and reported that they had not found the six missing animals. Our course has been along a little valley with small plateaus until we crossed the creek formed by the spring, and after traveling a short distance, we entered a rocky, hilly country [and traveled over it] until we reached a beautiful plain with good grass, several low hills, and some evergreen oaks. A long distance to the north there is an extended range of hills, and to the south there can be seen a grove of trees along the Colorado River. To the north was a hill with two peaks which the Indians said was called the Eagle's nest [La Casa de la Aguila]. We traveled in that direction until we climbed a range of extensive hills, and from there we saw a great plain with much grass, where there is a river which descends to join the Colorado. Having arrived at its banks, [we found the river] delightful both for its beautiful location as well as for its groves of very tall walnut trees; it seems like a paradise, had abundant water with much fish, and nearby there are extensive plains covered with grass. The Indians say that at about 9 or 10 leagues, the water comes gushing out of a rock. It [the river] flows north northwest and east east south [!]. In our course we found many buffaloes [in this day's march]. The Indians killed several, and the troops carried the meat to camp to cure it. Night fell without any other unusual incident. [Bexar copy only: 8 leagues]

April 20

This day dawned without incident except that the *cavallada* of the Colony stampeded, and part of it was found with the *cavallada* of the New Kingdom of León. After the horses were cut out, there were 18 animals missing, and some troops have gone in search of them. We did not set out on the march, for the need of resting the *cavallada,* which is run down, and because this place is suited to condition them, and [also because] the troops can provide themselves with meat, and should not reach a state of want as long as there is a remedy. Five soldiers and one corporal have gone out together to hunt meat; night fell without their having returned. At 8 o'clock in the evening, the Comanche Indian who had come from San Antonio as guide with the expedition, complained that he had lost an iron chain that he kept in a stable [or mounted on a quirt] because of which the adjutant was ordered to question the sentries, where was found the guilty soldier from the company of Don Matías Cantu, which is attached to the company of Don José Agabo de Ayala, called Faustino Lozano. When this fact was proved, I ordered assembly to be sounded, and the soldiers formed a circle. The soldier was brought in by a corporal and two privates as guards, placed in the center and his case recited. [Then] he was given twenty-five blows with a slender stick by the same corporal for his punishment and an example for the troops. He was then placed in the guardhouse until further orders [should be given].

## April 21

This day we continued in camp. At midnight it was reported that the hunters had returned, without unusual incident, bringing a large quantity of meat, which was ordered cured without waste; then, [several pages missing from the Bexar copy to almost the end of the entry for April 26] after the guard was changed, there was a drill by the companies, and, that finished, the hunters left and returned with meat at sunset. On this day, Captain Don José Agabo de Ayala, accompanied by the adjutant and two soldiers, left to examine the source of the river, skirting it and stopping on it at various places, because it has many very convenient watering places and wide plains, extensive in places; it is loaded with red silt, and in other places the water reached the level of the land. Both banks are excellent, with much pasture, forming some beautiful meadows walled in by easy-to-climb hills with a good view to the distance of 2 leagues from the encampment to the south. Ascending a hill that dominated the country and gave visibility to the northwest, a very large grove [was seen]. Another river flows southwest to northeast, which they said was the Colorado, and by information of a soldier traveling in the company, he knew also from where the water of this river on which we are encamped comes, which is 2½ leagues away. The hunters arrived with meat, and there was no other unusual incident.

April 22

On this day we remained camped in the same place in order to dry the meat and so that the animals may finish recovering [feeding up]. Yesterday Chief Chiojas arrived with his family, without bringing any news, and he returned to his village after having spoken with Cordero, and afterward there arrived various Indians from the above mentioned chief, and they brought no other news than that they had come to visit their companions. At night there occurred no unusual incident in the encampment or in the location, but at midnight an Indian arrived who said he came from a campaign; he speaks Castilian, and he gave information of having been in many settlements of Durango, Coahuila, and New Mexico, for he was born there. For those reasons he would be a very excellent person to have as a guide from here to the said New Mexico, and he told me that this river is not that of El Horrido, as I said before, but the Río Verde. There was no other incident. Night fell.[12]

April 23

This day dawned without other incident during the night than that of the stampeding of the *cavallada* of the New Kingdom of León and Bexar, but it was rounded up and added to that of the Colony, without loss. At 7 o'clock in the morning, Cordero, accompanied by four soldiers, the best of the squadron, left to visit the tribes in another village that is northwest of us about 3 leagues, where they have called a meeting by order of General Cordero; and at 4 o'clock in the afternoon they returned without any news. The soldiers say that it is a village larger than that of Cordero's, and shows a multitude of Indians. This day there was a review of arms and munitions, and the obligations of the soldiers and those of the guard were read. Five veteran soldiers left to kill buffalo. Night fell with no unusual incident.

April 24

This day, after hearing mass, we left the said encampment [and traveled] across country with plains and good grass, with very little mesquite, until we arrived at the village of Chief Chiojas, which is situ-

[12] The captain is getting a little automatic in his entries. The Indian arrived at midnight, and, after they questioned him, "night fell."

ated in an arroyo that the Indians call that of De Almagre. It flows, as is seen from the camp, to the southwest and "by the east to the northeast"; is well supplied with water, a great deal of forest with tall groves of walnut trees. Its beaches are of small mounds of stones; the view is level on all sides as far as the eye can reach. Upon arriving at the said village, we noted that not one Indian came out to receive us; as Cordero observed, it was a village of more than two hundred tents, but I considered that it might be [either] fear or lack of courtesy as practiced by Cordero. But after being encamped on the said river, as if from the north of the village, all kinds of Indians swarmed out to visit us, and I observed that they were more discourteous and stupid than the people of Cordero who had passed near our encampment. Because he knew that some Indian chiefs [?] were planning to steal the horses, it was ordered immediately to double the guard of the horses and mules. No further incident has occurred. 2 leagues

April 25

On this day there was no departure because we had to parley with the Indians who gathered in this village, and to appoint the guides who are to go with our expedition. Night fell without incident. This day we gave a small gift to the Indians, as had been done with Cordero, which also was delivered to Cordero in order that it be distributed through him, and there was a drill by the companies. In the afternoon we went to the village of Chief Chiojas, where assembled all the chiefs and the rest of their *bolos* and Chief Cordero, and by means of our interpreter I made to them a long and clear speech that our arrival was with the object of inviting them to visit us, to let them know the love of our king and father toward them, the loyalty and fidelity that we bear him; that they should observe the same, that they should not trade with any other nation that may come to induce them, for their [any other nation's] object is none other than that of afterward turning them from their loyalty to us; [I asked them] if they knew if any Americans from other nations have entered their lands and if they knew if they had a trading post; to which they responded, first, that they were satisfactorily informed of everything, for they considered themselves Spaniards and believe everything that comes from us, and without accepting anything from other nations; and, second, that they know nothing about what was asked them. It caused a great parley to take place; they spoke of all that we imposed on them, and that they were faithful to everything, likewise to us, that just like the defenders against the enemies, they would do the same. Afterward there was a discussion of the guides for our trip, which was left for them to discuss among themselves. And on the following day they decided those who should be most useful for the places in which we had to travel, and at the same time of good conduct and loyal to their nation—the best qualities required for this task—to which we agreed. Upon completion of everything expressed, we withdrew to our encampment, accompanied by Cordero, with no incident other than that upon our arrival we found one of the sick men from the company of Lieut. Luciano Garcia, named Rafael Mansilla, very ill with pain in the side, for which reason the chaplain immediately went to confess him. No other incident occurred, and night fell.

April 26

Today we remained in camp in the same place awaiting what was mentioned yesterday. During the night, nothing unusual occurred except that the sick man, mentioned before, continued very ill, and because of that, the chaplain went to hear his dying confession and grant him absolution according to the papal bull. At night of this day, Captain Agabo de Ayala went out with an escort of 8 men and a corporal to reconnoiter the pasture lands, and three hours later he returned with nothing unusual, after having found it to be very good pasture as far as the Colorado, which he reconnoitered. This day [also] 7 soldiers went to hunt, and [Bexar copy picks up here again] they returned with meat, with no unusual incident. At sundown a very ominous thundercloud appeared in the northwest, which *al esclarecerse* turned into a norther so violent that it seemed to be a hurricane of the worst kind ever experienced [with] lightning and thunder. Night fell without unusual incident.

April 27

Today we remained in camp in the same place to wait for the guides [to tell us] where we should spend the night. It continued to rain, and there was a norther so violent that it tore some of the tents to shreds; it blew until midnight, when it abated completely. The day dawned clear. The aforesaid soldier died at 9 o'clock, and was buried in the afternoon. At sundown a storm [*frolundada*] commenced to blow towards the southeast and to the northeast, and it started lightening and thundering, but it did not amount to a great deal. At midnight, however, it changed to the north, and then returned to the southeast, and [finally] blew from all directions. Such was the fury of it that the tents were of no value, and all the troops were swimming in it, and at that hour the weather became calm, but very cloudy. Without anything further occurring, today we all wrote to Bexar to report our situation.

April 28

At dawn today the road was muddy [*mojada*] because of the great storm of water and wind during the night, and very cloudy and dark on the horizon, and threatening rain; consequently, we did not set out. The *cavallada* of the Colony stampeded, and at dawn half of them were missing;[13] therefore, [some soldiers] went to search for them, and at 8 o'clock brought back a band of 24 animals; an Indian reported that they were looking for the others. At 10 o'clock a heavy rain and windstorm came up from the north, and lasted until noon, when it cleared up the same day. In the afternoon, the Indians paraded on horseback. Both the Indians and the horses were greatly adorned and painted with very strange figures. They seemed dressed like Moors on a holiday in our towns. They ride and galloped around the camp, and finally dismounted. The men looking for the *cavallada* reported that they had found all but six animals. Night fell with no unusual incident.

April 29

Today dawned clear, and we set out according to the arrangements made previously. During the night the *cavallada* of the New Kingdom of León stampeded [again?], but they were all found upon our departure except six animals belonging to New Santander and two belonging to the New Kingdom of León. Therefore, one corporal and six men were left to look for them. Today's march took us over level ground and some very high and open ground, with a few scattered small hills that formed mesas. There were passes among the [hills], and some

[13] The *cavallada* ought to be getting trail broke by now. One wonders if it was as run-down as the captain has been saying.

patches of mesquite trees; there were several small *cañadas* and some dry creeks.[14] At half a league from where we set out, we crossed a creek that flows into the Almagre, and on seeing it, it flows west northwest to east southeast. It is thickly wooded along its side, and does not carry much water. Night fell with no unusual incident other than the appearance of the men who remained to hunt the strays. 10 leagues

April 30

Dawn came today with no unusual incident during the night, and so we set out on our way. As we traveled, the men arrived and reported that they had brought back only four animals, and that three had been lost, and they had not been found because of the darkness. They lost one lance and broke one musket while the horses were on the run.[15] We continued on our way, traveling along the said creek over level ground covered with mesquite trees. On the north side of the creek there are some low hills, and that is true on the south side. There was a passageway between the hills, and we traveled through it. The weather was threatening; therefore we tried to get close to the creek. We camped on a high place, and immediately it started to rain, and the lightning was furious. Nothing else unusual occurred. The creek was still running in the same direction as it did yesterday. It continued to rain until noon, but cleared up in the afternoon. No unusual incident occurred, and night fell. All these creeks flow on the same course [to the same river?]. 1 league

May 1

This day dawned without any unusual incident having occurred during the night. After mass we marched over a level plain through a valley formed by the hilly country that runs north and south, and there were passes to the west and north, formed by some round hills that afforded a very good view. Captain Don José Agabo de Ayala climbed to the top of one of them, which was located in the middle of the valley; it is very high and commands the view to a great distance. All he could see from there were hills in every direction. And from there on, we began to march over hilly country [Bexar copy: and high plains covered with grass. We finally came down to a small plain near

[14] He says, *arroyos secos,* so now we have: dry water course.

[15] For a run-down bunch of horses, this is the wildest *cavallada* in Texas.

the river, surrounded by hills] on all sides. According to reports obtained from the Indians, these rivers are the branches that make up the Colorado, which is the one we sighted last night. Two hours later we crossed it, and we continued to travel parallel with another [river] that was visible at a distance of two leagues, running from north to south. The one we followed runs in the same direction we are traveling, to the point where we crossed it. On its banks, as aforesaid, we camped. No unusual incident occurred during our trip except that Captain Don Cayetano Quintero became ill, and it was necessary for him to remain behind with 20 men. After we reached the place where we pitched our camp, and after having given the necessary orders, Captain Don José Agabo, accompanied by the adjutant and two soldiers, set out with food [for Captain Quintero]. After having traveled 1 league, they encountered him; he was much better. They took him to camp, where, after taking certain medicines, he recovered completely. No other unusual incidents occurred before nightfall. [Bexar copy adds this: No other unusual incidents occurred this afternoon. Four soldiers were hunting to get meat for the Indians. These rivers are very beautiful because of the large number of trees near them, good and palatable water, good watering places, and grass that grows abundantly near the water. This is the best soil I have seen. No other unusual incident occurred; before night fell, the soldiers who had gone to hunt having returned without unusual incident.] 8 leagues

May 2

Dawn came today without anything unusual during the night. We continued on our way along the aforesaid creek, or headwaters of the Colorado. The terrain was like that of the previous day; all hills. We climbed a hill from which we could see a great distance of 1 league around. From there we could see more hilly country the same distance away among high peaks. Captain Ayala [Bexar copy says Captain José Agabo] climbed a peak from which he could see a long distance. All he could see from there was hilly country, but the hills were low, and the creeks that form the headwaters of the said [Colorado], where we slept. We crossed it about one hour after our departure by a crossing that ran northeast and southeast [?], and from there we continued along the other [creek], which joins it immediately [Bexar copy: near the place from where we set out] and flows in the same direction. We traveled along that creek until we camped on its banks [Bexar copy: at 11:30] on the level ground covered with mesquite trees. Many buffaloes have been sighted today; therefore, the soldiers were given permission to go hunting. Some of the buffalo came right into our camp, and after they had gone by, a soldier reported that he had seen Indian sign along the creek. Consequently a party [of soldiers] was immediately sent out to investigate the direction taken by the Indians. Three hours later they returned and reported that the trail was several days old, and that it led to an old village, where they found a horse that had been speared and whose hide was almost dry. No other unusual incident occurred except that at sundown one of the soldiers who had been hunting about 3 leagues from camp reported that some Indians had told him that their village was near there. While they were giving the information, an Indian on horseback, with a lance and carbine, came up and said he was a Comanche and belonged to the band of Chief Tuerto, one of those who were in our company with Cordero, and he dismounted and commenced to talk to the Indian guides. All the hunters returned, and night came without any other unusual incident. 5 leagues.

## May 3

Dawn came today without any unusual incident during the night, and we set out. As we were leaving, an Indian from the village arrived to look for the Indian who arrived here yesterday, and who had stolen his horse and arms; this [latter] Indian was left on foot, and he turned out to be a Yamparica and not one of El Tuerto's band, as he claimed yesterday. On our way, we had no unusual incident. We traveled over a plain, where the soil was very loose and there were many holes, several groves of mesquite trees, flat hills, and small mountains, and it was all the same as far as the eye could see. After we had traveled 2½ hours, we crossed the said creek, along whose bank we had been traveling, and continued along it on the north side until we camped at its source on a high plain. The creek is densely wooded, and there is a fairly high mesa near it in addition to a *castillo* [battle fort, lookout point] where we set out a sentry to watch from our camp, since it dominated a large area. Today an infinite number of buffaloes was seen in the arroyo; there was a watering place and a field that gave it the appearance of a great hacienda, and as far as one could see, the country was covered with buffaloes. Consequently, our people profited greatly. In the afternoon, an Indian guide with two soldiers went to scout for water for the following day, and when they returned they reported that there was not enough water even for the men. Consequently, it was decided to set out in the afternoon in order to reach the next day's water hole. The Indian mentioned above arrived, and continued to travel with us. During the afternoon there was a heavy hailstorm which covered the country. We climbed up on a mesa to reconnoiter, but a strong windstorm drove us down. This mesa is very extensive and forms a plaza about ¼ league in extent. The night was clear, and nothing unusual happened. [Bexar copy adds: We are at the headwaters of the aforecited creek, which is the source of the branches of the Colorado River. At the place where we are camped, it runs southeast. The reason for our failure to continue traveling over the mesa is that there are no water holes toward the north, which is the direction we must take. Therefore, it is necessary for us to go around it until we strike water flowing from the north, to continue to our destination.] May God take care of us. 3½ leagues

May 4

Today we remained in the same place until 1 o'clock in the afternoon. At that time we set out in order to spend the night at a place from which we could reach water the following day. We traveled over level ground, which had a few flat hills and open ground with a few patches of mesquite. In the distance we could see hills that looked like flat ranges.[16] At 4 o'clock we turned and passed by a small spring of water which we did not like because it had very little water in it; it is located in a small arroyo and in a thickly wooded section. We continued to travel to gain distance, although we stopped on a high place covered with chaparral. There was no unusual incident in the day's travel. 6 leagues

May 5

Dawn came today without unusual incident during the night. We continued to march over an open plain, treeless as far as the eye could

[16] It appears this may have been somewhere in the area of present Snyder, Texas.

see. Some low hills and a pass could be seen at a distance. The ground was very red, something like red ochre. At 10 o'clock we crossed an arroyo which had many turns from its source; it flowed from the north, and its shores and banks were of red ochre; it was dry. Floods had reached its highest banks, which extend back for some distance, but I believe the floods come only when it rains. A half hour after we crossed said creek, we went through the previously mentioned pass and hills, which run northwest and are very beautiful. We continued to travel over level ground, which had a few patches of mesquite trees, until we descended into a wide arroyo covered with red sand and running northwest to southeast. The banks are high and water was in pools, which the animals drank easily. For the troops, holes had to be dug, and drinkable water was thus obtained. We continued toward the north across a plain covered with many pools of water, mesquite, and chaparral. One hour after we had pitched our camp, two Yamparica Indians arrived. They said that the village of their big chief was located behind the hills mentioned yesterday. One of them said he was the son of the big chief, who was eager to see and to know his brothers from Bexar. Therefore, I ordered Lieutenant Cadena with 4 men to go with the Indians to [visit] the big chief to get acquainted with him. At the same time, one of the guides and 2 men went to scout to find a better location to camp and to await the big chief with his people. We continued, with no unusual incident. Night fell. 8 leagues

May 6

Day came today without anything unusual during the night, and we traveled along the said creek to improve our camping ground. We stopped near a high promontory next to a high, rocky bluff of red earth. We camped there to wait for Lieutenant Cadena together with the big chief and his Yamparica Indians. Nothing unusual was experienced in this short distance. Upon arriving there, I had the companies assembled, and since we are beginning to experience a scarcity of water, and the *cavallada* was greatly run down when it was kept together [because a large group of animals needs to spread out over a large area to find enough grass], I decided to have each company handle its own *cavallada* separately, and to have each [such] *cavallada* guarded by one corporal and 6 men. In this manner, the *cavallada* would suffer less while traveling as well as at the water holes. Consequently, today I issued this general order. In the afternoon, Lieutenant Cadena and the 4 solders who accompanied him, returned, together with the big chief and Sanbanbi [Sabarbi], a Yamparica, and two of their Indians. They were well received. They said that their village was located a short distance from this camp to the west east [?]. These [Indians] rejoiced to see us, and made us understand they had a great love for the Spaniards of Bexar and a great desire for friendship with them. They stayed in our camp that night, where they rested, with no unusual incident. 1½ leagues

May 7

This morning came with nothing unusual having occurred during the night. We remained in camp at the same place to rest the *cavalladas* and to discuss the object of our expedition with the Yamparicas, and to get information about the route to our destination in order to learn where water and grass might be found, and where hills might be found [for seeing a long distance] in order to enable us to succeed in reaching our destination. To this effect, they [the Yamparicas] agreed that on the following day we should get together to discuss these matters. Today, inspection of arms and ammunition was held, and the penal laws and the duties of sentries were read to the troops. Today [also] I placed Lieutenant Luciano Garcia under arrest in the company that he commands, while Don Manuel de Alanis of the same company was placed in charge of administrative and fiscal matters of the company. Today the commandant of the *cavallada* of the first company of the Colony reported that the *cavallada* had stampeded during the early-morning watch; thirty animals were missing. [Troops] immediately went in search of them, and all were recovered by the afternoon. Before dark, the Yamparica Indians withdrew to their village, taking leave of us cheerfully They said that on the following day they would see us in their homes. Night fell with no unusual incident.

May 8

This day dawned with nothing unusual having occurred, and after mass was said, we started over high and level ground covered with red sand. Many mesquite trees [grew] in the valley formed by the elevations. We reached the village of the previously mentioned big chief

Isambanbi [Sanbanbi], located on an elevation on the shore of a creek that runs north northwest and empties into the one from which we came. The place is level and has much grass and many mesquite trees. Upon our arrival, the big chief and the other chiefs of the tribe came out to meet us. They were very well dressed, but they wore very unusual clothes: long red coats with blue collars and cuffs, white buttons, yellow (imitation gold) galloons; one was dressed in ancient Spanish style: a short red coat, blue trousers, white stockings, English spurs, an ordinary cornered hat worn cocked, a cane with a silver handle shaped like a hyssop. Others wore red neckties; they wore sashes made out of otterskin, adorned with beads and shells; their hair was nicely braided and trailing on the ground; they were painted with chalk and red ochre. After having received them cordially, we moved north of the creek and there we had them dismount and sit in a shade that had been prepared for them. They were given refreshments, and then we talked for about an hour, after which they took leave of us and returned to their lodges. We told them to continue visiting us in order that we could show our friendship and loyalty for them. They were very grateful and showed signs of being very pleased at having met and being with us. Night fell with no unusual incident. 4 leagues

May 9

Dawn came today with very stormy weather—strong wind, rain, lightning, and terrible thunder. This morning the adjutant went to the village with the Indian interpreter to offer small gifts to the big chief Ysambanbi from the stock of presents we brought with us, as shown by the list of distribution. Four soldiers went out with one of the Indians [Bexar copy: guides] to look for an Indian woman belonging to this village, who is reported to be in a village located near this camp, which is under the jurisdiction of the aforementioned Ysambanbi, who gave orders for her return. The adjutant and the two chiefs began a discussion of the object of our mission, and they were made to understand that it was the will of our king for them to live [at peace] and not to consort with any enemy tribes in these parts of the country. They were well apprised of these [wishes] as well as of the [fact that they had a right to expect] loyalty and honest dealings from us, which we owe to them. They displayed a deep understanding and promised to be faithful in their friendship; they also set us right concerning the Indian settlements as far as the Red River. They offered us a guide in addition to the two that we had, so that we would not suffer for lack of water—for the land is very different from what I had imagined; according to the map, there is a great difference. At 1 o'clock the two chiefs and our adjutants withdrew to our camp. The weather continued very disagreeable, with thunder, and threatened a heavy rain. The Indians and two captains of militia were given something to eat, the [regular] meals having already been finished. It continued to rain heavily, and the arroyo arose so much that it cannot be crossed. Much thunder. Night fell without any other unusual incident except that the Indian and four soldiers have not returned.

May 10

Today we did not continue the march, as stated in a general order, because the Indian and 4 soldiers have not returned. We attributed it to the heavy rains and the overflowing streams. The night continued to be calm, and no other unusual incident occurred. The Indian and 4 soldiers returned. [Bexar copy adds: Daybreak came with calm weather, and the creek continued to rise; it carried much reddish water heavy with sand, and was not drinkable.] The soldiers were given permission to go hunting. They returned without anything, as they were unable to find any buffaloes. The day continued to be very warm and calm; the creek began to recede. North of the camp it flows to the west, and has many turns. No unusual incident occurred in the afternoon other than that the 4 soldiers and the Indian guide did not return. [A few sentences above he says they did return.] Today very few Indians have come to our camp because the large amount of rain and water in the arroyo have prevented their doing so. Consequently, we have had some rest, for [when they are here,] they hardly let us eat or sleep or do anything, as they are very curious, going uninvited into the tents and walking around among the troops. The captains have waited upon them as much as the facilities of the trip would permit, spending more on the Indians than on themselves. Nothing new happened.

May 11

This day dawned without the occurrence of anything unusual during the night, and so we continued our march. At the time of breaking camp, the 4 soldiers who had been reconnoitering the scattered villages, and who still were missing, returned [to camp]. Today we traveled over high country and a few small valleys covered with mesquite trees until we reached a creek. We encountered a few low hills, many arroyos [Bexar copy: rocky ledges, bluffs, and cliffs. We looked for a descent, and, having arrived at an arroyo, we went down into the creek channel on the south side. The bluffs were made of flat rock and gravel. The north bluff as well as the bank and the shore of the arroyo are made of red sand. The water flowing in it was reddish and undrinkable. We looked for a ford and found a good one,] at which we crossed our pack train, the troops, and the *cavalladas,* without incident. We camped on the north side of some low hills in the vicinity of which was a village of the aforementioned band, and they [the Indians] were very happy and simple, from whom it was learned that they call this arroyo La Arena—and so also is this land [sandy] that we must travel; the water is very salty, making it necessary to dig wells to draw water for the people.[17] 6½ leagues

[Bexar copy: We looked for a ford and found a good one, and drove our loaded mule train across it; the troops and *cavallada* also crossed it without incident. We camped on the north side of some low hills, which were surrounded by *cañadas,*[18] as a more comfortable place could not be found, since all the terrain is as we have described it. Toward the east northeast from our camp we sighted a village located near the same creek, about ¼ league away. It is under the jurisdiction of the big chief Ysambanbi, and has fifteen tipis. There was another (village) of the same Indians in the vicinity toward the west northwest; it was the one previously reconnoitered by the soldiers mentioned before, and they reported that there were twenty-seven lodges in it. Thus night came with no unusual incident other than the fact that several Indians of the aforesaid village paid us a visit; they were very simple and friendly, and from them we learned that this creek is called

[17] Obviously they are in gypsum country; there is a Sand Creek running into the Double Mountain Fork of the Brazos, near present Post, Texas, and this seems to fit the description.

[18] *Cañada* is another word whose proper translation gives us trouble; it means glen or valley, but "glen" is not a Texas word, and "valley" is too broad a term. Perhaps it is an arroyo with less broken ground and more vegetation.

La Arena (sandy)—and so also (sandy) is the land over which we traveled; and the water is very salty. It was necessary for us to dig wells to draw the necessary water for the men. 6½ leagues]

## May 12

Dawn came today without incident during the night. Therefore, after leaving one corporal and eight men in this place to wait for three soldiers who went to look for a horse that strayed from the last place, we continued on our way. We traveled over high and level ground, covered with flat hills, and a few *cañadas* covered with mesquite trees. There was an infinite number of arroyos and *cañadas;* [Bexar copy: some of them were carrying a little water because it had rained recently]. Thus we continued until we ascended an elevation from which we sighted an extensive plain and a strip of mesquite trees a long distance away. The guides said that there was nothing [but plains] ahead, and that it was impossible for us to go across during the day without exposing our men and animals to die of thirst.[19] It was decided to travel in a different direction, along some *cañada* with water, which the guide had examined, and [which were] covered with grass and a few mesquite trees; the rainwater was very good. The ground where we pitched camp [was red]. No unusual incident occurred on our route. After we had pitched our camp, an Indian guide went out to locate water where we could camp tomorrow. At 3 o'clock the corporal and soldiers who had remained to wait for the three men who went out to look for a horse, which they found, returned. A short while later the Indian guide returned and reported that he had found some water for tomorrow. No unusual incident. 4 leagues

## May 13

Today dawned with nothing unusual having occurred. We continued to travel over a high and level country, covered with red sand and some clumps of mesquite trees that were high and thickly wooded; there were several *cañadas*[20] formed by the beginning and ending of elevations. [Bexar copy: After traveling a short distance, we crossed said elevations and reached an extensive plain, with many small lakes

[19] At last they have sighted the Caprock of the Llano Estacado.

[20] *Cañada* now seems to be an enclosed meadow.

and pools of rain water. There were some clumps of mesquite trees and small cottonwoods; the place is a delightful valley, about 1 league in extent in every direction; its length was cut short by an elevation, very large and level, which we climbed. We again descended to another level, very delightful, that had similar *cañadas* and much water and grass, and a few mesquite trees toward the edges. As the Indian guides reported that if water should be found farther on, it would be merely by chance, as there were no water holes, we decided to camp on an elevated plain with a commanding view near a] *cañada* that held much rain water, and they run from the north to the west. [Immediately] an Indian guide went out in search of a water hole for the following day. He returned and reported that he had found plenty of water a long distance away. Night came with no unusual incident except that a soldier of the New Kingdom of León, who was attached to the company of Don José Agabo de Ayala, was seriously ill with syphilis.[20a] After he was treated with some medicine, he was confessed today. [Bexar copy: As soon as he reported to me, I sent him to his captain, who should give him some kind of medicine. He gave his confession today.] 5½ leagues

May 14

Dawn came today with the unusual incident that the officer of the guard reported to the dawn watch that he had heard a commotion in the *cavallada*. Consequently, one soldier from each company was immediately sent out to see what was going on. One of them returned within the same watch and reported that the *cavallada* of the New Kingdom of León had stampeded, but they were now quieted down and accounted for. When they went to the other *cavalladas,* in compliance with their orders, they learned the unusual incident that the *cavallada* of the Second Company of the Colony had stampeded and not a single animal remained but those of the fatigue party. The Yamparica Indians had stopped them; their village was composed of twenty-nine tipis, and from their village the stampeded horses were incorporated with the other band that had been rounded up by the troops. Night fell without novelty, although a corporal and 5 soldiers were still looking for the lost animals.

[Bexar copy: . . . the *cavallada* of the Second Company of the

[20a] Tsk, tsk.

Colony had stampeded, and not a single animal was left. Consequently, some troops were sent out immediately to determine the best way to find them and to capture them. The situation remained this way until 9 o'clock, when a report arrived concerning the said stampede. It was reported that forty-two animals had been found; that all the troops had joined the escort of said *cavalladas,* composed of twenty-four men, and had gone out to follow the trail; and that they were certain all the *cavallada* was together because of the broad trail they were leaving, and because no other trail had been found. Matters remained in this condition until noon, and we did not set out for that reason. At 2 o'clock the soldiers of other companies, who had been looking for the *cavallada,* returned with the report that the *cavallada* had been overtaken at the village of the Yamparica Indians, where it had been captured.[20b] The village was composed of twenty-nine tipis. From that place, the *cavallada* was taken and incorporated with the other groups that had wandered away. Ten animals were lost. Consequently, I ordered the troops guarding them to look for the lost animals, an equal number of troops replacing them.] Night came with no unusual incident other than the fact that five men and a corporal were still looking for the lost animals.

## May 15

Dawn came with the unusual incident that during the dawn watch [*cuarto de modorra*] three figures that looked like men on horseback were sighted on a nearby hill where the *cavallada* of the First Company of the Colony was located.[21] As soon as the report sent by the commandant of the [company] was received, orders were issued to the *cavalladas* and *muladas*[22] to have all the men mounted and remain in a state of utmost vigilance, and to report without delay the least incident that should be noticed. The same order was given to the sentries and guards. As soon as daylight came, a party of troops was sent out to reconnoiter the fields. They returned with the report that no enemy

[20b] From the fact that these animals should be thoroughly trail broke by now, and that these horses stampeded in the direction of the Indian village (!), it seems obvious that the Indians stampeded them this time, if not several times before—either with the idea of getting away with a few head or in anticipation of getting a reward for holding them, or both.

[21] By this time we can be sure that the Indians were behind most of those stampedes.

[22] *Mulada* is a drove of mules.

trails had been found. After mass, we set out on our route. We traveled over an elevated land with bare cliffs. [Bexar copy: over clumps of tall grass (*sacatones*), and through several *cañadas* and arroyos covered with mesquite trees, until 10:30, when we climbed some low, rocky hills of red soil] that ran from east to west. A short distance after we had descended the first hills, we reached level ground, but there were several red bluffs. [Bexar: We passed along the foot of the aforesaid hill on the northwest side, and] We continued on our way over level ground covered with grass, and camped on a plain with many pools of rain water. [Bexar: No unusual incident occurred on the route except the fact that] One corporal and 5 soldiers with an equal number of horses were left behind to wait for those who were looking for the strays. [Bexar: so that, as they joined them, all of them should come to camp.] At sundown the aforementioned soldiers arrived without anything unusual having occurred. [Bexar: with eleven animals; four were lost.] 7 leagues

May 16

This day dawned with the incident that in the dawn watch, an Indian arrived at the camp, who was taken to the adjutant, and said he came from the village of Chief Ysambanbi[22a] in search of a horse that was in the village of the big chief of the Yamparicas. This day two Indians left us for their village in the neighborhood of the camp. In this manner, night fell, with nothing new. 9½ leagues

[Bexar copy: Dawn came today with the unusual incident that during the dawn watch (*cuarto de modorra*), the corporal in charge of the *mulada* of the Colony reported that an Indian had been found in his camp; he was taken to the corporal of the guard, who made his report. The adjutant went with the interpreter to ask the Indian what he was looking for, and when he was questioned, the (Indian) said that he was a member of the band of Chief Ysambanbi, and that he was on the way to the village of the big chief of the Yamparicas, that is nearby, in

[22a] This chief, as Sabanbipit, was mentioned in the great peace treaty with Anza in 1786, and thus displays unusual longevity for a Comanche chief. Later in this journal it will appear as Ysambanbi, which probably is closer to the correct version; *ysa* is the Comanche word for Wolf, a favorite prefix in Comanche names, and Ysambanbi might mean Handsome Wolf. In 1786 he led eighty warriors against the Apaches; in 1808 he showed typical Comanche scorn for the Spaniards.

search of a horse belonging to his chief. We feared, however, that he might cause some trouble in the *cavallada*, and he was made to understand, in a very kind way, that it would be better for him to sleep in the guardhouse, and that he should continue on his way the following day. We traveled over high and level ground until 9 o'clock, when we began to cross an infinite number of creeks, bluffs, *cañadas*, and open prairies. Sometimes, in order to descend, it was necessary to open a path with our pickaxes and crowbars, because of the depth and steep elevations. We thus continued to climb up and down arroyo-beds until 10:30, when we climbed an elevated plain, (along which we traveled) until 12 o'clock, when we descended to a rim of small hills, which were covered with rocks, creeks, and bluffs. Before going down, we sighted a smoke to the west, about ½ league away. Therefore, an officer and 10 men were immediately sent to reconnoiter. They returned and reported that they had found three fires and the signs of tipi poles, where it seemed that a small village had been located; that the Indian trail led to the west into the hills. We camped, and about thirty minutes later three Indians arrived and said that they were subjects of the big Yamparica chief named Quegue, and that they were out looking for buffaloes. We asked them to dismount, and they stayed with us, talking with the Indian guides, who, they said, were acquainted with them. On our route we found no water save that in the first creek and the pools of rain water found here. At 4 o'clock in the afternoon the above-mentioned Chief Quegue arrived. He had a cane, and a medal with the picture of our king tied around his neck,[23] and was accompanied by some Indians of his council. They were cordially received by the militia captains, who gave them their dinner. The Indians were very well pleased, as they were very needy. At sundown the Indians withdrew to their village, which they said was a short distance to the east, but Chief Quegue remained with us and gave orders to his people to break camp and move near to our camp. Night came without anything unusual. 9½ leagues.]

## May 17

This day dawned without anything unusual having occurred. We remained in camp because the Indian chief and his companions begged us to do so in order that they could have the pleasure of having all

[23] Probably received from Lucero or Martin.

their people know us and visit us; they said that they wished to eat with us. [Bexar copy: because they were very needy today; they promised that they would freely give us information of any dangers, with the knowledge of which we would be able to continue on our way and fulfill our mission. We experienced nothing unusual. In the morning, the guards of the *cavallada* and *mulada* were relieved, and at 10 o'clock the band of the aforesaid chief arrived.] They were given a few presents that we had for that purpose, as recorded in the lists of distribution. They encamped their band on the southeast side of our camp, at a distance of a musket shot. The village is composed of thirty lodges. At noon Chief Quegue assembled all his Indians; they were given their dinner by the two militia captains, and they were also given something to smoke. After this was done, they were approached with the proposition that they give us a guide in order that we could continue on our expedition, because the guides we had, had become gravely ill. At the same time, he said there was no Indian who might be willing to become a guide, because the land, which is very steep and rocky and difficult, without doubt would cause a thousand losses to the *cavallada* and *mulada* on account of the increasing scarcity of water and the impassable road.

[The two copies have been substantially alike up to this point, but now the Bexar copy has much additional material: The wife of the most experienced and intelligent of the two guides we had was seriously ill, and therefore it was possible that he would be unable to continue on the trip; the other Indian was also sick, and even if he were not, he was not capable of guiding us because he had no knowledge whatever of the land and water holes. Although we made several proposals and offered to pay the chief for their services, it was not possible to obtain one of them. They said that the direction in which we wanted to travel and to reconnoiter had a great many obstacles, and that there was no water; that they believed it would be impossible for us to travel without losing most of our *cavallada* and *mulada*. Finally, they said that under no circumstances would they be able to risk any man to be a guide. They were rebuked and asked why, since they were our allies and since they knew how well they were treated by us, and the friendship shown by our government, they could not compel some of the Indians to go with us as guides. He answered through the interpreter that he had no authority to do so, and that their laws were very different from those of the Spaniards; that this was what he had told his confederates, but that if there was anyone who wished to volunteer, he could go, and that if he wanted a guide to Santa Fe, there were several ready to go at once;[24] but that they were aware of the positive risk in going over the route. Thus we remained until nightfall without any unusual incident. It was decided not to set out in the morning.]

## May 18

[Entries are missing from the Guerra copy for May 18 to June 17; therefore, the entries for the next thirty-one days will be from the Bexar copy alone.]

Dawn came today without any unusual incident having occurred during the night. We stayed in camp in order to see if the Indian woman would recover, as it was not possible to travel without an experienced Indian guide—who said he would continue [with us] the following day whether or not his wife recovered. At 8 o'clock this evening [, however,] they brought the said Indian woman from the village where they had taken her to give her medical attention, because she said she was completely recovered. At about 10 o'clock a tornado began to blow from the west; it was so violent that it was necessary to take down the tents and take refuge in a trench behind the baggage of the mule train, and even there it was difficult to bear the force of the dust, which made it look like the end of the world. It began to decrease at sundown, and the night was clear and calm, without unusual incident.

## May 19

Day broke without unusual incident. We set out and traveled over high plains; at the end of the plain, we descended to a creek bottom filled with gravel. Having crossed it, we continued to travel up and down slight elevations until we came out to another high, level plain. At the end of this plain, we again descended to gravel creek bottoms, and went over high hills, until we reached an extensive valley covered with trees in a canyon that is formed by a little caprock to the west; the trees are found at the foot of the caprock; at the bottom of the canyon there is a creek with white sand and clear, fresh, running water;

[24] Typical Indian double-talk.

it flows from northwest to southeast, and comes from a point in the valley [*abra*] formed by yesterday's hills in the west. We camped near this creek on the plain running to the south. Nothing more unusual happened except that the sick Indian woman was left in the village of Chief Quegue because she became worse, but the Indian guide cheerfully continued with our company. Night fell with nothing unusual. 11 leagues

May 20

Dawn today came with no unusual incident. At 7 o'clock we set out, and traveled over a large canyon formed by two caprocks on the west, which run in the same direction. We traveled to the east.[25] It has bluffs not very high, red, but in some places white. It is as broad as an 18-pound shot [range]. After we had traveled a short distance, and after we had crossed the canyon twice, we sighted a small spring of water toward the mesa to the west. Captain José Agabo, the adjutant, and the chaplain went out to reconnoiter, and on the summit they found a spring of water and a very beautiful cave [so big] that twelve men could stand in the entrance. It was narrow toward the interior, which was all painted with various colors and figures by the Indians.[26] The captain, the adjutant, and the chaplain carved their names on it. After they had reconnoitered it, they returned to join the squadron. We continued along the same canyon, following the banks of the river, which were thickly covered with cottonwoods. A small flowing creek with very little water joined the river, and we traveled along the creek. We camped in the valley, without having experienced anything unusual. At nightfall a Caddo Indian arrived from the village of Chief Quegue and said that he wanted to go with us on his way home in order not to travel alone. He had no equipment other than his horse and saddle, and had no weapons. He said his trip to the Comanche [village] had been to parley for peace—in which he had succeeded. 8½ leagues

May 21

Dawn came today without anything unusual having occurred. We continued to travel along the same canyon, which was very narrow,

[25] He must mean west.

[26] Perhaps this cave can be identified by somebody who knows the area. It should be somewhere in the broken country between Dickens and Quitaque.

with rocky ledges on both sides about fifty *varas* high and with several most uncomfortable bluffs. We continued to travel in this manner until noon, without unusual incident. At 12 o'clock seven Indian men and one woman arrived. They said they were on their way to fight the Lipillanos [Lipans or Llaneros?]; all had lances, and four had muskets. They came from the village of Chief Quegue, and remained in our camp that night in order to go with us the following day. Inspection of arms and ammunition was held this afternoon; missing cartridges were replaced; the laws concerning the duties of soldiers were read, as well as those regarding punishment.[27] Night fell with no unusual incident. 3½ leagues

May 22

Dawn came today with no unusual incident having occurred. We stayed in camp until noon in order to set out in the afternoon and spend the night at a point from which we could reach a water hole tomorrow. We set out at 12 o'clock, and, although it was late, we traveled toward the north. Leaving behind the rims that form the canyon, we began to travel over plains so immense that the eye could not see their end. There was nothing but grass and a few small pools of rain water, with very little water, and some dry holes, on these plains;[27a] where we camped, it was necessary to drive stakes for the horses of the guard and for precaution.[27b] No unusual incident occurred other than the fact that I became sick in one eye; therefore, the expedition started, [while] I remained at the place with an escort of ten men and one sergeant, to wait for the sunset so that I could continue on our route.[27c] Night fell, and we were without water, but at 8 o'clock I arrived at the camp, no unusual incident having occurred.[27d] 8½ leagues

[27] There is no doubt that Amangual was familiar with the signs of Indian trouble.

[27a] Buffalo-wallows.

[27b] Perhaps here is an explanation of the origin of the name *Llano Estacado* (Staked Plain). In broken country, obviously the Spaniards kept their horses together with the aid of the topography, but up on the plains, where there is no topography, they had to use stakes.

[27c] Obviously afflicted with a form of sunburn not uncommon on the Llano, similar to snow blindness and very painful.

[27d] He is now at last on the Llano Estacado, and it seems that he must have meant that he was traveling west rather than east. If so, the canyon that best fills the bill seems to be the north canyon west of Quitaque.

May 23

Dawn came today without anything unusual having occurred, and we continued on our way, traveling over the same plain in the same manner as yesterday, until 12 o'clock, when we arrived at a slight elevation. We descended some *cañadas* where we found some small, bare hills, which extended down to a creek named El Blanco,[28] where there are some springs of water. There was an Indian with two women at the first spring, who said they were hunting. We continued on our way, traveling over some deep creeks and steep red bluffs. A windstorm came up from the west, so violent that it was almost impossible to bear it until we descended into a very deep arroyo where there were some springs of water. We camped on a grassy plain surrounded by hills that form a caprock on both sides of the creek. We placed our advance guards on hills commanding the area, and night came without unusual incident. Note on the twenty-third: The wind was so strong that it almost blew the men off the horses. Whenever a [mounted] man's hat was blown off, it was almost impossible to retrieve it. There was an instance in which it blew off the hat of a soldier of the company of Captain Quintero, and he was not able to catch up with it, and thus he lost it. 9½ leagues

May 24

Dawn came today with no unusual incident, and we continued on our way. Climbing up some cliffs, we began to travel over a great plain, similar to the one we traveled over yesterday; it has very little grass. We traveled along the creek that runs in the same direction, and stopped on an elevation near the said plain. No unusual incident occurred en route. In the afternoon, [however,] turbonada [a strong wind] from the southwest and west, threatening rain. In this manner, night came without unusual incident. 4½ leagues

May 25

Dawn came today with no unusual incident. Consequently we continued on our way, traveling over plains so extensive that the horizon was tiring to the eye. We traveled all day over this kind of land, and

[28] This is Tierra Blanca Creek, which runs into the Prairie Dog Town Fork of Red River, and they must now be in the vicinity of Canyon, Texas.

found some dry lakes that showed signs of accumulating much water in time of rain. It could be seen that there is usually much grass during the rainy season, but at this time it has been trampled by a large number of buffaloes, which, in time, have exhausted [eaten up all] the grass. Furthermore, there has been such a severe drouth that today the plains are so burned up and clean that we have not found in all our route the least blade of dry grass or weed. This condition was no noticeable that it caused great astonishment. We continued traveling until about sundown, when we reached some small hills where, *a la hora que señala la tabla,* we pitched camp. At that place there were buffaloes as far as the eye could see. Night came without incident. 18 leagues

May 26

Today we remained in camp in order to rest the troops, the *cavallada,* and the *mulada,* inasmuch as the day's journey has been long and hard, and the sun has been hot that the majority of the soldiers had their legs so sunburned that it was necessary to use pads dipped in lime water on them. Furthermore, it was the day of the Ascension of our Lord, and therefore it was necessary to remain here for mass, which was celebrated with the usual ceremony. After mass, the unassigned troops were given permission to go hunting, and they went. No unusual incident occurred that afternoon, and night came on without incident except that [it was reported that] 3 men were missing; either they had gone to sleep or they were lost.[29]

May 27

Dawn came today with no unusual incident, and we continued to travel, after leaving one corporal and 6 soldiers to make smoke signals for the three men. At the time of [our] departure, these [men] were sighted traveling over some small hills. The ground over which we were traveling was a level plain until we arrived at some grassy hills, which had a clump of green trees at one end, and an abundance of pools of water; there were some permanent springs, but the water sank [into the earth] a short distance away. We camped in this place, but before we dismounted, Captain Don José de Agabo, the adjutant, and Captain

[29] It is an item remarkably similar to George Wilkins Kendall's entry: "It was now discovered that two of our men were missing; . . . it was impossible . . . to go back in search of them." Loomis, *Texan-Santa Fé Pioneers, ix–x.*

Quintero, with the Indian guide, climbed a small hill and sighted a rim of trees a long distance to the north. The Indian guide said it was the Red River,[30] and that the hills they saw were across the river. In this manner, night came without incident. The creek where we camped runs northwest, and according to its direction, it empties [it must empty] into the aforesaid Red River.[31] 8 leagues

May 28

Dawn came today with nothing unusual. It commenced to rain, and we decided not to set out until the weather should improve. As the clouds went away, we continued on our way, traveling over low hills. Nearby we found a spring of water that flows over a clear plain. At 12 o'clock we reached a number of deep creeks that caused us to go up and down in every direction; there was an infinite number of red bluffs. We finally descended a narrow creek that had many trees, pools of water, and seeping springs of permanent water. We crossed it and camped on the north bank. Two parties of men, each of one corporal and eight men—one of them in charge of a sergeant—went out to reconnoiter the country as far as the Red River on both sides, because of there being near this camp a creek, also wild grapes and wild Castilian rose bushes. In this manner we remained until this hour, which is 5 o'clock, with no unusual incident. Night fell as the parties of soldiers that had gone out, returned without having found anything unusual. 8 leagues

May 29

Dawn came today with no unusual incident. We remained in camp, since it rained all night, and everything in camp and all the equipment got wet, because we wanted to let everything in the camp get dry, and because we had to wait for a party of troops composed of one sergeant, one corporal, and ten men, who went out this morning to explore the country to the banks of the river. The weather continued to threaten rain, but it was very calm. Mass was held for the troops today, as it was Sunday. After mass, the party returned with the report that nothing suspicious had been found, and since the weather had cleared up, orders were given to start out. But before the *cavallada* could be brought up,

[30] The Canadian.

[31] About the only creek that fits this description is East Amarillo Creek, due north of Amarillo.

the sky was again covered with clouds, and it commenced to rain. Therefore, our departure was prevented, a new order [was issued] for the regulation of the march, as shown by the general orders of this date. In the afternoon it stopped raining, and it did not rain any more until sundown, when it again started raining and continued until the dawn watch. This creek has many turns, but its direction is toward the Red River, west northwest to east southeast. In this manner, night came without unusual incident. 4½ leagues

## May 30

Dawn came today with the unusual incident that the *cavallada* of the First Company of the Colony had stampeded, and half of them were missing. Consequently, steps were taken to find them. We remained in camp, waiting for the return of the *cavallada* and in order to give time for the ground and the clothes of the troops to get dry, since it had rained all night. As the *cavallada* was found at noon, we started out toward the river, traveling over very difficult terrain with many hills, *cañadas*, creeks, bluffs, cliffs, and precipices, with a great many impossible conditions. It was necessary for the unassigned troops to use crowbars and pickaxes to make a path up and down for the train, which was traveling with extreme difficulty; it was almost necessary for the muleteers to take the baggage in their arms and to make an infinite number of turns looking for the best terrain for us to travel over, until we reached the banks of the Red River [Canadian]. At that point, where we camped, the river flows as far as the eye can see from west to east. It is narrow, shallow, and close to the surface of the ground, with low banks, the highest being about one *vara*. There were very level, grassy plains on both sides. The water, as well as the ground around there, is red. Two parties of troops were sent out to patrol and reconnoiter the ground on both sides of the river. At sundown they returned and reported that nothing unusual had been found. In this manner, night came. 6 leagues.

## May 31

Dawn came today without incident, and we continued to travel along the banks of the river, which runs in the same direction as yesterday. After we traveled a short distance, the river channel and the grassy plains began to close in, so that the river touched the foot of the hills, and it was necessary for us to climb those [hills]. Because of the impassable route, we had to open a difficult road for the *mulada* and the *cavallada*. Today's route lay over hills, creeks, bluffs, and precipices that were so difficult that it would be impossible for a soldier on horseback to go through without the fatigue work of the troops. Nevertheless, as we found ourselves deep in this place, and moreover, as there was no way to help it, we worked to overcome the impossible and to attain the objective of our expedition. We continued traveling over the same kind of terrain. One of the scouts reported that he had found the trails of animals, signs of tipi poles, and a fire of the previous day, [which indicated that Indians] had slept there. Consequently, a subordinate officer and a party of men went from the vanguard to reconnoiter and to follow the train to ascertain what kind of people were making it. The train continued to travel over the most passable uphill and downhill slopes until 12 o'clock, when we climbed down with great difficulty into a canyon of the river, where it has a deep channel. We continued to travel until we reached a slight elevation, where we camped without incident. After we had pitched camp, a party of troops went to explore the country. The officer who, while we were traveling, had gone out to follow the trail [torn], [found?] [or arrived accompanied by] one Comanche Indian man and two Yamparica Indian women, who had been left behind [at the spring] on the twenty-sixth. In this manner, night came without further incident. 6½ leagues

June 1

Dawn today came without unusual incident. We continued to travel a short distance from the river; we could not travel along its banks because we could not find a way for the mule train and the troops. We traveled near the river until 9:30 o'clock over low hills until we again reached the river at a point where steep bluffs made it necessary for us to open a road by means of crowbars, axes, and pickaxes.[32] We continued to travel over hills, and after we had traveled a short distance, three men on horseback were sighted running away on the other side

[32] On three different occasions he has mentioned using crowbars and pickaxes to make a trail—on May 16, May 30, and June 1. One wonders why such strenuous work should have been necessary for mounted men and a mule train.

of the river to the north. Therefore, a detachment from the vanguard went out to reconnoiter, and found them to be settlers from the jurisdiction of Santa Fe who were hunting. When the detachment learned that they were not suspicious, it returned and joined the squadron. We passed a small elevation that forms a grassy plain near the river; soon thereafter, five men and one Frenchman who said his name was Don Pedro, arrived. They said they were settlers of the town of Santa Fe and that they had come out with permission from the governor of that capital to look for buffaloes for meat. In the afternoon the five men withdrew to their camp, which was near ours, [but] the Frenchman remained to spend the night with us. He stated that this territory is very peaceful; that this river is the Colorado, which is otherwise known as the Red River, but that it does not flow by Natchitoches; and that a long distance from here it joins the Napestle, and both of them join the Mississippi; and that the river we passed on the twenty-second of May was the Natchitoches [Red] River, and that we had reached its source. Thus night came without unusual incident. 2½ leagues

June 2

Dawn came today without incident, and we continued on our way, traveling along the river over terrain with creeks and low hills and the river's watershed. After we had traveled a short distance, some men were sighted, who were found to belong to the same party we met yesterday. We were informed that troops were traveling along the river to meet us. Among these men there was one named Manuel Martínez,[32a] who said he was interpreter to the Indian tribes, and that he was hunting with the Indians of the San Miguel del Bado missions. They told us that by crossing the river to the north side where it was flat, we would find a road over which we could travel, and that it was impossible to travel the way we were going without great difficulties with our train because of the creek and bluffs. Consequently, at 8 o'clock in the morning we crossed the river and traveled along its banks in the direction of the plateau; the river runs in the same direction. Thus we traveled until we reached the place where the aforesaid Indians and soldiers were camped, and, since there was much grass there, and a spring of water, we camped there. No other unusual incident occurred

[32a] Small world.

on the route. The aforesaid soldier told us that he had explored the river together with Lieutenant Don Facundo [Melgares],[32b] and that the water of this [river] exhausted itself in the sand, and that the bed was dry; and that it was not the one that flows to Natchitoches; that the source of this [river] was in the Sierra Blanca, but that two days' journey away it was impossible to travel on horseback; and that [even] on foot it was not possible to go down to the river to get a drink; that the small amount of water in it was rain water; that farther on, the river was formed by several creeks that enter it, and all of them have their source in the aforesaid Sierra Blanca, which is four days' journey from this place; and that its route lay over mountains that cause it to have an impassable depth. Thus night came without further incident. 6 leagues

June 3

Dawn came today without unusual incident. Therefore, we continue to travel on our way along the river on a level, sandy plain and many sand banks that form elevations and depressions. To the south there are some hills and bluffs that run in the direction of the river bed, which has many turns and a deep and narrow channel with high bluffs. We went down an open road or grassy plain where we found some clumps of cottonwood, and from there we could see many hills to the west; we camped in a meadow covered with grass. A short while later, a settler of the province of New Mexico arrived and said that he was at the head of 120 men who had come hunting with permission from the governor of the province. He reported that it [the party] had had no unusual incident on its route. They remained in our camp all afternoon and gave us information about the route. Late that afternoon they returned to their camp. Thus night came without further incident. 5½ leagues

June 4

Dawn came today without incident, and we continued on our way, traveling along the river, accompanied by the soldier Manuel Martínez and the resident Indians who were with him, over difficult terrain consisting of hills and rocky bluffs. The *mulada* and the *cavallada* traveled with great difficulty, and received many injuries, as a result of

[32b] The traffic gets heavier.

which many horses and mules were lame. After having traveled three hours, we crossed the river at a place where it turns to the south, and continued to travel on the other side in the same direction over very difficult terrain; it was necessary to make special arrangements in order not to experience any unusual incident with the *mulada*. After crossing over a large crest or mesa, we continued traveling over hills and creeks and dry *cañadas* along the river. We reached a place where we found some ditches that had been dug in the form of trenches. According to information given us by the settlers who were traveling with us, this was the work of the Yamparica Comanche Indians, who had dug them in order to defend themselves against the Quitaray Indians.[33] These were shaped in a circle; there was a moat and palisade of pickets, and one small bastion in the center, and signs that there had been bigger ones there.[34] We continued on our journey, traveling over a plain. A short distance from there we camped on the banks of the river, which runs in the same direction, and which runs through a very narrow and deep canyon. Thus night came without unusual incident. 6½ leagues

June 5

Dawn came today with nothing unusual, and after mass we continued on our journey, traveling over very bad country consisting of hills and creeks and stretches of rocks along the river. We followed a canyon containing many rocky mesas, as there was no other route. Despite our care, the *cavallada* and the *mulada* received many injuries. [We traveled] until we reached the place known as La Cinta, where we pitched our camp. Our Indian guide and the settlers of this country told us that it was impossible to continue traveling along the river with the train, and that even on foot it would be impossible to reconnoiter it;[35] and that the train could travel only over the road to Bado. Nevertheless, a party of 20 men under two sergeants was sent out to reconnoiter the river and route in order that we might continue to travel

[33] We cannot identify the Quitaray Indians in Hodge. This must be one of the very few instances in United States history in which Indians entrenched themselves to fight.

[34] They were to find a similar fortification later in the Sierra Blancas in southeastern New Mexico. These are the only references we have ever seen to fortifications by the Plains Indians.

[35] It sounds like the Angosturas, or Narrows, of the Canadian River; cf. George Wilkins Kendall's account in *Narrative of the Texan Santa Fé Expedition*.

that way if it should be found possible to do so. Thus night came with no unusual incident other than that a strong wind came up from the south; it was almost unbearable. It blows generally every day in this country. Night came without further incident. 5 leagues

## June 6

Dawn came today with no other unusual incident than the fact that all the troops and baggage were wet because it rained all night, and it was severely cold and windy. Mass was held a little late in order to give time for the ground to dry out. For that reason, and in order to wait for the return of the party of troops that went out yesterday, we did not start. The gale continued to blow violently. Today I gave Captain Don José Agabo de Ayala permission to send a sick soldier to the capital of Santa Fe in charge of Manuel Martínez, a veteran soldier and interpreter, so that the governor, if he so desired, might make arrangements to give him medical attention. The soldier was given 8 pesos in cash, 1 peso in cigarettes, 3 rations of flour, 2 horses, and all his baggage and clothes; a list was made of everything. A copy, together with a receipt given by the soldier Manuel Martínez, was kept by the captain. At 11 o'clock that night, the party we were waiting for returned and reported that it was impossible to continue on our route because of the large number of creeks and precipices, and because there was no water hole for the train or even for one single animal. Thus night fell.

## June 7

Dawn came today with no unusual incident except that the river was on a rise, and some of the *cavallada* of the Colony which was on the other side of the river could not get across. For that reason, and as there was much grass, we deferred our departure until we made arrangements to get the *cavallada*. The men and equipment crossed over on rafts made out of buffalo hides.[36] No other accident occurred than the fact that one horse was killed by a lance which by neglect was left at the chute [*aisladero*] made for the *cavallada* to go down to the river. After that duty was concluded, orders were given to set out at 2 o'clock; and we traveled over hills with corn patches [*lomas satosas*],

[36] This is the only reference we have seen to the bullboat in Southwestern documents.

and some plains. At 6 o'clock I arrived with the ten men and sergeant with whom I had remained behind because my eyes were sore and the strong sunlight hurt me during the day. At 8 o'clock that night I gave orders for 20 men and two sergeants to be prepared with food supplies for three days so they could reconnoiter the territory and its watering places. 4½ leagues

June 8

[Bexar copy:]

Dawn came today without unusual incident. The detachment went out at reveille, and at 8 o'clock, two other detachments consisting of one corporal and seven soldiers each, went out with orders to reconnoiter the ground everywhere around here and to report any suspicious trail. Four additional soldiers went out to reconnoiter the water holes up the road. The last patrols to go out returned without unusual incident. The four soldiers returned at 5 o'clock in the afternoon to report that a short distance from the place where we were camped, there were watering-places for the train. At the same time, a terrible rainstorm came down from the northeast; it was accompanied by wind, hail, and lightning, and was so violent that we were unable to resist it in the tents. We spent the night on foot and in the water. There was no unusual incident other than the fact that one of the patrols that went out to reconnoiter toward the west did not return.

June 9

Dawn came today without any unusual incident other than the fact that one mule was killed while bolting with a veteran soldier. At 7 o'clock the aforementioned party returned and reported that a long distance ahead there was grass and water along the road for the *cavallada*. In the afternoon a storm appeared to the south which came down in the form of rain and some thunder. After a while it cleared up. Thus night came with nothing unusual other than the fact that a party consisting of one sergeant and twenty soldiers which had gone out in the morning of the eighth to reconnoiter the river had not returned.

June 10

Dawn came today without incident, and we remained in camp because the party mentioned yesterday had not yet returned. At 6 o'clock two parties of troops went out to reconnoiter the country, and they returned at 10 o'clock without incident. At 12 o'clock the party that had set out on the eighth, returned and reported that they had traveled along the river as far as possible on horseback; it was so difficult that it was believed impossible for travel even on foot. They also reported that all the ground from this camp to the place they reached was very difficult because of the large number of creeks, rocks, bluffs, and the deep channel of the river, to which no approach or watering place was located. There was very little grass; and [they said] that it was impossible for our train to travel over that terrain. In the afternoon a wind and rainstorm came up. A short while later it became calm, and night fell without further unusual incident. I gave orders to the effect that thirty men and one lieutenant should be ready at dawn tomorrow with supplies for three days.

June 11

Dawn came today without unusual incident, and at that hour I set out with thirty men and one lieutenant as escort to reconnoiter all the ground already explored by all the patrols previously sent out. After my departure, [the troops] broke camp and traveled over good country along the creek, which they crossed to the north side at 9 o'clock; they traveled up and down over barren country and some mesas to the south. After traveling a short distance, we camped on one bank on a level elevation, without any trees of any kind [*desengeño claro*]; there was a large mesa to the south, and to the north all mountains, and to the west, mesas. This creek was narrow and resembled an irrigation ditch, but it had no running water—only some deep pools. Thus we remained the rest of the day, without other unusual incident than the fact that Don Gregorio Amador, adjutant *alférez,* took sick with fever. Consequently, he did not go out to reconnoiter the river. In the afternoon two parties, consisting of 6 men and one corporal, were sent out to reconnoiter the country. They returned without unusual incident. Night came with rain, violent wind, and thunder.

June 12

Dawn came today without incident, and mass was held with the troops in attendance in the usual manner. After mass, two parties of troops went out to reconnoiter the country. The weather continued to be threatening, and the sky was covered with clouds; it was drizzling. The two parties of troops returned without incident, and thus night came with nothing unusual. 8 leagues

June 13

Dawn came today without incident, and mass was held in the usual manner. At 9 o'clock I arrived with the party of troops that was accompanying me, having experienced no unusual incident on the route, and having reconnoitered the river as far as possible; I did not go any farther because it was impossible to do so. Nevertheless, I sent the officer I had with me with half the troops in order that he might reconnoiter as far as possible on horseback and then on foot. I remained in camp with the rest of the troops in a narrow ravine formed by the hills where the river disembogues. A short time after the officer had set out, a heavy rain, accompanied by a terrific hailstorm, began to fall, and it was necessary for us to move our camp because of the flood that came down the river. We had hardly moved out when it became almost impossible for the vehicles to get out;[37] the same fate overtook the party of the officer [who had gone ahead.] The weather became calm, but as he could not travel over 3 leagues on horseback, he gave orders to continue on foot. He left the *cavallada* under guard, and continued to travel along the river over many extremely difficult places consisting of crags and slippery places where the men usually had to crawl on all fours, risking their lives. As it was not possible to go any farther, the [officer] gave orders to return to the place where I had camped. They found the river on a rise and were compelled to cross it on rafts, with a great deal of difficulty; the horses were swum across. As they did not find the camp where they had left it, they feared that some misfortune had befallen us. However, thinking that perhaps their

[37] Here is the explanation for their use of pickaxes and crowbars. For the first time we learn that Amangual had wheeled vehicles in his train—which certainly was a new test of the country. We do not know whether they were two-wheeled or four-wheeled, but, in any event it is more difficult to travel with wheeled vehicles than with horses and mules. The most noticeable omission in this journal is the lack of any reference whatever to the Caprock. Several hundred feet high, it could be ascended by horses and mules only at established points, where trails had been made by the Indians. For wagons, there were only one or two such *puertas* for a long distance on the eastern rim.

failure to find me was due to the flood, he continued traveling until he sighted our camp. Upon arrival, he reported what had occurred, and the commandant decided to withdraw, for it was not possible even to sight the river, for there was a distance of approximately 18 leagues to the impassable ground explored. The direction of the river was to the northwest.[38] At that point we left the river, and remained in camp because we intended to start out on the final stretch of our expedition. Thus night fell without incident. 4½ leagues

June 14

Dawn came today with nothing unusual, and we continued traveling in the direction of the first mission to be found in the province of New Mexico. Having concluded the expedition, and in order to fulfill the instructions of Don Antonio Cordero,[39] governor of the province of Texas, we continued to travel over a level plain until we arrived at some small hills that form several *cañadas* and some low hillsides. We remained there until 9 o'clock in the morning, when we traveled up an elevation and sighted the rim of the mesa to the south and west and north, which appeared to be very broken and rough. Captain Don José Agabo climbed one of the hills, and sighted a range of high mountains to the northwest, whose summits were covered with snow. We continued to travel over the elevations and over some watersheds until we reached a creek that carries much water and has many trees. It flows from a mountain lying to the west. We crossed it going to the south, where it joins another creek that carries a current of water. Both these rivers join to form the Gallinas River. There we camped without mishap, and night came with nothing unusual. 6 leagues

June 15

Dawn came today without incident, and we continued to travel over a plain until 9:30, when we entered a very narrow canyon formed by the mountains. After having traveled a short distance, we arrived at a slope over a declivity that was very steep and rocky, where we passed

[38] Between Conchas Dam and Sabinoso?

[39] Lieutenant Colonel Manuel Antonio Cordero y Bustamante was governor of Texas from October, 1805, to 1810. He apparently overlapped Manuel Salcedo's appointment for the purpose of instructing Salcedo. In 1810 he returned to Coahuila as governor until 1817.

until we went down to a level plain and continued traveling toward the west. We then reached some hills that we climbed and went down in the *cañadas* and creeks, with heights found everywhere. There are many rocky elevations and depressions where we traveled through a valley and an opening formed by very high mountains on the west and north, which are the same that I wrote yesterday were covered with snow. We continued traveling along this place until we went down to a river named Miguel del Bado. We camped about a league from it, and the settlers thereof came to visit us. Night came without unusual incident. 10 leagues

June 16

Dawn came today without incident. Mass was celebrated because it was the First of Corpus. The settlers and troops were present in the customary manner. After mass, I issued orders for one corporal and four soldiers to go to the town of Santa Fe to report our arrival to the governor in order that he might communicate to us any orders he might have from the commandant-general so that we could carry them out according to the instructions of our commandant. Thus night fell without incident.

June 17

Dawn today came without incident. We remained in camp, waiting for the return of the corporal and the soldiers who went out yesterday. Thus night came. At 8 o'clock two soldiers arrived with an official letter from the governor; those two soldiers were sent by Captain Don Dionicio Balle, who was camped in the Pecos mission. At this hour I issued orders to set out tomorrow morning. Thus dawn came without incident.

June 18

[At this point we pick up the Guerra copy again, with references to the Bexar copy when the two are different:]

Today dawned without incident, and we undertook our march, crossing the Pecos River across inhospitable rocky land, with arroyos and hills, along a mountainside thickly wooded with spruce- and fir-trees, which is situated to the south of the Sierra Grande, until we arrived at the Pecos mission, where we camped. A short distance from there, we found a small spring of water in a creek of white sand. The river was half a league to the north. Thus night came with nothing unusual. 9 leagues

June 19

Dawn came today without incident, and after mass, we continued to travel over very difficult and rocky land, heavily forested, which had many arroyos that form a very narrow canyon with many slopes until we arrived at the point of the Sierra Nevada, from a height of which may be seen a great vista, with a very high range to the west and another to the south, and from that elevation at a short distance could be seen the town of Santa Fe. In this same place was waiting the squadron under the command of the interim governor. The troops retired to another plaza very large, surrounded by walls and very comfortable rooms, in which were assigned two barracks for each company and to the officers, who were to choose the best rooms. In this manner, night fell without incident. 9 leagues

[Bexar copy: . . . we could see the town of Santa Fe. The detachment was ordered to stop at the point, and a soldier was sent to report our arrival to the ad interim governor. The soldier returned after a short while with orders for us to go to the capital. We entered it at 2 o'clock in the afternoon, traveling over a level street until we reached the main plaza of the town. The squadron was there formed in parade formation, and the aforesaid ad interim governor ordered the troops to go to another large plaza, which was surrounded by a wall and which had some comfortable barracks. Two tiers of barracks were assigned to each company, and the officers were told to select the best quarters. Thus night fell with no unusual incident. 9 leagues]

[The Guerra copy has the following note on the inside cover:]

Notes

There is counted by this diary from Bexar to Santa Fe 196 leagues in the direction of the trip.

| | |
|---|---|
| From March 30 to May 19 | 51 days |
| March suspended | 17 days |
| Days actually on the march | 34 days |

*The "Notes" present some interesting figures—quite unlike ours. By our count, Amangual's little army actually traveled fifty-two days*

*and covered 368 leagues, or 957 miles, and the average daily mileage is 18.4—which is not bad at all for a large force with wheeled vehicles in wilderness country.*

*Amangual certainly encountered a full bill of typical West Texas and Panhandle spring weather, and the similarity of his trip across the Llano with that of Kendall, thirty-three years later, is astonishing.*

*Amangual gives us a vast amount of information on the country, the weather, and the Indians—and incidentally reveals himself as a man who was no novice around Indians, for he recognized all the signs of their presence: stampedes, strange riders on hilltops, strange visitors in camp for no particular reason, and Indian signs at an old camp—and he understood the danger after a rain. He invariably took precautions. He used scouts effectively, and recognized the value of Indian guides. It is also noticeable that on occasions when alarm was indicated, he alerted the troops by having them inspect their firearms and put in fresh charges, by reading the orders of the guard, and by reading the laws and the penalties. He lost animals to the Indians, but no men.*

*He has mentioned three documentary items that have not turned up so far: the general orders, the list of distributions (to the Indians), and the "table." We can only speculate concerning the nature of the last item.*

*He stayed in Santa Fe for three months, and then set out on the return trip, going by way of El Paso and San Elzeario.*

### *Diary of Francisco Amangual from Santa Fe to San Elzeario, September 20–October 21, 1808*[40]

### Return

[Bexar copy only has this identification: Diary of the journey made from the town of Santa Fe to the town of San Elzeario.[41]]

[40] We continue with the Guerra copy, collated with the Bexar copy.

[41] San Elzeario is spelled many different ways: San Elceario, San Elizario, and others—and it is difficult to determine which is correct. Since "San Elzeario" is consistent in this document (it appears four times), perhaps this version is as good as any. The fort or presidio at San Elzeario was founded in 1773, and was moved away sometime between 1808 and 1814, according to some authorities. The town of San Elizario, Texas, is now across the river from the original site of the presidio, but originally was on the Mexican side. The town was not moved, says Rex Strickland; the river changed its course.

September 20, 1808

We set out from the town of Santa Fe at 8 o'clock in the morning, and at mid-day crossed the river, and at 1:30 we entered a canyon between two high slopes, which runs until it joins that of the North [the Río Grande] at a small settlement that they call the settlement of Río Abajo. This river flows from Santa Fe to its mouth to the west southwest.[42] At 4 o'clock in the afternoon we passed Santo Domingo mission, and at 5 o'clock we reached a place ½ league from San Felipe mission, where we camped on the left bank of the Río del Norte [the Río Grande]. There was nothing unusual today except that two militiamen of the First Company of the Colony deserted, and another militiaman of said company broke his musket. 11½ leagues

September 21

We set out from said camp at 8 o'clock in the morning, and shortly passed the mission of San Felipe. At 11 o'clock [we passed] the place known as La Angostura; at mid-day that of Bernadillo; at 2 o'clock the settlement of Sandía; at 3 o'clock we stopped at a pleasant wooded place on the banks of the river. Our route from Santa Domingo has always been downward along the river and inclined to the south 5½ to 8 degrees. Night fell without incident. 9½ leagues

September 22

We set out from this camp at 8 o'clock in the morning and traveled along the said river. [Bexar copy: At 9:30 we passed the settlement of San Felipe de la Almeda; at 3½ at noon (?) we crossed the town of Albuquerque] and at 4 o'clock we reached a grove of cottonwoods, where we stopped, with nothing unusual having occurred except that one of the two deserters from the militia was found in the *cavallada* at dawn, and one of the muleteers ran away from the Company of la Bahía last night. Course, 5½ degrees east. 10 leagues

September 23

At dawn today the second militiaman who deserted the day of our departure was found in the *cavallada*. Yesterday afternoon two drummers deserted, one from the First Company of New Santander and the

[42] Perhaps he means east southeast.

other from the company of the New Kingdom of León, and during the night, two soldiers, one from the First Company of New Santander and the other from the Second Company. At 7:30 in the morning we set out from the above-mentioned camp and continued along the river, shortly passing the settlements at Ysleta, which are located on the right bank of the river; at 11:30 we passed the place known as Valencia; and soon after noon we passed the settlement of Tome; at 2 o'clock we reached a camping place on the banks of the river. The turns of the river are so minor that our route is still to the south, 5½ degrees east.[43] This morning as we started out, we found the trail left by the two militiamen deserters, having taken some animals. I immediately ordered the captain, a subordinate officer, and 25 men to follow them, and they found that the trail was of two saddled horses and two led mules. They followed the trail until their last horse was exhausted, without overtaking the two deserters. On their return, they discovered that a soldier of the militia whose horse had been the first to give out, had climbed a tree to see if his companions were returning, and had fallen and broken a leg. At 8 o'clock the party returned. No other unusual incident occurred. 8½ leagues

September 24

We set out from said camp at 8:30 in the morning, and soon passed through the settlement of Belén, which is located on the right bank of said river. At 4 o'clock in the afternoon we arrived at Sevilleta, where we camped with no unusual incident. 10 leagues

[Bexar copy: I shall remark here that from Santa Domingo mission to a point 2 leagues before reaching the settlement mentioned above, the country is overlooked by a hill of slight elevation and shaped like a mesa; at that point it joins a high range of mountains, which seem to come from the northwest. The range, which is extremely high, follows the left bank of the river, sometimes 1, 2, or 3 leagues from the river. The plain between the mountains and the banks of the stream is very fertile and is well cultivated, as much as proximity of the Apaches and small number of settlers permit. 10 leagues]

[43] It is noticeable that Amangual now uses compass directions. Either the commandant-general's orders received at Santa Fe were to this effect, or Amangual for the first time was able to obtain a compass—or both.

September 25

This morning the *cavalladas* were separated. We camped here in order to divide the troops into two detachments; one to continue the campaign, the other to accompany the mule train. Night fell with no unusual incident.

September 26

The *cavalladas* for the detachment to go on the campaign were detached and the troops were chosen, and all necessary provisions were made so that the troops could move out promptly in the morning. We continued camped in the same place.

September 27

We set out from Sevilleta at 9 o'clock in the morning. Having found the trail of the stock stolen by the Apaches on the 4th of this month, we followed it to the east until 11 o'clock, and to the southeast until a few minutes after noon. At that time we entered a very narrow and rocky hill section of the country; we continued traveling to the south until 5 o'clock in the afternoon, and stopped when we got out of the hills. At 6:30 we entered a level plain in order not to let the enemy see the dust raised by our *cavallada.* We continued to travel toward the south over the aforesaid plain, and at 1 o'clock in the morning we reached a water hole, but, as the water was not drinkable for the *cavallada*, we left the mules, inasmuch as they were exhausted by the forced march, and we continued going to the southeast with the troops until we arrived at Sierra Oscura, where we made a dry camp [camp without water] at 4 o'clock in the morning without further incident. 21½ leagues

September 28

We set out from said place at 7 o'clock in the morning, traveling along the foot of the mountains to the northeast, and reached a pool of water before 8 o'clock. I decided to wait there for the mules—which arrived at 11 o'clock. At 3:30 I ordered a detachment of 50 men, one captain, and one subordinate officer to find the road we have to travel and to reconnoiter the range. At 4 o'clock we set out, traveling along the aforesaid range of mountains to the east for about 300 paces; then entered a canyon that runs to the east south. We continued to travel in this direction until 5:30, and our direction after leaving the canyon was to the south. This canyon is named Canyon of the Piedra Parada; there is in its center a *cañada* with many pools of rain water. Until 10 o'clock we traveled to the south over an almost impassable and very dangerous road; we went up and down hills and mountains over very rocky trails, and three mules were exhausted on said route. At 10 o'clock our route gradually began to turn from south to west, and continued to do so until about 11:30, when we arrived at a place without water, and we stopped there because the mules were very tired. 8½ leagues

September 29

We set out from said place at 10 o'clock in the morning, traveling over very rocky and rough hills, with a general direction to the southwest. We camped about 3 in the night [!] near a rain-water pool. [Bexar copy only: Half an hour after we set out, the road turned to the south and then gradually to the southeast. At 7 o'clock we set out in that direction (and continued) until we went down to a valley, where we found the party that had gone to reconnoiter the ground, and which had returned with no unusual incident. We camped about 9 o'clock near some pools of rain water that were not sufficient to water the *cavallada*. The guides went out to explore the country, and half a league to the southeast they found another large pool of water, where we decided to spend the night. We went there, and at 3 o'clock in the afternoon we camped in the aforesaid place. We sighted a cow, and I gave permission to one corporal and eight soldiers to kill it. Said cow was found to be one of those stolen at Sevilleta, and it had been wounded with a lance].[44] Night fell without incident. 4 leagues

September 30

We set out from said place at 2:30 in the morning in order to conceal our *mulada* from the enemy [the Indians] in case it should be found in the Sierra Blanca.[45] We traveled along the Sierra Blanca in the

[44] They were at Sevilleta on September 24, but he did not report any theft then. It is interesting to note that the Indians did not bother to butcher his cow; within historical times, few Southwestern Indians would touch beef when horse meat was available.

[45] The Sierra Blanca Mountains are in the Ruidoso area, about half-way between the Río Grande and the Pecos. His men, traveling east, have just crossed the Jornada del Muerte.

direction bearing to the east until 5 o'clock in the morning at which time the road turned to the east northeast; and at 6:30 it turned to the northeast, and at 8:30 to the north. We continued in that direction over very bad lands until 9:30, when we suddenly changed our direction to the east, and traveled in that direction until we had crossed them, at 10 o'clock. At that time we reached the spring known as Santa Paula, where we camped without further incident. 10 leagues

Note

The bad lands is a stretch of ground about four hundred *varas* wide that runs from north to south between two ranges of mountains, the Oscura and the Blanca. This bad land seems to have been a volcanic [deposit] in its entire extent; it is impassable except over a trail made by the Indians. The rocks, calcined by the heat [of the volcano], look like an iron mine, and the trail by which we came offers a horrible precipice on both sides at every step.

October 1, 1808

We set out from said camp at 1 o'clock in the afternoon, and traveled to the east northeast until 3 o'clock, when, having reached the foot of the mountains, we took a direction veering to the east. We traveled in that direction over rough and hilly country until 8 o'clock, and that night we reached a place without water and made a [dry] camp with no other incident. 8½ leagues

October 2

We set out from said place at 7 o'clock in the morning, bearing to the southeast, and entered a section of hilly country that was very difficult and dangerous. At 9:30 we climbed a range of mountains, and continued traveling to the south, and, following the same direction, we descended until we reached the banks of the Sierra Blanca River, which we crossed, and traveled downstream along its bank. We camped on its banks at 11 o'clock in the morning; the river flows from west to east. One hour before setting out from the camp, I had sent the *alférez* with a party of 20 men to reconnoiter the ground and to see if they could find any enemy sign. Before we set out, said party returned, having observed nothing. 4 leagues

October 3

We set out from said camp at 7:30 in the morning, and traveled about 500 paces to the east, and then turned to the southeast by south. At 9:30 we crossed a creek of running water that comes from the Sierra Blanca, which runs from west to east, and continued our march to the south. [Bexar: We went up a hill and continued to travel to the south] over hills covered with grass and many trees. At 11:30 we reached the last river of Sierra Blanca, which we crossed, and then camped on its banks. This river, like the others we have found, runs from west to east. Upon our arrival I sent one lieutenant with a party of 30 men to reconnoiter the mountains and to explore the land to see if he could find the trail of the enemy. At 3 o'clock in the afternoon said party returned without unusual incident. 4½ leagues

October 4

This morning the guides went out to spy on the Indian villages, and at 8 o'clock we set out from said camp, taking a southerly direction, and traveling over hills thickly covered with trees until we arrived at the San Mateyito River at 1:30 in the afternoon. This river runs from the northeast to the southwest, and we continued to travel along its right bank over rough and rocky hills. At 5 o'clock that afternoon we camped on one of those hills. Direction, southwest. Night fell without unusual incident. 10 leagues

October 5

We stayed in said camp all day, but at 6 o'clock in the afternoon we set out, keeping along the river until we reached a place, where, flowing out onto the plain, the water was lost in the sand. We crossed and stopped on its left bank at 7:30 in chaparral of *frenos* [or *frunos*] and cottonwood. No other unusual incident. Made 1½ leagues

October 6

We stayed in camp all day in said place, and at 6 o'clock in the afternoon I sent a lieutenant with a party of 22 men and guides to spy on the villages. Night fell with no incident.

October 7

We stayed in said camp until 6 o'clock in the afternoon, when we left, reaching a stopping place where the water of the River of Our Lady of Light disappears in the sand. [Bexar copy: . . . until 6 o'clock in the afternoon, when we set out, traveling to the south southwest. After having traveled for half an hour, we passed the train, but waited until dark to conceal the dust raised by our *cavallada* from the enemy. Soon after 7 o'clock we continued our journey, traveling a very uneven road, and on our route, a horse fell down a bluff. We were able to get him out with the aid of ropes and a great deal of work on the part of ten men. Half an hour later, at 10:30, we reached a place where the River of Our Lady of Light disappears in the sand.] We were still on horseback when a boy named Juan Cristobal [Bexar copy: about 10 or 12 years old,] came out of a clump of chaparral, where he had been hiding. The Indians had carried him off as a captive [from Sevilleta] on the fourth of last month. [Bexar copy: The boy told us that he had run away from the Apaches five days before while they were rounding up their *cavallada* to move their village to another location. This unfortunate boy miraculously escaped the vigilance of a multitude of Indians.] His body was covered with lacerations that gave evidence of cruelty of these barbaric Indians, who, having no pity on him despite his tender age, had whipped him cruelly at every turn. [Bexar copy: This boy was named Juan Cristobal Padia. He had lived for five days on a few piñon nuts that he had gathered before leaving the woods.]

Upon arriving at the aforesaid place, we joined the party that had gone out yesterday to spy on the villages. One corporal and 6 men of said party had gone out on foot to reconnoiter the *sierra,* and at 8 o'clock in the morning, the corporal and 6 soldiers who had gone out as spies returned and reported that they had found the village abandoned by the Indians. Following the trail of the [Indian] *cavallada,* they had learned that the Indians had left the *sierra* on the east, and that they had gone in the direction of another *sierra,* which may be seen at a distance. At 8:30 a party consisting of one corporal and 10 men went out in pursuit of the fresh trail left by one mounted Indian, found yesterday, who had come to harvest some corn and tobacco that he had planted on the bank of the river. At 11 o'clock in the morning, we set out from said camp and traveled along the *sierra* of Our Lady of Light. We continued to travel toward the south over terrain covered with many liveoaks and rocks. At 2 o'clock in the afternoon we arrived at the foot of the Sierra del Sacramento, where the spies reported that they had seen a trail a few days old going up the mountain. [Therefore,] I decided to send an *alférez* with a party of 33 men to follow the trail. This was done at 3 o'clock in the afternoon. The rest of the troops remained in that place without water. No further unusual incident. 10½ leagues

October 8

At 8 o'clock in the morning the corporal and 10 [6] men who had gone out yesterday as spies, returned. They had found the abandoned village of the Indians, and, following the trail of the *cavallada,* [Bexar copy only: they found that the Indians had gone out of the *sierra* to the east; they seemed to have followed that direction to another *sierra* that may be seen at a distance.

[At 8:30 a party of one corporal and 10 men went out, following a fresh trail of a mounted Indian who yesterday came to harvest some corn and tobacco that he had planted on the banks of the river. At 11 o'clock we set out from said camp and traveled along the *sierra* of Our Lady of Light. We traveled toward the south over terrain having many rocks, liveoaks, and wooded places.[46] At 2 o'clock in the afternoon, we reached the foot of the Sierra del Sacramento, where the spies reported they had seen a trail a few days old going up the mountain. Therefore I ordered an *alférez* with a party of 35 men to follow said trail. The rest of the troops remained in camp without water.] Night fell without further unusual incident. 10½ leagues[47]

October 9

At 8:30 in the morning the party that went out yesterday to reconnoiter the trail of the mounted Indian returned and reported that they had followed it until 10 o'clock at night over a very dangerous and almost impassable road. [Just before dawn,] since the trail was three days old, the place was very far away from the camp; the camp was without water, and as there was no hope of finding any water soon, the officer in command decided to come back, [which he did without unusual incident.] We set out from said place at 9 o'clock, traveling along the *sierra* toward the south, and at 11 o'clock [we reached the mouth of

[46] Some unexplained repetition here.

[47] Originally in the Guerra copy, but deleted.

a canyon,] where we camped without unsaddling our horses to wait for those who had gone to reconnoiter said canyon [where we were camped] to ascertain whether there was any water in it for the *cavallada*, having learned that there was no water; therefore, at 3 o'clock we continued, traveling in the same direction until, at 5 o'clock, we reached the mouth of the said canyon, where flows San Marcos Creek, with a little water. This creek comes down from the Sierra of the Sacramento, and flows from east to west 400 *varas* before reaching said point. The troops guarding the *cavallada* found hanging from a [fairly tall] tree [ten] *tercios*[48] of dried meat, and another [*tercio*] in a liveoak a short distance away [to the west]. [When] I received the report, I went in person to examine the tracks of the Indians who had left the meat there, [and there] were those [tracks] of 34 Indians, and I immediately ordered a party of 50 men on foot and one captain to ambush themselves in the said place [to conceal themselves in the woods]. I myself, with 23 men on horseback, went to another place a short distance away. As no unusual incident occurred during the night, both detachments returned at 6 o'clock in the morning to the camp, where most of the troops had stayed under the command of a lieutenant.[49] 5 leagues

October 10

We set out from said place at [3?], following the trail of the Indians; it was ascertained that there were more than 70 men of them on horseback and 4 on foot. At 4 o'clock we stopped the train without dismounting behind a low hill that was located in the middle of the plain about 3 leagues from the foot of the Sierra del Sacramento. At 6:15, it having already become dark, we continued traveling over the plain; at 3 o'clock in the morning, we reached the Sierra de San Nicolas, where we camped on the banks of the spring of San Francisco de Borga, which comes down from said *sierra* and flows from west to east. On this route, one mule was exhausted. Our route was always to the west southwest. 15 leagues

October 11

This morning the spies went out to reconnoiter the *sierra* [de los

[48] Quarters?

[49] In the Bexar copy, two or three different handwritings may account for some duplication. These duplications do not occur in the Guerra copy.

Organos[50]], and at 5 o'clock in the afternoon, as the grass was very poor for the *cavallada,* we took the train down to the plain and camped at the foot of the *sierra,* about 500 *varas* to the south of the said spring of water. Night came without further unusual incident. [3½ leagues]

October 12

Last night at 9 o'clock, the corporal and 5 soldiers who had gone to reconnoiter the Sierra de los Organos returned without any other unusual incident than that of having followed the trail of the Indians until they made sure that they [the Indians] had watered their *cavallada* at two springs of water that came down from the *sierra.* We continued traveling toward the pass of San Agustin, which is located between the sierra and the above-mentioned Sierra de los Organos. At 6:30 we set out from said camp and traveled toward the south along the foot of the Sierra de San Agustin until 10 o'clock, when we turned to the south southwest and a little later to the southwest. We continued in this direction until at noon we reached the foot of the Sierra de los Organos. We camped on the edge of the spring of San Augustin. Upon arriving there, I sent one *alférez* with 20 men to look for water. Said officer found that there was very little water and that it was very difficult to water the animals. At 4 o'clock in the afternoon, one captain went out to reconnoiter the *sierra* with a party of 80 men to learn whether any Indians or their families have remained [were to be found there]. Night came without unusual incident. 7 leagues

October 13

At 10 o'clock last night, [the party of] the captain who went out to reconnoiter the *sierra* returned. He reported that he had found a village recently abandoned by the Indians. They had made a trench of rocks there,[51] and a large corral for their *cavallada.* Said captain followed the trail and found that it led to a place [pass] between the Sierra del Rescate and the Sierra de San Agustin, and the Sierra de los Organos. He returned to the camp without unusual incident. 9 leagues

[Bexar copy additional: This morning I decided that the Indians who were fleeing from us were part of those who had perpetrated the robbery in Sevilleta, and decided to pursue them. To this end, I selected

[50] Now the San Andres Mountains.

[51] See entry for June 4.

a party of 89 men and ordered the selection of the best horses; we left the rest of the horses with the train in charge of the lieutenant, with orders for him to go to the river and join the main train, which was under the command of Don José Agabo de Ayala, militia captain. At 10 o'clock we set out from that place and traveled to the northwest until we reached the foot of the Sierra del Rescate (Ransom Range) and San Agustin, which we climbed, and reached the top in the early afternoon. We continued traveling deeper into said *sierra* and the San Nicolas *sierra,* over hills covered with rocks and over very dangerous trails, until 4:30 in the afternoon, when the trail turned to the west. At 5:15 we reached the spring of water where we observed that the Indians had watered their *cavallada* two days before. We camped there without further unusual incident. 9 leagues]

October 14

We set out from said camp at 6:30 in the morning and continued to follow the trail of the Indians to the north northwest. At 7:15 we reconnoitered a place between two hills at the foot of the range where the Indians had spent the night before last. We continued to follow the trail to the north until 9 o'clock, and to the east in a canyon in the Sierra de las Pitacas; at 9:15 we sighted some Indians running away on foot along the ridges, driving their *cavallada* and families before them, while another party of Indians on horseback seemed to be spying on us from the summit of a hill. I ordered the men to dismount, and, leaving 14 men to guard the *cavallada,* I went up said hill with the remaining 74 men. The Indians ran away, but I pursued them as far as I could, but these Indians, forewarned, waited for us behind rocks, and began to rain bullets and arrows upon the men. The great difficulty encountered by our men at every step because of our unfamiliarity with the terrain, and the great advantage that the Indians had—who even threw rocks down upon us from the top of the *sierra*—[Bexar copy: obstructed our troops in such a manner that, after attacking them for three hours, I ordered a retreat. I left one soldier dead from the Company of the New Kingdom of León, and one corporal and one soldier of the Second Company of New Santander, two soldiers of the Second Company of said province, and two veterans were wounded.

[Although the shouts and screams of the Indians indicated that many of them died in that encounter, I can give no definite account of their losses. At 1 o'clock in the afternoon we retreated in good order, and, after having doctored our wounded and watered our horses, I held a review of arms and ammunition. I found that there were missing the musket, lance, cartridge belt, and package of cartridges[52] of deceased Vicente Hurtaita, four lances of the wounded militiamen, and two of the veterans,[53] and two muskets of José Benegas and Antonio Nañes, wounded militiamen.

[We set out at 3 o'clock, traveling through the same canyon through which we had entered the mountains, and we continued traveling over the plain to the west southwest] until 4:30, when we made a dry camp. Night fell with no further incident. 5 leagues

October 15

We set out from said place at 4 o'clock in the morning and continued to travel toward the southwest [Bexar copy: west southwest] until 9:30, when we arrived at the Río Grande del Norte, and camped at the place known as Robilledo [or Robledo]. At 3 o'clock in the afternoon, the main train under command of Captain Don Agabo de Ayala went through our camp. It came to a stop 1 league farther down the river, where we joined it at 5 o'clock. Night fell with no further incident. 7 leagues

October 16

We set out from said camp at 9 o'clock in the morning and traveled along the left bank of the river toward the south, ¼ southeast. At noon we encountered a party of troops under the command of Lieutenant Don José [Arvio y] Salas, who said that he was from the garrison of Santa Fe. At 2 o'clock in the afternoon we arrived at El Bajio [Bexar: El Brazito], where we joined the party that had gone out on a cam-

[52] Packaged cartridges were in use in the 1600's, and consisted of a proper quantity of powder and a lead ball wrapped together in a trapezoid of paper. At firing, the soldier in battle usually tore off the top of the paper with his teeth, poured the powder into the barrel, and then rammed home the bullet (which was packaged with a bullet patch). In 1816–17 the U.S. Army prepared such cartridges in packages of ten. See Carl P. Russell, *Guns on the Early Frontier*, 243–48.

[53] Veterans apparently were regular army men, while militiamen were volunteers for the campaign.

paign, and which had stayed behind under the command of Militia Captain Don Cayetano Quintero. 6½ leagues

October 17

We remained in camp in said place in order to hold a review of the *cavallada*. No unusual incident occurred during the day except that the boy we found in the Sierra of Our Lady of Light was returned to his father.

October 18

We set out from said encampment, following the left bank of the river, until we reached the place known as Los Esteros, where we camped, without unusual incident. 4½ leagues

October 19

We set out from said place at 7:30 in the morning. At 9 in the morning we ascended the range and continued our way toward the east, ¼ northeast. We arrived [there is no more for this day in the Guerra copy].

[Bexar copy: . . . at 7:30 in the morning, traveling along the river to the south ¼ to the southeast (!). At 11 o'clock we encountered the *situado* of the Company of San Elzeario. I decided to leave our *cavallada* there in the number of 626 animals with a guard of 40 men under command of one officer.[54] I continued traveling with only the loaded mules until we reached the place known as Las Borregas. At 3 o'clock in the afternoon we camped with no further unusual incident. 8½ leagues]

October 20

We set out from said place at 8:30 in the morning. At 11 o'clock we crossed the river, and just before noon we went through the town of El Paso. We continued traveling to the south, ¼ southeast. At 2 o'clock we reached the edge of the farming area of said town, where we camped with no further incident. 8 leagues

October 21

We set out from said place at 11 o'clock in the morning, and continued to travel to the south, ¼ south. At 3:30 we reached the Presidio

[54] It now appears that his animals must have numbered over eight hundred.

of San Elzeario, where, having distributed the troops to the quarters assigned them, we camped without further unusual incident. 5 leagues

[Bexar copy only]:

Private Nepomuceno Martinez, of the Company of the New Kingdom of León, was put under arrest for having shown insubordination in matters of the service and for having thrown a knife that pierced the cartridge belt of Carabineer Vizente Cabrera of the Bexar Company, while under his orders.

*Captain Amangual has proved himself quite a soldier. With a large body of men and somewhere near one thousand animals, he descended the Río Grande from Santa Fe, cut across the deadly lava* malpaís *to the Sierra Blancas, encountered Indians all the way, properly divided his forces into several parties, and finally took out after the Indians to punish them for stealing his animals. And in a wild and unfamiliar country—the enemy's home ground—he fought them with the loss of only one man, then retreated in order. It will be noted that never did he lose control of his force; he personally went with the party to chastize the Indians; he returned to the Río Grande, got his forces all back together, and went on to San Elzeario. No small achievement.*

*He was on the road thirty-two days, on all of which but four he was moving, for a total of 236 leagues, or 614 miles—an average of twenty-two miles a day. He reached San Elzeario on October 21 and would be there for eighteen days before starting the final lap of his trip.*

### *Diary of Francisco Amangual from San Elzeario to San Antonio, November 8–December 23, 1808*[55]

Journal of the expedition made from the Presidio of San Elzeario to the Capital of Bexar:

#### November 8

[The Guerra copy has no entry until November 11; therefore, we shall follow the Bexar copy for a few days:]

We set out from the Royal Presidio of San Elzeario with two friendly Apache Indians as guides at 9 o'clock in the morning, traveling to the southeast. Just before noon, we crossed the Río [Grande] del Norte, and rested on its banks without unsaddling our horses. At 1

[55] The Guerra copy has no entry until November 12.

o'clock we continued traveling along the said river to the south southeast until 6:30, when we camped on its banks at the San Antonio crossing [*abrevadero*]. Night fell with no unusual incident. 11 leagues

November 9

We stayed in camp all day because one corporal and 6 men had been left behind to wait for the Chihuahua *correo*. They arrived at 6 o'clock without unusual incident.

November 10

We set out from said camp at 11:30, traveling to the east, and at 6 o'clock in the afternoon we reached a place facing the Sierrita Blanca, without water, where we camped [dry] without further unusual incident. 8 leagues

November 11

We set out from said place at 7:30 in the morning. At 9 o'clock we ascended the range and continued to travel always to the east ¼ northeast. By 11:30 o'clock at night we reached La Salina with no other unusual incident having occurred on the route except that three horses were exhausted; one from the First, another from the [Second] Company of New Santander, and the other belonged to the company of the New Kingdom of León. We camped near two pools of sulphur water, with a large amount of copperas.[56] 21 leagues

November 12

[Guerra copy resumes:] We set out from the said place shortly after the noon hour, traveling to the east over a plain. At 5:30 we reached the foot of a ridge [*serranía*] that joins the Sierra de Guadalupe on the north, and there we stopped without water. No unusual incident happened other than that one mule [of the Second Company of New Santander] was exhausted. 7 leagues

November 13

We set out from said camp at 8:30 in the morning, going east, ¼ northeast. At 9:30 we climbed up the range to the east over a very rough and rocky trail. On going down, the trail gradually turned from east to north, and after traveling over a very broken ground, at 3 o'clock

[56] This seems to put them at Salt Lake, in western Culberson County.

in the afternoon we reached the foot of the Sierra de Guadalupe on the east. There we camped between two hills on the bank of the San Martin spring of water without further unusual incident. 7 leagues

November 14

We set out from said place just after the noon hour, and traveled to the east. At 5:30 we reached le Ciénega [the Marsh] on the shores of which are beautiful water holes; the water holes found to the west are heavily charged with sulphur and copperas; the others are less and less until one reaches the last on the east, which has clear fresh water. There we stopped, and night fell without any unusual incident. 8 leagues

November 15

We set out [from the said camp] at 8:30 in the morning over a good road to the east, ¼ northeast. At 1 o'clock we stopped on the banks of the Cottonwood Arroyo[57] without unusual incident. 6 leagues

November 16

We set out [from said place] at noon and continued along the left bank of the aforementioned creek toward the east northeast. At 4 o'clock in the afternoon we camped there with no unusual incident. 5 leagues

November 17

We set out from said place at 9 o'clock in the morning and continued along the left bank of the Arroyo of the Cottonwoods toward the east northeast. At 10 o'clock we crossed it and continued traveling to the east until noon, when we reached the banks of the Pecos River.[58] We then traveled along its banks downstream to the south southeast until 2 o'clock in the afternoon, when we found a watering place for the *cavallada* and camped by it.[59] On the route, nothing unusual occurred save that one horse of the Company of the New Kingdom of León was exhausted. 7 leagues

[57] Present Cottonwood Draw.

[58] It appears that they left Cottonwood Draw and followed one of the smaller water courses that lead into the Pecos at about Arro. The Pecos is in such a deep canyon that crossing places are few; therefore, he may have descended the river to what later became known as Horsehead Crossing.

[59] He seems to have found a crossing place a little below the present town of Pecos.

November 18

We set out from said camp at 10 o'clock in the morning, and continued to travel along the Pecos River to the south southeast, and at 1 o'clock in the afternoon, having found a good watering place, we camped on its bank. [Bexar copy: On the route, one horse of the Company of Bexar was exhausted.] Night came without further unusual incident. 4 leagues

November 19

This morning the two guides bade us good-by to return to San Elzeario.

We set out from said place at 9 o'clock in the morning and continued to travel along said river to the southeast, ¼ south. At 9:30 we crossed the river [Bexar copy: and continued on our way in the same direction until 4 o'clock in the afternoon, when, having found a good watering place, we stopped to camp,] without unusual incident. 9 leagues

November 20

We set out from said camp at 9:30 in the morning, and continued along said river to the southeast, ¼ south, until 4 o'clock [Bexar: 4:30] in the afternoon, when we stopped on its bank, with no unusual incident except that one horse [Bexar copy: of the Company of the New Kingdom of León] was exhausted. 10 leagues

November 21

We remained in camp all day in said place in order to let the *cavallada* and *mulada* rest. Night fell with nothing unusual.

November 22

We set out from said place at 9 o'clock in the morning, and continued to travel along the Pecos River to the southeast until 3 o'clock in the afternoon, when we arrived at the watering place of de las Conchas, where we camped, having experienced no unusual incident in all the day [Bexar copy: other than the loss of one (torn) belonging to one corporal of the Company of la Bahía (of "which the said corporal was carrying"), which was lost in the river.] 7½ leagues

November 23

We set out from said place at 9 o'clock in the morning, traveling along the Pecos River to the southeast, ¼ east, until 4 o'clock in the afternoon, when we reached the watering place of Pope San Clemente. Shortly before arriving there, we found a trail [Guerra copy ends; Bexar copy begins:] a fresh trail of Indians. I ordered one captain and 30 men to reconnoiter it, and they found that the Indians, while running away, had dropped some containers of meat. As it was impossible to overtake them before nightfall, the [men] returned to camp. On the route, one horse of the Company of New Kingdom of León was exhausted. 10 leagues

November 24

[November 24 is missing from both copies; November 25 and 26 are missing from the Guerra copy. There are again several changes of handwriting in the Bexar copy.]

November 25[60]

[Bexar copy:]

This morning one horse of the Bexar Company died. We set out from said place at noon, traveling toward the east along the river, and at 3 o'clock we camped on its bank at the watering place of Santa Catarina. No other unusual incident occurred. 3½ leagues

November 26

[Bexar copy:]

We set out from said place at 9 o'clock in the morning, traveling along [torn] to the east southeast until 1 o'clock . . . noon. We camped on its banks . . . watering place of San José. On the route, one horse of the Company of the New Kingdom of León and one of the Second Company of New Santander were exhausted.

I shall remark that since the seventeenth, when we crossed the Pecos River, we have been traveling over a level plain with few live-oaks. Today at 11 o'clock we entered a very beautiful valley between two low ranges of hills resembling a mesa, through which the said river runs. 5 leagues

November 27[61]

[Guerra copy resumes:]

At 3 o'clock in the morning there came a violent rainstorm with

[60] There is no entry for November 24.

[61] The Guerra copy continues in another handwriting.

thunder and lightning. At 11 o'clock it cleared up, and we remained in camp at said place all day in order to dry out the baggage. Night fell with no unusual incident.

November 28

[Bexar copy: This morning the musket of a militiaman of the Company of the New Kingdom of León was broken when he fell off his horse.] We set out from said camp at 9:30, course to the south, ¼ southeast. [Bexar copy: At 10:30 we joined the party that went out on the twenty-fourth to follow the trail left by some Indians. The militia captain who was in command of said party, reported that he had followed the trail until dark yesterday, but then, realizing that the Indians were one day ahead of him, he decided not to go any farther, for it would be impossible to overtake them. We continued traveling, the river winding little by little from the east ¼ southeast to south ¼ southeast; we turned (with it); we followed this last fixed course (southeast ¼ southeast), until 2:30 in the afternoon, when we camped at the watering place of San Juan,] without unusual incident except that twelve horses were exhausted. 7½ leagues

November 29

We set out from said place at 9:15 in the morning and traveled along the river to the south, ¼ southeast. At 11 o'clock we saw three Indians [run away] on horseback on the other side of the river, and I sent one lieutenant and 15 [13] men to reconnoiter. He advised me that they were Comanches of Chief Cordero who were on a campaign against the Apaches. [Bexar copy: At noon (torn) it became imperative for the train to go through. We went up the hill to the east, ¼ southeast, until 2 o'clock in the afternoon, when we camped at the watering place of San Andres. At 4 o'clock the lieutenant and the party that had gone out to find the Indians returned and reported that they had found the village abandoned, with eight fires still burning, and he was certain the Indians were Comanches who were hunting in that region. At 8 o'clock in the evening there came to this place three Comanches, and told us that they were from the village of Chief Cordero, and that they belonged to a party that was out on a campaign against the Apaches.] They promised to furnish us with guides who would take us to the village of the said Cordero. No unusual incident occurred. 6½ leagues

November 30

At 9 o'clock the Comanche guides arrived, and at 9:30 we set out from this place and traveled until we reached a bank of the Pecos River. [Bexar copy: . . . at 9:30 we set out from the said (torn) we climbed the hill . . . following always the. . . . We arrived at Las Uvas Creek shortly before noon. This creek, which carries much fresh water, flows from north northeast to south southwest, and empties into the Pecos River.] We camped on its bank without further incident. 3½ leagues

December 1

We set out from said camp at 10 o'clock in the morning, traveling along the right bank of Las Uvas Creek to the north northeast. At noon we rested near its headwaters, and continued to the east northeast until we arrived at the Water Holes of Leona, where we stopped at 4 o'clock in the afternoon, without further unusual incident. 8 leagues

December 2

We remained in camp in said place in order to let the *mulada* and the *cavallada* rest. Night fell without incident.

December 3

We set out from the said place at 9 o'clock in the morning, traveling over a level plain. [Bexar copy: to the northeast, ¼ east, over a level plain with liveoaks.] At 1:30 in the afternoon we reached San Francisco Xavier Lake, having experienced no unusual incident except that one mule of the First Company of New Santander was exhausted. 5 leagues

December 4

We set out from said camp at 9 o'clock in the morning, traveling toward the northeast, ¼ east. At 2 o'clock in the afternoon I sent two soldiers with the interpreter to inform the Indian Chief Cordero of our arrival and to ask permission to pass through. At 4 o'clock said chief came to meet us alone, because the *cavallada* of the Indians was [grazing] a short distance away. At 5:30 we reached the banks of the Almagre

Creek, where we camped. We left two mules of the Company of Bexar and two horses of the Company of the New Kingdom of León dead on the route.[62] 11 leagues

December 5

We remained in camp there in order to let the *cavallada* and the *mulada* rest. Night fell without incident.

December 6

We continued encamped in the same place for the same reason as yesterday. [Night fell without unusual incident.]

December 7

This morning we exchanged twenty-one of the most exhausted horses for others in order not to lose them on the trip. Four mules and four horses were left in care of Chief Cordero.

We set out from the village at 9:30 in the morning, traveling toward the east, ¼ southeast. Just before noon we crossed San Lucas Creek, which carries very good running water; it flows from the west southwest to the east northeast and joins Almagre Creek. We camped on its bank without further incident. 3 leagues

December 8

Dawn came today with rain, and it continued to rain all day, so we stayed in camp in said place. Nothing unusual.

December 9

We set out from said camp a little before noon, course to the east, ¼ southeast, and at 4:30 in the afternoon we camped on the right bank of a creek that had many water holes above the headwaters of the Verde River. The creek runs from the south southwest to the east northeast. Night came without further unusual incident. 5½ leagues

December 10

We set out from said place to the east, ¼ southeast, over some low hills that were covered with rocks. At 5:30 [Bexar copy: 5] in the afternoon we reached the creek of Nuestra Señora de Loreto, where we camped without unusual incident. 6½ leagues

[62] It is a country that always has been hell on women and horses.

December 11

We set out from said place at 9:30 o'clock in the morning, traveling toward the east, and at 2:30 in the afternoon we reached the head-waters of San Saba River, where we camped; at 6 o'clock in the afternoon seven Comanche men and one woman arrived; they said they were members of Cordero's band. Night came without unusual incident. 6 leagues

December 12

We set out from said camp, traveling along the left bank of the river to the east; on our route we crossed the river six times. At 3 o'clock in the afternoon we reached the abandoned presidio of San Saba. [Bexar copy: On the route we found 20 Indians in a camp; they were also members of the band of Cordero. No other unusual incident occurred.] 6 leagues

December 13

We set out from the said place at 9:30 in the morning, always traveling along the said river to the east, until [torn] we left and continued traveling to the southeast until 1:30, when we left the road about 300 *varas* to the east, where we found the two springs of Santa Lucia: we camped there, without further incident. 4½ leagues

December 14

We set out from said camp at 9 o'clock in the morning, traveling to the southeast. At mid-day we climbed up a low hill, and continued to travel over hilly country covered with rocks until 3 o'clock in the afternoon, when we reached the banks of the Río de los Llanos, about 1 league above the crossing that we had forded on our way from Bexar. On the route, [the stock of] the musket of a militiaman of the Company of New Kingdom of León was broken. 7½ leagues

December 15

We set out from said camp at 9:30 in the morning, and forded the river at a crossing where there were many rocks, and it was very difficult to cross. Until 1 o'clock in the afternoon we traveled over very rocky and hilly country, our course corrected to southeast, ¼ south. At 1 o'clock we went down to the plain and traveled to the south southeast until 4 o'clock in the afternoon. [Bexar copy: We reached the creek (torn) where we camped, without having experienced anything unusual.] 10 leagues

December 16

Early this morning the poor, run-down, and exhausted animals set out from the camp in the care of one sergeant and 12 men to travel by slow stages. This procedure will be followed until they reach Bexar.

This morning the soldier Juan Govea of the First Company of New Santander was placed under arrest because he was insubordinate in matters of the service to [Bexar copy: and because he clubbed] Corporal Francisco de León of his company.

[Bexar copy: We set out from said camp at 9 o'clock in the morning, traveling to the southeast. At 2 o'clock in the afternoon we reached the headwaters of the Pedernales Creek, and continued along said creek to the east. After crossing it four times, at 4 o'clock we camped on its right bank. No unusual incident. 9 leagues]

December 17

We set out from said place at 9 o'clock in the morning. Shortly thereafter we crossed the creek and continued to travel along it to the east until noon, when we stopped. [Bexar copy . . . again we left it (torn) our direction to the southeast. At 1:30 o'clock . . . Arroyo Blanco, and at . . . camped on the bank of (the Arroyo de) San Cosme . . . without further unusual incident.] 8 leagues

December 18

This morning Private Faustino Lopez was placed under arrest for insubordination in matters of the service and for having threatened with his weapons Corporal Francisco de León; both are of the First Company of New Santander.

We set out from said camp at 9 o'clock in the morning, traveling toward the southeast, ¼ east. At 10:30 we reached the headwaters of San Francisco Arroyo, and continued traveling to the southeast until at 1:30 o'clock in the afternoon we reached the Guadalupe River at Santa Cruz crossing, where we camped, without having experienced any unusual incident on the route other than the fact that one horse of the

Bexar Company, which had been sick several days, was completely exhausted. 5 leagues

December 19

We remained in camp to hold a review of the *cavalladas* and to let them rest.

December 20

We set out from said camp at 9 o'clock in the morning, course to the southeast, and arrived at Arroyo de los Balcones and stopped on its right bank. [Bexar copy: . . . toward the southeast and arrived at Arroyo Balcones . . . another Arroyo Balcones, and at 3 o'clock in the afternoon we reached the Arroyo Cíbolo.] We crossed it and camped on its right bank without further unusual incident. 7½ leagues

December 21

We set out from said camp at 10 o'clock in the morning, traveling southeast. At 2:30 o'clock in the afternoon we reached Arroyo de León, and we camped at the place known as Puerto Viejo without further incident. 6 leagues

December 22

We set out from said camp at 10 o'clock in the morning, toward the southeast. At 3 o'clock in the afternoon we reached Arroyo del Novillo and camped in the place known as la Cañada de Don Juan Martin. No further incident. 6½ leagues

December 23

We set out from said camp, course to the southeast, at 9:30 in the morning, and at 11 o'clock we arrived at the Presidio of San Antonio de Bexar without further incident. 1½ leagues 124[!]

FRANCO. AMANGUAL

It is a copy.
[Bexar copy: FRANCO. AMANGUAL *(rubric)*]

*Amangual made the arduous crossing in the Pecos country, a vast, arid wilderness of salt cedar and greasewood that Charles Goodnight later called "the graveyard of the cowman's hopes," and lost only twenty-seven animals on the crossing, which in itself might be con-*

*sidered evidence that he was an* hombre de campo. *A loss of only twenty-seven out of eight hundred was quite a feat. He did, of course, leave twenty-nine animals with Cordero, but those were not lost. All in all, Amangual as a commander was a fitting companion for Vial as an explorer.*

*On this last leg, Amangual traveled thirty-seven days, rested six; covered 263 leagues, or 684 miles, for an over-all average of 18.5 miles a day—and showed once more than he knew how to travel in wilderness country.*

*His totals for the round trip: 121 days of travel, 867 leagues covered, 2,255 miles covered; average number of miles a day over all, 18.8. His route to Santa Fe was 200 miles shorter than Vial's first one.*[63]

*Amangual quite likely was promoted to lieutenant colonel after this expedition. He married for the second or third time in about 1810, and he died on May 19, 1812.*

*Thus, within eighteen years, there were four westward crossings of the Llano Estacado—all relatively unknown to historians: two by Pedro Vial, one by José Mares, and one—the tough one—by Francisco Amangual with 200 men, 800 animals, and wheeled vehicles in his train.*[64]

*The roads had been opened to Santa Fe—but it would not be Spaniards who would benefit from them. Those who would use them would be the restless Anglo-Americans. They were already coming overland, and within a very few years they would start pouring down the Santa Fe Trail that Vial had blazed in 1792. New Mexico would receive them and their gray-canvassed wagons, but New Mexico would not change very much—far less than might be expected from twenty-five years' contact with the bullwhackers. A hundred and sixty years after Vial's time, New Mexico would still be predominantly Spanish in customs and language.*

[63] A map was made of Amangual's journey, and apparently was in existence at least as early as 1835; see Bolton, *Guide*, 261; Wheat, *Mapping the Transmississippi West*, I, 252. There is a copy in the Bancroft Library.

[64] These four crossings make my statement on p. 14 of *The Texan-Santa Fé Pioneers* that the first westward crossing was made in 1841, a monumental error.

# XIX
## *The End of a Long Trail*

Pedro Vial, on a hunting trip from Santa Fe, met Amangual on June 1. Shortly after that, he must have gone on another short expedition, for on September 25, 1808, José Baca, of Santa Cruz de la Cañada, gave a receipt that reads as follows:

> I received from the *alférez* of the Company of Agua Verde, Don José Alaria de Arze, the sum of 24 pesos, 6½ *reales*, to divide among the Indians of my jurisdiction who went on the expedition of Don Pedro Vial—which correspond to 6½ *reales* for each one. [I shall] make the legal distribution of which I must, with the proper receipts to the *alcalde de primer voz* of Santa Fe, Don Juan Rafael Ortiz, according as said official has advised me by the order of the *ad interim* governor of this province, Don Alberto Maynez—all of which, so that it be legal, I affirm by my signature at Santa Cruz de la Cañada on September 25, 1808[1]

However, by the time of that receipt, it appears that Pedro Vial was far away, for on September 14, 1808, Meriwether Lewis, governor of Louisiana Territory, issued a license to P. Vial to hunt (trap) on the Missouri River.[2] No other evidence on this subject has turned up—but Vial's name is missing from the New Mexican records until November, 1809.

Over the years with which we are concerned, there are many scattered records of payment made to interpreters, and Vial's name appears

[1] José Baca, Santa Crux de la Cañada, September 25, 1808, New Mexican Archives, doc. 2165.

[2] Thomas M. Marshall, *The Life and Papers of Frederick Bates,* II, 32.

first in 1791, when he signed a receipt for 23 pesos, 2 *reales,* in payment of the 6 *reales* per day assigned to him.[3] The sum named in the 1791 receipt would equal thirty days' pay at the rate given. He signed another for the same amount on March 31, one on May 31, one on June 30 for 22 pesos, 4 *reales* (?), one on July 31 for 23 pesos, 2 *reales,* one on December 28 for 21 pesos, and one on December 31 for 23 pesos, 2 *reales.*[4] All these sums were charged to the Peace and War Account.

His next appearance is in 1809–10, in a file of receipts by individuals who enjoyed a pension[5] and wages that were paid out of the Peace and War Account, as shown in the following items: "Pedro Vial earned 6 *reales* daily, and the order that validated it had been cited by the predecessors [of the governor] who . . . this account, and from November 1, 1809, until October 31, 1810, 273 pesos, 6 *reales.*"[6]

In the same file, José Jarvai, interpreter to the Pawnee nation, had been assigned 20 pesos a month, according to an order of June 12, 1805.[7] The total for Jarvai (Chalvert) is listed as "120-0-0," or 120 pesos.[8]

We find the next important reference to Pedro Vial on October 2, 1814, when he signed his will, which was written in these words:

> In the name of all-powerful God and of the Blessed Virgin Mary, Our Lady, conceived without the stigma of original sin, amen.
>
> Know all those who see this my will, that I, Pedro Vial, a Frenchman, resident of this capital of Santa Fe, finding myself sick but possessed of my whole and sound judgment, make and order this my testament freely in the following form:
>
> First. I say that I believe and confess in the ministry of the Blessed Trinity, Father, Son, and Holy Ghost, Three Persons Divine, and the

[3] Pedro Vial, receipt, Santa Fe, January 31, 1791, Provincias Internas, Vol. 204, f. 342.

[4] All in *ibid.*, scattered through f. 342 to 408.

[5] A fixed sum paid annually by the government.

[6] If he spent the winter on the Upper Missouri, he was back by the following November; he was paid for 365 days.

[7] On May 28, 1805, Chalvert had offered to work for half-pay, and on the expedition of 1805 he had assumed that he was working for ten pesos a month, but now it appears that the commandant-general had the grace to set his salary at twenty pesos a month only two weeks after Chalvert's offer. It appears also that perhaps Vial and Chalvert were together for the year, inasmuch as each one is getting a year's pay.

[8] This document is in the New Mexican Archives, doc. 2298.

one true God. I believe in our Holy Mother Church, and I confess and as a [*quanto un*] Christian Catholic must believe and confess, and in this faith and creed, I want to live and die as my God might be pleased to call me to him. I order this my testament on the following terms:

First: I commend my soul to the Almighty who created it and redeemed it with His sacred blood, and my body to the earth from which it was formed—which is my wish, that it be shrouded in whatever is available, and that it be interred in the cemetery of the Military Church, and that my interment may be modest.

Item—I direct that *a las mandar forzosas* two *reales* to each one.[9]

Item—I declare that I have not been married nor have any heir who could oppose or impede the bequest to my only and legitimate heiress of all that I shall declare in the following; I name her name, María Manuela Martin, as the one to whom I give the power so that she may enjoy the fruit of it all with the blessing of God and of me.

Item—I declare as my property, the house of my residence, which is composed of seven rooms, and a piece of land that it has in front; a silversmith's chest, an anvil, three large files and four small, one saw, one pair of forceps, some scissors, three hammers, *unas valencitas*, an auger, a chest of drawers without escutcheon [*un cajón sin chapa*], another of the same with locks, one mattress, old, one blanket, old, one serape, old, one *cuero de re*, two *fauretes*, three *cajas de molde* [candle molds? ], one *luy*, one jar of iron, useless.

Item—I declare that I owe Don Francisco Ortiz, storekeeper, 60 pesos; to Don Diego Montoya, 45 pesos, 6 *reales;* to Don Antonio Ortiz, 35 pesos; to Don Manuel Gallego, 12 pesos; to Doña Voledad Olguin, 7 pesos, 7 *reales;* to Corporal Ramon Sánchez, 4 pesos; to Doña Concepción García, 12 pesos; of all of which I here testify that I owe, and that it is my will, that of the remainder of my goods, that all be paid, toward which they shall place it at auction, adding the payments on my salary that are due me on my account, for which I give them the legal year or more time as needed by my executors so that they may comply with it and may give due fulfillment to this my will.

Item—I name that there is due to me [from] the resident of La Ciénega [? ], Antonio Romero, a fat ox as attested by the receipt as-

[9] This is a bequest required by law, similar to the modern bequest of one dollar to each person disinherited.

signed with the number 1; Doña María Miguel Baca, 45 pesos and 4 *reales* for a cure that I have [given] to her husband, now defunct.[9a]

Item—I name as my executors: first, Don Francisco Ortiz, the tobacconist; second, Don Francisco Ortiz, whom I beg for the love of God, that he carry out and execute all that I have ordered in this my testament, which, for its greater force and validity, I sign in the presence of Sergeant José Antonio Alarid,[10] whom I beg to place his authority and judicial [*de esto judicial yo*]. The said sergeant declares that I interpose and am interposing all that is conferred on me by law. I attest that I know the one authorized to sign it, and I sign it myself, together with two assisting witnesses who presented the said authority. Done in the presidio of Santa Fe, October 2, 1814.

PEDRO VIAL [*faint rubric*][11]
JOSÉ ANTONIO ALARID [*rubric*]
Assisting Witness: COR? FRANCO. ORTIZ [*rubric*]
Assisting Witness: JOSÉ TAPIA [*rubric*][12]

Curious are the ways of life and of death, for this man who had by himself covered more ground than any other man of his era, who had talked down more Indians, who had learned more about western geography than any man of his time, died possessed of pitifully few items of value, and named a tobacconist as the executor of his will. Interestingly, too, he says that he has never been married, and has no heirs—though in 1795 he was said to have children. Those children would nearly all be of age by the time of his death—but it is possible, mortality rates being what they were in those days, that none of the children survived him.

Vial must have died not long after he signed the will in October,

[9a] Is this an indication that Vial had practiced medicine?

[10] He and Vial had been in charge of the expedition of 1806.

[11] It is signed with a different pen with a very heavy point, or else he was in bed and let his weight push the pen hard against the paper. It is also written a little too high, into the text, but the old flare is there; it does not quaver or falter, and the rubric is the same except that it is not as deftly formed. Curiously enough, the pen sputtered on his signature in Santa Fe in 1793 (as a quill pen might well do under the pressure of his sweeping strokes), and the pen sputtered all the way through his will, but on his signature it was very firm.

[12] The original of the will, signed Oct. 2, 1814, is in the Bureau of Land Management at Santa Fe. It is cited as Document 1063 in *New Mexican Archives*, I, 315, and at that time was in the Museum of New Mexico.

for in August, 1815, Francisco Ortiz filed an accounting, listing the goods left by Vial and the prices at which they were sold.

Inventory of the goods and effects left by Don Pedro Vial, and the prices at which they have been sold:

| | | | | | | |
|---|---|---|---|---|---|---|
| Firstly, to Don Salvador Martin, a *yunque* [a pair of cloth-shearer's shears?] at 6 pesos, 2 *reales*, some bellows at 7 pesos, 1 *real*, and a small spoon, and some pieces of copper at 4 *reales* | | | | 13 | 7 | 0 |
| Don Rafael Serrasino, a small saw and some files | 4 | 0 | 0 | | | |
| An ink-well | 1 | 0 | 0 | | | |
| 3 *Mantillitos* (small saddlecloths?) | 3 | 5 | 0 | 16 | 5 | 0 |
| 1 [pair] small tongs and *muelles* [springs?] | 3 | 0 | 0 | | | |
| 1 chest of drawers with key | 5 | 0 | 0 | | | |
| Don Francisco Ortiz, some spectacles | 0 | 6 | 0 | | | |
| Two seals and a *cravebel* [?] *viejo* | 1 | 2 | 0 | 06 | 4 | 0 |
| 1 small pot | 1 | 4 | 0 | | | |
| 1 chest of drawers of wood | 3 | 0 | 0 | | | |
| Don Mariano Mestas, some small hand-tongs | | | | 00 | 6 | 0 |
| Don Ysidro [?] Rey, two old books | 0 | 6 | 0 | | | |
| 1 auger | 1 | 0 | 0 | 01 | 6 | 0 |
| Armo. Manuel Sena, the drawers for molding | 1 | 6 | 0 | | | |
| 1 *me—ia* | 1 | 4 | 0 | 03 | 6 | 0 |
| 1 old chest of drawers | 0 | 4 | 0 | | | |
| Don Ysidro, some old *balancitas at* | | | | 00 | 5 | 0 |
| Ramon Apodaca, the small boxes and the molds | | | | 02 | 0 | 0 |
| Don Francisco Montoya, 1 chest of drawers with key | | | | 05 | 0 | 0 |
| The *moldejor* [illegible] | | | | 00 | 6 | 0 |
| The old man Antonio Romero, 1 *buy* [?] for which he paid | | | | 12 | 0 | 0 |
| For which was collected from their [illegible] that I had *vencidos en* [illegible] *á Gr.* | | | | 05 | 2 | 0 |

| | | | |
|---|---|---|---|
| One house of his residence sold at | 100 | 0 | 0 |
| Total | 168 | 7 | 0 |

Ortiz noted that the 45 pesos said to be owed Vial by Doña Miguela Baca was not acknowledged by the woman, since her husband had died fifteen years before without telling her about it, and especially since Vial had never asked her for it before. Vial's estate therefore did not produce enough money to pay his bills. He listed about 176 pesos in debts, and when his estate was liquidated, his creditors accepted payment at the rate of 57 pesos for 60 pesos of indebtedness, and gave receipts in that proportion. The house and land were liquidated to produce the amount actually paid, and María Manuela Martin actually received nothing.

Thus passed Pedro Vial, a man who may have been the first white man on the headwaters of the Missouri River—the man who made the first overland trip from San Antonio to Santa Fe; the man who made the first overland trip from Santa Fe to Natchitoches; the man who made the first transit of the Santa Fe Trail between Santa Fe and St. Louis.

He left his land and his seven-room home to a woman who is otherwise unexplained, but his liquid assets were not enough to pay his debts. He left no legal descendants. But for some twenty-six years he had served Spain in her losing fight to preserve her New World empire against the driving Anglo-Americans. He might have served Spain far better if the imponderable higher levels of Spanish officialdom had used him better—but that is an idle speculation.

Already, in 1814, the restless Anglo-Americans were trying to turn Vial's trail into a road of commerce, and it would be only seven short years until William Becknell would lead his mule train down the Trail and establish commercial traffic on what was to become the best-known highway in the Western Hemisphere. He would be followed by Josiah Gregg, James Wylie Magoffin and his brothers, the Corderos of Chihuahua, Doctor Connelly, the Aulls, Albert Speyer, George Frederick Ruxton, James Josiah Webb, and many others—but they all would follow the path blazed by Pedro Vial, the Frenchman they called Manitou.

✠✠✠

# *Bibliography*

## Published Material

### Books

*(Includes only items cited in the text)*

Abernethy, Thomas Perkins. *The Burr Conspiracy*. New York, Oxford Press, 1954.

Almada, Francisco R. *Gobernantes de Chihuahua*. Chihuahua, 1929.

Alvord, E. W., and C. E. Carter. *The New Régime (Illinois Historical Collections*, XI) Springfield, 1926.

*American State Papers*. 32 vols. Washington, Gales & Seaton, 1832–61. *Indian Affairs* 2 vols.; *Foreign Relations* 6 vols.

Bancroft, Hubert Howe. *History of Arizona and New Mexico* (Vol. XVII of the *Works)*. San Francisco, History Co., 1889.

———. *History of the North Mexican States and Texas* (Vols. XV and XVI of the *Works*). San Francisco, History Co., 1886, 1889.

Bandelier, Adolph F. A., and Fanny R. Bandelier. (Charles W. Hackett, ed.) *Historical Documents Relating to New Mexico, Nueva Vizcaya, and Approaches Thereto, to 1773*. 3 vols. Washington, Carnegie Institution, 1937.

Bartlett, John Russell. *Personal Narrative of Explorations and Incidents in Texas, New Mexico, California, Sonora, and Chihuahua, Connected with the United States Boundary Commission During the Years 1850, 1851, 1852 and 1853*. 2 vols. New York, 1854.

Bolton, Herbert Eugene, ed. *Athanase de Mézières and the Louisiana–Texas Frontier, 1768–1780*. 2 vols. Cleveland, Clark, 1914.

———. *Coronado on the Turquoise Trail*. Albuquerque, University of New Mexico Press, 1949.

———. "French Intrusions Into New Mexico, 1749–1752," *The Pacific Ocean in History* (H. Morse Stephens and Herbert E. Bolton, eds.). New York, Macmillan, 1917.

———. *Guide to Materials for the History of the United States in the Principal Archives of Mexico.* Washington, Carnegie Institution, 1913.

———. *Texas in the Middle Eighteenth Century.* Berkeley, University of California Press, 1915.

Burpee, Lawrence J. *The Search for the Western Sea.* 2 vols. Toronto, Macmillan, 1935.

Carroll H. Bailey, and J. Villasana Haggard. *Three New Mexico Chronicles.* Albuquerque, Quivira, 1942.

Carter, Clarence Edwin. *Great Britain and the Illinois Country, 1763–1774.* Washington, American Historical Assn., 1910.

Castañeda, Carlos E. *Our Catholic Heritage in Texas 1519–1936.* 7 vols. Austin, Von Boeckmann-Jones, 1936–58.

Catlin, George. *North American Indians.* 2 vols. Philadelphia, Leary, Stuart and Co., 1913.

Caughey, John W. *Bernardo de Gálvez in Louisiana, 1776–1783.* Berkeley, University of California, 1934.

Chambers, Henry E. *Mississippi Valley Beginnings.* New York, G. P. Putnam, 1922.

Chapman, Charles E. *Catalogue of Materials in the Archivo General de Indias for the History of the Pacific Coast and the American Southwest.* Berkeley, University of California Press, 1919.

Chittenden, Hiram M. *The American Fur Trade of the Far West.* 3 vols. New York, Francis P. Harper, 1902.

Claiborne, W. C. C. *Official Letter Books of —, 1801–1816.* 6 vols.; Rowland Dunbar, ed., Jackson, Miss., 1917.

Coues, Elliott, ed. *The Expeditions of Zebulon Montgomery Pike.* 3 vols. New York, Francis P. Harper, 1895.

———. *History of the Expedition Under the Command of Lewis and Clark.* 4 vols. New York, Francis P. Harper, 1893.

———. *The Journal of Jacob Fowler.* New York, Francis P. Harper, 1898.

Cox, Isaac Joslin. *The Early Explorations of Louisiana. (University Studies,* Series II, Vol. II, No. I [January–February, 1906].) Cincinnati, University of Cincinnati Press, 1906.

Davis, W. W. H. *El Gringo.* New York, Harper's, 1857.

Denhardt, Robert M. *The Horse of the Americas.* Norman, University of Oklahoma Press, 1947.

Dodge, Richard I. *Our Wild Indians.* Hartford, Worthington, 1882.

Doniol, Henri. *Histoire de la Participation de la France à l'Établissement des Etats-Unis d'Amérique.* 5 vols., Paris, 1886–92.

Douglas, Walter B. *Manuel Lisa,* with hitherto unpublished materials annotated and edited by Abraham P. Nasatir. New York, Argosy-Antiquarian Press, 1964.

Drumm, Stella, ed. *Luttig's Journal of a Fur Trading Expedition on the Upper Missouri, 1812–1813.* St. Louis, Missouri Historical Society, 1920. (New edition by Nasatir [New York, Argosy-Antiquarian Press, 1964.])

Duffus, R. L. *The Santa Fé Trail.* New York, Longmans, Green, 1930.

Dunn, William Edward. *Spanish and French Rivalry in the Gulf Region of the United States, 1678–1702.* (University of Texas *Bulletin No. 1705; Studies in History,* No. 1, Austin, University of Texas Press, 1917.

Fisher, Lillian Estelle. *Background of the Revolution for Mexican Independence.* Boston, Christopher Publishing House, 1934.

Folmer, Henri. *Franco-Spanish Rivalry in North America, 1524–1763.* Glendale, Clark, 1953.

Fortier, Alcée. *History of Louisiana.* 4 vols. New York, Goupil & Co., 1904.

Gannett, Henry. *Boundaries of the United States and of the Several States and Territories (Bulletin No. 13* of the United States Geological Survey). Washington, Government Printing Office, 1885.

Garrett, Julia Kathryn. *Green Flag Over Texas.* Dallas, Cordova Press, 1939.

Gayarré, Charles. *History of Louisiana.* 4 vols. New Orleans, Hansell & Brothers, 1903.

Gómez del Campillo, Miguel. *Relaciones Diplomáticas Entre España y los Estados Unidos.* 2 vols. Madrid, Instituto Gonzalo Fernández de Oviedo, 1946.

Green, Thomas Marshall. *The Spanish Conspiracy.* Cincinnati, Robert Clark, 1891.

Gregg, Josiah. *Commerce of the Prairies.* (Max Moorhead, ed.) Norman, University of Oklahoma Press, 1954.

Grinnell, George B. *The Cheyenne Indians.* 2 vols. New Haven, Yale University Press, 1923.

Hackett, Charles Wilson. "Policy of the Spanish Crown Regarding French Encroachments from Louisiana, 1721–1762," *New Spain and the Anglo-American West.* Lancaster, Pa. 1932.

Haggard, J. Villasana. *Handbook for Translators of Spanish Historical Documents.* Austin, University of Texas Press, 1941.

Hammond, George P., and Agapito Rey. *Narratives of the Coronado Expedition, 1540–1542.* Albuquerque, University of New Mexico Press, 1940.

Haring, Clarence Henry. *The Spanish Empire in America.* New York, Oxford University Press, 1947.

———. *Trade and Navigation Between Spain and the Indies.* Cambridge, Harvard University Press, 1918.

Hart, Stephen Harding, and Archer Butler Hulbert, eds. *Zebulon Pike's Arkansas Journal.* Denver, Stewart Commission, 1932.

Hatcher, Mattie Austin. *The Opening of Texas to Foreign Settlement, 1801–1821.* (University of Texas *Bulletin No. 2714* [April 8, 1927].) Austin, University of Texas Press, 1927.

Hill, Roscoe R. *Descriptive Catalogue of the Documents Relating to the History of the United States in the Papeles Procedentes of Cuba Deposited in the Archivo General de Indias at Seville.* Washington, Carnegie Institution, 1916.

Hodge, Frederick Webb. *Handbook of American Indians North of Mexico.* 2 vols. (Bureau of American Ethnology *Bulletin 30*). Washington, Government Printing Office. 1912.

———. "The Narrative of Cabeza de Vaca," *Spanish Explorers in the Southern United States.* New York, Scribner's, 1907.

Hollon, W. Eugene. *The Lost Pathfinder.* Norman, University of Oklahoma Press, 1949.

Houck, Louis. *A History of Missouri.* 3 vols. Chicago, Donnelley, 1908.

———. *The Spanish Régime in Missouri,* 2 vols. Chicago, Donnelley, 1909.

Jablow, Joseph. *The Cheyenne in Plains Indian Trade Relations, 1795–1840.* (Monograph of the American Ethnological Society, Vol. XIX.) New York, J. J. Augustin, 1951.

Jackson, Donald. *Letters of the Lewis and Clark Expedition, With Related Documents, 1733–1854.* Urbana, University of Illinois Press, 1962.

James, James Alton. *The Life of George Rogers Clark.* Chicago, University Press, 1928.

James, Thomas. *Three Years Among the Indians and Mexicans* (Walter B. Douglas, ed.). St. Louis, Missouri Historical Society, 1916. *Ibid.* (A. P. Nasatir, ed.). Philadelphia, Lippincott, 1962. *Ibid.* (Milton Milton Quaife, ed.). Chicago, Lakeside, 1953.

Kendall, George Wilkins. *Narrative of the Texan Santa Fé Expedition.* New York, Harper, 1844.

Kinnaird, Lawrence. "American Penetration Into Spanish Louisiana," *New Spain and the Anglo-American West.* Lancaster, Pa., copyright by George P. Hammond, 1932.

Lafora, Nicolás de. *The Frontiers of New Spain* (Lawrence Kinnaird, ed.). Berkeley, Quivira Society, 1958.

Larpenteur, Charles. *Forty Years a Fur Trader.* 2 vols. (Elliott Coues, ed.). New York, Francis Harper, 1898.

Loomis, Noel M. *The Texan-Santa Fé Pioneers.* Norman, University of Oklahoma Press, 1958.

Lowery, Woodbury. *A Descriptive List of Maps of the Spanish Possessions, . . . 1502–1820.* Washington, Government Printing Office, 1912.

Lyon, E. Wilson. *Louisiana in French Diplomacy, 1759–1804.* Norman, University of Oklahoma Press, 1934.

McCaleb, Walter F. *The Aaron Burr Conspiracy.* New York, Dodd, Mead, 1903.

Manning, W. R. "Nootka Sound Controversy," American Historical *Annual Report for 1904.*

Margry, Pierre, ed. *Découvertes et Établissements des Française dans 'lOuest et dans le Sud d'Amérique Septentrionale, 1614–1754. Mémoirs et Documents Originaux Recuillis et Publiés par Pierre Margry.* 6 vols. Paris, 1879–88.

Marshall, Thomas Maitland. *A History of the Western Boundary of the Louisiana Purchase, 1819–1841.* Berkeley, University of California Press, 1914.

——— ed., *The Life and Papers of Frederick Bates.* 2 vols. St. Louis, Missouri Historical Society, 1926.

Mathews, Catharine Van Cortland. *Andrew Ellicott, His Life and Letters.* New York, Grafton, 1908.

Michaux, F. A. *Travels to the West of the Allegheny Mountains.* London, Crosby and Hughes, 1803. (Reprinted in Reuben G. Thwaites, *Early Western Travels,* III.)

Moorhead, Max. *New Mexico's Royal Road.* Norman, University of Oklahoma Press, 1958.

Morfi, Fray Juan Augustín. *History of Texas, 1673–1779.* (Carlos E. Castañeda, trans.) 2 vols. Albuquerque, Quivira, 1935.

Nasatir, Abraham P., ed. *Before Lewis and Clark.* 2 vols. St. Louis, Historical Documents Foundation, 1952.

———, and Walter B. Douglas. *Manuel Lisa.* New York, Argosy-Antiquarian Press, 1964.

Page du Pratz, Le. *Histoire de la Louisiane.* 3 vols. Paris, 1758.

Pérez, Luís Marino. *Guide to the Materials for American History in Cuban Archives.* Washington. Carnegie Institution, 1907.

Peyton, John Rozée. *The Adventures of My Grandfather.* London, 1867.

Reprinted in *New Mexico Historical Review*, Vol. IV, No. 3 (July, 1929); ed. by F. W. Hodge.

Phares, Ross. *Cavalier in the Wilderness*. Baton Rouge, Louisiana State University Press, 1952.

Pichardo, Father José Antonio. *Pichardo's Treatise on the Limits of Louisiana and Texas*. 4 vols. (Charles Wilson Hackett, ed.). Austin, University of Texas Press, 1931–46.

Priestley, Herbert I. *The Mexican Nation*. New York, Macmillan, 1923.

———. "The Reforms of José de Gálvez in New Spain," *The Pacific Ocean in History* (H. Morse Stephens and Herbert E. Bolton, eds.). New York, Macmillan, 1917.

———. *José de Gálvez*. Berkeley, University of California Press, 1916.

Richardson, Rupert N. *The Comanche Barrier to South Plains Settlement*. Glendale, Clark, 1933.

Riley, Franklin L. "Spanish Policy in Mississippi After the Treaty of San Lorenzo," American Historical Association *Annual Report for 1897*.

Robertson, James Alexander. *List of Documents in Spanish Archives Relating to the History of the United States, Which Have Been Printed or of Which Transcripts Are Preserved in American Libraries*. Washington, Carnegie Institution, 1910.

———. *Louisiana Under the Rule of Spain, France, and the United States, 1785–1807*. 2 vols. Cleveland, Clark, 1911.

Rowland, Mrs. Dunbar. *Life, Letters, and Papers of William Dunbar*. Jackson, Miss., Press of the Mississippi Historical Society, 1930.

Russell, Carl P. *Guns of the Early Frontiers*. Berkeley, University of California Press, 1957.

Rydjord, John. *Foreign Interest in the Independence of New Spain*. Durham, N.C., Duke University Press, 1935.

Shepherd, William R. *Guide to the Materials for the History of the United States in Spanish Archives*. Washington, Carnegie Institution, 1907.

Sibley, John. *A Report From Natchitoches in 1907* (Annie Heloise Abel, ed.). New York, Heye Foundation, 1922.

Stoddard, Amos. *Sketches, Historical and Descriptive, of Louisiana*. Philadelphia, Mathew Carey, 1812.

Surrey, N. M. Miller. *Calendar of Manuscripts in the Paris Archives Relating to the History of the Mississippi Valley to 1803*. 2 vols. Washington, Carnegie Institution, 1926.

———. *The Commerce of Louisiana During the French Régime, 1699–1763*. New York, Columbia University Press, 1916.

Tabeau, Pierre-Antoine. *Narrative of Loisel's Expedition to the Upper Mis-*

*souri* (Annie Heloise Abel, ed.). Norman, University of Oklahoma Press, 1939.

Teggart, Frederick J. "Notes Supplementary to Any Edition of Lewis and Clark," American Historical Association *Annual Report for 1908*. Vol. I.

Thomas, Alfred B. *After Coronado*. Norman, University of Oklahoma Press, 1935.

———. "Antonio de Bonilla and Spanish Plans for the Defense of New Mexico, 1772–1778," *New Spain and the Anglo-American West*, Vol. I. Copyright by George P. Hammond, 1932.

———. *Forgotten Frontiers*. Norman, University of Oklahoma Press, 1932.

———. *The Plains Indians and New Mexico*. (Vol. XI of the *Coronado Quarto Centennial Publications*). Albuquerque, University of New Mexico Press, 1940.

———. *Teodoro de Croix*. Norman, University of Oklahoma Press, 1941.

Thwaites, Reuben Gold, ed. *Original Journals of the Lewis and Clark Expedition, 1804–1806*. 8 vols. New York, Dodd, Mead, 1904.

Turner, Frederick Jackson. "Correspondence of Clark and Genêt," in American Historical Association *Annual Report for 1896*, I; *Correspondence of the French Ministers to the United States, 1791–1797*, in American Historical Association *Annual Report for 1903*, II; *The Mangourit Correspondence . . .* , in American Historical Association *Annual Report for 1897*.

Twitchell, Ralph E. *The Leading Facts of New Mexican History*. 5 vols. Cedar Rapids, Torch Press, 1911–17.

———. *The Spanish Archives of New Mexico*. 2 vols. Cedar Rapids, Torch Press, 1914.

Tyrrell, J. B., ed. *David Thompson's Narrative of His Explorations in Western America, 1784–1812*. Toronto, Champlain Society, 1916.

Vérendrye, Pierre Gaultier de Varennes, Sieur de la. *Journals and Letters* . . . (Lawrence J. Burpee, ed.) Toronto, Champlain Society, 1927.

Villiers du Terrage, Baron Marc. *Le Découverte du Missouri*. Paris, 1925.

———. *Les Dernières Années de la Louisiane Française*. Paris, 1905.

Webb, Walter Prescott, editor-in-chief. *The Handbook of Texas*. 2 vols. Austin, Texas State Historical Assn., 1952.

Wesley, Edgar Bruce. *Guarding the Frontier*. Minneapolis, University of Minnesota Press, 1935.

Wheat, Carl I. *The Spanish Entrada to the Louisiana Purchase*, 1540–*1804*, and *From Lewis and Clark to Fremont, 1804–1845*. (Vols. I and

II of the series, *Mapping the Transmississippi West, 1540–1861* [5 vols.].) San Francisco, Institute of Historical Cartography, 1957–58.

Whitaker, Arthur Preston. *The Mississippi Question, 1795–1803.* New York, Appleton-Century, 1934.

———. *The Spanish-American Frontier, 1783–1795.* Boston, Houghton-Mifflin, 1927.

Wilkinson, General James. *Memoirs of My Own Times.* 3 vols. Philadelphia, 1816.

Winship, George Parker. "The Coronado Expedition, 1540–1542," Bureau of American Ethnology *Fourteenth Annual Report,* Part 1. Washington, Government Printing Office, 1896.

Worcester, Donald E., ed. *Instructions for Governing the Interior Provinces of New Spain, 1785, by Bernardo de Gálvez.* Berkeley, Quivira, 1951.

Yoakum, H. *History of Texas.* 2 vols. New York, Redfield, 1855.

United States Government Documents

Abert, James William. *Report of Lt. J. W. Abert on His Examination of New Mexico in the Years 1846–47, House Executive Document No. 31,* 39 Cong., 1 sess. Washington, 1848.

Emory, William H. *Report on the United States and Mexican Boundary Survey, House Executive Document No. 135,* 34th Cong., 1st sess. Washington, 1857–59.

Periodicals

Abel, Annie Heloise. "A New Lewis and Clark Map," *The Geographical Review,* Vol. I (1915–16), 329–45, and maps.

Aiton, Arthur S. "The Diplomacy of the Louisiana Cession," *American Historical Review,* Vol. XXXVI, No. 4 (July, 1931).

Bierck, Harold A. "Dr. John Hamilton Robertson," *Louisiana Historical Quarterly,* Vol. XXV, No. 3 (July, 1942).

Bloom, Lansing B. "The Death of Jacques D'Eglise," *New Mexico Historical Review,* Vol. II, No. 4 (October, 1927).

———. "The Governors of New Mexico," *New Mexico Historical Review,* Vol. X, No. 2 (April, 1935).

Bolton, Herbert E. "New Light on Manuel Lisa and the Spanish Fur Trade," Texas State Historical Association *Quarterly (Southwestern Historical Quarterly),* Vol. XVII, No. 1 (July, 1913).

———, ed. "Papers of Zebulon M. Pike, 1806–1807," *American Historical Review,* Vol. XIII (July, 1908).

———. "The Spanish Abandonment and Reconstruction of East Texas, 1773–1779," *Southwestern Historical Quarterly*, Vol. IX, No. 2 (October, 1905).

———. "Spanish Activities on the Lower Trinity River, 1746–1771," *Southwestern Historical Quarterly*, Vol. XVI, No. 4 (July, 1913).

Bonilla, Antonio. "Bonilla's Brief Compendium of the History of Texas, 1772," Elizabeth Howard West, ed., *Southwestern Historical Quarterly*, Vol. VIII, No. 1 (July, 1904).

Caldwell, Norman W. "Tonty and the Beginning of the Arkansas Post," *The Arkansas Historical Quarterly*, Vol. VIII, No. 3 (Autumn, 1949).

Carter, Clarence E. "The Burr-Wilkinson Intrigue in St. Louis," Missouri Historical Society *Bulletin*, Vol. X, No. 4, Part I (July, 1954).

Chapman, Carl H. "The Little Osage and Missouri Indian Village Sites, ca. 1727–1777 A.D.," *The Mississippi Archaeologist*, Vol. XXI, No. 1 (December, 1959).

Corbitt, Duvon Clough. "The Administrative System in the Floridas, 1781–1821," *Tequesta*, Vol. I, No. 2 (August, 1942).

Cox, Isaac Joslin. "The Louisiana-Texas Frontier," *Southwestern Historical Quarterly*, Vol. X, No. 1 (July, 1906).

———. "The Louisiana-Texas Frontier, II," the *Southwestern Historical Quarterly*, Vol. XVI, No. 4 (April, 1913), Vol. XVII, No. 1 (July, 1913), and Vol. XVII, No. 2 (October, 1913).

———. "Opening the Santa Fé Trail," *Missouri Historical Review*, Vol. XXV, No. 1 (October, 1930).

Crichton, Kyle S. "Zeb Pike," *Scribner's Magazine*, Vol. LXXXII, No. 4 (October, 1927).

Diller, Aubrey. "Maps of the Missouri River Before Lewis and Clark," *Studies and Essays in the History of Science and Learning* (1946).

Espinosa, José Manuel. "The Legend of Sierra Azul," *New Mexico Historical Review*, Vol. IX, No. 2 (April, 1934).

Faye, Stanley. "The Arkansas Post of Louisiana: French Domination," *Louisiana Historical Quarterly*, Vol. XXVI, No. 3 (July, 1943).

———. "The Arkansas Post of Louisiana: Spanish Domination," *Louisiana Historical Quarterly*, Vol. XXVII, No. 3 (July, 1944).

Folmer, Henri. "Contraband Trade Between Louisiana and New Mexico in the Eighteenth Century," *New Mexico Historical Review*, Vol. XVI, No. 3 (July, 1941).

———. "Étienne Véniard de Bourgmond in the Missouri Country," *Missouri Historical Review*, Vol. XXXVI, No. 3 (April, 1942).

———. "The Mallet Expedition of 1739 Through Nebraska, Kansas, and

Colorado to Santa Fé," *The Colorado Magazine*, Vol. XVI, No. 5 (September, 1939), 163–73.

———. "Report on Louis de St. Denis' Intended Raid on San Antonio in 1721," *Southwestern Historical Quarterly*, Vol. LII, No. 1 (July, 1948).

Garraghan, Gilbert J. "Fort Orléans of the Missouri," *Missouri Historical Review*, Vol. XXXV, No. 3 (April, 1941).

Golley, Frank B. "James Baird, Early Santa Fé Trader," Missouri Historical Society *Bulletin*, Vol. XV, No. 3 (April, 1959).

Goodwin, Cardinal. "A Larger View of the Yellowstone Expedition," *Missouri Valley Historical Review*, Vol. IV (1917–18).

Hackett, Charles W. "New Light on Don Diego de Peñalosa," *The Mississippi Valley Historical Review*, Vol. VI, No. 3 (December, 1919), 313–35.

Hale, E. E. "The Real Philip Nolan," *Publications* of Mississippi Historical Society, Vol. IV (1901).

Hamilton, Raphael N. "The Early Cartography of the Missouri Valley," *American Historical Review*, Vol. XXXIX, No. 4 (July, 1934), 645–62.

Hammond, George P., ed. "The Zúñiga Journal, Tucson to Santa Fé," *New Mexico Historical Review*, Vol. VI, No. 1 (January, 1931).

Hill, J. J. "Spanish and Mexican Exploration," in *Utah Historical Quarterly*, Vol. III, No. 1 January, 1930).

Harper, Elizabeth Ann. "The Taovayas Indians in Frontier Trade and Diplomacy." Part I (1719–69), *The Chronicles of Oklahoma*, Vol. XXXI, No. 3 (Autumn, 1953); Part II (1769–79), in *Southwestern Historical Quarterly*, Vol. LVII, No. 4 (October, 1953); Part III (1779–1835), "*Panhandle Plains Historical Review*, Vol. XXVI (1953).

Hatcher, Mattie Austin. "Conditions in Texas Affecting the Colonization Problem, 1795–1801," *Southwestern Historical Quarterly*, Vol. XXV, No. 2 (October, 1921).

Hill, J. J. "Spanish and Mexican Exploration," in *Utah Historical Quarterly*, Vol. III, No. 1 (January, 1930).

Hodge, Frederick W. "The Jumano Indians," *Proceedings* of the American Antiquarian Society at the Annual Meeting, April, 1909.

———, ed. "A Virginian in New Mexico," *New Mexico Historical Review*, Vol. IV, No. 3 (July, 1929), 239–72.

Jackson, Donald. "A New Lewis and Clark Map," *Bulletin of the Missouri Historical Society*, Vol. XVII, No. 2, Parts I and II (January, 1961).

King, Grace. "The Real Philip Nolan," *Publications* of the Louisiana Historical Society, Vol. X (1917).

Kyte, George W. "A Spy on the Western Waters: the Military Intelligence Mission of General Collot in 1796," *Mississippi Valley Historical Review*, Vol. XXIV, No. 3 (December, 1947).

Liljegren, Ernest R. "Jacobinism in Spanish Louisiana, 1792–1797," *Louisiana Historical Quarterly*, Vol. XXII, No. 1 (January, 1939).

Marshall, Thomas M. (ed.). "Journals of Jules de Mun," Missouri Historical Society *Collections*, Vol. V, No. 2 (February, 1928).

Moore, R. Woods. "The Role of the Baron de Bastrop in the Anglo-American Settlement of the Spanish Southwest," *Louisiana Historical Quarterly*, Vol. XXXI, No. 3 (July, 1948).

Nasatir, Abraham P. "An Account of Spanish Louisiana, 1785," *Missouri Historical Review*, Vol. XXIV, No. 4 (July, 1930).

———. "The Anglo-Spanish Frontier in the Illinois Country During the American Revolution, 1779–1783," *Journal* of the Illinois State Historical Society, Vol. XXI, No. 3 (October, 1928).

———. "The Anglo-Spanish Frontier on the Upper Mississippi, 1786–1796," *Iowa Journal of History and Politics*, Vol. XXIX, No. 2 (April, 1931).

———. "The Anglo-Spanish Frontier in the Iowa Country, 1797–1798," *Iowa Journal of History and Politics*, Vol. XXVIII, No. 3 (July, 1930).

———. "Anglo-Spanish Rivalry on the Upper Missouri," *Mississippi Valley Historical Review*, Vol. XVI, No. 3 (December, 1929), and Vol. XVI, No. 4 (March, 1930).

———. "Ducharme's Invasion of Missouri, an Incident in the Anglo-Spanish Rivalry for the Indian Trade of Upper Louisiana," *Missouri Historical Review*, Vol. XXIV, Nos. 1, 2, 3 (October, 1929, January and April, 1930).

———. "The Formation of the Missouri Company," *Missouri Historical Review*, Vol. XXV, No. 1 (October, 1930).

———."Government Employees and Salaries in Spanish Louisiana," *Louisiana Historical Quarterly*, Vol. XXIX, No. 4 (October, 1946).

———. "Jacques Clamorgan: Colonial Promoter of the Northern Border of New Spain," *New Mexico Historical Review*, Vol. XVII, No. 2 (April, 1942).

———. "Jacques D'Eglise on the Upper Missouri, 1791–1795," *Mississippi Valley Historical Review*, Vol. XIV, No. 1 (June, 1927).

———. "John Evans, Explorer and Surveyor," *Missouri Historical Review*, Vol. XXV, Nos. 2, 3, 4 (January, April, July, 1931).

———, and Ernest B. Liljegren, eds. "Materials Relating to the History of the Mississippi Valley," *Louisiana Historical Quarterly*, Vol. XXI, No. 1 (January, 1938).

Parish, John Carl. "The Intrigues of Doctor James O'Fallon," *Mississippi Valley Historical Review*, Vol. XVII, No. 2 (September, 1930).

Reeve, Frank D. "Navaho-Spanish Diplomacy, 1770–1790," *New Mexico Historical Review*, Vol. XXXV No. 3 (July, 1960).

Scholes, France V. "The Supply Service of the New Mexican Missions in the Seventeenth Century," *New Mexico Historical Review*, Vol. V, No. 2 (April, 1930).

Thomas, A. B. "An Anonymous Description of New Mexico," *Southwestern Historical Quarterly*, Vol. XXXIII, No. 1 (July, 1929).

———. "The First Santa Fé Expedition, 1792–1793," *Chronicles of Oklahoma*, Vol. IX, No. 2 (June, 1931).

———. "San Carlos: A Comanche Pueblo on the Arkansas River, 1787," *The Colorado Magazine*, Vol. IV, No. 3 (May, 1929).

———. "Spanish Expeditions Into Colorado," *The Colorado Magazine*, Vol. I, No. 7 (November, 1924).

———. "Governor Mendinueta's Proposals for the Defense of Mexico, 1772–1778," *New Mexico Historical Review*, Vol. VI, No. 1 (January, 1931).

Turner, Frederick Jackson. "Origin of Genêts Projected Attack on Louisiana and the Floridas," *American Historical Review*, Vol. III (1898), 650–71.

———. "Documents on the Relation of France to Louisiana, 1792–1795," *American Historical Review*, Vol. III (1898), 490–516.

Voelker, Frederic E. "Ezekiel Williams of Boone's Lick," Missouri Historical Society *Bulletin*, Vol. VIII, No. 1 (October, 1952).

Wesley, Edgard B. "A Still Larger View of the Yellowstone Expedition," *North Dakota Historical Quarterly*, Vol. V, No. 4 (July, 1931).

Whitaker, Arthur Preston. "The Retrocession of Louisiana in Spanish Policy," *American Historical Review*, Vol. XXXIX, No. 3 (April, 1934).

White, Leslie A. "Punche: Tobacco in New Mexico History," *New Mexico Historical Review*, Vol. VIII, No. 4 (October, 1943).

Whittington, G. P. "Dr. John Sibley of Natchitoches, 1757–1837," *Louisiana Historical Quarterly*, Vol. X, No. 4 (October, 1927).

## Unpublished Material

Bjork, David Knuth. "The Establishment of Spanish Rule in the Province of Louisiana, 1762–1770." Doctoral dissertation, University of California, 1923.

Coughlin, Francis Ellen. "Spanish Galleys on the Mississippi, 1792–1797." Master's thesis, Claremore Graduate School, 1945.

Folmer, Henri. "French Expansion Toward New Mexico in the Eighteenth Century." Master's thesis, University of Denver, 1939.

Kinnaird, Lawrence. "American Penetration Into Spanish Territory, 1776–1803." Doctoral dissertation, University of California, 1928.

Martin, Lloydine Della. "George Victor Collot in the Mississsppi Valley, 1796." Master's thesis, University of California, 1935.

Nasatir, Abraham P. "Indian Trade and Diplomacy in Spanish Illinois." Doctoral dissertation, University of California, 1926.

Nuttall, Donald A. "The American Threat to New Mexico, 1804–1822." Master's thesis, San Diego State College, 1959.

Ruíz, Ramón Eduardo. "For God and Country, the Northeast Frontier of New Mexico to 1820." Master's thesis, Claremont Graduate School, 1948.

Thomas, Marjorie Oletha. "The Arkansas Post of Louisiana, 1682–1763." Master's thesis, University of California, 1942.

# Index

The text for *Pedro Vial and the Roads to Santa Fe* has been set in 11½-point Caslon on the Linotype. This machine-set face is a faithful reproduction of the original letter designed by William Caslon, one of England's great type designers. The paper on which the book is printed bears the watermark of the University of Oklahoma Press and has an effective life of at least three hundred years.